D0206064

Theoretical Logic in Sociology

At first, therefore, logic must indeed be learned as something which one understands and sees into quite well but in which, at the beginning, one feels the lack of scope and depth and a wider significance. It is only after profounder acquaintance . . . that logic ceases to be for subjective spirit a merely abstract universal and reveals itself as the universal which embraces within itself the wealth of the particular. . . . The system of logic is the realm of shadows, the world of simple essentialities freed from all sensuous concreteness. The study of this science, to dwell and labour in this shadowy realm, is the absolute culture and discipline of consciousness.

G. W. F. Hegel,
Science of Logic

Theoretical Logic in Sociology

Volume Four

THE MODERN RECONSTRUCTION OF CLASSICAL THOUGHT: TALCOTT PARSONS

Jeffrey C. Alexander

University of California Press
Berkeley • Los Angeles

University of California Press
Berkeley and Los Angeles, California

Printed in the United States of America

1 2 3 4 5 6 7 8 9

Library of Congress Cataloging in Publication Data
Alexander, Jeffrey C.
Theoretical logic in sociology.

Includes bibliographical references and index.
Contents: v. 1. Positivism, presuppositions, and current controversies——v. 4. The modern reconstruction of classical thought, Talcott Parsons.
1. Sociology—History—Collected works. 2. Sociology—Philosophy—Collected works. 3. Sociology—Methodology—Collected works.
HM24.A465 1982 301 75-17305
ISBN 0-520-03062-1 (set)
ISBN 0-520-04483-5 (vol. 4)

CONTENTS—OVERVIEW

Volume Three
THE CLASSICAL ATTEMPT AT THEORETICAL SYNTHESIS: MAX WEBER

Volume Four
THE MODERN RECONSTRUCTION OF CLASSICAL THOUGHT: TALCOTT PARSONS

THE MODERN RECONSTRUCTION OF CLASSICAL THOUGHT: TALCOTT PARSONS

Contents

VOLUME FOUR

THE MODERN RECONSTRUCTION OF CLASSICAL THOUGHT: TALCOTT PARSONS

Preface to Volume Four

Theoretical Thought and Its Vicissitudes

The Achievements and Limitations of Classical Sociology

In the first three volumes of this work I made certain statements about the nature of science and the relationship of its components, the status of contemporary theoretical debate in sociology, the qualities of good theorizing, and the role of interpretive readings in social-scientific theory. I also conducted, from the perspective of these initial questions and arguments, an investigation into the theoretical logic that informed the work of sociology's classical founders: Marx, Durkheim, and Weber. I hope, of course, that readers of the present volume will have read its predecessors. As the finale of a long work, this concluding volume, ineluctably, builds upon the earlier ones, particularly since I seek to demonstrate that the thought of the present subject—Talcott Parsons—can be understood only in the context of dialogue with Marx, Durkheim, and Weber. Nonetheless, many readers of this volume will not, in fact, have read the preceding works, and for this reason I will try to offer here an overview which can function, if even in a limited way, as a framework within which to place the present volume. For those familiar with the earlier volumes, this discussion is unnecessary, but they may still find it a helpful review of the status and implications of my general argument.

In volume 1, I conducted two simultaneous polemics. First, I argued against the positivist persuasion in contemporary understandings of science, evident not only among philosophers and sociologists of science but among its practitioners as well. The crucial proposition of the positivist persuasion, I argued, is that factual statements can be ontologically separated from nonfactual statements or generalizations. From this central tenet, the other components of the positivist persuasion follow: the notions that philosophical or metaphysical issues play no essential part in a true empirical science, that theoretical disputes must be decided by reference to crucial empirical experiments alone, that methodological techniques of verification or falsification are of critical and ultimate importance. In opposition to these positivist tenets, I suggested that general as well as specific thinking is crucial to science, and I defined this "theoretical" as contrasted to "methodological" or "empirical" logic as the concern with the effects of more general assumptions on more specific formulations. Throughout these volumes, the focus is upon this more general concern with theoretical logic.

My second polemic was directed against theoretical arguments that have occurred within the antipositivist framework itself. I argued that recent debates in sociological theory have sought to reduce theoretical argument to one or another particular set of nonempirical commitments. Theoretical empiricism has, for example, sought to reduce sociological theory to assumptions about methodology, conflict theory to assumptions about the relative equilibrium of the empirical world at a specific time, antifunctionalist critique to assumptions about the nature of scientific models, and ideological criticism—practicising a "strong program" in the sociology of knowledge—to the political components of a theorist's perspective.

I have proposed, to the contrary, that science be conceived as a multilayered continuum, one that stretches from the most general, metaphysically oriented presuppositions to more specific ideological assumptions and models, to still more empirical assumptions and methodological commitments, and finally to empirically related propositions and "facts." Each of these levels, I insist, has relative autonomy vis-à-vis other kinds of scien-

Figure 1

THE SCIENTIFIC CONTINUUM AND ITS COMPONENTS

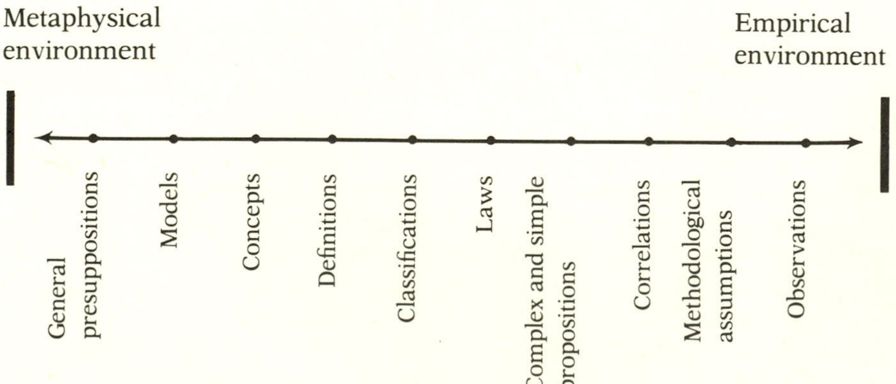

tific commitments, although each is powerfully interrelated to others at the same time. It is the task of *theoretical* logic in sociology to explicate what each of these commitments entails and how they are interrelated. Only with such a differentiated understanding of science, moreover, can the dichotomy of idealist versus positivist, or materialist, understandings of science be resolved, for with this understanding it becomes clear that every scientific statement is the product of the interaction between pressures from the empirical and the metaphysical environments. Figure 1 is my schematic representation of the scientific continuum.

As part of this second polemic I stressed a further point: not only have recent theoretical arguments been reductionistic, or conflationary, but taken together they have usually ignored the most generalized elements of social-scientific argument. I called these elements "presuppositions" and defined them as the assumptions any social scientist makes about the nature of human action and how it is aggregated into patterned arrangements.

These presuppositional assumptions address the problems of action and order. First—and here I must unfortunately simplify complex issues which were treated earlier at some length—action can be defined either in an instrumental, rationalizing way or in a manner that pays more attention to nonrational, normative, or affective components. The former takes the materialist path, the latter the idealist, although there is also, of course, the possibility for a more integrated and synthetic, or multidimensional, position. Second, theory must also adopt an orientation to order. Are social arrangements the results of individual negotiation or do they present themselves as collective structures that have sui generis, or emergent, status? Individualistic approaches often reveal important elements of empirical interaction, but they ignore the invisible parameters within which such action takes place, parameters which, indeed, often inform the substance of action itself. If one takes the collective course, on the other hand, action remains vitally important, for assumptions about the nature of action will determine how such collective order will be described. In line with the idealist approach to action, collective order has often been given a normative hue. This position has the advantage of allowing collective structures to be combined with the voluntary agency of individuals, for normative order rests upon internal, subjective commitments. Yet taken by itself, this approach exaggerates the responsiveness of the collectivity to subjective concerns. But if action is assumed, in the name of greater realism, to be instrumentalizing and rational, collective structure will be described as external and material; if motives are always calculating and efficient, action will be completely predictable on the basis of external pressure alone. Subjectivity and the concern with motive drop out: order is then viewed in a thoroughly deterministic way. These two solutions to the problem of collective order form the traditions of *sociological* idealism and *sociologi-*

cal materialism, traditions that must be sharply separated from idealism and materialism in a purely epistemological sense. Of course, once again, there remains the theoretical possibility that more synthetic and multidimensional understandings of collective order may be achieved.

It is within the contexts of these various polemics that I introduced certain technical arguments which might at first glance elude readers of the present volume alone. These are: (1) the dangers of "conflation" in scientific argument, (2) the importance of multidimensional thought at the most general presuppositional level, (3) the dangers of "reduction" within this presuppositional level itself. Within the context of the preceding summary, however, these technical points should now be more accessible. (1) Conflationary arguments attempt to make each of the components of the scientific continuum primarily dependent on one particular differentiated commitment. Thus, "conflict sociology" is conflationary, as are so many of the arguments for "critical sociology" and the arguments for or against "functionalist sociology" (see my references to these reductionist strategies above). (2) Within the presuppositional level—the most general and ramifying level of scientific reasoning—I insist on the theoretical power of multidimensional thinking over either its idealist or materialist counterparts. Critical benefits accrue to both forms of one-dimensional thought, but there are also debilitating weaknesses which make each, taken by itself, theoretically unacceptable. (3) I suggest that one-dimensional thinking has often been camouflaged by a form of reductionism within the presuppositional level itself: the reduction of the problem of action to the problem of order. Sociological idealists and materialists often argue—in fact, almost invariably—that a collective rather than individualistic approach can be achieved only if action is perceived in an instrumentalist or normative way. This reduction is false. The questions of action and order are themselves relatively autonomous, although once decided they profoundly affect one another. Normative and instrumental understandings of action can both be collectivist, and, conversely, they can both inform individualistic thought.

I made other arguments in volume 1. Most importantly, I suggested that nonpositivistic thought need not be relativistic, that it can attain its own kind of objectivity. I also argued, in the Prolegomena to volume 2, for the critical importance in social-scientific argument of the interpretation and reinterpretation of classical work. "Readings" of the work of dead theorists, or of completed and past theoretical statements, is in the nonconsensual world of social science a fundamental means—though, of course, not the only one—of establishing the validity of certain general orientations.

These assertions, which for polemic and clarity's sake were put as sharply as possible and here are being reproduced in an unforgivably foreshortened way, may have seemed tendentious. I hope that the intervening discussions, in volumes 2 and 3, have demonstrated that they are not. "Philosophical" and "humanistic" issues do seem to matter even for the most distinguished exercises in social science: every empirical fact, every propositional statement, is, after all, informed though not completely determined by much more generalized concerns. Two scientists might observe the same revolutionary movement, and even agree that it was a revolutionary movement, but they would explain it differently if they disagreed about the nature of human action and how such individual actions are aggregated to form social order. Other kinds of general concerns, of course, also affect their explanations—ideological evaluations, models of social system parts, methodological philosophies and specific techniques, expectations about empirical equilibrium and disorder. I hope to have succeeded in demonstrating, however, that while each of these different levels comes into play, while each is relatively autonomous and of possibly determinate influence in any specific situation, it is the most general level of presuppositional commitment that is the most ramifying and decisive for the analytic structuring of empirical life. It is decisions made on this level that cause the most critical shifts in social-scientific work; the power or weakness of presuppositional understanding—more than any other scientific commitment—places the blinders on social theory or offers the resources for its critical achievements.

These conclusions summarize my detailed examination of the scientific thinking of the founders of modern sociology. I hope to have demonstrated, in the first place, that this thinking is not of only antiquarian concern. It should be clear that the empirical matter they dealt with, the propositions they offered, and the models they built are still the life and stuff of contemporary sociology. These classical figures grappled with problems which continue to obsess their students and followers, whose writings—in more or less direct lineages—form the major bulk of contemporary sociology. It would not be difficult, indeed, to demonstrate from any advanced sociology text that the most current debates on the most specific subjects are still structured by—among other factors—the presuppositional arguments that were first articulated and sociologically specified by Marx, Durkheim, and Weber. In fact, in a casual and informal way, I made the beginnings of such a demonstration in volumes 2 and 3, for in the course of my analyses I discussed, perforce, fundamental issues in almost every specialized field of sociological thought: collective behavior and law; social change and science; education and religion; organization and stratification; social psychology and deviance; ethnicity and social change; urban sociology and modernization; socialization and politics; the sociology of the family, of work, and of economic life.

My goal, however, has not been to examine empirical issues per se but to illuminate the distinctively theoretical concerns upon which they rest, to contribute further to our thinking about the presuppositions that so often place insuperable barriers on more empirical work. This analysis has revealed, above all, that while it is relatively easy to express epistemological multidimensionality, it is much more difficult to translate this commitment into a sociological form. Multidimensional thought is necessarily complex; the temptation to simplify, to slip back into linear thinking, is correspondingly great. The temptation appears in a variety of disguises. Reductionist theory seems tempting for reasons of clarity and for reasons of ideology, because of intra- and interdisciplinary conflicts, because of the persistent and nagging error of conflation which seems to demand that one or another presuppositional position necessarily accompany a commitment at another level of the scientific continuum. And in the end, one-dimensional thought is always conducted in the name of empirical reality itself, for the effect of each of these more generalized pressures is to make the scientist "see" in a one-dimensional way. Scientific integrity, then, seems often to demand the negation of multidimensional thought. But this demand can never be legitimate; no matter what the initial appearance, our understanding of empirical reality is eventually impoverished if a vital dimension of social life is blocked from our theoretical consciousness.

The failure to achieve multidimensionality, however, has its most persistent cause in the difficulties and confusions of general theoretical logic itself, and it is to this problem that I have really devoted these volumes. Each of the classical theorists committed himself to a collective understanding of social order, yet the uncertainty of his conception of action made this social order difficult to define. Marx began with a normative and voluntaristic approach to revolution and change, in which critique was essential and in which the subjective alienation of reason and the desire for its reconciliation were the central mechanisms for social life. But the encounter with the radicalism of his day and especially the science of political economy initiated far-reaching changes in Marx's work: instrumental action now seemed the appropriate form for any analysis of the capitalist period. Alienation changed from a source of critical subjectivity to a rationalization for its theoretical elimination. Marx could then conceive collective order only in external and coercive terms. From this transition, sociological materialism was born, and with it an enduring sensitivity to the external dimension of social constraint. But so too was an antivoluntaristic theory with all its fateful implications.

Durkheim was from the beginning committed to avoiding what he justly regarded as this utilitarian error. He sought to combine a recognition of individuality and voluntarism with the necessity for social order and control. The history of his early writings, however, is the record of his failures to make this intention into a scientific reality. Because of his difficulties in conceiving of the individual actor in an analytical rather than a concrete way, because of his tendency to conflate empirical equilibrium with collective order, and because of a continuing residue of utilitarian thinking about action itself, Durkheim's first great work adopted—ambivalently, to be sure—a theory of instrumental action and external order. When the obvious "pathology" of the capitalist division of labor abolished the deus ex machina by which Durkheim had thought voluntarism could still be maintained, and when critical reaction brought home to him the truly deterministic theoretical structure he had actually wrought, Durkheim recoiled from this quasi-Marxian adventure. He now sought persistently to subjectify order, and he rediscovered the notion of culturally interpenetrated and solidary individuals from his earliest work. His revelation about the true nature of religious life allowed him to reformulate these insights in a more systematic and elegant way, and in the last two decades of his life he developed a theory of society that in every significant respect was the mirror image of Marx's. Durkheim understood more acutely than any before him the subjective and voluntaristic aspects of modern life; this understanding allowed him to solve the riddle of the fate of religion in a secular world. It was upon a religious model that the great successes of idealism were forged, but it was this same model that was also responsible for its greatest failings. Religious fervor must deal with the limitations of the human soul, but there are more external and material barriers to action that are equally obdurate, and these orders sociological idealism finds hard to explain.

The limiting assumptions of these sociological founders confined their thought in rather narrow ways. The fact that in some sense they "knew better" created pressures that burst the formal barriers of their science altogether. Marx managed to be extraordinarily consistent in his explicitly scientific writings, although not completely so, but his more informal political work—his pamphlets, letters, and speeches—reveals an effort to achieve a more synthetic scope. The residual and peripatetic nature of these efforts leaves them theoretically confused; Marx could not "theoretize" the elements whose existence he informally recognized. Durkheim, too, was forced to recognize at least the existence of the elements he had striven so hard to overlook in his formulations of scientific theory. He admitted that "utilitarianism" existed in the pathological interstices of modern life. Yet although in crucial ways it played havoc with moral solidarity, such utilitarianism still could not really be explained, at least not in a systematic rather than residual way. For material facts were always individual in Durkheim's later work, never social and collective in their sociological status.

The limits of one-dimensional theory are even more strikingly revealed in the schools that these founders of the major sociological traditions established. Under the guise of homage and obeisance to the master's work and memory, Durkheim's most distinguished followers tried to reconcile his religious theory of society with the telling obduracy of "material" facts, with class stratification, group conflict, market pressures, and the bureaucratic state. The most important Marxists moved just as persistently in the other direction. Their commitment to the voluntarism of revolution, combined with their sensitivity to continuing academic criticism, made them search for a way to voluntarize and subjectify Marx. The history of these revisionist efforts is extraordinarily interesting and each has contributed powerfully to elements of multidimensional thought. Each, however, has ended in failure, for as long as the effort is made to squeeze these broader insights into the narrow framework of the founder's work there is no escape from profound intellectual contradictions. To avoid contradiction, new starting points would have to be firmly established.

Weber initiated the fundamental steps in this direction. With one foot rooted in the traditions of Realpolitik and materialism, Weber was not seduced by the exclusively normative thinking that so engaged Durkheimian thought. Yet Weber's other foot was firmly planted in the soil of German Idealism. He understood the process of subjective signification and the spiritual world within which it was necessarily rooted. He was just as unlikely, therefore, to allow his salutary hardheadedness to be transformed into the kind of obsessive "realism" that so often characterized Marxian thought. Weber's attempt at multidimensionality reflected his fundamental theoretical insight into the analytic rather than concrete status of action's material and ideal environments. He realized that if these pressures were viewed as analytic references of every act rather than as the exclusive determining factors, then the materialist and idealist traditions could be transformed into a third, much more inclusive, theoretical whole. The individual would be free to the degree that he could refer to larger symbolic ideals, yet he would be constrained by the simultaneous reality of his external, material environment.

In a series of historical works of unprecedented empirical scope, Weber laid out the formal and substantive frameworks within which such a multidimensional tradition could be pursued. In the end, however, he never fully succeeded in laying to rest the materialism which had diminished his earliest work. Weber was afraid of materialism but he was afraid of idealism more. His explicitly political sociology became an exercise in instrumental action and external order, profound and responsive to the relative complexity of political life but reductive and mechanistic all the same. Durkheim had used his model of primitive religious life as the basis for explaining modern society; in Weber's case, it was an instrumental political sociology of traditional society that was transferred to the modern terrain. Weber viewed the modern world as without a religious soul; he felt no compelling reason to search for the secular equivalents of religious action and faith.

Contemporary sociology is stranded at the various stopping points of this classical work. Some sociologists echo the argument for unadulterated instrumentalism and determinism. Others argue for voluntarism and purely subjective control. Some engage in compromise formations that ambivalently reflect the confusing ambiguities which can also be found in classical thought: the vagueness and uncertainty of the founders' early thought, the contradictions of their transition periods, the aggressively asserted uncertainties of their followers and revisers. But the fundamental challenge that Weber laid down remains to be taken up. Sociology must learn to combine the genuine insights of both Durkheim and Marx, and it can do so only on the presuppositional ground that Weber set forth. The idealist and materialist traditions must be transformed into analytic dimensions of multidimensional and synthetic theory. In this fourth and final volume I turn to the writing of Talcott Parsons, the only modern thinker who can be considered a true peer of the classical founders, and examine his own profoundly ambivalent attempt to carry out this analytic transformation.

Chapter One

THEORETICAL CONTROVERSY AND THE PROBLEMATICS OF PARSONIAN INTERPRETATION

No matter how intellectually refined its argument, there is undoubtedly a charismatic power that adheres to the work of a great social thinker, a quality that raises to a heightened pitch the normal level of confusion and irrationality produced by generalized conflict in the social sciences. In defense against such a powerful intellectual center, there emerges alongside the usual thrusts and parries of serious theoretical combat an antagonistic tradition of misinformed, often trivial, sometimes grossly distorted commentary that attempts to present itself, and is partly accepted, as critical truth. At the same time, the attractive power of this center is such that those who follow the thinker prove unable to present an objective critical evaluation of his intellectual contributions. Only with the passage of time, as the center loses its immediate power, can a perspective that is both critical and appreciative be attained and the thinker's permanent contributions to intellectual tradition be properly assessed.

We can observe this tortuous path of assimilation in the reception of each of the theorists examined in the preceding volumes of this study. Marx's work, of course, immediately polarized the European intellectual community, creating a band of zealous "Marxist" followers on the one side, and a skeptical, anti-Marxist academic audience on the other. Only as this initial dichotomization subsided were Marx's insights incorporated into the mainstream of intellectual work and, at the same time, were revisionist "Marxists" finally able to present openings—albeit highly camouflaged ones—to established "bourgeois" theory, creating in the process the kind of cross-cuttings in general theoretical logic I described in volume 2, chapter 10.[1†] Because of the depressed condition of postwar German scholarship, the reception of Max Weber's work follows this pattern less precisely, although one can clearly detect what might be called the epigoni phenomenon in the Weberianism of the succeeding decades.[2] An entire generation would elapse before Weber's basic insights could be incorporated into the intellectual tradition, before the profound revisionism could emerge that inevitably separated many of Weber's most important insights from the overarching, systematic conceptual framework upon which Weber himself had insisted.

But this process seems particularly striking, and particularly relevant to the present discussion, in the case of Durkheim. As a forceful figure intellectually and personally, Durkheim created a powerful sociological school which followed "Durkheimian" theory in a manner that greatly extended its scope and application. While in fact highly revisionist, these Durkheimians were ostensibly merely loyal expositors. As a result, these immediate followers did little to articulate the foundations of Durkheim's thought or to clarify its critical weaknesses.[3] At the same time, "Durkheimianism" was subject to a barrage of what was often distorted and tendentious criticism, directed not only toward Durkheim's theoretical conceptions but in addition to his ideological involvement in the reconstruction of the French republic.[4] Only in the late 1930s and 1940s, with the work of sociologists like Parsons, Merton, and Gurvitch, and anthropologists like Radcliffe-Brown, Evans-Pritchard, and Lévi-Strauss, and, indeed, after the decline of almost all literalistic "Durkheimianism," was the attempt begun to reappropriate Durkheim's theoretical work. And only in the 1970s was the debate about his ideological perspective sufficiently separated from reductive argument and from the sterile radical-conservative dichotomy to enable the more humanitarian and progressive impetus of his work to be understood.[5†]

This dynamic of theoretical assimilation is particularly relevant when we consider Talcott Parsons, for as the only contemporary theorist among our four subjects his work remains stuck in the middle of this unfolding process. Among sociological theorists after the classical period, Parsons' theoretical contributions alone rank with those of Marx, Durkheim, and Weber. This contention underlies all of my ensuing analysis, whether favorable or critical. Yet today, more than ever, Parsons' status as a major figure is widely disputed. For the quarter century following the Second

NOTE: In addition to the citation of sources, the backnotes include numerous substantive discussions—refinements of points that occur in the main text and digressions about relevant issues and secondary literature. To enable the interested reader to turn immediately to this substantive annotation, I have distinguished these substantive notes by marking them with a dagger[(†)] following the note number. A ribbon bookmark is provided to facilitate such referral.

World War his intellectual prestige increased enormously, and a large number of distinguished followers—revisionist "Parsonians"—emerged to clarify his theory's anomalies, to extend its scope and range of application. In the mid-1960s, however, Parsons' intellectual fortunes suffered an abrupt reversal, and the fifteen years following have witnessed an intensification of self-consciously "anti-Parsonian" criticism, pursued along ideological as well as theoretical lines. According to much of this criticism, the earlier sociological tribute to Parsons was thoroughly misguided: his work not only falls far short of classical status but is probably unworthy of further theoretical consideration.

Intellectual distinction, however, is not identical with universal popularity.[6†] To the contrary, it is the very breadth of the controversy surrounding Parsons' work that underscores its general and long-range significance. Marx and Durkheim sparked similarly virulent debate. This Parsons controversy has taken two forms. On the most generalized level, it is not an exaggeration to observe that over the last forty years major theoretical debate in Western sociology has been mediated through Parsons' theories; further, every major theoretical innovation—exchange theory, ethnomethodology, conflict theory, even certain forms of revisionist Marxism—has been initiated through a reinterpretation of one segment or another of Parsons' theoretical corpus.[7†] Long, complex, often casuistic arguments have been launched over the validity of "Parsonianism" as a theoretical alternative to Marxism, Weberianism, Durkheimianism, symbolic interactionism, and phenomenology, despite the fact that the polemics of such "interpretive" readings have usually remained implicit.[8†] On a more specific level, controversy within most of the principal empirical subfields of sociology has, at one point or another, focused on a particular set of "Parsonian" propositions, whether or not such alleged configurations accurately represented Parsons' own thinking.[9†]

Surely, then, these critical barbs are also bouquets of a peculiar sort. In fact, lurking beneath the surface of even the most antagonistic critique there persists theoretical homage to Parsons' stature. In the midst of condemning Parsons as the high priest of sociological conservatism, Friedrichs describes him "as one of the most sophisticated minds that American sociology has produced."[10] While devoting the major portion of his magnum opus to what he views as the intellectual and moral bankruptcy of the Parsonian effort, Gouldner simultaneously calls our attention to "the intrinsic significance of Parsons' theory as theory."[11]

> There is no other work by an academic sociologist today that is as relevant to the entire galaxy of important theoretical issues. . . . If he himself does not directly deal with every important theoretical problem, he brings us to its threshold. . . . [H]e was and still remains the intellectual anchor of academic sociological theory in the modern world.[12]

When, therefore, Turner writes that "while few appear to agree with all aspects of 'Parsonian theory' rarely has anyone quarreled with the assertion that he has been the dominant figure of this century," he has got hold of an important and neglected part of the truth.[13] Social scientists have quarreled, and bitterly, over Parsons' ultimate significance, but it is precisely the intensity of this quarrel that lends credibility to the claim for Parsons' permanent relevance.

Further evidence for this claim can be found in recent indications that a more balanced sort of critical assessment is in the process of emerging, as thinkers of different theoretical and political traditions have returned to Parsons' work and argued for the legitimacy or centrality of its central concerns. Most of this trend has thus far occurred outside the United States, outside, that is, the area of the most immediate and personal confrontation over Parsons' work. In England, Percy Cohen's *Modern Social Theory* constitutes a critical appreciation of Parsons' thought that deftly steers among the land mines of postwar debate; Ken Menzies' *Talcott Parsons and the Social Image of Man*, while supporting the individualist critique of Parsonianism, is singularly successful in isolating Parsons' theoretical concerns from his empirical and ideological ones; in *Social Order, Reform, and Revolution*, Bob Jessop launches a radical socialist critique of the liberal approach to social change on the basis of a sophisticated reinterpretation of Parsonian systems theory; Dick Atkinson directs his radical critique of "orthodox sociology" at the troika of Parsons, Marx, and Weber, who "may all be thought of as founding fathers of sociology"; and Stephen Savage concludes his ambitious Althusserian interpolation by praising Parsons for having "sought to answer questions where others had not even seen the possibility of a question."[14] In Quebec, Guy Rocher has produced a plausible, sympathetic reading of the systems aspect of Parsons' work, carefully separating it from its anti-socialist animus which Rocher himself does not share.[15] In France, François Bourricaud has published a major interpretive account that retrieves and restates key elements of Parsons' work in important new ways; François Chazel has written an appreciative if still somewhat conventionally distorted account of Parsons' central position in Western sociology; Alain Tourraine has incorporated much of Parsonian functionalism, as a counterweight to Marxism, into his analysis of the "production of society"; and the so-called "structuralist Marxism" of Althusser, Poulantzas, and Godelier has borrowed heavily from Parsons' functionalist conceptualization in its revision of Marxian theory.[16†] In Germany, Niklas Luhmann has tried to re-create a Parsonianism more attentive to contingency if, paradoxically, even more dependent on "systems"; Wolfgang Schluchter has attempted to reconceptualize Weber's historical rationalization theory in what are fundamentally Parsonian concepts; Richard Münch has written a series of powerful interpretive essays which seek to reestablish the neo-Kantian vitality of

Parsons' work; and Jürgen Habermas, who in most respects is in sharp dialogue with each of these German colleagues, has made extensive use of Parsons' systems and evolutionary theories, warning his fellow Marxists that "although the interest in Parsons' theory has slackened since the mid-1960's . . . no social theory can be taken seriously today which does not—at the very least—clarify its relationship to Parsons' " and suggesting that "whoever deludes himself about this fact allows himself to be captured by contemporary issues instead of rationally confronting them."[17†] In Holland, Hans P. M. Adriaansens' sophisticated overview of Parsons' corpus tries to demonstrate that "it offers the prospect of systematization of the present chaotic state of social scientific theory with all its schools, movements and perspectives and their utterly vague relations one to the other."[18]

Finally, some of this rapprochement has been expressed within the United States. In bracketing the ideological question, Harold Bershady's *Ideology and Social Knowledge* produces new insight into the epistemological foundations of Parsons' meta-methodology. By stepping outside the either/or dichotomy of the recent literature of polemic and defense, Jonathan Turner has demonstrated a significant overlap between Parsons' propositions and those of his critics'—conflict, exchange, and symbolic interactionist theory. And the radical political economist Herbert L. Gintis has synthesized elements of Parsons and Marx in presenting a framework for an anticapitalist approach to welfare economics.[19†]

In short, although the perspective provided by the passage of time is simply not available for any contemporary examination of Parsons' work, we can already see emerging a pattern of evaluation that bears a remarkable similarity to the vicissitudes experienced by Durkheim's corpus. It seems likely that the dialectic of acceptance, critique, revision, and assimilation will also be the fate of Parsons.

What follows here is a contribution to this assimilative and revisionist task. I will argue that Parsons' most fundamental theoretical contributions have been badly misunderstood—by recent critics, by long-time Parsonians, and even by those who have begun the long-term work of theoretical sifting and winnowing. Like the theories of the classical sociologists who preceded him, Parsons has suffered from the interpretive errors of conflation and reduction, errors which, as we have seen in earlier volumes, permeate contemporary theoretical logic. Indeed, his work has been even more vulnerable to such misinterpretation precisely because it has been so intimately interwoven with recent debate.[20†]

Critics and supporters alike have conflated the autonomy of different levels of Parsons' thought. Judging from purely positivist standards, a host of commentators have focused exclusively on the most specific, empirical strand of his work, refuting or verifying "Parsonianism" on the basis of carefully planned "crucial experiments."[21] At the other extreme, Parsons' interpreters have often dismissed the empirical, or "objective," segment of his work as negligible, arguing from a sociology-of-knowledge perspective that the only really significant level of his theory is the ideological. Accordingly, such critics reduce the other segments of Parsons' formulations to reflexes of his political or social position.[22]

Between these two extremes of reductionism, interpreters have purported to explain Parsons' theory by conflating it with more intermediate levels of the sociological continuum. Some relate the objectionable aspects of Parsons' theory to his methodological choices. If Parsons had only been more of a positivist, his critics argue, his theoretical problems would have been resolved.[23] For his sympathizers, it is, on the other hand, this very commitment to the nonempirical that is held to produce Parsons' great insights at the other levels of his theory.[24]

Much more widespread is the contention, obviously more prevalent among his critics, that the determining assumptions in Parsons' work are those which produce his propositions about empirical conflict or harmony. An entire school of contemporary sociology has learned the false lesson that it is from Parsons' commitment to "equilibrium" that his other theoretical positions derive—his acceptance of systemic models, his conservative ideology, his normative presuppositions, even his anti-empirical methodology.[25] If conflict rather than harmony is supported, so goes this critique, the other elements of Parsonianism would disappear.

Finally, at the most general level attained by such conflationary interpretation, Parsons is presented as the "functionalist" par excellence. From his decision to adopt models that are systems, all else is said to follow. Functionalism is the basis of his conservatism, his opposition to conflict, his antipositivism, his idealism.[26] Similarly, many of Parsons' followers find in his functionalism the master key to the significance of his other theoretical insights.[27]

It is unfortunately on one or the other of these conflationary levels that the identity of "Parsonianism" has gradually taken shape in the sociological collective conscience. Still, some of Parsons' interpreters have addressed a more general level of analysis, offering the possibility for a truly effective critique or defense. Virtually without exception, however, these possibilities have not been realized.

One group of critics sees Parsons as patently idealist, as paying no serious attention to the material conditions that impinge on individual voluntarism and the realization of internalized norms.[28] Other critics, arguing from a different presuppositional animus, attack Parsons as not voluntaristic enough, as submerging voluntarism in an anti-individualistic, deterministic theory that views free will as completely inhibited by external constraints.[29] Ironically, Parsons' sympathizers have often endorsed the idealist evaluation of Parsons, arguing that his normative emphasis, far from being a disadvantage, represents the most important element in his work.[30] Other followers have maintained, to the contrary, that throughout his work Parsons has maintained a strong, consistent multidimensionality.[31]

In the following pages I will try to avoid the Scylla and Charybdis of Parsonian critique and defense. Confusion in the interpretation of Parsons' work results largely from conflation and reduction. My analysis will separate the different levels of Parsons' thought. More importantly, this analysis will focus attention on the level in Parsons' thinking that is most general in its scope and most decisive in its significance: his presuppositions. Parsons' positions on the basic presuppositional questions powerfully shape his formulations at every other, more specific level of analysis. They are most responsible for what is distinctive about his thought. As in the discussions of Marx, Durkheim, and Weber, in volumes 2 and 3, we will see that Parsons' success depends on the degree to which his theory meets the criterion of multidimensionality, and that his failure can be measured by the extent to which he departs from it.

Throughout, my analysis will compare Parsons' presuppositional solutions directly with those of Marx, Durkheim, and Weber. Despite the enormous contemporary focus on Parsons' work, and the manner in which Parsonian structural-functionalism has served as a continual foil for the theoretical arguments of contemporary Marxian, Durkheimian, and Weberian schools of thought, the fact remains that no full-scale comparison exists between Parsons and his classical predecessors. While implicit contrasts between Parsonianism and Marxism have been the critical stock in trade for several decades, these debates have occurred beneath the camouflage of the arguments about empirical conflict and systemic models. With one or two partial exceptions, therefore, no detailed, explicit comparison of Marx and Parsons exists.[32†] Similarly, while Parsons' work has even more often been related to elements of Durkheim's and Weber's theories, there are no extended discussions of Parsons and Durkheim, or Parsons and Weber.[33†]

By providing new perspectives on the old Parsons debates, new explanations for recurrent anomalies in Parsons' work, and explicit connections between Parsons' theory and the sociological classics, I hope to contribute to the task that has barely begun—that of establishing the nature of Parsons' permanent contribution to social thought. Insofar as this interpretive reading involves revision as well, as any creative theoretical argument inherently must, I will present my interpretation in such a way that this "revisionism" is plain to see.

Chapter Two

THE EARLY PERIOD

Interpretation and the Presuppositional Movement toward Multidimensionality

1. PERCEPT AND PRECEPT: POSTPOSITIVIST ASPECTS OF PARSONS' META-METHODOLOGY

Contrary to sociological conventional wisdom, Parsons' work was always empirically oriented, addressing the empirical literature on an extraordinarily wide range of topics. In this he resembles Weber more than Durkheim. At every point in his career, his "general theory" writings were interspersed with essays on specific empirical topics. Further, the observations expressed in these essays functioned as implicit points of reference throughout his more generalized work. The two bodies of material, in other words, are fully consistent with one another.[1†] It is possible, in fact, to draw a direct connection between the progression of Parsons' empirical knowledge and the significant stages of his theoretical evolution. His interest in the historical origins of capitalism and knowledge of macro-economics, for example, informed his early writings through the publication of *The Structure of Social Action*. Subsequently, almost half of his *Essays in Sociological Theory* relied on his empirical insights into the roots of the international crisis that produced Fascism and the Second World War, while direct observations of medical practice helped generate the pattern-variable schema toward which most of the rest of that collection was directed. *The Social System* can be viewed as integrating the preceding material with Parsons' involvement with psychoanalytic theory and practice, his knowledge about various types of deviant behavior, and his readings in cultural history. Finally, the breakthrough into his later four-function analysis coincides with Parsons' exposure to the Harvard small group research, particularly to Bales' systematic observations on task-oriented groups.[2†]

Taking a somewhat different approach to Parsons as an empirically oriented sociologist, one could organize his output according to the special fields of empirical sociology, viewing his contributions as kinds of supra-empirical generalizations. Certainly this is the way Parsons' theorizing has been utilized by his students and followers, whose own work has usually consisted in the creative elaboration, specification, and extension of Parsons' writings on a particular empirical area.[3†] Rocher has recently taken exactly this approach to presenting Parsons, dividing his empirical essays into an even dozen special subfields: industrialization and Western society, the radical right, bureaucracy, professions, education, social stratification, kinship and the family, mass society, illness and deviance, religion, sociology of knowledge, race and ethnicity.[4] In this connection it should be stressed that it has actually been Parsons' contributions to empirical subfields that have often been the main targets of his critics.

It is absurd, in other words, to claim that Parsons' work has nothing "empirical" about it, to pretend that it is, somehow, purely "definitional" or purely "conceptual," all form and no content. Those who make this charge fail to understand the inherently two-directional nature of science and, more particularly, Parsons' own consistent interest in empirical problems. Actually, once this side of his work is understood, Parsons' "theory" often meets the stringent "empirical" criteria formulated by his positivist critics. Insisting, for example, that "fully elaborated categorial systems should resemble incipient theories," M. J. Mulkay, an empiricist, goes on to argue that such incipient theories should "provide unexpected insights into empirical relationships as well as [offer] empirical generalizations of various degrees of adequacy . . . at various levels of abstraction."[5] This, indeed, is precisely what Parsons accomplished.

And yet the term "empirically oriented" should no more be taken as synonymous with "empirical" than should Weber's notion of "economically-oriented action" be confused with economic activity itself. There must, after all, be some reason for Parsons' reputation as a "general" theorist. Though empirically directed, his essays have not in fact been empirical generalizations in the true empiricist sense of that term; nor, despite the close connection between the expansion of Parsons' empirical knowledge and the stages of his theoretical development, has the former actually created the latter.[6] For sociological investigation, like science generally, is a multilayered enterprise. While Parsons was always sensitive to the patterns of the empirical world, he consistently separated the empirical inputs to scientific formulation from the more generalized. In his concern for the empirical, he self-consciously focused on the more general. This differential focus characterized his work from the beginning.

An argument for the relative autonomy of generalized, nonempirical elements in social science represents one of the two central themes of Parsons' first important work, *The Structure of Social Action*. Perhaps the most significant analytic history of social thought in the twentieth century, this book remains Parsons' most sophisticated discussion of his meta-methodological position. From the outset, he is very clear about his antipositivist stance. "It is fundamental," he asserts in the Introduction, "that there is no empirical knowledge which is not in some sense and to some degree conceptually formed." And he dismisses as inherently untrue "all talk of 'pure sense data,' [and] 'raw experience.' "[7] His point of departure is Whitehead, whose *Science and the Modern World*, in Parsons' words, "so beautifully exposed under the name of 'the fallacy of misplaced concreteness' . . . [the] 'deep rooted errors' of a scientistic perspective on the natural sciences."[8†] In contrast to both positivist doctrine and Western common sense, the objects of scientific statements are not empirical in a concrete, sensual sense. "Any particular . . . concrete phenomenon or unit must be thought of not as a property in this [concrete] sense," Parsons warns, but rather "as capable of description in terms of a particular combination of . . . general properties."[9] As such, science is concerned with analytic, not concrete, elements.

> It is these general attributes of concrete phenomena relevant within the framework of a given descriptive frame of reference, and certain combinations of them, to which the term "analytical elements" will be applied.[10]

It is in the light of this insight that Parsons later praises Pareto for "includ[ing] the element of theoretical abstraction in his concept of fact itself" and for his understanding that "the facts themselves are . . . observations 'in terms of a conceptual scheme.' "[11] This antipositivist, "analytic" emphasis is a refrain throughout all Parsons' subsequent work.

Yet, because he acknowledges the nonempirical, analytic status of "facts," Parsons does not feel compelled to adopt an anti-empirical, merely antipositivist position. He remains thoroughly committed, as Weber was, to the notion of scientific objectivity and to value neutrality. Indeed, Parsons feels that Weber is still too anti-empirical, and he rejects Weber's view that concepts are "useful fictions." This view, Parsons asserts, is too relativistic, and he believes that Weber's notion that "scientific concepts . . . are not reflections of reality" was an exaggeration, too much of a "conscious reaction against . . . empiricism." As such, while Parsons is willing to acknowledge an "element of truth in this view," he rejects it as ultimately "untenable."[12†] He argues, by contrast, that good analytic theory can, somehow, be true empirically, describing this middle position as "analytical realism." Analytic realism, Parsons asserts, avoids "the objectionable implications of an empiricist realism"; at the same time, he argues, it provides a position that is "in an epistemological sense, realistic."[13] While we will see that this notion produces some troubling inconsistencies in his later work, it is still vital for illuminating the anti-idealist tone of Parsons' analytic emphasis.

> As opposed to the fiction view it is maintained that at least some of the general concepts of science are not fictional but adequately "grasp" aspects of the objective external world.[14]

> It is a philosophical implication of the position taken here that there is an external world of so-called empirical reality which is not the creation of the individual human mind and is not reducible to terms of ideal order . . .[15]

Although "systems of scientific theory are obviously not this external reality itself, nor . . . a direct and literal representation of it," Parsons argues that "for certain scientific purposes they are adequate representations of it."[16]

Parsons, then, is not an anti-empirical thinker. As compared with Marx or Durkheim, or even Weber, however, he was extremely self-conscious about the two-directional nature of science. Marx buried his presuppositional assumptions beneath his ideological commitments and his "empirical" discoveries about the laws of capitalist development. Weber, despite his greater sophistication, presents his concepts as somehow derived from the "typical" qualities of empirical reality. Durkheim, whose attention to generalized issues permeates his entire work, chooses for the most part to articulate his presuppositional position under the guise of empirical fact. Parsons does not. Sensitive to the autonomy of generalized elements, he discusses them independently of more empirically-related questions. In doing so, he achieves greater clarity about such "theoretical" concerns, and he succeeds in solving problems in general theoretical logic that perplexed the classical founders. It is precisely these generalized solutions that make Parsons' more empirical work significant. His illumination of this empirical world does not depend on methodological techniques for gaining more accurate observation. Rather, accepting—for the most part—observations provided by others, Parsons reorders the material according to his more general resolution of crucial theoretical problems.

Like Marx, Durkheim, and Weber before him, Parsons has been influential because he created new linkages among the intellectual tendencies of his time. Although his work represents an original formulation, it is no more fashioned from whole cloth than were the classical theories. Parsons recognizes this fact. "Although their terminology may differ," he wrote in 1968, the theory "long used by the author [has] also, in substance, [been used] by very many others."[17] What did differentiate Parsons from his contemporaries was the success of his efforts at clarifying theoretical logic. On this basis, his work has managed, at least in part, to avoid the limitations of classical sociology and its contemporary practitioners. It is to the nature of these generalized solutions that we now turn.

2. PRECEPTS AS PRESUPPOSITIONS: THE SYNTHETIC INTENTION

Parsons has a specific name for the "analytic elements" that must inform any social science. He calls them the "frame of reference." A science's frame of reference, he contends, has a phenomenological status in Husserl's sense.[18] Concrete empirical elements, which may be called "the *values* of analytical elements," are subject to variation.[19] Precisely because a given empirical element has a "*specific* content," it may or may not play a part in any particular scientific statement.[20] The status of the "frame of reference" could not be more different. As the frame for empirical analysis, its elements have a general, not a specific, content; they are constant, not subject to variation.

> The action frame of reference . . . involves no concrete data that can be "thought away," that are subject to change. It is not a phenomenon in the empirical sense. It is the indispensable logical framework in which we describe and think about the phenomena of action.[21]

The frame of reference, then, concerns the levels of science more closely related to what I have called the metaphysical end of the scientific continuum (see fig. 1, in Preface). Yet there are, as I indicated in volume 1, a number of different levels of such metaphysically oriented assumptions. By couching the issue as simply empirical versus nonempirical, Parsons does not explicitly tell us to which level the frame of reference corresponds. When we examine his argument closely, however, the answer is clear. His "frame of reference" is a presuppositional formulation. By it he intends to address the problem of action. "It is impossible even to talk about action," he writes, "in terms that do not involve a means/ends relationship." All action "consists essentially in the irreducible framework of relations" between ends, means, conditions, and norms.[22] It is clear, therefore, that Parsons' frame of reference encompasses at least one basic presuppositional issue. It also, we will see, addresses the second fundamental question—that of order[23]—although Parsons himself fails sufficiently to differentiate one question from another.[24†]

On both these questions of action and order, Parsons tries to pursue a synthetic position. He seeks to combine the partial presuppositional solutions of Marx, Durkheim, and Weber in a manner that resolves the basic conflicts of sociological epistemology: materialism versus idealism, and individualistic nominalism versus anti-individualist realism—or sociologism. Although not always successful, and, indeed, not always unambiguously pursued, this synthesis was for Parsons a vitally significant goal.[25†] To miss it is not only to miss the breadth of Parsons' theoretical ambition but also the significance of his accomplishment; as Robin Williams, a former student of Parsons, once attested, Parsons' goal was no less than "the development of a conceptual scheme . . . that could subsume at a certain level of abstraction *all* knowledge about social conduct."[26]

Critics who perceive Parsons' work simply as an attempt to construct a one-dimensional idealism cannot possibly perceive the internal drama and tension of Parsons' theoretical development. At the end of *The Structure of Social Action*, Parsons makes the following claim: "There are no group properties that are not reducible to properties of systems of action and there is no analytical theory of groups which is not translatable into terms of the theory of action"[27] He can pursue such a grand design only by establishing a multidimensional epistemological framework, the existence of which is assured by his inclusion of ends, means, norms, and conditions in his frame of reference. "It is impossible," he writes, "to have a meaningful description of action without specifying all four."[28] Before this epistemological commitment can be evaluated, however, it remains to be specified in a sociologically relevant way, which Parsons does in his critique of utilitarian social theory. Though we will see later that this critique has elements of an "abstract negation" in Hegel's sense, a significant part of it is truly dialectical, a "concrete" negation that embraces utilitarianism's positive contribution while rejecting its limitations.

2.1. THE MULTIDIMENSIONAL APPROACH TO ACTION

The Parsonian emphasis on "action" has often been mistaken for an emphasis on a particular kind of empirical conduct. Sorokin's and Znaniecki's early critiques, for example, completely misunderstand the term's level of generality and the sociological-epistemological debate within which it was defined. Parsons' statement that action has goals was taken by Sorokin as an emphasis on the concrete actor's persistence and consistency; Znaniecki similarly saw it as neglecting variations in the actor's subjective understanding of his goals and intentions.[29] Later commentators, such as Martindale and Pope, misconceived Parsons' "action" emphasis, by contrast, as denoting self-consciousness and individuation.[30] Parsons himself encouraged such misconceptions by particularizing the action concept in his own presentation, by insisting on calling his total theory the "theory of action" and by identifying it with Weber's often nominalistic invocation of the term. Yet Parsons' actual usage is far more generalized. For him, all social theories are theories of action, in that each rests upon an implicit epistemological conception. In what is essentially a paraphrase of Parsons' position, Rex puts the matter well: "The 'hypothetical actor' is a theoretical construction and statements about his motivation [e.g., the epistemological assumption] have empirical implications."[31] Despite the problems in his own self-presentation, Parsons clearly understands the generality of the action question. It was, after all, self-consciousness about general nonempirical issues that led him to make action such an explicit theoretical focus. The misinterpretation is due, then, more to his critics' own errors of "misplaced concreteness." Whether an empirical, concrete action is conscious or unconscious, creative or conformist, accidental or consistent is not Parsons' concern. What he does argue is that all of these actions can be seen as involving a certain kind of sociologic-epistemic orientation.

Parsons' discussion of action, as it occurred first in *The Structure of Social Action* and throughout most of the rest of his work, was designed to traverse the pitfalls and to combine the successes of Durkheim and Weber, and, more indirectly, of Marx. He admired Durkheim's emphasis on norms and religion, but criticized his idealism. He applauded Weber's attempt to combine idealism and materialism, yet rejected the tendency toward rationalism in Weber's analysis of industrial society. As we will see, it is impossible to comprehend Parsons' theoretical development without understanding Durkheim and Weber, and, equally important, Parsons' interpretation of them. As the great poets, according to Harold Bloom, suffer from a hidden anxiety about the influence on them of their most important predecessors, so does Parsons vis-à-vis Durkheim and Weber.[32] As poets "read" their illustrious progenitors in a manner designed, unconsciously, to justify their own imaginative autonomy, so Parsons reads Durkheim and Weber. Radical critics, like Gouldner, have insisted that Marx is Parsons' primary animus. Certainly, Marx's general position forms an omnipresent background and continuous foil for Parsons' thought, though much more in its presuppositional than its ideological sense. Yet it is Durkheim and Weber that constitute Parsons' primary and direct theoretical adversaries. It is through them that he deals with the basic epistemological issues of sociology and against them that he produces his own theoretical presuppositional position.

Despite their great differences in intellectual position, the early Durkheim and Weber were alike in at least one respect. Each began his career by demonstrating, to one degree or another and with more or less ambivalence, the inadequacy of a purely instrumentalist position, particularly as this position was specified in classical economics. Parsons followed much the same path. Beginning in 1928 with the publications from his Heidelberg dissertation and continuing through 1937 with the publication of *The Structure of Social Action*, Parsons produced a series of critiques of the dominant economic writers of the day, American, German, Italian, English. His purpose was to criticize the rationalism of the economic frame of reference, and he accomplished this in a theoretically self-conscious manner. Basically, he demonstrated that the very depth of each theorist's insights forced an acknowledgement of the role of nonrational elements. Yet, as economists, they could so acknowledge these only in a "residual" way. As Parsons explains his critical strategy in the 1937 volume:

> Every system, including both its theoretical propositions and its main relevant empirical insights, may be visualized as an illuminated spot enveloped by darkness. The logical name for the darkness is, in general, "residual categories." Their role may be deduced from the inherent necessity of a system to become logically closed.[33]

Residual categories, then, are empirical elements that theories cannot logically account for. How do residual categories intrude, therefore, into theoretical accounts that strive for consistency?

> If, as is almost always the case, not all the actually observable facts of the field, or those which have been observed, fit into the sharply, positively defined categories, they tend to be given one or more blanket names which refer to categories negatively defined, that is, of facts known to exist, which are even more or less adequately described, but are defined theoretically by their failure to fit into the positively defined categories of the system.[34]

Ironically, it is "in the work of the ablest and most clear-headed proponents of a system," Parsons argues, that "these residual categories will often be not merely implicit but explicit, and will often be quite clearly stated."[35]

In his series of early critical essays, Parsons focused on the tensions that forced these economists' theories to define noneconomic, normative elements as residual categories—Adam Smith's "moral sentiments," Ricardo's "habits and customs of the people," Marshall's "wants adjusted to activities," Veblen's "instinct for workmanship," Sombart's "spirit of capitalism."[36] He concluded that the instrumentalist approach to action was overly narrow, that it placed "an overwhelming stress upon one particular type [of norm], which may be called the 'rational norm of efficiency.' "[37] Parsons did not deny the epistemological relevance of subjective orientation for the economists, but he emphasized that at least in one systematic and self-contained part of their work they adhered to subjectivity only of a particular type.[38†] This conclusion, and the theoretical framework which established it, were the fruits of Parsons' labor in the decade preceding *The Structure of Social Action*.

Parsons might have continued to demonstrate the inadequacy of an instrumental framework, perhaps in a more direct and empirical, less interpretive way. He did not choose this path. Despite his admiration for Durkheim, he did not want to follow the French theorist down the road to what he called the "crucial experiment" style of theorizing.[39] Instead, Parsons chose to construct an explicit analytic framework that would precede any subsequent, more specific analysis. By constructing a self-consciously multidimensional theoretical framework, the residual formulations of the economists could be avoided. To such a purpose he devoted *The Structure of Social Action*.

Though he never stated his ambition quite so baldly, it was possible, Parsons believed, to construct a synthetic approach to action that could avoid the necessity to resort to residual categories of any kind. For him, this challenge involved two different kinds of presuppositional tasks. First, he must isolate the central presuppositional mistakes of the economists' instrumentalist approach, which he had now characterized as the "utilitarian frame of reference." Their error, Parsons believed, involved the assumption that actors resemble scientists, that they approach every goal by the empirically most efficient path.

> The common element in the great majority of attempts to reach intellectually sophisticated formulations of the concept of rationality is the view that action is rational in so far as it may be understood to be guided on the part of the actor by scientific or, at least, scientifically sound knowledge of the circumstances of his situation.[40]

This perception creates a significant problem, particularly because "from the point of view of the actor [according to these theorists], scientifically verifiable knowledge of the situation in which he acts becomes the *only* significant orienting medium."[41] Given the assumption "that there is no alternative selective standard in the choice either of means or ends," action becomes essentially involuntary.[42]

It is precisely here that Parsons finds another drawback to the instrumentalist position, on yet another level of the scientific continuum. We have seen, in the preceding section, that Parsons objects to positivism because it eliminates all nonempirical self-consciousness from social science. He now connects this to a more substantive criticism: positivism provides crucial ammunition for an instrumentalist approach to action. Rarely, we have seen, is an important theorist's methodological commitment irrelevant to his presuppositional position, and Parsons is no exception. The utilitarians, he argues, were not only rationalists but positivists as well.

Having identified this double error, Parsons conflates the methodological and presuppositional levels of the utilitarian position. "Positivism" and "rationalism" become interchangeable; throughout *The Structure of Social Action*, Parsons refers to positivism as if this methodological position necessarily implied presuppositional rationalism, and vice versa. This confusion, though leaving Parsons' own presuppositional discussion basically unscathed, has seriously hindered a number of subsequent interpretive analyses.[43†]

Parsons, then, like Durkheim and Weber before him, intends to avoid establishing scientifically guided instrumental efficiency as the exclusive normative orientation of action. Throughout *The Structure of Social Action*, he criticizes such a position, particularly by emphasizing the autonomy of the religious variable in the analyses of Pareto, Durkheim, and Weber. Yet Parsons will not make Durkheim's mistake and simply turn utilitarianism on its head. Any satisfactory approach to action must avoid idealism, and this is the second great task that he sets for his synthetic attempt. His intention to distance himself between the two extremes is clear. In exclusively rational action, he writes, "causal relations" concern only the "role of conditions and means." In the idealist tradition, however, there are only "meaningful relations." Elements of meaning still "condition action in one sense, but not in the same sense. Their role is normative."

> Just as positivism eliminates the creative, voluntaristic character of action by dispensing with the analytical significance of values, and the other normative elements by making them epiphenomena, so idealism has the same effect for the opposite reason—idealism eliminates the reality of the obstacles to the realization of values. The set of *ideas* comes to be identified with the concrete reality.[44]

Durkheim made just such an error, for he "is found explicitly stating that society exists only in the minds of individuals."[45] In contrast to this, the normative, or value referents of action must not be the exclusive focus of theoretical attention.

> The effect of this tendency of Durkheim's thought is to regard the aim of sociology as that of studying the systems of value ideas *in themselves,* whereas the position put forward [here] . . . calls for a quite different study, that of these systems *in their relations to action.*[46]

Parsons intends, therefore, to combine ideal and material referents. "Action must always be thought of," he argues, "as involving a state of tension between two different orders of elements, the normative and the conditional."[47] Yet the task of making this combination is not an easy one, as we have seen from the difficulties with which Marx, Durkheim, and Weber struggled to translate epistemic multidimensionality into sociological form. Weber, of course, was the more successful. Why will Parsons succeed where Weber failed? Parsons' answer to this presuppositional question is based, once again, on the advantages of his meta-methodological understanding of science. Parsons rejected Weber's ideal-type approach, we saw earlier, because of its implied relativity; we now see that there were other reasons for this rejection. Parsons believes that the "type" conceptualization led Weber to an overly instrumentalist perspective on action. Parsons connects his methodological critique to Weber's presuppositional position. Weber's "hypostatization of ideal types," Parsons writes, "breaks up . . . the organic unity . . . of concrete historical individuals." It creates "a 'mosaic' theory of culture and society, conceiving them to be made of disparate atoms." When applied to Weber's "use of the rational norm," such "reification" is "the source of . . . his objectionable 'rationalism' and of the iron-bound character of the process of rationalization that is such a prominent feature of his empirical work."[48]

Ten years later, in his extended Introduction to his co-translation of Weber's *Theory of Social and Economic Organization*, Parsons makes this connection more specific. He complains that Weber's division of social action into the ideal types of *Zweck* (or instrumental) and *Wert* (or value) rationality creates the appearance that a given empirical action can be completely instrumental: "The use of the ideal type concentrates attention on extreme or polar types . . . [and] minimizes the elements which link the type in question with other elements of the structure of the same system."[49] In other words, by trying in an overly empiricist manner to relate his concepts directly to individual action, Weber's definitions do not "give an adequate description of any concrete act." In the ideal-typical framework, *zweckrational* actions are not considered to have normative, or value, elements. The result is that "elements which may well in some instances be integrated with the rational elements in a system [e.g., value elements], are pushed into conflict with it."[50†] Parsons illustrates this problem with reference to Weber's discussion of bureaucratic rationality. Weber's definition of bureaucratic administration, that it is "essentially control by means of knowledge," implicitly recognizes, Parsons believes, a mixture of voluntary and coercive authority. Yet Weber, because he was committed to conceptualizing bureaucracy as a concrete entity rather than as an embodiment of different analytic elements, chose to define bureaucracy simply as coercive authority. In doing so, Weber "has thrown together two essentially different types which, though often shading into each other, are analytically separate," and has "overemphasize[d] the coercive aspect of authority and hierarchy in human relations."[51]

Contrary to Weber, Parsons holds that there is no "rational" or "nonrational" action as such: "a 'purely rational' act or system is a contradiction in terms—it is not 'objectively possible.' "[52] Rather, the concepts *rational* and *nonrational* should apply to elements of any action, not to different actions themselves. With such an analytic rather than concrete approach to the problem of action, Parsons moves beyond the dichotomization of instrumental and normative which plagued significant parts of Weber's work, and expands upon the relatively unconscious "analytic synthesis" that characterized Weber's theorizing at its best. For Parsons, value elements will always impinge on action's condition-determined efficiency; and, vice versa, pressures toward efficiency will always condition other normative considerations.[53†]

By thus approaching the central presuppositional questions in an analytic rather than concrete way, Parsons can carry the understanding of action not only beyond Durkheim's idealism but beyond Weber's own synthetic attempts. It is this analytic-presuppositional emphasis, not an emphasis on individualism or idealism, that distinguishes Parsons' famous analysis in *The Structure of Social Action* of the "unit act." Every action, Parsons asserts, involves subjective ends. It is the actor's effort to achieve his ends, or goals, in the face of his situational environment that constitutes the voluntaristic element of action. As a result of this voluntary effort, the situation may be viewed as involving two different kinds of elements, means and conditions. The latter refers to the material elements which are out of the actor's control, and, therefore, coercive. The former identify the material elements which the actor can control. Finally, between means and ends there are norms, subjective elements that regulate the actor's effort toward conditions.[54†] Within this frame of reference, Parsons need not choose between instrumental or normative connections. On the one hand:

> The means employed cannot, in general, be conceived as . . . dependent exclusively on the conditions of action, but must in some sense be subject to the influence of an independent determinate selective factor. . . . What is essential to the concept of action is that there should be a normative orientation.[55]

On the other hand, Parsons points to the distance between normatively induced effort and the realistic possibility of individual achievement. To measure this distance, he holds that analysis must focus on the material elements of the situation.

> As so far defined, an end is a concrete anticipated future state of affairs. But it is quite clear that not this total state of affairs but only certain aspects or features of it can be attributed to normative elements, thus to the agency of the actor rather than to features of the situation in which he acts.[56]

In important respects, therefore, *The Structure of Social Action* provides a clear and firm presuppositional foundation for a multidimensional approach to action.

> Action must always be thought of as involving a state of tension between two different orders of elements, the normative and the conditional. . . . Elimination of the normative aspect altogether eliminates the concept of action itself and leads to the radical positivist position [i.e., to sociological materialism]. Elimination of conditions, of tension from that side, equally eliminates action and results in idealistic emanationism. Thus conditions may be conceived at one pole, ends and normative rules at the other.[57]

What remains for Parsons is to combine this approach to action with an approach to order, to discuss how unit acts become aggregated to form societies.

2.2. THE MULTIDIMENSIONAL APPROACH TO COLLECTIVE ORDER

Critics have usually misunderstood Parsons' interest in the problem of order. His treatment of order has been linked to his decision to assert equilibrium, to a conservative interest in the status quo, to an antivoluntarist bias, and to an idealist orientation.[58†] While the first two of these charges are simply conflationary—attempting to reduce presuppositional issues to empirical and ideological questions—the latter two involve fundamental distortions on the most generalized level. As such, these last two issues will occupy a good deal of our attention for the remainder of this chapter.

To begin with a revealing paradox: those who argue most strongly that the main thrust of Parsons' order theory is anti-voluntary often at the same time exempt his early work from this criticism. The stated grounds for this exemption is that Parsons' early focus on the "unit act" constituted an individualistic approach to social order.[59] I will dispute the specifics of this claim shortly, but let us first recall some general, contextual points. It has been my contention throughout these volumes that recognition of the uniqueness of the individual and the existence of free will does not preclude simultaneous emphasis on the collective nature of social order. In a typical empirical situation the supra-individual context of any action is decisive for the social arrangements of which such action is a part. Considered from the perspective of a single actor, therefore, collective order as such is not a matter of negotiation at any given point. For these reasons, the dispute over the "individual" versus "society" should actually be considered an argument over levels of preferred analytic attention. There is no inconsistency in focusing, for a given scientific purpose, on the process of individual negotiation and choice while acknowledging, at the same time, the collective network within which such choices must be made. This is, for example, clearly the position of Weber, who despite his frequent focus on the individual is not the nominalist that many have taken him for. It is also, I will argue, Parsons' own position in his early writings.

In *The Structure of Social Action*, Parsons' focus on the unit act does not imply an individualistic approach to order. Rather, as indicated in the preceding section, this focus provides a simplified and clear-cut format for talking about the problem of action, for differentiating action's normative and instrumental components. The unit act, in other words, is an abstraction, an "analytic" exercise. In the conclusion of *The Structure of Social Action*, Parsons remarks prophetically that "it will be asked whether breaking up concrete phenomenon into parts or units . . . is a process of abstraction at all." Against this possibility, he hastens to assure his readers that "the answer is that it is precisely so in so far as the phenomenon in question is organic [i.e., collective]," and "is preeminently true of systems of action as they have been treated in this study." On these grounds, he concludes that the "isolation of the unit act" has been a "conceptual" one, "a process of abstraction."[60] It has indicated neither the isolation of the concrete individual, nor presented an individualistic approach to order.

Once again, as in his analysis of action, Parsons links this presuppositional position to a nonpositivist approach to science. If the theorist views the individual as a "concrete unit" rather than as an "analytic one," the presuppositional position would, he believes, inevitably be biased towards an individualistic perspective on order: "By assuming that a concrete system as a whole is made up only of units of this character we get the picture . . . that the concrete action systems being studied are *simply* aggregates of such . . . unit acts."[61] This is the great danger in the empiricist approach to the individual. "If the conceptual scheme is not consciously 'abstract' but is held to be literally descriptive of concrete reality," this must result in a "failure to state anything positive about the relation of [individual] ends to each other." The implication would necessarily be "that there *are* no significant relations, that is, that ends are random in the statistical sense."[62]

The Structure of Social Action, in fact, is a polemic against such an individualistic assumption of random ends. Its true subject is the "emergent properties" that Parsons believes to be inevitably involved in any individual interaction. While "it is true," he acknowledges, "that in the last analysis all . . . systems are 'composed' of unit acts," such a last-instance argument is as fallacious in this case as in every other.

> It does not mean that the relation of the unit act to the total system is analogous to that of a grain of sand to the heap of which it is a part. . . . Action systems have properties that are emergent only on a certain level of complexity in the relations of unit acts to each other. These properties cannot be identified in any single unit act considered apart from its relation to others in the same system.[63]

Individualistic approaches, then, are empirically unable to clarify the true causal relationships of social life.

> Limiting observation of the concrete phenomenon . . . to the properties that have a place in the unit act . . . leads to indeterminacy in the theory when empirically applied to complex systems. This indeterminacy, a form of empirical inadequacy, is the fundamental difficulty of atomistic theories.[64]

Atomistic theories ignore the supra-individual aspects of order, the arrangement of individuals into patterns on some basis other than individual negotiation. Only a more collectivist theory can correct this "empirical" error. It is by such a process of reasoning that Parsons arrives at his famous and controversial focus on the problem of order.[65†] Clearly, it is the problem of "the randomness of ends" with which he is concerned,[66] not, in the first place, with problems of ideology, empirical harmony, or idealist versus materialist orientations.

Parsons' polemical target is the same as that of Marx, Durkheim, and Weber: individualistic theory. And his concern throughout *The Structure of Social Action* is with what the nature of a collective order shall be. Once again, his primary focus is utilitarian theory, particularly classical economics, which he describes as "the theoretical action system characterized by these four features, atomism, rationality, empiricism, and randomness of ends."[67] There exist, Parsons believes, two possible collectivist emphases, "normative order" and "factual order." While he endorses each approach for its ability to transcend individualism, he argues —at least in one important strand of his work—that each is inadequate when considered in isolation from the other.

Parsons describes the factual order as implying a "set of uniformities," the "uniformity of behavior of things."[68] Above all, it is "the antithesis of . . . randomness or chaos."[69] Why call this approach to collective order "factual"? Because it refers to the order established by the instrumental calculation of action's external conditions. It is, in Parsons' words, a form of "natural determinism,"[70] one that assumes the actor has access to his situation only through proto-scientific rationality: "Factual order . . . connotes essentially accessibility to understanding in terms of logical theory, especially of science."[71†] Within utilitarianism, the most common, if implicit, example of such factual order is the emphasis on the economic "power" of the market.[72]

In part 1 of *The Structure of Social Action*, Parsons describes how theorists of the rationalist tradition broke through the individualism of classical economics and emphasized, explicitly, the force of collective factual order. Following Elie Halévy, from whose "artificial identity of interest" he derives the notion of factual order, Parsons describes Hobbes as the great precursor of this factually-oriented tradition.[73†] "Hobbes saw the problem [of order] with a clarity which has never been surpassed," Parsons writes, "and his statement of it remains valid today."[74] Hobbes realized that a "purely utilitarian society [i.e., a rationalist and individualist one] is chaotic and unstable, because . . . [of] the absence of the [normative] limitations on the use of means."[75] For this reason, in Hobbes' theory "the concept of power comes to occupy a central position in the problem of order,"[76] and Hobbes was forced to accept the necessity of the Leviathan.[77] It was in this Hobbesian, collectivist tradition that later theorists criticized the individualistic assumptions of classical economists. Ricardo, for example, recognized and incorporated supra-individual disparities of wealth as market disturbing mechanisms.[78] Malthus' critique was more direct. Purely individualistic economic competition, he argued, must always be limited by population growth, a feature of the collective order. Moreover, the latter would prove disastrous unless regulated "within the proper *institutional* framework," consisting of such collective forces as marriage, property distribution, and moral restraint.[79†] Marx took this emphasis even further. "The permanent importance of the Marxian exploitation theory," Parsons writes, lies "in the fact that, starting as Marx did from the element of class conflict, the center of his attention was on [collective] bargaining power. Thus in a particular case he reintroduced the factor of differences of power into social thinking that had been so important in Hobbes' philosophy."[80†]

Although Parsons' focus on instrumental collectivist, or factual, order becomes less central in the remainder of *The Structure of Social Action*, for a variety of significant reasons which I will discuss later, its importance is by no means forgotten. In part 2, Parsons praises Pareto, for example, for his emphasis on the role of force and fraud in human relations. "Force and fraud," he writes approvingly, are basic "means of getting something done," means that are peculiarly instrumental: "They are means which, whatever their differences, have one important factor in common—the absence of certain limitations on the choice of significant means imposed by ethical considerations."[81] The role and significance of such factors, Parsons concludes, has, quite wrongly, "been very seriously minimized by the 'liberal' [i.e., individualistic] theories."[82]

The same emphasis appears in Parsons' discussion of Weber. He praises Weber for seeing through the individualist fallacy of classical economics, warning that "the logical simplicity of a system of economic theory that excludes coercion should not be allowed to obscure the enormous importance of coercion in actual economic life." Weber, he believes, "is not subject to this criticism. He had a deep, almost tragic, consciousness of the importance of coercion in human affairs."[83] Parsons points to Weber's discussions of capitalist bureaucracy, technology, and class relations as examples of his emphasis on collective instrumental order.[84] He argues, moreover, that Weber's sociology of religion was "never meant to establish that other than religious elements have not to a highly important degree been involved in the . . . development of a religious ethic itself."[85] In fact, Parsons views his own secondary analysis of Weber's writings on religion as an attempt to set forth typical examples of the different ways in which Weber "held [such] nonreligious elements to be involved."[86]

Parsons' discussion of instrumental collective order, then, succeeds in going beyond the "empirical inadequacy" of individualist theory. Particularly in his critique of classical economics, his analysis parallels in important respects the one presented by Marx nearly a century before.[87†] This kind of instrumental collective order is, indeed, a necessary presupposition of any social theory. It is not, however, sufficient, and must not, Parsons believes, become the exclusive focus of a one-dimensional analysis. To the degree it becomes so, "factual order" solves the randomness problem at the expense of voluntarism, for it envisions only an "efficient" relation between means and ends. Such indeed has been the case with the rationalist tradition of collectivist thought. "On positivist [i.e., rationalist] grounds," Parsons argues, "there was only one possible way of escaping . . . [the] unsatisfactory limitation [of individualistic theory]": [88]

> If ends were not random, it was because it must be possible for the actor to base his choice of ends on scientific knowledge of some empirical reality. But this tenet has the inevitable logical consequence of assimilating ends to the situation of action and destroying their analytical independence.[89]

By so undermining the analytic autonomy of the subjective element, the multidimensional aspect of order is lost.

> The action becomes determined entirely by its conditions, for without the independence of ends the distinction between conditions and means becomes meaningless. Action becomes a process of rational adaptation to these conditions.[90]

This is Parsons' famous "utilitarian dilemma": in rationalist theory "either the active agency of the actor in the choice of ends is an independent factor in action, and the element must be random," or, on the other hand, "the objectionable implication of the randomness of ends is denied, but their independence disappears and they are assimilated to the conditions of action, that is to elements analyzable in terms of nonsubjective categories."[91]

In articulating this dilemma for the first time, Parsons achieved a significant breakthrough in the history of social thought, making conscious and explicit the logic that has informed theoretical strategy since the origins of social thought in ancient times.[92†] Far from attempting to legitimate idealism, a common critical charge, this argument attempts to preserve a "conditioned" voluntarism. The principal contribution of Parsons' argument consists in the crucial translation of conventional epistemological categories into a sociological frame of reference. Although Parsons himself never puts the issue with this kind of clarity, it is clear that what he is demonstrating is that the critical problem for social theory is not whether multidimensionality is articulated epistemologically, but, rather, how this framework becomes utilized in social explanation. Such utilization depends on two points: first, on the content of the normative element; second, on whether actions are linked collectively or individually. What creates "sociological materialism," Parsons implicitly understood, is not the elimination of norms in *fact,* but rather their elimination in *effect,* through their instrumentalization. He realized, further, that this consequence was not visible in individualistic rationalism, which could still appear to be voluntary; it became visible only in collectivist rationalism.

Instrumentalist thinking, then, moves back and forth between two poles. In the attempt to address the randomness problem, it moves in the collectivist direction. Yet, "Hobbes' solution," that of exclusive factual order, negates freedom. It is the insight into this danger that pushes instrumentalist theory back in the individualist direction, with all the latter's inherent inability to address the collective aspects of order. This vicious circle can be broken, but only by ensuring the independent status of the normative aspects of collective order, by defining some of action's normative constraints in a noninstrumental fashion.

To indicate how this might be done is Parsons' principal project in the latter sections of his first book. As in his critique of the instrumentalist approach to action, Parsons combines analytic argument with a kind of ersatz history, describing how normative elements gradually moved from their residual status in utilitarian theory to a more positively defined position in post-utilitarian thought. Early in the work, he demonstrates that Locke's contract theory, unlike that of Hobbes, had succeeded in maintaining voluntarism because it contained the hidden, anti-instrumentalist assumption of human "reason." And what does Locke's natural reason mean?

> Essentially that men "being reasonable" ought to, and in general will in pursuit of their ends subordinate their actions, whatever these may be, to certain rules. The essential content of these rules is to respect the natural rights of others, to refrain from injuring them. *This means that the choice of means in pursuit of ends is not guided solely by considerations of immediate rational efficiency.*[93]

Locke's theory, in other words, contains a "normative component not indigenous to the utilitarian system," and it is this that allows for "the stability of Locke's particular type of individualistic society."[94] Ostensibly, Locke's theory "minimized the importance of the problem of order"; implicitly, however, it did address the order problem by compromising its commitment to rationalism. In this, Locke's work became the basis for the essentially fallacious theoretical logic of classical economics, an orientation which, Parsons writes, "for two hundred years evaded the Hobbesian problem [of collective order]."[95]

Marshall and Pareto emerge in Parsons' discussion as the eventual critics of such Lockean residual categories as natural reason. Though Marshall's "activities" represented a positive acknowledgment of the noninstrumental elements of action, he remained fully within an economic framework.[96] Pareto went beyond this with his clear-cut articulation of residues, derivations, and sentiments. Still, even he did not develop an adequate analysis of the internal differentiation of the normative order, one which in any real sense could balance his powerful, multicausal analysis of market rationality.[97]

Only Durkheim and Weber, Parsons believed, thoroughly transformed the rationalist position, incorporating normative elements fully into their theories. In his view, Durkheim's early use of the *conscience collective* "reraise[d] in a peculiarly trenchant form the whole Hobbesian problem."[98] For Durkheim, Parsons writes, social order "concerns not only the conditions under which men act in pursuit of their ends but enters into the formulation of the ends themselves."[99] Weber also brings "the ultimate-value element" directly into the heart of his theory, into his institutional analysis by the notion of legitimate political order, into his religion analysis through his theory of charisma.[100]

By now, the multidimensional intention of Parsons' approach to collective order should be clear. Much like Weber and Durkheim before him, in his earliest essays Parsons started with critiques of instrumentalist theory and, from this base, advanced basically ad hoc arguments for the relative autonomy of normative order. With the publication of *The Structure of Social Action*, however, Parsons went beyond the generalized analyses of either Durkheim or Weber by developing a more sophisticated, analytically explicit understanding of the presuppositions of sociological analysis. With this framework he successfully clarified important elements in both theorists' work, evaluating their strengths and weaknesses according to the standard of collective order and multidimensionality. It is true that Parsons labels his synthetic alternative a "voluntaristic theory," yet he does so, at least in part, to preserve an element of subjective voluntarism, not to claim that action is exclusively voluntary. The key word in the following statement is "exhaust."

> As opposed to all types of positivistic [i.e., rationalistic] theory the basic tenet of the voluntaristic is that neither positively nor negatively does the methodological schema of scientifically valid knowledge *exhaust* the significant subjective elements of action.[101]

Parsons' point is that "insofar as subjective elements fail to fit as elements of valid knowledge," insofar, that is, as norms are not simply instrumental, "the matter is not *exhausted* by the . . . dependence of these elements on those capable of formulation in nonsubjective terms."[102] "The voluntaristic system," Parsons concludes, "does not in the least deny an important role to conditional [factors] . . . but considers them as interdependent with the normative."[103] On these grounds, the idealist approach is unequivocally rejected, for in it "the role of the conditional element disappears, as correspondingly at the positivist [i.e., instrumentalist] pole that of the normative disappears."[104]

3. LATER REFINEMENTS OF MULTIDIMENSIONAL ORDER

Despite this early abstract understanding of multidimensionality and despite this accurate insight into the specific elements in Weber's and Durkheim's work that reflected such an order, Parsons' theoretical vision in his first great work was decisively limited. His analysis of order never reached anything like the clarity that he had achieved in his analysis of action. For action, he articulated the sociological epistemology of the unit act, a fundamental formulation that quickly attained classical status in modern theoretical discussion. For order, however, Parsons could go no further than to talk about "webs of means-ends chains" as constituting normative and factual force.[105] The asymmetrical development accurately reflected, perhaps, the greater intellectual sophistication in the 1930s period of individualistic modes of thought. But for whatever reason, it would take Parsons fifteen years to move substantially beyond this position and about three decades to present a formulation of multidimensional order approaching the sophistication of his unit act analysis. Although my discussion has been largely chronological, and in the main will continue to be so, my concern is primarily an analytical, not a historical one. Parsons' articulation of the order presupposition proceeded over a number of years; the ensuing analysis concerns these later refinements.

3.1. GENERALIZATION-SPECIFICATION

The most presuppositionally oriented publication of Parsons' middle period was the long essay written with Edward Shils, "Values, Motives, and Systems of Action," which formed the theoretical centerpiece for the interdisciplinary *Towards a General Theory of Action.* Parsons and Shils return here to Parsons' earlier concern with the order problem. Although they utilize a new "systems" language, the focus remains on the issue of random versus patterned action.

> The most general and fundamental property of a system is the interdependence of parts or variables. Interdependence consists in the existence of *determinate* relationships among the parts or variables as contrasted with *randomness* of variability. In other words, interdependence is *order* in the relationship among the components which enter into a system.[106]

They go beyond Parsons' earlier analysis, however, in clarifying the link between order's factual and normative strands. In regard to the latter, they return to Durkheim's "symbolic" solution to the Hobbesian problem, which we might briefly recall here. While Durkheim's concern was to transcend individualism, he wanted to do so on a subjective basis, for it was *conscience* that held significance for him, not material wealth as such. "Individual consciences are closed to each other," he writes; "they can communicate only by means of signs which express their internal states." The key to transcending individualism, then, is the symbol. "If the communication [is to be] established between them . . . the signs expressing them must be fused into one single and unique resultant."[107]

Following this lead, and combining with it the subsequent work of symbolic theorists such as Charles Morris—himself a follower of George

Herbert Mead—Parsons and Shils introduce the term "generalization" to emphasize how symbolic order is directed against the notion of discrete individuals: "Communication through a common symbol system . . . presupposes generalization from the particularity of the given situation of ego and alter, both of which are continually changing and are never concretely identical over any two moments in time." Symbolic generalization, in other words, creates categories rendering individual orientations comparable which, if viewed concretely, would appear to be simply divergent and would, therefore, indicate randomness. Normatively, this randomness is negated by some thread of common meaning.

> When such generalization occurs, and actions, gestures, or symbols have *more or less the same meaning* for both ego and alter, we may speak of a common culture existing between them, through which their interaction is mediated.[108]

"A 'way of orienting,' " they add later, will "be systematic and not a random occurrence if the various persons within whom the way of orienting occurs are controlled by the same . . . symbol system." If this occurs, "symbolization allows 'interpersonalized' generalization."[109]

The central polemic point, once again, is against randomness. Interpersonal connections are stressed rather than purely personal ones; a notion of interpersonal generality is substituted for one of discrete persona. By definition, symbolism overcomes individualism. Yet there is something more. Symbols tend inherently to be organized in patterns. As Parsons later writes:

> The "conventions" of the symbolic system must be observed if there is to be effective communication, just as in the case of language. It is not possible by *arbitrary whim* to give an expressive act "any old meaning" and still be understood.[110]

Symbolic "conventions" represent the collective arrangements, the order, of the normative sphere. This presuppositional message is forcefully articulated in Parsons' essay on culture in *Theories of Society*, a decade later.

> Orientations to objects are conceived as *structured* or, in the term commonly used in the cultural context, "patterned." In other words, there are elements of "consistency," "order," or "coherence"—between orientations to different *discrete* objects and classes of objects.[111]

Cultural interpenetration, then, has nothing to do with social integration in the sense of social harmony or cooperation.[112†] It concerns problems of meaning, not institutional arrangements. In creating this distinction, Parsons and Shils have begun to articulate the link between normative and factual order. To clarify this presuppositional point, they emphasize the analytic/concrete distinction of Parsons' earlier meta-methodological discussions. The elements of generality and interpersonal identity, they argue, are an analytic dimension of every concrete relationship. As such, these "cultural" components must be differentiated from the more directly "social" dimensions of order, which represent other analytic elements. It is this notion that Parsons and Shils are trying to articulate when they write, somewhat elusively, that "symbols which are the postulated controlling entities . . . are not internal to the system whose orientations they control."[113] Parsons later makes this analytic differentiation more forcefully. "The *generalization* of meaning," he writes, "emancipates a symbol from being bound to the particularities of context."[114] Social context and cultural meaning must be conceptually distinct.

> A symbol must be an object with sufficiently *generalized* meaning so that [it] can fit into . . . patterns of great diversity and do so in such a way that the . . . symbols are not dependent for their meaning on *particularities* of the context of use.[115]

Or, in the same essay:

> The structure of cultural meanings constitutes the "ground" of any system of action, as distinguished from the set of situational conditions to which its functioning is subject.[116]

Parsons wants to emphasize, in other words, that collective orders are not simply dichotomous, do not merely occur "side by side." Normative order is "generalized," and the factual order of situational conditions "specifies" these general meanings in accordance with the functional exigencies of social scarcity. This new conceptualization is a powerful one, far more suggestive than the approaches Parsons made in *The Structure of Social Action*. It continues to inform Parsons' work throughout the remainder of his career. Nevertheless, it still does not resolve the presuppositional problem of order with the neatness and theoretical simplicity that Parsons achieved in his earlier analysis of action.

3.2 THE CYBERNETIC CONTINUUM

Parsons finally achieved this sophistication only with his formulation, in the 1960s, of the "cybernetic hierarchy." This part of his work has also been widely misinterpreted—as merely attempting a technical analogy and convergence with information theory, or as simply providing a new shape for his purported commitment to idealism. But Parsons' use of cybernetic theory is not necessarily either of these. For its most important meaning, we must look, once again, to the presuppositional problems that preoccupied Parsons throughout his career.

Figure 2

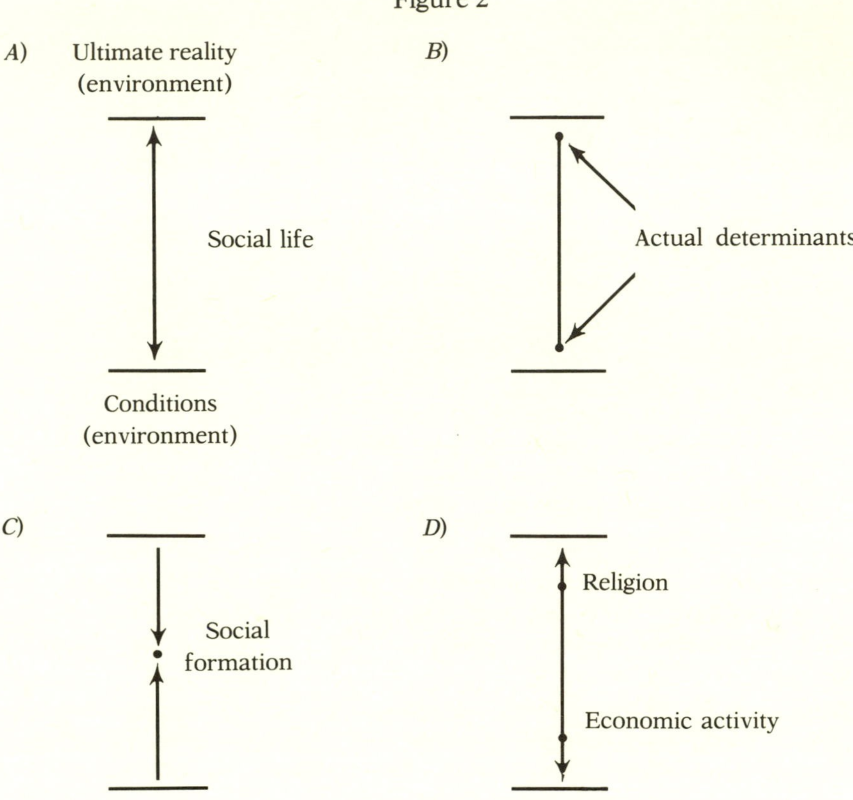

A)
Ultimate reality
(environment)
Social life
Conditions
(environment)
B)
Actual determinants
C)
Social
formation
D)
Religion
Economic activity

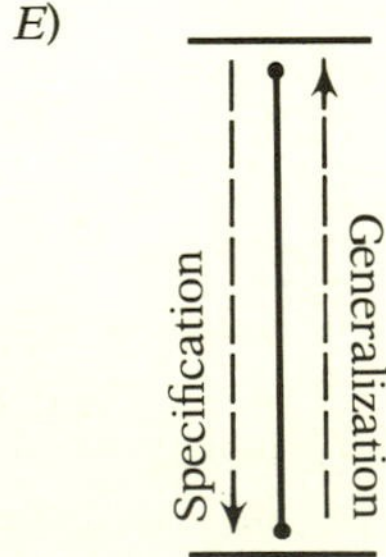

E)
Specification
Generalization

Parsons now defines the symbolic and conditional orders of his earlier discussion as the two cybernetic "environments" of action.

> The two environments within which action systems function [are] the physical-organic environment, relations with which are mediated in the first instance through the behavioral organism, and the environment we have called "ultimate reality," relations with which are mediated through the constitutive symbol systems . . . of the cultural system.[117]

Every concrete action is oriented to both environments, and a necessary but not sufficient logic holds. (See fig. 2, *A*.) On the one hand, orientation to the subjective environment of ultimate reality can never be "adequately legitimized by necessities imposed at lower levels of the hierarchy of control—e.g., that things *must* be done in a specific way because the stability or even survival of the system is at stake."[118] On the other hand, orientation to the material, conditional environment is necessary because "in so far as physical factors are not controllable we must adapt to them or human life will disappear."[119]

Although this cybernetic language of "levels of control" offers a potential for misuse, it does not necessarily imply any causal priority. Organically related conditions are "lower" only in the sense that they are closer to nature, farther from the "higher" qualities of spiritual life.[120†] Similarly, factors related to ultimate reality are "controlling" rather than conditional only in terms of the manner in which they influence action, not in terms of their greater causal impact. Since normative factors affect action through changing motivation, they depend on strategic "information" rather than on "energy" for their collective force. On the other side, since factors relating more to the organic environment affect action by establishing external conditions, they depend more on energy than on information.[121]

In terms of providing analytic refinement of his earlier efforts, the crucial point Parsons makes is that the cybernetic hierarchy is a continuum. Again, Parsons returns to his connection between meta-methodological and presuppositional considerations. Although a concrete causal factor may look as if it is simply a conditional or symbolic force, it is analytically neither one alone. To indicate this, Parsons makes the crucial distinction between action's environment and its determinant. While ultimate reality and the physical-organic world "are the environments of action," Parsons asserts that, in fact, they are environments "standing above and below the . . . factors that *control* action in the world of life."[122†] If either environment were an actual controlling or determinate factor, order could be caused by one or the other alone. Instead, the determinants that actually control action are conceptualized as touching neither environmental pole. They are located on a continuum that stretches between the poles but includes neither (see fig. 2, *B*). This distinction is the key to Parsons' definition of the actual end-points of the causal continuum. The human organism must be distinguished from the "physical-organic environment," a term that applies to the entirety of the natural world.

> Below action in the hierarchy stands the physical-organic world. . . . As humans, we know the physical world *only* through the organism. Our minds have no direct experience of an external physical object unless we perceive it through physical processes and the brain 'processes' information about it.[123]

"Similar considerations apply," Parsons adds, "to the environment above action—the 'ultimate reality' with which we are ultimately concerned in grappling with what Weber called the 'problems of meaning.' " The prototypically symbolic factor of control, namely "ideas," must be distinguished from the ideal environment itself: " 'Ideas' in this area, as cultural objects, are in some sense symbolic 'representations' . . . of the ultimate realities, but are not themselves such realities."[124] Because neither pole actually determines action, every point on the cybernetic continuum must be some combination of both symbolic and instrumental orders.

Each social formation, then, represents, in presuppositional terms, a compromise formation (see fig. 2, *C*). Our common-sense designation of instrumental and normative order is a terminological convenience which does not, strictly speaking, describe concrete reality. It represents, rather, an evaluation of relative position on the continuum, one which remains, nonetheless, multidimensional. Thus, for example, economic and religious systems remain multidimensional combinations of differentiated social forces despite their usual status as the ideal-typical material and ideal forces (see fig. 2, *D*). By separating environment and determinant, Parsons demonstrates that it is proximity to a pole, not identification with it, that produces such social-scientific designations of material and ideal orders.

This cybernetic formulation clearly articulates with Parsons' generalization-specification language. Parsons argued earlier that the element of generalization, or symbolization, is not the only relation of institutions or actors to one another. In every instance, this element is, in addition, specified by conditional pressures. Generalization, in other words, refers to a "direction" on the cybernetic continuum, to the movement that flows from conditions toward ultimate reality. Correspondingly, specification refers to the opposite movement, from ultimate reality toward conditions (see fig. 2, *E*).

3.3. BEYOND THE CLASSICS

With these conceptualizations, Parsons finally articulated the problem of order with the same power and elegance that characterizes his discussion of the unit act. Like that earlier schema, the cybernetic formulation and the logic of generalization-specification are presuppositional in their intention. They do not refer to causation in any particular historical context. They certainly do not argue that the influences of both environments are "equal" in any concrete sense. To the contrary, as extremely generalized arguments their purpose is to complete the translation into sociologically relevant categories of a certain epistemologic position. In this Parsons has succeeded where the other classical theorists, who also accepted a multidimensional epistemological position, usually failed.

Neither Durkheim nor Weber, from whom Parsons draws in both these formulations, was able to produce this kind of multidimensional framework. In *The Elementary Forms of Religious Life*, for example, Durkheim saw that the religious or sacred properties of objects were not determined by their intrinsic properties but by the manner in which they were symbolized. Despite this insight, however, Durkheim remained committed to a concrete approach to the division between material and ideal elements. Some types of objects were sacred, others profane. Economic activity was usually not religious; to the contrary, it sapped the normative fiber in a manner that could be countered only by reimmersion in ritual life.[125†] More broadly speaking, of course, Durkheim's sociological idealism eliminated the possibility for synthesis at any level of conceptual sophistication. Weber, as we have seen, came closer to this synthesis. In important elements of his work, particularly in his discussions of class ethics, religious development, and urban politics, he presented empirically the kind of analytic synthesis that Parsons has outlined. Yet in other, equally significant parts of his work, Weber suffered from the ambiguity that I have called "dichotomization" and that Parsons himself related to Weber's methodological error of ideal-typing.[126†] In this strand of his work, Weber handled economic and religious action as concrete and independent factors, throwing them together in a "laundry list" style without attempting to conceptualize their actual interrelation. His sociological materialism, of course, only exacerbated this tendency.

Marx's theory suffered from similar problems. In fact, the cybernetic schema not only overcomes difficulties we discovered in Marx's own work but also helps to resolve one of the thorniest contradictions in the Marxist interpretive literature. Marx viewed man in capitalist society as primarily engaged with one environment, that of nature. On this basis, Engels, in his *Anti-Dühring*, interpreted Marxism as a "dialectic of nature" which included theories of the physical sciences. This position has recently been challenged by those who contend that Marx's position is not as deterministic as such a direct relationship to nature would imply, that Marx's notion of epistemological praxis demands the inclusion of a voluntary, subjective element, of the "human" as well as the natural world. These critics point out that for Marx the relationship between human beings and the natural environment is never direct, but always mediated by some humanly constructed institution. Thus, although Marx emphasizes the determinacy of economics, this is a "social" not a natural cause.[127†] In Parsons' terminology, this interpretation argues that Marx recognized the separation of determinant and environment. This major debate within Marxism, in other words, is precisely over the status of nature as environment or determinant. Engels and the generation influenced by him were not as sensitive to this distinction as recent Marxist interpreters.

The problem remains, however, that Marx does continually "naturalize" his determinism, portraying action "as if" it were directly determined by the conditional environment.[128†] This is because he failed to postulate, at the other end of his implicit cybernetic continuum, a correspondingly independent position for ultimate, symbolic reality. If this does not exist, action is defined in a purely instrumental manner and causation is, in effect, reduced to its purely conditional form. For this reason, Marx never explicitly drew the distinction between nature-as-determinant and nature-as-environment. Engels' problem, then, is an understandable one, for Marx did not successfully translate his multidimensional epistemology into sociological form. For the problem of collective order, Parsons' cybernetic schema clearly articulates the criteria that any such attempt must meet.

This issue leads us to a final consideration. A common criticism of Parsons by the behaviorist and materialist schools is that his synthetic effort is dualistic, that it posits an ideal realm completely separate from and irreconcilable with the realm of material conditions. This charge is made against Parsons' early works, for example, by Scott.[129] It is also made against the later theory, as when Heydebrand describes the cybernetic continuum as postulating a "non-dialectical," "eternal order" of ideas.[130] Such critics counterpose this supposed idealism to some form of naturalism. It is now clear that this charge ignores one of the principal building blocks of Parsons' entire theoretical effort. Dualism is exactly what Parsons has sought to avoid—by arguing that determinant and environment are separated, and that material elements effect action through the "specification" of symbolic generalization rather than through some mechanized overlay of "coercive force."[131†]

Parsons has produced a dialectical, not a dichotomous, position, one that may be viewed as building upon and going beyond the work of Weber and the early Marx. Ideal and material elements are independent variables only in an analytic sense, for concretely, in any given empirical instance, there is an ineluctable interdependence. Surely, in this strand of his work Parsons has proposed a naturalistic approach to the world of values, one that is anti-emanationist and self-consciously opposed to Durkheimian idealism. In *The Structure of Social Action*, in fact, Parsons is explicitly critical of Durkheim because "[his] epistemology thinks in terms of a rigid dualism: objective-subjective, phenomena-idea."[132] What Parsons finds objectionable is precisely the notion that "if a thing does not fit into one half, by definition it must belong to the other, since there is no further alternative."[133] To find such an alternative was exactly the goal that Parsons set for himself and which, we have seen, he accomplished to a significant extent.

4. SYMBOLIC ORDER AND INTERNALIZATION: LATER REFINEMENTS OF THE VOLUNTARISM PROBLEM

Parsons' critics view his emphasis on the unit act as evidence of his early individualism. The preceding argument has sought to establish, to the contrary, that the major theme of Parsons' early approach to order is one of "emergent properties," and that his attention to the unit act, instead of implying individualism, is perfectly compatible with his collectivist critique of the randomness of individual ends. We are now in a position to address a closely related critical charge, namely, that Parsons' emphasis on supra-individual order, when it does occur, is antivoluntary. I will argue that Parsons' emphasis on collective order is complementary to a voluntarist emphasis. In doing so, I will focus on the last strand of Parsons' intellectual synthesis, psychoanalytic theory, and upon the connections he established between psychology and classical sociological thought.

To fully appreciate Parsons' reconciliation of order and voluntarism, we must first acknowledge the contradictory quality of his treatment in the early part of *The Structure of Social Action*.[134†] Parsons' argument about voluntarism is at this point fundamentally ambiguous. Even while he articulates the collectivist framework I have ascribed to him above, he also introduces, particularly in the important second chapter, a more radically free-will approach.[135†] "Conditions" are defined not simply as the material, antisubjective elements of the actor's situation, but as referring also to all situational elements that the actor qua individual cannot personally alter.[136] Although Parsons does not explicitly assert this, such "givens" logically include ideal as well as material elements. This position implies a different, more individualistic definition of "normative" than the understanding discussed thus far.

It is true that Parsons' general approach to the concept "normative" is consistent throughout *Structure*: he defines it as referring to elements that provide freedom vis-à-vis the conditions of action. But according to the now expanded definition of conditions, such "normative" or free elements would no longer refer to all ideal elements as such. Instead, "normative" would now refer only to those ideal elements that allow the individual actor to change his position vis-à-vis all temporally prior—i.e., supra-individual—constraints, including ideal as well as material ones.[137] If Parsons had consistently maintained this position he would have been forced to approach all collectivist order as per se antivoluntary, and his argument would have remained grounded in the very individual/society dilemma it was intended to transcend. We have seen, however, that this was not the case. Alongside this extreme position, Parsons constructed a more truly collectivist framework, one which provided him with the theoretical resources for embracing voluntarism in a more modified form.

The passage in which Parsons first sought to resolve this early ambiguity and move toward a more consistently collectivist stance reveals the difficulties of this early position. While it is his insight into the importance of supra-individual order that leads him to discard the individualistic position, the reasons he offers for the collective status of normative elements indicate that he may, in fact, consider them external, or conditional, to the acting individual. "When the attempt is made to generalize about total *systems* of action in terms of the functional interrelations of [acts]," he warns in the second chapter, "the problem of the discrimination of the roles of normative and non-normative elements" becomes increasingly complicated. It is true, he acknowledges, that "from the point of view of a single concrete actor in a concrete situation the effects . . . of the actions of others belong in the situation, and thus may be related to the action of the individual in question in the roles of means and conditions." This kind of demarcation would reinforce the more radically voluntaristic approach in which all situational givens would necessarily be "conditional." Yet Parsons now argues that this is precisely what must not be done, for "in estimating the role of the normative elements in the total system of action in which this particular actor constitutes a unit, it would obviously be illegitimate to include these elements in the situation for the system as a whole." While still allowing that ideal elements may be external to any given actor, then, Parsons now insists that, nonetheless, they are not external to the collective environment, that is, to the social system of actors considered as a group: "For what are, to one actor, non-normative means and conditions"—if the actor's own individual viewpoint is adopted—"are explicable in part, at least, only in terms of the action of others in the system."[138]

Parsons' argument, then, is as follows. To focus only on creative, free-will innovation would force the analyst to remain mired in the purely individual and idiosyncratic, for what is an external and coercive norm for any particular actor will have been, at some earlier point, the fruit of another actor's creative innovation. Every subjective nonmaterial element, in other words, carries this double message. Faced with the option of describing every collective element as conditional, and foregoing, thereby, reference to the implications of subjective versus objective action, Parsons chooses to define collective ideal elements as per se voluntary.

But this argument, as it stands, is fallacious. Virtually all collective elements, both material and ideal ones, at some point originated from the actions of individual actors. To make this fact of "human origin" the criterion of normative status would, if logically applied, once again blur the distinction between ideal and material elements. Parsons has referred to collective order because in this strand of his early argument he is becoming implicitly aware of what he has explicitly discussed elsewhere in these early pages—that the unique quality of normative elements emerges only at the collective level. Yet he still cannot state precisely what this quality is: to be simultaneously subjectively related to human volition and collective and supra-individual.

By the beginning of the third chapter of *The Structure of Social Action*, however, the weight of Parsons' early argument has completely shifted from the pure to the modified position. Introducing Hobbes as "the first great example of deterministic [i.e., antivoluntarist] thinking in the social field," Parsons notes that Hobbes "is almost entirely devoid of normative thinking." His explanation for this fact, and it is a crucial one, is that Hobbes "sets up no *ideal* of what conduct should be, but merely investigates the ultimate *conditions* of social life."[139] Parsons then defines these ultimate conditions as power phenomena, particularly force and fraud.[140] Conditions, in other words, are now clearly material elements, while norms refer to ideals that govern conduct. This is the position that Parsons maintains, with great consistency, for the remainder of his long work. It is the major point in his discussion of the "radical anti-intellectual positivists"—Malthus, Ricardo, Marx, and the Social Darwinists—and the same position informs the individual theoretical analyses that form the substance of the rest of the book. "It must never be forgotten," Parsons warns in a discussion of norms that occurs in the middle of the work, that norms are "phenomena of a very peculiar sort." Whether or not a norm is actualized "depends upon the *effort* of the individuals acting as well as upon the conditions in which they act."[141] Parsons concludes that "this active element of the relation of men to norms, the creative or voluntaristic side of it," is precisely what creates their radical distinction from the elements of the actor's situation, the 'conditional' elements."[142†]

The insight that has allowed Parsons finally to resolve his early ambiguity is the distinction between the concrete and the analytic individual, which was discussed at some length in section 2. The key point here is that although any ideal element may be external to the individual, in the sense that it is part of the extra individual environment, it is not external in the concrete sense. For the concrete empirical actor, the location of determinate ideal elements is within: they are internal to action. This is the reason norms can affect action in a noninstrumental, noncoercive manner. Parsons' individualistic critics cannot perceive his reconciliation of voluntarism and collective order because they fail to recognize this analytic/concrete strategy.

This insight is elaborated in Parsons' critical approach to the antivoluntaristic qualities of Durkheim's work and the antidote he discovers in the psychoanalytic theory of internalization. Throughout most of *The Structure of Social Action*, the individualist critics argue, Parsons views collective order as an external, anti-individual phenomenon, and, conversely, he conceives of voluntarism only in a purely individualistic form.[143†] Implicitly, of course, this interpretation identifies Parsons with Durkheim, for Durkheim is regarded by such critics as the quintessence of an antivoluntary theorist.[144] Despite the fact that he and Durkheim are similar in a number of ways, this is a gross distortion of Parsons' fully developed position on the order question. Indeed, Parsons is actually engaging in a major polemic against Durkheim. Far from following Durkheim in his awkward identification of collective order as "external" to the individual, Parsons forcefully rejects Durkheim on precisely this point. Once Parsons had arrived at his insight that supra-individual order cannot be considered inherently anti-voluntary—an insight achieved only after some initial confusion—he simply could not accept the Durkheimian analysis that makes it appear to be so.

Parsons believes that Durkheim articulated normative collective order in a clear and unambiguous manner from the very beginning of his career. What Durkheim did not succeed in clarifying was that these "constraining" collective forces were, simultaneously, the basis for voluntary activity. In finding the reasons for this oversight, Parsons stresses a meta-methodological point, just as he did in his critique of Weber's presuppositional errors. Durkheim, Parsons asserts, was not sufficiently sensitive to the analytic/concrete distinction. In discussing the relation between the "individual," on the one hand, and normative "social" force on the other, Durkheim portrayed the individual as if he were the concrete individual of everyday empirical interaction and the social as if it were a tangible, literally coercive force.

> [This] is the view that the "individual" which is the unit of synthesis and the "society" which results from it are concrete entities, the concrete human being known to us, and the concrete group.[145]

This positivist inclination to concrete, "objective" facts forced Durkheim to identify "subjectivity" with an "unscientific" method.

> The distinguishing characteristic of the empirical element [for Durkheim] is its objectivity, its independence of the subjective inclinations, sentiments, or desires of the observer. A fact is a fact whether we like it or not. As he says it offers "resistance" to any alteration on the part of the observer. A fact is precisely distinguished by the criteria of exteriority and constraint—it is from scientific methodology that these criteria have been derived.[146]

This confusion was exacerbated further, Parsons believes, by Durkheim's misunderstanding of the individual problem. For despite his rejection of utilitarianism's rationalist emphasis, he accepted, at least in the early part of his career, the utilitarian notion of the individual as a randomizing variable: "[Durkheim] accepted the most fundamental basis of utilitarian thought—the subjectivity of individual wants in the peculiar sense pointed out, involving the assumption of their random variation."[147] These blinders, according to Parsons, explain why Durkheim never succeeded in linking the collective normative element to voluntaristic activity.

Parsons believes, nonetheless, that despite these limitations Durkheim gradually became aware of such a link, and he describes Durkheim's thought as marked by a tension between the increasing clarity of his basic understanding and the limitation of his theoretical vocabulary. Discussing Durkheim's later lectures, *Moral Education*, for example, Parsons notes that despite the anti-individualistic form of his argument, Durkheim had realized by that time that "in so far as the actor maintains an attitude of moral obligation toward it [i.e., the supra-individual world], the norm to which his action is oriented is no longer exterior in the same sense. . . . It becomes a constitutive element of the individual personality itself. Indeed, without this moral element there would not be what we mean by human individuals, personae, at all."[148] In *The Elementary Forms of Religious Life*, Parsons believes, Durkheim finally began to overcome some of these limitations. This is particularly clear in Durkheim's ritual theory, in which he moved toward reconciliation of voluntarism and collective order by emphasizing that normative behavior involved active, intentional activity.[149] "This whole aspect of Durkheim's thought," Parsons writes of the ritual theory, "points in the direction of . . . a process in which the concrete human being plays an active, not merely adaptive, role."[150†]

Parsons, then, does not repeat the mistakes he finds in Durkheim's work. Because his greater methodological sophistication allows him to clarify the analytic/concrete distinction, he remains free of the positivism that often forced Durkheim to portray normative order as antivoluntary. But beyond this point *The Structure of Social Action* does not go. When writing it, Parsons knew he must avoid Durkheim's errors, but he did not yet know precisely how. He had developed the abstract terminology with which to criticize Durkheim, but he had not yet developed the substantive theoretical language to provide a positive alternative. Basic questions remained unanswered. What mechanisms allowed collective forces to achieve an "internal" position? In what manner could factors be both social and constitutive of the concrete individual?[151†] In solving this riddle, Parsons perhaps took a cue from the typically enigmatic response that Durkheim had given his critics in the second preface to *The Division of Labor in Society*. In response to charges about his antipsychological bias, Durkheim protested that he was not against psychology per se but only its individualistic form. Sociology, he assured his readers, could be called a "collective psychology."

To develop this perspective Parsons turned to the psychoanalytic theory of introjection, according to which parental figures can be "internalized" by the personality. In *The Structure of Social Action* Parsons had mentioned Freud's introjection theory twice in a passing way, and in his own second preface, written a decade later, he expressed regret about the book's "relative neglect of the psychological aspects of the . . . conceptual scheme," a neglect that created a "major one-sidedness of the book."[152] Freud believed that through an affective charge parental figures became introjected to form permanent parts of the child's personality. He applied this general conceptualization primarily to the particular case of Oedipal crisis and its resolution, the process that produces the superego. Parsons adopted this analysis, but, characteristically, immediately abstracted it beyond its immediate empirical application. Perceiving its basic epistemological implications, he described it as a "solution" to the presuppositional task of reconciling voluntarism and collective order. There is, he writes, a convergence between Freud and Durkheim:

> Freud's discovery of the internalization of moral values as an essential part of the structure of the personality itself constituted . . . a crucial landmark in the development of the sciences of human behavior. . . .The formulation most dramatically convergent with Freud's theory of the superego was that of the social role of moral norms made by . . . Durkheim.[153]

Freud's introjection became Parsons' "internalization," and an apparently psychological process revealed its sociological meaning.

Earlier Parsons had used the notion of symbolic generalization to extend Durkheim's analysis of the nonrandom ordering quality of symbolism. He now uses the psychoanalytic notion of internalization to go beyond Durkheim in interrelating symbolism and voluntarism. Freud enabled Parsons to perceive that every act of symbolic generalization is also an act of individual internalization: "A pattern is internalized . . . so long as it generalizes the relations among objects."[154] In this critical statement Parsons actually makes two distinct points. On the one hand, he is arguing that an individual's relationship to the symbolic order involves the same kind of process that, according to psychological theory, allows personalities to become autonomous and voluntary—that is, the formation, through internalization, of the superego. On the other hand, he is asserting that the achievement of such psychological voluntarism involves a symbolic component, that it is not simply instrumental behavior toward material objects. "Although physical and cultural objects have . . . features in common," Parsons and Shils write, "there is a crucial set of differences which center on the fact that *cultural* objects can be internalized and thereby transmitted from one action to another." In contrast to the material elements of conditional order, "the cultural object is a pattern which is reproducible in the action of another person."[155] Without the presuppositional insight into normative behavior, in other words, the psychological theory of internalization would be impossible: "It is this 'transferability' from the status of object to the internalized status and vice-versa which is the most distinctive property of [symbolism]."[156]

Using Parsons' substantive theoretical language, social theory may now talk of individual desire, individual commitment, and individual action without in any way endorsing, as Durkheim feared it would have to, an atomistic, nonsocial emphasis. Once the phenomenon of internalization is understood, it becomes perfectly clear why concrete empirical individuals are not "individuals" in the analytic, randomizing sense. Concrete individuals actually are formed through object internalizations. "Only in the figurative sense," Parsons and Shils write, "does an individual *have* patterns of value orientation. In a strict sense he *is*, among other things, a system of such patterns."[157] The autonomy of the personality is actually generated and protected by object internalization. Obviously, then, symbolic generalization—which is achieved through internalization—cannot be in conflict with individual voluntarism. By demonstrating that the psychological focus of psychoanalysis—the greatest "individualistic" theory of the twentieth century—is simultaneously social, Parsons has solved the riddle of Durkheim's "collective psychology."

As will be seen later in the discussion of Parsons' more specific formulations, this presuppositional clarity allows him a flexibility that Durkheim never achieved. Without creating Durkheimian paradox, Parsons can accept Durkheim's emphasis on the empirical individualism of modern society and his ideological emphasis on the "cult of the individual." By adopting the notions of generalization and internalization, Parsons can articulate in more empirical and generalized terms the position which Durkheim expressed in his secularization of the processes of religious life: that the achievement of individualism in an ideological sense depends not on the lack of constraint per se but on the type of constraint. Thus, socialization itself insures voluntarism in a presuppositional sense, but it is the particular nature of this socialization that determines whether the internal motivation so constructed will allow freedom in an ideological sense.[158†]

The commonplace criticism, advanced for example by Dennis Wrong,[159] that Parsons' joining together of Durkheim and Freud reveals his commitment to empirical conformity could not, therefore, be wider from the mark. In the first place, this charge misunderstands Parsons' presuppositional logic itself: he draws on Freud to indicate how normative order promotes voluntarism rather than the anti-individualistic determinism that remained a distinctive residue in Durkheim's account. In the second place, this criticism is radically conflationary, identifying a presuppositional position on order with empirical and ideological positions that must remain separated—a separation that Parsons' own clarification was, in part, actually designed to allow. Moreover, the point that such criticism usually implies, that Parsons' later acceptance of Freudian internalization presented a sharp break with the "early" Parsons of the *Structure of Social Action* period, is equally incorrect.[160†] Not only can explicit references to internalization theory already be found in that early work, but Parsons himself clearly believes that adherence to internalization is consistent with the early position. Some early confusion aside, Parsons believed from the outset that the normative aspects of collective order produced voluntarism. His later incorporation of psychoanalytic theory represented simply a more successful manner of expressing this notion. The emphasis on internalization, then, is a means of preserving the voluntary, "individualistic" element of action, not of eliminating it.

Concrete approaches to the individual assume that voluntarism rests entirely on the individual's differences from others, and it is interesting that although Parsons rejects this notion as a general principle he accepts the common-sense view that such empirical differences permeate social life. At certain points, in fact, he emphasizes that internalization in no way mitigates them. Such empirical individualization is a product of the same factors that locate any social process: time and space. First, since individual life is chronological, an actor, even if considered as the sum of previous internalizations, will face any new situation with freedom vis-à-vis the sanctions he encounters, whether material or ideal. Second, since every individual life necessarily passes through a different social space, each individual personality will be different from every other, simply by virtue of encountering a different field of internalizations. As Parsons expressed this notion later in his career:

> [Although] his learned behavioral system (which I shall call his personality) shares certain broad features with other personalities, [his behavioral system] will be a *unique variant* of the culture and its particular patterns of action.[161]

Perhaps the best articulation of these two points is found in a universally ignored section in the Parsons and Shils essay entitled "Individuality." This consists in a compact argument for the position that internalization does not eliminate the distinctiveness of individuals from one another, that a "system of internalized 'values' is not the *only* constituent of personality."[162] Parsons and Shils argue, first, that in any given situation an "ordered pattern" is not all of one piece but represents, rather, variation within an acceptable range. As a result, even elements internalized in common may vary greatly; moreover, they will include not only this admitted variation, but other deviant orientations to action as well. Second, even when personalities "have been exposed to the 'same' experiences as other persons," individual idiosyncracies and accidents of birth will create "influential source[s] of variation." These include not only things like birth order of children but also the wide range of individual organic differences. "The upshot of these considerations," they argue, "is that though in a fundamental sense personality is a function of the institutionally organized [value patterns,] in an equally important sense, it cannot be even approximately fully determined by this aspect of its structure."[163]

Over and above the differences induced by time and place, Parsons emphasizes the fact of free will. By a simple analytic device that parallels the symbolic interactionist distinction between the "I" and the "me," free will can be reconciled with the notion of personality as internalization: at any given moment, the actor can take himself as well as the external world as an object. As Parsons and Shils state this position:

> From the point of view of any given actor, *his own* personality (i.e., his system of action or any part of it which is larger and more extensive in time than the action he is performing at the moment) may be an object.[164]

Thus, although common sense "lays *all* the stress on the *difference* between ego and alter as two separate entities," an emphasis with which the more analytic theory of internalization and generalization obviously disagrees, Parsons and Shils argue that internalization theory still "accepts this difference as fundamental."[165] In essence, they argue, "we are *analytically* splitting the concrete self into two components, the self as actor and the self as object."[166] Free will exists; its existence, however, does not prevent patterned, nonrandom order.[167†]

In the conclusion to chapter 2 of *The Structure of Social Action*, Parsons wrote that he hoped his argument would "show a way of transcending the old individualism-social organism [and] social nominalism-realism dilemma which has plagued social theory to so little purpose for so long."[168] He took a significant step toward accomplishing this goal with his clarification, in that work, of the analytic/concrete distinction and his critique of Durkheim. He essentially completed the task when he later incorporated internalization theory. Parsons' individualist critics have missed this solution because they have not accepted the presuppositional position involved. In making this interpretive error, moreover, these critics have missed what should actually be the crucial theoretical question concerning voluntarism. As Parsons realized from the beginning of his career, it is not the existence of constraint that prevents freedom but the kind of constraint.[169†] Later, he also came to realize that the freedom provided by the inclusion of normative order can be clearly perceived only through an understanding of the process of internalization. In a formal, presuppositional sense, therefore, recognition of these internalized normative elements is recognition of voluntary action. To prove anything beyond this—to demonstrate, for example, that any action also attains freedom in a substantive sense—requires investigation of the particular character of that action's internal and external constraints. To pursue this insight requires specification of Parsons' presuppositional formulations, particularly as they articulate with an ideological standard and an empirical theory of social change. Such developments become the focus of my discussion in later chapters.

5. CONCLUSION: "SYSTEMATIC THEORY" AND ITS ECUMENICAL AMBITION

My analysis of Parsons' most basic orientations has been made without reference to functionalism, political consensus, or ideology; the omission of these more specific levels of scientific commitment has, indeed, been critical to the entire analysis. Perhaps more than any other sociological theorist, Parsons was conscious of the sui generis character of theoretical formulation and, particularly, of the status of presuppositions as an independent level of sociological analysis. Parsons' early work is devoted principally to this most generalized level. Only in his later work, which is examined in subsequent chapters, does he begin to articulate this multidimensional position with more empirically oriented levels of the sociological continuum.

It is this articulation that makes Parsons' "systematic theory" systematic. Systematic theory has been a controversial notion in sociological debate throughout most of this century, and it has often been debated without explicit definition. Shortly after *The Structure of Social Action*, Parsons himself defined it as "a body of logically interdependent generalized concepts of empirical reference" in which "every logical implication of any combination of propositions in the [theoretical] system is explicitly stated in some other proposition in the same system."[170] Although this definition as such exists purely on the meta-methodological level, as a commitment to a certain notion of science, it would be a mistake to accept it simply at face value. Characteristically, Parsons has linked his methodological position to certain substantive presuppositional implications. His systematic theory does not consist simply in logically interrelated propositions; it reflects, rather, a formal attempt to connect such propositions to explicit presuppositional commitments. The "logical interrelationship" among variables that Parsons carries on throughout his work has presuppositional roots; it is an attempt to articulate presuppositional commitments with the more specific levels of the sociological continuum. Every significant aspect of Parsons' systematic conceptualization is intended, whether consciously or not, to clarify the implications of his general position for commitments at each of the other levels of sociological analysis—for commitments to a liberal ideology, for commitments to functional models, for various empirical perceptions of social development and social process.[171†]

This understanding of systematic theory provides us with clear-cut standards by which the ultimate success of Parsons' effort may be judged. Parsons' theory is not an attempt, contrary to the claims of some critics and supporters alike, to generate all sociological knowledge from "first principles." It attempts, instead, to demonstrate the roles of such first principles at every relatively independent level of thought. He is successful, therefore, to the degree that he shows how a multidimensional position contributes to the solution of long-standing sociological problems, how it can shape and make more effective theoretical formulations at the level of model, ideology, concept, and proposition. In this process, as noted in the first pages of this chapter, Parsons uses massive amounts of empirical data, but he does so, in the manner of the classical theorists, to illustrate, to elaborate, and to specify his fundamental theoretical commitments. He does so, like Kant, in order to demonstrate how these fundamental categories are imbedded in the real world. In the process of such specification he continually produces new empirical insights and new directions of empirical research. This too follows the classical example. Weber certainly did not invent the Protestant ethic thesis, nor did Durkheim first discover the relation of suicide to secularization. What both theorists did, rather, was to place these well-known phenomena in a more general context, one that demonstrated their full theoretical relevance.

At its best, therefore, Parsons' theory is intended to introduce theoretical ecumenicism on a grand scale.[172†] From the very beginning, his aim was to produce a theory that would end the need for continued theoretical conflict. By "avoiding the 'factor' type of theorizing" that polemically adopts one partial presuppositional position over another, Parsons wrote in 1945, a true synthesis would transcend the "division of the field into warring 'schools' of thought."[173] "Every school," Parsons wrote, "has some solid empirical justification but equally each . . . involves insuperable difficulties and conflicts with other interpretations of the same phenomenon." The result is that "professional pride and vested interests get bound up with the defense or promotion of one theory against all others and the result is an impasse." Parsons' intention was to end that impasse by embracing, in the manner of a truly dialectical transcendence, the positive elements in each school while avoiding their errors.

I will argue in the following pages that to a significant degree Parsons accomplished this task. Still, he fell far short of total success. Certainly the war between the schools continues unabated, with no less noise if with somewhat more sophistication than when Parsons addressed the situation more than three decades ago. If this were classical drama rather than social theory, one might find the source of Parsons' failure in his hubris. Since we are concerned with theoretical argument, we must examine the limitations of his generalized logic. Before doing so, we need to determine the nature and extent of his success.

Chapter Three

THE MIDDLE PERIOD

Specifying the Multidimensional Argument

Several years after the publication of *The Structure of Social Action*, his first and most general book, Parsons stated that the goal of his future work would be to discover the "essential categories" in terms of which "empirical description can be determinate."[1] Fifteen years later, he called attention to the fact that the more empirically oriented quality of his theorizing in this intervening period meant that it must be evaluated as a relatively autonomous phase of theoretical development. "From the legitimacy of these [earlier] assumptions on the most *general* level," he wrote in reference to arguments he had made in *The Structure of Social Action*, "it does not follow that the much more *specific* ways in which I have built them into a more detailed conceptual scheme must be accepted." That acceptance, he acknowledged, would involve "several further steps."[2] Whether one wishes to take these "several steps" depends, of course, on how one evaluates this distinctive phase in Parsons' work. It is to this more specifically oriented "middle period" of his development that we now turn.

1. "SPECIFICATION" AND THE STAGES OF THEORETICAL DEVELOPMENT

In examining Parson's movement toward specification, we must be sensitive to the two-directionality of that process. Every less general level of analysis involves new and independent commitments, yet each continues to be informed by his more general multidimensional presuppositions. Parsons' formulation of "functional theory" provides a case in point. In order to specify his presuppositions, Parsons had to embrace some particular model of society. "The structure of social systems cannot be derived from the 'frame of reference,' " he wrote in 1945; "it requires functional analysis."[3] This constituted an independent choice, for a wide range of different models would have been consistent with Parsons' presuppositional multidimensionality; among these, he chose the "functional system" model. Still, the autonomy of this choice was relative: not just any functional system would do. Thus, in discussing Weber's rejection of functionalism, Parsons emphasizes the great variability within the "functional" rubric. For Weber, Parsons writes, "functionalism" implied a number of different theoretical choices, all of them negative: the exclusive attention to "the external conditions of the survival of organisms," the "reification of collectivities as organisms or as cultural totalities," and the "tendency to attempt to reduce the subject-matter of [sociology] . . . to biological terms."[4] But such orientations, Parsons contends, are not inherent in a functional model; they reflect, rather, the impact of the more general presuppositions which are brought to bear on functional analysis. Weber's objections to functionalism were based on the fact that he did not sufficiently separate these two levels in his critique.

> He did not perceive that starting from the frame of reference of subjectively interpreted individual action—which he himself used so extensively—it was possible for functional analysis to develop a generalized outline of social systems of action.[5†]

In formulating his own functional model, then, Parsons would not make such mistakes; the model he employed would be consistent with his presuppositional solutions to the general problems of order and voluntarism.

The same kind of two-directional interactive process holds for the development of every level of Parsons' theoretical specification, not only as he outlines his theoretical model but also as he develops his conceptual system, elaborates his crucial definitions, and produces his empirically oriented classifications. The propositional implications of Parsons' discussions, and they are enormous, also are informed by the presuppositions of his early work.[6†]

If specification describes the overall course of Parsons' later development, it does not imply some sort of logical, step-by-step development from first principles, despite certain strong and often quite destructive tendencies on Parsons' part to present his work in this vein. More accurately, as Parsons himself put it, his theoretical development resembles the case method by which common law emerges: an overarching legal apparatus is gradually, and haltingly, developed by the bringing of general principles to bear upon an often bewildering variety of specific cases.[7]

The course of Parsons' post-1937 development is, in fact, highly uneven, moving forth and back along the scientific continuum. This work can be divided into several distinctive stages. There is a definite "middle period" in Parsons' development, covering the years 1938 through 1951, yet within this period there are further clearly distinguishable phases. There is an early mode of theorizing in which Parsons paid relatively little analytic attention to his functional model. The fruits of this earlier period were the essays written between 1938 and 1950 and published in *Essays in Sociological Theory*. Parsons focused here on elaborating general concepts in relation to concrete institutional analysis—for example, on the pattern-variable schema and its relation to the political, economic, and cultural changes that threatened the vested interests of class, sectional, and religious groups. Moreover, he worked almost exclusively with concepts provided by others, particularly by Marx, Weber, Durkheim, and Freud, selecting among them according to his own presuppositional solutions. Yet in the course of this middle period there quite clearly emerged a "later" and more sophisticated phase of Parsons' thought, a phase which was publicly presented only in the two major monographs published in 1951, *The Social System* and *Towards a General Theory of Action*. In these works, Parsons' model level becomes much more explicitly developed, with a consequent partial shift in focus from social institutions to the nature of the system in which they are embedded. Yet Parsons' use of "system" language remained limited—for example, to the personality-society-culture vocabulary I will describe below. The Parsonian conceptual system reached its most elaborate development in this phase of his work, with the extensive analysis of "allocation and integration" and their articulation with the pattern variables, the tripartite system division, and the deviance paradigm. In his "late" period, Parsons made great strides on the model level, succeeding with his "four function" scheme in directly incorporating into his idea of the social system his most general presuppositional logic. Maintaining enough of the conceptual apparatus from his previous development to make this new systems language empirically relevant, Parsons outlined his most effective analyses of institutional analysis, social change, and life-cycle development.[8†]

Parsons' critics have often unfavorably contrasted his "general" theory with Merton's "middle range" theory, arguing, as Gouldner once did, that while Merton "feels that empirical operations are necessarily involved in the very admission of elements as parts of the social system," Parsons believes empirical operations to be irrelevant.[9] That Merton himself applies such strictly empirical standards is, I have indicated in volume 1 (pp. 11–15), open to doubt. On the other hand, that Parsons utilizes none at all is simply wrong. Middle-range theory comes in all shapes and sizes. As Parsons specifies his general assumptions, his work necessarily enters the middle range. Indeed, it is this very interaction of the theoretical with the empirical that will be at the center of our attention in the remainder of this chapter.

2. THE EMPIRICAL ESSAYS AND THE PATTERN-VARIABLE CRITIQUE OF INSTRUMENTAL RATIONALITY

Parsons' early empirical essays are perhaps the most widely read and easily assimilated writings of his entire corpus, in large part because they rely more heavily than his later work on the familiar conceptual apparatus of his classical predecessors. He reorders this inheritance, at least in part, along multidimensional lines, and, in addition, produces certain distinctive conceptual innovations. Yet most of this early work, for all its preliminary achievement, is more fully developed later on. Either it is more effectively elaborated in later publications of this middle period—as in *The Social System*'s pattern-variable discussions and its interweaving of personality, society, and culture; or it can most effectively be analyzed as particular cases of these later analyses—as his early essays on social change stand in relation to his later formulations of the deviance paradigm. Most of my analysis of these essays, therefore, will await these subsequent discussions. I will, however, briefly discuss the origins of the pattern-variable schema, which has been the subject of much recent controversy and misunderstanding.

The pattern-variable analysis originates in Parsons' first two empirical essays, "The Professions and the Social Structure" and "The Motivation of Economic Activities," published in 1939 and 1940 respectively. These essays have often been viewed as simply derivative of other theoretical, empirical, and ideological positions. They have, for example, been seen as mere applications of Tönnies' *Gemeinschaft/Gesellschaft* dichotomy; as mere extensions of Parsons' direct empirical observation of medical practice;[10] and as an ideological apologia for the ethics of the business class and the medical profession.[11] All these influences are involved, to be sure. What is more decisive, however, is the manner in which Parsons utilized the essays to specify his presupposition that action is ordered, in part, by collective, normative pressures.

In both essays, Parsons starts by criticizing a distinctly "utilitarian" perspective. The economic and utilitarian orientation of thought that dominates modern Western society, he writes, postulates a sharp contrast between business practice, defined as purely rational, self-interested profit seeking, and the "liberal professions," typically viewed as disinterested, morally regulated activities that are "survivals" from traditional guilds.[12†] Parsons disagrees strongly with this dichotomy. Medical practice is as "rational" in its way as business, he insists, but it can be so perceived only if an instrumental approach to rationality is overcome. Parsons accomplishes this by defining rationality as "part of a normative pattern," as induced not simply by situational exigencies but by normative ones as well.[13] Rationality, he believes, rests upon two particular kinds of normative patterns. One sanctions "specificity" over "diffusiveness," the other "universalism" over "particularism." Despite this common rational patterning, of course, business and medical practice still differ from one another, but Parsons can now argue that this divergence is not simply an issue of conditionally induced "efficiency" versus normative "morality." While both activities necessarily face the "efficient" pressure of external conditions, the contrast between them lies in the normative patterning of this efficiency toward "self-interest" versus "disinterest."[14] Differing on this element, business practice patterns its efficiency primarily toward profit making, medical practice more toward the curing of illness.[15†]

In both cases, the emotional satisfaction of the concrete self is a focus of motivation, as are the pressures of the institutional environment a source of coercion. In both professions, then, action is in this sense self-interested and efficient. The specific rationality of this self-interest and efficiency, however, is decided by the cultural element of normative definition. In discussing the dichotomies of specificity/diffuseness, universalism/particularism, and self-interest/disinterest, Parsons has identified three dimensions of individual choice that collective norms must pattern. These are the first three "pattern variables." Later, Parsons will add affectivity-neutrality and achievement-ascription to this list. His basic point, however, remains the same. Situational exigencies are filtered through normative constraints. Parsons has developed criteria that bring to bear on the institutional relations of a single society the conclusions of Weber's historical and comparative critique. Rationality is not inherently instrumental. Because conditions are mediated by norms, rationality is variable, not just historically but institutionally as well.

3. EMPIRICAL SPECIFICATION OF MULTIDIMENSIONALITY IN THE LATER-MIDDLE WORK

More than any other single work, *The Social System* has identified "Parsonian" theory. But for a book of such universal recognition, its general framework has rarely been discussed. More importantly, when this framework has become the focus of analysis, it has almost universally been misunderstood as the quintessence of sociological idealism. I will demonstrate that, to the contrary, *The Social System* contains an important and highly successful strand of distinctly multidimensional analysis.

3.1. PERSONALITY, CULTURE, SOCIETY

The first chapter of *The Social System* addresses the problem of sociological epistemology and tries to elaborate an empirically oriented, synthetic approach. Parsons emphasizes the divergence of the actor's orientation from the objects of his orientation. These objects—some social, others physical, and still others cultural—actually perform different roles in the means/ends schema. Physical objects are always means, cultural and social objects may be means or ends.[16] It is on the basis of these initial distinctions that Parsons moves away from the concrete individual actor and the action problem as such, and in their place presents his more fundamental vision of social life as divided into three analytically distinct realms: the personality system, the social system, and the cultural system.

While the systems aspect of these concepts introduces the element of supra-individual order, at this stage of his discussion Parsons utilizes them more as intermediate points between purely individual action and its aggregation. He speaks about collective systems but still employs the "action" language of the individual means/ends problem. In fact, he has derived the systems distinction from his earlier differentiation of objects and orientations. If the actor's orientations are differentiated from objects, he argues, "various elements of the situation come to have special 'meanings' . . . as signs . . . which become relevant to the organization of his expectation system."[17] In other words, because expectations must be organized independently from objects, cultural orientations have a special role. Since, in turn, objects themselves, particularly the social and physical, are differentiated from orientations, social interaction must occur. With social interaction, individual behavior becomes subject to "functional imperatives" produced by "the pressures of scarcity of time, opportunity, and resources in the object situation."[18] This scarcity produces the distinctive level of organization Parsons calls the social system. Finally, because the concrete carriers of orientations and often the objects themselves are organisms, their interaction must be related to gratification. Since in the human world such gratification becomes structured through object internalization, organic necessity becomes "represented" through socially related need-dispositions.[19] The organization of individual feelings about objects, then, is separated from the organization of both external objects and their symbolic definition. In systems language, the operations of cultural and social systems are subject to the satisfaction of socially constructed but independent personality needs. In this culture, society, and personality-system schema, Parsons has moved from the problem of individual action toward the problem of order. He has done so by refining his earlier vision of action as composed of symbolic components, scarce conditional exigencies, and individual intentionality.

In his subsequent discussion, Parsons introduces divisions among each of these three system levels. Personality expectations can be cognitive, cathectic, or evaluative; cultural orientations are cognitive, appreciative, or value oriented; social action may be instrumental, expressive, or moral.[20†] On the basis of these divisions, Parsons can make two distinctive points, both of which bring his analysis closer to the order problem and, in the process, elaborate and specify his more general presuppositions. First, by homologizing the patterns of each system, Parsons emphasizes the possibilities for complementarity among cultural themes, personality needs, and institutional structures. Without some such complementarity, no nonrandom, orderly social arrangements would exist. Second, by this analytic division Parsons also emphasizes that this order will be neither exclusively instrumental nor exclusively normative. Even if a particular expectation, orientation, or action is dominant in a given situation, it cannot simply eliminate the other two. For example, in instrumental kinds of action systems or institutional arrangements, cognitive orientations and expectations have primacy. Yet as Parsons and Shils write in "Values, Motives, and Systems of Action," the contemporaneous essay that presents a parallel argument to *The Social System*:

> Instrumental actions are [still] subsidiary in the sense that the desirability of the goal is given by patterns of value orientations, as is the assessment of [the expressive] cost which is felt to be worth while to pay for its realization (i.e., the sacrifice of potential, alternative goals). But *given* the goal and the assessment of permissible sacrifice, the problem of action is instrumental, and is to be solved in accordance with given standards of efficiency. It becomes a question of what the situation *is*, and this is answerable in cognitive terms.[21]

In other words, the organization of situational conditions is the *most* significant arbiter of action in instrumental systems, yet these conditions still can pattern action only within the cultural orientations and psychological expectations established by particular expressive and moral structures.

Parsons concludes his discussion by emphasizing the irreducibility of the three systems to one another. Collective order, it is true, depends on a certain complementarity among the three system levels and among each of their three components. Nonetheless, not only the divisions within each level but the separations among the levels remain. If this seems a surprising conclusion in the light of the common criticism of Parsons' middle-period work as unappreciative of conflict and strain, it should be recalled that one of his primary targets throughout *The Social System* and *Towards a General Theory of Action* is the "culture and personality" school of anthropology. He believed that this approach greatly overemphasized the "fit" between cultural orientation and personality expectation, ignoring the intervening level of the social system and the overwhelming barriers it presents to complete integration:

> The clear recognition of the independent variability of these two basic modes or levels of orientation [i.e., personality and culture]

> is at the very basis of a satisfactory theory in the field of "culture and personality." Indeed it can be said that failure to recognize this independent variability has underlain much of the difficulty in this field, particularly the unstable tendency of much social science to oscillate between "psychological determinism" and "cultural determinism." Indeed, it may be said that this independent variability is the logical foundation of the independent significance of the theory of the social system vis-à-vis that of personality on the one hand and of culture on the other.[22]

Parsons intends to avoid this trap. "From the fact of a given 'psychological' cathectic significance of an object," he warns, "one cannot infer the specific appreciative [i.e., cultural] standards according to which that object is evaluated, or vice-versa."[23] Compared with the personality-level problem of cathectic significance, a "symbolic system has modes of integration of its own, which may be called 'pattern consistency.' " The result of this systematic divergence is that, despite their relative complementarity, the demands of personality and culture do not fully mesh: the "norm of pattern consistent integration of a cultural system can be only *approximately* realized, because of strains arising out of the imperatives of interdependence with motivational elements."[24†] This same lack of synchronicity occurs between the personality and the social system,[25] and is even more clear between social system and culture. While there is, inherently, an element of cultural generalization among institutional parts of a social system, there can never become complete congruence.

> Evaluative orientation confronts situational events which may be both "reinterpreted" and creatively transformed, but only within limits. The recalcitrance of events, particularly the . . . scarcity of means or resources, imposes certain functional imperatives on action. There is no necessity, and certainly little likelihood, that all the facts of a situation which in a pragmatic sense must be faced can be dealt with by the actor in accordance with all the canons of a given value system. The various value systems will be differentially selective as to which facts fit and which do not, and how well or how badly, but there will always be some facts that will be *problematical* for every value system.[26]

"Problematic facts," Parsons and Shils continue, "are those which it is functionally imperative to face and which necessitate reactions with value implications incompatible with the actor's paramount value system."[27†]

In this discussion, Parsons has clarified the relation between his presuppositional logic and more empirically oriented considerations. Cultural systems produce generalization via internal congruence with personality and social systems. Each system, in turn, has its own autonomy and is subject to its own internal constraints. The reasoning is deceptively simple, but before Parsons articulated it the problem seemed enormously complex. Only four years before these late-middle-period publications, Pitirim Sorokin, one of America's most sophisticated thinkers, had approached the same Gordian knot in his *Society, Culture, and Personality*. Yet despite the title, Sorokin's book dealt with these recondite issues only in an indirect, simplistic way. Sorokin failed because he had not integrated the general logic of cultural studies and psychoanalytic theory with his social-system theory, nor had he adopted the Weberian synthesis as his standard of theoretical evaluation. The distinctiveness of Parsons' accomplishment is emphasized by Clifford Geertz, who comments on the culture-social system distinction that he himself subsequently elaborated.

> Until Talcott Parsons, carrying forward Weber's double rejection (and double acceptance) of German idealism and Marxist materialism, provided a viable alternative, the dominant concept of culture in American social science identified culture with learned behavior. [It was thought that] *social* phenomena were explained by [simply] redescribing them as culture patterns . . . [In contrast,] the workability of the Parsonian concept of culture rests . . . on the degree to which the relationship between the [differentiated] development of symbol systems and the dynamics of social process can be circumstantially exposed.[28]

3.2. ALLOCATION AND INTEGRATION

Later, in chapter 4 of *The Social System*, Parsons moves from this preliminary discussion to a more direct specification of multidimensional order. The social system, Parsons asserts, faces two basic problems: allocation and integration. Allocation concerns the "economic" aspects of social life, broadly defined as those processes most directly patterned by scarcity. Parsons and Shils describe this in the following way:

> When a plurality of individual actors are each oriented in a situation to gratify sets of need-dispositions, certain resultant phenomena are inevitable. By virtue of the primordial fact that the objects—social and nonsocial—which are instrumentally useful or intrinsically valuable are scarce in relation to the amount required for the full gratification of the need-dispositions of every actor, there arises a problem of allocation: the problem of who is to get what, who is to do what, and the manner and conditions under which it is to be done. This is the fundamental problem which arises from the interaction of two or more actors.[29]

Specifically, these scarce resources are allocated through society's role structure. Parsons defines three different kinds of allocative tasks: the allocation of personnel, facilities, and rewards. Each of these, in turn, relates to different combinations of the social system's instrumental, expressive, and moral modes of action, and each, in addition, draws upon cultural and psychological as well as such specifically social resources.

The first allocative problem, that of distributing personnel, is related primarily to expressive action keyed to the criteria of age and sex. In institutional terms, such action is directly linked to family structure, though it manifests itself also through the personality system. But personnel allocation depends, in addition, on the more instrumental social-system processes of appointment and market competition. These expressive and instrumental processes, in turn, produce strong pressures for a certain type of moral regulation of personnel allocation, namely, for the pattern-variable orientations of "achievement" rather than "ascription."[30]

The second allocative problem concerns the provision of facilities for these personnel, the access to crucial "means" which include, Parsons emphasizes, both physical and social objects. This issue of control and power over facilities raises in a more concrete institutional form the presuppositional problem that Parsons earlier called the "Hobbesian question"—whether instrumental action must be ordered by some form of supra-individual control. Although Parsons' collectivist answer leads him to consider the issue of possessions and their distribution,[31] he believes that the decisive issue in the allocation of facilities is not economics but power. The significance of power in any social system is determined by its extent of "generalization," that is, the differentiation of power in an autonomous institutional form like the state.[32†] This generalization depends on three criteria: first, the breadth of the exchange network, a purely instrumental, quantitative matter; second, the incidence of universalistic as opposed to particularistic norms, a moral problem which itself is significantly dependent on the extent of exchange; third, successful restraint in the use of political means. If no limits on use exist, Parsons warns, no one would have any power. Whereas economic power is a matter of more or less, political power and its generalization involves the issue of higher and lower; it is, therefore, hierarchical and coercive.[33] These Hobbesian considerations are the central ones in Parsons' discussion of facilities allocation.

The third allocative problem is the distribution of rewards, or what Parsons calls the "economy of expressive orientations."[34] Once again, Parsons defines the problem by the unique combination of cultural, social, and psychological needs it presents. Whereas the facilities problem arises from the combination of cognitive needs and orientations with scarce instrumental resources, the rewards problem emerges from cathectic needs interacting with scarce expressive resources and appreciative orientations. Arguing that an actor's cathexis necessarily involves a selection among different possibilities,[35] Parsons emphasizes that these cathectic choices are socially ordered: "The conditions on which ego has a right to a certain [cathectic] attitude . . . on alter's part cannot be left unstructured and random."[36] Cathexis is organized by allocation of the rewards of prestige and loyalty. These rewards mediate, therefore, between personality and social systems.[37] They do so in the guise of an array of "expressive symbolism" that is integrated with the other allocative tasks.[38] To illustrate this process, Parsons describes how the cross-cutting of the pattern variables "affectivity/neutrality" and "specificity/diffuseness" produces the variegated symbolic reward clusters of receptiveness, approval, esteem, and love.[39] These pattern-variable combinations are produced by the interaction of general cultural tendencies, the particular allocative exigencies of personnel and facilities distribution, and the cathectic needs that produce the need for a "reward" process in the first place. These four kinds of expressive symbols organize the allocation of loyalty and prestige.

Alongside allocation, every social system faces the "integration" problem, which Parsons also calls the problem of institutionalization. The challenge of integration is to control the more instrumental and functional processes of social allocation by linking them to the value elements in the culture's orientation. In this way, "moral action" becomes institutionalized in the social system alongside instrumental and expressive action. Such institutionalization involves two different kinds of processes. There is, first of all, the process of socialization, which draws upon the appropriate elements of the personality and cultural systems. It is because of socialization that the allocation of personnel, facilities, and rewards does not have to contend with the most extreme kinds of divergence between the needs of personality, culture, and society.[40] "The process of socialization in the family, school, and play groups, and in the community," Parsons and Shils write, "focuses need-dispositions in such a way that the degree of incompatibility of the active aspirations and claims for social and nonsocial objects is reduced."[41]

Institutionalization, however, integrates not only by forming the actor's voluntary will but also by utilizing coercive, instrumental elements of the social system. "Social integration," Parsons and Shils write, "however much it depends on internalized norms, cannot be achieved by these alone." They insist that "it requires also some supplementary coordination" from explicit prescriptions and prohibitions.[42] These are carried out by authoritative "enforcement" and "interpretation"—both of which are designed to limit the pursuit of individual and organizational private interests at the expense of collective needs. This task is accomplished through formal and informal sanctions, specifically through leadership, both administrative and repressive, and through binding, legitimate authority.[43]

In this complex analysis of social allocation and integration, Parsons has simultaneously relied upon and greatly elaborated his personality-society-culture analysis.[44†] Even as presented in this severely abstracted form, it should be evident that Parsons has greatly extended the earlier, classical attempts at multidimensional interweaving.[45†] Introduced in Parsons' earlier *Essays* and elaborated in *The Social System* and *Towards a General Theory of Action*, the allocation-integration schema has gone a long way toward rendering his general presuppositional position in more specific terms.

3.3. THE BASIC STRUCTURAL FORMATIONS OF SOCIETIES

Thus far Parsons' discussion in *The Social System* has dealt with social processes in a purely abstract way. In chapter 5 of that work, he takes another step toward specificity by utilizing his conceptual schema to explain the kinds of institutional complexes that develop in actual social systems. Institutional variation, Parsons believes, is produced by the interaction of psychological and cultural exigencies with the functional pressures of social integration and allocation.

Parsons attempts first to explain the universality of relatively nuclear and concentrated kinship systems: why biologically related groups are the primary modes of status ascription and the principal socializing agencies; why women have been the traditional socializing agents; and why these socializing kinship groups are also the typical location of adult sexual relations and the object of stringent sexual taboos.[46] Since the cultural demands of social life are complex, Parsons argues, great plasticity must be built into the human being and extensive time will be necessary for acculturation. When this fact is combined with the organic-sexual substratum of personality, the connection between biological relatedness and socialization is clear: only a few, indeed probably only biologically related, persons would be willing to devote themselves to meeting the organic needs of a child over an extended length of time. An instrumental, technological fact—the lack until recent times of any substitute for breast feeding—explains the women's key role in this process. Finally, a personality variable, the postadolescent's "deeply rooted need for adult attachments which can serve as substitutes for his infantile attachments," explains why this biologically related socialization unit also becomes the locus of adult sexual relations and the incest taboo.[47†]

Parsons turns next to the question of why, even within otherwise highly differentiated societies, the distribution of instrumental facilities so consistently coincides with expressive reward structures.[48] In the first place, given any cultural valuation of achievement, the division of labor will differentiate among degrees of instrumental competence. This evaluative factor will be matched by the inevitable hierarchical differentiation of organizational responsibility, which occurs for purely objective instrumental reasons. For both cultural and functional-instrumental reasons, therefore, within any given organization unit there is an "inherent tendency to allocate greater facilities to those on the higher levels of competence and responsibility."[49†] To relate this intra-organizational convergence to the typical overlap of facilities and rewards outside the organizational context, Parsons turns to the third component of order—to personality—and to the dimension of orientation he has not yet considered—expressivity. He emphasizes that the actor's expressive needs are not fulfilled by the instrumental and moral institutions of occupational life. The result is that the actor simultaneously establishes diffuse affective attachments and loyalties to kinship units. But this presents a peculiar problem, for the expressive solidarity generated within the kinship unit is "of such a character that if certain facilities and rewards are available to one member, they will have to be 'shared' with the other members."[50] From this, Parsons argues that the allocation of expressive rewards must generally overlap with the distribution of instrumental facilities.

Parsons follows a similar analytic strategy when considering why, in a given society, force becomes territorially centralized.[51] First he asks the basic question why there is a centralized state at all, and refers back to his earlier discussion of allocation, which established force as the ultimately effective means. Since force is physical, he continues, it inevitably tends to be linked to a territorial location. There is also an integrative element to the existence of the state, for "it is safe to say that no paramount integrative structure of a society could perform that function effectively unless it were intimately tied in with the control of power relations in general and force in particular."[52] The most effective structure that fulfills both this integrative need and the allocative ones as well is the state. Yet its historical emergence depends not only on such long-term demands. It is related, in addition, to instrumental factors like the technology and organization of force and the degree of bureaucratization of the army.

Finally, there is the problem of the universal existence and pervasive scope of religious belief.[53†] Parsons first posits fundamental, insoluble human problems. On the biological level, there is the inevitability of death. On the social-system level, there is the chronic frustration that "results from the empirical impossibility of complete integration of any *value*-system with the realistic *conditions* of action."[54] Yet in themselves these tensions do not create religion. They must interact with both the psychological level, where fears of death and the frustration of internally cathected values intensify anxiety over object loss, and with the cultural level, where the fact of undeserved suffering creates an unbalanced "moral economy." Religion presents a solution to these multileveled problems. It does so by integrating expressive symbolism with cognitive expectations and moral valuations.

It must be recognized that this series of empirical "explanations" takes place at a high level of generality. Parsons is attempting here the same kind of sweeping theoretical discussion that so occupied Marx, Durkheim, Weber, and Freud. And while it is possible to take issue with the ideological implications and empirical reasoning of Parsons' assertions, one cannot overlook the extraordinarily supple multidimensionality of his achievement. By interweaving personality, society, and culture with the exigencies of allocation and integration, Parsons' explanations of basic social forms can account for greater complexity than those of any of his classical predecessors.[55†]

3.4. THE PATTERN VARIABLES IN SYSTEMIC CONTEXT

Parsons' multidimensional analysis in the *Social System* culminates in an analysis of the two basic complexes of social structures that occur in every society.[56] In analyzing what he calls the ascriptive and achievement complexes, he is continuing the discussion of pattern variables begun in the *Essays in Sociological Theory*. At the same time, he is linking them more firmly to the social rather than the cultural level of analysis.

For the "ascriptive complex," Parsons begins with the "kinship cluster" and its emphasis on the primary biological givens of age, sex, and birth order which render familial interaction diffuse and particularistic. Because it is evaluated primarily according to diffuse and particularistic standards, the overwhelming proportion of the child's status position will be ascribed rather than achieved. This situation has a number of ramifications. First, because families also constitute units of residence, biological relatedness becomes connected to territory, and "community" therefore becomes linked to ascription rather than to achievement, at least for family members not engaged in outside occupations. Second, kinship groupings will aggregate not only by common territory but by common biological ancestors as well. In this way, the ascription of kinship is transferred to ethnic groups. Third, insofar as hierarchical status rather than horizontal ethnicity becomes the basis of kinship-unit cohesion, social class becomes the ascriptive carrier. Given the exigencies of the kinship structure, then, there is an "irreducible minimum of commitment" to ascriptive pattern variables.[57] "Membership in the four types of groupings, kinship, community, ethnic, and class, should characterize every individual actor in every society."[58] Together, these memberships form an enormous complex of recalcitrant inequality.

In his discussion of the countervailing "achievement complex," Parsons combines his analysis of five non-kinship institutional "clusters" with the allocation/integration dichotomy to explain the origins of more egalitarian and responsive patterns.[59] He first identifies the ecological cluster, which "in the instrumental case [is] a market nexus, in the expressive a network of 'purely personal' friendships."[60] Instrumentally oriented organizations present a second, more structurally elaborated component. The need for integration enhances the importance of the power-territoriality-force nexus, the third structural cluster, which can expand only at the expense of community and ethnic groupings. Such integration needs also supply important pressures for the growth of differentiated cultural orientations, particularly for the growth of a church religion, which constitutes the fourth cluster. The allocative exigencies that stratify facilities and rewards according to functional exigencies contribute additional pressure and present the fifth institutional grouping of the achievement complex. With the growth of these five institutional groupings, Parsons writes, "a premium is placed on achievement criteria over ascription. Similarly, there is much more scope for universalism, and . . . affective neutrality."[61] Although these institutions are always opposed to the ascriptive groupings, it is only in industrial society that "they overshadow all except the broadest bases of community and of ethnic belongingness."

The patterns of orientation that Parsons has here identified originate in the tensions among the multilayered orders of the social system. This analysis has a psychological and social slant that complements the more cultural analysis of the *Essays*. Taken together, they provide the foundations for a multidimensional approach to the crucial pattern-variable complex.

3.5. CONCLUSION: THE SOCIAL SYSTEM *AND ITS CRITICS*

Although there is another side to *The Social System* to which we will turn at a later point, in the parts noted here Parsons has succeeded in finding empirical referents for his broad synthetic presuppositions. He manages to specify these general ideas in a series of conceptual distinctions, definitions, and classifications that have strong propositional ramifications. Throughout this development, his argument is strikingly multidimensional.

On the basis of this evidence, the judgment by the critics of this middle-period work seems badly off balance. For Lockwood, *The Social System* was "highly selective in its focus on the role of normative order," giving virtually no attention to the "factual substratum."[62] Dahrendorf agreed with this judgment, describing the book as being concerned solely with values and integration, with no reference whatsoever to coercion. For Parsons, Dahrendorf wrote, "units of social analysis ('social systems') are essentially voluntary associations of people who share certain values."[63] Mills soon added his assent: "The whole of Parsons' book . . . transform[s], by definition, all institutional structures into a sort of moral sphere."[64] And Blake and Davis utilized the work to illustrate what they termed "normative determinism," which "takes the fact that norms are meant to control behavior as the basis for assuming that they do control it."[65]

In such critical evaluations we hear nothing of those aspects of Parsons' argument we have just presented—the tripartite division into personality, societal, and cultural systems; the economies of instrumental and expressive actions; the exigencies of social allocation and integration. We learn nothing about the structural variations, instrumental and normative, that the interaction of such pressures produces, or the complexes of value patterns that result. We do not, I think, because of the peculiarly polemical nature of "readings," a subject to which we have often returned in the course of these volumes. Each of these critical evaluations, indeed, is an argument for an instrumentalist perspective, either a relative or an extreme one. Despite his formal commitments to multidimensionality, Lockwood's analysis does not actually embrace the autonomous dimension of normative order.[66†] Dahrendorf, it turns out, utilizes Parsons merely as a polemical starting point for "coercion theory." Mills argues that all moral phenomena are, in reality, simply legitimations for instrumental power.[67†] Blake and Davis, despite their own commitment to normative analysis, discount, apparently on ontological grounds, the very existence of broad social values. It will be seen later in my discussion (chs. 8, 9) that these critics do have a point. But distorting the truly multidimensional elements of Parsons' theory does this point no service.

4. THE CHANGE THEORY AND THE VICISSITUDES OF WESTERN DEVELOPMENT

The "conflict school" in contemporary sociology emerged in large part as a critique of the theory of social change that Parsons developed during this middle period.[68†] Its critique accused Parsons of a static, idealist bias that ignored issues of process, conflict, and change. While Parsons' attitude toward change is complex and often ambiguous, this evaluation is certainly incorrect.[69†]

4.1. THE GENERAL MULTIDIMENSIONAL THEORY

The most general treatment of conflict and its repercussions occurs in *Towards a General Theory of Action*. This discussion, in fact, can be read as a powerful argument against the conflationary notion that a given presuppositional position implies either empirical social conflict or cooperation. To the contrary, Parsons and Shils argue that the very social processes that meet functional needs—particularly the allocation of facilities and rewards and the maintenance of cultural orientations—become the sources of instability both in the genesis of conflict and in its control. This was already clearly implied when they emphasized the lack of complementarity among social, psychological, and cultural systems. Here it becomes explicit. On the level of values, strains can emerge because of inadequate socialization. But in a more systematic sense, tendencies toward value alienation are "endogenous": "There cannot be a society in which some of the members are not exposed to a conflict of values."[70] Strains also can emerge from the social system level, "from [particular] changes in the situation of the social system in relation to nature or to other systems." More systematically, however, "the allocative process always produces serious strains by denying to some members of the society what they think they are entitled to . . . "[71] Finally, given the phenomenon of internalization, both these strains necessarily produce internal personality conflict as well.

> Very frequently the most important internal as well as external conflicts are not between obligations imposed by a general collective value system and "self-interest" but between the obligations of different roles, that is, between the constituent, more or less specific, need-dispositions in the superego. The actor is put in the position of having to sacrifice one or the other or some part of each. This is an authentically internal personality conflict, and not merely a conflict over the possible "external" consequences of sanctions . . . [72]

Every conflict, in other words, is psychologically overdetermined. In combination, such strains may "deaden the motivation of actors to role fulfillment and [cause] their apathetic withdrawal." On the other hand, if they are "associated with an identification with a collectivity or a class of individuals who come to identify themselves as similarly deprived," a much more active and rebellious response will ensue.[73]

In response to these "problematic facts," mechanisms of social control are invariably brought into play, corresponding to the integrative mechanisms that balance allocation. They are necessarily multidimensional in their composition: how else could they "match" the sources of strain? Underlying any attempt at social control is the problem of value consensus. The weaker the consensus, the more other mechanisms must be brought into play. "One of the most prominent and functionally most significant" of these other mechanisms, according to Parsons and Shils, "is the artificial identification of interests."[74] Formulated originally in Elie Halévy's analysis of the political reform strategy of anti-individualistic Benthamite utilitarianism, this notion of creating an "artificial identity" is a crucial one. In adopting it, Parsons and Shils simply define the process in a multidimensional rather than an instrumentalist way. Social authority tries to create the identification of interest not only through the manipulation of the "allocation of facilities," as the utilitarians imagined, but also through "rewards [that] can redirect . . . motivational orientation[s] by offering them objects that are more easily cathected."[75] If these attempts at reintegration fail, there remain the possibilities of "insulating" disruptions through such processes as the creation of subcultures or "contingent reintegration" through the therapeutic treatment of deviance, as in the case of psychotherapy for mental illness. Insofar as these processes fail to reintegrate, social conflict intensifies and structural change occurs.

4.2. RATIONALIZATION, ANOMIE, AND REVOLUTION

The early essays which Parsons collected in *Essays in Sociological Theory*, and which rely more heavily than the later-middle-period work on an inherited conceptual scheme, similarly emphasize the presuppositional basis of conflict and strain. In one of his earliest contributions to the *Essays*, for example, Parsons warns against the tendency in common-sense thinking to "exaggerate the integration of social systems."

> For purposes of sheer comparative structural study this need not lead to serious difficulty, but when dynamic problems of directions and processes of change are at issue, it is essential to give specific attention to the elements of malintegration, tension and strain in the social structure.[76]

In fact, more than half the essays Parsons wrote between 1939 and 1950 deal directly with such malintegration, tension, and strain. They do so in a distinctive manner, one that applies Parsons' abstract reasoning to a particular empirical problem.

Combining the change theories of Weber and Durkheim with his own presuppositional position, Parsons first presents an analysis of the strains inherent in recent Western development. The underlying process is what Weber called rationalization, which Parsons believes must be cultural as well as social. Science presents one of the most important rationalizing forces, an inherently dynamic element that progressively undermines traditional beliefs. Connected to science and simultaneously to other, more instrumental pressures, technology has an even more unsettling effect on the concrete circumstances of human life. Bureaucratization, contractualism, and the growing differentiation of what Parsons would later, in *The Social System*, call the achievement and ascriptive complexes represent other rationalizing processes which he discusses at some length. Finally, critical thought promotes an antitraditional "frame of reference for determining the proper attitudes of 'reasonable' men toward the social problems of the day."[77†] As more specific manifestations of these trends, Parsons cites such factors as the economic instability of market systems, rural-urban migration patterns, the growth of fad and fashion cycles in every area of social life.[78]

Parsons moves beyond this neo-Weberian analysis, however, not only by maintaining, as Weber did not, the multidimensionality of rationalization but by integrating this analysis with Durkheim's anomie theory, as modified by its connection with Freud. In the face of antitraditional disruption, Parsons contends, value orientations become either insufficiently specific or internally ambiguous. Since value commitments correspond to internalized object cathexis, such orientational confusion generates object loss and, therefore, expectational anxiety. The result is "generalized insecurity" and "free floating aggression," prime prospects for displacement onto "relations or symbols only remotely connected with their original sources."[79]

These strains produce social polarization, in which, according to Parsons' scheme, projective fantasy both reinforces and distorts the instrumental and moral conflict between the "traditionalistic" and "emancipated" elements of the national community. It is important to make explicit a point that implicitly informs Parsons' entire discussion, namely, that such polarization is as horizontal as it is vertical. It is not simply that rationalization and anomie create divisions between hierarchical groupings, but that they intensify conflict within them as well: there are traditionalistic and emancipated elements among the lower, middle, and upper classes. These pressures trigger movements toward social control, and legitimate authority attempts to reintegrate the national community through appeals to consensus and through the manipulation of facilities and rewards. At this point, the crucial variable becomes the structure of this authority, that is, the society's hierarchical order, particularly the arrangement of social classes and the vertical problem of dominant and subordinate groups. To articulate this factor, Parsons brings into his argument a multidimensional version of Marxian analysis.

He begins by asserting the "inherent hierarchical aspect" of economic class relations in all industrial, not just capitalist, society. This hierarchicalization occurs both because of pressure for efficiency generated by the economy of instrumental action and, in addition, because of the demands for equalization of status among kinship members generated by the economy of expressive needs.[80] Still, such vertical differentiation need not undermine the possibilities for societal integration or for the authoritative social control processes that depend upon it. By itself, the division is a "latent conflict." Whether or not it will contribute to social polarization depends on whether the "[stratification] system does [or] does not succeed in developing adequate control mechanisms."[81] This coping must contend with certain distinctive exacerbating factors. On the instrumental side, the discipline and authority of impersonal organization creates opposition, an endemic problem intensified by the "general tendency for the strategically placed, the powerful, to exploit the weaker or less favorably placed."[82] On the expressive-cathectic side, the polarity of high and low is increased by the psychological consequences of an individualistic occupational system, the arrogance of winners and the resentment of losers. This in turn relates to the way in which such attitudes, combined with family income and living conditions, create early socialization that positively handicaps lower-class individuals.[83]

The crucial question is the degree to which such strains produce class-related cultures, the "differentiation of attitude systems . . . to a greater or lesser degree around the structures of the occupational system."[84] To the degree that this does occur, communication across group lines is impeded and "the tendency to develop a hiatus may become cumulative." In such situations, social control of the polarization produced by the rationalization-anomie-projection cycle becomes impossible: authoritative attempts at reintegration are no longer acceptable. What can mitigate such class-cultural polarization? There are, first, standard mechanisms like the organization of reward allocation and integrative structures like the law. But in addition to these, Parsons emphasizes a number of other particular factors: the supra-class impact of national, religious, and moral solidarity; the cross-class impact of ethnicity; the insulative mechanisms that conceal or diffuse differences in rank, reward, and competence.[85] Above all, however, he emphasizes the more general inclusive factor of how the "precapitalist residues of the old class structure [get] tied in with the consequences of the developing industrial society."[86] This historical fact, the relation of the old class structure to the new, will determine the effectiveness of the reintegrating factors he has described.

It is not, then, industrialization or rationalization itself that creates social revolution and the breakdown of social control, "but its pathology and the incompleteness of its development."[87] If the necessary mitigating factors—social, cultural, and psychological—do not occur, societal authority will be unable to counteract the general processes of polarization—both vertical and horizontal—that accompany rationalization and anomie. While in the nineteenth century such breakdown appeared to herald the advent of left-wing socialism, in the twentieth it is radical right-wing movements that more often result. Fascism, Parsons wrote in 1942, "is at least as deeply rooted in the social structure and dynamics of our society as was socialism at an earlier stage."[88]

Parsons therefore applies his theory of Western development and its vicissitudes to the mass movements of the radical right, particularly though not exclusively to the German case.[89] In Nazism, the national community was severely divided and reintegrating social control impossible. Parsons considers the ultimate cause of this situation to be the distortions created by Germany's pre-industrial past. As instrumental factors, he emphasizes the tenacity of Prussian feudalism, the continuing power of the Junker military class, and the fact that the modern German state necessarily emerged under, rather than against, the aristocracy. For these reasons, neither the German bureaucracy nor the bourgeoisie ever gained any democratic autonomy of their own. On the cultural level, Parsons describes the reinforcing impact of Lutheranism, with its other-worldly attitudes and its relatively passive acceptance of state authority. In addition, peculiar familial structures became associated with the tensions of these more "public" structures, particularly the exaggerated emphasis on male domination and female submission. Finally, Parsons incorporates the psychological level by defining "typical" German traits—the formalism of social relations, the emphasis on titles, the romantic and spiritualized orientation to nature and *Volk*, the military ethic of the community of brothers—as expressive symbols that functioned as cathectic outlets for the strains such precapitalist arrangements engendered.[90]

Given this situation, the "disorganizing effects" of late-nineteenth- and early-twentieth-century rationalization struck Germany particularly hard.[91] Because of the past structures, the inevitable polarization, both vertical and horizontal, was unusually intense. Because significant cultural groups in Germany were more conservative and traditional than their counterparts in other Western societies, the German "rationalistic," or "emancipated," cultural leaders were exaggerated in their response. Parsons argues, for example, that "the German labor movement was considerably more extreme in the rationalistic direction than its counterparts in the Anglo-Saxon countries." As a result, their political program "came to be formulated in terms of the strict Marxist ideology which, above all, required drastic repudiation of traditional religious values."[92] The result, of course, contributed to further polarization, for it "undoubtedly made it easier for the labor movement to be defined as 'dangerously radical' to the rest of the population."[93] Similarly radical cultural divisions occurred in every area of German life.

This "ideological definition of the situation," Parsons emphasizes, was "necessarily in the closest interdependence with the psychological states and the social situation of the people to whom it appeal[ed]."[94] It overlapped, in the first place, with the vested, "real" interests of diverse and opposing groups, the urban-rural and capitalist-labor splits, the difficult competitive position of the lower middle class, the insecurity of the feminine role, the particular strains in the position of youth, the discrimination against German Jews.[95] The polarization was also overdetermined by the unconscious attempts of these groups to compensate for the very anxiety which their anomic situations had produced.

> Being insecure they tend[ed] to "overreact" and both positively and negatively to be susceptible to symbolizations and definitions of the situation which are more or less distorted caricatures of reality and which are overloaded with affect. . . . The pattern tends to bear conspicuous marks of the psychology of compulsion.[96]

During the Weimar period, for example, the German left, broadly defined, engaged in "compulsively distorted patterns of extreme emancipation" which were "highly provocative to the more traditionalized elements." At the same time, from the right, aggression was "turned toward symbols of the rationalizing and emancipated areas which were felt to be 'subversive' of the [traditional] values [in] an exaggerated assertion of and loyalty to these traditional values."[97] Parsons calls this latter reaction fundamentalism.

In the face of this multilayered complex of polarization, effective social control and reintegration were unlikely. Still, the final dissolution of the German national community depended on a specific sequence of historical events.[98] Through political intrigue and the financial influence of the older elites,[99] the Nazis were able to capitalize on these events and become the carrier group for the traditional elements in German society.

> "Fundamentalist" sentiments . . . crystallize[d] about phenomena symbolic of the extremer forms of emancipation in defining what was dangerous to society. The coincidence in Nazi ideology of the Jews, capitalism, bolshevism, anti-religious secularism, internationalism, moral laxity, and emancipation of women as a single class of things is strongly indicative of this [polarized] structuring.[100]

4.3. THE DEVIANCE PARADIGM: REFORMULATING STRAIN AND ITS CONTROL

Parsons' chapter on social change in *The Social System* covers the same ground he worked out in the *Essays*, though in substantially less empirical detail.[101] He discusses the crucial role of vested interests in creating polarization and the social impact of rapid cognitive development, particularly in socially disruptive technological changes. He also introduces some new variations on the general themes covered in his essay with Shils. For example, in analyzing the transformation of the Bolshevik movement after the Russian revolution, he focuses on the tension between the utopianism of communist values and the pressures generated by Russia's need to maintain the "empirical institutional clusters" that he had earlier identified as basic to the functioning of any social system—the centralization of political coercion, uniform socialization, the integration of facilities and rewards, and generalized "religious" orthodoxy.[102]

Rather than in this formal discussion of change, however, it is in *The Social System*'s analysis of deviance that Parsons introduces significant new elements into his theory of change. We have seen that in his essay with Shils, Parsons presented the therapeutic control of deviance, or "contingent reintegration," as the last and least important element in the social control of strain and conflict. In *The Social System*, this element becomes transformed into Parsons' major paradigm for social control, subsuming the authoritative "appeals to consensus" and the "artificial identification of interest" that were central to the theory presented with Shils. This deviance paradigm has consistently been misinterpreted as a psychological or individualistic approach that radically deemphasizes large-scale and institutional change.[103] Yet while Parsons has borrowed the formal logic of the patient-psychiatrist interaction, the deviance paradigm can, in principle, be utilized in a multidimensional way.

In fact, the deviance model can be seen as providing a more systematic format for Parsons' earlier analyses of change and control. It posits, first, an equilibrium-disrupting strain, the source of which, Parsons emphasizes, is situational—either social or cultural—but in either case external to the individual actor or institution.[104] In response to this pressure, the actor develops deviant motivation, in which compulsive conformity or nonconformity overdetermines the differences between acting units and creates polarization.[105] The ensuing social control, directed at affective, instrumental, and cultural levels,[106] is differentiated by Parsons into four separate processes: the manipulation of rewards, the denial of reciprocity, permissiveness, and support.[107]

It would not be difficult to apply this model to Parsons' analysis of the origins of Nazism—to the interaction among the strains that generated it, the psychological needs that distorted its expressive symbolization, and the efforts at social control that failed to provide authoritative reintegration. Yet such ad hoc analysis is unnecessary. Long before the deviance paradigm had ever been explicitly formulated, Parsons had already applied essential aspects of this theory of control to the case of Nazism. This effort, "The Problem of Controlled Institution Change," illustrates the multidimensional origins and potential of the deviance model.

Parsons' intention in this essay is to describe how the Allies could transform postwar German society, an alteration which meant, for him, returning Germany to the "normal" development course followed by the Northern European democracies. He begins by noting that while most analysts of this problem have pressed for transforming the "typical German character structure which predisposes people," he believes a more "situational" focus to be more appropriate.[108] He recommends, first, a drastic "manipulation of rewards," namely, the compulsory suppression of the Nazi party and the Junker class. This step is necessary, he explains, not only by virtue of these groups' instrumental power but also because of the authority of their moral traditionalism.[109†] The suppression of the Junkers could be accomplished either through direct compulsion, by force, or through indirect inducement, by eliminating their economic base. The Nazification of the civil service and business class, Parsons continues, could be dealt with indirectly. If the "precapitalist" base of support for the radical right were eliminated, more democratic stratification patterns and class orientations would gradually assert themselves.[110] He emphasizes, further, the psychological need for "permissiveness" in this reconstruction process, for any harsh action would encourage the defensive and projective distortion that characterized Nazi ideology. If, on the other hand, the Allies guaranteed order and security, the anomic basis for extreme anxiety would disappear. Finally, although ideological conservatism would undoubtedly prevail initially over more liberal attitudes, the denial of all "reciprocity" for conservatism, by withholding moral, affective, and physical support, would be an effective, if indirect, deterrent to conservatism in the long run.[111]

In considering how more direct, positive measures of redirection could be assumed—"support," in the terminology of the deviance paradigm—Parsons warns, once again, against an overemphasis on purely subjective pressures.

> The view so common among Americans that it is "conversion" to democratic values which is the key to bringing Germany "around" is one of the most dangerous misconceptions currently in the air.[112]

He rejects the family, educational system, or government as institutional foci for reform. Either they are inaccessible, or their manipulation would produce psychological overreaction. Instead, Parsons recommends a focus on the economic system, particularly on reforming the occupational system by making it more responsive to equality of opportunity and functional criteria of achievement rather than to more traditional, ascriptive pressures. If industrial expansion is encouraged and the earlier barriers that exacerbated vertical division removed, the other major causes of social polarization would be mitigated. For example, by providing greater security for the husband, the upgrading of occupational status would reduce the need for harsh paternalism in the home and would provide, as well, a wider scope for female independence.[113] Similarly, by changing the economic and cultural situation in which the government acts, the latter's traditionalistic animus would gradually dissolve.[114]

Ten years later, in an essay written after the actual publication of the deviance paradigm, Parsons once again demonstrated the model's multidimensional potential, its continuity with his earlier change essays, and its analytic relevance to crucial contemporary problems.[115†] In this essay, entitled "Social Strains in America," he utilized the approach to analyze the causes of McCarthyism and the prospects for its amelioration. As for causes, Parsons posits a situational conflict. The particular American patterns of rationalization and anomie have produced widespread reluctance to assume "national" obligations. This has been particularly manifest in the pervasive resentment, for both moral and instrumental reasons, of the older, established eastern elite that traditionally offered national leadership. The economic shift westward, for example, exacerbated sectional divisions among upper-class groups. Immigration and rural-urban migration created ethnic animosity among other class segments, particularly within the lower middle class. The failure of business and agriculture in the Great Depression, and the ensuing regulatory legislation, created a hostile and distrustful attitude toward national government, intensifying the individualism of certain groups of farmers and businessmen.

In opposition to these fragmenting national developments, however, the postwar international environment, particularly the cold war, produced an urgent "need to mobilize American Society to cope with a dangerous and threatening situation." This mobilization could succeed only by subordinating private to public interest. This contradiction between national and international development, Parsons believes, placed further strains on the more traditionalistic, less secure segments of American society.

McCarthyism was, Parsons asserts, the reaction to this situational strain. Analyzing it as the psychologically overdetermined effort to resolve structural tensions, he explicates the key expressive symbols of the movement. The focus on loyalty, for example, resolves ambivalence by allowing traditionalist groups to combine exaggerated patriotism with aggression, for while they imputed disloyalty to others, it actually was doubts about their own national loyalty that was generating their anxiety. Communism was another multivalent symbol, allowing the internal and external sources of strain to be neatly tied together. Through this vehicle, radically "emancipated," left-wing groups could be made scapegoats, as could the liberal, more established elites and institutions. Once again, this aggression could be projected outward while the underlying insecurity that these traditionalistic groups felt about their own commitments could be simultaneously assuaged.

By such a process of strain, conflict, and reinforcement, McCarthyism increasingly polarized American society. In order to reidentify interests and to restore consensus, authoritative social control had to be activated. "The problem," Parsons writes, "is in essence a matter of political action, involving . . . questions of leadership—of who, promoting what policies, shall take the primary responsibility.[116] Such responsibility, the key factor in all integrative processes, would encourage wider governmental participation among citizens and, at the same time, support the strengthening of central government.[117]

Social-control processes had not worked, Parsons believes, because no such national authority existed. The assumption of national responsibility was impossible because there was no group for whom "traditional political respect is ingrained."[118] Since at least the 1930s, the business elite had been discredited, and no other group had risen to take its place. Parsons argues that, in the long run, crises of the McCarthyite type can be resolved and national integration restored only by the development of a new, "functional" governmental elite. Primarily, this would involve the creation of two relatively cohesive groups: politicians, who could act and direct opinion in the national rather than sectional interest; and administrators or civil servants, who could effectively carry out the national will. This political elite, however, necessarily would work closely with intellectuals, religious leaders, and segments of the business community.

4.4. CONCLUSION: THE CHANGE THEORY AND ITS CRITICS

As I mentioned earlier, the change theory of Parsons' middle period is particularly interesting because it provided the polemical basis upon which "conflict theory" was constructed. I will later examine the legitimate aspects of such conflict critiques. At this point, however, it is important to emphasize the dimensions of conflict theory which are fundamentally ill conceived. Dahrendorf, in his influential early book, for example, writes that Parsons' " 'array of concepts' is . . . incapable of coping" with social situations that do not manifest "(1) Stability, (2) Integration, (3) Functional coordination and (4) Consensus."[119] Mills concurred, arguing that in Parsons' theory "the idea of conflict cannot effectively be formulated."

> Structural antagonisms, large-scale revolts, revolutions—they cannot be imagined. In fact, it is assumed that "the system," once established, is not only stable but intrinsically harmonious.[120]

Gouldner's early critique is somewhat more nuanced. Acknowledging that two of Parsons' essays, on American social strains and controlled institutional change, deal quite effectively with change and conflict, he asserts that they can do so only by enlisting a number of "*ad hoc* concepts and assumptions" from Freud and Marx that are "nothing less than bewildering," given the true nature of Parsons' work.[121]

On the basis of my preceding discussion, such interpretations can only be described as thoroughly misleading. Parsons' perspective does not focus on integration alone, nor does it assume consensus. To the contrary, it effectively articulates some of the most basic social antagonisms.[122†] Moreover, this change theory is firmly rooted in Parsons' more general empirically-oriented work and in the multidimensional presuppositions that inform it. Beginning with an emphasis on the tension between normative and factual levels, the change theory develops clear notions about the social, cultural, and psychological patterns of strain, about conflict, and about the inhibitions on social control.[123†] Moreover, Parsons' work in this area is not addressed simply to "modernization" or "development" in some abstract sense. Taken together, his writings present a sustained inquiry into the particular national patterns of Western development and the threat to this development posed by the radical right.[124†] In conducting this inquiry, Parsons built upon the contributions of Weber, Durkheim, and Marx. He utilized them, however, only after filtering them through his own original multidimensional synthesis.

Chapter Four

THE LATER PERIOD (1):

The Interchange Model and Parsons' Final Approach to Multidimensional Theory

1. INTERCHANGE AND ITS PRESUPPOSITIONAL LOGIC

In 1953, with the publication of *Working Papers in the Theory of Action,* the form of Parsons' theory, though not its fundamental presuppositional substance, underwent a radical transformation, emerging as the "four-function model" or "interchange theory."[1†] Parsons now focuses his attention more exclusively on the model level. By reformulating his model of society as a functioning system, he tries to relate social process to interchanges between what he regards as the four basic dimensions, or "subsystems," of society.

1.1. THE PROBLEM OF INTERPRETATION

As with the early and middle phases of Parsons' theoretical development, the later phase of his work has been pervasively misinterpreted by sympathizers and critics alike. First, it has been conflated with every significant level of the scientific continuum. Certain commentators, for example, insist that "interchange" derives directly from Parsons' methodological commitments, though their conception of what these are diverge widely. For Wallace, interchange represents an "a-priori specification" of empirical fact, another example of Parsons' effort to take sociology away from theories of the middle range.[2] To Mulkay and Menzies, on the other hand, the scheme's specificity indicates precisely the opposite: it is the direct result, they contend, of Parsons' movement toward positivism.[3] Bershady also locates the relevance of interchange in Parsons' meta-methodology, though he views the latter as an "analytic" position rather than as simply positivist or antipositivist.[4]

Other interpretations see interchange as rooted in Parsons' empirical concern about the maintenance of social stability. Mulkay notes, for example, that "no functionalist imperative dealing with change is included" in Parsons' four functions,[5] and Harry M. Johnson describes the functional problems as "those which must be met to maintain social continuity."[6] Still others, like Dahrendorf, Giddens, Heydebrand, and Gouldner, associate the scheme with specifically ideological objectives.[7]

By far the most pervasive and significant conflationary error, however, is the belief that the interchange scheme derives simply from Parsons' commitment to the functional model itself. Sklair, a critic, views this late innovation, the "cornerstone" of Parsons' sociology, as being based on the later Parsons' more sophisticated understanding of systems and functions.[8] Menzies similarly sees interchange as derived, in part, from Parsons' ambivalent preference for systems analysis over the examination of problems of meaning.[9] Parsons' supporters often make the same kind of conflation. For Benton Johnson, interchange can best be thought of as "processes that constitute the imperatives of any system, from a simple two-person interaction to the most complex modern society."[10] Devereux similarly views the scheme as derived from purely systemic considerations of model choice, as does Rocher.[11]

If Parsons' interpreters manage to avoid such conflationary errors—if they recognize what I will argue is the scheme's true level of generality—they often do so only to reduce interchange to one presuppositional pole over another. Mulkay, for example, takes the position that Parsons' interchange is a form of instrumental exchange theory, representing a radical shift away from Parsons' earlier focus on normative action.[12] Wolin agrees, arguing that with interchange Parsons equates collective order with the utilitarian notions of the classical economists.[13] Much more common, however, is the position that interchange represents an idealist construction. For Wallace, every dimension of this model is located in the normative realm.[14] Martel, a more sympathetic commentator, also sees interchange as merely extending and refining an organicist, holistic approach.[15] Gouldner, though rarely mentioning interchange as such, makes essentially the same point.[16]

In what follows, I will argue that none of these interpretations captures the essence of Parsons' most important contribution.[17] Though indicating a new direction, interchange follows what is by now the familiar preoccupation of Parsons' theory. It is generalized and presuppositional in its primary reference, continuing in a different form his earlier efforts to specify his general commitments. Interchange is Parsons' final and most significant approach to theoretical ecumenicism, to his hope of producing a multidimensional and synthetic sociological theory.

1.2. THE LIMITATIONS OF PARSONS' MIDDLE-PERIOD THEORIZING

The problem of the origins of the interchange model, while a separate task from determining its theoretical meaning, can nonetheless provide us with insight into Parsons' initial intentions. If the model was developed, for example, in response to non-presuppositional considerations, it is less likely to have important presuppositional implications. For reasons that will be elaborated only later in this book, Parsons obscured the origins of interchange in a web of misleading camouflage. At one time or another, he related the inspiration for interchange to logical deduction from the pattern-variable schema, to the empirical discoveries of Bales' small-group research, and to his recognition of the formal homologies between sociological and economic theory.[18] His interpreters, quite understandably, have often cited these same, essentially obfuscating explanations.[19†] The true origins of interchange, however, are to be found in the problems Parsons encountered as he sought to specify his general presuppositional commitments. Interchange provided Parsons with a new mold in which to reshape his long-standing theoretical interests.

But why was any new approach necessary? In his middle-period work, Parsons accomplished great things. Nonetheless, though these achievements were real enough, by the end of the middle period Parsons' conceptualization was in important respects actually inhibiting his presuppositional purpose. As I indicated in the earlier discussion of *The Structure of Social Action*, from the very beginning of his career Parsons associated his presuppositional multidimensionality with the transcendence of empiricism. Only by developing concepts corresponding to analytic rather than concrete elements, Parsons believed, could he clarify the degree to which any empirical phenomenon combined both material and normative factors. Yet a number of the basic concepts he developed in *The Social System* actually indicate an empiricist bias. "Allocation," for example, refers to the concrete processes of distribution, not to an analytic dimension—the distributive—of various concrete activities. Thus, he defines allocation by pointing to activities involved in the actual distribution of emotional and instrumental rewards. "Integration," similarly, refers to the actual operation of the legal system and governmental authority, not to the integrative aspects of laws or government in an analytical sense.

In other words, the two most important social processes that Parsons has identified in the middle period are in important ways concrete rather than analytic. It is not surprising, then, that Parsons' discussion of them is beset by the kinds of theoretical problems that he had earlier linked to theoretical empiricism. In crucial respects, for example, allocation and integration are not sufficiently differentiated. Though they are defined by Parsons in terms of separate empirical processes, they actually overlap with another. Is socialization integrative or allocative? Parsons defines it as a prime example of integration, and socialization as the cathectic organizer of expressive symbols certainly places brackets around conflict over the redistribution of power, a function that is obviously integrative. Yet, in fact, socialization also helps produce the attitudes and skills of personnel. It must, therefore, simultaneously be viewed as an allocative process. As such, it creates the labor power whose needs are at the center of the very conflict that integration is supposed to control. Socialization can be both integrative and allocative because these latter processes *actually* refer to more general analytic dimensions of order than to the concrete processes Parsons formally identifies. He defines these basic processes, therefore, in an overly specific way. Fundamental concepts should be more generally defined; they should relate more closely to Parsons' presuppositional, analytic focus.

The Social System, therefore, exhibits some characteristics of the "type theorizing" that Parsons always sought to avoid. An elusive quality of atomism permeates its discourse; elements and processes of social structure are forcefully analyzed but not sufficiently interconnected. The problem is not, as Parsons' empiricist critics would have it, the giant outpouring of conceptualization—any broadening of empirical specificity entails greater conceptual detail. It is, rather, that these conceptual flights, with the exception of the generalized culture-social-system-personality distinction, are not built upon fundamentally analytic conceptualizations of multidimensional structure. Because they are not, Parsons' conceptual complexity often appears ad hoc, and it often is.

The innovations of Parsons' later period address themselves to this problematic situation. In order to coordinate a wide range of empirical variables, Parsons was forced to simplify his basic conceptual structure.[20†] Good scientific theories must handle complex phenomena, but they must do so in an elegant way. To achieve this combination, Parsons returned explicitly to analytic considerations. His focus shifted to the relation between the presuppositional and model levels, to the connection, that is, between multidimensionality and functional systems. In formulating the model of society as composed of interchanges among four fundamental dimensions, Parsons abstracted his most basic conceptual analysis from any specific empirical characterizations. Though he would never fully recover the tactile, empirical feel of his earlier work, this new effort came much closer to achieving his true theoretical ambition.

Parsons' transition to interchange theorizing, therefore, constituted an effort to contend with these earlier unresolved problems. It was not a question of discovering the data of small-group research, of working out the logical implications of the pattern-variable schema, or finally recognizing the homologies of economic and sociological analysis. While establishing such connections probably helped Parsons personally to bridge these contrasting stages of his theoretical career, they were not fundamental in creating the transition itself. It was the pressure from his commitment to presuppositional synthesis that forced Parsons to abandon much of his early conceptualization. It is not surprising that interchange, initiated for a generalized purpose, is intended to have a fundamentally presuppositional effect.

1.3. THE FOCUS OF INTERCHANGE: REFINING THE MULTIDIMENSIONAL MODEL

We will approach interchange not through the actual stages of Parsons' own presentation of his insight but rather by examining the model's relation to the cybernetic continuum, the most effective formulation of Parsons' approach to multidimensional order.[21†] On the basis of this conceptualization (illustrated in fig. 3), Parsons found he could realign the culture-society-personality schema.[22] By abstracting and schematizing their arrangement, this diagram clarified the levels of generality and specificity among the systems of Parsons' middle-period conceptualization. It also emphasized, more clearly and forcefully than before, their two-directional dialectical relation. The personality system, for example, can now be seen as drawing upon, or mediating between, the resources of the social system on one side and the organism on the other. The cultural system, though it more directly faces "ultimate reality," is conditioned also by the exigencies of social interaction, which bring into play the needs of personality and organism.

But Parsons' most important focus was the social system itself, bordered on one side by the symbolic environment of the cultural system, on the other by the conditional exigencies of personality and organism (see fig. 4). He reasoned that the same pressures that differentiate the cybernetic continuum into these four primary systems—that produce the social system as a differentiated level of organization—would continue to operate within the confines of the social system itself. The social system, Parsons argued, is divided into cybernetic levels of generality and specificity. These must involve, he realized, the most basic analytic components of the concrete processes he had discussed in the middle period. To identify them, he turned back to his earliest analysis of components of the unit act: means, goals, norms, and conditions. From each of these elements, he generalized to a dimension of collective social order (see fig. 5).[23†]

By focusing on basic analytic processes, this new formulation eliminated the disturbing conceptual redundancy of the earlier analysis.[24] Instead of intermixing authoritative power, value consensus, and legal mechanisms, "integration" now refers simply to norms. While "allocation" had earlier focused on a variety of different kinds of instrumental and quasi-instrumental processes, the new formulation differentiates

Figure 3

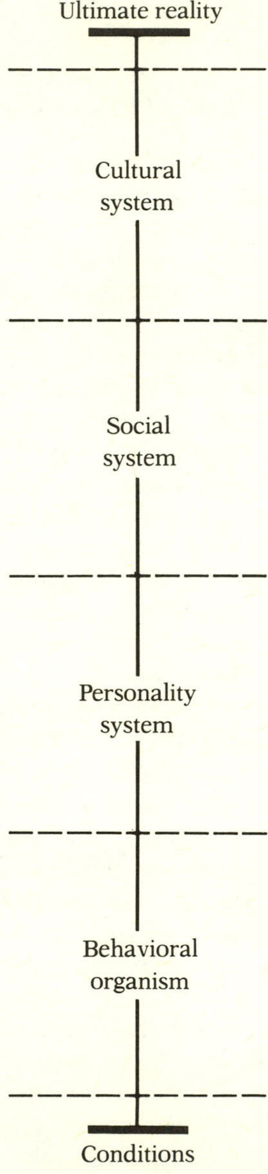
Ultimate reality
Cultural
system
Social
system
Personality
system
Behavioral
organism
Conditions

Figure 4

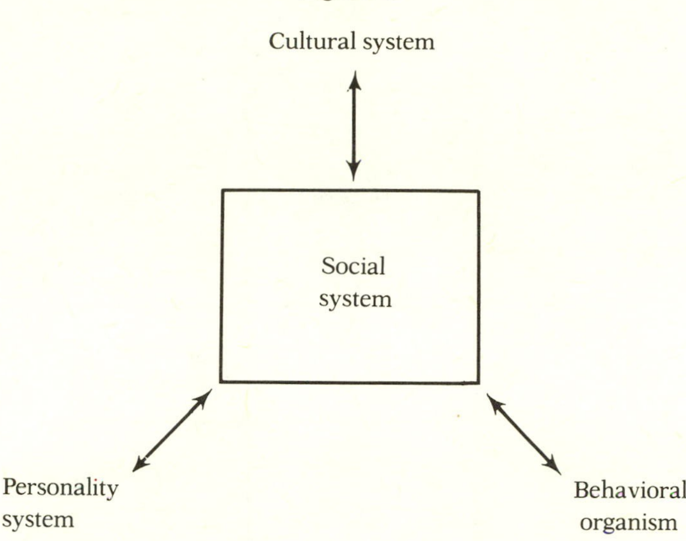

politics and economics, defined simply in terms of the contrasting levels of goals and facilities. "Rewards" had earlier referred both to basic social components, like symbols, and to complex institutional processes, like prestige satisfaction. Now the symbolic aspect of social-system life is identified as an independent dimension, pattern maintenance, which also includes the moral element that in the middle period had been an ad hoc element of both allocation and integration.

The interrelationship of these dimensions follows the general logic of the cybernetic continuum. Perhaps Parsons' most innovative proposal is his differentiation of the "value" sphere of pattern maintenance (L) from the cultural system itself. Because of its social-system focus, pattern maintenance is concerned only with the value patterns that actually become part of empirical conduct. It does not include all the "patterns of meaning" extant in any society, patterns which are part of the cultural, not the social, system.[25†] At the other end of the continuum, the adaptive dimension (A) articulates society's restrictions on the realization of these values, limits that are inherent in the relation of action to the conditional environment. As compared with the internalized constraint of pattern maintenance, adaptation takes the form of external constraints that force action to assume an instrumental focus.

Between these extremes, Parsons identifies two intermediate positions. Like adaptation, goal attainment (G) also represents a focus on effectiveness vis-à-vis external conditions, yet it does so in greater proximity to more general cultural definitions of the situation: "A system of goals . . .

Figure 5

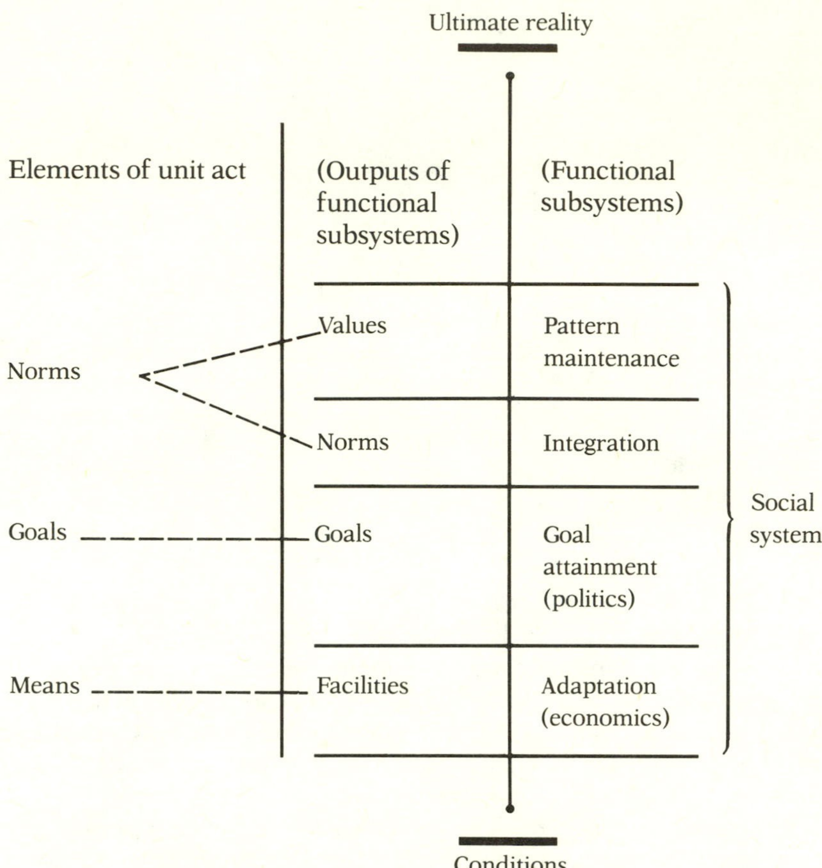

must have some balance between integration as a system and flexible adjustment to changing adaptive pressures."[26] Finally, the integrative dimension (I) delineates noninstrumental elements that are more specific than general values. More influenced by the pressures of goal attainment and adaptation, integrative norms are oriented to the task of maintaining solidarity in particular situations.

By returning to his earliest analysis of action and his later cybernetic refinement of order, Parsons has provided the basis for simplifying and clarifying his conceptual specification of collective order. Despite the functional language, the presuppositional roots of this "four system" model are clear. It formulates, in a sociologically relevant way, an epistemological alternative to materialism and idealism. As Parsons writes in his important "Outline of the Social System":

> The problems of social integration and of pattern-maintenance stand in a different relation to the motivation of the individual than do adaptation and goal-attainment. The latter two are concerned primarily with the mechanisms of "rational" orientation to the conditions of action. . . . The former two, on the other hand, have to do with "nonrational" factors, that is, those involved in the operation of *internalized* values and norms.[27]

The four functional dimensions, in sum, represent increasing degrees of autonomy vis-à-vis the determinacy of external material conditions.[28†]

Is there, however, any way to conceptualize the simultaneous multilayered interaction of these dimensions with one another? If not, we could still be left with simply a more finely graded version of type theorizing. It was precisely to establish such interaction that Parsons formulated his model of societal interchange. In doing so, he replaced the linear continuum with a two-dimensional plane (see fig. 6).[29†]

Figure 6

THE FOUR-FUNCTION MODEL

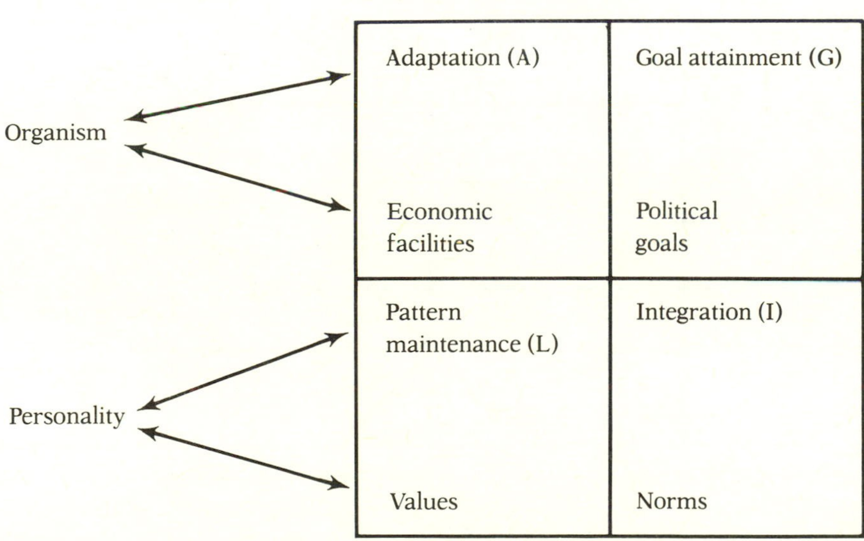

Functional relationships are no longer conceived as linear, as connecting two dimensions alone; they can now be visualized as occurring among all four dimensions simultaneously. This model of simultaneous interrelationship is "interchange" (see fig. 7).

With interchange, Parsons' formulation of collective order achieves the abstract simplicity and elegance of an effective scientific model while encompassing the full multidimensional complexity of real social causality. Political institutions, for example, are viewed as the product of independent political action interacting with values, norms, and facilities (see fig. 8). Yet each of these latter dimensions, the normative, for example, in turn depends on inputs from the others, one of which is politics itself (see fig. 9). The analysis of any single subsystem, in other words, cannot be isolated from the analysis of any other, and it is impossible to simplify social causality in a one-dimensional way.

As compared with his middle-period work, the interchange model much more effectively links Parsons' presuppositional solution to analytic rather than concrete elements. The model's dimensions are defined not by reference to some actually existing organization, but in purely analytic terms.

> It is incorrect, as we have pointed out repeatedly, to identify any concrete class of organizations or their orientations with any one

Figure 7

INTERCHANGE

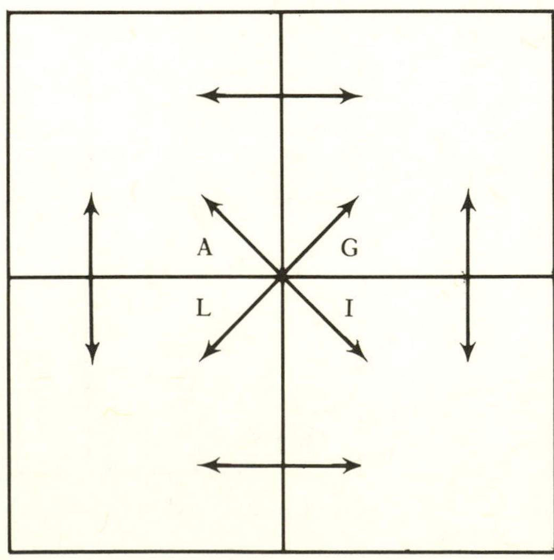

Figure 8

POLITICAL INTERCHANGE

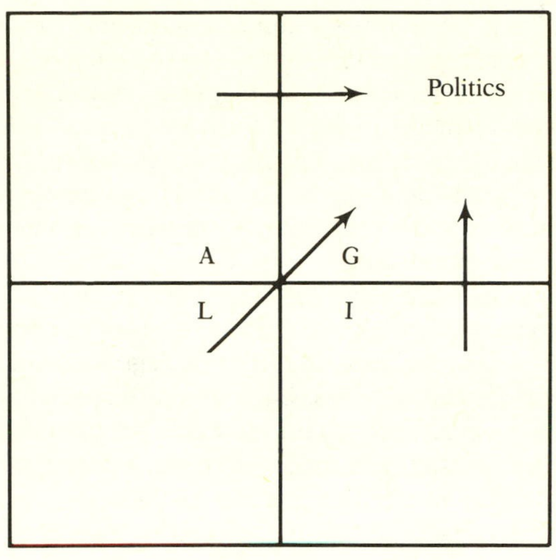

Figure 9

INTEGRATIVE INTERCHANGE

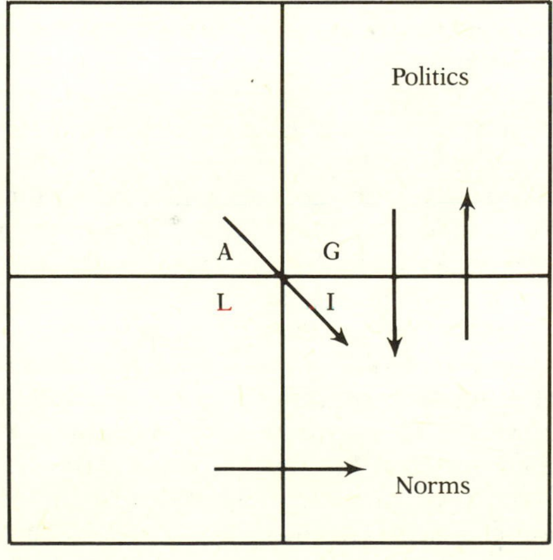

> functionally differentiated subsystem. . . . In principle every concrete organization participates to some degree on [*sic*] all four functional subsystems. . . .[30†]

Every empirical institution must adapt to conditional exigencies in order to gain facilities, form goals to mediate between such exigencies and the value commitments of its members, integrate its social process around norms, and relate all these processes to more general values. There are economic aspects of churches and political aspects of factories. No matter what its concrete focus, no empirical unit is one-dimensional. On presuppositional grounds—for, that is, analytic reasons—every unit must exchange with all four dimensions.

Still, every model must also be specified empirically and ideologically, and the interchange model takes particular shapes in concrete historical situations. Institutions specialize, to different degrees, in economic, political, normative, and value spheres. Each of these specialized institutions, depending on its empirical make-up, depends on certain highly specific inputs from other units. These inputs, in turn, become the object of attempts at control and usurpation among institutions, actors, and social groups. Boundary relations often involve intensive competition and social conflict.

Only by so specifying interchange does Parsons' model become explanatory in an empirical sense. In this specification, empirical and ideological judgments must be made. Are corporations primarily adaptive, market-oriented institutions, or do they function also as goal-attainment structures, regulating the market politically through oligopoly and monopoly? What are the interchanges between goal attainment and integration that characterize a socialist as opposed to a capitalist society? Every utilization of the interchange model, in other words, involves both general and specific levels of analysis.

This introductory presentation of Parsons' later work opposes a number of basic misperceptions which have developed over the years. Given the main thrusts of the secondary interpretation, two points are most important. First, interchange does not exemplify the logic of "functionalism." Interchange is, indeed, a "model" of a "functioning system," but to view its distinctive properties as deriving from Parsons' insight into "systems" per se puts the cart before the horse. The key to this particular system model is that it specifies Parsons' more general epistemological multidimensionality. Parsons does, of course, speak of these dimensions as "subsystems." He even describes the differences between the four dimensions in terms of the need for subsystems to maintain their "boundaries" vis-à-vis their environments. But one must insist on the fact that the boundaries between A, G, I, and L (see figs. 6–9) are not simply the manifestations of abstract system functions. They represent, rather, the demarcations between different degrees of instrumental and normative order.

Exchange over these boundaries, therefore, is not carried out because "systems" must inherently carry out "input and output" relations with their "environments," but rather because Parsons' multidimensional position demands the interrelation of instrumental and normative exigencies.

Equally significant, interchange cannot be reduced to presuppositional idealism, as many critics have attempted. In fact, the fundamental basis of interchange could not be more misconstrued. The model does, of course, extend normative factors into every dimension of social life, but, in principle, it just as consistently traces the permeation of instrumental pressures for efficiency. Without the notion of multidimensionality, interchange would not be *interchange.*

Perhaps the best illustration of these points can be found in the connection between interchange theory and Parsons' continuing dialogue with Weber, Durkheim, and Marx. With interchange, Parsons liberates sociological theory from the base-superstructure straitjacket that plagued not only Marx but his classical antagonists as well. The problems with classical theory rest, in the end, on its concrete rather than analytic approach to social causality. Only in such a concrete framework can an action or institution be classified as either "economic" or "cultural," as either base or superstructure. By formulating a much more analytic approach to social order, Parsons breaks through such dichotomizing, dualistic constraints on theorizing. Institutional orders are autonomous and interdependent. They differentiate not according to whether they are more or less "real," but according to their differentiated positions on one continuous causal continuum.[31†]

The following discussion of Parsons' specific applications of interchange theory will demonstrate that the model provides significant advances over the formulations of each of these earlier theorists. By systematizing the interaction of instrumental and normative factors, interchange allows Parsons to avoid the residual categories and presuppositional simplifications that undermined the triumphs of classical thought.

2. ECONOMICS AS INTERCHANGE: ELABORATING THE CRITIQUE OF CLASSICAL ECONOMICS

Throughout *Economy and Society,* which Parsons co-authored with Smelser and which represents his most significant application of the interchange schema to economic life, there are implicit a variety of neo-Keynesian empirical and ideological assumptions. Though certainly not insignificant, these are not the original aspects of Parsons' treatment. *Economy and Society* is, above all, a presuppositional tour de force, an attempt to utilize interchange to carry through a radical critique of the individualist and utilitarian assumptions that inform contemporary, neo-classical economic thought.

Parsons and Smelser use the model, first, to establish the relation between the adaptive subsystem and its environments. "Those who control factors of production," they write, must be induced to "utilize or permit utilization of these resources for economic purposes."[32] Each factor of production—labor, capital, organization—is linked to outputs from the extra-economic subsystems, from pattern maintenance, goal attainment, and integration, respectively. In effect, money is traded for appropriate values, norms, and power. In this process, instrumental considerations are vital, for each party naturally "seeks to make the best possible bargain." Still, given the logic of interchange, such demands are also regulated by more normative considerations. Furthermore, this exchange cannot be an individualist one: it is regulated by supra-individual, collective forces.

The discussion of the pattern-maintenance–adaptive interchange provides perhaps the best illustration of this concern. While the process involves an exchange of labor for wages, Parsons and Smelser warn against a rationalist or individualist analysis: "Labor does not enter the labor force from a completely undifferentiated state."[33] To incorporate the facts of cultural generalization and psychological internalization, they conceptualize a "resource chart" for the production of labor. Composed of seven levels of increasingly specific "trained capacity," ranging from the relatively unformed socialization of early life to the concrete utilization of labor in a production setting, the sequence spans both pattern-maintenance and adaptive dimensions.[34] It can now be seen that it is not with the supply of labor as such but rather only with the fourth stage of this supply sequence that the economic analysis of labor supply is usually concerned. This stage represents the individual's transition from "value" to "adaptive" activities, and here, indeed, there is the "sensitivity to short run economic sanctions" that such labor-force analysis typically assumes.[35]

Because he faces the adaptive environment, then, the worker "must adapt his actions [to] limiting conditions" and be constrained "by the kinds of goods he sells and the terms he must accept." Yet because this worker is, at the same time, emerging from the dimension of values, this instrumental exchange also "involves a higher level of symbolic generalization," one that "defines the 'meaning' of [his] primary goal objects." The very willingness to supply labor depends, in part, on the "valuation of the function performed."[36] Parsons and Smelser treat the trade union, for example, as addressing both these concerns. In its adaptive function, it compensates for the "relative bargaining disadvantage of the individual worker." In its relation to the other boundary, to the pattern-maintenance dimension, however, unions perform "semi-ritual" functions for the worker's personality, helping to "integrate the individual worker and his household into a larger collectivity."[37]

In their analysis of the integrative and goal-attainment interchanges, Parsons and Smelser follow this same double-pronged critique. Insofar as economic norms are "independent of the particular positions of the contracting parties and of the particular resources" involved, they constitute inputs from integration to adaptation.[38] These inputs may be formal rules—for example, laws allowing individual rather than familial control over the disposal of labor power. They may also be informal, and by this Parsons and Smelser refer to the factor of "organization," defined as the creation of new normative arrangements by economic entrepreneurs. Neither of these factors, they argue, can be systematically accounted for by the neoclassical approach.[39†] There must, of course, be adaptive "returns" for such inputs, which Parsons and Smelser describe as economic outputs that allow integrative institutions "control over instrumental conditions."

In discussing the economy-polity relation, the crucial point Parsons and Smelser make is that control over capital funds is a political, not an economic, decision: "The creation of credit is primarily an exercise of power." It involves, in other words, a kind of coercive control different from the instrumental "inducement" of economic life. In return for this input of power over capital, the economy supplies the polity, through taxation, with control over crucial instrumental facilities.[40] Once again, Parsons and Smelser emphasize the generalized aspect of this argument. It constitutes "a radical departure from traditional economic analysis which, because of its inability to differentiate goals from facilities, treats the supply of capital funds as directly dependent . . . on interest."[41] Moreover, this interchange is not simply a rational one, in either the political or the economic sense: Parsons and Smelser detail how the symbolic aspects of government interest rates are crucial to investor confidence in the economy.[42]

This discussion can provide only the briefest sketch of Parsons' and Smelser's argument, particularly of the manner in which they incorporate complex empirical materials. Still, the basic structure of their argument is plain. The interchange model has pushed them in a distinctive direction, and while the empirical-ideological assumptions of "Parsonian" economic analysis are relatively malleable, this interchange framework is not. In conclusion, two points are particularly apparent. First, although Parsons and Smelser continually use systems language, their position obviously has a fundamentally more generalized, presuppositional orientation. Second, a good part of this presuppositional argument is clearly multidimensional. When, three years after the publication of *Economy and Society*, Gouldner criticized Parsonian systems theory for "excluding all 'material elements,' " he never so much as acknowledged the existence of the interchange model.[43] To do so would necessarily have blunted the sharp edge of his critical remarks.[44†]

Finally, as in his earlier theoretical efforts, Parsons has oriented his presuppositional position to the problems he perceives in Weber, Durkheim, and Marx. In this sense, *Economy and Society* directly addresses the issues Parsons raised in his earliest interpretive work. By arguing within his synthetic interchange model, Parsons in his later economic analysis can avoid the residual categories that he exposed in the work of the classical economists and their critics. By analyzing integrative and value inputs, for example, Parsons incorporates the "non-contractual" elements that Durkheim emphasized.[45†] Further, he utilizes the Freudian internalization-socialization theory to differentiate the specific issue of worker motivation from contract regulation in a way that Durkheim could not. On the other hand, by simultaneously focusing on the interchange between these factors and economic sanctions, Parsons can account for the Marxian emphasis on scarcity that remained residual for Durkheim. At the same time, Parsons, like Weber, offsets Marx's economic reduction by separating economic factors from organizational, legal, and political ones. This synthesis, moreover, is far from eclectic: it is informed by a highly refined analytic model that is itself presupposed by an intensely self-conscious effort at epistemological synthesis.

3. POLITICS AS INTERCHANGE

Parsons' later political theory has been subject to a series of conflationary and reductionistic interpretations. Labeling this work as typically "functionalist," for example, Gouldner claims that Parsons simply "define[s] power as legitimate" in itself.[46] Viewing it as typically idealist, Rex argues that Parsons ignores anything other than "value systems," suggesting as an alternative view that "there are many transitional points between actual coercion and legitimate rule or rules by consent."[47] In a similar vein, Giddens suggests that Parsons is unable to connect his abstract political typologies to actual conflict between interest groups.[48] Finally, stressing Parsons' commitment to an empirical equilibrium, Dahrendorf asserts that Parsons' rejection of the zero-sum approach to the distribution of power[49] renders him incapable of analyzing political conflict.

Although it will be seen later in my analysis that such critiques are not by any means totally without foundation, any realistic and objective assessment of Parsons' political theory reveals that they have drastically distorted its most important contribution. Parsons' later political theory is not exclusively normative or static. Nor is it uniquely systems oriented. It is none of these things because this political theory is organized around the interchange model, which was designed to specify Parsons' broader multidimensional intention.

3.1. REFINING THE MULTIDIMENSIONAL CONCEPTUALIZATION

Parsons' later definitions of power take their cue from the logic of interchange, utilizing it to focus on the tension between force and legitimacy. In the first place, power is instrumental: "Power and wealth have in common that they are both generalized categories of 'means,' i.e., of 'capacities' to get desired things done."[50] For this reason, power must be viewed as having an important coercive aspect. An individual has power, then, if he can effectively "carry out his intentions, regardless of [another person's] wishes—not necessarily against them, but independently of them."[51] At the same time, however, power has a more intermediate dimensional position than wealth. It is concerned with goals, not just facilities. More directly than purely adaptive economic processes, therefore, power must be concerned with normative and value commitments. Because it results from this interaction of instrumental and more general pressures, power needs legitimation. In defining legitimation, for example, Parsons is careful to indicate its more intermediate, conditionally oriented status relative to the "value" dimension.

> Legitimation thus is the set of criteria by reference to which "adherence" to a pattern of values is translated . . . into implementing action—it is, that is to say, the *action* which is legitimated.[52]

Perhaps the best indication of Parsons' insistence on power's multidimensionality is his treatment of force. Force would appear to be the prototype of instrumental power, the conditional base line beyond which the application of power cannot go. Yet this is not true, Parsons contends. As a form of power, force is inherently multidimensional: "The use and threat of force have a set of symbolic meanings that define a penumbra of effect extending well beyond their direct instrumental influence."[53] If power itself is a kind of cybernetic continuum, so is force. "It is possible to construct," Parsons argues, "a scale of degrees of forceful deprivation of effectiveness-potential."[54] At one extreme, force is actually no more than "deterrence," which amounts simply to threats and warnings. In other words, though associated with force, deterrence is not strictly coercive, for it remains, like most exercises of power, dependent to some degree on the voluntary will of the dominated. In fact, only by nullifying "action" itself, Parsons believes, can force become truly coercive, for only in this manner is intentionality, or will, prevented from confronting the situational environment.

Parsons defines power, then, in a multidimensional manner, and he uses this definition to establish a continuum of transitional points between voluntary and coercive accession to rule. This argument is neither specifically functionalist nor idealist; rather, it builds upon and refines the synthetic presuppositional orientation of his earlier work. Similarly, it is this presuppositional commitment, not some inability to envision empirical conflict, that defines Parsons' opposition to the zero-sum approach to politics. As Parsons defines it, zero-sum is the notion that "any gain on the part of A must by definition occur by diminishing the power at the disposal of other units B, C, D."[55] In political analysis, in other words, zero-sum represents the empirical equivalent to the Hobbesian approach to action and order.

Parsons conducts his critique of this position through a series of complex arguments in a number of different essays, but his basic point is simple and clear. Zero-sum is true only if theory accepts a one-dimensional, exclusively instrumentalist position. If action is conceived as controlled only through the conditional environment, then the actors in the struggle for political power can be viewed as completely discrete individuals among whom no "interpenetration" exists. In this situation, any power increase must necessarily be linked to a particular individual interest. If, on the other hand, symbolic generalization among individuals is accepted, increases in power need not necessarily detract from the power of any particular individual, for such increases may be "felt to be in accordance with valid norms and may apply to situations which are felt to 'call for handling' at the level of heightened binding commitments." In such situations, Parsons believes, political leaders "can mobilize the binding commitments of their constituents in such a way that the totality of commitments made by the collectivity as a whole can be enhanced."[56†]

3.2. POLITICS AND THE COMBINATORIAL PROCESS

After using the general logic of interchange to conceptualize power, Parsons uses the model itself to specify power empirically. Once again, we will see that this more specific Parsonian treatment is linked neither to idealism, nor to a reified systematicity, nor to a commitment to empirical stability.

Parsons defines power as dependent on a number of supra-political inputs, which he calls factors of "capacity" and "opportunity." Capacity refers to inputs from the economic dimension, which allow power to "command . . . the facilities necessary for effective action." Opportunity, on the other hand, refers to inputs from the internal, more general exigencies, that allow "access to the support of those units that have somehow become . . . dependent on the output of the units in question."[57] If power has inputs of support without capacity, it will not be effective. If, on the other hand, it has inputs of capacity without support, it will not be authoritative.[58]

In the course of various essays, Parsons elaborates each of these interchanges in some detail.[59] Because of his emphasis on the relative autonomy of each input, the tension between instrumental and normative aspects of power pervades these discussions. In his analysis of the economic-political exchange, for example, Parsons emphasizes mutual self-interest. The polity allows capital improvement in the economy to "improve its [own] level of adaptation,"[60] Parsons asserts, and he cites feudalism as an instance in which conflict ensued between state and economy because the shrinking economic "base of mobilizable resources"—for example, taxes—"seriously impaired" the power of centralized bureaucratic regimes.[61] Similarly, in discussing normative inputs to politics, Parsons differentiates "support" from "interest demands." While support supplies government policy with a relatively diffuse legitimation, interest demands refer to the specific policies lobbied for by particular groups, which are considered normative because they represent, as such, neither economic inducements nor, as yet, political power.[62] The crucial point in this theoretical differentiation is Parsons' view that the relation between these two inputs revolves around their contrasting levels of generality. Particular policies, if implemented, will "impinge differentially, not equally," thus "imposing varying obligations . . . and reallocating resources"; it is because of this, Parsons believes, that "inherent integration problems arise"—a belief that he articulated in a different form in his earlier allocation/integration dichotomy.[63] To justify this inequality, political leadership must create, through normative persuasion, more diffuse support. It is in the tension between these two potentially conflicting kinds of normative inputs that the integrative significance of political parties lies. For while political parties campaign on "specific issues that are close to the level of . . . advocacy of policies," they usually try to connect these demands to the "symbolization at higher levels of generalization" about which "supra-party consensus exists."[64] This higher-level symbolization, in turn, draws not only upon norms but upon values; an input of "legitimation" from the pattern-maintenance sphere completes the interchange through which power is produced.

This normative-factual interrelation is further complicated by Parsons' argument that politics is itself an independent dimension. Politics involves, in other words, an active, "combinatorial" component. An individual, group or institution achieves power only to the degree that these factors of economic capacity, support, and legitimation are effectively brought together. "Good administration and policy making . . . 'make' power," Parsons writes, "just as production 'makes' . . . goods and money."[65] It is this "process of transformation of the non-political factors" that distinguishes "what is wanted" from "what is merely available."[66] In utilizing this exchange schema to conceptualize the historical origins of the English parliamentary system, for example, Parsons emphasizes not only the suprapolitical inputs—the independent economic position of the English gentry, the common-law tradition of extragovernmental norms, the religious tradition of nonconformity—but also the series of creative political acts, from the Long Parliament to the Glorious Revolution, without which the new democratic structures could not have been born.[67]

Finally, far from being rooted in a static analysis, Parsons locates the sources of political strain and conflict in the very tension between the generalizing and specifying pressures that constitute political interchange. Given the diversity of particular social interests, he believes, "it is objectively impossible for government to satisfy all the demands presented to it." Moreover, given the very generality of normative support and value legitimation, many of these unmet demands will be legitimate ones, for a political situation "always involves a major excess of legitimate . . . demands over capacity to satisfy them."[68] But if legitimate demands cannot be met, support will be withdrawn. To the degree that an imbalance occurs between inputs and outputs, political instability ensues, for in "the long run the balance-of-power potential depends upon capacity to exchange power for the media of societal subsystems adjacent to the polity."[69] Given feelings of illegitimacy and grievance, power will be unable to conduct these crucial exchanges. But if sufficient inputs to power do not occur, even less power will be forthcoming and further withdrawals will be made by power's dimensional environments. If these deficits are serious enough, there will be a downward spiral toward the use of force. Eventually, revolutionary countermovements will develop.[70†]

The combinatorial process itself, in other words, creates instability. Far from overlooking political conflict, Parsons' theory of interchange is, at least in part, designed to clarify it.[71†]

3.3. BEYOND THE CLASSICS: PARSONS' DURKHEIM-WEBER SYNTHESIS

Karl Deutsch has described Parsons' interchange analysis of politics as having opened "a path to a more fundamental reinterpretation of power than has been possible since the days of Hobbes and Locke."[72] While this evaluation may not apply to Parsons' theory in toto, it is clearly true that the multidimensional aspects of this later theory offer the potential for resolving significant and long-standing issues in the study of politics. When applied to empirical problems, it is flexible enough to follow the fluid nature of the legitimation-coercion dynamic, incorporating phenomena from the most mundane and specific to the most general. At the same time, the theory addresses the concerns of classical political theory, which emphasizes the transcendent elements of political life, its normative focus and the ethical concerns of its participants. The interchange analysis is sensitive to such factors, moreover, without crossing over into purely speculative, nonempirical forms of theorizing or into a purely voluntary approach to political life.[73†]

But my concern is presuppositional, not empirical, and, once again, the best approach to the significance of Parsons' theoretical contribution is to trace the relationship between his political theory and that of the classical theorists with whom he carried on a continual dialogue. For Parsons has, in fact, developed his political analysis largely to resolve problems he discovered in the theories of Durkheim and Weber.

For Durkheim, politics involved the dialogue between representative institutions of the state and the symbolic collective conscience. Through this dialogue, specific democratic normative commitments would emerge from the inchoate general will. In producing this theory, Durkheim superseded the instrumentalist view of the state, and in this Parsons closely follows his French mentor. In differentiating the pattern-maintenance and normative dimensions of politics from the explicitly political and adaptive ones, Parsons accepts the Durkheimian injunction. He is determined to avoid the "tendency to exaggerate the empirical importance of power by alleging that it is only power which 'really' determines what happens in a society,"[74] and his analysis of power's value and normative interchange clarifies the general/specific dialogue Durkheim had emphasized. For Durkheim, however, this is where politics ended. His sociologically idealist theory had no room for the state's instrumental, coercive face. Parsons' interchange theory does not follow Durkheim along this road. Instead, Parsons turns at this point to Weber.

It would not be inaccurate to describe the achievement of Parsons' political theory as the integration of Weber's political sociology with his sociology of religion. I have argued earlier (in vol. 3) that while Weber's religious studies stressed the political ramifications of different religious beliefs, his political studies used legitimation and coercion in an almost purely instrumental way. Stretched between Machiavellianism and religious inspiration, Weber's important efforts at multidimensional interrelation too often ended in dichotomization and reduction. This problem is reflected both in Weber's general definitional discussion of power, which continually confuses feelings of legitimation with the factual legality of authority, and in his empirical discussions, which too often focus on the Hobbesian dynamics of domination rather than normative legitimation.

By postulating interchanges between the polity and its three environments, Parsons provides a framework for resolving these dilemmas. The simultaneity of interchange and the analytic rather than concrete status of the four-function model supersede Weber's dichotomization of political action. Moreover, the continuum from compulsion to voluntary authority provides an alternative to Weber's definitional problems. Most important, Parsons' model illuminates the fundamental connections between Weber's formulation of political development and his analyses of religious, legal, and economic change. Among his contemporaries, Parsons was the only theorist who went beyond Weber in this way.[75†]

This relationship between Parsons' and Weber's political sociologies has been difficult for interpreters to perceive. For Parsons' instrumentalist critics, there simply is no complementarity; they view Parsons as merely idealizing Weber's original materialist bent. On the other hand, critics who appreciate the multidimensional element in Parsons' political sociology have not been able to recognize the antagonistic relation between the two theorists.[76†] Both these interpretive errors, ironically, derive from Parsons' denial of any opposition between Weber's political sociology and his own.

My earlier discussion (vol. 3, e.g., ch. 4, secs. 1, 3) described Parsons' influential interpretation as contending—quite falsely—that Weber had successfully integrated his analyses of political action and religious belief. Now, after examining Parsons' own political theory, we can recognize an extraordinary circumstance: in so interpreting Weber, Parsons denied his own originality. There are, it seems, two reasons for such an anomaly. One involves an issue in the sociology of knowledge: the kind of antagonism to traditional authority that intellectual originality requires often produces a certain anxiety.[77] Weber always functioned as the most important legitimation for Parsons' emphasis on the importance of multidimensionality. Yet, at the same time, only by overcoming Weber could such multidimensionality in fact be achieved. By denying any difference between himself and Weber, then, Parsons could both absolve himself from the guilt of rebellion and sustain himself in his own theoretical quest. The second, not unrelated reason for Parsons' denial rests on the methodological level, in his linear, "accumulationist" view of scientific growth. By reading back into Weber much of what he himself discovered, Parsons could view his own work simply as one more link in the steady evolution of social scientific theory. Yet, in truth, only by imbedding Weber in the matrix of Parsons' more dynamic model does Weberian political sociology take a truly multidimensional form.[78†]

4. INTEGRATION AS INTERCHANGE: "SOLIDARITY" BEYOND IDEALISM

Far from being derived from some abstract notion about the nature of functional systems or from an attempt to define the basis of social stability, Parsons' later analysis of integration has its origins in his continuing effort to specify his multidimensional image of society. Once again, it is the interchange model that supplies Parsons with the crucial theoretical resources for this task.

4.1. INTEGRATION DEFINED: SOLIDARITY AND THE LOGIC OF INTERCHANGE

Parsons' initial definition of integration relies on interchange's general logic. In contrast to the external, conditional focus of politics and economics, the integrative subsystem structures internal obligations of loyalty and solidarity. But the norms through which solidarity and loyalty are established are not simply anti-instrumental; they are also, in some sense, "anti-ideal," since they are differentiated from the dimension of "values" by their greater sensitivity to particular conditions. More than the consensus created by values, the solidarity generated by norms is likely to result in concerted social action. Solidarity, Parsons writes, implies that people share a "common fate" in terms of their actual life circumstances.[79]

Parsons follows this definition, for example, in his analysis of voting. Although voting obviously has political effects, Parsons argues that for the individual it has primarily integrative significance. As such, it assumes an "intermediate" dimensional position. Parsons supports this proposition by contending, first, that the issues involved in voting are too numerous and complex to be solved by the kinds of rational, cognitive processes upon which instrumental action depends.[80] In making their decisions voters need more generalized, nonconditional references. Given the "pressure to make commitments" that voting involves, and the inability to justify these in a rational way, voters will rely on "beliefs that can give meaning to the commitment."[81]

These beliefs, however, do not refer to the most highly generalized level of value consensus. Voting, after all, is still closely related to specific economic and political considerations; the beliefs that govern it, therefore, must be rooted in more conditionally structured associations than value groupings. It is rather as members of solidary groupings that individuals vote. Shared political belief, in fact, occurs more frequently in the family; it is less frequent in associations generated by religions and classes that are too generalized or too conditionally related to induce solidarity.[82] This conclusion should not be surprising, Parsons believes, because the family is society's core solidary group. Members of a family, in contrast to members of either more or less generalized associations, share the same fate, "belonging together . . . on such a basis that . . . ego could not have an interest in trying to deceive alter."[83]

4.2. THE NATURE OF SOLIDARY INTERCHANGE

This definition of solidarity provides the basis for Parsons' new specification of the interchange model. Like economic facilities and political goals, integrative norms are in a sense "produced" by interaction with their dimensional environments. Norms can be viewed as indicating membership in a "community of solidarity," an association composed of individuals who have internalized the same norm.[84] In this respect the normative inputs to economic and political production, discussed above, represent the impact of the economic or political actor's simultaneous membership in another kind of associational grouping. While less instrumental than the economic or political collectivity in which his action concretely occurs, the actor's membership in this solidary association is equally binding.[85]

Parsons believes that the nature and scope of any norm, as well as the solidary community it implies, are produced by inputs from society's non-integrative environments. On the one hand, because concerted action is vitally affected by its instrumental ability both to adapt to external conditions and to achieve specific goals, the range of solidary loyalty must in part be "a function of factors deriving from the economy and the polity."[86] On the other hand, such instrumental pressures by themselves would promote atomism rather than solidarity. In studying integration, any consideration of such conditional actors must be supplemented by attention to inputs from pattern-maintenance institutions. The structure of any normative community, Parsons argues, depends in part "on the relative valuation of the functions in the larger system of the solidary groupings we are talking about."[87]

4.3. THE HISTORICAL PRODUCTION OF CITIZENSHIP SOLIDARITY

Parsons' analysis of solidarity and interchange goes into extensive empirical detail. In fact, he devoted an entire monograph, *The System of Modern Societies*, to an interchange analysis of national solidarity in Western societies. Identifying the integrative dimension of the nation states as the "societal community,"[88] Parsons is concerned with the transition from a particularistic societal community to a universalistic one, a process which he views as synonymous with the growth of citizenship.

Parsons' first problem is to locate this transition within the framework of his general analysis of solidarity. Throughout most of the postfeudal period, he believes, the national societal communities of Europe remained particularistic, identified with the solidarity of the group that ruled the nation—a class, religious, organizational, or ethnic group whose rule was articulated through some dynastic family. Only in the late eighteenth and nineteenth centuries did the societal community begin to define belonging in terms of the more universalistic ties of citizenship.[89] As citizenship became the dominant solidarity, it provided the possibility that more particularistic groups, groups with antagonistic economic, ethnic, religious or political interests, would still share some overarching commonality.

In early modern society, the strongest foundation of solidarity was found where the three factors of religion, ethnicity, and territoriality coincided with nationality. In fully modern societies, however, there can be diversity on each basis—religious, ethnic, and territorial—because the common status of citizenship provides a sufficient foundation for national solidarity.[90]

After so defining citizenship, Parsons employs the multidimensionality of interchange to trace its historical development. The evolution of universalistic solidarity, he believes, depended on the unique solutions offered by Western society to the systemic problems that impinged on integration—the structures Western societies developed to cope with the conditional pressures of adaptation and goal attainment, and the patterns they created to define cultural reality. In response to these distinctive developments, more universalistic forms of solidarity were gradually constructed.

According to Parsons' analysis, the new definition of religious community established by the early Christian church constituted the most significant value input to this integrative development. By conceiving of itself as a voluntary association, Christianity "freed the religious community from previous territorial and ethnic ascription."[91] In contrast to the Jewish identification of religious solidarity with a national covenant, Christianity promoted a sense of religious belonging that was separate from any political commitments.[92] It thereby generated indirect pressure for defining the secular national community in a similarly differentiated way. Limited by the conservative economic and political forces that feudalized Europe, this cultural input was still strong enough, Parsons argues, to ensure that the particularistic definition of the feudal societal community should receive only secondary legitimation. At the end of the Middle Ages, the universalism of the original Christian promise became prominent once again, this time, during the Reformation, in an even more radical form.[93]

Furthermore, Parsons uses interchange to reject a one-dimensionally idealistic position. For, in his view, while these long-term cultural developments were necessary to establish a universalist solidary, they were certainly not sufficient. To indicate the other, more conditional factors involved, he launches into a detailed analysis of the concrete historical situation in post-Reformation Europe.[94†] For example, the societies of the Counter-Reformation, despite their Christianity, produced relatively particularistic societal communities. Parsons accounts for this by pointing to the military problems created by the difficult frontier conditions of many southern and eastern European societies, their internal ethnic multiplicity, and their frequent lack of cohesive territoriality. Such factors, combined with the regeneration of Catholicism, produced the alliance of monarchy, church, officialdom, and aristocracy that undermined the autonomy of the rising urban classes.[95†]

Only in societies where the Reformation took hold, in Parsons' view, did a more universalistic societal community have any real chance to develop. England provides him with the major illustration of such success and, once again, he uses interchange to clarify the complex historical process. In terms of the value input so crucial for universal solidarity, only in England were the integrative implications of the Christian community even approximately realized. In turn, Parsons argues that this could occur only because the English civil war gave political legitimacy to the nonconformist aspects of the Protestant faith.

Parsons' discussion, in fact, emphasizes the crucial importance of political developments in supplementing value inputs to the "production" of citizenship. If such universalistic norms are to inform actual conduct, they must be capable of binding enforcement.[96] Such political support could be forthcoming, of course, only if the structures of national solidarity and political authority were sufficiently complementary. The emergence of political absolutism in the early modern period, for example, greatly facilitated the expansion of solidarity from the local to the national level. Yet because it linked membership in the national community with loyalty to a particular national leadership, absolutism later proved a barrier to any further movement toward universalism.[97] Broader definitions of national community, therefore, had to wait for inputs from democratizing political developments. Only with the spread of the franchise could membership in the societal community finally be separated from the allegiance to a particular government as such.

The development of such a democratic franchise occurred first in England, and Parsons devotes considerable space to tracing its origins. In so doing, he is applying an interchange approach to politics as one part of his broader interchange analysis of solidarity. Without the systematic clarity provided him by this model, such complexity would be impossible to articulate in a systematic way. Parsons first discusses England's unusual ethnic homogeneity as an integrative input to democratic development. In turn, he relates this to the political and religious forces that virtually eliminated English Catholicism, particularly the spread of Puritanism and the political repression of Catholics by the English monarchy. An equally important source of democratization was the historical strength of the English system of parliamentary representation, a factor Parsons links to England's unusual class structure, particularly to the fate of its aristocracy.[98] In the early transition to absolutism, the crucial challenge had been to overcome the localistic, familial nature of aristocratic rulership. Both France and England accomplished this during the struggles of the Reformation, which "nationalized" the aristocracies by forcing them to ally with national administrative and military authority. But whereas in the French case this process completely undermined aristocratic independence, the English aristocracy retained its autonomy. It was able to do so for a number of political and military reasons, particularly the unity the aristocracy had forged in the struggle against William the Conqueror, together with the physical isolation of England which allowed this strength to be maintained. As the institution of aristocratic representation, the English parliament, therefore, remained powerful throughout the consolidation of national power. Parsons believes this institution was fundamental to the emergence of citizenship because representation necessitated the separation of government membership from membership in the national community. England's tradition of "extra-governmental" common law and the independent status of its legal professionals reinforced this separation. Eventually, as the aristocratic character of parliamentary representation gave way, a democratic franchise evolved. As England began to incorporate rising groups into Parliament regardless of their economic, religious, or ethnic identity, its political system was universalized. By such interaction of religious, integrative, political, and class factors, therefore, a political input emerged that was complementary to a universalistic societal community.

Parsons now returns to his broader analysis of English solidarity as such. He emphasizes the importance of the tremendous expansion of English trade alongside the other inputs he has discussed from religion and politics. By allowing the separation of economic status from family, land, and ethnicity, the commercialization of the English gentry undermined the particularistic definitions of community membership.[99] Moreover, by commercializing the peasantry, this development disposed of a force that in other nations formed a fundamental barrier to the expansion of national solidarity.

In conducting this analysis of the development of citizenship, Parsons utilized the multidimensional logic of interchange to define a universalistic solidary community. Subsequently, he measured historical developments by their contribution to such integration, focusing on religious, political, and economic factors in turn. Although Parsons treats integrative developments as independent variables in this historical process, at no point does he make this analytic isolation concrete. In his discussion of multilayered interchanges, integrative developments are always carefully linked to their dimensional environments.

4.4. THE INTERCHANGE THEORY OF INTEGRATION AND THE LIMITATIONS OF PARSONS' CLASSICAL PREDECESSORS

In terms of his long-range synthetic goal, Parsons' interchange approach to integration represents a tremendous accomplishment, more original and potentially more significant than his discussion of either economics or politics. On the basis of his multidimensional presuppositional critique, Parsons has utilized interchange to illuminate an empirical variable that has been treated largely as an epiphenomenon by materialists and idealists alike. Parsons' critics have ignored this accomplishment. In their essay on the treatment of norms in contemporary theory, for example, Blake and Davis claim that Parsons' idealism forces him to subsume norms entirely to values.[100] Making a similar error, Heydebrand examines the monograph just discussed, *The System of Modern Societies*, and concludes that it presents a purely cultural, antimaterialist account of citizenship solidarity.[101†] Both these critiques miss the multidimensionality which lies at the very heart of Parsons' analysis. At the same time, Parsons' focus on norms as distinct from values has been only sporadically appreciated by his "Parsonian" followers.[102†]

To appreciate fully Parsons' contribution, we must place it in the context of his dialogue with his classical predecessors. As with the political and economic theories, Parsons has built his approach to integration upon the work of Durkheim and Weber. Yet, as in these other discussions, he has also clearly gone beyond them in significant ways.

The concept of solidarity comes, of course, from Durkheim. Yet, as I tried to demonstrate in volume 2, except in parts of *The Division of Labor in Society* Durkheim never successfully analyzed solidarity in a multidimensional, dynamic way. Certainly, he shared Parsons' enthusiasm for a universalistic solidarity oriented to the norm of "individualism" as opposed to solidarity dominated by particular, specific values. This argument, indeed, was central to his effort to demonstrate the relevance of his symbolic analysis for a secular, democratic society. Yet for Durkheim this effort was organically tied to an argument for a presuppositional emphasis on values and sacred commitments in a generic sense.

Parsons, in contrast, takes his argument for citizenship beyond Durkheim's idealism. The very notion of solidarity attains a clarity in Parsons' treatment that Durkheim's original analysis did not allow. For example, where Durkheim often vaguely identifies concrete group solidarity, broad symbolic consensus, and concrete individual cooperation, Parsons clearly differentiates solidarity from value agreement, and both of these, in turn, from kinds of political cooperation. This is made possible through interchange, which enables Parsons, unlike Durkheim, to systematically relate solidarity and its nonsolidary environments.[103†]

As in his analysis of politics, the interchange model allows Parsons to resolve the weaknesses in Durkheim's argument by incorporating elements of Weber's. His strategy, in effect, is to place Durkheim's analysis of solidarity within the context of Weber's analysis of religious, economic, and political development. In his own historical discussion of citizenship, Parsons relies heavily on Weber's insights into Western religion and law; he also follows Weber in emphasizing the significance of the decentralized aspects of Western feudalism. Weber's discussion of the origins of the modern bureaucratic state, as well as his specific discussion of the causes of English democracy, breaks down into political and economic Hobbesianism (see, e.g., my argument in vol. 3, ch. 4). Parsons' analysis of bureaucracy and English democracy does not, and we can now understand why: while following Weber's emphasis Parsons also systematically embraces the autonomy of the solidarity dimension. If interchange allows him to save Durkheim by incorporating Weber, the same process works also in reverse. By accepting Durkheim's emphasis on the autonomy of solidarity, the interchange model allows Parsons to salvage Weber's work from his own damaging reductionism.

Parsons' discussion of citizenship allows us to see that it was in part because Weber could not conceptualize the solidary mediation between religious, economic, and political development that he was forced to dichotomize and historicize his discussion of Western development. Where Weber describes religious, political, and economic factors as having an impact and then effectively withdrawing from the historical stage, Parsons sees each factor as leaving a precipitate of more universal solidarity. It is through this changing solidarity that these factors continue to affect historical process.[104†] In other words, if Weber had conceived the impact of religious, economic, and political factors more in terms of an interchange than an either/or dichotomy, he may have been led, as Parsons was, to an emphasis on the intermediate level of social integration.[105†]

Speculative support for this hypothesis can be found in the fact that Weber's only fully realized multidimensional political study is *The City*. What distinguishes this analysis from his others is the demonstration that against the background of its religious legacy Western political and economic developments produced an urban structure bounded by universalistic laws. This separation of the legal definition of community membership from particularistic class and political affiliations, Weber believes, allowed Western urban conflict to generate its unique mixture of reform and universal franchise. In Parsons' terms, of course, legal phenomena are indicators of societal solidarity. Because Weber did not conceptualize solidarity, he could not visualize an "ideal" force that was sufficiently specified to regulate economic and political conflict. As a result, he could not generalize from *The City*, and this essay remained unintegrated with his other, more Hobbesian accounts of Western development.

Such a presuppositional innovation would also have helped resolve other troubling incongruities in Weber's work. If solidarity had become a theoretical resource, Weber would not have been forced to instrumentalize either the legal apparatus of capitalist society or the political process of the democratic state. He would, in addition, have more successfully connected his analyses of status and community in "Class, Status, and Party," and in this manner he could have related his discussion of status conflict to broader value dimensions rather than only to the specific, quasi-instrumental issues he chose to discuss.

A failure to differentiate the solidarity dimension undermines Marx's analysis in a similar way. As was shown in volume 2 (esp. ch. 6), despite his frequent reference to the universalizing aspects of capitalist society, the mature Marx actually discusses this phenomenon only in terms of the rationalizing expansion of the capitalist market. Moreover, instead of considering the market's integrative impact as an independent factor, as Parsons does, Marx only discusses this impact in order to argue that there is, in fact, no solidarity at all, that technical instrumentalism is the only universal in capitalist society. It is for this reason, contrary to certain recent interpreters, that Marx does not refer to the solidarity created by the expanding division of labor as an explanation for increased class consciousness. He would have been able to do so only if he had envisioned solidarity as an independent dimension of social life, a perception that ran contrary to his presuppositional inclinations.

These considerations lead to a final point of comparison. Parsons' own study of solidary variation, influenced by his ideological assumptions and empirical vision, was confined to the historical growth of citizenship. Yet the theory Parsons developed could well be used to study shifts in the integration of a single unit within a limited time span—for example, the intensification or dissipation of class, ethnic, or religious solidarity in a crisis situation. In a more generalized way, therefore, Parsons' solidarity theory may be conceived as presenting an implicit theory of association, an interest which was explicit in Marx's and Durkheim's discussions of the origins of group cooperation. Their theories present antithetical approaches to association. For Marx, class consciousness is the by-product of rational interest; for Durkheim, solidarity is the result of effervescence and the circulation of ideas. Parsons' more multidimensional approach would allow this either/or dichotomy to be broken down. For example, a class's group consciousness could be viewed as dependent not only on the structuring of that class by economic exigency, as Marx would have it, but also on the degree to which the concurrent exigencies of politics, solidarity, and values produced "associational groupings" congruent with this economic division. On the other hand, while for Durkheim solidarity could be achieved only in opposition to economic organization, in this Parsonian view the two could be seen as complementary.

Such a conceptualization would also provide a happier conclusion to the abruptly terminated analysis of the association/community dichotomy that so seriously mars Weber's essay "Class, Status, Party" (see vol. 3, ch. 5). While Weber noted here that classes could become communities, he made no links between this analysis and his later discussion of the status order. Only if integration is viewed as an independent dimension can economic communities be clearly seen as status groupings that have converged with the economic division of labor between owners and producers. Ordinarily, it is the pluralization and cross-cutting of status groups that fragments economic communities into associations. Yet the sources of this integrative fragmentation would, in the terms of Parsons' interchange theory of solidarity, be inherently multidimensional.

5. INTERCHANGE AND THE RESPECIFICATION OF PARSONS' VALUE THEORY

Parsons' value theory has been one of the most widely distorted aspects of his work. It is not an exaggeration to say, for example, that Gouldner's entire polemic rests on his assertion that Parsons emphasizes values in order to obliterate the effects of realistic, instrumental conditions. Such an identification of the value theory with idealism is shared, in fact, by most of Parsons' critics. They often, however, disagree about whether this presuppositional problem is itself the most fundamental. For many, like Dahrendorf and Rex, what is alleged to be Parsons' exclusive emphasis on values derives from his concern for equilibrium. Parsons views values, they claim, as consensual and homogeneous. Other critics, and sympathizers as well, view the value emphasis as being tied directly to Parsons' functionalist commitments. Functional models, it is held, inevitably overemphasize the role of values. I intend to show that Parsons' value analysis is neither so reductionist nor so conflationary.

5.1. VALUE INTERCHANGE AND THE DIFFERENTIATION OF SCOPE

Parsons utilizes interchange to respecify the multidimensional value analysis of his middle period. In becoming differentiated from cultural patterns as such, Parsons argues, values are specified into more socially realistic "priorities and allocations" that are connected more directly to socially "proper occasions and relationships." There always remains, of course, the "normative tension between the actual state of affairs and that conceived, in value-terms, to be desirable."[106] Still, to be realistic "factors in the regulation of the interaction between actors and objects in the *social* process," values must be compromises between cultural patterns and more conditional pressures.[107] They are produced by interaction between the universe of a society's culture meanings, on the one hand, and the disposition of its solidary communities (the integrative dimension), the arrangements by which its political goals are pursued (the goal-attainment dimension), and the nature of the facilities it provides for economic adaptation (the adaptation dimension), on the other.

Parsons introduces the notions of scope and responsibility to specify further this tension between the ideal and the real.[108] In more complex societies, institutions are differentiated in terms of their social responsibilities—families from firms, parties from parliaments, laws from traditions. It is because such "complex action systems cannot be 'governed' by a single undifferentiated value," Parsons writes, that "a shift from the cultural system level . . . to the social system . . . involves not only the question of . . . specification of the cultural pattern but also the differentiation of types of substantive context to which it is relevant."[109] Values become specified, in other words, not only by "conditions" per se but by relevant institutional contexts. In this way, they become restricted in "scope." In complex societies, it is usually the particular scope of a general value, not the value itself, that provides the ideal reference for any given social action.[110]

By focusing on this restriction in scope, Parsons' value analysis concerns itself primarily with what he calls "functional values," and by this he does not mean to suggest empirical equilibrium, systems analysis, or an antimaterialist causality. Functional values, rather, are the patterns that emerge from the mediation between the social system's specific dimensional exigencies and more general cultural patterns.[111†]

5.2. "RATIONALITY" AND THE UNIVERSITY: INTERCHANGE, VALUE SPECIFICATION, AND CONFLICT

Parsons and his colleagues have written extensively on the effects of the institutional specialization of value scope, particularly as this phenomenon can be formulated through the theory of value interchange and functional values.[112] The following discussion concentrates on Parsons' and Platt's *The American University* because it is not only the most self-consciously analytic discussion of this type but also the most elaborately empirical.

The modern university is organized around the value of cognitive rationality, which Parsons and Platt view as a specification from the more general rationality pattern. To emphasize the latter's cultural rather than social quality, they define it as the inclination toward "instrumental activism" that has "underlain the development of Western civilization through its Christian heritage."[113] They examine Western development in terms of the social opportunities that emerged for implementing instrumental activism. In doing so, they are describing the differentiation of rationality's scope. In principle, this pattern was compatible with a number of different courses of institutional development. In fact, the first great movement toward institutionalization was economic rather than intellectual or even political. It was, Parsons and Platt reason, far easier to implement such a revolutionary value in the realm of physical objects than in symbolic or even social relations.[114]

Only after substantial economic and political rationalization was the scope of rationality finally specified in a more distinctively cognitive direction, toward a concern with truth rather than economic or political effectiveness. Although Parsons and Platt give credit to the "realistic" factors involved in this development, they also emphasize the significant cultural complementarity between the economic, political, and cognitive forms of rationality.[115] They point out, for example, that in the late nineteenth century members of the same urban upper-class groups, often members of the same family, moved freely between the newly formed universities and the more traditional institutions of economic wealth and political power.[116] It was, they argue, through interaction between the more general cultural inclination toward rationality and changing economic and political exigencies, themselves influenced by the rationality pattern, that the modern American university system—with its emphasis on both research and teaching—was first established in the late nineteenth century. With the establishment of this university system, cognitive rationality had "become a *differentiated* value system with substantial autonomy vis-à-vis other subsystems."[117]

After so utilizing interchange to trace the origins of the cognitive rationality value, Parsons and Platt devote the remainder of their book to analyzing the multidimensional process by which this autonomy is maintained. They describe the challenge to cognitive autonomy in terms of the logic of interchange: while the university's primary operation is directed to the value sphere, it must still deal effectively with specific conditional exigencies and maintain, as well, satisfactory relations with more general, purely cultural currents.[118] The university must, in other words, gain "inputs" from more economically adaptive institutions, from structures that specialize in goal attainment, from societal solidarities, and from the cultural system. In gaining this support, however, the university risks becoming a supplicant by subordinating its own goals to these other dimensional needs. If this were to occur, the autonomy of the cognitive rationality value would be lost: the university would become dominated either by other, noncognitive definitions of rationality—the "rationalities" of economic, political, or integrative life—or by antirational patterns in the cultural sphere.

Specializing in the production of values undermines an institution's ability to control facilities and goals. The university has had to rely, therefore, on considerable economic subsidization. It has also depended on the coercive powers of the state—for example, in enforcing legal guarantees of academic freedom. Both these inputs, however, create tensions with respect to the university's independence. "What kind of outputs," Parsons and Platt ask, "can offset the financial deficits involved in the operations of the typical university?" In a similar vein, they warn that "academic autonomy . . . depends on the academic system generating outputs which are valued from relevant political points of view."[119]

Parsons and Platt describe outputs to economy and polity in terms of the relative material and ideal position of each output. The most important output the university can supply, they believe, is simply the value of cognitive rationality itself.[120] To the degree that economic and political actors are internally committed to cognitive rationality—to the degree they view it simply as desirable in itself—they will perceive their own contributions to the university as immediately reciprocated. The second return the university generates is more closely related to the instrumental interests of the recipients, though it is still primarily valuational. It concerns the contribution that cognitive rationality makes to the "rationalities" that guide political and economic performance. Cognitive standards, Parsons and Platt insist, are vital to effective economic and political action. While it is true that politics and economics depend on "goals [that] are defined by primarily noncognitive interests," they also depend on means that are cognitively rational and efficient.[121] Business and government rely on disciplined "intelligence" to provide technology and administration. Such intelligence also reinforces the rationality of the constituency demands upon which democratic government depends.

Other outputs from the university, which Parsons and Platt call "services," relate still more directly to instrumental political and economic interest. The most direct, of course, are the kinds of contractual relations that often tie the university to polity and economy. Much more significant services, however, are supplied by the "applied professions" of social work, engineering, medicine, and law. These service professions "reorganize [cognitive] knowledge in terms of its relevance to the practical goals and interests which the professions serve."[122] On the one hand, they respond to specific conditional demands, attempting to achieve "concrete practical goals where serious interests of their clients are at stake." Yet because such "competence has to be grounded in bodies of theoretical knowledge," they remain connected to the university's more generalized cognitive concerns.[123]

Through this series of successively more instrumental outputs, then, the university attempts to balance its dependence on more conditional structures. The potential for disbalance, for unequal exchange and the conflict it produces, is omnipresent. For example, the practical interests to which the university contributes may turn out to be incompatible with its commitment to cognitive objectivity. In the period since World War II, Parsons and Platt argue, this is precisely what occurred in the relation between the university and the "military-industrial complex." Because of the university's dependence on the American government's political and economic patronage, the propaganda needs of America's war policy began to threaten the university's ability to carry out its cognitive concerns.[124]

This same kind of tension exists between the university and the dimension more general than itself, the cultural system. The importance of cognitive rationality must be "legitimated," Parsons and Platt believe, by noncognitive cultural patterns. If expressive symbols and the artists who pattern them do not acknowledge the importance of the university's "humanistic scholarship," such scholarship will be difficult to carry out.[125] Similarly, the university needs support from religion, whose "constitutive symbolism" must recognize the importance of intellectual insight in defining ultimate reality.[126] For the social sciences, cultural legitimation is more closely connected to the moral aspects of culture. Parsons and Platt call this moral input ideology, or social criticism, distinguishing it from theology by virtue of "its concern with the existing or potential society that is inherently part of *this* world."[127] To be fully legitimate, cognitive rationality must be viewed as complementary to the task of social criticism.

To protect the independence of its cognitive focus, such supports to the university must be balanced by returns. The university's most vital output, once again, is the cognitive rationality value itself, which reciprocates cultural support to the degree that a society's expressive, moral, and religious actors share a cognitive focus. In contemporary America, for example, religious and moral patterns are sharply scrutinized for their consistency with scientific truth. In this way, they are as dependent on cognitive rationality as this value is dependent on them.

As in the university's interchanges with more conditional dimensions, Parsons and Platt identify a concrete group as an intermediary in this university-culture exchange. Playing a role like that of the applied professions, "intellectuals" mediate between cognitive rationality and its cultural legitimation.[128] Intellectuals, in this scheme, are not simply academics. While they are unusually sensitive to cognitive standards, they are more committed than the pure academic to the need for integrating these standards with expressive, moral, and religious concerns. This university-culture interchange can become imbalanced, then, to the degree that cognitive concerns are perceived as incompatible with expressive, moral, and religious ones. Precisely because the intellectual is a generalist who "wants to tap concerns not congruent with cognitively specialized interests," the balance is a delicate one.[129] While more romantically inclined intellectuals may judge cognitive standards as irrelevant to "true" artistic expression, morality, or religion, more rationalist intellectuals may view such noncognitive culture as irrelevant to the pursuit of knowledge. Such perceptions are highly vulnerable to the shifting currents of contemporary events.

Finally, the university depends for support on the structure of social solidarity. Cognitive rationality can be produced only if the structure of the "college environment . . . closely approximates the universalistic societal community," with its "commitment to pluralistic basic rights and voluntary association."[130] If the societal community were particularistic, the university would be pressured to subordinate its analysis of reality to the perceptions of particular interests, to surrender the universal reference upon which cognitive rationality depends. But while the university depends on a universalistic societal community, it can provide this community with some important inputs in turn. Parsons and Platt detail a number of ways in which cognitive rationality is "formally congruent with universalistic basic rights."[131] The theoretical aspect of scientific knowledge, for example, allows actors to generalize beyond particular cases. Similarly, the independence of cognitive reasoning from other dimensional constraints makes it inherently antihierarchical and egalitarian.[132]

This university-solidarity interchange is conducted at a number of different levels. Parsons and Platt focus particularly on the relation between university and undergraduate community. An entering freshman class, for example, is integrated in a particularistic way, combining "a diffuseness of belonging . . . with a fierce loyalty that overrides all competing claims to solidarity."[133] Such integration, they believe, presents a significant barrier to learning, to internalization of the cognitive rationality value. As the freshmen are gradually incorporated into the more universalistic college community, there is the "differentiation of [such] peer group solidarity and the acceptance of participation in plural involvements."[134] Only to the degree this broader inclusion occurs can the university's output of cognitive rationality be produced. In such an interchange, tremendous opportunities for imbalance and conflict exist. If universalistic solidarity is not sufficient, the university will be unable to provide cognitive rationality. At the same time, if the university does not allow initially diffuse affective ties, it would be unable to attract potential members or to socialize them when they arrive.

5.3. THE VALUE THEORY AND ITS CRITICS

Far from being inherently committed to empirical equilibrium, the value theory produces a fluid and subtle approach to conflict and integration. In fact, it clarifies the difference between presuppositional concerns about values and their role in empirical conflict or stability.

By perceiving the multidimensionality of social life, Parsons has been able to tease apart the closely intertwined issues of pattern disintegration from social conflict. First, by indicating how institutional responsibility differentiates value scope, Parsons emphasizes the differentiation of values, not their homogeneity. Given this condition of differentiation, there is continual conflict among functionally specified values. Despite this conflict, however, the more general value-pattern may still be "integrated."[135] Specific value conflict can occur, then, in the midst of general value agreement. *The American University*, in fact, is keyed to this very insight. Parsons and Platt argue here that maintaining cognitive rationality's autonomy—maintaining, in other words, the "integration" and integrity of the cognitive rationality pattern—inherently involves tension and conflict between the university and the groups representing other dimensions, groups like the professions, economic and political interests, intellectuals, and undergraduates. Value disintegration will occur only if this conflict produces such imbalanced interchange that the autonomy of cognitive rationality is undermined.[136]

A second common criticism, that Parsons' value theory is "functionalist," simply misses the main point.[137] It is rather Parsons' focus on the presuppositional tension between generality and specificity, or the tension between instrumental and normative approaches to rationality, that is always central to his analysis.

It is because of this focus that Parsons' value theory also manages to avoid an inherent idealism. It is, indeed, by bringing together normative and "factual" concerns that he defines the relationship between institutional responsibility and value scope. Similarly, the tension between cognitive rationality and the conditional pressures of politics, economics, and solidarity forms a vital part of his analysis of the university.

5.4. MULTIDIMENSIONAL VALUES AND THE DIALOGUE WITH DURKHEIM AND WEBER

The true presuppositional focus of Parsons' value theory is revealed, once again, in the nature of his animus toward his classical predecessors. Value interchange must be seen as an attempt to resolve the problems Parsons perceived in the reductionist approaches of Durkheim and Weber.

Durkheim emphasized in *Moral Education* the centrality in modern society of rationality as a value (see vol. 2, ch. 8). This emphasis represented a crucial part of his later critique of instrumental rationality. But while tying education to moral rationality, Durkheim submerged instrumental rationality to moral education and, more generally, to purely symbolic and sacred constraints. Partly as the result of this treatment, the interplay between moral and instrumental rationality is missing from the later part of Durkheim's work.[138†]

Parsons takes over Durkheim's emphasis on moral rationality and its role in education. But by analyzing it in terms of interchange, Parsons can accept this emphasis while avoiding Durkheim's idealist slant. In so expanding his analysis, Parsons once again broadens Durkheim by incorporating the breadth of Weberian analysis.

Rationality was, of course, central to Weber's theory. Particularly in his discussion of the origins of religious rationality, but also in his accounts of political and economic rationalization, Weber carefully interwove broad cultural currents with more specific political, economic, normative, and intellectual developments. In a certain sense, Parsons' interchange analysis of rationality simply formalizes this multidimensional method.

Yet Weber's vision of rationality in the modern world was sharply disjunctive with his historical analysis. While rationality played a substantive role in the premodern world, in the modern it is, for the most part, portrayed as only formal, as connected primarily to purely instrumental orders. In addition to the ideological and empirical reasons for this shift in Weber's focus, his tendency toward sociological materialism also played a major role (see vol. 3, chs. 4, 5). On the basis of Parsons' more consistent multidimensionality, the specifically theoretical problems in Weber's analysis can now be more clearly understood.

Weber could not envision the interplay between general values and their specification. Rationality was sustained, for him, only as long as it maintained its direct alliance with the broad cultural pattern of religion. He believed that once the organic unity of culture disintegrated, rationality as a value no longer could regulate action. When economic production, political administration, legal norms, and the intellectual-scientific community became separated from one another as well as from moral, religious, and artistic concerns, rationality became a purely instrumental, non-normative orientation. For Weber, there was no interpenetration between the original rationality value and these now independent spheres. He could see no relation because his theoretical blinders forced him toward the dichotomization of norms and conditions. The rationality value could be maintained only if it were part of one organic unity. Surrounded by relatively autonomous social and cultural spheres, the value was unattached and without social significance.

Because of his own more successful theoretical resolution, Parsons was able to see the fallacies in Weber's vision and, more importantly, could correct them. As institutional responsibility becomes more complex, general values do not simply disappear. Instead, they become more differentiated in scope. As institutionalized in the university, the cognitive rationality value does have its own distinct location, separated from other spheres. It nonetheless maintains links through mutual interaction. Cultural knowledge remains partly disciplined by cognitive concerns and, conversely, cognitive concerns often reflect broader humanistic cultural values. Similarly, economic and political exigencies have not completely instrumentalized rationality; actually, conditional forces still draw upon a variety of more substantively rational values. The very efficiency of conditional forces, in fact, depends in part on the strength and continued production of the value of cognitive rationality.

Parsons' interchange theory thus breaks free of the faulty theoretical logic that—along with ideological and empirical commitments—limited Weber's vision of modern rationalization. Parsons provides a methodology for connecting Weber's historical analysis of rationality to a complementary vision of contemporary society. In accomplishing this, he dynamizes Durkheim's emphasis on the crucial importance of rationality as a fundamental value in contemporary life.[139†]

6. GENERALIZED MEDIA THEORY: CONCRETIZING INTERCHANGE ANALYSIS

Parsons initiated his interchange theory to specify his multidimensional presuppositions while avoiding the empiricist tendency toward the "concrete" that marred his middle-period work. As he succeeded in developing a more thoroughly analytic specificity, however, Parsons returned to the challenge of concreteness. With his conceptualization of "generalized media," he tried to connect interchange directly to the action of concrete individuals and collectivities without sacrificing the sophistication of his multidimensional model.

6.1. MEDIA AND MULTIDIMENSIONALITY

By generalized media, Parsons means the most fundamental "commodities" that actors use to get results in social action: money, power, influence, and value commitments. Unlike the "products" of interchange noted in the preceding pages, each of these media is something concrete, an object that is more or less consciously manipulated in the give-and-take exchange of social life. Parsons confuses the issue by using some of the same terms—power and value commitments—to refer to both media and products. Nonetheless, he clearly means to differentiate the two by their level of concreteness.[140†] Whereas the media are objects to be manipulated by collective and individual actors, the products of interchange form the invisible networks within which such attempts at manipulation take place. Through its products, interchange provides the fundamental "structurings" of social order. The products of interchange constitute analytical "dimensional pressures"; the media, in contrast, refer to actual "things."[141†]

Adaptation, for example, results from the interaction of a society's value patterns, normative arrangements, and goal capacities with the instrumental-efficient pressures of its environment. The result, a society's "adaptive structure," represents a social "dimension," an abstract pressure that limits the possibilities of its social arrangements. Money, in contrast, is a concrete social object that represents this adaptive capacity in a particular social interaction. While it is obviously connected to such adaptive capacity, the use of money is not the only way in which the adaptive dimension has impact. Adaptive pressures can also structure solidary groupings through a range of indirect, dimensional processes. Rationalized economic production and market oriented classes, for example, are adaptive pressures that constrain individual cooperation. Such effects are a "product" of interchange. However, adaptive pressures can also be brought to bear on solidarity in a more direct, interactional manner: through the manipulation of money. This occurred, for example, when English laws of primogeniture forced the early breakup of extended families, or when, in the early stages of industrial capitalism, financial competition between urban and rural groups over the money supply polarized American farmers and workers. In such cases it is the generalized medium of adaptation, not simply dimensional pressure, that is at work. As compared with such adaptive pressure, money is a concrete and specific "sanction," applied self-consciously in attempts at struggle and domination.

The same is true for other media. Strictly speaking, the product of the goal-attainment dimension is not power but a certain "political structuring" of the social order, a structuring that reflects a particular capacity to relate general values to specific conditions. Thus, an absolutist political structure, by creating obedience to a kinship group, limits the possibilities for a universal solidary community. This restriction is a "product" of political interchange, but it is not concrete. On the other hand, political power, in a concrete sense, can be used to structure solidarity, as when new administrative policies, like urban renewal, create new group alliances and conflicts. This political power is a medium; it is a concrete, manipulatible expression of goal-attainment capacity.

When actors use media they are limited by the general products of interchange. Solidarity is not a medium; it is a dimension of social order produced by the mutual constraint and reinforcement of different types of collective exigencies. Influence, by contrast, is a factor that can be manipulated in concrete interaction. Individual and collective actors can exchange influence for power or money. Yet influence still relies on, and is limited by, the underlying structure of social solidarity. "The user of influence," Parsons writes, "is under pressure to justify his statements . . . by making them correspond to norms that are regarded as binding on both parties."[142]

The media illustrate a concrete level of social interchange. Actors may, for example, try to expand the impact of their social values by bringing themselves or their collectivities to more preeminent symbolic positions. To do so, they exchange the medium of value commitments for money, influence, and power. With each input they can broadcast their value commitments more powerfully. The exchange of commitments occurs, for example, when a charismatic religious leader proselytizes an important solidary group. By "spending" his commitments, the leader gains solidarity with the group's members, and the latter, in turn, by spending their influence have gained a new set of religious commitments. By spending his commitments, the value leader has gained influence: "The individual [with his value commitments] . . . no longer 'goes it alone' but adopts associational status, which gives him expectations of solidarity with fellow members of the community or collectivity in question."[143] The exchange of these value commitments, of course, is limited not only by the nature of the other media but by the structure of the pattern-maintenance system itself.

While the media are more concrete than dimensional products, they remain, nonetheless, intimately related to the more abstract processes of interchange. Indeed, the media can be seen as "representing" the results of interchange in concrete interaction. For Parsons, they form a language that provides concrete communication between societal subsystems. He writes, for example, that money is "an evaluative medium . . . for judging the 'rationality' of production policies." Because money is used in concrete exchanges between economic and noneconomic actors, "factors of production . . . have to be 'translated' into the terms relevant to . . . processes that can minimize costs."[144] Money becomes, therefore, the concrete representation of adaptive effectiveness. A unit's "solvency," or profitability, indicates its ability to master the adaptive pressures of the situation, its ability to successfully exchange adaptive outputs for inputs from other dimensions.

Influence "represents" the effectiveness of solidary production in a similar way. For an influential actor to generate consensus for a universalistic position, the interchange process must have produced a relatively universalistic integrative structure. If it has not, the attempt at achieving universalistic influence will fail, for it will not be able to justify itself by reference to mutually binding norms.

In conceptualizing just how such "representation" occurs, Parsons turns to a more elaborate definition of the media themselves. A medium, he believes, represents the effectiveness of interchange in the relationship that exists between its own "symbolic" and "real" components. Parsons views every medium as being composed of a base, or "intrinsic persuader," and a generalized element, or "code": "Every symbolic medium must link a 'resource base' with a cultural level of code and symbol."[145†]

A medium's base is an actor's ultimate sanction in trying to enforce compliance. The base of money, for example, is "inducement," the actual provision of real goods or services. The base for influence and value commitments is harder to identify, since their subjectivity means there exists no source of final enforcement in an instrumental sense. For influence, Parsons describes an actors' reference to face-to-face solidarity as the ultimate persuader. For commitments, he identifies "invocation of guilt."

A medium's generalized, code element makes it a *legitimate* representative of such real factors. Authority, for example, provides the generalized code for power. An authoritative political figure, therefore, can wield power without having to invoke his ability to enforce binding decisions. Similarly, because of money's acceptability as symbolic legal tender, it can be exchanged without providing evidence of the real goods and services it can command; and an actor who is influential need not try continually to demonstrate the actual resources of solidarity upon which his influence ultimately rests.

The advantage of such a "symbolic-real" conceptualization is that variation in the medium provides a specific and clear-cut indicator of the effectiveness of the interchange process: "It funnels tensions generated at particular points in the system into the functioning of the medium itself, notably into confidence or lack of confidence in its [the medium's] stability, an attitude on which its general acceptability depends."[146] If interchange goes well, the symbolic element of the medium is strong and effective. Actors will accept the code in lieu of real goods. Such acceptance facilitates the interchange process; social production is expanded; more "real" commodities are produced. On the other hand, if production is ineffective, the symbolic aspects of a medium will not be acceptable. Instead, potential recipients demand intrinsic resources, and the expanded potential of the medium is lost.

For example, if value production is effective, an actor will be "charismatic": new value commitments will be more easily accepted by those exposed to his persuasive power. Cultural innovation will be facilitated and new ideas will proliferate. If, in contrast, value production is failing, new commitments will be less easily accepted; some kind of "intrinsic" proof of their consistency with older, more traditional values will be demanded. Cultural innovation will decline. Similarly, if only intrinsic economic inducements are acceptable, or if political coercion must continually be brought into play, the interchanges that produce economic facilities and political power will also be minimized.

To articulate this symbol-base dynamic, Parsons introduces the conceptualizations of "trust" versus "barter," and "inflation" versus "deflation." Social trust exists to the degree that interchange is effective. If trust is maintained, a medium's symbolic code will be acceptable. To the degree that only the intrinsic base becomes acceptable, social interaction becomes a process of barter: exchange can occur only through the trading of real, specific goods. Barter is a more primitive and limiting style of exchange than the more generalized exchange that rests on trust.[147†]

Exchange moves toward barter if there is an imbalance between a symbolic code and its base, an imbalance that is created by sufficient inequality, or instability, in a dimension's inputs and outputs. Trust in a medium must ultimately be reciprocated with "real," not just symbolic, results, and to provide such results a subsystem's outputs must command equivalent inputs. If appropriate inputs are not forthcoming, an actor will be placing more trust in a medium than is justified by the effectiveness of its functional referent. In such situations, the medium's value will become inflated. Its promises cannot be kept. Inflated power will not produce the expected results; inflated values will turn out to be inauthentic; inflated money will not be exchangeable for goods and services. Eventually, trust is withdrawn. In a barter situation, a medium is deflated; its true value cannot be realized because interaction is reduced to "intrinsic" exchange.

Parsons and Platt use this media schema, for example, to formulate the crisis of the American university in the late 1960s and the 1970s. Prior to the late 1960s, they assert, the value of cognitive rationality had been inflated, so that the society expected far greater returns from such rationality than the university could realistically deliver. When the expected returns were not forthcoming, trust was withdrawn, and the value of cognitive rationality underwent drastic deflation. As a result, the university could not use its medium to acquire the inputs necessary for successful functioning. As the university's effective production of cognitive rationality decreased, its economic, political, integrative, and cultural supports were withdrawn. This withdrawal created the higher education "crunch" of the 1970s.[148]

With the notion of the generalized media, Parsons introduced another theoretical level into his interchange theory. By concretizing this analytic model, he further dynamized it, making it still more fluid and flexible. It becomes even more clear that balances, imbalances, and conflict are rooted not only in the structural qualities of systemic interaction but in the efforts of individual and collective actors to expand their dimensional positions and to enforce compliance with their will. This concretization, moreover, introduces greater contingency into interchange analysis. Media "entrepreneurs" do not necessarily have to follow the general course of systemic interchange. By creative and resourceful innovation, they can try to alter the balance of inputs and outputs, redress an inflated or deflated medium, and reshape the balance between its symbolic and intrinsic components. In this way, media analysis contributes further to the clarification of social conflict provided by the theory of interchange.[149†]

6.2. MISINTERPRETING MEDIA THEORY

As will be seen later in the discussion (ch. 9), Parsons' treatment of the media is fraught with ambiguity. This fact, to be sure, helps to explain the misinterpretation to which the theory has been subject from its inception. A more important explanation, however, is the close relationship between media theory and Parsons' interchange model. It is not surprising that the same misunderstandings which have distorted the interpretation of interchange have also plagued the perception of media analysis.

Parsons' critics and sympathizers alike have subjected media theory to drastic interpretive conflation. Its primary inspiration has been linked, for example, to Parsons' attempt to explain, or to legitimate, empirical equilibrium; hence the emphasis, these interpreters point out, on generalized trust over barter.[150†] It has also been viewed as derived primarily from the model level, either from Parsons' commitment to generalizing the economic model and its monetary medium, or from his insight into the nature of functional systems.[151] Still others have connected media to Parsons' ideological conservatism, arguing that his extensive use of market economic analogies reflects his acceptance of the imperatives of economizing and scarcity that are particular to capitalism.[152]

It is certainly true that Parsons' use of media theory has been affected by his commitments at each of these levels. The technical language of media analysis is borrowed from economic theory, and the inflation/deflation schema is designed to illuminate the threats to social stability. Media theory is, after all, an attempt to concretize empirically Parsons' more general and abstract conceptualization. As such, it must engage empirical and ideological levels. But the logical roots of this specificity refer primarily to presuppositional issues. Perhaps more directly than any other segment of Parsons' later writing, media theory returns for its inspiration to basic sociologic-epistemic questions. By focusing on the trade-off between "symbolic" and "intrinsic," media theory reformulates the "problem of action" in a much more empirically specific manner than his earlier writings. Of course, a medium's intrinsic base is not necessarily instrumental, in a literal sense, but the logical form of this argument is clearly derived from the instrumental/normative dichotomization of action. Similarly, by focusing on the difference between generalized interaction and barter, Parsons returns to the argument over the "problem of order." True, even media barter is still symbolic activity—it occurs, after all, within the context of a cultural system—but in discussing barter's disadvantages Parsons closely follows the outline of his earlier critique of individualist, "discrete" approaches to interaction. Without comprehending this presuppositional focus at the center of Parsons' concern, it is impossible to appreciate the structure of his media analysis.

Many analysts have, of course, recognized the generalized reference of Parsons' argument. Yet there is a strong tendency to regard these presuppositions as idealistic. Sympathizers extol the media as conceptualizing a purely symbolic language which controls the instrumental aspect of concrete interaction.[153] Critics attack the theory for the same emphasis, objecting that it ignores the material elements of concrete interaction and substitutes a psychological focus on trust and confidence for structural explanations of conflict.[154†]

It seems quite apparent, however, that media theory, in principle, makes neither of these errors. It is, rather, an extension of the multidimensionality of Parsons' interchange analysis. In addressing the action question, media theory posits a continuum from more intrinsic to more normative persuasion. In discussing order, it posits a tension between generalized, voluntary order and the more coercive potentialities of institutional or individualistic barter. Moreover, Parsons locates the constraints that determine these trade-offs in the balance between instrumental and normative orders established by societal interchange.

6.3. MEDIA ANALYSIS AND CLASSICAL THEORY

Once again, the most compelling evidence for the multidimensionality of Parsons' efforts lies in the way that he utilizes media theory to bolster his long-standing debate with classical social theory. This strategy is particularly striking because he is dealing here with concrete individual exchange, which for classical theory represented the prototypical social relationship. In fact, media theory is not just a dialogue with Durkheim and Weber. It takes on classical theory in each of its presuppositional forms.

In the first place, media analysis confronts the utilitarian theory of rationalistic individualism, a position Parsons attacks through his confrontation with George Homans' exchange theory, the approach which has been so central in reintroducing classical utilitarian ideas to contemporary sociology. Parsons rejects Homans' utilitarian identification of instrumental action as the most elementary form of social life. While he acknowledges that "there *are* elementary principles of economics [as a] discipline," he asserts that "these are most emphatically not elementary principles of social behavior." To the contrary, Parsons argues that the phenomenon of generalized media illustrates behavior's nonindividual and nonrational elements.[155†] In a related critique, he also takes issue with Homans' utilitarian view of money as the sine qua non of rational sanctions. "Homans speaks of money," Parsons complains, "as if it were hardly different from any other [valued] physical object." Media theory proposes, however, that money has elements that are symbolic as well. In fact, "in its developed form, [money] has no 'value in use' as the classical economists called it whatever."[156]

Media theory is also designed to present an alternative to rationalist theory in its collectivist form, a critique that is particularly interesting when applied to Marxism. In the early chapters of *Capital*, Marx discusses at great length the two forms of commodities in capitalist society, the phenomenal and the real.[157] The prototypical commodity, of course, was money. Given his instrumentalist inclinations, Marx contended that the phenomenal form of money was a device that served merely to camouflage the commodity's real, utilitarian value, that is, its value in actual use. Money's ability to function as a universal medium of exchange—an ability based on its "phenomenal" acceptance as symbolic legal tender—was sustained solely because this universality was efficient for the market; it had nothing to do, in Marx's view, with any general properties of social interaction. Marx maintained that the only *really* valuable aspect of a commodity was its use value, which corresponded not to symbolic ideas but rather to the concrete characteristics that gave the commodity its actual utility. Marx insisted, moreover, that money was the only such symbolically universal commodity in capitalist society, and that its very convertibility into other kinds of particular commodities indicated the extent to which capitalism had made social exchange completely instrumental.

Parsons' media theory runs directly counter to Marx's. Money's symbolic form, Parsons contends, is as real as its metallic base. In fact, it is from the symbolic, generalized element of money that its most important use value is derived. Furthermore, not only does money's universal convertibility not instrumentalize the rest of social life, but money does not even represent the only such universal medium. Power, influence, and value commitments are equally important mediations between collective order and individual interaction, and even in capitalist society they present equally significant objects of possession and manipulation.[158†]

As an antidote to such rationalist approaches, Parsons has obviously incorporated into his media theory the normative collectivism of Durkheim. Within the Durkheimian tradition, the anthropologists Malinowski and Mauss developed their conceptions of "generalized exchange"—particularly in reference to noninstrumental gift giving—to confront the rationalist approaches to exchange of Spencer and the English Utilitarians. Parsons takes over this symbolically generalized approach, but his broader theory of interchange links it much more systematically to multidimensional exigencies.

It is because of this connection to interchange theory that Parsons' media analysis can avoid the idealism which derives from Durkheim's concentration on purely generalized, quasi-sacred action. When he mentioned instrumental action at all, Durkheim sharply separated it from symbolic activity. Parsons, in contrast, closely interrelates them, by describing media as continually inflating and deflating the relation between instrumental base and symbolic code.[159†] Undoubtedly, this emphasis came to Parsons from Weber, particularly from the latter's analysis of the problematic legitimacy of political power, its dependence on the interplay of force and belief. Media theory generalizes this Weberian analysis to each of society's four subsystems. Further, by linking this discussion of concrete sanctions to the analytic level of interchange analysis, media theory avoids the reductionism to which Weber's analysis of political legitimacy was continually subject.

It was in 1789 that Bentham introduced the term "sanction" into Western social discourse. There were, he considered, four fundamental ways "of giving a binding force to any law or rule of conduct"—the physical, the political, the moral, and the religious.[160] Yet these sanctions were differentiated from one another, Bentham believed, only in the sources from which they issued: sanctions were physical if deriving from nature, political if originating with legal authority, moral if residing with the community at large, and religious if evolving from God. In terms of their mode of relating to action, Bentham asserted that these four sanctions were one. Each achieved its effect through the manipulation of pleasure and pain. In fact, he reasoned, political, moral, and religious sanctions might as well be reduced to the physical.

While a good part of sociology since Bentham has discarded his language, it has not yet dispensed with his presuppositional point. Sanctions, it is widely believed, must, somehow, be "real." By avoiding this reductionist trap, and its idealist counterpart as well, Parsons' media theory makes a crucial contribution to social thought.

Chapter Five

THE LATER PERIOD (2)

Socialization, Social Change, and the Systemic and Historical Bases of Individual Freedom

With interchange theory, Parsons moved significantly beyond his earlier attempts to specify a multidimensional position. This analysis of his later work runs contrary, of course, to the conventional wisdom that it is resolutely idealist. I have argued instead that interchange not only outlines multidimensionality at the institutional level, but does so more effectively than the major theoretical efforts of classical sociology.

In addition to the widespread objections to Parsons' supposed idealism, there is another major critical response to his later work. It is raised not only by the materialist polemic against "functionalist" theory but by the nominalist critique as well. The argument here is that Parsons has created an "order theory." Because he has eliminated the tension between norms and facts or, so the nominalist reasoning goes, between individual and society, Parsons has created a theory unalterably committed to social stability: to the harmonious conformity of individual will with collective imperatives, to the harmonious equilibrium among social groups and institutions.

I have, of course, referred to such charges throughout the preceding analysis, particularly as they are linked to arguments about the centrality of Parsons' idealism or the significance of his functionalist commitments. One major problem of such criticism is that it is conflationary. To endorse collective order on the presuppositional level is not to support order at the empirical level, that is, order as equilibrium. Nor does the acceptance of symbolic internalization imply any commitment to individual conformity. Furthermore, neither of these presuppositional positions, nor any commitment at the level of model or empirical proposition, produces any particular ideological vision, any particular commitment to one approach to individual freedom over another. Moreover, in addition to conflating these various levels of analysis, these arguments also make fundamental errors in theoretical logic itself. As I have indicated at some length in chapter 2, far from detracting from the conceptualization of individual autonomy, symbolic internalization provides the basis for any effective approach to it. Indeed, this presumption is at the heart of Parsons' empirical account of individual socialization. It is also, as will be seen, fundamental to his analysis of social change. In both of these segments of his later theory, Parsons' "voluntaristic" presupposition is specified as empirical individuation, as increasing self-conscious control over the external and internal elements of an individual's environments. In his socialization theory, Parsons places a multidimensional analysis of this empirical process within a perspective that views the life cycle as a bridge between the normative and conditional institutions of society. His change theory historicizes this account by connecting individuation to an anti-organicist account of differentiation in institutional development. In both these later efforts at specification, Parsons continues his decisive reformulation of classical theory.

1. THE LATER SOCIALIZATION THEORY: MULTIDIMENSIONAL PROCESS AND VOLUNTARY BEHAVIOR

It is not surprising that Parsons' socialization analysis has undergone the same kind of misinterpretation as the interchange concept.[1†] For example, critics argue that socialization is important to Parsons because of his commitment to empirical equilibrium. According to this view, Parsons believes that socialized individuals will not engage in disruptive conflict. Socialization theory is also viewed as inherently related to Parsons' model choice: since functionalism, it is alleged, must make every institutional unit "fit" organically into a system's imperatives, socialization comes to play a vital role. These approaches complement the reduction of another, more ideological argument: given Parsons' opposition to social protest and the assertion of individual rights against authority, he must portray individuals as "over-socialized."[2]

In the background of each of these conflationary interpretations there lies an implicit assumption, namely that Parsons' socialization theory prescribes conformity and passivity vis-à-vis the collective order. This view becomes explicit in those analyses that more directly address the most generalized level of Parsons' work. The socialization approach is antivoluntary, it is charged, because Parsons emphasizes the role of values and internalization, thereby eliminating the independence of the individual actor. Closely related to this reading is the contention that Parsons' socialization theory is simply one more example of his idealism. According to this critique, the theory ignores "conditions" in at least two ways. First, socialization involves only the interaction between cultural values and personality. Second, if individuals are well socialized, the coercive aspects of the collective order become superfluous.[3†]

We will see later that these interpretations, often proposed by Parsons' supporters as well as his critics,[4] accurately reflect certain weaknesses in Parsons' approach to socialization. Still, they ignore the theory's most significant contributions. They reflect, as often as not, the conflationary bent of contemporary debate. More importantly, they indicate an inability to understand certain vital issues in general theoretical logic. In what follows, I will demonstrate the overarching presuppositional reference of Parsons' socialization discussion. I will indicate, in addition, the multidimensionality of his vision of the socialization process and his emphasis on the voluntarism it produces.

1.1. THE "RESOURCE CHART" AND THE DOUBLE CRITIQUE

In comparing Parsons' later discussion of functional exigencies to that of the middle period, it is relatively easy to see interchange as providing a framework that includes the earlier references to the task of "integration" and to the instrumental and expressive aspects of "allocation."[5†] The relationship between interchange and personnel allocation—the final allocational task that Parsons identified in his earlier work—is not as readily evident. In fact, however, Parsons' later work reformulates "personnel allocation" as well. If the family is primarily a "pattern maintenance" institution, Parsons reasons, then personnel allocation involves a kind of dimensional passage, from the child's earliest training in the pattern-maintenance sphere to the adult's achievement of an occupational position in the dimensions that are more conditionally, instrumentally oriented. In formulating this passage, Parsons specifies his earlier, more general analysis of internalization by articulating it with his interchange theory.[6†]

Parsons accomplishes this integration by describing personnel allocation as the "production" of a peculiar kind of resource: human beings. To trace this human production and its multidimensional course, he develops the "Resource Chart."[7] We have briefly discussed this scheme in the analysis of economic interchange in the preceding chapter.[8†] The chart formulates the stages by which motivation develops from its most general unformed condition to the more specific and differentiated form of adulthood. In the process, the individual actor moves from the institutions of the pattern-maintenance system, through various life-cycle stages, and into an adult occupational role. The first three steps of the Resource Chart, which occur within the pattern-maintenance dimension, cover the relevant aspects of pre-adult socialization. The fourth step represents the labor market, the individual's transition across dimensional boundaries to his participation in a work setting. The remaining three stages correspond to the utilization of this socialized human resource in the particular institutional context. Parsons' theory of socialization, therefore, focuses on the first phases of this allocation process.

Parsons bases his empirical analysis of socialization on his presuppositional solution to the "individual problem" which I have outlined in chapter 2, a solution which involves the double critique of Durkheim and Freud. I have already discussed at some length how Parsons utilized Freud to correct Durkheim's theoretical errors. Durkheim knew that moral sanctions ordered individual actions, and he recognized their internal location. Yet, although he effectively employed the metaphor of religion, he did not understand precisely how such internalization could actually occur; for this reason, he continually referred to moral sanctions as coercive and as external to the individual. These problems in Durkheim's analysis, Parsons believed, could be resolved only through Freud's notion of object introjection.[9] By "Freudianizing" Durkheim, Parsons could conceptualize a psychological process of social internalization.

But to "psychologize" Durkheim, Parsons had first to "socialize" Freud. In fact, Parsons believed that Freud's own epistemological framework was as great a barrier to reconciliation as Durkheim's, and for much the same reason. Freud's presuppositions were, for the most part, positivistic and individualistic. Because of these deficiencies, orthodox Freudian theory is inclined toward two fundamental errors. First, it tends to exaggerate the instrumental rationality of the healthy personality. Second, it perceives the individual in a concrete rather than analytic way, describing only discrete, separated relations among individual actors. Parsons mounted a fundamental attack on this Freudian epistemology, a critique that parallels his earlier response to social utilitarianism in *The Structure of Social Action.* Such a presuppositional criticism, Parsons believed, was a necessary prelude to any truly successful empirical analysis of socialization.

Parsons' challenge was direct: he had to reconcile Freud's assumptions about ego rationality and the externality of objects with the critique of instrumentalism and the subject/object dichotomy which provided the underpinnings of his own work. In Parsons' view, Freud himself had facilitated this task by creating the essentials of a postutilitarian psychoanalytic theory in his account of super-ego formation. The problem, as Parsons saw it, was that Freud could not extend this fundamental analysis of internalized moral standards to the need for internalized cognitive and expressive symbols as well.[10]

Freud was not sufficiently sensitive to the inherent difficulties of human communication, to the need for the symbolic mediation of individual interaction. He did not see the perception of reality as problematic for healthy actors: "Freud's view seems to imply that the object, as cognitively significant, is given independently of the actor's internalized culture, and that super-ego standards are *then* applied to it." Parsons takes issue with such a utilitarian understanding: "The [cognitive] constitution of the object and its moral [i.e., superego] appraisal are part and parcel of the *same* fundamental cultural patterns."[11] Furthermore, if the objects that compose factual reality must be symbolic, then the organizing capacity of the ego cannot be derived simply from "adaptation" to external conditions, a proposition that Freud had strongly endorsed. Rather, the ego itself must have an internal, cultural component.[12] Parsons argues that each of the personality's components, even the id, is as much a symbolic orientation as a biological impulse or adaptive response.[13]

In Parsons' later work, this Durkheim-Freud synthesis underlaid every aspect of his analysis. Any discussion of culture implied an internal personality structure; conversely, any analysis of personality implied the impact of cultural patterns. Parsons accomplished a fundamental critique of Freud's presuppositions. While in no way implying that personality is harmonized with society and culture, this critique does break down the rigid utilitarian dichotomization of individual and society that so marked Freud's metapsychology. Parsons severed the link between symbolization and neurosis. "Identification" need no longer be considered simply in a pejorative way, as a process inimical to individual well-being. Collective action, in other words, is not necessarily "group psychology," as Freud used the phrase. If the very elements that give the personality autonomy, the ego and superego, are built up through social internalizations, then individual voluntarism and collective order are indeed reconcilable. It is from such presuppositional considerations that Parsons develops his theory of the socialization of autonomy.[14]

1.2. EXTERNAL CONSTRAINT, VALUE INTERNALIZATION, AND FREEDOM

If interchange supplies the "space" of multidimensionality, socialization identifies the "time." With interchange Parsons makes the case against instrumentalism by cross-cutting the conditional and normative sectors of institutional life. With socialization, he makes the same point in terms of the individual life-cycle. As individuals move through the life cycle toward an occupational role, they become exposed to increasingly more conditional, more instrumental collective arrangements. Parsons' socialization theory contends, however, that for each new situation, the actor also cathects a new mode of normative internalization. Thus, by emphasizing the interplay between conditional and normative inducements to change, Parsons' theory of socialization remains consistently multidimensional.

According to Parsons, each of Freud's psychosexual crises are social and cultural crises as well. Each is initiated when the developing child is placed in new objective conditions to which he or she cannot adapt.[15] The anxiety created by this adaptive failure can be resolved, Parsons asserts, only by new object internalizations, which correspond to the personality elements of ego and superego. These new internalized objects supply the child with more adaptive "standards of what are and are not legitimate expectations of his own [and his parents'] behavior.[16]

Internalization is achieved by applying affect to culture. Since culture is generalized, Parsons reasons, personality development can also be described as involving a process of generalization.[17] The initial stage of oral dependency, for example, only partly rests upon biological needs for gratification. It involves also a distinctive learning process. The infant must learn to "interpret" the mother's tones, expressions, and gestures in an appropriate way. Gradually, the child generalizes from specific acts to a "pattern" of "meaningful" parental behavior. Henceforth, attitudinal signals by the mother are sufficient to induce the infant's cooperation in the nursing process; direct, physical manipulation of the relation is much less necessary.[18]

The oral stage, in other words, involves communication; this achievement allows the child to gain some freedom vis-à-vis external pressures.[19] Not only does he learn to be much more responsive to the parent's wishes, but he learns how to demand a response on his own. A new piece of common culture has been produced, but so has a new part of the personality, for, in Freud's terms, oral dependency indicates a stage of ego development. Further personality development involves the same cycle of increased autonomy: deprivation, anxiety, generalization, and internalization. While physical objects are lost in personality development, the old cultural expectations and knowledge are unconsciously retained.

Parsons emphasizes the autonomy provided by socialization by arguing that general roles, not specific commitments, are its most important products. By internalizing new and more complex attitudes at each stage of personality development, an individual learns what to expect from the basic situations of adult life.[20†] In the pre-Oedipal situation, for example, the child learns how to love and be loved and how to utilize diffuse emotional expression for both domination and submission. In the Oedipal stage, with the crisis produced by identification with the opposite-sex parent, the child, particularly the male, learns more abstract orientations: instrumental performance, self-esteem, and cooperation.[21] Each of these orientations, Parsons contends, derives from a specific familial role with which the Oedipal child has been involved: from the competition with father, the successful repression of castration anxiety, and the post-Oedipal cooperation with siblings. "The essential point," Parsons writes, "is, that . . . the child himself *becomes* all of these . . . types of objects" he encounters in family interaction. On the basis of this identification, he "becomes capable of assuming [these] roles in his interactions with others."[22]

These early patterns supply frameworks for later, adult relationships by the psychological process of "substitution."[23] Parsons explains, for example, how the male child's "ambivalent orientation to the father can be symbolically generalized" as the "prototype of a source of authority."[24] Substituting earlier paternal internalizations for objects encountered at a later point in the life cycle, the adult may genuinely respect social authority. But given the element of fear in that earlier relationship, this authority is rarely loved. What's more, for those authorities which force reluctant compliance, this early ambivalence will find an outlet in strong resentment, in the adult's "burning sense of injustice." By such generalization and substitution, the new and complex situations of adult life are "matched" with appropriate internal guidelines. In this way, despite the new and complex conditions of adulthood, an important element of individual autonomy is preserved.

Alongside such general "role orientations," socialization also imparts "value standards" which are similarly generalized and abstracted from particular commitments. The structural configuration of each sequence in the life cycle, Parsons believes, presents a life view that corresponds to different cultural patterns, or pattern variables. As long as a child's activity remains within the nuclear family, for example, it is impossible to escape cultural particularism, for in this situation the child "has no need to discriminate the universalistic and particularistic categories of role definitions."[25†] Thus, "to an adult, a boy's father is only one instance of the universalistically defined category of 'man,' " but "to the oedipal boy the discrimination of 'father' and 'man' has not yet been made." Nor, Parsons adds, has the discrimination been made between "mother" and "woman," "brother" and "boy," "sister" and "girl."[26] Only when the child's world "includes the nuclear family but also extends beyond it" is universalism possible.[27] The most important such institution is the school, where "intrafamilial standards" are superseded because "the child is put in explicit comparison with children who represent a sample of the families in the community."[28†]

A similar process occurs in the transition from ascription to achievement values. In the nuclear family, the child's status is ascribed: "I do such and such because I am a male child." With the child's entry into peer-group culture, status becomes more responsive to actual achievement. The peer group, contrary to the family, is an environment in which "superiority-inferiority relationships are not institutionally ascribed."[29]

This aspect of Parsons' socialization analysis suggests that values develop not through some purely intellectual, cognitive acculturation but through the structure of the psychological interaction itself. More universalistic standards depend on psychological maturation, on the existence, therefore, of longer and more complex socialization. Since universalistic and achievement values are significantly activistic, it is clear that collective arrangements, through socialization, can indeed produce an increased capacity for autonomy and self-control. This conceptualization involves a blending of Freud with Durkheim and Weber. The notion that anxiety is produced when new structural arrangements create deprivation is surely Weberian. Membership in new solidary groups, however, allows this anxiety to be alleviated by value internalization—a conception derived from a Durkheimian emphasis. Finally, because such internalizations result in further personality individuation, the individual can henceforth create structural arrangements and solidary groups in a more voluntary manner. This last understanding is clearly derived from Freud himself.

1.3. SOCIALIZATION THEORY AND PARSONS' DEBATE WITH THE CLASSICS

As with other aspects of Parsons' work, it is possible to evaluate the socialization analysis simply in terms of its empirical accomplishments. As compared with traditional socialization theory, for example, Parsons stresses that it is "relationships," not specific values, that are internalized. These general orientations provide autonomy not because they involve the actor in specific commitments but, instead, because they provide standards by which he can create and evaluate future interactions.[30†] A second empirical innovation is introduced vis-à-vis traditional personality theory. As compared with the main thrust of traditional psychoanalytic theory, Parsons stresses the role of external object relations, a position to which certain strands of Freudian theory have paid increasing attention in recent years.[31†] Only with such an "object relations" theory, Parsons believes, can psychoanalytic theory be satisfactorily combined with social analysis. Parsons' socialization theory also presents important supplements to Piaget's discussions of cognitive development. Parsons links the types of cognitive shifts Piaget describes to alterations in moral and affective development, and he relates changes in all three dimensions to characteristics of the larger social system.[32†]

These empirical achievements are embedded, however, in Parsons' more general presuppositional solution to the "individual problem." His overall understanding is that individual autonomy and normative order are reconcilable through the phenomenon of internalization. It seems that the critical equation of Parsons' socialization theory with an emphasis on conformity is based not simply on misreading but on a polemical misunderstanding of the general theoretical issues involved. Given their own nominalism, it is no wonder that Parsons' critics cannot see the voluntarism of his approach.[33†]

But the nature of Parsons' achievement can only be fully appreciated by understanding its role in his long-standing argument with his classical predecessors. It is possible to argue, for example, that Weber's rationalistic reduction of modern life could occur only because he utterly failed to comprehend the nature, even the existence, of early socialization. Weber could perceive the role of normative, internal elements only insofar as action was overtly influenced by a powerful religious culture. In traditional society, of course, religion played an important role in every institution. When Weber looked to modern society, where more differentiated institutions usually have no direct relationship to religious codes, he could no longer perceive individual action as related to internal values. Accordingly, voluntarism disappeared from Weber's analysis of contemporary society.

Weber lacked an understanding of the manner in which early socialization mediates between the individual and cultural norms, not only in traditional but in modern life. Modern bureaucracy may not be explicitly normatively directed, but given the fact of childhood socialization its members simply cannot be the purely instrumental automatons that Weber was inclined to describe. Of course, this failure on Weber's part can be linked to a presuppositional problem; his instrumentalist inclinations encouraged him to view the individual bureaucrat or modern economic actor in a concrete rather than analytic manner.

Parsonian socialization analysis also helps resolve the problematics of Marxian dualism. Marx's base-superstructure division, like all rational collectivist theory, relies on a concrete rather than analytic approach to the individual.[34†] All social forces are viewed by Marx as external to individual volition. The individual cannot be viewed analytically, as a carrier of internal value commitments. Parson's socialization theory, in contrast, allows such an analytic perspective to develop. The quality of an individual's action within any institution—for example, the degree of rationality in an office setting—can be understood as partly determined by value elements internalized prior to such institutional involvement. Parsons' socialization theory of the "production" of human resources offers the multidimensional alternative to Marx's reductionistic approach to the "reproduction" of labor power.

The irony of Marx's insistence that despite collective pressures individuals make their own history is that Marx's individual is epiphenomenal. What allows the individual to act over and against material forces? Marx cannot say. Socialization theory resolves this anomaly by "filling in" the historical individual. Individuals make their history insofar as they can bring internalized value commitments to bear on economic conditions in innovative and creative ways. This understanding indicates the incongruity of the base-superstructure dualism. How can the base determine the superstructure when it is socialized individuals who make economic innovations in the first place?[35†]

I have already discussed at some length the relation of Parsons' socialization theory to the problems in Durkheim's and Freud's analyses. Durkheim was thoroughly aware of the need for some theory of sequential value formation that would parallel the individual's life cycle. He wrote in *Moral Education*, for example, that "school should serve as an intermediary between the affective morality of family and the more severe morality of civil life."[36] But in discussing the nature of this transitional morality he could write only of a moral pedagogy that combined rationality and discipline. With socialization theory, Parsons can describe the process by which such moral civility is created without appearing, as Durkheim often did, to sacrifice the voluntarism upon which it is based.

Compared with Durkheim, Freud was relatively unaware of the need to complement his personality theory with an analysis of moral and symbolic development. Still, the independent role of object relations in personality development becomes increasingly significant in Freud's later writings on ego psychology. With his socialization theory, Parsons demonstrated that such object relations are not simply a matter of personality alone. If Durkheimian value analysis is also psychological, Freudian personality theory is, necessarily, also a theory of cultural development.

2. THE LATER CHANGE THEORY: DIFFERENTIATION, ADAPTATION, AND FREEDOM

If Parsons' later theories of interchange and socialization do indeed represent an original theoretical synthesis of the concerns of classical theory, we would expect a similar kind of innovation in his later treatment of change. This change theory does, in fact, present an important advance. Instead of syncretizing the historical analyses of Marx, Durkheim, and Weber, as in his middle-period work, Parsons' later writing presents an outline for surpassing the classical theories with a true analytic synthesis.

In contrast with the concreteness of the earlier work, Parsons' concern here is to define historical change at a fully generalized level. He does this by developing a model of change as "differentiation." As societies differentiate, he contends, the institutions associated with the different dimensions of society—with the functional demands of adaptation, goal attainment, integration, and pattern maintenance—become separated from one another. In the process, each develops the capacity to mobilize the resources of other systems and to assert an independent, though partial, regulation of them. In less differentiated societies, single structures perform a number of different functions; for example, kinship units may be the source of economic production and legal regulation, or political structures may also serve as religious institutions. The more differentiation develops, the more different functions will be performed by individuated specialized units.

In one sense, of course, this change theory derives directly from the interchange model itself. The very conception of what "differentiates" depends on Parsons' vision of multidimensional order. But while interchange describes the fundamental dimensions that structure all social behavior, including social change, the relation between the abstract, universal model of interchange and historically specific institutional development is open. In developing differentiation theory, Parsons specifies the model's relation to history. He argues, moreover, not only that social interchange will follow a specific historical pattern; he also asserts that it will have a certain historical meaning. Social differentiation, in his view, increases a society's adaptive potential and, at the same time, broadens its scope of individual freedom. But by giving his formal theory such substantive historical coloration, Parsons makes certain assumptions that are independent of his general commitment to the interchange model per se.[37]

2.1. THE IDEOLOGICAL SPECIFICATION

Parsons himself has never acknowledged the significant ideological element in his differentiation theory. His critics, for their part, have recognized this component, but they have usually distorted it. Indeed, the controversy surrounding Parsons' ideology closely resembles the confusions over his socialization theory, and for good reason: in both cases, it is voluntarism which is at stake.

To say that Parsons places himself in the liberal tradition of Western political thought does not say very much in itself, although certain ideological critics would question even this. Parsons believes that differentiation brings greater individual freedom and, as long as it is consonant with such liberty, greater equality. Still, what strain of Western liberalism does Parsons uphold? To what particular conception of freedom is he committed?

In his formal presuppositional work, of course, Parsons discarded the individualistic position of nineteenth-century liberal utilitarianism. In this substantive theory, however, he embraces at least part of it: he believes that the concrete individual actor must be the reference point for any normative political theory. Thus, when Parsons asks what freedom for the individual implies, he adopts the anti-Romantic, rationalistic perspective. Freedom entails individual separation and conscious self-control vis-à-vis the actor's internal and external environments. After this point, however, Parsons and moral utilitarianism part ways.

Parsons, unlike the utilitarians, believes that the individual is never really independent of collective order, in either its symbolic or material form. Individual autonomy, therefore, is not a matter of whether or not collective constraint exists. It concerns, rather, a qualitative matter, namely, the nature of the constraints themselves. Parsons addresses this question by turning to the collectivist strands of Western libertarian thought, and developing a synthesis of rational and normative collectivist approaches to individual freedom. This is, on an ideological level, the same ecumenical course he followed in his presuppositional analysis.[38†]

Both the Western traditions of critical idealism and materialism, it can be argued, define individual freedom as dependent upon different kinds of institutional, or collective, differentiation. Within the socialist materialist position, where freedom means individual control over the external environment, the most significant strand of Marx's mature theory identifies structural "fusion" as the source of capitalism's inequity and domination.[39†] Negatively stated, Marx believed that freedom could be achieved only by divesting the economic structure and its dominant class of their undifferentiated control over the other institutional dimensions of social life. In a positive sense, Marx believed that an autonomous electorate, represented in the state, should be able to assert its control over the economy; that law should become the expression of an independent sense of "right" rather than simply reproducing extant property arrangements; and that, in general, there should be an increase in the free competition of ideas and in the range of opportunities for individual activity.[40] In addition to Marx, of course, there have been other significant formulations of this socialist approach to freedom as increased differentiation, the most important of which extend the conception more explicitly to the noneconomic dimensions of social life. Perhaps the most significant of these are Robert Michels, with his theory of the democratic competition of elites, and T. H. Marshall, who emphasizes the "social" aspects of citizenship.[41]

Another Western intellectual tradition emphasizes the connection between individual freedom and differentiation on the normative, ideal level. Its premise is that individual autonomy, defined as the ability for self-conscious control over the internal environment, occurs to the degree that spiritual and ethical issues are transcendent over earthly concerns. This position has been articulated by such diverse traditions as the Judaic and Christian notions of divine law and the natural law tradition of the French Enlightenment; by the Protestant notion that the sanctity of the individual conscience depends upon the achievement of a "universal otherhood"; and in the various conceptions of freedom as tied to the autonomy of secular intellectual thought, from the Greeks and the Humanists to Bacon.[42]

It is out of these three conceptions of individual liberty that Parsons forged his version of the liberal ideal. From utilitarian liberalism he assumes his commitment to individual rationality and self-conscious control. From the two collectivist traditions, materialist and idealist, he conceives his understanding of the forces which this emancipation must confront.

There is a clear correspondence between this proposed ideological synthesis and the presuppositional arguments with which Parsons has been primarily concerned. On the presuppositional level, it will be recalled (see e.g., ch. 2, sec. 2), Parsons is particularly critical of three positions: the nominalist emphasis on an individualistic approach to collective order; the idealist emphasis on internal over external collective constraints; and the exclusively external focus of materialist analysis, which effectively eliminates voluntary action. In proposing his ideological synthesis, Parsons implicitly connects evaluative judgments to each of these generalized, theoretical positions. By ignoring the impact of collective social forces, he argues, individualistic theories risk the "social" obtuseness of nineteenth-century liberalism and laissez-faire. By postulating only instrumental action and external order, he believes, Marxist theory potentially tolerates antinormative, nondemocratic coercion. Finally, by ignoring the conditional, instrumental constraints on individual action, idealist theory tends toward abstract utopianism or complacent conservatism.

By grounding his perspective on individual freedom in his more general presuppositional synthesis, therefore, Parsons intends to avoid these ideological pitfalls. This ecumenical ambition is clear from the term he applies to his normative ideal: "institutionalized individualism." With this standard, Parsons establishes two sources of moral evaluation. First, historical changes are "progressive" if they contribute to the individual's "freedom from previously constraining limitations." This "enhanced capacity at the individual level," however, must meet a second requirement: it must develop "concomitantly with that of social and cultural frameworks for organization and institutionalized norms."[43]

Parsons navigated this delicate course between individualist and collectivist, rationalist and normative moralities from the very beginning of his career. In one sense, this struggle took the form of a lifelong debate between Parsons and his Christian inheritance. Parsons' family roots lay in the Social Gospel movement of the American Middle West, a tradition which in the face of the abuses of early industrialism rejected the individualism and privatism of earlier American Protestantism for an emphasis on political activism and reform. It is possible to see this legacy at work in Parsons' first book, *The Structure of Social Action.* Parsons accepts here the utilitarians' emphasis on voluntarism while rejecting their individualistic and rationalist understanding of what it entailed.[44†] Moreover, while he traced the roots of these objectionable elements in utilitarianism back to the Protestant Reformation, he also argued that only by adding a "religious" element to action could these negative elements be superseded.

A similar cross-cutting permeates the ideological analysis of Parsons' middle period. For example, he embraces the pattern-variable norms of universalism, specificity, achievement, and affective neutrality, which in addition to their presuppositional relevance should also be seen as normative commitments to the ideal of a secularized Protestant ethic. However, while this cultural pattern articulates the standard of rationality and individual self-control, its very existence amounts to the denial of an exclusively rationalist or individualist position. The values are, after all, supra-individual patterns that inspire action through internalization. Further, they are normative elements, not simply the result of efficient adaptation to circumstances.

In the later period, when Parsons' discussion of the pattern variables abates, he turns to a focus on the normative ideal of "instrumental activism." Defining this pattern as rationalistic and activistic, he insists that it differs from earlier American Protestantism only in its lack of explicit religious commitment to a supernatural order.[45†] Once again, in other words, Parsons' complex relationship to the Puritan heritage is evident. While the substantive content of his ideal is neo-utilitarian, its presuppositional implications indicate his sensitivity to the need for collective and "religious" dimensions of social order.[46†]

This pattern of ideological synthesis and compromise represented by Parsons' commitment to "institutionalized individualism" also reflects the more concrete political sensibilities, commitments and antipathies generated by his involvement in the politics of the twentieth century. Three concrete political positions functioned as ideological foils for Parsons throughout his careeer: American conservatism, the radical right, and the radical left. Each of these political positions violates his understanding of the requisites for individual freedom, and in one form or another every article and essay he wrote contributed to the counterargument he proposed.

Parsons views American conservativism as the quintessence of individualism, and he attacks the ideology in two forms. From his very first published essays, he criticizes laissez-faire capitalism and the belief, still so influential in America, that the market—unregulated by overarching values, political organization, or social solidarity—should determine the distribution of goods and services. It is true, he agrees, that the economic differentiation indicated by the market allows more individual control, but this control must itself be regulated in a multidimensional and social manner.[47†] Parsons' other conservative target is religious fundamentalism, the generic term he applies to those literalistic theologies that foster mistrust for collective agencies and exclusionary prejudice against "immoral" segments of the social community. Parsons views fundamentalism as inimical to social reform and to the expansion of scientific rationality upon which it depends. He considered American McCarthyism as a prime example of such traditionalism.[48†]

On the other hand, Parsons always forcefully reacted against fascism, the ideology of the radical right, and communism, the ideology of the radical left, on the grounds of their anti-individualistic collectivism. He treated fascism as an extension of fundamentalism, as a reaction against differentiation that while idealizing the primitivism of an earlier, highly fused social order tried to effectuate this vision through the power of a differentiated, totalitarian state. The case of communism was more ambiguous. In addition to his criticism of its extreme collectivism, Parsons rejected its radical version of emancipation. While he accepted the egalitarian thrust of its principles, he could not accept the antinormative, antireligious framework within which they were embedded. Differentiation would bring emancipation, but it would do so only within the context of some kind of individualized, secular civic religion. The rationalism of the communist ideal, Parsons believed, would appeal only to an avant-garde minority; it would ultimately polarize and alienate the great majority.[49]

On the non-communist radical left, Parsons was suspicious of what he viewed as a latent individualism, an "anarchistic" utopianism which he found, for example, in C. Wright Mills' "Jeffersonian" conviction that institutional constraint, in the form of social elites, was inherently iniquitous.[50] A differentiated society, Parsons believed, would, despite its pluralization, continue to rely on elites, though they would be of a functional rather than a hereditary caste. An extreme individualism, whether of the left or right, would interfere with the trust that even a critical and democratic relationship to authority demanded.

For his own position, therefore, Parsons tried to combine the emancipation of the left with the sensitivity to tradition of the right. Though he found quite acceptable the democratic socialism of T. H. Marshall, his own version of progressivism was prototypically "American." He embraced Roosevelt's New Deal and Stevensonian liberalism, applauded activistic social reform and accepted with equanimity the regulated, Keynesian capitalism of the Welfare State.[51†]

Parsons' ideological critics, then, have not only erred in their effort to reduce Parsons' theory to political values, but they have, for the most part, distorted these values themselves. Parsons is not an "organicist," and neither is he an "individualist." He can be labeled a "conservative" only if we adopt the most present-minded, antihistorical framework. Parsons lifelong polemic against the nominalism and utilitarianism of the Anglo-Saxon democratic tradition resembles Durkheim's, and his synthetic counterproposal, despite its greater theoretical clarity, has proved almost as difficult for critics to understand.[52†]

2.2. THE EMPIRICAL SPECIFICATION

By itself, this ideological specification is still not sufficient to convert Parsons' abstract interchange model into a substantive theory of social change. Parsons' liberalism helps explain the form historical differentiation takes; it does not, however, explain why such changes will actually occur. To approach the latter question, Parsons must make some crucial empirical commitments. Differentiation, he argues, increases the "adaptiveness" of social systems and subsystems. More differentiated states are more efficient, and because they stand a higher chance of survival, they will be "selected," in an evolutionary sense, over the course of historical time.[53]

Despite the controversy generated by such an openly Darwinian approach, this empirical criterion is actually a familiar one in historical sociology.[54] While the classical sociological theorists would disagree with Parsons about the results of this selection process, they shared his view of the process itself. For Marx, the capitalist economy became dominant because it could respond to economic adversity by rapidly adjusting the organic composition of its capital. Such increased efficiency, he believed, provided it with an unparalleled competitive advantage. For Durkheim, organic solidarity depended, in part, on the growth of the division of labor, an adaptive alteration of the formerly segmental social organization in response to increasing population density. Similarly, Weber's explanations of movements toward patrimonialism and feudalism depended on assumptions about their empirical adaptiveness. In the course of history, Weber believed, these two basic forms continually had been "selected" because of their intrinsic political effectiveness.

Parsons' differentiation theory, then, specifies his interchange model empirically as well as ideologically. At every evolutionary stage, systemic adaptiveness and individual freedom are interwoven.[55†] For purely empirical reasons, Parsons believes, freedom will not—in the long run—be able to expand in ways that are detrimental to systemic effectiveness. For moral reasons, he believes, such adaptiveness ought not to increase at the cost of individual freedom or decreased equality.

Parsons makes this double reference throughout his historical discussions. For example, although the institutional developments he defines as historically "universal" ostensibly are chosen purely for their empirical contribution to adaptive capacity, it is evident that Parsons also views them as steps toward the liberation of the individual actor.[56] While such an ideological point is relatively easy to see in discusssions of such developments as economic markets, universalistic legal norms, and democratic associations, Parsons makes the point in his analyses of stratification and bureaucratization as well. As compared with the later growth of stratification, he argues, early class formation introduced innovation and individual mobility, and encouraged more universalistic evaluations of competence. Similarly, he emphasizes the moral relevance of bureaucratization; it could have developed, he argues, only with the individual's "broad emancipation from ascription."[57]

The same kind of simultaneous empirical and ideological reference occurs in Parsons' later, more systematic analysis of these historical universals as components of the more abstract "evolutionary process." In this later conception, he defines differentiation as involving "adaptive upgrading," "inclusion," and "value generalization." While he argues, for example, that value generalization is necessary to ensure the stability of structurally diversified systems, he emphasizes at the same time that this generalization also facilitates religious toleration and the achievement of more individuated forms of cultural commitment.[58]

2.3. DIFFERENTIATION AS A CONCRETE SOCIAL PROCESS

2.3.1. "Structural" Change versus Deviance

Differentiation is initiated by social strain, which Parsons defines as any force that disrupts the relation between a unit and its environment. Strain can originate from any dimensional source—from economic, political, integrative, or cultural factors—and involves, in interchange terms, an imbalance in the boundary relationships between subsystems.[59] In any social system, two responses to strain occur. On the part of the acting unit, intensified psychological anxiety produces the "generalization" of value commitments away from specific orientations geared to immediate role performance.[60] With this generalized response, social conflict occurs, as the affected unit tries to combat its deteriorating situation. The second response to strain originates in the unit's environment: the legitimate authorities of the broader system initiate social-control processes to bring the unit back into line. If such controls are successful, the strain and generalized response will be viewed merely as episodic deviance. Ineffective control efforts, however, indicate that the source of strain is deeply rooted in the very structure of the system.[61†]

To resolve such "structured" strain, new, more differentiated and adaptive structures must be developed. This is structural differentiation, and it occurs through a variety of mechanisms. First, new resources and opportunities must become available, both objectively, as in the provision of rewards for innovation, and subjectively, as when communications media broadcast messages that legitimate new forms. Simultaneously, competing authorities will apply a range of sanctions—political, economic, legal—in an effort to direct the emerging structural changes in the directions which they prefer. Finally, new and more inclusive norms will emerge to integrate the new units with more established structures.

If differentiation succeeds and the structural sources of strain are eliminated, psychic anxiety will abate, values will be respecified, and equilibrium restored. The new structures will not only be more empirically adaptive, but will provide more freedom for the individual as well.[62]

2.3.2. Historical Development as Social, Psychological, and Cultural Differentiation

The emergence of the economic market system has always represented for Parsons the prototypical illustration of structural differentiation, interweaving increased adaptation and individual autonomy with a multidimensional approach to the process of change itself. While he acknowledges that technological innovation was basic to the Industrial Revolution, he takes the expansion of the market as the more crucial causal factor.[63]

Markets allow factors of production to be combined strictly according to standards of economic efficiency. It is because of markets that the economic system can command and regulate society's noneconomic resources for economic purposes.

Parsons describes markets as differentiating over the course of several centuries in response to the strains of European expansion and the opportunities this expansion provided for an entrepreneurial middle class. The ability to respond to these opportunities, he emphasizes, depended on certain unique features of Western development: the legal and military autonomy of the merchant cities; the checks and balances between church and state that prevented political authority from inhibiting the growth of the middle class for noneconomic, political reasons; the legacy of Roman contract and property law that encouraged individual financial responsibility; and the transcendent, activist values that characterized Western religion.[64] By the nineteenth century, markets had developed sufficiently to allow the kind of purely economic control of labor, physical facilities, organization, and financial capital upon which industrialization depended.

Yet this nineteenth-century capitalism still represented an incomplete economic differentiation. Composed primarily of family-owned and -directed enterprises, its principal units of production were fused with kinship criteria.[65] This limitation inhibited the accumulation of capital and, by placing ascriptive barriers on economic mobility, limited the efficiency of economic management. This situation was gradually transformed, Parsons believes, by the differentiation of ownership from control, and the concomitant rise of joint-stock companies to accumulate capital.

This phase of the differentiation process was initiated not only by the strains produced by undercapitalization but also by the self-interested group conflict that had developed toward the end of the nineteenth century between the new group of professional managers and the old economic leadership represented by family ownership. The strain produced psychological anxiety, generalized ideological debate, and social conflict—for example, Veblen's pleas for "expert management" and the "social engineering" movements of the Progressive era. In response, new material and ideational opportunities emerged and new legal arrangements were created. Gradually, the more impersonal arrangements of twentieth-century capitalism emerged. The maintenance of this new structural arrangement, which sharply differentiated ownership from control, depends upon the complex input and output arrangements that Parsons and Smelser describe in *Economy and Society*.[66†]

In contrast to such economic development, Parsons views political differentiation as creating the structural apparatus for a society to define and enforce self-conscious goals. This development obviously enhances system adaptation, because the resources of other dimensions can be increasingly regulated and coordinated in more strategic fashion. This increased capacity is achieved through the creation of specifically political organs which specialize in executive administration, like bureaucracies, in the mobilization of support, like political parties, or in the articulation of grievances, like constitutions and courts. At the same time, Parsons believes that such political differentiation also increases the potential for individual freedom, as government membership and responsiveness become separated from positions and commitments in other functional systems.

In European history, the first crucial political differentiation was the development of absolutist kingships. Despite their relative autonomy, however, the fusion of such governments with kinship and lineage greatly limited their flexibility and responsiveness. The transition to representative and democratic forms, which occurred first in England, involved the further differentiation of government from lineage, class, and other particularistic groupings.

Faced with the enormous strains that disequilibriated every post-Reformation European nation, England alone was able to modernize its aristocratic system of parliaments in the course of a relatively continuous transition to democracy. The relative ease of this differentiation, Parsons believes, was guaranteed by a number of historically idiosyncratic factors.[67] First, the island's physical isolation and the unusual unity of its aristocracy limited the emerging kingship's military expansion. Second, the early commercialization of one part of the English aristocracy created status conflict and a source of "objective dissatisfaction" with the old order. Finally, this dissatisfaction was culturally legitimated and disciplined by Puritan religious nonconformity and legally protected by the English tradition of common law and the traditional independence of England's professional legal community. Given this pattern of opportunities and sanctions, the English middle classes could respond to the strain of transition in an innovative rather than reactionary manner, creating more differentiated and representative political structures.[68†]

Given Parsons' interchange model, it is not surprising that he insists that these processes of political and economic differentiation were necessarily intertwined with changes in solidarity. The differentiation of the societal community—a process which he also calls "inclusion," or the "production of citizenship"—occurs when membership in the national solidary community becomes independent of the individual's position in any nonsolidary subsystem. While a gradual movement toward such differentiation occurred throughout historical development, Parsons is primarily concerned, once again, with the modern West.

The strains that produced the first real differentiation of the societal community were widespread throughout early modern Europe. These can be described, most generally, as resulting from the tension between modernizing and traditional elements in the economic, political, and religious spheres. The restructuring of integration in response to these strains depended, however, on the existence of very specific patterns of opportunities and sanctions. Such patterns simply were not available in the central and eastern European countries of the Counter-Reformation, where social development had been "frozen" into the relatively fused forms of political absolutism, aristocratic domination, agricultural and barter economies, and particularistic versions of Christianity. In contrast, the countries of the northwest, particularly England, responded to these strains by internal reform, not by retrenchment. In the Counter-Reformation countries, there was the attempt simply to "suppress" the disequilibriating strain; in the countries of the northwest, there was the attempt to "resolve" it. England's greater flexibility depended, in turn, on its commercialization of agriculture and the strength of its markets, on its development of more representative government, and on English Puritanism's more universalistic version of Christianity.[69†]

Though perhaps the most significant step toward integrative differentiation was the establishment of "civil" or legal rights for all members of the national community, Parsons follows T. H. Marshall in suggesting that the full differentiation of solidarity involves the movement toward "social rights" as well. Any truly independent national "community" depends, in other words, on the minimum protection of its members against the basic economic and biological threats to individual autonomy. The basic exigencies of life—health care, unemployment insurance, housing, education, and so on—should be provided to all members of the community regardless of their achievement or position in other functional spheres.[70]

Parsons emphasizes that such integrative differentiation, though fundamentally dependent on other functional developments, retains its own causal independence in turn. It represents, as do the others, structural changes produced by institutions and groups in particular historical situations. Rome, for example, developed its impressively universalistic legal norms because of the particular interaction between the exigencies of imperial administration and the impersonal conceptions of the Stoic philosophy of nature.[71] Yet this integrative differentiation actually produced more conflict instead of resolving it, for the other dimensions of Roman society could not supply complementary degrees of functional flexibility and individual freedom. The later patrician political structure fused wealth and military power with kinship, and in Roman culture neither the imported Classical philosophy nor the religious cults and sects could provide the empire with the necessary transcendent symbolic legitimation. Given such limitations, the legal, formal incorporation of individuals into the Roman community never became "inclusion" in substance.

Parsons finds another example of such uneven development in the American record on assimilation. Any effectively differentiated community must, of course, guarantee membership independent of the biological criterion of race. Yet this extension of solidary membership depends on the particular kind of inputs that the integrative system receives. While American Negroes were legally granted full citizenship after the Civil War, this equal status was effectively nullified by the segregating impact of geographical, economic, political, and religious discrimination. So the radical incompatibility between integrative and nonintegrative dimensions proved intolerable. Eventually, more particularistic legal rules developed to formalize this inferior status. In contrast, those immigrant groups not distinguished by race could capitalize on their legal rights and progress in other spheres to fully implement their integrative status.[72]

Parsons believes that these historical developments in society were thoroughly intertwined with changes in culture and personality. For most of his career, he described the evolution of values as a movement toward "universalism." Universalism promotes flexibility, critical judgment, and reform because it demands that all particular traits be evaluated according to a broader, more general set of principles. Value universalism, in other words, is itself a form of differentiation: it creates distance between cultural norms and the object of cultural judgment.[73]

In his later differentiation theory, however, Parsons describes this value change as a process of "generalization." In the earlier, traditional societies, social values were derived from the commitments imposed by a particular religion. With increased differentiation, religious "denominationalism" became established, and social values increasingly were legitimated by the secular moral community of the nation. As social differentiation proceeded still further, even this secular moral community became too restrictive a reference. The modern nation-state includes a vast range of functionally differentiated, often conflicting values. It must reconcile symbolic patterns—specific religious, national, and political beliefs—which previously had exerted an absolute monopoly on moral legitimation:

> At one stage only "good Catholics" could be full citizens of many Western societies; at the height of nationalism . . . only "good Frenchmen," understood in an ethnic-cultural sense, could be full citizens. . . . More recently, only "good members of the working class," with a presumptive eligibility for membership in the Communist Party, could be full citizens.[74]

To cope with this new situation, fundamental value referents must be couched at still higher levels of generality. They develop more abstract ways of codifying social obligations. This generalization can occur only if basic social values refer neither to a specific religion nor to the secular national community as such, but rather to the moral autonomy of the individual person.[75†]

Parsons views this value differentiation as involving a multidimensional complex of historical factors. Cultural legitimation becomes strained in the first place simply because differentiation on the social level inevitably produces new, "unexplainable" social conflicts. But the specific cultural content of the extant symbolic pattern contributes to this strain in traditional values. The moral controversy surrounding the problem of usury in the commercial revolution in the early modern period, for example, involved both the cultural strictures of Christianity and the social needs of the emerging bourgeois groups. Eventually, Christian ethics became more generalized. Brotherhood no longer depended as much on specific kinds of economic behavior. Financiers could now take interest while maintaining their religiosity.[76]

Cultural and social differentiation both produce increased individual autonomy. They can do so, Parsons believes, only because they are connected to complementary psychological developments. In psychoanalytic terms, individual independence depends on increased ego autonomy and on the control over unconscious affective dependence on early object attachments. Modifying the Freudian theory, Parsons places this developmental schema into sociological terms: psychological autonomy is directly related to the social and cultural distance an individual travels away from his family of origin and from its diffuse, ascriptive character of parental authority.[77] Portraying the psychological issue in this way allows Parsons to see that the requisites for ego autonomy mesh with the opportunities provided by cultural and social differentiation. After all, as differentiation increases the separation between a functionally specific nuclear family and other institutional areas, social and parental authority do in fact diverge. In this process, the authoritative sources of traditional sanctions come into conflict, with the inevitable result that ascriptive legitimations become more difficult to enforce. As cultural values become more abstract and individuated, the particularistic loyalty values associated with passive obedience are more difficult to maintain. The individual is forced to become more responsible and active.

Parsons formulates this interrelation in explicitly psychoanalytic terms. In the first place, differentiation increases individual autonomy because the growth of extrafamilial institutions and groups provides increased opportunity for rebellion, separation, and neutralization of early object relationships. But the actual situation is more complex. Along with the separation and object loss produced by differentiation, there develops a pattern of extended socialization. Between childhood and adulthood there emerges a graded series of transitional institutions—the peer group, the elementary-school classroom, the high school, the university. In each of these, the child, adolescent, or young adult is exposed not only to the strain of object loss but, simultaneously, to the opportunity for new cathectic attachments. In each case, these new attachments are more universalistic than earlier objects. The new authorities are less loving, more neutral and impartial; the new communities are less fused and more pluralistic. Each new internalization, therefore, demands that the personality structure become more generalized, more able to cope with divergent and complex object situations.

In terms of actual causal analysis, Parsons becomes quite specific. In discussing the timing of the child's entry into elementary school, for example, he emphasizes that only with the onset of psychosexual latency can the child's eroticism be brought under control.[78] It is appropriate, therefore, that schooling, the first real nonascriptive experience, should begin only at this stage in the life cycle. Parsons observes that in the earlier elementary grades, schoolteachers tend to resemble the mother, not only in their female sexual identity but also in terms of their diffuse affectivity and in the relative particularism which still infuses their relationship to the student. Gradually, schoolteachers become less like parents and more like the impersonal authorities of adult society. As compared with the high-school community, for example, the solidarity of the university is much more complex, egalitarian, and individualistic.[79] Parsons emphasizes that the elementary classroom, the high school and university—even the peer group—are available only in societies that have achieved certain levels of social and cultural differentiation.[80†]

Differentiation theory, therefore, provides a historical perspective for Parsons' more general multidimensional analysis: societal interchange always occurs, but this general model can become rooted in separate concrete institutions only after considerable historical development. Given a multidimensional perspective on order, culture must always be defined as "generalized" from concrete objects, but it becomes distinctively so only with cultural differentiation; similarly, if internalization is to occur at all, personality growth necessarily involves a certain generalization, but this "learning" becomes still more abstract and significant with the lengthening of the socialization process.[81†]

This relation between historical and presuppositional multidimensionality also applies to Parsons' conceptualization of the generalized media of interchange. It is relatively easy to see the relationship between historical development and the creation of differentiated media. Although individuals always invoke sanctions in concrete interaction, the media can become specialized into the distinctive commodities of wealth, power, value commitments, and influence only as a society's own subsystems actually become separated and relatively independent. It is more difficult, however, to see why these differentiated media must necessarily be "generalized." Is there any link between differentiation and such "generalization" on the social level?

Parsons argues that there is. Once again, he relates the impact of differentiation both to increasing empirical effectiveness and to the expansion of individual freedom.

The "symbolization" of media is necessary, Parsons believes, in order to realize the potential efficiency gained by a differentiated system. If media exchange were simply "intrinsic"—if, for example, political institutions could gain obedience only through coercion, or if economic organizations could induce cooperation only by providing real goods and services—resource production would be a clumsy, slow-moving process indeed. The generalized element of media, in other words, provides a streamlined "language" for conducting concrete interaction.

But even more important to increased effectiveness is the "trust" that such generalized symbolism implies. While differentiation brings a social system greater flexibility and responsiveness, the very act of separating a system's component parts exposes it to potentially great instability. In a differentiated situation, individuals and institutions must mobilize and coordinate resources from segments of society that are unknown to one another. Moreover, the institutional authorities themselves—corporate managers, political officials, influential leaders—are as often as not unknown quantities to the very groups they are trying to affect. Finally, the very independence and flexibility of each social sector means that empirical exchanges can no longer be regulated by the "traditional" givens of ascribed norms.[82†] Only if the media of exchange can generate trust, if they can mobilize or plug into some functionally specific consensus, can societal production occur without the continual, crippling withdrawal of resources by participating groups and individuals.[83†]

Not surprisingly, Parsons argues that media generalization also has moral implications. The existence of trust, for example, means that creative individuals are allowed greater freedom and autonomy. Further, simply by facilitating cooperation among diverse individuals and groups, trust contributes to a more inclusive, cosmopolitan community. In the process, Parsons believes, it also lessens the possibility for the kind of social polarization and extremism that is inimical to individual liberty.[84]

Like the differentiation process in general, then, Parsons views the emergence of generalized media as creating the possibility for achieving both the morality of "institutionalized individualism" and the empirical fact of increased systemic effectiveness. If the media are fully generalized, he believes, freedom can be realized without excessive individualism; innovation can occur without radical instability; democracy can be achieved without debilitating atomism; and leadership and reform can occur without the abuse of power and the factionalization of the societal community.

2.3.3. *Differentiation as a Conflict Theory*

This analysis of the "generalized" component of exchange media presents an introduction to Parsons' thinking about the nature of conflict in a differentiated society. Given the separation of individual and institutional actors, and the lack of ascriptive regulation, conflict can only increase as differentiation proceeds. After all, even the generalization of media creates the potential for destabilizing "deflation" and "inflation." But while the *amount* of conflict varies directly with the degree of differentiation, its *severity*, Parsons suggests, varies inversely.

As Parsons sees it, conflict becomes less severe for the same developmental reasons that it becomes more frequent. For example, the growing differentiation of normative and value spheres from economic and political power increases conflict by encouraging opposition to authoritative economic and political positions. Thus, political dissatisfaction becomes much more frequently expressed because democratization separates political decision-making from the solidary processes that mobilize demands and support. First, it becomes impossible for any government simply to handle the plurality of interest demands. Equally important, it becomes legal, indeed informally mandated, for constituencies to withdraw support in response to political dissatisfaction.

But while differentiation encourages such specific opposition, it insulates a more general level of normative support, and the integration of the national community itself, from the kind of polarizing divisions such conflict produces. The very independence of a solidary community from particular political and economic membership generates a normative agreement that potentially cuts across more specific divisions of interest. Only a differentiated solidary community can create "rules of the game" that prevent interest conflict from exploding into civil crisis. Writing about American presidential elections, for example, Parsons argues that while political parties campaign on divisive particularizing interests, they usually are forced to connect these demands to elements of supra-party consensus.

"There is, to a fair degree," he believes, "a common framework both of institutional norms and of cognitive definition of the situation." This framework guarantees "fair agreement across party lines on the characteristics of the candidates and the relevant criteria to judge them, on what the major issues of the campaign are, on various expectations for the future."[85]

Differentiation also limits the severity of conflict by generating certain kinds of elites.[86] Although the very existence of structural differentiation indicates that established authorities have been unsuccessful in re-equilibriating social conflict, the strains which produced this conflict can still be of widely varying intensity. Can strain be resolved by reform or can the necessary differentiation only be produced through revolutionary restructuring? The answer to this question, Parsons believes, depends on the relative flexibility of social elites. If they are fused with the structures that have created the strain, elites will be less flexible; they will identify with the very authorities whose actions they must try to reform. Such vested interest in the status quo naturally radicalizes conflict. On the other hand, if powerful elites operate independently of authorities which are responsible for the disfunctional structure, reform efforts are bound to be facilitated. The ability to respond positively to social conflict, in other words, depends on the distance between society's strategic elites and its malfunctioning institutions.

Parsons argues that differentiation produces precisely this kind of independence among social elites. As institutional sectors become functionally autonomous, elites become functionally specialized, their status differentiated not only from kinship but from position in other institutional sectors as well.[87] Thus, in his controversial critique of Mills' "power elite" thesis, Parsons argues that the homogeneity Mills proposes simply does not exist.[88] Mills, Parsons asserts, has ignored the role of competence in economic management, the regulatory impact of legal norms and the judiciary on political and economic life, the independence of political parties from both governmental and economic interference, and the independent religious legitimation and normative support upon which political activity depends. Mills has ignored, in other words, the effects on elite formation of structural differentiation.[89†]

2.4. *DIFFERENTIATION AND THE "CONFLICT CRITIQUE"*

In 1956, Lewis Coser could write the following: "While to an earlier generation of American sociologists, 'laws' of social change, structural variability, and an analysis of what later theorists called 'functional alternatives' were of central concern, these questions, although not totally neglected in Parsons' work, are peripheral to him."[90] As should be clear from the discussion in chapter 3, this was not an accurate evaluation even of Parsons' middle-period work. Whatever validity it had for Parsons' change theory before 1956, however, it is still less descriptive of his later writing. Analysis of the "laws" of social change, structural variability, and functional alternatives has permeated Parsons' ideologically and empirically specified theory of historical differentiation.

The other principal charges leveled at Parsons by the proponents of the "conflict" school also thoroughly disregard the achievements of his differentiation theory. For example, Coser and other critics have accused Parsons of adopting a purely negative view of conflict. They argue that he treats intra-system conflict only as deviance, that he treats it only as debilitating for the system as a whole. As an alternative, Coser proposes that conflict "contributes to the emergence of new norms."[91]

> A flexible society benefits from conflict because such behavior, by helping to create and modify norms, assures its continuance under changed conditions. Such mechanisms for readjustment of norms are hardly available to rigid systems: by suppressing con-

> flict, the latter smother a useful warning signal, thereby maximizing the danger of catastrophic breakdown.[92]

Is this not precisely the line of reasoning that differentiation theory itself proposes? In fact, Parsons' theory not only proposes this argument but elaborates it in at least as systematic and historically grounded a form as "conflict theory."

Again, in the 1950s and early 1960s these critics scored *The Social System* for failing to develop any theory of structured change and conflict, for relating nondeviant strain and conflict purely to extrasystemic "intrusions" and historical accident.[93] Yet so much has differentiation theory reversed this tendency—which was, even at that, only one strand among others—that the critics of "functionalist" change theory today argue that it is actually too "structural" and "internalist," that it neglects extrasystemic factors and minimizes the role of accident.[94†]

Perhaps the most effective illustration of this paradoxical contrast between differentiation theory and the conflict critics can be found in Dahrendorf's well-known argument in *Class and Class Conflict in Industrial Society.* Dahrendorf asserts that Parsons' "consensus theory," which he views as identical with functionalist and idealist theories, gives no consideration to conflict and its differential impact on industrial societies. I have argued, to the contrary, that Parsons has developed such a theory. In fact, because of its multidimensionality, this theory illuminates the differential effects of conflict more effectively than Dahrendorf's own.

In examining conflict in "post-capitalist" society, Dahrendorf argues that institutional "pluralization" has increased at the expense of "superimposition." The increasing isolation of the industrial sector, he believes, has diluted not the frequency of class conflict but its intensity.[95] This, of course, is exactly the point of differentiation theory itself, not only as it has been explicitly presented in Parsons' later work but implicitly in his earlier change theory as well.

Yet a significant contrast between the two approaches remains. In his analysis of pluralization, Dahrendorf fails to distinguish the nature of the nonindustrial spheres which "pluralize" the social system. Nor has he described the process of their historical formation. For example, he blurs together the integrative and political pressures on economic life.

> In capitalist society . . . the lines of industrial and *political* conflict were superimposed. . . . Clearly, the relations between industry and *society* are close in all modern societies. [However,] in post-capitalist society industry and society have, by contrast to capitalist society, been dissociated. . . . If it is correct to speak of an "economic citizenship" side by side with the "*political* citizenship" . . . then this very distinction hints at the separation of the spheres of industry and *society.*[96]

But what is "society"? Is it political or solidary? Surely, economic life could not be isolated effectively if politics constituted the society's only noneconomic dimension. Could citizenship be simply political, could it be constituted by the legal right to vote alone? These questions remain unanswered. Later in his argument Dahrendorf gives a crucial role in the pluralization process to noneconomic and nonpolitical developments like secularization, science, prestige solidarity, and socialization.[97] The nature of these developments, however, remains thoroughly residual in his discussion.

This ambiguity occurs in Dahrendorf's theory of pluralization because it is not systematically multidimensional. A rationalist bias pervades his work. His insistence that only vertical and instrumental conflict is "really" important leaves him theoretically unprepared to analyze the very normative factors which he later emphasizes as crucial to a pluralist situation. In contrast, Parsons' change theory not only embraces the ideological and empirical assumptions of differentiation but places them in a firmly synthetic framework. As a result, his analysis of the isolating effects of historical pluralization is significantly more illuminating.[98†]

These criticisms by conflict theorists, it must be allowed, emerged before the explicit formulation of Parsons' differentiation had proceeded very far.[99†] The irony, of course, is that the charges gained currency just as this theory was beginning to be seriously elaborated, not only by Parsons himself but by a generation of students. In 1970 Gouldner still wrote about the "oneness" of Parsons' social world, about Parsons' "pre-Keynesian sociology" which is "moored in an earlier image of a social order held together by spontaneous processes."[100†] Certainly such elements can be found in Parsons' later work, and in the chapters following I will demonstrate the problems they create. But just as clearly, such analysis ignores entirely a fundamental aspect of Parsons' late historical theory, which emphasizes the differentiated complex of modern social processes, as well as the existence of self-conscious, functionally specific forms of social control.[101†]

2.5. REFORMULATING THE CLASSICAL THEORIES OF CHANGE

I have discussed Parsons' later change theory in terms of its empirical and ideological assumptions, arguing that its complexity and sophistication compare favorably with the stereotypes of the conflict critique. I have also emphasized, at every point, the significance of the theory's presuppositional foundations. But, once again, the most effective way to gain perspective on Parsons' theoretical achievement is to personalize its polemical intent, to place it within the context of Parsons' lifelong argument with his classical predecessors.

Differentiation theory clearly owes much to Durkheim. Parsons credits Durkheim with formulating the ideological ideal of "institutionalized individualism," and, indeed, he faithfully follows Durkheim's premise that ideological individualism must be combined with collectivist presuppositions. Like Durkheim, moreover, Parsons continually turns his polemic against theoretical individualism into a powerful critique of conservative, laissez-faire ideology. It will be recalled, however, that Durkheim's polemic produced some fundamental confusions. While Durkheim realized that symbolism could produce individualism, his presuppositional problem with the "individual" prevented him from consistently connecting collective symbolism to a moral emphasis on the freedom of the concrete individual. Durkheim feared that by emphasizing individual choice he would undermine his collectivist commitment. This problem also affected his analysis of pathological individualism, for he frequently described anomie and egoism as if the individual were entirely cut loose from any symbolic control.

Because Parsons handles the individual/society dilemma with a much surer hand, he can allow the norm of individual freedom to consistently inform his theory of social change. He can focus on the processes that produce such freedom without the danger of being forced into an individualistic analysis. Similarly, he can discuss pathological anomie and maintain his focus on collective force.

On the more empirical level, Parsons' change theory follows the dialectic of generalization and differentiation that Durkheim left hanging in his first book, *The Division of Labor in Society.* In this work, Durkheim conceived both factual and normative lines of development, although he could conceptualize no relationship between them. Even this dichotomized multidimensionality was abandoned in his later writing, although the cultural aspect of secular generalization is brilliantly defined. Parsons takes up this latter theme of value generalization and combines it with considerations of structural development in a manner that Durkheim never approached. He could do so because in this as in so many other parts of his work Parsons filled out Durkheim's theory with Weber's more multidimensional analysis.

"We should like to reformulate the process of rationalization," Parsons and Smelser wrote in *Economy and Society,* "as the tendency of social systems to develop progressively higher levels of structural differentiation."[102] This is precisely what Parsons accomplished. For Weber, rationalization was a process that affected every dimension of social life—every cultural pattern, from religion and art to morality and science, every social activity, from economics and politics to law, education, and the conception of self.[103] But Weber's conception of the end results of this rationalization process destroyed the multidimensionality of his historical analysis: rationalization became instrumentalized, and he described bureaucratic economic and political structures as dominating normative and personal concerns. With his differentiation theory, Parsons directly confronts this reductionist approach to rationalization. He does this first on the ideological level: his more optimistic form of Enlightenment liberalism makes him much less equivocal about the possibilities for realizing individual freedom in industrial and differentiated society. More importantly, he confronts Weber's rationalization theory with his more thorough commitment to presuppositional multidimensionality.

By formulating differentiation theory, Parsons argues that the characteristics Weber associates with modernity can be articulated more effectively through a multidimensional analysis than through the instrumentalized model that Weber describes. Parsons' differentiation theory can potentially reconcile the three antagonistic components of Weber's work: the comparative studies on religion, the historical-political sociology, and the sociology of contemporary industrial society.

Parsons makes this case for each of the spheres that Weber describes as instrumentally rationalized. The flexibility and autonomy of modern economic life need not imply, Parsons believes, the utter domination of noneconomic society by market imperatives; rather it may be seen as involving a process of differentiation, as allowing the economic subsystem a relative autonomy while it remains, nevertheless, firmly embedded in, indeed dependent upon, extra-economic exigencies.[104†] Similarly, just as interchange provides an alternative to Weber's theory of politics, so differentiation theory supplies an alternative explanation for bureaucratic and democratic authority. Far from indicating the triumph of the iron cage, the ascendance of bureaucracy may be viewed as reflecting the need to coordinate functions that have actually grown increasingly autonomous. As such, bureaucratization can contribute to an expansion of individual freedom rather than to its reduction.[105†] Similarly, the impersonality of authority need not imply deracination and lifeless control; it can be seen as indicating, rather, the differentiation of politics from arbitrary control, from its fusion with the nonpolitical pressures of religion and kinship.[106]

In the same manner, the formalism Weber described as characterizing modern law can be viewed as derived from the universalism of the modern societal community; it can be seen as indicating integrative differentiation, not the subordination of solidary sanctions to economic and political efficiency.[107] Again, Parsons' theory of functional elites not only systematically extends the implications of Weber's class-status-party division, but relates it, in a manner that Weber simply could not, to ongoing, multidimensional social processes. Similarly, Parsons' theory of the media which these elites control—the media of money, power, influence, and value commitments—supplies a mitigating framework for Weber's instrumentalization of modern status and power conflicts. While Parsons agrees that these sanctions are indeed "commodities," he emphasizes that they are not sui generis. He describes them, in a way that Weber does not, as closely related to more fundamental social processes in which solidarity and cultural patterns are as significant as adaptive and political constraints.

Differentiation theory reformulates Weber's notions of religious development in the same way. The movement Weber described toward transcendence and abstraction, Parsons argues, is actually a movement toward the differentiation of religious values from more social constraints.[108†] Secularization, therefore, does not imply the end of religious and cultural development; it represents rather the continuation of differentiation in the cultural sphere. Generalized codes continue to affect social regulation. They do so, however, while allowing and encouraging more functionally specific values to regulate differentiated institutions and social groupings.

Finally, Parsons' change theory puts into a much broader perspective what is perhaps the overarching theme of Weber's historical theory, namely, his assertion that social effectiveness and individual freedom are directly related to the separation of each institutional activity from the immediate influence of "sib" ties. For Parsons, differentiation is a master term that indicates movement away from functional fusion with kinship in every sphere—from clan-based ancestor worship in religion, from family-based guilds in economic life, from patriarchy and lineage-based kingship in politics, from clan justice and caste particularism in the integrative sphere.

Parsons was able to achieve this transformation of Weber's work in part because he incorporated Durkheim's much more penetrating understanding of the continuity of sacred values in secular society. Yet an equally important reason was his acceptance of Freud's much more sophisticated understanding of the basis of individual freedom. Parsons could thus understand, in a way Weber could not, that autonomy requires a sustained process of normative socialization, that it depends upon a web of internalizations which Weber's instrumentalized view of modern life could not sustain.[109†]

Yet by using psychoanalytic ideas to expand Weberian, and Durkheimian, theory in this way, differentiation theory also brings Parsons into direct conflict with Freud. He argues with Freud that the personality is not historically invariant, that it is tied to external developments and complexities which not only have internal ramifications but are affected by the changing personality in turn. In effect, Parsons puts into concrete empirical form the historical counter-theme that Freud only partly developed, that secularization and the growth of scientific rationality correlate with the historical development of ego functions. In differentiation theory, Parsons connects the Freud of *The Future of an Illusion,* with its stress on the emergence of historical adulthood, to the Freud of *Totem and Taboo* and *Moses and Monotheism,* with their less reductionistic insight into the relation of religion and personality despite their mistaken insistence on historical repetition.[110] Moreover, by translating Weber's institutional analysis into a theory of extended socialization, Parsons connects these meta-psychological treatments to the more empirical analyses of Freud's clinical essays on individual ego development.

By linking Freud and Durkheim with Weber, Parsons utilizes differentiation theory to argue that Weber's pessimistic, instrumental vision was mistaken.[111†] Freedom and inefficiency are not necessarily antithetical.

Chapter Six

THE METHODOLOGICAL ERROR(1)

Neopositivism and the Formalization of Parson's Theory

Throughout most of the preceding five chapters, I have insisted that Parsons is not the man his opponents have perceived, nor, in many cases, the figure his supporters have lauded. It would be strange, however, if either were completely in error, if they had created their distortions out of completely whole cloth. In fact, as in the interpretations of Marx, Durkheim, and Weber, the problems and confusions in interpretations of Parsons do not, finally, emerge from polemical misreadings and errors in theoretical logic alone. They respond to central equivocations in the theory itself. Up to this point, for reasons that will soon become evident, I have drawn a deliberately analytic portrait of Parsons' work. While it presents one current of Parsons' theorizing, alongside this current there run several others. Taken in its "concrete," empirical totality, Parsons' theory contains contradictory strands. Like Weber's, it is confusingly, and frustratingly, "multiple" in its identity.

In the 1945 essay in which he formulated the course of his future theorizing, Parsons set out two standards for his work. First, theory must be synthetic in its presuppositional orientation. Second, it should seek to articulate and synthesize the positive aspects of previous empirical and theoretical writing. Instead of trying to establish sociology from "first principles," Parsons' theory would bring unity to sociology by demonstrating the role of first principles at every level of sociological analysis.[1] To a striking degree, unparalleled in post-Weberian sociological theory, Parsons succeeded in these tasks. Still, the temptation to depart from such stringent and elevated standards is great. To maintain a synthetic aim is consistently to resist any presuppositional bias, to maintain an objective, multidimensional orientation rarely achieved in the history of sociological thought.[2†]

Similarly, the commitment to refrain from the effort to rebuild sociology from first principles must confront the overweening ambition that stimulated the uncovering of these principles in the first place. What great theorist has been able to abjure such temptation?

It should not be surprising, therefore, that Parsons failed to meet the standards which he set for himself, and that, indeed, he failed as often as he succeeded. Still, this failure is no less objectionable for being understandable. The chapters which follow will show that Parsons continually falls from synthesis back to a partial, "factor" kind of theorizing. Moreover, at least by the time of his middle-period work, Parsons' approach is often far from ecumenical: he continually strives to separate "action theory" from all previous approaches to sociology, and to develop, in fact, an entirely "new" sociology. In his factor theorizing, Parsons overlays his multidimensional analysis with a reductionist and highly damaging form of sociological idealism. In his attempt to generate "action theory" from first principles, he reifies his systematic theory by casting it into the language of formalism; through such formalism, he tries to generate theory at each level of the sociological continuum from the "logic" of his own, more general formulations.

Parsons had an ecumenical ambition. He professed the desire to end the war of sociological sects. Yet he failed in this ambition, failed so drastically that his very intention has been open to doubt. Was it only the inability of others to accept the true word that caused his failure—their ignorance, or their stubborn resistance? Surely, Parsons and some of his followers would have us believe so. But Parsons' failure to convince goes beyond simply the bad faith of others. For like many ostensibly ecumenical figures, he sought also to be a prophet. Though he would have liked to end theoretical conflict, he was, throughout, highly sectarian and combative in his own right. He would eliminate sects only to build in their place a new church. But to be both priest and prophet is an impossible task.

1. METHODOLOGICAL AMBIVALENCE: THE OBJECTIVIST BIAS IN PARSONS' ANTI-EMPIRICIST APPROACH

Parsons' problem begins with a profound methodological ambivalence. This may be described, somewhat ironically, as a confusion of the very distinction between the analytic and the concrete reference of social theory upon which so much of his theoretical accomplishment rests.

In chapter 2, I examined the important advances that Parsons made in the meta-methodological issues that inform social science, particularly in *The Structure of Social Action*. Building upon Whitehead, Parsons anticipated the position proposed by Kuhn and other postpositivists three decades later. This adumbration is particularly true for Parsons' emphasis on the sui generis character of theoretical problems and his insight into the crucial role of theoretical anomalies and residual categories in scientific growth.[3] Indeed, Parsons formulated these insights at about the same time that Koyré made his historical revision of scientific development and Polanyi, Toulmin, and Hanson began their radical philosophical investigations into the scientific method.[4†]

Yet though Parsons anticipated elements of the postpositivist position, it seems clear, at least in retrospect, that he was unable to arrive at a consistent perspective. While the general direction of his meta-methodological thinking is correct, tension remains between his theoretical attention and a continued commitment to empiricist analysis, a tension that was never entirely resolved. This incomplete resolution damages Parsons' subsequent work, revealing an ambivalence about the relation between theory and fact that affects his entire self-conception as a sociological "theorist."

This paradox appears first and most clearly in *The Structure of Social Action*. Parsons asserts that theoretical argument is independent of empirical discoveries, and that the insights he produces in *Structure* are of a thoroughly analytic sort.[5†] At the same time, however, he argues that these theoretical discoveries are also empirical and factual ones. Though "neither is the cause of the other," theory and facts "are in a state of close mutual interdependence."[6] In social as well as in natural science, Parsons asserts, "the imminent development of the logic of theoretical systems" must inherently occur "in relation to [the discovery] of empirical fact."[7] For all practical purposes, then, theory and fact are one and the same. If, in Kant's terms, theory reveals the synthetical a priori, Parsons claims here that theory is, simultaneously, the synthetical non–a priori.[8] He believes that his analytic discoveries are, in the end, concrete.

In so arguing, Parsons avoids the full implications of his anti-empiricist assertion that theoretical argument actually does occur independently of factual discovery, for the corollary of such an assertion is that highly successful theoretical frameworks can and often do fundamentally "distort" empirical perception. Certainly the empirical world consists of independent patterns, but at any given point in time these patterns need not be accurately reflected even in a sophisticated and highly explanatory scientific theory. Parsons argues, to the contrary, that, despite its analytical autonomy, successful theory accurately reflects the empirical patterns themselves.

This confusion is revealed in an incongruous way. Alongside his anti-empiricist argument, Parsons simultaneously adopts certain central propositions of the empiricist position. Indeed, given the incomplete nature of his methodological resolution, he is ineluctably led to such propositions.

Throughout *Structure*, Parsons maintains that the theoretical development he analyzes also represents the deepening of empirical insight. The historical movement from rationalism to normatively sensitive, multidimensional theory, he argues, is based not on some underlying shift in the intellectual climate of European thought but, rather, on empirical discoveries, on a "revolution in empirical interpretation."[9] For example, alongside his subtle and intricate discussion of the confusion in Durkheim's thought between individualistic and social explanations of order, Parsons tries to argue that these problems occurred because Durkheim's theoretical understanding of order lagged behind his empirical observation. Durkheim's initial critique of Utilitarianism, Parsons maintains, was based upon a "clearly perceived state of *fact*," that order was internal, collective, and voluntaristic. It was only because of "facts which he . . . found to be incompatible" with individualistic and rationalistic assumptions that Durkheim's anti-Utilitarian theory was produced.[10] As Parsons paraphrases Durkheim's early insight: "Hobbes . . . was *factually* wrong."[11] What created problems in the early part of Durkheim's career was his "fail[ure] to carry the codifications of the [Utilitarian] *conceptual* scheme . . . far enough to do justice to the *factual* insight already arrived at."[12] "Though his *empirical* observation quite definitely" was correct, he simply "did not clearly grasp the distinction in *theoretical* terms."[13]

In keeping with this positivist faith in the conjunction of theory and fact, Parsons' perspective on the development of social science is strictly an "accumulationist"one.[14†] A scientific theory succeeds because it has expanded the range of factual knowledge beyond the capacity of its predecessor. Theories are discarded because they are not based upon accurate empirical observation. The implication of this position for Parsons' argument in *Structure* is that individualistic and rationalist theories were discarded because they were "immature."

> It is but natural that in the early stages of development of a theoretical system its adherents should work with the simplest conceptual scheme which seems adequate. It is only with the accumulation of factual knowledge and the more refined and subtle working out of logical implications and difficulties that the more complex possibilities are brought into consideration. *At the stage of development closest to the common-sense level there is generally found an atomistic tendency in scientific theories.*[15]

But if nonatomistic theory is simply empirical, if it relies simply on factual advances and discoveries, why should Parsons bother to spend more than 700 pages arguing its analytic rather than empirical validity? He can, of course, justify this effort only by acknowledging the independence of theoretical argument. But he cannot fully accept this justification because in the end he refuses to abandon fully the positivist—or, in more technical terms, the logical empiricist—perspective.[16†]

The paradox of this "accumulationist" position places a new light on an argument that represents one of *Structure*'s major themes: that the agreement to be found in Marshall, Pareto, Durkheim, and Weber about voluntarism actually represented the historical "convergence" of European sociological theory. Parsons never demonstrates this argument by reference to the actual historical situation, nor could he have done so. Had sociological thought never embraced a normative or multidimensional position before the beginning of the twentieth century? Certainly French Romanticism and German Historicism had been explicitly anti-Utilitarian. And has there not been influential individualistic and rationalistic theory subsequent to the emergence of this turn-of-the-century convergence? Indeed, Parsons' contemporary theoretical adversaries have been theorists of the rationalistic and individualistic variety. Far from representing any new agreement on the nature of empirical reality, this convergence among Parsons' four European writers was, at least in part, purely a generational phenomenon, produced by the coalescence of distinctive cultural, political, and economic developments in certain sectors of West European society.[17†]

Why, then, did Parsons attempt such an unlikely argument? He did so in order to claim for his theoretical argument an empirical status. "Convergence," for Parsons, is equivalent to empirical verification.

> It goes without saying that this convergence, if it can be demonstrated, is a very strong argument for the view that *correct observation and interpretation of the facts* constitute at least one major element in the explanation of why this particular theoretical system [i.e., "action theory"] has developed at all.[18]

Of course, without Parsons' faith in the identification of fact and theory, this contention would be absurd. Given this faith, however, convergence becomes an extremely convenient demonstration of empirical validity. Parsons can claim empirical proof for what is essentially a purely theoretical argument. He can achieve verification without actually referring to any empirical facts.[19†]

It is not surprising, therefore, that in concluding *Structure* Parsons maintains that by successfully mounting his theoretical argument he has also verified it empirically.[20] Instead of accepting the work as an analytic argument about the theoretical logic of Durkheim and Weber, Parsons claims that he has conducted an empirical inquiry into their thought, an inquiry that is "as much a question of fact as any other."[21] He argues, incongruously, that the preceding analysis of Durkheim and Weber, which has resulted in "the critique of positivist theories," has "followed [in part] from their new empirical discoveries and insights."[22]

Parsons misunderstands the nature of his great book. A grand exercise in theoretical persuasion, it is a thoroughly normative argument about the nature of "good" theory, conducted according to certain exquisitely illuminated a priori commitments. Yet Parsons will have none of this. His argument must be accepted because of the "evidence" he has presented; it must be taken as "objective" in the positivist, not the postpositivist, sense.[23†] He would steer us away from the nature of his presuppositions while, all the time, actually taking them as the principal focus of his own theoretical attention. What we are ready to acknowledge as an intellectual and analytic tour de force, Parsons would have us applaud as chaste scientific experiment.

This profound ambiguity permeates Parsons' subsequent work. In his penetrating essay in *Theories of Society*, for example, Parsons comes closer than at any other point in his career to articulating an internally differentiated, two-directional conception of science. "The higher order premises" in scientific theory, he writes, "are the 'primitive' concepts *which are not subject to empirical validation* but are assumed to underlie the *meaning* of the problems."[24] He insists that this "frame of reference"—the principal subject of *Structure*—is not, in fact, strictly "scientific": "These premises lead into the logical and epistemological problem areas where science has its major direct connections with philosophy." In the strict sense, he argues, "[scientific] theory is a body of interrelated generalized propositions about empirical phenomena *within* a frame of reference."[25]

But in this very same year, 1961, Parsons replied to Max Black's empiricist critique of his work by arguing that his frame of reference was, in fact, thoroughly empirical. Referring to his presupposition about action—"that action . . . is fundamentally oriented to the problems of meaning in the symbolic-cultural sense"—Parsons posits "the *empirical* status of [this] assumption."[26] As for his position on the order problem—"that order in systems of action is grounded in normative controls"—Parsons describes this as "a very basic empirical generalization."[27] Finally, alleged scientific convergence is cited as proof of empirical validity, and Parsons discusses recent physical and biological "discoveries" about the cybernetic control of living systems and advances in brain physiology and linguistics.

But are the components of Parsons' frame of reference derived from objective empirical observation, or from philosophical argument about the problem of meaning as applied to sociological analysis? Do the empirical insights of science occur *within* a frame of reference, or do they actually *create* it? Parsons himself is undecided. This ambivalence reverberates through every level of his theoretical work.

2. FORMALISM AS THE RESOLUTION OF PARSONS' METHODOLOGICAL AMBIVALENCE

One immediately obvious repercussion of this confusion in Parsons' methodological self-consciousness is the legitimation it offers to his empiricist critics. In the altercation with Black to which I have just referred, for example, it was precisely the ambiguity in Parsons' early statements that provided grist for the philosopher's empiricist mill. With Parsons' blessing, Black could point to the generalized formulations of Parsonian theory and ask, "Do they arise from previous empirical research?"[28] Of course, they did not, and Parsons' strenuous objections that they did could serve only to undermine further critical understanding of the fundamentally nonempirical nature of his theoretical contribution. Certainly, in the preceding chapters we have seen ample evidence for the empirical *relevance* of this contribution. This relevance, in turn, shows the error of those positivist interpreters who would dismiss Parsonian theory simply because it cannot explain and predict in the manner of more specifically propositional work. Yet in his own often expressed belief that generalized theory should not only be empirically relevant but also, somehow, directly empirical, Parsons himself gave credence to such ill-formed criticism.

There is, however, an even more debilitating, if less direct consequence of Parsons' methodological confusion. Above and beyond the inconsistencies in his specifically methodological statements, there are far-reaching repercussions affecting his theoretical activity as a whole. The charge that Parsons' theory is simply "abstract conceptualization" clearly is false.[29] But that his work contains a disturbing amount of superfluous, purely formal abstraction cannot be denied.

While Parsons believes, in principle, that his work should be simultaneously empirical and theoretical, generalized and specific, we have seen in the preceding chapters that, in fact, he concentrates almost exclusively—and quite legitimately—on the more generalized elements of the scientific continuum. This dilemma pushes Parsons relentlessly toward the very "premature closure" for which he once so chastised Pareto.[30] In one dimension of his work—the strand I have reconstructed and interpreted in the preceding chapters—Parsons realizes clearly that his theoretical synthesis cannot directly subsume sociology's "special theories," those specific, middle-range generalizations and propositions which constitute the discipline's empirical subfields. These areas are, he realizes, simply too empirical and specific. It is in response to this realization that Parsons restricts his focus to the level of presupposition and model, and to the formulation of crucial definitions and general classifications. Yet there is another, cross-cutting dimension of Parsons' writing, in which he rejects such propositional *relevance* and tries, instead, to achieve truly propositional status.

But to achieve anything like a propositional form, Parsons must stretch his generalized theory far beyond its intended shape. To resolve his methodological dilemma, he must, in effect, reach both ends of the scientific continuum; he must do so, moreover, with a theory that is basically oriented to one end over the other. In the attempt to force his theory to perform this impossible task, Parsons' theoretical efforts become dangerously distorted. Alongside his more balanced and differentiated contribution, there emerges a decidedly one-directional form of analysis.

Though always empirically sensitive, Parsons does not, after all, ever engage in the most specific and directly empirical forms of sociological analysis. As a result, his work never achieves the range of concrete variation and the propositional complexity that analysis must embrace at more specific levels of the scientific continuum. Parsons can, therefore, achieve his goal of empirical specificity only by a kind of theoretical fiat: by moving unilaterally from theory to fact. He has no other choice. Without deriving his formulations at specific empirical levels from directly empirical calculations, Parsons must "deduce" them from his more general, less empirical work. This proclivity for theoretical deduction—or formalism—rests like a dense fog over the length and breadth of Parsons' work. It functions as camouflage, obscuring the theorizing that lies beneath it—the theorizing that represents the truly important aspects of Parsons' contribution.

Unfortunately, this tendency toward "deductivism" intensifies with Parsons' theoretical development. Alongside his increasing theoretical sophistication we can trace a growing insensitivity to the differential, basically generalized quality of his accomplishment. Increasingly, Parsons compares his conceptual apparatus, even his frame of reference, to the definitions, models, and equations of the physical sciences, particularly to those of classical mechanics. In his 1945 essay on the prospects of sociological theory, he is still somewhat equivocal. While expressing a desire to make sociological theory approximate the physical formulas which relate such things as energy, mass, and velocity, he acknowledges such precision and specificity to be an impossible task for social science theory.[31] By 1951, however, with the publication of *Towards a General Theory of Action* and *The Social System*, Parsons has become more ambitious. "Action theory" can now be viewed as a conceptual scheme that achieves for social phenomena the same specificity and inclusiveness which the concepts of classical mechanics—"space, time, particle, mass motion, location, velocity, acceleration"—have achieved for physical ones.[32] Both these conceptual schemes, Parsons now believes, have "sufficient complexity . . . to duplicate, in some sense, [actual] empirical systems."[33] The goal of both social and physical theorizing, Parsons insists, is to combine these specific concepts in a "systematic theory," and he defines systematicity in a manner strikingly different from the approach presented in my earlier analysis.[34†] Instead of referring to the systematic analysis of presuppositional implications at every level of the scientific continuum—the goal that, at least implicitly, informs one strand of his work—Parsons here defines theoretical systematicity simply as formal precision. Systematic social theory will resemble, as closely as its social subject permits, the mathematical equations of classical mechanics.[35] It will become systematic to the degree it becomes "a logically complete system of dynamic generalizations which includes *all* the elements of reciprocal interdependence between the variables of the system."[36]

Still, even in 1951, this remained a goal that Parsons did not believe his conceptualization had yet achieved. Action theory, he admitted, had reached the stage only of a "categorial system"; it had not yet become a "theoretical system" which could state the relations between the conceptualized elements in a precise manner. Sociology could not yet, in other words, produce the "laws" of a "social mechanics" which would place concepts into empirically related equations and from which concrete empirical patterns could be deduced with minimal additional specification.[37]

As Parsons viewed the situation in 1951, such further systematization was blocked because his concepts were not sufficiently empirically specific and precise.[38] In fact, however, precisely the opposite was the case. Parsons' middle-period work could not become formalized and deductive because it remained too close to the empirical world, too concrete (see ch. 4, sec 1.2, above). Though he had transcended his early, more direct reliance on the concepts of Durkheim, Weber, Marx, and Freud, his later middle-period theory was still insufficiently analytic. His key concepts were still enmeshed in empirical processes and structures. The kind of abstract elegance and simplicity necessary for a sociological equivalent to classical mechanics simply did not exist.

Ironically, all this changed with the breakthrough to interchange theory that initiated Parsons' later work. In fact, of course, this development was actually achieved by an "upward" movement on the scientific continuum. As Parsons' attention shifted further away from the empirical world, he more successfully reconceptualized his multidimensional synthesis on the level of model.[39†] Yet Parsons himself interpreted this development in the opposite manner, as a breakthrough to a more empirically precise and specific form of conceptualization. Interchange, he believed, presented the fundamental "laws" of social life;[40] it provided "testable propositions" that awaited only "measurement and mathematical tasks."[41] With interchange, sociology had progressed beyond mere categorial conceptualization to the precision of mechanical equations. "It seems clear," Parsons writes, "that we are working in and with a genuine *theoretical* system, crude and incomplete as . . . its development undoubtedly is."[42†]

What are the principal laws of this new theory? They are none other than the postulates outlining the four social dimensions and their interrelation: "four . . . propositions with reference to the direct interchanges . . . between the four primary functional subsystems."[43] As I have indicated above, this interchange idea actually emerged from Parsons' ability to reformulate presuppositional multidimensionality in terms of a functional model. But Parsons has now lost sight of his argument's basically nonempirical reference. The complex intermediate processes—involving levels of qualitatively different concepts and specifically empirical work—that would be necessary actually to relate interchange successfully to the propositional level are ignored. True, Parsons does not believe that interchange is itself empirical: he argues, rather, that like the equations of classical mechanics it is so empirically directed, specific, and precise that empirical processes can be directly derived from it. "It will certainly in time be possible through its use," he predicts, "to derive a whole series of hypotheses for the treatment of empirical problems."[44] Parsons now speaks of the "operational application" of interchange to "particular problems" and of the possibility, finally realizable, of "integrating [all] available data . . . in relatively strict theoretical terms."[45]

Interchange is presented by Parsons as providing the theoretical equations from which more completely empirical formula can be formally deduced. The stage of empirical "codification" has now arrived. Far from being limited to only the more generalized dimensions of the scientific continuum, therefore, interchange is, in Parsons' view, just as fully directed to the empirical side. In fact, interchange describes empirical processes at every level of social life:

> The theory covers the whole range of microscopic-macroscopic levels: for example [for personality systems] from the S-R-S system level to the total personality, [and for social systems] from the experimental small group to the total society. . . . This claim is fundamental to the whole status of the [interchange] scheme; disproof of it would be extremely damaging.[46]

By the mid-1950s, Parsons was convinced that sociological explanation should proceed exclusively within the interchange model, that through its logical manipulation (with the addition of some minimal empirical specification) all important empirical propositions could be derived.[47†] We have seen that the great synthetic power of interchange did indeed allow Parsons to make signal advances beyond his classical predecessors and his contemporaries as well. But by couching this breakthrough in the language of empiricism, Parsons mystified it. Paradoxically, it was with interchange—his potentially most important contribution to wider sociological discourse—that Parsons' theoretical development became increasingly inturned and self-referential, increasingly separated from developments in non-Parsonian sociology. The very success of his theoretical development had finally allowed the dangers of his methodological confusion, always latent, to become fully manifest. With interchange, Parsons turned decisively from ecumenism to theoretical imperialism, from synthesis and bridge building as a conscious theoretical strategy to the tactics of theoretical exclusivity. It is not accidental that interchange, despite its great promise, is the aspect of his theory least integrated with ongoing sociological practice.

The interchange model should have provided a matrix by which sociologists could become more self-conscious and sophisticated about the multidimensional elements in their more empirical work. Instead, Parsons tried to use it as the basis from which such analyses could be formally derived. From the outset, this effort was doomed. The parallel between interchange and classical mechanics rests upon a fundamental misperception. "Action theory" nowhere achieves anything like the precision and predictability of such physical laws. Simply to approach this goal would involve exactly the kind of specifically empirical studies and independent intermediate conceptualization that Parsons consistently eschewed.

This formulation points to the difference between Parsons' formalist approach and his efforts at "empirical specification" which I have analyzed throughout the chapters preceding. "Specification" implies a two-way process. In making this effort, Parsons sought to relate his generalized interchange model, or, for that matter, his presuppositional notions of internalization and voluntarism, to empirical data whose independence he explicitly acknowledged. He established this relatedness by developing intermediate levels of conceptualization. One example is the middle-level arguments of his socialization theory, which, while clearly informed by presuppositions about the tension between ideal and material elements and about symbolic internalization, involved, at the same time, a number of independent empirical arguments.[48†] Another example is his later approach to change as differentiation. This theory involved a number of independent ideological assumptions and a distinctive empirical understanding about the course of historical events. Parsons combines these elements with the analytic sophistication provided by his model of institutional interchange. Finally, this balanced, two-directional kind of specification is certainly reflected in many of the arguments Parsons advanced for interchange theory itself. In establishing his analysis of political interchange, for example, he utilized the general multidimensional model of the social system as a guide, but he combined this with a number of independently derived complex propositions about the structure of political action—for example, with propositions about the nature of interest group and political party behavior and about the structure of constitutionalism. In making arguments about solidary interchange, his approach is similar. While he "articulates" his argument about the movement from ascriptive to universalistic integration with his multidimensional model, in no sense is the former "deduced" from the latter.[49†]

In the formalistic strand of Parsons' later argument, this pattern is reversed. Interchange itself is viewed as an empirical formulation. Given this initial position, Parsons' subsequent effort is devoted to "deriving" lower-level arguments directly from the model and presuppositional levels themselves. Although some additional empirical specification is necessarily included, the impact of such nongeneralized, "external" reference is minimized. The fundamental theoretical movement is portrayed in a decidedly one-directional way.

In a certain sense, therefore, Merton's critique of Parsons was correct.

I argued earlier that Merton did not sufficiently recognize the need for generalized theory in social science.[50†] It is also true that he ignored the significant elements in Parsons' work that succeeded in differentiating the autonomy of different levels of sociological analysis. Still, Merton did correctly perceive the dangers in Parsons' formalism. Increasingly, Parsons did indeed try to deduce empirical propositions from general concepts without reference to intervening, middle-range formulations. While Merton tended to reduce the autonomy and certainly the significance of generalized analysis, Parsons evinced a strong tendency to do exactly the opposite, to undermine the autonomy and importance of middle-range conceptualization.[51]

As Parsons lost track of the generalized locus of his most important theoretical reasoning, his formalism became increasingly esoteric. "Parsonian" theorizing became riddled with curious analogies and inordinately elaborate classifications. In his desperate effort to reach both sides of the scientific continuum, Parsons established purely logical, often casuistic connections between different levels of analysis. Such efforts at theoretical rationalization camouflaged the truly significant elements in his theoretical development.[52†]

This neopositivist formalism does not occur in one part of Parsons' later writing rather than another. It represents, rather, a continual refrain. Analytically rather than "concretely" located, it is interwoven with Parsons' more differentiated specification in every piece of his later work, in every book, every essay, every discussion that utilizes interchange to engage in more specific empirical argumentation. Parsons is no more able to distinguish his two approaches to more specific argument than he can separate the empiricist from the postpositivist strands of his meta-methodology. That is, of course, precisely the point.

3. NEOPOSITIVISM AND PARSONIAN RHETORIC: ANALOGIC ISOMORPHISM AND INTERNAL MANIPULATION

Parsons contends that interchange embodies specific empirical properties at every level of societal analysis, from the most macrosocietal level to the most microscopic. But Parsons must establish these properties without himself engaging in independent, empirical research. He accomplishes this through certain distinctive forms of argumentation, rhetorical devices that are undoubtedly familiar to anyone who has ever confronted a "Parsonian" argument.

The most basic strategy represents a form of argument by analogy, in which Parsons establishes the "isomorphism" between interchange and other, more specific levels of scientific analysis. Isomorphism implies direct, one-to-one connections between elements in qualitatively different classifications, or species. Parsons' proclivity for "analogic isomorphism"—the term is Baldwin's[53]—could, of course, be considered simply a matter of rhetorical style, like Durkheim's "petitio principii" or the synecdoche of Freud and Marx.[54] But style usually reflects substance. This was certainly true of Durkheim, whose rhetoric clearly reflected his presuppositional problems with the individual/society dichotomy and his commitment to a one-dimensional form of theorizing. It is true for Parsons as well. By establishing interchange through analogy and isomorphism, Parsons points to more established empirical sciences and to already verified empirical propositions as "proof" of interchange's own empirical status. There is an element here of Parsons' earlier convergence argument. Other disciplines have carried out detailed empirical investigations. Other levels of human life have been extensively researched and intensively explained. If interchange is isomorphic with these disciplines and subfields, it must itself have an empirical status.

Three analogies played particularly important roles in Parsons' later work. The first, a physical-science reference, was invoked extensively in the first published papers on interchange, although rarely referred to again. Throughout *Working Papers in the Theory of Action*, published in 1953, Parsons advances the claim that interchange is isomorphic with the laws of thermodynamics. This is not just a metaphorical argument for interchange's empirical relevance but an assertion that the two theories actually have a similar substantive content. Constructing elaborate physical analogies, Parsons tries to couch his discussion of social interchange in the language of thermodynamics. Pattern maintenance becomes the "principle of inertia," adaptation and integration operate according to the "principle that action and reaction tend to be equal in force and opposite in direction," and dimensional interchange is described as triggered by the "principle of acceleration," which asserts that "changes of rate of process must be accounted for by . . . an 'input' of energy from a source outside the unit [or] an 'output' of some sort from the unit."[55†]

The second major analogy, which plays a similarly important role in the early formulations but occurs also in a number of subsequent analyses, refers to the macrosocial implications of small-group behavior. In the late 1940s, Robert F. Bales developed a scheme to classify the communications among members of work groups as primarily instrumental-adaptive or integrative-expressive. In presenting interchange for the first time, Parsons claimed that the model was built directly upon—in fact, that it simply reformulated—Bales' empirical research. More often, however, Parsons argued that the interchanges which he had independently "discovered" in macrosocial processes were directly isomorphic with the processes Bales had described in his small task-oriented groups.[56]

Only several years after the actual inception of interchange theory did Parsons introduce his final and undoubtedly most significant analogic "explanation." Interchange, he proclaimed, was isomorphic with the input-output flows established by macro-economic analysis. When Parsons had first introduced the interchange approach to social systems, in *Economy and Society*, he did not make such a conflationary claim, suggesting merely that economic theory should be viewed as "consistent with" the general theory of social systems. Soon afterward, however, he advanced the much more radical claim that interchange theory was actually a generalization from macro-economic insights. "Fortunately for sociology," he wrote in *Theories of Society*, "our sister discipline, economics, has developed and refined a theoretical model of this [social] process of factor-combination that is capable of generalization."[57] All the essentials of interchange—the problem of boundaries, reciprocity and disbalance, inputs and outputs—were now reformulated as formal analogies with this economic theorizing.[58†] The most striking such reformulation occurs in Parsons' media analysis. He often discusses his media theory as if it were based, indeed, on purely analogic reasoning, with no presuppositional or empirical reference whatsoever. "The primary model [for media theory]," as Parsons never tired of repeating, "was money," and in a typical introductory statement he describes media theory as simply an effort "to match these [monetary] traits with cases which though formally similar, had a different content."[59] The isomorphism between interchange and economics becomes increasingly esoteric; Parsons creates intricate diagrams and charts which, as "technical appendices" to essays and books, establish for each noneconomic medium its homologous "value code," the "form" in which the medium presents this value (including both a "product form" and "factor form"), and the "circular flow" for each medium, with the respective criteria for "solvency," "credit," "inflation," and "deflation."[60]

The argument here is not that Parsons makes no positive use of analogies. The problem, rather, is that he often makes analogies the prime reference point of his explicit theoretical reasoning. In doing so, he "empiricizes" his theoretical work, obscuring its generalized reference. This is most obvious in his use of thermodynamics. Interchange is not, in fact, about the "energy" of particles; it is an analytic formulation of the ideal/material synthesis as applied to the structure of total societies. "Pattern maintenance" has to do with values, not inertia; the latter implies an empirical resistance to change that has nothing to do with sociological epistemology. The integrative dimension, similarly, has no necessary connection to an "equal and opposite reaction." Referring to processes at a certain symbolic level, integrative developments may be neither equivalent nor opposite to those in other dimensions. More importantly, of course, these analogies are not relevant in principle. Physics refers to processes far removed from those of social systems.

But the contention that interchange reflects Bales' empirical analysis of small groups is equally wide of the mark. In the first place, Bales' studies were themselves far from being simply empirical; they were, in fact, highly influenced by Parsons' preceding theoretical work. Second, Bales' classification referred to communications, not necessarily to actions themselves. Finally, and most significantly, the claim of isomorphism takes attention away from Parsons' own fundamentally presuppositional intention. Interchange uses Parsons' multidimensional synthesis to model social action along the symbolic-conditional axis. Bales' categories apply, rather, to the dichotomy between opinion (instrumental-affective communication) and emotion (integrative-expressive). *Both* these modes of expression are symbolic, integrative activities; neither is directly adaptive in a material sense. It is easy to see that such a dichotomization would have been highly suggestive to Parsons, particularly in its use of a grid to conceptualize analytic properties in a spatial way.[61] But such an imagistic relationship hardly establishes an isomorphism between small groups and societies.

Similarly, no matter how useful economic analogies were to Parsons' later development, and there is no doubt they were extremely useful, it is sheer formalism for him to suggest that interchange amounts to no more than a generalization of economic analysis. Historical chronology itself makes this contention unlikely. After all, Parsons had worked with interchange for several years before he ever applied it to economic analysis.[62] More importantly, however, interchange is more than anything else a refutation of economic theory, not a generalization from it. It utilizes the formal input-output model, in a rather ironic manner, precisely to make variable what macro-economics takes as constant. This economic analogizing, moreover, is not only misleading but often technically inaccurate. For example, confidence in money as a medium—the economic concept which so often provides the technical reference for Parsons' media logic—is not the same as confidence in power. Monetary confidence means simply the acceptance of money as a legal tender; the economic system within which this money is acceptable may still be highly unproductive, inflationary or deflationary. Despite his attempt at formal isomorphism, Parsons conceives confidence in the political medium, to the contrary, as directly related to the effectiveness of system functioning; political trust or confidence in the power medium means not only that the medium itself is acceptable but that there is a reciprocity and balance between political demands and political outputs.[63]

Separated from its generalized reference, Parsons' insistence on these economic analogies leads him away from substance into casuistic, purely formal argumentation. For example, to "match" the economists' traditional factors of production—land, labor, capital, and organization—with the three noneconomic subsystems outlined by interchange theory, Parsons proffers the implausible explanation that "land" must be considered to be functionally equivalent, in societal analysis, to values.[64] Hence, since Parsons argues that values are latent rather than manifest, he can proceed to ignore land as a factor in economic interchange. Only if land is so eliminated can he maintain formal isomorphism: the four factors of production must be reduced to three. In this way the pattern-maintenance dimension of interchange can "logically" be identified with the factor of labor power.

Though analogic isomorphism represents Parsons' primary rhetorical device for establishing the formalistic precision and empirical status of his interchange analysis, there is a second rhetorical mode that cannot be overlooked. One might call this approach "internal manipulation." Parsons rearranges an earlier, more empirical piece of his work according to some retrospectively convenient but purely ad hoc criterion, and then argues, on purely logical grounds, for continuity between this earlier, now reconstructed, analysis and the interchange paradigm. He asserts, for example, that the fundamental logic of interchange was actually contained in his discussion of the pattern variables. The latter, it will be recalled, were significant elements in Parsons' middle-period theory and performed a number of important theoretical functions. First, as general cultural choices that pattern all normative order, they indicated the noninstrumental elements in even the most conditional action. On a more empirical level, the differential combination of these patterns indicated the cross-cultural, trans-historical variation in cultural matrices, particularly in the degree to which different cultures encourage activism and freedom of choice.[65†]

But as Parsons moved into his later analysis, these original functions of the schema were obliterated. He argued that the pattern variables had "really" been about the four dimensions of functional interchange. To demonstrate this convergence, he conducted a series of internal, purely logical manipulations. He argued, first, that the pattern-variable combinations of "achievement-specificity" and "ascription-diffuseness" actually referred to external conditional and internal normative order respectively.[66] He offered a similar interpretation for the other combinations. "Universalism," he contended, clearly applies to problems of adaptation and pattern maintenance, while "affectivity" and "particularism" relate to goal attainment and integration. Having thus established the "true" meaning of the pattern variables, Parsons could now describe interchange as a logical deduction from this earlier, more empirically specific analysis. The four dimensions of interchange, he asserted, were developed simply by cross-cutting the four basic pattern-variable combinations.[67†]

But such reasoning is purely ad hoc. To argue for this continuity, Parsons must pull his earlier analysis entirely out of its original context. The pattern variables, as they were conceived not only by Parsons but by several generations of students, refer primarily to normative analysis, not to organizational exigencies. Moreover, they refer to certain specific empirical tendencies, not to epistemological arrangements. Can the pattern-maintenance dimension of a system not be institutionalized around ascriptive rather than achievement-oriented norms? Can the integrative dimension of a society not produce particularistic as well as universalistic associations? Simply to ask these questions is to demonstrate the violence Parsons has done to his earlier formulations. Presuppositionally, the pattern-variable analysis functioned to indicate normative references; empirically, it pinpointed cultural variation.[68†] In neither case did the variables supply the kind of generalized, overarching epistemological framework that the interchange model was intended to create. In the effort to provide interchange with an empirical pedigree, Parsons has confused levels of analysis and formalized a theoretical transition which should have been explained in a more substantive way.[69†] Interchange is no more logically deducible from the pattern-variable schema than it is isomorphic with physics or small-group behavior.

There is abundant evidence that this neopositivist reliance on analogy and internal logic contributed enormously to the critical misunderstanding of Parsons' interchange schema. Accepting the identification of these strategies with interchange that Parsons himself established, commentators have elided criticisms of both into attacks on the interchange schema. As refutations of analogic and internal logic, these critiques are, in themselves, often penetrating and lucid. That they cannot, however, also function as legitimate evaluations of interchange is a failure not entirely of the critics' own making. It was Parsons who first set the decoys by which they were deceived.

The alleged isomorphism between interchange and thermodynamics, for example, has been a red flag inviting positivist misunderstanding. Thus, the operationalist Lundberg applauded interchange as indicating Parsons' return to the physical science model. On the other hand, Catton, another leading figure in the operational wing of the positivist persuasion, welcomed Parsons' positivist intention but rejected interchange on the grounds that Parsons based the model upon an inaccurate reading of Newtonian mechanics. In terms of his argument about physics, Catton is correct; if Parsons had indeed generated interchange by close physical analogy, this would constitute a sharp challenge. In fact, the argument is much more an attack on Parsons' methodological pretensions than on his actual theoretical argument.[70]

Similar problems affect Parsons' isomorphism with small-group behavior. Accepting this argument at face value, Wagner quite legitimately criticizes interchange for a fundamental "displacement of scope," arguing that Parsons has ignored the kind of emergent properties that develop in the transition from small groups to large-scale societies.[71] This would be a telling criticism of the model if Parsons had, in fact, generated interchange from Bales' empirical discoveries of small-group life. But Parsons' own neopositivist claims notwithstanding, this was far from the case.

The same kind of dynamic applies to those interpretations of interchange which have taken Parsons' analogy with economic theory at face value. Gamson, for example, reviews a number of Parsons' most important papers and concludes that "Parsons' contribution to political sociology rests largely on the extended use of a very rich analogy between the economy and the polity." While Bliss C. Cartwright and R. Stephen Warner also view the economic analogy as central, particularly to Parsons' media analysis, they argue that the isomorphisms are often false or misleading, that Parsons has misapplied technical economic terms like solvency, deflation, and circular flow. On these grounds they dismiss media analysis as misdirected.[72] But the terms of such debates are misplaced. Since economic analogies are not, in fact, the fundamental source of either interchange theory or media analysis, their evaluation cannot constitute grounds for either acceptance or rejection of Parsons' later work. This is true, moreover, despite Parsons' insistence on the primacy of such analogic reasoning.

But the serious interpretive difficulties created by Parsons' rhetorical choices are best illustrated by the confusion he has generated with his claim that interchange has been deduced, through internal manipulation, from the pattern-variable scheme. Dubin, for example, initiated what has become a long and tendentious series of arguments by suggesting that interchange is invalid because it leaves the subjective concerns of individual interactions behind and focuses, instead, on supra-individual system imperatives. In other words, interchange was not, as Parsons had claimed, actually derived from the original pattern-variable schema. Parsons' "Response to Dubin," not surprisingly, constitutes a prototypical example of his casuistic style, presenting a series of formalistic arguments to justify an internal deduction which was, in truth, never really made.[73] The pattern variables actually make generalized arguments by presenting a scheme for classifying the types of normative order that regulate individual action. The generalized aspect of interchange theory, to the contrary, approaches the material/ideal debate at the model level, concentrating on macro–societal analysis. By failing to emphasize the entirely different domains of these two conceptualizations, Parsons encouraged the entirely false criticism that, with interchange, his work had moved from a focus on interaction and meaning to a focus on objective, anti-individual "systems."[74†]

Ironically, Parsons' claim to have derived interchange from the pattern variables has also encouraged the completely opposite criticism, namely, the argument that interchange represents a purely normative model. This criticism would, of course, be eminently sensible if the model had actually been derived from a system of normative classifications like the pattern variables. Savage, for example, cites Parsons' derivation of interchange from the pattern-variable schema to argue for a fundamentally idealist tendency in Parsons' later work: "The effect is to deny the concept of system . . . as a theoretical instrument designating specific modes of organization, and to reduce it to a cultural pattern."[75] Wallace places interchange completely in the phenomenal realm, despite his recognition that the model could, potentially, present a synthesis that cross-cuts exclusively material and ideal approaches.[76] Similarly, while Menzies recognizes that Parsons is confused about the relation between the pattern variables and functional dimensions, he accepts, in large part, what he views as Parsons' principal contention—that "the functional dimensions are a classification of action in terms of the *meaning* of the action."[77] In fact, to formalize this close relationship between pattern variables and interchange, Menzies suggests renaming the functional dimensions to reflect more clearly their purely symbolic purpose.[78] This interpretive problem, however, is not confined to Parsons' critics. One of his students, Mayhew, argues that actors "adopt [the various] pattern variable choices according to . . . the specialized functional contribution of the subsystem."[79] It will be seen in the chapters following that there are, indeed, important grounds for making such a normative interpretation of interchange, for there are significant idealist strands throughout Parsons' work. Yet this normative emphasis in no sense is based upon Parsons' "derivation" of interchange from the pattern variables, a claim whose formalist inspiration misses completely the model's more generalized reference.

Chapter Seven

THE METHODOLOGICAL ERROR (2)

The Neopositivist Strategy and the Conflation of Presuppositional Logic with Specific Commitments

In chapter 6, it was seen that Parsons' proclivity for argument by analogic isomorphism and internal manipulation reflects a fundamental confusion about the levels at which his theoretical argument is directed. His formalism can, in fact, be viewed as theoretical conflation. By formalizing his argument, Parsons argues that he has deduced a more specific level of analysis from a more general one. In so doing, the relative autonomy of different levels of scientific analysis is eliminated: they are "conflated" with one another.[1†] Given his methodological dilemma, a conflationary strategy offers Parsons certain distinct advantages. By identifying lower, more specific levels of analysis directly with more generalized ones, he can argue that the latter are, in effect, empirical and specific. Conflation provides the methodological vehicle to legitimate Parsons' imperial ambitions. He can then argue that every other level of the sociological continuum can be derived from his more generalized formulations. To demonstrate how he pursues this strategy is the purpose of the present chapter.

1. FORMALIST CONFLATION AND THE MODEL LEVEL: INTERCHANGE AS FUNCTIONALISM

Although following sections will show that this conflation applies not only to models but to empirical propositions and ideological statements as well, Parsons' conflation of presuppositions with model commitments has undoubtedly been the most overt expression of his methodological strategy. There is an important strand of his work in which Parsons argues that his theory is derived from systems qua systems. Instead of presenting his systemic models as specifications of his more general presuppositional commitments, he presents his presuppositional insights as derived from systemic models. In this way, Parsons' systems analysis can be viewed as dependent upon the accuracy of his insight, most assuredly empirical, into the nature of systems per se.

When Parsons first introduced his "systems" approach, in his major theoretical essay of 1945, he was quite clear about the proper relation between models and presuppositions. While models were necessary to specify "frames of reference," the latter must be arrived at by an independent process of analysis. Any analysis of systems, then, must occur within prior frames of reference.[2†] By the 1950s, however, when his utilization of systemic models had become much more explicit and, indeed, more successful, Parsons' attention to this distinction had waned. In *The Social System*, where the banner of structural-functionalism was most stridently raised, Parsons is ambiguous. He begins the book with a chapter on his frame of reference, and in the chapter following argues that another functional approach, that of Aberle et al.'s "functional requisites," is overly objectivist. Yet even here, Parsons' argument is as much that Aberle et al. have erred because they have mistaken the true nature of systems as it is an argument that they have used a systemic model to specify overly instrumental presuppositions.[3]

Once Parsons has formulated interchange, his conflation of presuppositions and model becomes much more explicit. It was with interchange, we have seen, that Parsons' methodological confusion reached its highest point. But if interchange can be represented as an empirical discussion, as Parsons' neopositivist line would have us believe, it can just as well be viewed as discourse about the laws of systems. Interchange occurs, Parsons now argues, because of the nature of systems per se: "Process in any social system is subject to four independent functional imperatives or 'problems.' "[4]

By the 1960s, this conflationary approach to interchange had become fully formalized despite the fact that it occurred right alongside Parsons' more differentiated application of the model commitment. Each of the interchange model's key terms—the "dimensions" of interchange, the "boundaries" between systemic dimensions, the "inputs" and "outputs" between different dimensional structures—is now presented as if it were derived from some inherent logic of systems rather than from Parsons' effort to model his analytic synthesis of instrumental-normative order.

In my previous analysis of interchange, it was demonstrated that Parsons established the boundary relations of a social unit by referring to its position on the cybernetic continuum, a position derived from the fact that every unit is "bounded" by certain symbolic and conditional environments.[5†] Parsons now argues that this boundary differentiation is actually contingent on certain empirical characteristics of systems. System survival itself creates a boundary relation, in that "a pattern is maintained which is different from the environmental state of affairs."[6] Systems maintain input-output relations with this environment not because of the reciprocal interaction of normative and conditional forces, but because, quite simply, that is what ongoing systems do.[7] As for the internal differentiation of systems, this again is a matter of purely "systemic" needs. If a system survives, there will be "related differentiation in internal structures and processes of a system," and these will, inherently, "match" the system's external relations to its environment, its boundaries and input-output relations.[8]

This exclusively model level of analysis is held to explain the general structure of interchange. Parsons applies the same kind of reasoning to his analysis of each subsystem. As for the vertical, top-bottom division of adaptation and goal attainment from pattern maintenance and integration, Parsons argues that this reflects the natural division of any system into functions which specialize, respectively, in external (extrasystemic) and internal (intrasystemic) exigencies. No mention is made here of the distinction between more instrumental and more normative responsibilities. For the horizontal, left-right division between adaptation and pattern maintenance, on one side, and goal attainment and integration on the other, Parsons introduces the distinction between a system's "instrumental" and "consummatory" activities. Systems, he argues, perform different functions at different times. Because "systems . . . must meet conditions and utilize environmentally available resources . . . through processes that are inherently time extended," the labeling of systemic functions should reflect this temporal fact. The left-right division, then, does not indicate different degrees of instrumental and normative position. Rather, "these categories designate *stages* in a sequence of temporal succession."[9] While adaptation and pattern maintenance "build up resources for future utilization," goal attainment and integration "actually put them to use, thereby destroying them through consumption."[10] Interchange, therefore, is produced by the "cross-classification of the two axes" representing basic system problems.[11]

With this exposition of interchange, Parsons has completed his conflation of system model and presuppositions. Yet he has succeeded only in a formal sense. Interchange is not, in fact, derived from such quasi-empirical insight. While the "external-internal" division of vertical functions seems plausible, this is only because the same terms—"internal" and "external"—also are utilized in the presuppositional distinction between instrumental and normative action. But this presuppositional reference completely contradicts the application of "external" and "internal" to the nature of "system" tasks per se. Pattern-maintenance values, for example, may develop as much to protect a society from extrasystemic threat, in either a symbolic or material sense, as to order intrasystemic relations. Similarly, the adaptive dimensions may be oriented as much to maintain certain intrasystemic facilities and arrangements as to combating outside threats. The point is that the nature of these interchange dimensions is not actually derived from such references to systemic activity as such. The value dimension is distinguished from the economic for fundamentally presuppositional reasons, and in these terms both are equally concerned with the "external" environments of any given system, those of "conditions" and "ultimate reality" respectively.[12†] Whether activities within these dimensions actually are directed toward threats that are internal or external to the concrete societies of which they are a part is, of course, an entirely empirical question.

The confusion is even more clearly pronounced in Parsons' attempt to link the left-right, horizontal division of interchange to systemic specialization of means versus ends. In terms of the major thrust of Parsons' work, of course, means and ends are presuppositional questions, not problems rooted in the nature of systems. But even if we accept, for the moment, the possibility of purely systemic derivation, Parsons' own classification of systemic means and ends is an arbitrary one. Pattern-maintenance values can, contrary to Parsons' assertion, certainly be viewed as supplying the ends of a system, for which goal-attainment political processes present the means. Parsons can justify a contrary classification, in fact, only by bringing in the issue of temporal sequence, arguing, for example, that pattern-maintenance activity is concerned with means because it occurs prior to political action. But whether adaptive or value-oriented activity occurs first is surely an empirical question, not a presuppositional or even model problem. Political conditions often necessarily precede value developments, as Parsons himself demonstrated in his argument that political democracy is necessary for the development of the value of "institutionalized individualism."[13†]

In stretching for this temporal reference, Parsons has anthropomorphized social systems and confused individual with social activity. Implicitly returning to the unit act analysis of *The Structure of Social Action*, he has described systems as if they were an "action" in which individuals must prepare "means" before they strive to realize their ends.[14†] Yet even in *Structure* the unit act was simply a convenient analytic abstraction for illustrating certain presuppositional points. Parsons never intended the concrete unit act to serve as a model of systemic, emergent properties. The confusion in his later work would be inexplicable if Parsons had not lost sight of the more generalized, presuppositional reference which scientific models must inevitably specify, albeit in a two-directional manner.

Parsons, then, often presents himself purely as a "functionalist," encouraging the very interpretation that has undermined critical understanding of his most important contributions. Parsons himself has reified his model commitment, setting it adrift from his more generalized assumptions. In doing so, he has forgotten his earlier injunction against Weber—that Weber dismissed functionalism as organicist or objectivist without realizing that functional explanations differ widely according to their informing presuppositions.[15†] By claiming to derive interchange from systems per se, Parsons himself has committed this same error. In making his argument that systems themselves reveal the structure of interchange, he ignores the fact that systems vary according to what presupposes any particular functional analysis. Parsons would take our attention away from "philosophical" issues to more purely empirical ones. But his "functionalism" is a conflationary argument, launched to resolve the tensions of his methodological dilemma.

2. FORMALISM AND PROPOSITIONAL CONFLATION: INTERCHANGE AS EMPIRICAL REALITY

In arguing that the presuppositional elements of his interchange analysis are actually derived from the nature of systems, Parsons has, in effect, gutted his central theoretical model: he has lost touch with the model's most important theoretical origins. The logic behind this conflation guarantees, moreover, that the model reduction will be only the first of several conflationary steps. Parsons has sterilized the model, after all, to purge it of philosophical, nonempirical properties. Cut off from its presuppositional moorings, interchange often assumes a kind of free-floating existence. Parsons uses interchange to conflate his general theory not simply with formulations at the model level but directly with empirical propositions themselves. Interchange, he argues, reflects, indeed is derived from, the detailed arrangements of empirical social life.

Before his "discovery" of interchange, such conflation between generalized and specific reasoning was impossible; Parsons' generalized concepts simply were not powerful enough to assume such an imperial task. His middle-period work, as a result, formulated a number of complex concepts over a wide range of intermediate levels of the sociological continuum. This is evident, for example, in his pattern-variable analyses of role differentiation and in his discussions of the institutional processes of allocation and integration. Because he was forced to utilize his general concepts simply as orienting and sensitizing cognitive maps, Parsons' work in this period often reflected the rich variation of the empirical world, as his penetrating analysis of medical practice in *The Social System* amply indicates.[16]

After the triumphant achievement of interchange, however, Parsons had a much more powerful generalized tool, and his approach to the empirical, propositional level changed accordingly. Interchange would allow him to "deduce," formally, every segment of institutional life. In the process of pursuing these deductions, Parsons becomes increasingly insensitive to the intervening levels which necessarily mediate between generalized and specific analysis. He engages here in a double reduction, from presupposition to model, and from model to proposition. Not only does he reduce presuppositional to systems language, but he views this systemic model as identical with certain specific propositions. Just as Parsons' presuppositional logic is presented as the reflection of systemic interchange, interchange now becomes the empirical operationalization of Parsons' presuppositions.[17†]

2.1. FREE-FLOATING EMPIRICAL FORMALISM

From the beginning of his later writings, Parsons often applies interchange to situations that have nothing to do with its presuppositional intent. He discovers empirical interchanges among variables which are unrelated to his normative-material synthesis; accordingly, he derives from interchange arguments that have, in fact, no theoretical justification.

The grand example of this debilitating strategy is the edifice Parsons constructs to formulate interchange at the level of "general action." In the middle-period work, his effort to specify multidimensionality produced the important distinction between psychological, social, and cultural systems as different analytic levels of any concrete analysis. With this division, Parsons could reformulate in a more empirical way the elements he had earlier identified as components of the unit act: personality provides intentionality and effort, culture supplies the normative element, and the social system organizes these according to the conditional constraints produced by the aggregation of individual action. It was from precisely this line of thinking, in fact, that Parsons later developed his notion of social-system interchange as being bordered on either side by culture and personality.[18†]

But with the analytic developments of his later work, Parsons felt compelled to reorganize this personality–social-system–culture relationship as itself an interchange relationship. If interchange did indeed reflect empirical behavior at every level, and if the interchange model could, in fact, provide the equations from which all social knowledge could eventually be deduced, then general action itself must be interchange process. Henceforth, Parsons presented his middle-period insight in the manner shown in figure 10.[19] In one sense, there is a certain plausibility to this diagram. Culture, society, personality, and organism are, after a fashion, differentially connected to action's organic and symbolic environments, although the relative positions, for example, of personality and society, are certainly open to doubt. But even this plausibility derives from the kind of cybernetic insight that is expressed perfectly well in Parsons' middle-period work: there is no need to formalize it in interchange terms. It is precisely in terms of this interchange framework, in fact, that this rearrangement of the original tripartite division cannot be legitimated. In what sense does personality supply the "goals" to which cultural and social systems are subordinated? Does personality "organize," or administrate, the operation of organism, culture, and society? Is it possible to conceive personality,

Figure 10

GENERAL ACTION AS INTERCHANGE

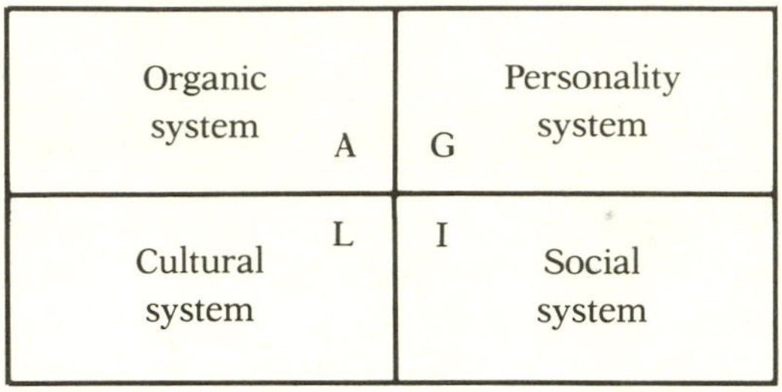

Organic system A	G Personality system
L Cultural system	I Social system

society, and culture as "producing" the human organism? Does the organism, in exchange for cultural products, supply facilities upon which symbolic patterns depend? Does the social system somehow supply normative regulations for the personality in exchange for the opportunity to realize its own goals? Simply to ask these questions suggests the kind of misleading reification that such an interchange model implies. There are indeed some interesting metaphors that develop from such theoretical play, but the argument as Parsons presents it is a purely formal one. It reflects neither the presuppositional reference of the interchange model nor the original empirical sense of the tripartite distinction.[20†]

2.1.1. Conflation in the Culture and Personality Theories

Given such architectonic formalism, it is not surprising that Parsons similarly reorganizes his empirical discussions of culture and personality. In the middle-period work, he distinguished between cognitive, expressive, and moral symbols in order to specify further the multidimensional interaction of symbols, scarcity, and psychological exigencies. As a scientific element, cognitive symbols represented the cultural reference that helped organize instrumental action. As an emotional element, expressive symbols provided the cultural reference for the cathectic element of action that represents both normative internalization and voluntary effort. As the normative element, moral symbolism represents the cultural contribution to normative action.[21†]

In the course of his later analysis, Parsons lost sight of his original, substantive reasons for this cultural division: these dimensions of culture were now deduced formally from the logic of the interchange diagram. Instead of viewing them as crucial contributions to a multidimensional conception, Parsons argues that the cultural patterns themselves constitute a multilevel interchange (see fig. 11).[22] Again, this argument gains nothing but formal precision. The patterns do not, in the first place, represent any hierarchy of material-ideal directions. Expressive patterns qua

Figure 11

CULTURE AS INTERCHANGE

Cognitive A	Expressive G
Constitutive (religious) L	I Moral

patterns are not more instrumental or efficient than moral ones, nor are cognitive patterns more material than expressive. More significantly, since they are not different epistemological dimensions of a single concrete entity, no interchange takes place among them: expressive patterns are not the product of moral and cognitive inputs, nor do they create organized goals to which these other symbols are directed. The length to which this search for formalism can go is indicated by the fact that Parsons now claims religion as a fourth cultural dimension, one which encompasses, or "constitutes" the other three. Yet religion is an empirical phenomenon, not an analytic one; while it may encompass each of the three dimensions, it certainly does not constitute an independent cultural focus in itself. It is not possible to escape the suspicion that Parsons adds constitutive symbolism to the cultural system because if he had not done so, the fourth box of interchange—latency—would have been blank. With such an empty cell, the veneer of formal deduction would have been destroyed. I would not deny that in the course of constructing and applying this model of cultural interchange, Parsons makes a number of illuminating points—for example, that historical development involves gradual cultural differentiation among the patterns of science, art, morality, and religion. Yet none of these insights is tied to, or even facilitated by, the manner in which he has encapsulated his cultural analysis within the camouflage of interchange.[23†]

This formalism detracts from most of Parsons' later analyses of culture. In his analysis of science in *The American University,* for example, Parsons relies heavily on the important distinction between frames of reference, theories, problem solutions, and facts. He discusses empirical disciplines in terms of their connection to these different levels of cognitive generality, and he analyzes the growing diversity of scientific disciplines as reflecting the growing differentiation among these levels. Yet because of his commitment to the empirical status of interchange, Parsons feels compelled to formalize this discussion by analyzing the four components as "subsystems"—adaptation, goal attainment, latency, integration, respec-

Figure 12

SCIENTIFIC KNOWLEDGE AS EXCHANGE

Facts A	G Problem solutions
L Frame of reference	I Theory

tively—of the "system of knowledge" (see fig. 12).[24] But where is the interchange between these "system" parts? Do facts and frames of reference exchange important material and ideal media? Are problem solutions the means of organizing and controlling theories, facts, and frames of reference? Do facts supply theories with some more instrumental adaptation vis-à-vis the material world? Again, on a purely metaphorical level, some interesting possibilities do arise from this imaginative leap. Yet intellectual inspiration could probably also be developed by relating the division of knowledge to atomic fission or to an internal-combustion engine, or, perhaps, to the metaphysical relationship between the seven circles of Dante's hell. Analogies do not represent actual theoretical relationships. The fundamental references of interchange have no direct relation to the components of knowledge. Both interchange and the elements of knowledge, however, are connected to Parson's presuppositional commitment to multidimensionality; they represent models and concepts which sensitize him to the levels of generality and specificity in any situation.

A similar formalism occurs when Parsons utilizes interchange to encapsulate the personality, though the problem is less significant because his writings on personality are a less consequential element of his work. In his later writings, Parsons presents the "structural theory" of psychoanalysis as a special case of interchange functioning (see fig. 13).[25] But this effort to match the logic of interchange with empirical propositions about personality process is bound to fail. In the first place, ego, id, and superego do not, in the strict sense, represent different levels of cybernetic generality. If anything, the ego would be more "specific" and "externally-directed" then either id or superego. Moreover, the functional relationship that Freud postulates between these structures simply does not correlate with the (presuppositionally informed) "functions" of interchange. While the id

Figure 13

PERSONALITY AS EXCHANGE

Id A	Ego G
L Identity	I Superego

may be close to organic life, it certainly does not play an adaptive role for the personality vis-à-vis the pressures of the material environment, either external or internal. In fact, it is the passivity and spontaneity of the id which creates, in Freud's terms, the necessary formation of the more adaptive ego and superego. And while it may be plausible to view the ego as not only adaptive but also as organizing and goal directed, it is also the ego, not the superego, which performs the personality's integrative function. Finally, there is, quite clearly, no multidimensional "production" of these personality structures in the way that Parsons' interchange model would imply. There is, for example, no way that the ego and superego can be viewed as producing the id.

Parsons has attempted these implausible formulations for formalistic reasons alone: unless interchange can be conflated with the psychological level, its universal empirical claims are open to doubt. But Parsons has eliminated the autonomy of psychological propositions, and in doing so he has done violence to both sides of the conflation, to the interchange model and to actual psychological reality. Nothing illustrates the purely logical character of this exercise better than Parsons' inclusion of "identity" in the personality matrix. In any empirical sense, of course, identity represents a phase of ego development, or, put another way, an element of the ego itself; it is not, in other words, an independent, functional dimension of personality. Though Parsons tries to justify this placement in empirical terms, it seems painfully clear that he has defined pattern maintenance as identity simply to "fill in" the empty fourth dimension. Unfortunately, from Parsons' perspective, Freud's observations produced only three basic functional dimensions, not four. Once again, the details of Parsons' actual discussion of personality and interchange produce a number of interesting, even important, insights; but they are produced despite the formal application of his model, not because of it.[26†] The interchange analogy may be a fruitful one, but it is mistakenly reified as the actual model of empirical patterns.

After evaluating Parsons' forays into culture and personality, I am in a position to reaffirm what was an implicit point throughout my earlier discussion of interchange: it is only in the social system that empirical structures mesh with the presuppositional dimensions of the interchange model. On the social system, A-G-I-L can be applied to the long-standing subject matter of economics, politics, sociology, anthropology, and social psychology without damaging in any way the integrity of their empirical status. In applying interchange to societal analysis at the institutional level, Parsons can specify his model without engaging in conflationary formalism. Economics, politics, integration, and value patterns do, in fact, represent different points on the material-ideal continuum. They can, indeed, be viewed as products of the simultaneous interaction among their institutional environments. But this should not, after all, be very surprising. For looking back over the history of Parsons' theoretical development, it was the social-system level that he had in mind all along. It was the origins and functioning of capitalism, democracy, legal formalism, and value rationality that focused Parsons' lifelong struggle with Marx, Weber, and Durkheim. Personality was important mainly because its inclusion, through the concept of internalization, contributed to this theoretical debate. Culture provided a focal point for similar reasons. From the beginning, Parsons believed that the resolution of his conflicts with classical sociology lay in the resolution of certain generalized problems: interchange represents, quite clearly, simply the final phase of this theoretical quest. Oriented toward generalized, presuppositional problems, this reconstituted system model was designed to mesh with classical debates over the history and functioning of social institutions.

But even at the level of the social system, Parsons' use of interchange has often lapsed into formalism. Not content to apply his model simply to national societies and institutional interrelations, Parsons' conflationary logic compelled him to pursue interchange from the most microscopic social level to the most international. In his effort to deduce every level of empirical analysis from his general formula, interchange once again becomes the vehicle for his free-floating formalism.

2.1.2. Conflation and Social-System Analysis

In pursuing this variant of empirical conflation, Parsons views all social life as organized into systems qua systems; the characteristic of all interaction, in turn, must follow the four dimensions into which "functional" needs inherently divide. The most conspicuous example of such treatment is Parsons' analysis of organization.[27]

Applying the deductive language of formalism, he describes his organizational analysis as "bring[ing] to bear a *general classification* of the *functional* imperatives" on the study of institutional life.[28] This interchange model of organization has a certain plausibility. As goal-attainment process par excellence, the policy-making elements of organization do not violate the spirit of interchange's political dimension. And because policy makers must grapple continually with their legitimation vis-à-vis general societal values, the pattern-maintenance dimension of organization is easy to find. After this point, however, the relation between Parsons' "application" and the actual theoretical logic of interchange becomes increasingly attenuated. In defining an organization's adaptive dimension, for example, he must identify the resources upon which organizations depend, resources which must be provided vis-à-vis the external, conditional environment. It turns out, however, that in Parsons' discussion these facilities include technological and administrative "traditions" and socialized labor as much as financial resources and instrumental support. As for integration, Parsons focuses mainly on what he calls the organization's "foreign policy," the problems of assuring compatibility between the organization and its surrounding units.

In making these arguments, Parsons has forced empirical facts into categories with which they have no presuppositional relation. First, there is no material-ideal continuum among the organizational activities he has identified as interchange functions. Organizational adaptation, as he describes it, involves as strong a normative reference as do his accounts of organizational goal-attainment and integration. In fact, organizational adaptation is defined as including processes, like the acquisition of technical skills and socialized labor, which in macro-social terms refer, more legitimately, to pattern-maintenance functions. Given this lack of cybernetic continuity, it is not surprising that the "boundaries" between these organizational dimensions have little to do with the epistemological references of Parsons' more generalized interchange model; they refer, instead, simply to empirically differentiated activities. Finally, Parsons can describe no "interchange" among the dimensions he has identified. The organization's finances and labor force (A), value patterns (L), and interorganizational relations (I) do not "combine" to produce the specific policies and goals of the organization (G). Such processual interchange makes sense only in terms of consistent presuppositional logic and, in addition, the kind of empirical reference points supplied at the level of total societies.[29†]

Because Parsons' fundamental theoretical attention is not, in fact, really focused at the micro-institutional level, this kind of social system conflation does not occur frequently in his work. Whenever he does focus on such issues, however, he does so in a similarly formalistic way. In *Economy and Society*, for example, he and Smelser move from the level of national society to an analysis of the interworkings of the economy as a system.[30] As a formal parallel to value commitments, they identify "economic commitments" as the economy's pattern-maintenance system.

These include, however, not just cultural and motivational inputs but also physical resources, an element which in presuppositional terms is "adaptive," not value-oriented. Similarly, for integration, Parsons and Smelser refer not to organizational norms but to the organizing skills of the entrepreneur, an input which may result in normative structures but certainly remains a rather arbitrary subset. Once again this formalistic application has distorted both presuppositional logic and empirical reality in turn. Although there certainly is factor exchange within the economic system, it is conflationary to assume it will follow the same logic as the social system as a whole.

In *The System of Modern Societies*, Parsons formalizes interchange by applying it not to micro-social analysis but rather to the international order. Taking seventeenth-century Europe as a "system," he arranges various countries into different functional categories. The northwestern nations, particularly England, France, and Holland, represent goal attainment because they were the most innovative and flexible in terms of contributing to further structural differentiation. As the center of the Counter-Reformation, in contrast, Italy played a pattern-maintenance role, opposed to all antitraditional developments. Prussia, with its military focus on the eastern front, and Austria, with its relatively pluralistic imperial solidarity, performed adaptive and integrative functions, respectively.[31] This analysis takes Parsons' formalism to its logical extreme. Not only do the connections have no presuppositional reference—did Prussia supply more material facilities to the European system than England or France?—but they make relatively little sense in terms of the system model itself. While the Austrian empire may have been internally pluralized, Parsons never indicates that it played a significant integrating role in Europe as a whole. Precisely because Italy was committed to maintaining its own traditional values, it was certainly not the cultural reference for the Northwest, a role any "pattern maintenance" sector would, by definition, have to have performed. Parsons' motivation for such categorization can only be his commitment to theoretical deduction. If international politics becomes his focus of empirical analysis, it must, somehow, be viewed as logically derivative from his systemic model. In doing so, Parsons further stretches his model beyond its original shape.

Parsons' conflationary societal analyses, like his later writings on personality and culture, usually contain significant insights. By insisting on placing them within the rubric of interchange, however, Parsons casts them into a formal framework that camouflages their nongeneralized, intermediate status. At the same time, the interchange schema is deprived of its own more generalized reference. By approaching empirical phenomena in these purely systemic terms, Parsons' conceptualization becomes arbitrary. Without the guidelines provided by the presuppositional references to means, goals, norms, and values, an empirical datum can be "located" in almost any functional box, and it often is. By taking this interchange model out of its presuppositional context, Parsons makes one of his most important conceptual discoveries appear to be purely formal conceptual baggage.[32†]

2.1.3. *Interchange as Empirical Chronology*

Up to this point, I have presented Parsons' use of interchange primarily in terms of his efforts to redefine psychological, cultural, and social phenomena as functional parts of empirical systems. In his analogic argument for the "empirical" origins of interchange in small-group theory, Parsons is similarly reductionistic. He includes a reference to empirical chronology, drawing a parallel between the functional dimensions and the "phase movements" of social groups. Bales, in his empirical studies, had found that the interaction in small, task-oriented groups alternated between more adaptive-instrumental periods and more integrative-expressive ones. These sequences, moreover, occurred in a predictable, sequential order. In his effort to parallel empirical and presuppositional arguments, Parsons claimed that functional dimensions occurred in a similar sequential order; indeed, he asserted that he had "discovered" interchange in part by observing these phase movements on the macro-level of the social sytem.[33] This assertion seems absurd if the dimensions, or interchanges, are conceived in their properly presuppositional, nonempirical perspective. It makes perfect sense, however, in terms of the kind of empiricist framework that Parsons' conflationary strategy implies.

It is not completely unexpected, therefore, to find this phase-movement concept in Parsons' later "empirical" applications of his interchange model. From the perspective of Parsons' imperial ambitions, the payoff, indeed, is rather significant: when he finds a sequential development in the empirical world, he can argue that this temporality "reflects" the phase structure of interchange. From here, it is only one short step to the argument that these empirical phenomena are, in fact, deducible from his generalized analysis. Interchange once again becomes an exercise in theoretical formalism and, in the process, the truly generalized reference of the model is significantly obscured.

The principal examples of such conflation occur in Parsons' important discussion of personality development and socialization in *Family, Socialization, and Interaction Process*. In chapter 5 (sec. 1.2), I presented Parsons' approach to psychosexual crises as phases in symbolic generalization. Each phase begins as an instrumental, conditional crisis for the child, and each is resolved when new symbols are developed to create new, more complex object attachments. The essentials of this process, it will be recalled, were derived from Parsons' presuppositional resolution of the Durkheim-Freud dilemma and specified by the empirical content of

Freud's developmental theory.[34†] Parsons himself, however, has no patience with references to such generalized reasoning. His learning theory must appear to be directly dependent on empirical fact, and he accomplishes this feat by formally deducing the theory from his interchange model.

There is, Parsons argues, a "convergence" between socialization theory and Bales' small-group analysis.[35] The phases of each socialization crisis, he believes, correspond to the temporal phases of the interchange scheme. The child's initial cognitive discrimination of crisis corresponds to adaptation, his sense of relative deprivation to goal attainment, his generalization of cathexis to integration, and his final cognitive generalization to latency.[36] But Parsons achieves this conflation only at the cost of both empirical and theoretical distortion. These learning phases are not so rigidly ordered in Parsons' empirical descriptions of learning; they are much more temporally intermixed. More important, perhaps, these "functional" dimensions have nothing to do with the presuppositions of interchange. They have neither a differentiated cybernetic reference, nor can they in any sense be viewed as reciprocally interactive, as exchanging media with one another. In fact, they have little relationship even to Parsons' purely systemic thinking. Learning does not constitute a system in any legitimate sense. Does relative deprivation, for example, play an organizing role in the "system of socialization"? It is hard to escape the conviction that, finding a time-ordered empirical sequence, Parsons has applied interchange to it for purely formalistic reasons.

He reifies his approach to social control in much the same manner—once again, primarily in the monograph *Family, Socialization, and Interaction Process*. I discussed earlier how in his middle-period work Parsons utilized psychotherapy as a model for social control, developing a theory of control as involving support, permissiveness, denial of reciprocity, and the manipulation of rewards.[37†] I argued that this theory specified Parsons' more general concern with the tension between normative and conditional order. With his discovery of interchange, however, Parsons rewrites this social-control paradigm. It actually presents, he now realizes, a sequentially ordered pattern of "functional" sanctions: permissiveness corresponds to social-control efforts at pattern maintenance, support to integration, denial of reciprocity to goal-attainment efforts, and the manipulation of rewards to adaptation. In each developmental crisis of the life cycle, each of these sanctions is involved in precisely this order: permissiveness must precede support, which in turn must precede the denial of reciprocity, and so on.[38] This temporal sequence of control (L → I → G → A) reverses the sequence of learning described above (A → G → I → L), and this reversal is not happenstance. For according to Parsons' empiricist logic, "convergence" is persuasive evidence of theoretical accuracy. Within a purely formalist logic, moreover, it makes perfect sense that what ends a crisis should be the reverse of what created it. Once again, this reduction does violence to both sides of the conflation. Empirically, such a rigid separation of sanctions would be disastrous for social control, as Parsons' own essays on European Fascism demonstrated with great clarity.[39†] Theoretically, this identification of social control with the logic of interchange is merely a metaphorical aperçu. For example, why would "permissiveness" correspond to integration rather than to pattern maintenance? Why would the authoritative "manipulation of rewards" not be political rather than adaptive?

Finally, Parsons converts his vision of the life cycle itself into these same arid categories. In my earlier discussion, I emphasized the presuppositional references of Parsons' life-cycle theory, how he views development as an individual's movement from security, affect, and the external control of childhood to the abstraction, conditional pressure, and voluntarism of adulthood. The transition is specified, I argued, through Parsons' translation of Freud's object relations theory.[40†] Yet Parsons must formalize this process; it must be geared to his scheme of temporal succession. Psychosexual development now becomes a "system," which, inevitably, has four components: orality corresponds to pattern-maintenance phase, the later period of "love" attachment to integration, latency to goal attainment, and genital maturity to adaptation. Little empirical justification exists for such a presentation. To establish this isomorphism, Parsons must amalgamate anal and phallic stages into one "integration" phase, and he must telescope "maturity" into a single undifferentiated movement. The scheme also plays havoc with the generalized logic of interchange itself. The epistemological reference, for example, is nonexistent, at least in the rigid form Parsons presents: earlier developmental periods do not involve a stronger orientation to values than does later ego adaptation. And, of course, there is no conception here of reciprocal interaction among different levels of multidimensionality.[41†]

A curious student of the interchange model once applied it to traffic accidents; Parsons himself, in one of his last published statements, related it to the cosmic underpinnings of the "human condition."[42] A theoretical model subject to such frenetic claims for universal relevance is bound to be emptied of substantive content. In his impossible effort to encompass every level of the scientific continuum simultaneously, Parsons applied interchange beyond the generalized, social-system context for which it was intended. Because of his conflationary reliance on "systems" exclusive of presuppositions, the writings of the later period appeared ever more "functionalist," and this functionalism ever more formalist and "anti" rather than "non" empirical. It is not true, as E. P. Thompson once asserted, that interchange is applied to empirical analysis simply by "filling in the boxes."[43] It is true, however, that such work must too often be appreciated in spite of the "boxes," not because of them.

2.2. *MULTIDIMENSIONALITY AS EMPIRICAL EQUILIBRIUM*

Though I have referred frequently to the implications of Parsons' theory for the treatment of stability and conflict, I have not discussed Parsons' actual positions as such. These orientations to stability and change are located on empirical, not generalized levels of analysis. I have strongly maintained, however, that an a priori acceptance of stability is not necessarily connected to Parsons' presuppositions, his functional model, his ideological commitments, or his empirical understanding of the process of social change. Parsons' actual position on stability and change is, in fact, ambiguous. Though he writes frequently about empirical strain and instability, his primary concern has been to delineate the structure of stable interaction and processes of restabilization. Thus, Parsons has never applied his later, theoretical schema to revolutionary conflict, though others have certainly done so.[44] And although his use of equilibrium as an analytical reference point implies no commitment to empirical stability,[45†] there is no doubt that he focuses, empirically, more on the control of disequilibrium than, for example, on the reform of exploitation. It could be argued, of course, that exploitation, too, produces disequilibrium, so that to control the latter implies reformation of the former; nevertheless, to focus on one over the other represents, as Gouldner has pointed out, a clear empirical choice.[46]

Still, the nature of this empirical choice is not my primary concern; I am concerned, rather, with the peculiar relationship Parsons establishes between this empirical question and the more generalized aspects of his work. There is a strong tendency, throughout Parsons' work, to conflate empirical questions about conflict and order with more generalized commitments. Parsons often claims, in fact, that his empirical tilt toward equilibrium is derived from the validity of his general presupposition and models. In other words, Parsons argues for equilibrium by a conflationary strategy.

2.2.1. Functional Interchange as Stability

As I have demonstrated at some length above, empirical "order" qua stability has nothing to do with presuppositional or model commitments.[47†] Certainly, systemic models represent the acceptance of order, but only when order is taken as collective organization in the presuppositional sense, as nonrandom social arrangements. Yet while Parsons often clearly recognizes this distinction, he just as often does not. His conceptualization is permeated by what might be described as a two-step conflation. He argues, first, for the identification of "order" at the presuppositional and model levels; subsequently, he identifies the "order" of systemic organization (the model level) with actual empirical equilibrium. Taking the first step of this reduction, Parsons often maintains that there is a necessary connection between the critique of "discrete" individualism—he equates such discreteness with randomness and an individualistic approach to the presuppositional question of order—and the articulation of this collective order in terms of a functional model. "The most general and fundamental property of a *system*" he writes, "is the *interdependence of parts* or variables." And he equates this property with "*order* in the relationships among the components which enter into a system."[48†] Just as frequently, he will then go on to identify this systemic order with equilibrium at the empirical level: "This order must have a tendency to self-maintenance, which is very generally expressed in the concept of equilibrium."[49]

Like Parsons' other conflationary arguments, this tendency to proceed automatically from one type of "order" to the next becomes more pronounced after the formulation of interchange theory. Defending the "empirical" status of his generalized argument, Parsons writes in 1961 that "if there are no uniformities involved in the interdependence of components, there is no scientific theory."[50] In this passage, he clearly refers to nonrandom order in the presuppositional sense: if action were completely individualistic, no prediction or structure would be possible. But Parsons goes on to conflate this argument with an empirical commitment to stability over change. It is not randomness that threatens the predictability of science, but empirical instability: "If no distinction can be made between conditions which favor stability and those which tend to a change in state away from the 'stable state' . . . there can be no such thing as a systematic empirical analysis."[51†] Empirical equilibrium implies systemic models, which in turn are based on the presuppositional critique of individualized, noninterdependent units: "The concept of equilibrium is a simple corollary of that of system, of the interdependence of components as interrelated with each other."[52]

But this conflation is not confined to an abstract discussion of "systems"; it reaches into the very heart of Parsons' analysis of the interchange model itself. The very differentiation of the dimensions of interchange, Parsons believes, depends on the empirical achievement of equilibrium. "Process in any social system," he and Smelser write in *Economy and Society,* "is subject to four independent functional imperatives or 'problems' *which must be met adequately if equilibrium and/or continuing existence of the system is to be maintained.*"[53] The internal differentiation of social systems, Parsons would have us believe, develops not because of any particular presuppositional assumptions but rather because of the system's search for empirical equilibrium.

Each of the four dimensions of social systems—which, I have argued, fundamentally derive from Parsons' solution of certain presuppositional dilemmas—is formally presented, at one time or another, as a solution to the problem of empirical stability. This is clearest, perhaps, in Parsons' earlier presentations. In *Economy and Society,* he and Smelser tie the pattern-maintenance dimension to the need for value stabilization, rather than simply to values as an "epistemological" referent of social life.

> A social system is always characterized by an institutionalized value system. The social system's first functional imperative is to maintain the integrity of that value system and its institutionalization. *This process of maintenance means stabilization against pressures to change the value system.*[54]

It was, undoubtedly, Parsons' commitment to the equilibriating aspect of values that induced him, in *Working Papers in the Theory of Action,* to label this dimension "latency."[55†]

The goal-attainment dimension is subject to the same debilitating reduction:

> A goal state . . . for a social system is a relation between the system of reference and one or more situational objects which (given the value system and its institutionalization) *maximizes the stability of the system.* Other things equal, such a state, once present, tends to be maintained, and if absent, tends to be "sought" by the action . . . of the system.[56]

In presuppositional terms, of course, this is thoroughly misleading; the basic properties of the "political" function—its intermediate position vis-à-vis symbols and conditions, its organizing capacity—have no intrinsic relation to stability.

Parsons even justifies adaptation, ostensibly the most disruptive of functional problems, in terms of his argument for empirical equilibrium. "Stability," he writes in *Working Papers,* "depends not only on the stability of the . . . 'commitment' to the goal, but also on the stability of the situational factors themselves in relation to the system."[57]

> Since this relationship cannot be presumed to "stay put" without processes of control and/or adaptation on the part of one or more of the member units, a major *task* [i.e., functional exigency] is imposed. . . . There must be diversion of some energy . . . into "instrumental" activity.[58]

The conflation of integration and empirical stability is, of course, much easier to accomplish. As Parsons and Smelser write in *Economy and Society:* "Integration is the problem of inter-unit relationships . . . by which the boundary relationships between the economy and other subsystems are adjusted."[59] The integrative dimension develops in response to the possibility that inter-unit relations will be "mutually obstructive and conflictual"; it occurs, therefore, "in the interest of [continued] effective functioning."[60] The presuppositional reference of integration, its intermediate, normative reference, is nowhere to be seen. Its definition, in other words, is accomplished in purely empirical terms.[61†]

Much like the conflation of interchange with systemic models discussed earlier in the present chapter (sec. 1), this confusion has greatly contributed to the controversy surrounding Parsons' work, particularly the later work. His sympathizers, for example, often accept this conflation, viewing "Parsonian" analysis not only as multidimensional but also as committed to empirical equilibrium. Devereux presents a series of ingenious empirical illustrations to demonstrate that the A-G-I-L schema can be derived from a system's efforts to maintain stability.[62] Similarly, Benton Johnson describes interchange as the "set of conditions that Parsons believes must be met if systems of action are to be stable and effective."[63] Harry M. Johnson, in turn, defines the very existence of pattern maintenance as dependent upon the continued "maintenance of units' commitments" to "dominant" values. He views "conflicting value systems in the same society" as a threat to the pattern-maintenance function rather than simply as a nonequilibriating specification of it, and he argues that the notion of a pattern-maintenance function remains relevant because even in disequilibrium situations antagonistic groups continue to strive for internal value stability.[64] For Parsons' critics, on the other hand, this conflation provides an opportunity to dismiss Parsons' interchange model on the grounds that it involves an inherently static bias. Its more generalized implications and empirical relevance need not, therefore, be considered. Thus, Chandler Morse writes in an early evaluation of the interchange model:

> One may . . . question the implied proposition that societies must "solve" the four functional problems in order to survive. As there is no criterion of "solution" other than the fact of survival itself, the proposition implies that mere survival may be taken as evidence that a society's value system and social structure are "functional."[65†]

On these grounds Morse rejects interchange as inappropriate. If Parsons himself rests the case for his generalized theory on the frequency of empirical equilibrium, his conflict critics must certainly be justified in doing likewise.

2.2.2. Symbolization as Stability

Another line of conflationary reasoning that Parsons periodically uses to assert empirical stability proceeds not from "model" but from presuppositional commitments. Here it is not interchange as such that guarantees equilibrium but rather the relationship the model establishes between empirical activity and the symbolic order. When seen in its properly presuppositional context, of course, the symbolic regulation of action has no necessary relation to any empirical condition. But in the conflationary strand of his argument, such a connection is precisely what Parsons intends to establish. If action is disciplined by symbolic inputs—by "pattern maintenance" or by "integration"—it will be in equilibrium. Parsons believes that in making a generalized argument he can also make an empirical one.

The most ramifying example of this reduction is Parsons' conflated approach to "institutionalization." There is a significant element in Parsons' work which defines institutionalization in a careful, fully generalized way: institutionalization indicates "intermediate," societally-oriented value commitments which are created through the interaction of broad cultural patterns with the scarcities of social-system life. The reference here, quite clearly, is to the same tension between normative and condition pressures that focuses Parsons' presuppositional concern. Within this generalized context, in fact, Parsons uses "institutionalization" to refer not simply to successful efforts at maintaining value consensus but to the coercive, often polarizing, efforts to reassert legitimacy in crisis situations.[66†] In the conflationary strands of his work, however, Parsons defines institutionalization not simply as a way of creating socially specific values but as a vehicle for establishing empirical equilibrium. "The main criterion of institutionalization," he now writes, "is that, ideally, the goal-interest of the unit coincides with the functional significance of its contribution from the point of view of the subsystem."[67] In other words, if institutionalization operates normally, it ensures that value commitments are completely complementary to the social system's functional demands.

The confusion in Parsons' discussion of voting illustrates how this kind of conflation can cross-cut his more differentiated argument. In my earlier discussion, I demonstrated that Parsons focuses on the normative regulation of voting—the "integrative inputs"—because he does not accept voting as a purely rational act.[68†] At the same time, decisions about voting are too situationally specific to be guided by generalized values. Hence voting's intermediate normative status. But in the same discussion of voting, Parsons implicitly negates this presuppositional reasoning by arguing that voting is normative because of the equilibrium needs of the political system. If stability is to occur, people must agree on basic principles, even while disagreeing on situational specifics. This agreement, he argues, is facilitated by the differentiation of the integrative "societal community" from the society's political apparatus. This conflationary strategy, in fact, is revealed by the very title Parsons has chosen for this essay: " 'Voting' and the Equilibrium of the American Political System."[69]

But Parsons has illegitimately identified empirical with presuppositional judgements. Whether or not the differentiated societal community contributes to empirical equilibrium depends on the specific historical situation. As Parsons himself demonstrated on numerous occasions, the societal community can be polarized and particularistic. The act of voting may be thoroughly regulated by norms, yet these norms may refer to opposing solidary groups. The problem here is that Parsons has eliminated the autonomy that must exist between empirical statements and presuppositional ones. Conflicting interests may be no less antagonistic for being rooted in norms and solidarities.[70]

In an argument that is closely intertwined with this problematic approach to institutionalization, Parsons often asserts a connection between social stability and the "generalization" of the interchange media. As was indicated in my earlier discussion, generalized media can, in fact, make a potentially great contribution to the equilibration of social conflict.[71†] "Generalization" itself derives, of course, from Parsons' specification of his presuppositional commitment to symbolization, and Parsons' point is that only if media are symbolically generalized can they create the trust that allows cooperation in a differentiated, relatively impersonal society. Generalized media, therefore, present the possibility for creating a cosmopolitan community without widespread polarization. But while generalization is necessary, it is not sufficient: none of these empirical consequences is guaranteed. Stability is still contingent on a series of more specific, empirical factors, on the relative transcendence of a nation's religion, on the historical relationship of its economy and polity, on its sectional divisions and ethnic homogeneity.[72†]

Throughout much of his later media theory, however, Parsons skips over these intermediate levels, moving directly from the fact of symbolic "generalization" to empirical stability itself. This jump is typified by Parsons' treatment of money, which is the initial analogy from which his media theory derived. The symbolic character of money, Parsons contends, indicates its institutionalization. "Under this general rubric of symbolic character," he writes, a monetary medium is to be "characterized by a state of institutionalization."[73] From institutionalization, in turn, Parsons argues for the media's positive, equilibriating functions: "The media . . . perform *regulatory* and *integrative* functions in that the [symbolic] rules governing their use define certain areas of *legitimacy* and the limits of such areas within which . . . systems of transaction can develop."[74] He makes this connection of money and legitimacy more specific by arguing that while "money can, of course, be used illegitimately through such channels as political bribery," this must be considered a "special case" rather than "constitutive" of the phenomenon of generalization.[75] But this argument is a highly conflationary one. The symbolic element of money can guarantee only its generalizability beyond particular, concrete commodities; how the medium is then employed—to finance social welfare and other equilibriating ameliorations or to bankroll political bribery, assassination, or revolution—is an empirical question. In either case, the medium is still "generalized," for it is acceptable as legal tender.

Parsons makes the same fallacious connection for each of his other media. Not content with "generalization" as the symbolic dimension of power, he must link political symbolization with empirical equilibrium. He argues, for example, that generalization of the power medium implies a "collective" reference, such that "power should be used . . . to act effectively with reference to the affairs of a collective system." This generalization implies, moreover, political legitimacy: "People who have power have legitimated rights to make and implement collectively binding decisions."[76] But both these claims camouflage particular empirical assumptions. Power can be generalized by individuals challenging legitimate systems: rebels still must gain the trust of followers and they still cannot produce "real" payoffs to more than a few of their followers at any given time. True, deflation of the power medium can promote increased conflict. But the generalization of power can just as well contribute to revolutionary conflagration, as when it helps legitimate the power of a charismatic rebel or vanguard party. The concept of generalized media simply is not specific enough to imply either of these empirical alternatives.[77†]

2.2.3. Interchange as the Antidote to Internal Fragmentation

The third and last kind of empirical conflation I will consider links Parsons' formalistic application of interchange to his identification of the model with equilibrium. I will argue that by applying the interchange model directly to empirical reality, Parsons avoids the problem of social groups and the conflicts they engender. In principle, of course, the use of interchange is perfectly compatible with such an empirical focus; it is group needs and relationships, after all, which structure the different functions. The model of social-system interchange is an abstraction, an aggregating device; it no more implies the absence of groups than macroeconomic indicators imply the absence of particular firms or sectors.[78]

In fact, Parsons does refer, on occasion, to the relationship between interchange and certain kinds of social groups, namely, those which "represent" each of the four functions to the "society" as a whole. Even on these occasions, however, he uses interchange to avoid focusing on the kinds of groups which produce conflict and division between social functions rather than within them. If each interchange dimension is, in itself, an unmediated empirical reality, then to describe group conflict within any single dimension would be highly contradictory; it would imply the need for intervening conceptualization between this model and empirical fact and would give to interchange an analytic and general rather than concrete and empirical status. Thus, while Parsons writes about the economy and the problems adaptation presents to the system, he does not write about the conflict between class interests that these adaptive pressures often induce. And while political problems and exigencies are a focus of his theory, *internal* political conflicts—between leaders and staff, for example—are generally ignored.

Once again, interchange is perfectly capable, in principle, of making such assessments. In *The System of Modern Societies,* for example, Parsons used the model to discuss class conflict between aristocracy, peasants, and bourgeoisie, political conflict between king and parliament, and internal ethnic and religious dissent. But this is a rare occurrence. For the most part, he is concerned only with conflict between subsystems, not within them, with "the conditions of balance between [the] flows" among subsystems.[79]

It is at least in part because of this strategy that Parsons' later empirical perspective on the social system stresses holism in an unrealistic wholeness. Conflict between subsystems may be intense, but if the subsystems' collective cohesion and internal legitimacy are assumed this conflict will not be truly fragmenting nor will social polarization be too extreme. *The American University* provides a good illustration of this, for while Parsons and Platt discuss at some length the tensions over subsystem boundaries they hardly mention the internal fragmentation that occurred within the functional subsystems themselves—for example, the divisions and conflicts between university groups with different "ideal interests."[80†]

If, for the moment, we bracket ideological issues, the source for this arbitrary commitment to equilibriating rather than disintegrating conflict can be traced to the neopositivist ambition that motivates Parsons' general conflationary bent. Because he must derive the structure of empirical conflict directly from the general, abstract interchange model itself, Parsons cannot allow autonomy to the intermediate, more specific levels of interaction. But interchange can be related to intra-system conflict only if additional specifications are made. Once the actual structures of each abstract function are given empirical substance, inter-system boundary exchanges will be seen to depend upon particular internal exigencies. Thus, in a late rather than early capitalist economy, class divisions will produce different kinds of tensions between state and economy. It is illegitimate, in other words, to derive the empirical perception of conflict from the general systemic outlines provided by presuppositional or model logic alone.[81†]

Once again, this tendency was much less pronounced in Parsons' middle-period work. When his general logic was less explicit and formally specified, he was usually forced to work "up" from empirical facts, particularly from the structure and relations of social groups. In his early essays on the radical right (ch. 3, sec. 4.2), for example, Parsons focused extensively on what he would later call intrafunctional tensions: on class conflict, strains between bureaucracy and military, tensions within religious patterns and between solidary groupings. Yet this very concreteness is the source of theoretical weakness in these early essays, for Parsons is unable to encompass these strains in an abstract, generalizable theoretical account.[82†] Yet, ironically, the very development of such a general conceptual scheme made him less able to articulate these strains. His later analysis of the radical right emphasized only interfunctional conflict, allowing relative consensus and stability within each functional sector. It is particularly in the lengthy "Postscript" to his essay on McCarthyism, for example, that Parsons attempted to "derive" the extremist movement directly from the general principles of his interchange model.[83†] In the process, his early emphasis on internal class and solidarity fragmentation now shifts to a focus on tension along the boundary between the political subsystem and the societal community. He argues that McCarthyism amounted to the withdrawal of integrative inputs to government, a withdrawal induced by conflict between the new political demands generated by America's increased military role, on the one hand, and the political tradition's distrust of big government, on the other.[84]

This failure to acknowledge the intermediate level of social groups presents another example of the more sectarian approach to theoretical debate that emerges in Parsons' later writing. Since most "conflict theories" operate at the level of concrete groups and institutions, the connections between Parsons' interchange analysis of strains and this important strand of contemporary theoretical argument became increasingly attenuated. Parsons insisted, in effect, that the analysis of collective behavior be conducted with interchange variables alone; his own "language" must be substituted for that of other sociologists. This enforced isolation created a significant focus of strain between Parsons and his most important students, who often reacted against this thrust by eschewing formalism and turning back to a consideration of social groups.[85†]

3. FORMALISM AND IDEOLOGICAL CONFLATION: INTERCHANGE AS THE GOOD SOCIETY

In chapter 5, discussing the central ideological and empirical specifications that structure Parsons' theory of change, I emphasized the independent status of each of these theoretical decisions and their autonomy, in turn, from Parsons' more generalized commitments. I will indicate in this discussion, however, that in an important strand of his writing the distinctions between these three levels of analysis are collapsed. This conflation has far-reaching consequences.

There is, in fact, a central irresolution in Parsons' synthetic approach to change. He is ideologically committed to a nonindividualistic liberalism, a normative goal he links to increased social differentiation. At the same time, he argues that structural differentiation occurs for "adaptive" reasons, that systems differentiate to gain more "efficiency." The relationship between these two assumptions is never clarified.[86†] One logical implication is that Parsons views increased empirical efficiency and normative freedom as congruent, that he believes an efficient system—operationally defined as a system that has resolved extant strain—is also one that has realized, or at least substantially increased, freedom for the individual actor. Though Parsons himself never makes such claims explicit—and there is no reason to believe he would have endorsed such a bald proposition if it were proposed in this way—the very possibility reflects a deep ambivalence in his approach to change.

If ideological virtue and structural differentiation are both tied to empirical efficiency and the resolution of strain, the "normative" and "real" dimensions of social theory are collapsed. If the present system is not violently conflictual and visible structural strain largely resolved, the system must be viewed as adaptive and efficient. Further, if it is adaptive, it must also be accepted as free, for voluntarism is tied to structural differentiation and increased efficiency.

It should not be surprising, therefore, that in the relatively stable period of postwar democratic capitalism, Parsons' theory evinced increasing satisfaction with the course of history. Despite his strong criticism of laissez-faire capitalism and advocacy of the welfare state, there was an increasing tendency in Parsons' social analysis to apply this ideological critique to the past rather than the present. In the course of this development, Parsons' ideological commitments gradually evolved from those of a dynamic and activistic liberalism to a more static and quiescent position, a movement in political, if not in theoretical, terms from a Benthamite liberalism to a more Burkean one.

Still, my concern in this discussion is not with Parsons' ideology per se, but, rather, with the fact that he does not argue for his ideological position in an independent manner. For Parsons conflates his ideological evaluations with empirical and theoretical commitments. Whether arguing from a dynamic or a quiescent position, he will not acknowledge that these a priori political principles play any role in his scientific judgment. Instead, he argues that his political evaluations are "provided" by his more generalized commitments and the more empirical developments they imply. Thus, although the perceptive reader can see Parsons' normative judgments quite clearly, Parsons himself never acknowledges their existence. Rarely does he argue against a competing theory on the grounds of ideological approbation; he contends only that it is true or false in theoretical/empirical terms.

Parsons' strategy, then, is conflationary, for he reduces one level of sociological analysis to another; and the motivation for this disturbing tendency, in this case as in the others we have examined, is the peculiar strand of neopositivism that permeates Parsons' work. In fact, the claims Parsons makes for theoretical objectivity rest not only on his conviction that his presuppositions "reflect" empirical reality—a conviction we have just examined in some detail—but also on his belief that these nonempirical commitments contain no political bias. It can now be seen that Parsons' identification of theory with fact has a further ambition. By producing "objective theory," Parsons intends to avoid the historicist fallacy, the relativism which views every social scientific theory as the product of its immediate political environment. His empiricism is a moral argument against the influence of morality on science. Like Popper, Parsons wants to save social theory from the ravages of historical relativism; he, too, adopts a meta-methodology that upholds the objective, ahistorical character of science.[87]

Unlike Popper, however, Parsons would accomplish this objectivity not by experiment and falsification but by a priori theoretical construction and formal deduction. It is not coincidental that shortly before the more sophisticated conceptualization of his later middle-period was about to appear—and in the midst of the darkest period of the cold war—Parsons warned his sociological colleagues, in his presidential Address to the American Sociological Association, about the dangers of ideological bias. "Social scientists," he argued, "are plagued by the problems of objectivity in the face of tendencies to value-bias to a much higher degree than is true of natural scientists." However, in what must have seemed to the more positivist members of his audience a rather peculiar solution, Parsons argued that the only true antidote to such value bias was to embrace a self-consciously theoretical sociology. Because of the great threat of value bias, "theory is even more important in our field than in the natural sciences."[88]

And, indeed, on the very first page of the interdisciplinary *Towards a General Theory of Action,* published the year following this statement, Parsons and his co-authors announce that they have moved substantially closer to this goal. As a point of departure for specialized work, "general theory . . . will facilitate the control of the biases of observation and interpretation."[89] Thus, although Parsons supplements Weber's "concrete" approach to theory with a more self-conscious analytic understanding, he remains a Weberian in a peculiar and important sense.[90†] For Parsons, science has three basic types of components: conceptual frames of reference, methodological commitments, and empirical statements. Since, at least in the empiricist strand of his work, he believes that the first and second of these elements are in some sense "consonant" with empirical statements rather than connected to a priori presuppositions, Parsons can endorse Weber's position that ideological assumptions not only should not but do not impinge on scientific work.[91†]

This neopositivist conflation of ideological with empirical and presuppositional judgments reaches its apogee in Parsons' later writings, when his theoretical scheme achieves its most powerful and supple form. While arguing, on the one hand, that interchange presents an important empirical discovery, Parsons also utilizes the model, implicitly, to make a series of ideological, evaluative arguments. He does this in two ways: indirectly, by arguing that the very existence of social interchange indicates a fully pluralistic and liberal society, and, more directly, by using interchange theory as an ideological weapon in political argument.

3.1. INTERCHANGE AS POLITICAL PLURALISM

Interchange articulates social divisions, or boundaries, that are rooted in highly general, essentially epistemological assumptions. They are valid without resort to empirical verification. But as I have emphasized throughout earlier discussions, whether these presuppositional divisions correspond to actual institutional separation, to "structural differentiation," is another matter entirely. Any such judgment depends on a series of much more specific, intermediate evaluations, a number of which I indicated in the discussion of Parsons' change theory (ch. 5, sec. 2).

In the conflationary presentation of his argument, however, Parsons eliminates these intermediate steps. Presuppositional division is held to reflect actual social differentiation. Concrete institutional relationships follow the "boundaries" established on purely analytic, presuppositional grounds. As a result, the historical specificity of differentiation theory is lost; Parsons' discussion moves from the subjunctive to the indicative, from "differentiation in American society would occur if . . ." to "American society is differentiated." In modern, contemporary society, Parsons implies, functional fusion is a thing of the past. Institutional dimensions do not dominate others, and development is not skewed in one functional direction at the expense of another. In such a situation, significant structural barriers to freedom do not exist or, at least, need no longer be systematically described. All this, of course, serves the larger interest of Parsons' neopositivist ambitions, for the nature of empirical differentiation can now be formally derived from the boundaries established by the generalized model of interchange. Parsons' work may be theoretical, but it is, once again, making empirical claims at the same time.

Such ideological conflation is particularly clear in Parsons' discussion of the boundary relation between economy and polity. Parsons consistently argued that the American polity exercises substantial, independent control over the nation's economic life.[92] He substantiates this assertion in a number of different ways. Empirically, he points to the regulatory acts of the New Deal, and the growing separation between legal ownership and actual managerial control in large corporations. In discussing neither of these controversial issues, however, does he offer sufficient empirical evidence to indicate the actual balance of power between public and private spheres. Rather, to "prove" the independence of politics from economics, Parsons repeatedly cites the differentiation of adaptation from goal-attainment functions in ongoing social systems. By merely specifying this model, he lays out their independent spheres of empirical control.[93] Thus, Parsons categorizes the provision of credit as a political, not an economic, decision, concluding from this that the economy depends on power inputs from the polity. He reasons, therefore, that polity indirectly controls capital formation and with it the provision of basic economic facilities. In return for this political input, the economy supplies the polity with control over purchasing power, for the polity needs economic facilities if its public goals are to be met. The government uses this money, in turn, to induce cooperation with its political goals.

Yet Parsons' identification of this generalized argument with empirical reality is conflationary, for it is made on purely analytic, not empirical, grounds. The economy and polity are not so differentiated in neocapitalist society. In fact, Parsons himself has offered compelling empirical evidence of relative fusion. Ironically, it is his quest for formal deduction that forces him to ignore this evidence and, in the process, to forgo a more accurate, independent specification of his multidimensional model.

In *Economy and Society*, Parsons and Smelser acknowledge that the political "credit creation" function is actually carried out not by government but by banks, and, one might add, by the self-financing corporations themselves.[94] This has two implications. First, while they do indeed have a political reference, decisions about capital creation are private, not public; thus, instead of being regulated by input from the solidary citizenship community, credit creation is regulated by market considerations which fuse political and economic criteria. The second implication results from the first. Because capital formation is not, in fact, dependent on "public" political decisions, the national government does not receive the kind of adaptive inputs it needs to function effectively. National governments, for example, rarely receive sufficient funds to achieve their public goals. If Parsons' interchange model is used to assess social change in a nonconflationary manner, therefore, it becomes clear that functional differentiation between state and economy is by no means complete; significant fusion remains, and certain distinctive strains can be linked to this fact.[95†]

By insisting on his conflationary strategy, Parsons can avoid making any explicit ideological comment on the socialism-capitalism controversy. Yet the argument can be advanced that a more "socialist" economy-polity relationship is implicit in his very adoption of structural differentiation as the criterion for freedom. If concrete institutional development is, in fact, to correspond more closely to the purely analytic distinctions of the interchange model, decisions about credit and, indirectly, capital formation must be more fully connected to public, governmental control. Though Parsons claims that the Soviet economy is overly politicized and "fused,"[96] it would seem more accurate to argue that, in certain respects, the Soviets' political control over investment is more rather than less differentiated, in the very terms which Parsons himself has set forth.[97†] While accepting uncritically the status quo of American economy-polity relations, Parsons has produced empirical evidence for a much more critical perspective; nevertheless, he claims, throughout, that no ideological judgment is being made either way.

This paradox is nowhere more clearly revealed than in the debate between Parsons and Karl Polanyi. The central point made by Polanyi and his co-workers, argued both analytically and historically, is that the economic market, while retaining an essential autonomy, should be strongly regulated by the community at large.[98] In reviewing *Economy and Society*, Polanyi's followers regaled Parsons and Smelser with the criticism that the interchange model implied isolation of the market from such supra-economic controls as social solidarity and government regulation.[99] In one sense, of course, this presents a gross misinterpretation of Parsons' model, which in fact separated social dimensions only in an analytic, not an empirical, sense. Indeed, while Parsons and Smelser acknowledged the empirical independence of market laws, they utilized the analytic differentiation of interchange theory to suggest that the capitalist economy was actually highly interpenetrated by noneconomic spheres and controls. This was essentially the position taken by Smelser in his forceful and lengthy response to the critical reviews. Arguing that the degree of market differentiation must be considered a matter for empirical and historical investigation, Smelser asserted that the results of Polanyi's empirical investigations could, in fact, be incorporated into the general interchange model.[100†] In another sense, however, the more critical interpretations made by Polanyi and his co-workers were correct, and Smelser's review missed the point. Parsons had used interchange in a conflationary way, identifying analytic with empirical points. With his formalistic logic, he had assumed, quite erroneously it turns out, that the neocapitalist economy is consistently regulated by political institutions representing an integrated national community. In fact, if Parsons had attended more closely to his own independent empirical insight, his conclusions would have closely resembled Polanyi's.[101†]

By conflating his analytic model of interchange with the actual conditions of economy-polity relations, Parsons' change theory avoids the difficult question of "degrees" of social differentiation, avoids dealing with the inescapable fact that differentiation is actually a process rather than an event. By simply equating interchange and empirical differentiation, Parsons undermines the historical specificity of his change concept. While differentiation may begin with some kind of formal separation—for example, the creation of a constitutional state—it only gradually makes interdependence and regulation more concrete and substantive. What precisely constitutes institutional "autonomy"? What political controls on economic life are enough to create economic regulation? While these are exactly the kinds of important questions that Parsons' differentiation theory elucidates, they are questions that his ideological conflation prevents him from answering.

Parsons' other major strategy for demonstrating the pluralism of modern, particularly American, society is to argue that adherence to a particular government has been separated from membership in the modern national community and from loyalty to legitimate national values. Once again, however, the conflation and formalization of his analysis produces a dangerous tendency to assume the completeness of empirical differentiation. In discussing the relation between societal community and state, for example, Parsons recognizes that inequalities of group position and political power present the critical problem for maintaining an inclusive societal solidarity: "Policies . . . impinge differentially, not equally, on members [of the community] . . . and impose varying obligations."[102] It is precisely because of this tension that "inherent integrative problems arise," the only response to which is political "justification," which Parsons defines as government "persuasion that the relevant [policy] is urgent for the collectivity as a whole and . . . that shifts in the benefit-burden balance . . . are fair."[103] The success of such persuasion obviously depends on the differentiation that exists between societal community and government: only if a real sense of national community exists that is separate from loyalties to particular governments can there be the conviction that a broad, public interest can be maintained while particular group interests are simultaneously advanced.[104]

But how does Parsons decide that such differentiation does indeed exist? His first strategy is simply conflationary: he points to the presuppositional fact of "influence" as an analytically independent medium of interchange. Justification will occur if political leadership "exercise[s] influence relative to important elements of the constituency."[105] After all, influence means, by definition, that "individual members must be *persuaded* (not coerced or induced) to vote for candidates and policies."[106†] But Parsons has confused generalized with empirical argument. The fact that the influence sanction produces voluntary behavior tells us nothing about whether this sanction is acceptable to large segments of the national community. Whether government action is felt to be coercive or is accepted in a voluntary way depends on the degree of social consensus, on whether the influence sanction is accepted by a large or small segment of the political community. Even if national solidarity were deeply factionalized and fragmented—and political action, therefore, coercive to large segments of the community—influence, by definition, would still be the medium by which political leaders would attempt to gain justification through voluntary compliance with their decisions. Parsons has certainly identified the technical medium of exchange involved in such polity-community transactions, and he has done so in a brilliant way. This generalized reasoning cannot, however, be substituted for empirical argument itself.

Parsons does make a second argument for the completeness of polity-community differentiation. He points here to the existence of legal democratic rights, to the universal franchise, the secret ballot, and laws against bribery and direct political coercion.[107] Through such protection of the voter, voluntary individual decisions now become the basis for leadership selection: the mobilization of political support is now legally separated from the exercise of power. Given such institutional developments, Parsons argues, "a more or less universalistically ordered normative system" is guaranteed.

Certainly, such constitutional processes of differentiation are terribly significant. As Parsons demonstrated in his discussion of seventeenth-century England, constitutionalism allows membership in the societal community to be separated from ascribed memberships in economic, religious, political, and ethnic groups.[108†] Yet this formal membership in no way implies the kind of equality between social groupings upon which widespread "community solidarity" depends. While Parsons' repeated reference to the historical nature of "inclusion" and to the expansion of the social aspects of citizenship indicates that he is aware of this problem, he never indicates how historically rooted exclusion continually tempers the guarantees of full community in even the most "modern" of contemporary societies. Certainly, even in legally egalitarian national communities significant ascriptive disparities contine to impinge upon the electoral process, often, indeed, to the extent of thwarting attempts to gain legitimate "justification" for more functional kinds of inequalities. Diffuse and ascriptive factors continue to affect solidary life, and the universalistic community is in constant tension with the solidary groupings that correspond to factional religious, economic, political, and ethnic divisions.[109†]

Though Parsons often recognizes such tensions, he never systematically incorporates such "particularism" into his contemporary analysis. Pursuing his formalist, deductive approach, he conflates the analytic divisions of interchange with empirical differentiation. In doing so, he converts theoretical into ideological argument.

Finally, though he spends significantly less time on the issue, Parsons makes a similar conflationary error in his analysis of the separation of political power from more general symbolic legitimation. This is clear, for example, in his analysis of the relationship between cognitive rationality and state power in *The American University.* In this work, Parsons and Platt present a convincing argument for the differentiation between state and university. They argue that the state is, in fact, regulated by certain relatively independent cultural values, some of the most important of which are institutionalized in the university. But they never discuss the tension in this relationship between such value "relevance," where state action is actually disciplined by cognitive nationality, and value "cooptation," where the government pays homage to this value only in a formal sense. Presumably, the differentiation of university and government is also a continuum, one which can encompass *degrees* of university autonomy and *variations* in the cognitive regulation of political action.

This same conflation occurs in Parsons' later discussions of constitutionalism. He argues that constitutional guarantees ensure that the symbolic legitimation of power is independent of the coercive power of the state. But surely constitutionalism refers to the universalism of only one strand of political culture. Cultural patterns that structure political legitimacy, even within constitutional systems, can range from relatively passive and submissive traditions to more transcendent and critical ones—that is, from symbols that are more fused with power to symbols that are more differentiated from it. For Parsons, however, it is sufficient to argue for differentiation per se, and more often than not he roots his argument for value autonomy simply in analytic presuppositional argument alone. Cultural legitimation controls government, according to this argument, because it is, by definition, more symbolically "generalized" than conditionally related goal-attainment activity. Although this conflationary tendency is less central in Parsons' earlier essays, it becomes particularly pronounced after his formulation of the interchange model.[110†]

The ideological impetus beneath this conflationary strategy is especially evident on those rare occasions when Parsons takes a positive view of structural fusion. Normally, he utilizes formalism to deny the existence of structural fusion in contemporary society; he will, however, praise such fusion if it maintains an institutional arrangement to which he is normatively committed. For example, by combining higher education with the activities of pure research, the American university "fuses" expressive with cognitive functions. Yet Parsons and Platt justify this "bundle," as they call it, by arguing for its far-reaching functional significance.[111] In fact, as Smelser has pointed out, this fusion may well have been an important factor not only in the strains which first created undergraduate unrest in the 1960s but in the rigidity that so often characterized the university's response.[112]

Parsons misperceives structural fusion because he conflates empirical differentiation with the existence of analytical interchange in a more generalized sense. Differentiation is a linear development. If the culture's cognitive dimension has become differentiated with the emergence of the modern university, Parsons reasons, the university's internal differentiation must be similarly complete. Only in this manner can formalism be maintained. Not only can Parsons deduce specific empirical patterns from more generalized assumptions, but in doing so he can camouflage the inevitable selectivity of his ideological judgments.

But Parsons' optimism about modern life can scarcely be suppressed. In the end, this buoyancy produces a neo-Utilitarian confidence in the complementarity of efficiency and freedom. True, social change involves great collective structures and significant noneconomic regulation. Parsons believes, nevertheless, that differentiation has produced "markets" for influence, power, values, and money which are, in the end, flexible and responsive, not oligopolistic or monopolistic.[113] The spheres of economic and political power, normative control, and value formation are not only differentiated but they are usually in balance with one another and mutually supportive. They distribute rewards according to individual merit and competition. With this rather utopian vision, Parsons neutralizes the tensions between individual and society and the polarizing conflicts of independent, competing functions, which his change theory has done so much to illuminate.[114†]

3.2. *INTERCHANGE AS IDEOLOGICAL CRITIQUE*

Parsons' argument from generalized interchange to empirical pluralism represents an important and debilitating ideological reduction of his theoretical analysis. But Parsons also utilizes interchange in an even more directly ideological way. He argues that critics of liberal *ideology* are incorrect because they have ignored crucial *theoretical* points. Because antiliberal critics ignore interchange theory, they cannot comprehend the true nature of contemporary life, particularly the high degree of structural differentiation that it presents.

The most striking and ingenious example of this ideological strategy occurs in *The American University*, when Parsons and Platt mount a simultaneous argument against the collectivist left and individualistic right. "Radicalism of both right and left," they assert, "functions to dedifferentiate . . .pluralistic differentiatedness by asserting . . . a single position, which unites goal-attainment orientations (the political component) with legitimation by undifferentiated value-commitments."[115] In their argument against this "fusion," however, Parsons and Platt treat these left- and right-wing critiques not as potentially problematic empirical analyses and normative evaluations but as misinformed presuppositional arguments. Left and right both believe, they contend, that particular economic systems produce particular political arrangements. For the Marxian radicals, capitalism inevitably produces liberal democracy; the conservative right, on the other hand, believes that any non-laissez-faire capitalism produces political dictatorship. Both ideologies, in other words, perceive only two active theoretical variables, politics and economics; furthermore, both view the relation of politics and economics in a highly deterministic way.

On these grounds, Parsons and Platt mount a purely analytical counterattack. Their crucial rejoinder is that, contrary to both critiques, societies contain a third significant dimension, the societal community. Capitalist and non-laissez-faire economies, therefore, do not produce political structures in and of themselves: their impact on politics must be filtered through the normative structure of the societal community. This, of course, represents simply a generalized statement of analytical pluralism. Parsons and Platt believe, however, that this assertion of analytical pluralism is at the same time an argument for ideological and empirical pluralism, that to demonstrate the analytic autonomy of the legal order is to prove, also, the independence of political democracy from the compromising pressures of the economic system. In this way they can conclude that political democracy is "bound up with structural pluralism": given the autonomy of the societal community, diverse group interests "can be integrated into a system of order that is not inherently repressive [i.e., not politically totalitarian] or exploitative [i.e., not economically laissez-faire]." Only the ideological center—"differentiated from both the radical left and the radical right"—has been able to articulate this more accurate vision of the modern pluralistic society.[116]

But this argument is based on a series of illegitimate jumps from generalized to ideological argument. True, without a differentiated societal community it is impossible to achieve the kind of universalistic integration upon which democracy depends. It is equally true that ideological extremists often fail to perceive this important point. What is not true, however, is that such extremists necessarily make one-dimensional analytic arguments. Left- or right-wing critics could very well utilize analytically multidimensional theory and still conclude, for specific empirical and ideological reasons, that political and economic functions are fused in late capitalist society. An analytically differentiated theory, in other words, does not mean that there is concrete empirical differentiation, that there is differentiation in fact. A radical argument that capitalist pluralism does not exist need not make any assumptions about the determinism of economic exigencies in an analytic sense. It may, in fact, accept an analytically differentiated model, focusing its critique on interchange imbalances and arguing that subsystem reciprocity, or pluralism, can be restored only by further empirical differentiation.

Parsons has tried, once again, to move directly from interchange to politics, refuting an ideological point by using what are essentially presuppositional principles.[117†] Parsons could have accomplished his critique in a nonconflationary way by arguing, instead, that these radical ideologies violate certain normative principles about freedom or make incorrect empirical observations about the course of historical development. But while such nonconflationary arguments are certainly made in the course of his theoretical career—as my discussions in chapter 5 (sections 2.1, 2.2) indicate—Parsons is obviously not satisfied with them. For only by eliminating these intervening steps can his generalized argument be at the same time fully specific and "objective."

Parsons employed this same kind of direct ideological conflation in his famous attack on C. Wright Mills' power-elite thesis.[118] The essay is particularly interesting because it is double-sided, simultaneously offering both a conflationary and a much more differentiated, less reductionistic critique. Thus, at several points in the essay, Parsons accepts, with qualification, a number of Mills' empirical observations about the interpenetration of American elites, acknowledging, for example, that the absence of an American "governing class" has allowed business and military groups a disproportionate role in government decision-making. But Parsons goes on to place these facts in a much more nuanced framework than Mills' neo-Marxist approach allows. As in his essay on McCarthyism (see ch. 3, sec. 4.3), he argues, first, that such strains must be viewed within the broader context of ongoing social differentiation and, second, that they are rooted not in some deterministic deus ex machina but in the historical and ideological peculiarities of America's national development.[119] In emphasizing such historical variations in structural differentiation, and particularly their importance on elite formation and responsiveness, Parsons continues the emphasis on empirical variation and dynamic liberalism of his middle-period work.[120†] Combining these emphases with his more sophisticated presuppositional framework, Parsons begins to construct a realistic approach to the modern limits on voluntarism that accepts the valid elements in Mills' critique while transcending the work as a whole.

But this balanced approach to Mills is cross-cut by a much more conflationary strategy. For Parsons also argues against Mills' ideological and empirical critiques by linking them to Mills' unacceptable, more generalized commitments. He argues, for example, that Mills' work is permeated by presuppositional individualism, that on "basically individualistic premises" Mills believes that any "social organization beyond the level of the family and the local community is a bad thing *en toto*."[121] It is on the basis of this generalized commitment, Parsons asserts, that Mills has pilloried America's power elite. If more collectivist presuppositions had been adopted, he argues, Mills would have adopted a more positive approach; he would have seen "that power, while of course subject to abuses and in need of many controls, is an essential and desirable component of a highly organized society." Parsons also attacks Mills' conceptualization on the level of model. Because Mills has no conception of power as an interchange process, Parsons contends, he has focused only on the "distributive," or output, side of the political system while ignoring the "production" side, or the inputs to power.[122] Because of this second generalized error, Parsons argues, Mills can write only about the power elite's negative face, for it is on the productive side that power gains inputs of symbolic legitimacy and normative support.

But these arguments assume a deterministic, deductive relationship between theory and fact. It is true, perhaps, that individualistic assumptions lurk beneath Mills' critique, although his collectivist emphasis on social classes certainly creates a strong theoretical counterpoint. But whether or not such presuppositional individualism exists, Parsons must still attack the power elite thesis in a directly empirical way. It is much more likely, as Parsons himself notes, that Mills is guilty of *ideological* individualism; yet once again, Parsons would have had to attack this directly—ideologically—without conflating it with his critique of presuppositional individualism. Parsons' attack on Mills for focusing exclusively on the distribution of power is a much more telling point, for Mills' rationalist bias forces him to instrumentalize legitimacy and blinds him to the voluntary elements of political legitimacy and support. But here, too, no logical deduction can be made from this more general problem to weaknesses in empirical and ideological argument. A sophisticated multidimensional theory—fully "Parsonian" in its differentiation of production and distribution—might still discover that American political power is monopolistic, that there is fusion among military, economic, and representative functions.[123†]

Still another example of such direct ideological conflation is Parsons' justification of inherited wealth. The allocation of economic position by family lineage presents, of course, a primary case of the ascription that Parsons' theory of structural differentiation is directed against. His opposition to ascription is, moreover, clearly as much ideological as empirical.[124†] For this reason, the differentiation of lineage and economic position is a continual focus of his historical work. He makes a great deal, for example, out of the gradual separation of large-scale property ownership, presumably inherited, from economic management, the process documented by Berle and Means.[125†]

In analyzing the contemporary situation, however, Parsons does not carry this analysis of family-economy differentiation beyond the problem of economic management itself. To continue the strict application of his differentiation theory would force him to adopt a critical attitude toward the fusion of family and economic position which remains, toward the still significant fact of inherited, ascribed wealth and its power to mitigate achieved, meritocratic status. Parsons, however, does not maintain such ideological consistency. While he clearly acknowledges that such unearned disparities exist, he argues that they are justifiable.[126]

This reversal constitutes a revealing example of the tension between Parsons' dynamic and quiescent liberalism. Much more interesting from the present perspective, however, is the conflationary manner in which he makes this argument. Without the ascribed inheritance of wealth, Parsons claims, socialization would be impossible. Socialization demands a minimum level of family stability and cohesion, and Parsons connects the wealth problem to the question of how this stability is to be maintained. If father acquires a certain level of control over instrumental facilities and economic status, he argues, the expressive demands of family life dictate that mother and children must be accorded equal access and status.[127†]

Surely, however, this argument misses the point. Status may be equalized within the socialization period without allowing the child to maintain this privilege into adulthood and, indeed, to pass it on to his or her own children. More fundamentally, monetary rewards outside the firm need have no direct relation to the allocation of instrumental facilities and status rewards within it. In the argument over inherited wealth, Parsons would have us believe, the very existence of societal interchange is at stake. Without some inherited privilege, the autonomy of the pattern-maintenance dimension would be eliminated. Once again, Parsons has conflated theoretical argument with ideological evaluation. It is not a matter of the autonomy of the pattern-maintenance activity but a question of how—according to what normative principle and in what empirical patterns—the pattern-maintenance process will be organized in a specific historical instance.[128]

3.3. IDEOLOGICAL CONFLATION IN THE GENERALIZED MEDIA

But probably the most succinct and direct instance of ideological reduction occurs in Parsons' analysis of the generalized media. It is in this media theory that Parsons most egregiously fuses efficiency and freedom. Without media generalization, he argues continually, differentiated systems will either dissolve or de-differentiate; this is the efficiency argument.[129] But, time and time again, he makes another, specifically ideological point: "without relevant generalization . . . ascriptive rigidity is almost inevitable."[130] Ascription, of course, is a pattern that Parsons has consistently identified with the lack of individual choice. Media generalization, then, is not only efficient but liberating. I have already criticized Parsons' argument that symbolic generalization produces empirical stability; I will deal here with his equation of symbolism with the maintenance of individual freedom.

Throughout Parsons' later writing on power there is a marked tendency to slide from analytic arguments about the nature of political generalization to arguments about the actual existence and desirability of substantive political rights.[131†] He writes, for example, that political generalization "becomes necessary in giving representatives power vis-à-vis their constituencies," arguing that without this separation of representatives and constituencies political dissent would be impossible: "Were the outcome [of the relationship between representatives and their constituents] a matter of pure political barter, there *could* be no dissident minorities."[132] In one sense, this reasoning is correct. In a just and stable order, freedom can, in fact, be maintained through indirect representation based upon symbolic generalization. In an unjust system, however, generalization and freedom may well be opposed to one another. In the limited parliamentary system of nineteenth-century Germany, for example, power was generalized in Parsons' technical use of that term: electors were separated from representatives, and powerful segments of the society trusted their political leaders. But the German political system was also relatively undifferentiated; family lineage and economic class were fused with political position, resulting in ascriptive access to these positions and a great reduction in political flexibility. In such a situation, the *deflation* of the political medium, that is, a *decline* in trust, must be the first step toward increased freedom; only the movement *toward* political "barter," represented by growing demands for a more direct equivalence between trust and rewards, would create a more differentiated political system.[133†]

General concepts about "symbolic generalization," therefore, tell us little about the relation of power and freedom. To produce an ideological evaluation of any situation, much more intervening analytic specification is needed. The possibilities for empirical variation are enormous. Thus, even in a relatively differentiated society, particular electoral rules may be decisive in determining whether power can be generalized or not. As compared with winner-take-all elections, for example, coalition systems encourage fragmentation and political barter. And beyond these empirical matters, any evaluation of political generalization and freedom must depend upon particular ideological commitments. If Parsons had a populist rather than a "representational" approach to democracy, generalization—which includes the independence of leaders vis-à-vis their constituents—would appear as a threat to freedom as often as its necessary foundation.[134†] The point here is not that such additional judgments are impossible to make, or that this additional complexity makes media theory trivial or unimportant. I contend simply that ideological arguments cannot be deduced from generalized concepts. Indeed, by embarking on such formalized reduction Parsons undermines the universality of his more generalized theoretical argument.

This strategy of ideological conflation is even more clear in Parsons' analysis of the influence medium. In his more nuanced and differentiated argument, it will be recalled, generalized influence is the ability to gain trust beyond the network of immediate associations, to create a symbolically generalized community beyond the concrete groups of actual interaction. On this basis, it is easy to see why generalized influence is so important in a pluralized society, where the inclusive solidary community must tolerate a variety of independent groupings.[135†] But Parsons is not satisfied with this argument alone; he asserts that generalized influence actually produces normative cosmopolitanism. The generalization of influence, he argues, refers not just to the process of symbolization but to the increased significance of certain symbolic patterns over others. The "intrinsic base" of influence, which refers to influence in its nongeneralized form, is not just any relatively narrower associational context, but a "*Gemeinschaft*," a diffuse solidarity, a particularistically organized community. Conversely, when influence is generalized, it creates universalism; it generates the kind of tolerance that a differentiated solidary community demands.[136] Generalized influence corresponds to "structural pluralism."[137]

But surely influence can be generalized in situations that are restrictive as well as those that are liberating. It may, for example, become the basis of vast particularistic solidarities, as in the revolutionary creation of a fascist society. Parsons has, of course, written of such episodes at great length, but most of these discussions occurred before his introduction of media terminology. In his haste to camouflage ideological arguments with more generalized ones, these discussions have evidently been forgotten.[138†]

The same kind of problem cross-cuts Parsons' treatment of the medium of value commitments. If commitments are generalized, the basic loyalty of symbolic leaders is taken for granted; trust is established and the continuous proof of value compatibility, which Parsons calls barter, is not required. In societies which are at all differentiated, such value generalization is obviously an important component in effectuating collective action, in maintaining equilibrium, and in increasing the range of individual choice. Just as value generalization is necessary but not sufficient for social stability, however, it certainly cannot, in itself, provide guarantees that individual freedom will in fact be attained. But Parsons clearly implies that it does.

In his change theory Parsons described one basic evolutionary process as "value generalization"; he refers here to the manner in which religious universalism and, eventually, secularization create cultural values that can tolerate diverse traditions.[139] In this substantive sense, value generalization implies decreasing polarization and cultural exclusion.[140†] But Parsons' argument becomes conflationary when he identifies this substantive conception with value generalization in the formal sense, for in the latter it refers simply to generalization of the symbolic medium of commitments. This is the strategy Parsons uses to identify medium generalization with increased freedom as well as increased trust. "Inflation" and "deflation" now become ideological, not just analytic terms. "The sharp ideological dispute between socialist and capitalist commitments," Parsons asserts, "constitutes a 'deflationary' movement within the development of Western society and its [value] commitment system." Deflated, nongeneralized commitments, then, represent ideologically unacceptable values: uncompromising value absolutism, fundamentalism, particularism, ascription.[141]

In making such an argument, Parsons has confused a number of issues. On the one hand, he is making a series of ideological judgments about what is morally good for Western society; on the other, he is conducting a historical argument about the empirical course of Western development. Neither of these points, however, can be derived from his much more generalized and analytic media theory. Parsons' conception of media emerges from his presuppositional synthesis, and more directly from his interchange model. It "specifies" each analytic interchange by showing how the fundamental dimensions of social systems can be concretized in individual and institutional interaction. But this specification is thoroughly abstract, and it implies no particular empirical outcome or structure. Indeed, religious fundamentalism, revolutionary socialism, exploitative capitalism—even fascism itself—all involve generalized value commitments and the creation of trust. Of course, they often involve also the deflation of certain value commitments, particularly the ones upheld by the moderate center which tries, either honestly or hypocritically, to represent "society" as a whole. But such value polarization depends on specific empirical conditions, for the moral legitimacy of the moderate center is certainly historically relative. In any particular case, the "deflation" of moderate, centrist commitments may actually present the only path toward the eventual expansion of individual opportunity and tolerance. Compromise and trust may, in certain situations, be retrogressive and "ascriptive." Parsons himself takes charismatic leadership as the prototype of value generalization,[142] yet it is precisely such charismatic behavior that so often deflates commitments to value moderation and stability in the modern world. Charismatic leadership can, nonetheless, not be used to deduce the desirability or empirical frequency of either generalization or deflation. By conflating generalized argument with empirical and ideological commitments, Parsons turns his own theory against itself.

3.4. IDEOLOGICAL AND EMPIRICAL CONFLATION: THE END OF HISTORY

By this point it should be clear that Parsons' ideological conflation dovetails with his empirical one. By reducing empirical to nonempirical judgements and normative evaluation to presuppositional assumptions, Parsons has produced a simplistic and distorted line of analysis which at every point cross-cuts his more sophisticated work. He presents history as a Hegelian "unfolding," in which the psychological, social, and cultural losses are always neatly balanced by the historical gains. Ideological fundamentalism, political dictatorship, economic exploitation, and solidary polarization—the negative faces of modernization to which his earlier writings devoted considerable attention—become, in his later work, increasingly residual. With the differentiation of societal community and state, resistance to progress is no longer systematically rooted; change and reform are more likely to occur than not.[143†] Conflict and discontent are created by the intellectuals, not by the strains which intellectual ideology symbolizes and articulates.[144] Parsons' accent is on the positive: modernization presents a consistent process of "upgrading" and "inclusion."[145] Institutionalized individualism is not a normative goal partly realized, but an empirical fact. The historical agenda has been achieved.

4. CONCLUSION: CONFLATION AND THE RIDDLE OF PARSONIAN CRITICISM

As many have noted, Parsons' rhetorical style is often vague and obscure.[146] Sympathetic critics, in fact, have gone so far as to suggest that this opacity itself explains the confusion and disagreement that surrounds Parsons' work.[147] But style is not sui generis, not simply an aesthetic issue. It is his conflationary strategy that has forced Parsons to stretch his conceptual vocabulary out of shape. His logic and conceptualization are so often vague because he has tried to use the same concepts to reach a number of different levels of analysis. By conflating his theoretical argument, Parsons undermined the precision of his theoretical language.

It is evident that, in matters much more important than stylistic, the portrait I have drawn in the first five chapters of this analysis differs significantly from the one drawn by Parsons himself, that it was, indeed, an interpretive reading and, as such, itself a certain kind of theoretical argument. In that earlier discussion, I sought to distinguish the different levels in Parsons' analysis; I presented his generalized analytic arguments and indicated how they were specified in his middle and later work. By interrelating empirical and ideological assumptions with model commitments and presuppositions, I argued, Parsons produced a series of complex concepts and classifications which were empirically relevant without being empirical themselves. This was as much an archaeological reconstruction as a presentation of surface fact, for Parsons' balanced and differentiated line of thinking is cross-cut, at every point, by his more conflationary reasoning about the role of scientific theory. Though committed to the independent role of analytic theory, Parsons could not forgo objectivity in the empiricist sense. To resolve this methodological problem, he became increasingly formalistic. Protected by his deductivist camouflage, he argued that his analytic presuppositions were "really" developed from the observation of concrete empirical systems, that they denoted empirical stability, that they identified the prerequisites for the good society. The riddle of Parsonian criticism can now be solved: the master of "analytic theory" himself committed the sin of "misplaced concreteness" on a truly massive scale.[148†] If we take Parsons at face value, he is often, in fact, the "functionalist," the "equilibrium theorist," the "ideologist" that his critics portray. He can achieve each of these identities, moreover, while maintaining his generalized, presuppositional emphasis. Parsons' critics, then, are correct; yet at the same time they are wrong. The part cannot be taken for the whole, even if Parsons himself would allow his critics to do so.

Chapter Eight

THE PRESUPPOSITIONAL ERROR (1)

Sociological Idealism and the Attack on Instrumental Order in the Early and Middle Work

In 1966, more than a decade into the writings of his late period, Parsons wrote that, under certain circumstances, "I am a cultural determinist rather than a social determinist."[1] From the theorist who throughout his career had proclaimed an ecumenical purpose, this is a rather astonishing statement. Why, after all, must a choice be made? Has Parsons' analytic theory not been devoted precisely to making just such a choice unnecessary?

Parsons promised a synthetic theory, one which would incorporate one-sided "factor theories" within a higher ideal/material synthesis—a theory which would continue Weber's transformation of the materialist and idealist traditions into analytic elements of a multidimensional perspective. While the preceding chapters do, I believe, demonstrate that the range of his multidimensional achievement was enormous, it must, nonetheless, be acknowledged that the achievement remained a partial one. Though Parsons was consistently critical of purely instrumental rationalism, his negation of it was often, in Hegel's terms, more abstract than dialectical: Parsons often simply negated instrumental rationality instead of incorporating it in a broader theory. At every point, in fact, Parsons' multidimensional theory is cross-cut by sociological idealism. In contrast to the contradictory strains in Weber's work, this ambivalence is not limited simply to one or another concrete segment of Parsons' writing: there is no opposition between a Parsonian political sociology and a Parsonian sociology of religion. In contrast to work of Marx or Durkheim, there is no early-versus-late Parsons in terms of significant presuppositional change. Rather, these opposing strands of Parsons' writings are intertwined throughout the length and breadth of his work.

1. IDEALISM IN THE EARLY WRITINGS: CONFLATING ORDER AND ACTION

Parsons' presuppositional logic is ambiguous, and this confusion lies at the heart of his first and perhaps still greatest book. In scrutinizing the densely argued pages of *The Structure of Social Action,* one cannot avoid the conclusion that Parsons is not sure whether he is arguing for a multidimensional theory or simply against an instrumentalist one. On the one hand, Parsons' analytic scheme clearly incorporates collective order in the conditional, instrumental sense, and he devotes a great deal of the first part of the book to tracing its articulation in the rationalist tradition of Malthus, Ricardo, Marx, and the Social Darwinists.[2†] He argues that the flaw in the instrumental solution to the order problem is that it can overcome individualistic randomness only by sacrificing voluntarism. At the same time, however, Parsons argues that this rationalist solution to order—what he calls the postulate of "factual" or material order—is actually no solution at all. Instead of arguing that rationalism resolves the order problem but that in doing so it must incur certain unacceptable costs, he contends that rationalism is in itself a randomizing approach. Instrumental theory cannot, in other words, resolve the problem of individualistic order.

Pursuing this latter line of reasoning—in what amounts to an anti-instrumentalist argument—Parsons adopts two different strategies. He argues, in the first place, that instrumental rationalism is inherently individualistic, a point which has a certain plausibility. By denying the possibility of internalization, instrumental theories cannot envision the symbolic interpenetration of individuals.[3] Yet to accept concrete individual separation is not to imply an atomistic, individualistic theory, for it can be argued that collective order is maintained, nonetheless, by some supra-individual external force. Yet despite his own, often forceful explication of this possibility for external order, Parsons just as often denies it. He treats Marxism, for example, merely as an interesting variant of "utilitarian *individualism.*"[4†] If instrumental rationalism cannot produce a truly collective theory, of course, the only solution to the order problem is to adopt a purely normative approach.

Though this form of argumentation occurs throughout *The Structure of Social Action,* Parsons also develops a more sophisticated justification for idealist reduction. He acknowledges that a factual or material order does exist but argues that it is nonrandom only in the sense that it presents action as ordered in a scientific, that is, statistically predictable, sense.[5] To be truly nonrandom—and Parsons implicitly is introducing here a second criterion—order must also bring stability. Factual order is unacceptable because the interaction it describes, though nonrandom, is fundamentally "precarious." This is the weakness in Hobbes' theory of the regulation of the "war of all against all."[6] "The *actual* situation," Parsons writes, referring here to his own version of empirical reality, "is not a state of war held in check by a coercive sovereign, but a state of relatively spontaneous order."[7] Spontaneous order, of course, is more stable than coerced order, for it is self-imposed through the internalization of norms. In this way Parsons can contend that Hobbes failed to resolve the order problem because he was "devoid of normative thinking."[8†] Theory can articulate order only if it describes cooperation as spontaneous and voluntary, for only in this way can "precariousness" be overcome. Once again, Parsons has presented a line of reasoning in which purely normative order is the only possible option. But in doing so, he has reduced the generality of his argument. Order now refers to a special kind of empirical situation. Action must not simply be collectively regulated—it must be normative as well. Moreover, not just any normative regulation will do; the collective norms must also produce empirical equilibrium.

On the basis of either theoretical strategy, collective instrumental order becomes a residual category: it is no longer among the central axioms of Parsons' theoretical logic. A good example of this more idealist logic occurs in Parsons' discussion of Locke, which also initiates the selective reading of the history of sociological thought that allows him to rationalize this reductionist strand of his argument.[9] Locke avoids the Hobbesian dilemma, Parsons writes, by postulating what Halévy called the "natural identity of interest." He notes that Locke could postulate this natural identity, however, only by implicitly assuming an overarching normative consensus about the rules of the game.[10] It is this implicit assumption that allows order to become a residual category in the individualistic tradition of classical economics. From this weakness in Lockean theorizing, Parsons draws the following conclusion: the only way to go beyond residual categories, to transcend the individualism of classical economics, is to make Locke's normative assumption explicit, to argue, as Durkheim was later to do, that economic life is ordered by value consensus. Yet surely this is not the only alternative to the individualism of classical economics. As Halévy himself pointed out in his analysis of Bentham, Locke's theory may also be countered by postulating an "artificial identity of interest": through external coercion or inducement, political and economic systems create supra-individual orders of their own. In this idealist strand of his argument, however, Parsons cannot acknowledge external coercion as a viable alternative, for it would violate his additional criterion that order must not be precarious. Parsons accepts only the Lockean approach to interest-identification; he argues, simply, that the residual status of "natural identity" must be replaced by an explicit theory of internalized norms.

Immediately after discussing Locke's position, Parsons embarks upon an extended historical analysis of "anti-individualistic positivism."[11†] In this discussion, which takes up the better part of a chapter, Parsons analyzes the reaction which developed within the instrumental-rationalist tradition itself against the individualism that had characterized Western thought since the seventeenth century.[12] As I emphasized in ch. 2, sec. 2, the analysis of this tradition serves to establish the instrumental factor in Parsons' multidimensional synthesis. Yet this grand synthesis, as I have begun to indicate, is cross-cut by a much more specifically normative argument. Parsons resolves this dilemma in a highly strategic manner: he qualifies the significance of anti-individualistic rationalism by placing this theoretical development within historical brackets. Implicitly, Parsons presents the logic of instrumental collectivism simply as one phase in the development of nineteenth-century thought.[13] With the turn of the century and the emergence of those thinkers to whom Parsons devotes the main body of his book—Marshall, Pareto, Durkheim, and Weber—the thrust toward theorizing in the rational tradition is said to have faded away. Once the more normative solution was discovered, it seems, the instrumental one simply was no longer necessary.

But this historical argument is surely contrived. In fact, Halévy, from whom Parsons claims to derive his historical sketch,[14] describes Western intellectual developments in an almost directly antithetical manner. While acknowledging the importance of the rationalist breakthrough in seventeenth-century secular thought, Halévy argues that the Western intellectual milieu remained significantly idealist and organicist through the early nineteenth century.[15] The collectivist rationalism that emerged in nineteenth-century English theorizing, therefore, represented less an end to instrumentalist thinking than a beginning, and Halévy devotes as much attention to the struggle Bentham and his followers waged against normative, organicist theorizing as he does to their attacks on their individualistic opponents within the rationalist tradition itself. From this perspective, the normative emphases of Parsons' fin-de-siècle theorists represented not so much the movement toward an ultimately satisfactory solution to order as one side of a continuing and much more ambiguous dialogue.[16] While Halévy's version of intellectual history has its own biases, it offers, nonetheless, a useful antidote to the retrospective rationalization proffered by Parsons. The validity of an exclusively normative approach to order cannot rest upon its historical triumph.[17†]

In this ambivalent attempt to legitimate an idealist presuppositional position, Parsons has committed several fundamental errors in theoretical logic. By arguing that collective order must ensure social stability, he has conflated empirical statements with presuppositional ones. As I have emphasized throughout these volumes, presuppositions about normative order provide no sure guarantee of empirical equilibrium, nor does the general postulate of instrumental order necessarily assume empirical conflict. If Parsons argues against factual order on the grounds that it denies voluntarism, this is a generalized, presuppositional argument; he cannot, simultaneously, then argue against it on the more specific grounds that it destabilizes social relations. Indeed, voluntaristic behavior may in some cases be just as destabilizing. The preservation of normative voluntarism, moreover, in no way excludes an equal emphasis on order's coercive aspects, a point, of course, that forms the backbone of Parsons' argument for the multidimensional approach.

The other major error Parsons commits involves the identification of rationalism with individualism. In arguing directly from his critique of the rationalist-individualist position to the justification of normative collective order, Parsons equates rationalism with atomism.[18] But in making this equation, Parsons effectively reduces the issue of "order" to the problem of "action."[19†] Because the crucial issue now becomes whether action is conceived instrumentally or normatively, the independent logic involved in the order question—exemplified by the movement within rationalism from an individualist to a collective stance—becomes trivialized and, indeed, epiphenomenal. If the rationalist theorists articulated a collective order, this is not really important; besides, if collective order is conceived in an instrumental way, it is not really order at all. Conversely, if theory moves toward a normative position, it will necessarily reject atomism, for a normative reference implies collective order. This implicit conflation of action and order, I have earlier argued, marks every attempt to legitimate one-dimensional social theory. It is not surprising, then, that although Parsons lauds Marx for his attack on individualism, he contends, nevertheless, that Marx made "no fundamental modification of the general theory of human social behavior."[20†]

If order is reduced to an epiphenomenon of action, such "fundamental modifications" must be reserved for theorists who have attacked the instrumental postulate. It is precisely for this reason that Parsons devotes so much of his attention in *The Structure of Social Action* to Durkheim and Weber. It is this same, basically conflationary, perspective that makes his interpretations of these thinkers so ambiguous.

In Parsons' analysis of Durkheim, for example, he confuses Durkheim's rejection of instrumental rationalism with his criticism of individualism. Thus, in discussing Durkheim's critique of Spencer, he presents him as dissatisfied with contract theory because of its individualism. In contrast to Spencer, Parsons believes Durkheim had a clear vision of the "uniformities of behavior," that is, of the way individual action is collectively ordered.[21] In the very next passage, however, he characterizes Durkheim's critique as an attack on Spencer's rationalism: "As has been pointed out, Durkheim's most fundamental critique of Utilitarian individualism was on the grounds of its inability to account for the elements of normative order in society."[22] Durkheim's position on order, in other words, is explained by his position on instrumental action. By implying that a normative theory presents the only alternative to an individualist one, Parsons neatly side-steps the intellectual tradition initiated by Bentham, Ricardo, and Marx.

Parsons also tries to justify Durkheim's excessively normative emphasis by conflating, once again, presuppositional order with empirical stability. Durkheim turned to normative order, Parsons asserts, because other options implied an unrealistic degree of social conflict. Durkheim thus correctly perceived the connection between moral commitment and social equilibrium; he realized, in Parsons words, that "the ultimate source of power behind sanctions is the common sense of moral attachment to norms—and the weaker that becomes, the larger the minority who do not share it, [and] the more precarious is the order in question."[23]

Protected by the camouflage of such conflationary reasoning, Parsons only equivocally applies a multidimensional standard to Durkheim's theory. We can now see that even his famous critique of Durkheim's idealism is highly inconsistent.[24†] In the first place, Parsons argues that Durkheim moves toward idealism only in his final work. I have indicated in volume 2 (chs. 7–8), to the contrary, that once Durkheim had abandoned the contradictory structure of *The Division of Labor in Society*, he was consistently committed to an exclusively normative approach. In fact, Parsons is not arguing here against Durkheim's sociological idealism: he is contesting idealism only in the purely epistemological sense. Parsons believes that Durkheim in *The Elementary Forms of Religious Life* adopts a neo-Kantian perspective that leads him to accept a priori mental conceptions as the basis of society, categories which operate outside time and space. If this path were actually followed, Parsons argues, sociology would not differ from literary interpretation; social values would be analyzed "in themselves" rather than in relation to the exigencies of human interaction.[25] Parsons' objection, in other words, is that Durkheim adopted a purely idealist epistemology, not that Durkheim overlooked instrumental action or coercive order. But it is perfectly possible to emphasize the reality of the world external to the individual mind—to discuss concrete human interaction and the relation of values to institutions—and still to theorize in a sociologically idealist way.[26†]

Although Parsons believes that Durkheim is not an idealist because most of his work "retains a place for the Utilitarian elements of action," he fails to scrutinize carefully the role such elements actually play in Durkheim's schema.[27] In so doing Parsons forgets his own earlier injunction against the rationalist position. The problem with Utilitarianism, he argued in the first part of *The Structure of Social Action*, is not that it actually eliminates normative elements but that by making them exclusively instrumental it effectively ignores their effect.[28] To fully understand the problem of sociological idealism, Parsons would have had to develop the inverse of this logic: the problem does not come from eliminating instrumental elements but rather from treating them as if they were fully regulated by nonrational commitments. But although this understanding is implicit throughout the multidimensional strand of his work, Parsons never articulates this logic in an explicit way. In terms of his self-conscious critical logic, then, the problem of sociological materialism receives far greater attention. This unequal emphasis is portentous of the strains that develop in his later writing.

The same strand of idealist reduction distorts Parsons' treatment of Weber. We have seen how in analyzing Weber's sociology of religion Parsons strongly asserts its multidimensional quality, particularly its interweaving of political structures and classes with religious rationalization. This reflects Parsons' own multidimensional bent.[29†] The recognition of this emphasis must now be balanced, however, against less synthetic aspects of Parsons' treatment. First, he ignores the unresolved tensions between instrumental and normative order that permeate even Weber's sociology of religion. More importantly, however, he completely ignores Weber's substantive political sociology, the historical discussions of the transition from patriarchal household to feudal and patrimonial systems which revolve almost exclusively around instrumental motivation and coercive force. Only by ignoring this discussion can Parsons construe Weber's political sociology as focusing on the problem of legitimacy in primarily moral and symbolic terms, as a problem in which the concept of charisma plays a pivotal role.[30]

The Structure of Social Action, then, constructs two agendas for social theory. In part 1, Parsons provides what amounts to a multidimensional framework for theoretical logic. Yet this synthetic standard is marred because the critique of materialism is much more explicit and self-conscious than that of idealism. Moreover, multidimensionality is applied in parts 2 and 3 only in a highly uneven way. Further, and most importantly, this multidimensional purpose is cross-cut by a contradictory, idealist interpretation of the history of the sociological tradition. Parsons repeatedly defines normative order as the preferable—if not the only—reference point for collectivist theorizing, and he presents classical theory as a progressive movement toward such a symbolic and normative emphasis.

The faults that Parsons finds with classical theory are, in this strand of his argument, more "methodological" than presuppositional. Durkheim's central problem was not his failure to relate norms to conditions but rather his inability to clarify the relation between norms and individuals. If Durkheim had taken a more analytic, rather than concrete, approach to the individual, he could have transcended the individual/society problem; such "analytic theory" would also have allowed him to avoid the embarrassment of epistemological idealism.[31] Weber, on the other hand, undermined his discussion of modernity by occasionally lapsing into a neo-utilitarian mode. Once again, Parsons turns to a methodological rather than presuppositional critique. If Weber had utilized an analytical rather than ideal-typical approach to action, he argues, such lapses could have been avoided. Moreover, such analytic theorizing would have allowed Weber to present his generally successful approach to normative order in the form of a self-conscious and cumulative theory of society rather than as a series of historical essays.[32]

In this second strand of his argument, then, Parsons' aim is to construct an analytic sociology that can more successfully articulate the presuppositional emphases of his classical predecessors. Insofar as he has characterized the latter as oriented primarily to normative order, his own theory seeks to become an analytically more sophisticated version of sociological idealism.

2. IDEALISM IN THE MIDDLE PERIOD: THE SOCIAL SYSTEM AS "GROUND" FOR CULTURE AND PERSONALITY

Parsons' middle-period work must be viewed, in part, as an attempt to provide just such an analytic resolution. Despite this ambition, however, the essays of the early middle period remain directly rooted in the conceptual structure of classical theory. Furthermore, Parsons is preoccupied throughout this early period with the empirical problems of international conflict and social reconstruction. For both these reasons, his idealist reconstruction of the sociological tradition upon more sophisticated analytic lines is much less distinct than it becomes in the later work. The tendency is present nonetheless, and it produces a disturbing, one-dimensional undertone for many of the individual essays.

For example, although the pattern-variable schema—certainly the major conceptual innovation of this period—is in no sense inherently opposed to a multidimensional focus, Parsons often treats it more as an alternative to instrumental-conditional order than as a modification of it. In only his second effort to conceptualize this scheme, "The Motivation of Economic Activity," in 1940, this idealist strategy becomes quite explicit. The problem with the rationalist approach to economic activity, Parsons writes, is that by dealing with exclusively instrumental self-interest it is "almost random" in its approach to the aggregation of individual acts. If one postulates only instrumental self-interest, he argues, "society could scarcely be an order" at all.[33]

While more specified empirically, this logic echoes Parsons' presuppositional argument in *The Structure of Social Action*. Economic activity is inherently individualistic; the only way to provide collective order is to focus on the kind of supra-individual constraint provided by norms. Yet, as in *The Structure of Social Action*, this is more of an argument for sociological idealism than an objective statement of the nature of presuppositional logic or actual empirical necessity. As Marx and Weber both demonstrated, rationalist theory can certainly structure instrumental self-interest in a collective way. By focusing on the organization of scarce means, it postulates particular forms of economic or political arrangements. Parsons ignores this option. Collective order, he implicitly argues, can be achieved only by organizing ends, not means. Economic order is accomplished by the normative pattern-variables of achievement, specificity, universalism, and affective neutrality. In one form or another, this argument is repeated throughout Parsons' subsequent work.[34†]

By his later middle period, Parsons had more fully established an independent conceptual scheme; his focus, in addition, was less tied to any particular empirical concerns. This idealist strand of his work became, as a result, much more pronounced.

The critical ambivalence in *The Social System* revolves around the relation of psychological, social, and cultural systems. The problem is already clearly revealed in the first chapter, where, it will be recalled, Parsons moves from a consideration of the problem of action, to the differentiation of action's objects into physical, social, and cultural types, and finally to the organization of these objects into the orders of personality, culture, and society.[35†] Although he formally allows each of these three types of objects to comprise both means and ends, he tends, in fact, to limit the status of means to nonhuman, physical objects alone.[36] Since it is human objects, of course, that form the principal focus of Parsons' study, this limitation legitimates inattention to the instrumental element in human affairs.

Correspondingly, despite his formal distinction between instrumental, expressive, and moral dimensions within each of the levels he has identified, Parsons focuses much more on the expressive and moral dimensions than on instrumental ones. It is true that the social system and its "scarce exigencies"—which produce pressure for the organization of needs and commitments—presents a vital point of theoretical reference; nonetheless, these exigencies are treated, in this chapter, in a distinctly secondary way. If the independence of the social system were not acknowledged, Parsons warns, no "real," extra-individual objects could be described, and society would be viewed as the perfect congruence between individual personality and cultural demands. If modern theory made such an error, Parsons believes, it would replicate the epistemological idealism he attributed to Durkheim. Parsons will not make this mistake: he recognizes the autonomy of the social level. As a result, he can avoid also a more modern failing: the facile, fundamentally idealist identification of symbolic patterns and psychological needs espoused by the "culture and personality" school of anthropology.[37†] Yet it is upon this primarily negative justification that Parsons' treatment of scarce societal exigencies concludes. Instead of making social system exigencies into active, independent variables in their own right, he usually conceptualizes them, in this introductory chapter, simply as providing the differentiated "ground" upon which psychological and cultural imperatives interact. True, the social system's independence guarantees that *epistemological* idealism will be avoided; but if this autonomy is conceptualized in a primarily passive way, the culture/society/personality trichotomy can still be used to elaborate idealism in a more *sociological* form.[38†]

In chapters 2 and 3 of *The Social System,* Parsons elaborates this sociologically idealist approach to the social system in greater detail. There are, he writes, two types of "functional requisites," those concerned with biological considerations like nutrition and physical survival and those that address more social kinds of problems which can be classified under the general heading of the "need to secure adequate participation."[39] This problem of participation, in turn, has two different aspects; participation can be achieved by expediency, "where conformity or non-conformity is a function of the instrumental interests of the actor," or through value commitment, in which internalization guarantees that conformity "becomes a need disposition of the actor's own personality."[40] Whereas in the multidimensional strand of his argument—as formulated particularly in the later chapters 4 and 5—Parsons refuses to make any choice between these modes of gaining participation, here he tilts sharply toward the normative pole. He argues that instrumental interest can secure participation "only in the limiting case"; the "predominant" form of participation is voluntary and value-oriented, occurring "relatively independently of any instrumentally significant consequences."[41] The problem of participation has become the problem of "motivation." The specifically social category of functional requisites must be viewed as concerned primarily with the integration of psychological cathexis and normative patterns.[42] "This integration of a set of common value patterns with the internalized need-disposition structure of the constituent personalities," Parsons now writes, "*is the core phenomenon of the dynamics of social systems.*"[43] On the basis of this idealist understanding of society's "core," Parsons now defines collective order entirely without reference to instrumental conditions. Although he acknowledges that "an integrated structure of action elements" must be defined "in relation to a situation"—it must, in other words, have a social-system referent—he argues that the aggregation of action, or collective order, consists essentially in the "integration of motivational and cultural or symbolic elements."[44]

In view of his earlier presuppositional confusion, it is not surprising that Parsons now conflates this presuppositional reduction with an empirical commitment to equilibrium. To focus on norms, he asserts, is to focus on the problem of empirical stability: instrumental activity is residual because continual instability and disruption is the exception rather than the rule.[45] When Hobbes suggests that men become enemies because they "desire the same thing which nevertheless they cannot both have," he argued from scarcity and instrumentalism to the likelihood of empirical conflict. Parsons has turned Hobbes' error on its head, arguing that if actors engage in normative, noninstrumental action their activities must be complementary.[46†] In opposition to the Hobbesian solution and its Benthamite and Marxian legacy, Parsons argues that modern sociology must pursue a more Lockean path. It can do so, however, only by marrying Durkheim with Freud, by combining the analysis of symbolic values with the "implication of modern psychological knowledge" about cathexis and internalization.[47] Modern social theory, in other words, should devote itself to elaborating the Durkheim-Freud synthesis; as far as Weber's legacy is concerned, theory can incorporate only the normative aspects of his work.

To begin this task, Parsons lays out in chapter 3 the basic empirical components of social systems. He starts with an ideal-typical relationship of instrumental exchange and enumerates four basic problems that such a relationship produces: cooperation, remuneration, access to, and disposal of, facilities.[48] These problems, he asserts, present the four basic points of societal differentiation, and, consequently, the principal foci for the distribution of social roles. But instead of following up this fourfold division by analyzing the dialectic of allocation and integration—the path he takes in the multidimensional strand of his analysis—Parsons defines sociology as being primarily concerned with the value orientations around which, he assumes, these instrumental tasks must become institutionalized: "The specifically sociological problem focus with reference to such a [differentiated] system . . . concerns the kind of value orientations which are institutionalized in it."[49] Social roles are now defined simply as specifications of these institutionalized value standards.[50] The basic structures of social systems, then, can be derived from value orientations; Parsons proceeds, in fact, to cross-tabulate the pattern-variable combinations—values like specificity-neutrality and diffuseness-affectivity—with the various instrumental and expressive exigencies they control.[51†] He concludes by affirming the centrality of the Durkheim-Freud synthesis: "The bases of differentiation," he writes, are "found in the motivational structure of an actor's orientation and in the cultural value-standards which are built into it."[52†]

In chapters 4 and 5, of course, Parsons' approach to social structure is very much different. Though he still is concerned with value patterns and normative solidarity, he combines these emphases with attention to the more instrumental aspects of allocation and integration.[53†] This switch of emphasis, however, poses a real threat to the continuity of Parsons' argument. There is a real sense in which he simply ignores the dissonance between these multidimensional and idealist treatments. Indeed, given his profound ambiguity, both strands of argument are internally coherent and stand quite effectively on their own.[54†]

But Parsons is committed to systematization and deductive logic, and he is bound to present at least some rationale for the bracketing of his multidimensional allocation-integration scheme. He does so by offering a distinction between relational and regulative institutions.[55] The first he defines as the core institutions concerned with value patterning and emotional control. Because some actors behave in ways that are "independent of the moral-integrative patterning of the social system," however, these relational institutions are not sufficient and regulative institutions become necessary. Regulative institutions concern primarily "ecological" processes,"[56] which Parsons defines as involving "a plurality of actors who are not integrated by bonds of solidarity . . . but who are [still] objects to one another."[57] Ecological processes, in other words, involve the dominance of instrumental order, and Parsons includes in this category every institutional situation that imposes order in an efficient way, including, particularly, the economic and political spheres. He argues, however, that such regulatory institutions must be viewed as peripheral to the fundamental processes of social systems, and in doing so he departs radically from the multidimensional focus of his allocation-integration scheme.[58] Parsons admits, of course, that political and economic activities can and do become the focus of significant social activity and that they have, as a result, been the objects of extensive sociological analysis. He emphasizes, nonetheless, that such activity operates only within parameters established by institutionalized values and motivations.[59] Any sociological treatment of economics or politics must take account of this fact.

In keeping with this tendency to bracket instrumental considerations, Parsons concludes his important multidimensional discussion in chapter 5 by reversing his field, returning to a one-dimensional, normative point of view. He argues that institutional differentiation is derived not from the interaction of normative and instrumental orders but rather from the elective affinities of cultural patterns themselves, affinities which, he believes, are articulated by the different pattern-variable combinations.[60†] Parsons was always profoundly ambivalent about the pattern variables and their role in his developing theory. When the patterns of specificity and achievement were first introduced in a "Note" in *The Structure of Social Action,* he used them simply to characterize in more precise terms Tönnies' *Gesellschaft,* a conception which, he argued, referred to the same kinds of instrumental and political phenomena described by Marx.[61] Parsons first used the pattern variables, in other words, to characterize "factual order." At another point in *The Structure of Social Action,* however, he introduces a third pattern variable, universalism/particularism, in the context of his Weberian analysis of social values as derived from comparative religious differences.[62] This treatment, in effect, established the other pole of Parsons' future pattern-variable analysis, for it treats values as prior patterns from which instrumental arrangements are derived.

This ambivalence is continued in *The Social System*.[63†] In chapter 4 and a good part of chapter 5, Parsons describes institutional differentiation as being derived from the interaction of material strains and cultural patterning. In these discussions, the pattern-variable combinations are employed to represent the input of cultural patterning and, even more importantly, to characterize the cultural implications of the institutional differentiation that finally emerges. This strategy is illustrated, for example, in the discussion of the ascriptive and achievement "complexes." Here Parsons used the pattern-variable designations to characterize two ideal-typical forms of association, and describes association as the result of interpenetrating psychological, organizational, and symbolic pressures.[64†]

In the idealist strand of his analysis, which includes not only chapters 2 and 3 but the latter part of chapter 5 as well, Parsons takes a far different approach to the pattern variables. Institutional differentiation is directly derived from different pattern-variable combinations, which in turn emerge from intrinsic symbolic affinities.[65†] In a purely voluntaristic fashion, Parsons argues here that it is individual *choices* which determine situations;[66] for example, he views "achievement" and "ascription" as inherent in the culturally defined qualities of internalized objects themselves. To discover whether an action or institution belongs in the achievement or ascriptive complex, he asks, in effect, "what do the objects involved *mean?*" The gist of Parsons' multidimensional analysis is now reversed, and value patterns are utilized to define the possibilities of scarcity and instrumental action. He argues that the instrumental complex of possessions and the ecological nexus of economic and political organization have become significant in modern society simply because of the emergence of universalistic and achievement orientations. [67]

It is on this basis—a concern for what is "logically possible" in cultural terms[68]—that Parsons proceeds to derive the principal "empirical clusters" of modern social institutions: he describes the basis of kinship collectivities, territorial organization, the centrality of political force, and the extension of class solidarity in an idealistic manner which significantly contradicts his earlier analysis of these same phenomena.[69] From an important element in his multidimensional theory, the pattern-variable scheme has been transformed into cultural hermeneutics. This is not to say, of course, that this hermeneutical strategy is not a major achievement in itself. In their idealistic form, the pattern variables provide a systematic classification of cultural tendencies and their sociological implications unparalleled in the history of sociological thought. They allow Parsons to establish law-like statements about cultural life that far surpass the idiographic quality which undermines the general relevance of most cultural studies. Even in this idealist effort, then, Parsons builds upon the achievements of Weber, although he does so in a one-dimensional manner that Weber would not endorse.[70†]

In an important sense, the remainder of *The Social System* may be viewed as an analysis of how these crucially significant pattern-variable combinations are sustained through the exigencies of social-system interaction. Since Parsons' idealist approach to the problem of normative order—what I have called his Durkheim-Freud synthesis—has both a psychological and a cultural dimension, his energy is devoted to describing the specific mechanisms by which societies integrate pattern-variable combinations with the personality and the cultural systems.

In the multidimensional aspect of his work, Parsons treats socialization as a transitional process between the earlier, value-oriented institutions and the later, more conditional environments of the life cycle, a process which guarantees that the later, more instrumental pressures will be mediated by at least some internal reference. In contrast, in the idealist strand of his thinking, where cultural patterns actually create basic social structures, socialization assumes a much more pivotal role. Although he acknowledges the existence of the "process of allocation of facilities and rewards," Parsons now argues that this process is interesting only "from the motivational point of view."[71] He believes, in other words, that the allocation of personnel overshadows the problems generated by the allocation of facilities and rewards. From this reductionist perspective, socialization not only allocates personnel by producing value internalization but, in a crucial sense, creates the social roles and institutions in which this personnel will later participate.[72] Beginning with a society's pattern-variable combinations, Parsons employs his theory of psychological identification to describe how these "social structures" become internalized.[73] To deal with the specific conditional challenges which the adult may encounter, he develops a theory of "secondary identifications" which demonstrates how generalized motivation is adapted to the complex actuality of social system life.[74†]

The other side of this exclusive concentration on learning is Parsons' exaggerated concern for the psychocultural aspects of deviance and social control. As I indicated earlier, Parsons' deviance theory can be understood in a distinctively multidimensional way.[75†] Since from a multidimensional perspective social order is normative as well as instrumental, disequilibrium is related to a variety of strains, both symbolic and conditional. In response to the normative violation and subsequent emotional reaction that creates deviance, social control mechanisms combine a range of coercive and symbolic sanctions and rewards. In the idealist strand of his work, Parsons distorts this account by placing deviance in the context of his twofold conflation of the order concept. "The crucial significance of this [deviance] problem," he writes, "derives . . . from two fundamental considerations," first, "the fact . . . that all social action is normatively oriented," and, second, that these norms must, to an important degree, "be common to the actors in an institutionally integrated . . . system."[76] Deviance, in other words, focuses on the problems that norms face in maintaining equilibrium.

Nonetheless, Parsons begins his substantive discussion of deviance by arguing that strains are, after all, produced by the social situation. The action of significant others is variable and unpredictable; more importantly, societies are rife with role conflicts that impose irreconcilable demands.[77†] But this characterization of the origins of these strains and their effects is shortly enmeshed in Parsons' reduction of collective order to the dialectic of Durkheim and Freud. "In the analysis of deviance," he writes, "we must focus on . . . the *orientation* of the individual actor . . . to the situation itself, including above all the significant *social* objects."[78] According to Parsons' idealist reduction, it will be recalled, social objects are only ends, never means.[79†] Parsons must, therefore, deal with conflicts between individuals and roles—the disruptions created by social objects—only as strains in the organization of ends, as the disruption of cultural patterns and internalizations rather than as the disorganization of means and the imposition of scarcity. Relating differential structural possibilities for deviance to different kinds of pattern-variable clusters, Parsons translates situational conflicts into pattern-variable strains.[80] The problems generated by industrial organization and bureaucracy, for example, are treated principally in terms of conflicts between the impersonal norms that regulate work and the personalistic norms that govern family life.

Since normative order rests upon internalized cathexis, the strains produced by cultural conflict are, in the first place, affective ones. Deviance begins, according to Parsons, when alter acts in a manner "frustrating" to ego. Alter blocks the gratification ego had obtained from alter's earlier attitudes, that is, the pleasure from his internalization of alter as a loving object or as a symbol of cathected values.[81] Parsons traces the impact of this affective frustration psychologically: it creates an ambivalence which takes the form of either compulsive conformity or alienation. Such compulsive conformity or alienation—in either an active or a passive form—then becomes structured in support groups and legitimated as deviant behavior.[82]

My intention here is not to minimize the empirical contribution Parsons makes by his complex and subtle interweaving of cultural and psychological variables.[83] Parsons demonstrates, for example, that normative abstraction and impersonality induce strain because they make communication highly ambiguous; that compulsive conformity—despite its invisibility to the casual observer—can be as serious a deviant problem as compulsive rebellion; and that deviance often "splits" motivation in such a way that different institutionalized demands can be fulfilled and denied by the same individual actor. In terms of social control, he calls attention to the crucial significance of emotional and cultural response; to the informal sanctions which usually make more formal measures unnecessary; and to the crucial role of "bridge" elements—the term he applies to individuals and institutions who are intermediate between deviants and established authorities and who can, as a consequence, effectively mediate the process of reintegration.

My criticism, rather, is a presuppositional one. These empirical insights are not sufficiently combined with a multidimensional approach. Too often, Parsons shunts "reality factors" into the status of residual categories. While he admits that questions of instrumental advantage, such as whether deviance "pays" and whether it is possible to "get away with it," inevitably enter the picture,[84] he argues that "from the point of view of the central dynamics of the social system they are not the core problem."[85] The real concerns of deviance theory "[are] to be found in the balance of forces involved in the building up and the counteraction of *motivation* to deviance," not to the forces that make deviance instrumentally advantageous.[86] Because Parsons has refused to consider situations where ends are stable—where norms are "realistically" internalized and cathected—and where it is the disorganization of means which creates deviance, his psychological reference appears to resemble the invidious caricature drawn by his critics. Since values are now an exclusive focus, and values are achieved only through cathexis, deviance can be described as an internal, not an external problem. It is tied to fantasy and the distortion of ends and goals, not to the realistic perception of the inadequacy of the available means.[87†]

Parsons' analysis of the left/right, radical/conservative polarization in Western society illustrates this tendency very well. In his earlier multidimensional analyses of social change, he concentrated as much on the objective forces of rationalization as on its psychological and cultural aspects.[88†] Now, however, he refers only to the "discipline" modern societies impose on their members, a factor which he relates to the influence of the pattern variables of affective neutrality, achievement, and specificity.[89†] In the light of the romantic-utopian elements which are a part of the cultural life of every modern society, he suggests, such discipline creates frustration and ambivalence. These emotions can be channeled in either an alienative or a conformistic direction. The alienative pole, which creates left-wing politics, is encouraged because the universalism of Western values makes it difficult for authorities to deny the legitimacy of the radical critique.[90] While this formulation is certainly not without empirical interest, by focusing exclusively on such normative and psychological concerns Parsons has offered an idealist explanation of political deviance. In line with his Durkheim-Freud synthesis and his normative reading of Weber, he has considered social-system scarcity merely as a passive ground for the interplay of psychological and cultural forces.[91†]

The same kinds of problems distort Parsons' treatment of social control. In his multidimensional work, Parsons used psychotherapy as a model to develop a typology of control sanctions, which he links to both normative and instrumental order. The sanctions of "permissiveness" and "support" are psychological and cultural, while the "manipulation of rewards" and the "withdrawal of reciprocity" refer to more instrumental political and economic forces.[92†] In this idealist strand of analysis, however, Parsons actually views social control as functionally equivalent to psychotherapy, thereby limiting such control to restoration of the motivational and symbolic elements of social order. While he acknowledges that "compulsion" and the "appeal to rational decisions through coercion or inducement" may deter deviance in certain instances, he argues that the "subtle, underlying motivational aspects" are far more important.[93]

Parsons now treats the four social-control sanctions as different modes of affect, corresponding to four different kinds of psychological reactions to strain.[94] In keeping with his focus on ends rather than means, social control becomes the resocialization of deviant motivation; and the importance of restructuring instrumental means and external opportunities becomes increasingly obscured. When he considers the political aspects of control, for example, he discusses the state apparatus only in its relation to the motivational problems of deviant citizens. Partisan, polarizing attempts to restore legitimacy are counterproductive because they simply reinforce aggressive fantasies of compulsive alienation. Impersonal, consensual leadership, in contrast, cannot be drawn into the vicious circle of deviant motivation; as a result, it can play a much more effective therapeutic role.[95] In his multidimensional analysis, Parsons viewed effective consensual elites as indications that structural factors had allowed the separation of social control from the sources of institutional strain.[96†] Now, however, the structural forces giving rise to different types of elites are much less important than the psychocultural environment to which they contribute.

Once again, my point is not that Parsons has failed to introduce interesting empirical propositions. In discussing the challenge of therapeutic control, for example, he analyzes such issues as the importance of the timing of therapeutic efforts, the role of institutional priorities, indirect sanctions, the insulation and isolation of deviance, and the self-control of deviance through ritual. My objection to such analysis, rather, is presuppositional. In his multidimensional discussion, Parsons argues that the first and most important defense against deviance is the authoritative restructuring of the "artificial identity of interest"; he treats the "contingent reintegration" presented by psychotherapy as an option not only less effective but less frequently resorted to.[97†] In his idealist analysis, this order is reversed. It is, after all, the Lockean "natural identity of interests" to which Parsons directs his attention in this idealist mode, and he illuminates this by focusing on normative and voluntary elements, not on instrumental and deterministic ones.[98†]

The remainder of Parsons' discussion in *The Social System* generally follows this idealist thrust. In chapters 8 and 9, he focuses on the cultural problem of organizing cognitive and expressive symbols. In the chapter following, the psychological and cultural points he has established become parameters for his examination of a specific interactional context—namely, the social system formed by the doctor-patient relationship. While his penultimate chapter on social change constitutes a return to the multidimensional theme, his concluding chapter can be read as an apologia that seeks to legitimate sociology as a discipline specializing in the reductionist program he has set forth in the earlier chapters.[99†]

Even in the idealist strand of *The Social System,* it should be emphasized, Parsons never ignores the existence of conditional order as such. To do so would be to engage in the very epistemological idealism which he consistently rejected since the beginning of his career. Rather, he acknowledges instrumental conditions as givens which—while not of independent interest in themselves—create "problems" which must be addressed by the psychological and cultural sources of normative order. While instrumental conditions cannot constitute a satisfactory solution to social order, they still must be controlled. That his idealism is sociological, not epistemological, can be seen from a central paradox in this strand of Parsons' work: while he rejects cultural "emanationism" and psychological determinism, he accepts, nevertheless, the existence of a "natural identity of interest" based upon the interpenetration of individuals by cultural symbols. The problem with cultural and psychological idealists from Hegel to Ruth Benedict, Parsons believes, is not that they accepted the dominance of nonrational factors but that they explained this dominance simply as the logical unfolding of *Geist* or the projective expansion of personality. In asserting such a relation between culture or personality and society, however, these theorists ignored the autonomy of the social system. In doing so, they sidestepped what Parsons views as the much more difficult problem, which is to explain not simply the workings of culture or personality but rather the mediating mechanisms by which both become institutionalized in complex social structures that serve ecological populations of strikingly diverse interests and activities.[100†]

Ten years after *The Social System,* Parsons repeated this objection. "Theories which have approached the philosophically idealist pole," he wrote in *Theories of Society,* "have continually been forced into postulating a mysterious process of emanation which, like Locke's identity of interest, becomes a name for a problem rather than a solution for it."[101] Parsons solves Locke's problem by making this mysterious process of normative order explicit. In place of the hidden, residual categories of classical economics, he describes in a detailed, empirically oriented way the congruence of society, culture, and personality.

3. CONCLUSION

Considered in its entirety, then, Parsons' middle-period work appears highly uneven and, indeed, internally contradictory. It is precisely this ambiguity that has eluded most interpreters. Lockwood and Rex, for example, who have produced the most articulate critiques of this phase of Parsons' normative reduction, view his work as consistently idealist, dismissing his multidimensional allusions simply as formal statements that are never substantively elaborated.[102] One group of Parsons' more sympathetic interpreters dismisses these attacks simply as "misreadings," arguing that Parsons maintains a consistent, multidimensional perspective throughout his work.[103] Other sympathetic readers, by a curious sort of convergence, actually accept the idealist reading of Parsons as valid, but view it as a positive and necessary solution to the problem of order. They, too, claim that Parsons' commitment to this position is consistent throughout his career.[104]

Beyond the false insistence on intellectual consistency, these interpretations are often motivated by presuppositional errors of their own. Lockwood and Rex actually use Parsons as a foil for their own theorizing, in which they reproduce a mirror image of the errors they have criticized in Parsons. While paying formal homage to multidimensionality, they tend to reduce order to its instrumental base and conflate the perception of empirical conflict with attention to material conditions.[105†] In a similar way, Parsons' sympathetic readers tend to confuse epistemological with sociological multidimensionality, defending sociological idealism as a satisfactory option simply because it takes cognizance of the objective world.[106†]

I have argued, for my part, that Parsons' work suffers from a fundamental ambiguity. His early and middle work often conflates presuppositional order with empirical equilibrium. More importantly, within the presuppositional level itself, the synthetic, objective standard of multidimensionality is never consistently maintained. These debilitating problems continue in Parsons' later work.

Chapter Nine

THE PRESUPPOSITIONAL ERROR(2)

Idealist Reduction in the Later Writings

The interchange model that Parsons develops in his later work is ineluctably multidimensional; his idealist deviation in no way affects the presuppositional nature of this formulation. It is rather when he applies or specifies the interchange model in social analysis that he tends toward an idealist reduction. Although, as I demonstrated in chapter 4, Parsons devotes considerable energy to utilizing interchange in a multidimensional way, he continually cross-cuts this application by deemphasizing the tension between the model's conditional and normative dimensions. Parsons demonstrates an alarming propensity to present "adaptative" and "goal-attainment" institutions simply as facilitating the realization of norms and values, neglecting their functional capacity for antithesis and negation vis-à-vis normative ideals. He tends, correspondingly, to portray norms and values as successfully controlling and regulating power and economics rather than as simply attempting to do so. Too often, indeed, the cybernetic hierarchy is presented as an empirical assessment of causal importance rather than as an epistemological description of analytic relationship.

IDEALISM IN THE LATER WRITINGS (1): INTERCHANGE AS THE ANALYTIC ARGUMENT FOR NORMATIVE ORDER

Parsons created interchange so that he could systematically differentiate integration and pattern maintenance from the more instrumental dimensions to facilitate theoretical synthesis. In this way, he made it clear that every concrete act is analytically multidimensional.[1†] Insofar as this differentiation becomes a means to focus exclusively on order's normative elements, the model's potential is perverted. Interchange then becomes merely an analytically more sophisticated approach to Durkheim's "crucial experiment," not an exercise in systematic theorizing.[2†]

1.1. ECONOMIC INTERCHANGE AS THE NORMATIVE ALTERNATIVE TO CLASSICAL ECONOMICS

In my earlier account I analyzed the way in which Parsons and Smelser utilized interchange to counter the individualistic notions of economic theory, describing the multidimensional, analytic interdependence of the economic and noneconomic factors of production.[3†] In this context, each boundary between economy and society is subjected to the tension and trade-off between the economy's outputs of money and conditional pressures on the one hand, and the less adaptive exigencies produced by the noneconomic dimensions of politics, solidarity, and pattern maintenance on the other. Yet alongside of, and, indeed, often dominating this balanced analysis, there runs a much more one-sided account. In this version, economy is subordinated to "society." In presuppositional terms, Parsons and Smelser ignore the multidimensional alternative to individualistic rationalism and devote themselves, instead, to demonstrating the importance of nonrational, collective regulation. In so doing, they follow the minimalist critique of classical economic rationality Parsons established in *The Structure of Social Action*, where he underplayed the instrumental, collectivist alternative and formulated the problem as a simple dichotomy between an individualistic economics and a normative sociology.

In terms of the pattern maintenance-economy exchange, I focused in that earlier discussion primarily on the relationship between money and labor power. But Parsons and Smelser actually deal also with a second exchange, the economy's provision of goods and services for the family's consumer spending. They are concerned here, however, only with one particular empirical problem: the fact that consumer spending does not vary directly with individual income. The classical economists, they argue, could not satisfactorily explain this problem, first, because they tended to ignore supra-individual constraint per se, and, second, because when they considered such constraint at all they could do so only rationalistically—in their focus on the interest rate as the principal explanation for variation in consumer spending.[4] Keynes made some progress beyond this point with his famous "consumption function," which stated that the proportion of spending declines as total income increases. Yet this remained simply an empirical generalization, indeed a residual category, within the context of economic theory.[5] The only way to break through this impasse, Parsons and Smelser argue, is to adopt the theoretical framework of interchange and to acknowledge that consumer spending is a pattern-maintenance decision, not an adaptive one.[6] It occurs in the family, and its primary function is not to satisfy biological needs. Yet sociologically more important than its simple pattern-maintenance location is the fact that consumption occurs "because man, as human personality, must be provided with the symbolic media for learning and implementing values in human relations."[7] Parsons and Smelser subsequently analyze in considerable detail the symbolic, familial exigencies around which consumption is organized, and they conclude that spending "varies in accordance with *value* changes," that, in fact, it "is relatively *invariant* in the face of moderate economic changes."[8]

Although producing a plausible and interesting answer to a particular empirical problem, Parsons and Smelser have limited their discussion of the consumption exchange to the terms established by the Durkheim-Freud synthesis. In terms of the action problem, they vastly underplay the role of instrumental rationality. Dismissing the "situational exigencies" involved in consumption as of only peripheral interest, they ignore, indeed, what is particularly "economic" about consumption.[9] What separates consumer spending, after all, from purely symbolic expression is the way it is influenced by its connection to instrumental, economic pressures. Because spending is subject to market considerations, this form of cultural expression is of a particular type.

This weakness in Parsons and Smelser's analysis also bears on their treatment of the "problem of order." Parsons and Smelser ignore the relation between consumer spending and what Halèvy called the "artificial identification of interest," that is, the way that this form of cultural expression is patterned not only by values but by the distribution of wealth and the peculiarities of the productive process. In this sense, they turn Marx's analysis of the reproduction of labor power on its head. Where Marx emphasized only the instrumental and biological sources of consumption, Parsons and Smelser discuss only the cultural and psychological. Marx's theory of consumption placed normative order in a residual category—"Besides the mere physical element of life the value of labor is in every country determined by the traditional standard of life."[10] Parsons and Smelser similarly slant their argument, treating adaptive considerations only in a negative way. In doing so, they echo the later Durkheim's emphasis on the normative and sacred over the instrumental elements of contract.

This bias cross-cuts the multidimensional analysis Parsons and Smelser provide for the wages-labor power exchange, which they conceptualize in terms of the "Resource Chart." The Resource Chart, it will be recalled, includes seven distinctive phases involved in the transformation of labor power from unsocialized motivation to actual participation in a productive enterprise.[11†] In terms of its multidimensional reference, this scheme is effective because it differentiates the instrumental from the symbolic aspects of resource utilization, "the sequence by which 'labour-power' is created," on the one hand, from the sequence by which it is "utilized in production," on the other,[12] or, as Smelser writes at another point, the distinction between the "motivation to work" and the "rewards to work."[13] The middle stage of this sequence is the labor market, which because of its intermediate position between pattern maintenance and organization is the phase during which actors are particularly sensitive to instrumental sanctions. Yet in their utilization of this model, Parsons and Smelser focus on the earlier stages of labor production alone, on the stages located in the pattern-maintenance system that refer to phases of preadult socialization. In doing so, they have concentrated on normative order, on the culture-personality matrix, at the expense of order's instrumental face. But it is the labor market that presents the prototypical situation where economic-class position and material resources are the decisive regulators of individual action. When Parsons and Smelser choose to focus primarily on the nonrational arrangements that precede this phase of material ordering, they reverse Marx's emphasis rather than follow the multidimensional alternative provided by the interchange model.

The same kind of problem undermines their discussion of the economy's other boundary relations. When they write, for example, that the integrative rules which regulate economic life are "largely independent" of specifically adaptive exigencies, they tend to take this as an argument for complete empirical autonomy rather than a presuppositional argument for the analytic separation of integrative inputs. Thus, in writing later about the important impact of the laws which sanction individual over familial forms of ownership, Parsons emphasizes the cultural basis of the transition to entrepreneurial capitalism. Similarly, by focusing on the "entrepreneurial function" in their analysis of the integrative sector's less formal inputs to economic life, Parsons and Smelser ignore what is at least an equally significant input, namely, the way in which class solidarity is structured by common productive position.[14†] They claim, furthermore, that the economic input to what they regard as the integrative phenomenon of stratification has primarily cultural implications, because "appropriate combinations of goods and services are necessary to symbolize a style of life adequately."[15] In doing so, however, they reduce adaptive to normative considerations; they ignore Weber's strictures about the impact of markets on status opportunities and, indeed, the nonsymbolic, instrumental aspects of status conflict in general.

Finally, although Parsons and Smelser's discussion of the polity-economy interchange brings power into a central position, they overlay this account with an idealist emphasis. Once again, they feel compelled to present the order problem as necessitating a presuppositional choice rather than interweaving coercive and voluntary pressures. While they recognize, for example, that political establishment of the interest rate has significance "as a direct reward," they must argue that it is "even more" significant as a symbol.[16] Most of their analysis, in fact, is devoted to tracing this normative effect of interest, and they ignore the ways in which interest rates structure instrumental conflict, for example, the farmer/worker antagonism described by Weber. As for the other side of this exchange, the economic provision of facilities to government, they underplay the dialectic between values and coercion that inevitably informs state procurement through taxation efforts or nationalization, minimizing the manner in which this process is affected by the nature of property ownership.[17†]

1.2. POLITICAL INTERCHANGE AS THE CRITIQUE OF INSTRUMENTAL HIERARCHY

In Parsons' later writings on politics, his multidimensional analysis provides a supple and dynamic approach to power as a continuum from material coercion to symbolic legitimacy. His interchange model articulates this vision by formulating politics as an autonomous dimension interacting with interest demands, with more general support and legitimation, and with more conditional facilities.[18†] Yet this multidimensional treatment is, once again, cross-cut by Parsons' continuing effort to specify sociological idealism.

Parsons' ambivalence centers on the role of the independent goal-attainment dimension itself, the dimension which through its "combinatorial" power is the central component in the political process. Parsons is reluctant to acknowledge the role which instrumental self-interest plays in such political activity, reluctant to recognize that while internalized values and support do, indeed, supply the general symbolic "frame" for political process, particular value positions will, at the same time, be manipulated by political actors in an instrumental way.

This tendency is clearly evidenced in Parsons' formal definition of power. Despite his recognition of force and coercion as the "intrinsic persuaders" of politics, he argues that power must always be considered in its "collectivity" references.[19] Power, he argues, "is the capacity to mobilize the resources of society for the attainment of goals for which a general 'public' commitment has been made, or may be made."[20] Instead of focusing equally on the political actor's self-interested effort to make particular goals appear collective, and on the self-interested striving of the political staff, Parsons shifts the burden of proof to those who would deny political legitimacy and the public and collective nature of political commitment.[21†] In cybernetic terms, his argument tilts toward the *value* reference of goals and away from the *conditional*. When this framework becomes the context for his discussion of political deflation and inflation, the analysis, not surprisingly, assumes a highly artificial quality. Power is described as in the first place legitimate. Only if this legitimation fails do coercion and force become involved. In this way, the simultaneity of material-ideal interaction which characterizes his multidimensional analysis is lost.

Finally, this reductionist strain also creates ambiguity in Parsons' critique of zero-sum theory, which so frequently has presented a target for critical attack. While it is certainly correct that the possibility for normative legitimation means that actor "A" may increase his power without taking power directly from "B," it is also true, nonetheless, that such an increase inevitably changes the distribution of power, making the relationship between "A" and "B" less equal.[22] Parsons can think otherwise only insofar as he identifies private interest with public power.

1.2.1. From Hierarchy to Collegiality

The most effective way to demonstrate how this idealist strain affects Parsons' specific analysis of political interchange is to piece together his extended discussion of horizontal and vertical authority.[23†] We will see that while this normative application of interchange, like Parsons' other excursions into sociological idealism, allows him to achieve striking empirical insights, at the same time it forces him to commit serious theoretical errors which ultimately detract from the persuasiveness of his general position.

Parsons focuses initially on intra-organizational power rather than on societal power as such. While acknowledging an inevitable tendency toward hierarchy, he protests that this instrumental, vertical aspect of authority has been overemphasized.[24] His own focus, therefore, will be a polemical one, namely, to demonstrate that normative order and horizontal authority are politically significant. It is interchange theory that allows Parsons to conduct this "crucial experiment." The weakness of hierarchical-instrumental theories, he contends, is that they view politics as a closed system.[25] Interchange theory, in contrast, demonstrates that politics is an open system, involved in important boundary relations with its nonpolitical environments: "The essential modifications of the hierarchical principle involved in bureaucratic . . . systems may be derived from the boundary exigencies of the system as expressed in [the] qualities of the inputs necessary for collective processes."[26] Not surprisingly, the inputs Parsons defines as relevant refer to the polity's need for integration with the larger society's norms and values.[27] While he briefly elaborates the constitutional and symbolic restrictions on hierarchy generated by the pattern maintenance system,[28] he devotes himself primarily to normative inputs from the integrative dimension. Parsons' idealism, one must remember, is of the sociological type; rather than eliminate instrumental conditions, he tries to elaborate mechanisms by which they are controlled. Since norms are more adaptive and specific than values, they qualify better for this task.

Parsons believes that the degree of coercive hierarchy in an organization corresponds to its dependence upon instrumental as opposed to normative kinds of internal controls. This can be correlated, in turn, with the kinds of labor utilized by an organization. If its labor force has undergone extensive socialization and has, as a result, internalized complex normative controls, the organization will follow a more voluntary path. This ratio of skilled to unskilled labor, and of voluntary to coercive organization, will be reflected in the membership criteria which an organization establishes. In interchange terms, membership requirements refer to the "boundary process" between political organization and normative integration: "The critical problem here concerns the relation of [the organization's] resources to the category of membership."[29]

The base line for procuring membership is the simple exchange of wages for untrained labor power.[30] In return for money, the untrained laborer accepts a purely vertical relationship to organizational authority. Yet even here, Parsons argues, the relationship is not purely coercive. Given the legal norm that makes labor formally free, the instrumental pressures on unskilled labor to accept membership are modified by its legal right not to accept a contract. Also, given a differentiated constitutional system, the employee maintains certain individual rights even after he has entered the organization.

The labor-polity exchange is more voluntaristic to the degree that an organization depends upon more technically competent or professional labor power. This is true, Parsons argues, because organizational authority delegates power only in exchange for the valued commodity of expertise—that is, for "facilities for [the] effective implementation of collective goals."[31] The likelihood of such exchange depends, in turn, on the culture in which the organization is imbedded. The less traditionalistic and more universalistic the culture, the more technical competence becomes the central expectation and the more labor becomes professionalized. Insofar as labor power must be trained and complex skills internalized, vertical authority gives way to more horizontal, voluntary control:[32] "The specialist must . . . be given freedom from intervention by authority in his own technical sphere."[33] To the degree that authority becomes horizontal, it is "associational" or "collegial" rather than hierarchical and bureaucratic.[34]

Parsons has now constructed a continuum of authority stretching from coercive, purely market exchange on one side to voluntary, purely collegial relations on the other. Collegial membership is decided by peer election rather than by appointment from above, for if qualified peers do not control the selection process, at least at important points, there will be no way to ensure that members have the required technical competence. Finally, although collegiality may be organized independently, as in a university faculty, it more frequently occurs as one dimension of bureaucratic organization. In such situations, professional membership in a collegial group—e.g., as accountants, engineers, architects—creates horizontal authority that cross-cuts the vertical jurisdictions of the bureaucracies within which these professionals spend their actual working days.

Subsequently, Parsons extends this normative analysis of bureaucratic-collegial tension to public authority. Mass political democracy represents collegial authority writ large. With enfranchisement, a certain kind of universalistic competence becomes the formal qualification for gaining membership in the political community: the full rights of citizenship must be granted to individuals in good standing without particularistic consideration of financial status or ethnicity. By "good standing," political membership is limited, as is all collegial membership, to persons who have internalized the appropriate norms and skills, who have not significantly deviated—as, for example, have "criminals" or the "insane"—from the standard of morality and rationality. The universal franchise means, therefore, that the political community can be normatively, rather than coercively, regulated, and that political power has, in some sense, been equalized, or "horizontalized," among community members. Because this polity depends upon voluntary commitment, its governors must be elected. Since the assumption of authority must be based upon voluntary election, candidates for political office can campaign only by appealing to common normative standards.

> Individual members [of the political community] must be *persuaded* [not coerced or induced] to vote for candidates and policies; and office holders must be *persuaded* to make policy decisions desired by their constituents. Justification of such decisions must be based on the more or less universalistically ordered normative system.[35†]

1.2.2. Political Idealism, the Classical Critique, and the Limits of Political Internalization

This analysis of private and public authority is typical of Parsons' idealist analysis. It is, in the first place, an ingenious empirical account, in which Parsons has used his important refinements of the idealist tradition—the Durkheim-Freud synthesis as articulated by his interchange model—to resolve certain issues which had remained perplexing for his classical predecessors. Most directly, perhaps, Parsons' analysis of organizations in which labor procurement extends beyond simple market transactions demonstrates the rationalistic limitations of Marx's perception of labor exchange and economic authority. Ownership of the means of production is not the only way to gain control over processes in the work place. As labor-power becomes more highly skilled, work relations become more voluntary.[36†] Weber criticized Marx for ignoring the importance of Protestant-inspired voluntarism in the transformation of property and labor into alienable commodities.[37†] Through his interchange analysis of the labor exchange, Parsons transforms Weber's historical criticism into a systematic theory of the role of voluntarism in productive organizations.

By bringing his conceptualization of the Durkheim-Freud synthesis to bear on the problem of political authority, moreover, Parsons can transcend the rationalistic tendencies of Weber's sociology of the modern state. Given his presuppositional problems, Weber could not systematically describe the manner in which "rational-legal" authority depended not simply upon the instrumental-efficient organization of action but also upon the internalization of constitutional norms and universalistic culture. Where Weber could see only a Darwinian party conflict and amoral plebiscitarian or Caesarist democracy, Parsons recognizes the normative context within which such antibureaucratic party conflict and voting must occur.[38†] While Weber recognized, in passing, the increasing role of evaluation and competence in bureaucratic organization, he could envision it as functioning only in the instrumental terms of contributing to modern conflict over status and prestige.[39†] Parsons, in contrast, with his sensitivity to the socializing role of education and to the possibility for internal and voluntary compliance with authority, can recognize the anti-hierarchical and noninstrumental elements in bureaucratic organization.[40†]

Yet Parsons achieves these empirical insights only at significant theoretical cost. Once again, the problem is not that Parsons simply ignores the instrumental aspects of political life. To the contrary, political "conditions" concern him greatly, as empirical forces that must be theoretically encapsulated by the nonrational dimensions of norms and values. Thus, although he acknowledges the role of instrumental, monetary sanctions in procuring membership, he pushes the discussion of membership back to considerations of normative order. For Parsons, it is ultimately, the socialized motivation of workers that determines the freedom of movement inside organizations and the freedom of choice allowed by the labor market.

By making a polemical argument for the significance of norms rather than a fully multidimensional analysis, Parsons deals with elements of external, instrumental order only as parameters, not as variables to be explained. Focusing in his organizational theory exclusively on issues of education and socialization, he can ignore the unequal power that coercively structures labor exchange, the issue that so preoccupied Marx, and underplay the coercive aspects of bureaucracy which were the focus of Weber's attention as well as that of Michels. Instead of offering a normative corrective to the rationalism of classical political sociology, Parsons here offers a normative alternative. He writes, for example, that "the consent of the employed to the discipline imposed upon him is . . . a condition of retaining his services."[41] But in this Lockean formulation, Parsons underestimates the crucial role that political and economic coercion play in artificially identifying interests. This bias even affects his analysis of the collegial form of authority itself. While he correctly notes that collegiality is in itself much more democratic than bureaucracy, he ignores the undemocratic, monopolistic aspects of collegiality in its relation to the broader society. This can be seen most directly in Parsons' discussion of professionals, where he applauds their autonomy from bureaucratic authority while overlooking their often particularistic relationship to the society at large. He could focus on the latter element, of course, only by balancing his discussion of normative organization with an equal emphasis on the instrumental aspects of collegial authority.[42†]

In his discussion of public power, Parsons undermines his subtle analysis of the voluntaristic aspects of politics by ignoring the tension between these elements and instrumental coercion, economic inducement, and intimidation. Concentrating almost exclusively on the franchise, he underplays the role of interest groups which he specified so accurately in his more multidimensional application of the interchange model.[43†] Whereas he pays close attention to the normative boundary of political systems, he systematically neglects the crucial significance of economic facilities in promoting effective political action and the role that self-interested political and solidary elites play in political interchange. If Weber's presuppositional reduction promotes the rationalization of political norms and values, Parsons reduces political power to the exercise of political influence.[44†]

1.2.3. Presuppositional Ambiguity and the Interpretation of Parsons' Political Sociology

This tension between normative and multidimensional elements in Parsons' political sociology further explains the paradoxes of Parsonian interpretation. While critics like Gouldner, Dahrendorf, and Giddens have correctly identified the gist of Parsons' idealist deviation, they do not comprehend the significance of the other side of his political sociology, its truly multidimensional strand.[45†] In direct opposition to this critique, Parsons' sympathetic interpreters often deny that his political sociology contains any ambiguity at all, insisting, to the contrary, that it is resolutely multidimensional.[46] Perhaps the only valid interpretations are those which are implicit in certain strands of Parsonian political sociology itself. While accepting Parsons' overall framework, these functionalists have moved to correct its normative reduction. In political science, Mitchell insists that the consideration of economic and stratificational inputs is decisive for evaluating the process of power production; Easton similarly affirms the nonnormative character of "interest demands," contrasting them with the more diffuse inputs of normative "support."[47†] In sociology, Eisenstadt has emphasized the role of specific groups in structuring political interchange and, particularly, how the "combinatorial process" is initiated by the self-interested activity of ambitious political leaders and groups.[48†] Similarly, Lipset and Rokkan have analyzed the impact of the integrative dimension on politics in terms of the tensions and demands generated by conflicting solidary groups rather than in terms simply of abstract normative support.[49]

1.3. THE TILT TOWARD PATTERN MAINTENANCE AND INTEGRATION: INTERCHANGE AND THE DISTORTION OF PARSONS' GENERALIZED CONCEPTS

Parsons accomplishes his idealist reduction of economic adaptation and political goal-attainment, it is clear, by placing an exaggerated emphasis on inputs from pattern-maintenance values and instrumental norms. This imbalance, however, is only one part of a much broader shift in emphasis. In the course of Parsons' later writing, indeed, subtle yet significant alterations occur in each of the key terms that inform his general conceptual scheme. These unacknowledged shifts blur his multidimensional focus.

There is, in the first place, a transformation in the presuppositional implications of Parsons' cybernetic hierarchy.[50†] Instead of an analytical statement about the interrelation between different types of control—control by symbolic information versus control by physical energy—Parsons takes the hierarchy as a concrete ranking of actual causal significance. Instead of utilizing the cybernetic analogy to facilitate a multidimensional argument, in other words, he employs it to argue for the unequal impact of normative order. Once again, instead of presenting a synthetic framework, Parsons implies that presuppositional choices must be made.

The language of "priority" is unmistakable. In his introduction to *Societies: Evolutionary and Comparative Perspectives*, for example, Parsons uses cybernetic logic to convert interchange into a one-way continuum. "A superordinate cultural orientation system," he writes, "is, above all, the *primary* source of legitimation for its [society's] normative order."[51] In discussing the political sphere, he asserts that "the priority of the societal normative order" is necessary because "physical force . . . must be controlled in order for the higher-order controls to operate."[52] Although Parsons recognizes that "such priorities do not preclude two-way relations," he makes his own preference clear when he applies this general logic, later in the book, to change in premodern societies. Throughout, the analytical clarification provided by cybernetic logic and the interchange model is employed not to create multidimensionality but to legitimate a normative emphasis. In this typically ambiguous statement, for example, Parsons shifts from an argument against exclusively instrumental determinism to an argument for the priority of normative elements.

> Basic innovation in the evolution of living systems does not occur *automatically* with increases of factors or resources at the lower (conditional) levels of the cybernetic hierarchy, but *depends on* analytically independent developments at higher levels.[53]

He concludes, unambiguously, that "within the social system, the normative elements are more important for social change than the 'material interests' of constituent units."[54] Yet while Parsons quite legitimately argues that "conditional factors cannot create a new order without *independent* innovation at a higher normative level," the same statement can be reversed, and must be, if a synthetic multidimensional position is to be maintained.[55] But Parsons refuses to make this corollary; in not doing so, he undermines the authority of his cybernetic scheme.

The other key conceptualization in Parsons' later refinement of his presuppositional position, the "generalization-specification" language, is similarly emptied of its multidimensional content.[56†] Instead of employing the distinction as an analytic vocabulary for interrelating symbols and conditions, Parsons argues that symbolic generalization precedes material specification in a concrete, temporal sense: "Normative patterns . . . define *programs* for the operation of the social system.[Such a program then] requires much greater specification before the level of particular goals is reached."[57]

Both these shifts in presuppositional emphasis are reflected in Parsons' reductionist approach to "institutionalization," the concept which defines the relation between culture and social systems. In his multidimensional analysis, institutionalization refers to the process by which social-system values are created by the cross-pressures of organizational scarcity and cultural patterns.[58†] In the idealist aspect of his argument, however, institutionalization implies the control exerted by values over conditions. Parsons uses this revised understanding in a polemical way, arguing that the determinism of instrumental interest must be replaced—not just complemented—by the voluntarism of the Durkheim-Freud synthesis.

> The general theorem of institutionalization [is] that the *interests* of participating units, that is what they *desire*, should be considered in conformity with the *standards* of desirability which are involved in the value patterns.[59]

Institutionalization now describes the normative regulation which controls instrumental action. The social system simply provides the ground upon which motivation and symbol intersect. Instead of emphasizing the challenge which norms pose to values, Parsons writes that norms are significant because they allow values to be enforced with "pragmatic consistency." Instead of challenging the validity of norms, situational exigencies complement them; they allow norms to develop "detailed and circumstantial content."[60]

In view of this approach to institutionalization, it is not surprising that the legal system assumes such a central position in Parsons' later work.[61†] For Parsons, laws represent moral proscriptions which are "circumstantially detailed" enough to control instrumental interest and political force. Legal enforcement, he asserts, is "concerned with the conditions of security of a normative order."[62] The other side of the legal question—the use of normative pronouncements for the ideological justification of material interest—is ignored. Parsons here produces a factor theory, not a synthetic analysis: "When used as [normatively-oriented] sanctions, force and other physical-organic factors contribute much more to the security of collective processes than they can as more 'conditional exigencies.' "[63†] Though he discusses the history of legal development at some length, it is the "downward" movement from values to norms, not the "upward" pressures on legal development from economic and political conflict, that occupies his attention.[64†]

Finally, if institutionalization is to assume such an idealist cast, Parsons can no longer define "structure" in a multidimensional way. Instead of identifying the different dimensional positions of the interchange model, structure now relates to normative order alone. Parsons' definition becomes a polemical reversal of the rationalist approach to structure as instrumental coercion. Structure orders voluntary, not coercive actions: "The most fundamental theorem of the theory of action [is] that the *structure* of systems of action *consists* in institutionalized . . . and/or internalized patterns of meaning."[65]

The true extent of this counterproposal is revealed by the conceptualization of the "four structural components" that surfaces periodically in Parsons' later writings. If these structural components were to be derived from a multidimensional interpretation of interchange, they would refer to values, norms, organizational goals, and economic facilities. Why, then, does Parsons define them as values, norms, collectivities, and roles?[66] The answer can be found in Parsons' idealist strategy: such a transformation allows "structures" to be viewed simply as different levels of normative culture, levels which correspond to adaptation—goal-attainment—integration—latency if the latter are conceived purely as levels of cultural specification. Interchange is used, in this case, merely to explicate different kinds of symbolic commitments. Parsons differentiates goal attainment from adaptation, for example, by arguing that "knowing the value pattern of a collectivity does not . . . make it possible to deduce its role composition."[67] And he defines society's most conditional dimension, adaptation, in a thoroughly idealist way. "The capacity to fulfill valued role-performances," he writes, "is the most generalized adaptive resource in any society."[68†]

Because of the polarization of Parsonian interpretation, the deep ambiguities that cross-cut his most general conceptualization have generally been overlooked. Parsons' critics, once again, see simply the ideal emphasis alone. For example, while Blake and Davis produce the best critical account of Parsons' reductionist approach to institutionalization, they ignore the contrasting multidimensional perspective from which, in fact, they drew much of their own critique.[69] Similarly, Heydebrand produces some penetrating objections to the one-directional movement of Parsons' cybernetic schema, but he fails even to acknowledge the existence of a more balanced approach.[70†] On the other side, those sympathetic to Parsons have also interpreted his key concepts as fundamentally consistent; they simply view them as complementary to their own orientations. While Toby agrees that Parsons' "cultural determinism" declaration was a "weak moment," he himself introduces an idealist slant in his discussion of Parsons' cybernetic hierarchy.[71] In an implicit attempt to resolve Parsons' ambiguity, Rocher adopts the Engelsian language of residual category, arguing that in Parsons' cybernetic hierarchy cultural elements exercise control over the social system "in the last resort."[72] Even Eisenstadt, while recognizing the "possible cybernetic centrality [for Parsons] of one component [e.g., values or culture]," argues that Parsons' cybernetic schema ranks factors only in terms of the analytical, qualitative mechanisms of regulation, not in terms of the priority of one factor over another.[73†]

1.4. THE REDUCTION OF VALUE INTERCHANGE: FROM "PRODUCTION" TO "IMPLEMENTATION"

In his later writings on values, Parsons used the interchange model to transcend the dichotomizing treatments of classical sociology. In the idealist strain which cross-cuts this later work, interchange becomes, in contrast, a vehicle to establish the causal priority of generalized values. This shift, of course, is simply the corollary of the idealization that affects Parsons' other central concepts, particularly the notion of "institutionalization."

1.4.1. Functional Differentiation as Value Specification

Alongside his effort to place values into the context of a synthetic theory, Parsons defines his task in a much more polemical way. His concern shifts from the "production" of values—a focus that highlights interdimensional interplay—to their "implementation."[74] Although he continues formally to recognize the distinction between these two processes, the process by which values are formulated, or produced, is now basically assumed. Value production becomes, for all practical purposes, a residual category. Interchange is useful, then, not because it traces the tension between the value dimension and its environments but because it outlines various paths toward value implementation. "The articulation between [value] commitment . . . and the concrete allocation of resources," Parsons writes, "involves the *use* of . . . factors of production."[75] The organizational aspects of social-system life—the "factors of production"—become a mere backdrop for the more precise articulation of normative order, or institutionalization.[76†]

Although "scope" and "responsibility" are concepts that, potentially, have a strong multidimensional application, they also prove highly useful for this reductionistic task.[77†]If general values become effective only after their scope is differentiated according to the actual functional specializations in any society, it is possible to argue that the tension between values and scarce functional exigencies can be eliminated. Because values are "compatible with a wide scope of action areas," Parsons asserts, a wide range of "differentiated *implementive* activities can be *legitimated*."[78] Even if adaptive pressures, for example, sharply challenge certain fundamental commitments, the notion of differentiated scope can be utilized to argue that these pressures do not really create cultural tension. Thus, the purely economic rationality that informs adaptation in a capitalist society can be viewed simply as a specification of the general rationality value.[79]

With his notions of scope and responsibility, therefore, Parsons can, in effect, circumvent the more instrumental, conditional spheres; he can now identify the pressures generated by other subsystems in terms of their respective value specifications alone.[80†] Perhaps the most disturbing attempt to pursue this strategy occurs in Parsons' discussion of the pattern-maintenance value of "instrumental activism," a commitment that he characterizes as particularly suited for economic adaptation. On the one hand, the formulation of this value presents a sophisticated formulation of how rationality has become abstracted and generalized in the course of American modernization, as compared, for example, with the more group-oriented, rather than instrumental activism of Russia or Japan.[81†] Yet Parsons also uses the value pattern in a reductionist way to "explain" the disproportionate power of the American economy. It is the "societal value system," he asserts, that "defines the relative importance of economic functions in the hierarchy of [social] functions."[82] The American value of *instrumental* activism emphasizes "the production of valued facilities . . . *whatever they may be*"; this "puts the primary [sociological] emphasis on productive activity in the *economy*."[83] Whatever pathologies result from such an emphasis on instrumental means rather than particular ends—and Parsons himself notes many of them[84]—they are problems generated by the value commitment itself; economic institutions, after all, simply implement these adaptive values.[85†]

In making this argument, Parsons' idealization follows what is by now a familiar path: he treats instrumental economic action as if it were purely voluntary, as if it were not significantly produced by the deterministic pressures of the external situation. He assumes, therefore, that economically induced strains are an inevitable outgrowth of the institutionalizing of value commitments rather than an external imposition that operates in tension with the pattern-maintenance sector. In doing so, however, Parsons fails to emphasize the manner in which institutional structures like markets or corporations, or different social groups like managerial elites or classes, limit voluntary behavior by "artificially" structuring instrumental interest. Once again Parsons has transformed Locke's residual category of "natural identity." Instead of bracing it with a reference to Hobbesian force, he simply makes explicit its connection to the internalization of culture.

1.4.2. The University as the Center of Society: Value Interchange as Value Conflict

Given its central focus on rationality, *The American University* offers a convenient illustration of how this kind of idealistic conceptualization affects Parsons' actual discussion of value interchange. In chapter 4, I discussed at some length the multidimensional aspects of Parsons' and Platt's analysis of the university. Using the interchange model, they trace the formulation of an independent societal commitment to cognitive rationality, its "institutionalization" in the multidimensional sense of the term. They also utilize interchange to analyze the tensions between this value commitment and the political, economic, integrative, and cultural exigencies of the university's environment. We are now in a position to see that this argument is cross-cut by a much more reductionistic approach.

Parsons and Platt are at least as inclined to view cognitive rationality as the natural unfolding of the more general cultural commitment to rationalism as they are to emphasize the more multidimensional pressures involved in this process of value production. Indicating a shift away from synthetic reasoning, they argue that "by whatever combination of forces, the process of development of a society follows the *direction* of the normative pressures exerted by its value system."[86] In discussing the impact of organization and scarcity on the West's increasing cognitive emphasis, they are profoundly ambivalent. For example, while they discuss the role of the capitalist class in nineteenth-century America in creating the first university system, they add, at the same time, that the significance of this class, like the university system itself, represents, in the long run, the working out of the Protestant ethic.[87]

In their analysis of the interchanges by which the university seeks to maintain its cognitive autonomy, Parsons and Platt often treat the problem of autonomy simply as value implementation, instead of focusing on the interdimensional tensions involved. This tendency is apparent, for example, in the continuum they construct to describe the more general and more specific outputs between the university and its environment. They describe the university's general "cognitive contribution" to political and economic action as an attempt to balance the corrupting influence of more purely instrumental and practical goals. They rarely, however, concern themselves with the actual importance of such instrumental forces in themselves, in terms either of specific issues, like financing and control, or with more diffuse instrumental pressures. It is because they do not analyze such tension between cognitive ends and instrumental means that their focus shifts to implementation; throughout *The American University*,

Parsons and Platt imply that if only the university could socialize students more effectively, the autonomous status of cognitive rationality would finally be assured.[88]

The same kind of contradictory message permeates their discussion of the university's more specific, quasi-instrumental outputs. While the significance of concrete contractual obligations is undoubtedly underplayed, the crucial distortion occurs in their analysis of the boundary relations established by the university's connections to the professions. They argue, quite plausibly, that professions are functionally significant because they create links between the university and the instrumental interests of the clients they represent—between the university and wealthy taxpayers, underprivileged welfare recipients, hospital patients, automobile consumers, corporations, churches, and so forth. The university tries to gain the support of such diverse social groups by providing the professions with valued cognitive output in the form of rational training. Yet the tension that such a boundary relation creates between value commitment and instrumental efficiency is hardly explored. It is the cognitive processes of professional socialization and training that receives most of their attention, not the instrumental pressures, generated both by professionals and their clients, which distort not only the application of professional knowledge but also affect what kind of knowledge is actually produced.[89] In focusing almost exclusively on the process of value implementation, this discussion clearly fails to realize its multidimensional potential.

Indeed, alongside their synthetic analysis of the university-society relationship, Parsons and Platt have, simultaneously, pursued an entirely different problem. The purpose of this idealistic strand of their analysis is actually to introduce a new approach to the integration of advanced societies. The university is at the center of the modern integration problem, they believe, because the crucial problem in modern life is to balance cognitive and noncognitive rationalities.[90] In their multidimensional discussion, Parsons and Platt define this balance as central to the university's relation to the noncognitive aspects of culture, a relationship which they view as mediated by intellectuals. In their idealist analysis, however, this cultural tension becomes the pivotal factor in the university's social-system boundaries as well. The crisis of the intellectuals has now become the crisis of modern society.[91]

The university suffers chronic imbalance in its relations with its institutional environment, Parsons and Platt believe, not because of tension between cultural commitments and instrumental demands but because of a long-term crisis in Western culture itself. In the process of secularization, claims to cognitive rationality have increasingly been promoted as viable substitutes for religious, moral, and expressive forms of truth,[92] e.g., the "scientific socialism" of Marx and Saint-Simon, the "scientific ethics" of Russell, Bridgman, Lundberg, and Skinner, and the perennial second-class citizenship of the arts in the intellectual community.[93] Parsons and Platt discuss the different types of cultural conflict that have marked this process of secularization, from the earlier debates between science and religion to the contemporary arguments about the relation between science and ideology and science and artistic expression.[94] They maintain that no matter what their particular form, these efforts to substitute cognitive rationality for other kinds of cultural answers have created wildly unrealistic expectations. Such value inflation was bound, eventually, to issue in the strong rejection of cognitive rationality itself.

The integrative crisis of modern society centers in the university because the institutional locus of this long-range cultural conflict has changed along with its specific form. Earlier debates occurred, for the most part, among unattached intellectuals. Today, they occur almost entirely among academicians.[95]As a result, it is the university's boundary relations, more than those of any other institutions, that reflect the spiraling cycle of cognitive inflation and deflation. Professionals' clients, for example, are dissatisfied because their primary "interests," which are practical and noncognitive, have been neglected.[96] The boundaries between the university and the economy and polity suffer for similar reasons. These interests attack the university because in subordinating explicit political and economic criteria to "scientific" validity they have relied upon the university's cognitive rationality for outputs it simply cannot produce.[97] The same kind of cultural disjunction has disrupted the university's relationship to the societal community, a boundary mediated by the undergraduate student body. The university's "output" to citizenship solidarity is ineffective because the deflationary reaction against cognitive rationality has made the socialization of university students much more difficult.[98]

By replacing conflicts between symbolic and instrumental interests with conflicts over different kinds of values, Parsons and Platt have shifted their focus from the interplay between culture and society to the internal dynamics of the cultural system itself.[99†] This constitutes a serious departure from Parsons' multidimensional agenda. Yet, despite its idealism, the empirical importance of this argument must not be ignored, any more than we may ignore Weber's political sociology because it underplays religion or Marx's class theory because it fails to deal with consciousness. It is true, of course, that there are other significant, indeed crucial, modes of integration in modern society. Nonetheless, by clarifying the role of cognitive rationality, Parsons and Platt have illuminated a critical aspect of modernity. They have suggested, in effect, that even the most secular society has strong elements of integration and, moreover, that such integration is achieved by the most secular morality of all, the idea of scientific truth. Cognitive standards present the religious, constitutive symbolism of modern society, and it is the university where this scientific religion resides: As Parsons remarks in another work published at about the same time, "The educational revolution has introduced mechanisms by which the new [cognitive] cultural standards are . . . institutionalized in ways that partly replace religion."[100] Indeed, emphasis on cognitive integration has increased step by step with the decline of religious belief,[101] with the result that contemporary morality, expressive values, even religion itself can now be accepted only if they are cognitively legitimated.[102] It is because of its role in establishing these new cognitive standards that the university has such pervasive integrative significance in the modern world, and, conversely, why instability in the university has such powerful social reverberations.[103†]

1.4.3. Value Idealism and Parsons' Debate with the Classics

In making this argument, Parsons has contributed further to his critique of the classical foundations of sociological value theory.[104†] It was only through his religious theory, for example, that Durkheim could connect morality to internal needs and, hence, to voluntary action. In arguing that science had divested religion of its cognitive component, Durkheim guaranteed, therefore, that his theory of symbolic internalization would be unable to explain fully the pervasive role of rationality in the modern world. True, Durkheim understood that cognitive rationality, rooted in education, formed an important moral, even sacred, principle in secular life, but because he lacked a true socialization theory he could explain the impact of rationality only by connecting it to moral discipline, a seemingly contradictory emphasis which seriously distorts the voluntaristic role that rationality plays in modern integration. While it was Piaget who first criticized this apparent emphasis on discipline, it was Parsons who provided the sociological theory that explained how a more realistic, voluntary approach to rational symbolic integration could be institutionalized. Parsons, then, carries out Durkheim's mandate, but he does so in a more theoretically sophisticated way.

At the same time, by focusing on the relation between cognitive and noncognitive rationality, Parsons has perceived the nonscientific roots of modern culture in a way that Weber could not. Even if those elements of the Protestant ethic most complementary to industrialization—the cognitive emphasis on efficient calculation, for example—have subsequently become differentiated from other aspects of morality, they remain, Parsons demonstrates, firmly rooted in cultural life. Moreover, contrary to Weber's implications, science is not unrelated to the maintenance of values; it is, in fact, an important symbolic commitment in its own right, one which itself requires extensive socialization. Indeed, in modern society science assumes a quasi-religious, moral power. It is hardly possible, therefore, that modern political and economic rationality can impose a purely environmental determinism, for they both depend in fundamental ways on a distinctive cultural standard and are, in fact, highly vulnerable to cultural disruption.

Still, *The American University*, like the rest of Parsons' work, aspires to an ecumenical position, and in this Parsons has failed. If a significant strand of his argument treats the institutionalization of cognitive rationality purely in cultural terms, the latent function of this argument, at least, must be viewed as factional and antimaterialist. Among the three modes of orientation Parsons described in his earlier work, cognition is the one most adapted to instrumental action. For this reason alone, any fully multidimensional analysis of cognitive rationality would have to focus, much more heavily than do Parsons and Platt, on the role that efficient demands and coercive pressures play not only in structuring but also in creating different modes of rational cognition.[105†]

While Parsons devotes himself to an analytic theory that can resolve Durkheim's idealism, he does not fully extricate himself from this idealism in a sociological sense. In his reductionist argument, he, too, deals with rationality purely on the value level, emphasizing, like Durkheim, that instrumental action is voluntary rather than coercive. While going beyond Weber in crucial respects, Parsons ignores Weber's insight into the corrupting pressures on scientific truth which emanate from modern political and economic structures. He also ignores the way these institutions can "artificially identify" interest in ways that contradict efforts to integrate society around the value of cognitive rationality.

1.5. IDEALISM IN THE INTEGRATIVE INTERCHANGE: SOLIDARITY AS THE CORE OF WESTERN DEVELOPMENT

There is, however, an important sense in which norms, not values, are the crucial focus of Parsons' later idealism. It is norms, after all, which are more situationally specified and more capable, therefore, of providing the kind of discipline for instrumental interests that a specifically sociological idealism demands. To make this argument for normative control, however, Parsons must abandon his approach to normative production as multidimensional exchange. Instead of pursuing the conditional limitations on normative integration, he now utilizes the analytic sophistication of the interchange model primarily to explore the independent solidary basis of norms and the way this base interacts with changing value patterns.

To trace the theory and practice of this strand of Parsons' analysis, we must return to his most important later work on normative development, *The System of Modern Societies*. It was noted earlier how Parsons concretizes here the notion of civil society.[106†] In demonstrating how the Christian idea of voluntary community gradually became secularized and institutionalized through the interplay of political and economic vicissitudes and cultural heritage, Parsons produces a multidimensional analysis that successfully resolves certain classical dilemmas. If we consider the book as a whole, however, we are forced to conclude that this synthetic and truly dialectical argument, though extremely powerful in its own right, presents an isolated line of analysis, one which is overshadowed by a more powerful idealist slant.

Though this short later work is formally about the system of modern "societies," it is much more concerned, in fact, with the system of modern solidarity. The reasoning by which Parsons arrives at this reduction is crucial, for it reveals the same errors in general logic that have been traced throughout this chapter. The societal community, he contends, is not just a solidary dimension of modern society; it is, rather, its "core."[107†] The crucial problem for social change, then, is the changing structure of solidary loyalties. Parsons justifies this assertion by a now familiar formula. First, he collapses the presuppositional questions of action and order, moving from a valid critique of individualistic theory to an illegitimate argument for the centrality of normative concerns.

> Individualistic social theory has persistently exaggerated the significance of individual "self-interest" . . . as an obstacle to the integration of social systems. [But] the self-interested motives of individuals are, on the whole, effectively channeled into the social system through a variety of memberships and loyalties.[108]

He proceeds, subsequently, to conflate the problem of empirical equilibrium with this presuppositional resolution of the order problem. "In cases of conflict," he argues, "the most immediate problem for most individuals is the adjustment of obligations among competing loyalties."[109]

This conflationary logic establishes the rationale for the idealist argument that occupies much of the remainder of the book. Solidarity is not only the crucial element in social change, it is also the most important element in establishing the causes of modern social conflict. More conditional dimensions of society intrude upon change theory, then, only insofar as they disrupt established patterns of loyalty or create new ones. The organizational elements of the social system are treated as "ground," while the "figure" is composed of the institutions of normative order. Political and economic interchange emerge in a rather peculiar form. Parsons defines politics as if it were simply the execution of normative commitments, designed to maintain the integrity of the societal community against external threats and administering power in the public interest.[110] The adaptive dimension is important simply because considerations of practicality are vital to any moral community.[111]

The imbalance in this initial theoretical chapter (ch. 2) is continued in the next, which presents an empirical discussion of the crucial developments in Western society from the decline of the Roman Empire to Post-

Reformation Europe. Not only is solidarity treated in this discussion as the crucial systemic dimension, but it is analyzed in a decidedly one-dimensional way. Parsons treats religion as the primary activating factor in integrative change, and he considers solidary problems, in turn, as the basic triggers for complementary shifts in political and economic organization.

While the Christian ideal of voluntary community provided the essential cultural resource for a differentiated solidary community, its institutionalization was prevented by the onset of the Middle Ages and the decline of the Roman Empire.[112] Though Parsons mentions the conditional sources of this breakdown—the disappearance of a monetary economy, for example, and the attack on centralized political authority by regional and tribal groupings—the focus of his concern is clearly on the "principles" that constituted what he calls the "institutional heritage" of Rome. These were rational law, the normative commitment to territorial organization, and the conception of an egalitarian "municipium" as the proper form of political participation.[113]

While population density, economic organization, and physical security are duly noted, Parsons describes the crucial conditional developments of this period as following, basically, from these Roman ideals. When the extreme decentralization of feudalism made it increasingly difficult to integrate various hierarchies of status and power, the "territorial principle" gained steadily.[114] Similarly, the autonomy of the European city developed from the interaction of Christian religious principles and the commitment to the Roman *municipium*.[115] In discussing political centralization and urban development, then, Parsons effectively ignores the instrumental pressures which preoccupied Weber, the military and political domination so crucial to absolutism and the economic and military conflicts that helped propel the urban guilds. Indeed, for Parsons it is actually religious developments, particularly the institutionalization of priestly celibacy, which brought about the bureaucratic differentiation of religious autonomy that, in his view, constituted the most important evolutionary development of this period.[116] After discussing the geographical differentiation of the European "system" along the four functional dimensions,[117†] Parsons concludes his analysis by returning to this cultural theme, discussing the intellectual innovations of the Renaissance and the religious institutions of the Reformation as further specifications of the earlier developments toward universalistic solidarity.

Parsons' presuppositional ambivalence is nowhere more strikingly illustrated than in the chapter that immediately follows this extended empirical analysis. For in this crucial fourth chapter this exercise in factor theorizing is interrupted by the strikingly multidimensional analysis described above.[118†] Yet as soon as this analysis of the early modern period of European history is completed, Parsons returns to his earlier approach; he continues to discuss social developments only as they present opportunities for increased solidary integration. In chapter 5, which focuses on the political and economic revolutions of the eighteenth and nineteenth centuries, Parsons treats industrialization in a perfunctory way as the "unfolding" of appropriate economic capacity. Market differentiation was inevitable, he believes, once membership in the legal community became differentiated from ascriptive kinship and political affiliations. Parsons emphasizes the complementary aspects of economic development vis-à-vis social values—for example, the growth of money as a generalized, impersonal medium of exchange, which contributed to the movement away from normative ascription. Because only the integrative, normative aspects of economic development draw his attention, Parsons ignores the challenge to expanded community which the expansion of instrumental structures created in the form of class conflict and domination.

Parsons takes more interest in the democratic revolution in France, but while this analysis is more original, it is, in turn, more strikingly reductionist. He abstracts away from the political aspect of the French Revolution, considering it mainly in terms of normative conflict and resolution. In a discussion which provides a historical referent for his idealist analysis of political interchange, Parsons argues that democratization occurred only after universalistic norms began to regulate membership in the political community. He approaches the Revolution, in fact, by analyzing the impact of the ideas embodied in the revolutionary slogan of "Liberty, Equality, Fraternity."[119] As compared with English developments, the distinctiveness of the French movement toward democracy can be found, Parsons believes, in the ambiguity of "liberty," a term which referred, for the French, to the freedom of the "people" rather than to the freedom of individual persons. In much the same way, "fraternity" represented a primordial symbol of early, diffuse loyalties transferred to the democratic nation. It is the conflict between these ideals, Parsons implies, which explains the unresolved struggles of the Revolutionary period. The collective emphasis on liberty sowed the seeds for later terrorism against political minorities, and the conjunction between equality and fraternity raised expectations for actual social equality before formal political freedoms were fully secured. Nowhere does Parsons interlink this analysis of normative order with an equal sensitivity to the social groups whose definitions of self-interest helped propel these conflicts, or to the political and economic exigencies which helped shape them.

In his final substantive chapter (ch. 6), while ostensibly discussing America as the lead "society" of contemporary social development, Parsons actually concentrates on the American societal community alone. Though he mentions briefly economic and class conditions, his historical argument gives causal priority to America's religious nonconformity and early ethnic homogeneity; in his discussion of the political factors involved, he elaborates in great detail the legal norms to which the early

American situation was subject.[120] The same imbalance characterizes Parsons' analysis of twentieth-century America, where he emphasizes the ways in which mass education and professional organization have created more egalitarian forms of integration. Political and economic exigencies are described as contributing to this solidarity in diverse ways. In discussing early American capitalism, for example, Parsons argues that universalistic community has been promoted by banking, which encourages broader monetization; by mass production, which creates wide distribution and provides incentives for the expansion of scientific knowledge; by the separation of technical management from property ownership; and by the unequal distribution of wealth according to technical competence and responsibility.[121]

The ideological purposes of this discussion are clear. The particularistic groupings that continue to structure modern solidarity, for example, receive short shrift.[122] In terms of the present argument, however, it is much more significant to see how Parsons has conflated these political evaluations with his presuppositional reduction. He has vastly underestimated the extent to which conditional exigencies create artificial identifications of interest, and by concentrating so overwhelmingly on the internal dimensions of interchange he has given American society a thoroughly voluntaristic slant. But modern societies, even the American one, are not simply Lockean. It is true that by analytically differentiating the solidary dimension, Parsons goes beyond the purely political, state-oriented analyses of citizenship promoted by Weber, Marshall, and Bendix in turn.[123†] But while American society may indeed have created strong citizenship loyalties, these sentiments must contend, at every point, with the fragmenting, particularizing pressures produced by the more instrumental exigencies of economics and politics. While the multidimensional element in Parsons' integration analysis recognizes this tension, it is finessed in his conflationary strand. Instead of synthesizing his great classical protagonists, Parsons chooses sides, forsaking Weberian power for Durkheimian morality.[124†]

2. IDEALISM IN THE LATER WRITINGS (2): GENERALIZED MEDIA AS THE NORMATIVE REGULATION OF SYMBOLIC EXCHANGE

In Parsons' multidimensional analysis, the media concretize his interchange model, representing the "commodities" employed by actors in actual situations. Indeed, each of the central antinomies in media theory—symbolic code and base, inflation and deflation, trust and barter—can be firmly rooted in Parsons' synthetic program.[125†] In the idealist counterpoint to this program, however, Parsons reverses his field, conceptualizing these concepts primarily as specifications of the normative order.

If a medium is to be an effective representation of multidimensional interchange, it must be conceptualized as facing both symbolic and conditional directions. Because of its symbolic dimension, it can provide a "language" that facilitates communication between institutional structures. The intrinsic base is necessary, on the other hand, if this language is to serve a distinctly social, rather than purely cultural function, for it is through its base that a medium is connected to the exigencies of scarcity. In the idealist strand of his argument, however, Parsons breaks this symbiotic connection, emphasizing symbolic code over and against intrinsic base. He justifies media analysis not by pointing to the way it represents multidimensional interchange but by arguing, simply, for the significance of symbolic language per se.

In a logical sequence that is presented time and time again in his later work, Parsons approaches media analysis by defining "action" as a symbolic activity. From this initial presuppositional distortion, he argues for the absolute centrality of language to any social interaction. He then presents media theory as the corollary of this need for symbolic language, writing, for example, that "to spend money is *only* to communicate a message."[126] This logical progression is exemplified in an early passage from his *Societies*:

> The type of process characteristic of social systems is what we call *interaction*. To comprise action in our sense, such process must focus on *symbolic levels*. This means, essentially, the linguistic level of expression and communication. . . . Furthermore, there are *symbolic media of interaction* other than language, such as money, which are probably better regarded as specialized languages than as essentially different orders of communication.[127]

Parsons has created a neat syllogism: if (1) interaction involves some symbolic media of exchange, and if (2) language is the most effective form of symbolization, then (3) media represent a symbolic language. But in making this argument, Parsons blurs the distinction between culture and social system. If the media are simply forms of language, then social processes are simply specifications of more general cultural forms, a status that denies the autonomy of specifically social exigencies.

If the symbolic code is so central and overarching, and if media are to continue to "represent" interchange, the relation between media and interchange must be distorted in a similarly idealist way. In fact, there is a strong tendency in Parsons' later work to trace the production of media to inputs from pattern maintenance and integration alone. He develops, for example, a new slant on the process by which media become viable means of exchange, the process he calls "credit creation." He contends that media become trustworthy—accepted on credit rather than on intrinsic grounds—only if they are infused with inputs from "higher" cybernetic sources. Media "support," Parsons argues, "comes only from calling on . . . various cybernetically higher forces."[128] This assertion reflects the distortion of cybernetic logic that permeates Parsons' reductionistic strategy. While it is quite possible to analyze the inputs to "credit creation" cybernetically, this viewpoint should actually lead to a focus on the tension between norms and conditions, not to a focus on the normative "control" of more conditional factors. Whether power is an acceptable medium—viewed as reciprocating inputs of support—depends not only on its normative authority but on the monetary inputs it receives from its adaptive environment. Much of the manipulation of power, or the "art of politics," depends on stabilizing the power medium by balancing these two inputs against one another. An effective politician or party can utilize a surplus on one side to compensate for a deficit on the other. In his multidimensional argument, Parsons understood this well; in the idealist version, this lesson is ignored.

Because Parsons now identifies media with cultural and subjective inputs alone, he equates media "generalization" with the symbolic legitimation produced by effective integration with norms and values. In the political case, for example, he equates the achievement of political generalization with inputs from the integrative dimension, with the successful exercise of political "influence."[129] The distinctive contribution of media now becomes their special formulation of normative regulation; through the rules which they formulate, media "define certain areas of legitimacy and the limits of . . . systems of transactions."[130] The inflation-deflation dynamic, accordingly, is related only to variation in normative inputs. This shift of emphasis is illustrated in the 1963 "Postscript" Parsons offers to his essay on McCarthyism, "Social Strains in America," which was written in 1955, before the media theory had evolved. In his earlier effort, he had described this crisis of political trust as, in part at least, the product of imbalance in America's economic, political, and cultural spheres.[131†] In this second attempt, he describes McCarthyism as a power deflation produced by the withdrawal of integrative support, which occurred, he believes, because the individualism of Americans left them culturally unprepared for the new and more demanding political responsibilities of the cold war.[132†] The same kind of distortion affects Parsons' analysis, in *The American University*, of the inflation of the cognitive rationality value; he focuses on the rationalizing effects of Protestantism and ignores almost entirely the impact of technological rationalization and political bureaucratization.

But important elements that Parsons associates with media generalization—for example, in the political case, flexibility vis-à-vis sectoral demands and the capacity to expand power beyond zero-sum—depend as much on economic capacity and instrumental political manipulation as on subjective normative and value inputs. If the political medium is symbolically legitimated, this can quickly be eroded by a failure to deliver actual services, a problem of "capacity" that can be generated by inadequate financial inputs to government. And, vice versa, insufficient symbolic legitimation can be remedied, and the political medium reinflated, if increased economic inputs or more effective political leadership allows the state to be more innovative and flexible. Trust, therefore, though associated with symbolic legitimation, should not be taken simply as a dependent variable in relation to it. A medium can move toward "generalization" by virtue of the strength of its conditional inputs alone. If power is effective, trust may be generated and the possibility for symbolic relegitimation may be significantly increased.

Parsons argues, finally, that the deflation of symbolic trust produces barter, defined as the kind of purely individualistic exchange that disrupts, indeed randomizes, social life. But this antinomy between symbolization and barter is unrealistic; it is more revealing of Parsons' idealist ambition than of actual empirical fact. Symbolic deflation can, after all, still leave intact collective control over resource distribution and exchange; such collective control must simply assume a more instrumental and coercive form. Parsons has here committed the error in theoretical reasoning that permeates his idealist logic. Conflating action and order, he treats normative structures as if they provided the only route to collective order. According to this logic, Parsons can argue that if a medium is symbolically delegitimated and action correspondingly instrumentalized, only individual order will be possible. He has ignored, once again, the possibility for artificially identifying interests.[133†]

As in the other aspects of his reductionist analysis, these presuppositional problems distort Parsons' dialogue with his classical predecessors. In the multidimensional strand of his media theory, Parsons confronts the individualistic exchange theory of classical economics by synthesizing the collectivist approaches of Durkheim and Marx. In the idealist strand, however, his critique becomes more purely Durkheimian, modifying this idealist legacy only by connecting it to the Freudian notion of internalization, a revision which allows it to be still more visibly voluntaristic. For example, while Parsons quite correctly criticizes Homans' belief that monetary exchange is individually structured, he himself describes the nonindividualistic sources of the market complex only in terms of economic norms and the socialization of economic motivation.[134] But in posing the choice as between Homans' individualistic rationalism and Durkheim's normative collectivism, Parsons ignores the entire thrust of Marx's work. Marx, after all, also mounted a collectivist critique of classical economics; he simply did so from a rationalistic rather than a normative perspective. Of course, as I argued earlier (ch. 4, sec. 6.3), the media theory implicit in Marx's analysis eliminates a commodity's symbolic code and insists, instead, on the exclusive importance of the intrinsic base. In doing so, however, Marx does outline the vital relationship between media and the structures of coercive power, a connection which media must "represent" as surely as they stand for more symbolic controls.

This Durkheim-Freud reduction is perhaps most directly formulated in Parsons' later attempts to generalize media theory to what he calls the "general action" level.[135] In this effort, Parsons is, ostensibly, simply elaborating his earlier differentiation of the four basic systems of action by identifying each with a specific kind of "product," or commodity.[136†] Thus, the behavioral organism produces "intelligence," the personality "performance capacity," the social system "affect," and the cultural system "definitions of the situation." Parsons argues that the relation between the social system and its organic, cultural, and psychological environments is structured by the relation among these four media. To gain necessary inputs of organic intelligence, cultural definitions, and motivated performance, the social system provides the other systems with structured opportunities for the gratification of affect.

But while Parsons and his students have utilized this general action interchange to illuminate important relationships between social system and personality, culture, and organism, their relative empirical success should not obscure the potential presuppositional problems involved.[137] Parsons identifies affect as "the generalized medium most definitely concerned with the mobilization and control of the factors of solidarity in Durkheim's sense."[138] In doing so, however, he describes the basic output of the social system in a manner that shifts attention sharply away from instrumental and organizational phenomena to variables that have exclusively internal references. In fact, taken together, the four action media present a picture of society as a solidary interaction in which continued stability depends solely upon actors' cognitive performance, cultural standards, and motivational commitments.

In a certain sense, of course, this picture is not inaccurate. Diverse "opportunities for affect" may, in fact, be viewed as the upshot of a given set of societal patterns, and in this sense the four general action media may illuminate the tensions involved in the social system's boundaries with the organic, motivational, and cultural systems that impinge on it.[139†] In a more strictly theoretical sense, however, the media can only be viewed as reflecting Parsons' familiar effort to treat the social system as "ground" for the cultural regulation of personality, the same effort that seriously distorts his much more elaborate treatment of media at the societal level. Indeed, once Parsons had formulated "general action interchange," it presented him with a continual temptation, for it allowed him to slip ever more securely into the synthesis of Durkheim and Freud, the synthesis which defines affective solidarity as the core of modern society.

The presuppositional ambiguity in Parson's media theory is reflected, as are the ambiguities in the rest of his work, in the interpretations offered by both critics and sympathizers. Once again, the tension in Parsons' writing produces a strange convergence between negative and positive interpretation. Parsons' more instrumentalist critics, like Gouldner and Giddens, ignore completely the multidimensional element in his analysis, arguing that media theory focuses exclusively on symbolic trust to the exclusion of more structural concerns.[140] Parsons' sympathizers, on the other hand, make the same one-sided interpretation, only this time in Parsons' defense. They applaud what they view as his consistently anti-Marxist, symbolic focus. Schwanenberg writes, for example, that the "generalized media are . . . the generalized mechanisms of the integrative function" of the social system.[141] Similarly, in the most elaborated and sophisticated defense of media theory, Baum defines media as "normative specification[s]."[142] Arguing that they reflect Parsons' overriding concern with "problems of communication," he suggests that "societal media can be understood best as functionally specialized yet generalized languages of trust."[143†] Defining media theory as "the analysis of symbolic mediation," Baum, in another work, engages in a detailed discussion of media inflation and deflation as generated by conflicts within a society's value patterns.[144†]

It is largely because of this mutually reinforcing dialogue that the most important presuppositional references of Parsons' theory have gone unrecognized. It is surprising, indeed, that any multidimensional examples of media analysis have survived intact.[145]

3. IDEALISM IN THE LATER WRITINGS (3): SOCIAL CHANGE AS THE EVOLUTION OF NORMATIVE REGULATION

Finally, if we consider Parsons' theory of social change in its entirety, we must conclude that it, too, is fraught with ambiguity. Yet Parsons' change theory differs from the other segments of his work in one important sense: its epistemological reference has a temporal cast. The change theory becomes increasingly idealistic in the course of Parsons' writing.

This progression is exemplified in the transformation of the concept "vested interests," which plays a central theoretical role throughout Parsons' career. In the writing of his early middle period, Parsons utilized the concept in a broad, multidimensional manner to refer to groups—political, economic, religious, and regional—opposed to social rationalization. Parsons argued that such groups, responding to a variety of normative and instrumental pressures, defined their self-interest in traditionalistic terms.[146†] In the writings of his later middle period, however, Parsons began to conceive such groups in a decidedly less synthetic manner. Though his change theory as a whole retained significant multidimensional elements, his approach to "interest" was deeply affected by the moral-psychological reduction which lies at the root of his presuppositional problem. Parsons now approaches traditionalistic groups in terms of the Durkheim-Freud synthesis: "Vested interests . . . fundamentally [represent] the interest in maintaining . . . conformity with institutionalized *expectations*," including the "interest in . . . love, approval, and esteem."[147] When he discusses the conservative opposition to industrial technology, for example, it is in terms of a group's vested interest in noncognitive, religious culture rather than in terms of its instrumental opposition to the new economic arrangements which increased technology helps produce. By the time of Parsons' later writings, the notion of "vested interest" has been transformed completely into value opposition; Parsons treats it as interchangeable with "fundamentalism" in the religious sense.[148]

This shift in "vested interests" indicates a more general movement that occurs in the course of Parsons' later writing on change. Alongside his multidimensional approach, where differentiation proceeds on each of the four cybernetic levels of the social system, Parsons develops a much more reductionist schema that portrays differentiation as a historical process of "learning." Although Parsons certainly does not believe that ontogeny recapitulates phylogeny in any precise sense, there can be no doubt that he has taken his socialization theory of individual development as the model for his idealist approach to history. In this idealist version, conditional factors like economic and political development can only create disruptive strains, not structural change itself. New world-historical stages, which include fundamental changes in political and economic structures themselves, can occur only if they are preceded by the creation and internalization of new normative patterns.[149] It is on the basis of the increasing rationalization of cultural life, Parsons believes, that social development, like individual development, can present a process of increasing adaptation to, and control over, the conditional aspects of collective existence. Historical change, therefore, is voluntaristic: "A change in the structure of a social system is a change in its normative culture."[150] In the light of this perspective, it seems only natural that the historical evolution of moral codes occupies so disproportionate a part of Parsons' theoretical attention.

3.1. VALUES AS THE MOTOR OF PREMODERN HISTORY

In his multidimensional analysis, Parsons indicates how economic and political differentiation have been crucial in facilitating the unusual cultural evolution that has characterized Western history. Insofar as he adopts an idealist strategy, however, the significance of political and economic factors recedes; change in values and solidarity assume a determinate importance.[151†]

Although this declension from multidimensionality can be followed in Parsons' shorter theoretical essays,[152†] it is demonstrated most powerfully in his two monographs on world history, *Societies: Evolutionary and Comparative Perspectives* and *The System of Modern Societies*. In these two works, Parsons places his focus on solidarity and value change within the context of a general theory of historical differentiation. As was noted in my earlier analysis of the idealist strand in *The System of Modern Societies* (sec. 1.5), Parsons devotes by far the greater part of his analysis of European development to changes in solidarity. In the earlier monograph on premodern history, *Societies: Evolutionary and Comparative Perspectives*, in contrast, it is religion, not norms, that becomes the focal point of Parsons' attention. He believes that it was differentiation in the pattern-maintenance system which formed the bedrock for later developments in the societal community. Differentiation of the societal community institutionalizes the morality of individualism, the principle that a person's political rights are based on membership in a universal community rather than on loyalty to any particular national, regional, ethnic, religious, or economic group. We might recall that Parsons is also concerned with this morality of individualism in his theory of social change as "value generalization," which refers to the ascendance of universalistic codes over more ascriptive, group-defined loyalty values.[153†] If pattern-maintenance changes are to precede integrative ones, value generalization must be the focus for any study of premodern society.

Since religious development is to provide the resources for later normative change, value change must gradually differentiate religion from its imbeddedness in "society," or, more precisely, from particular social obligations. The symbolic sources of legitimation must, in other words, become increasingly separated from the institutional bases of power. At the same time, the symbolic understanding of community must be redefined as a collectivity separated from the nonsocial levels of action, from the biological, the psychological, and the cultural. Parsons believes that these purely symbolic developments—religious differentiation and the resymbolization of community—constitute the foundations for all other premodern developments. According to his idealized understanding of cybernetic causality, cultural symbols provide the "codes" by which more structural resources are organized and revised.[154]

In primitive society, Parsons writes, the "we" reference of a society's symbolization has a direct connection to the supernatural world, for the community's ancestors were believed to be divine.[155] It also interpenetrates with the biological world, a fusion exemplified by totemism, in which animal figures simultaneously represent divinity, ancestor, and society itself. The biological and religious worlds, in turn, are fused with the social-organizational order through the institution of kinship, which provides the central status criterion in primitive societies. Parsons believes that religious ceremonies provide a striking illustration of this multilevel fusion, for in rituals members of primitive society act out their deep unconscious connections to ancestors, gods, and animal life. Incest is often a crucial element in these ritual ceremonies, and Parsons regards incest as the sine qua non of fusion between organism and society. He believes that this symbolic commitment to incest demonstrates the extent to which the particularistic association of kinship constitutes the core of the societal community. It is because of this close interpenetration between religion and the other levels of action that primitive societies allow little possibility for social creativity, freedom, or conflict.

In archaic societies, symbolism becomes more cosmological.[156] This involves, most importantly perhaps, the development of literacy, for religion once it is written down can be elaborated in a more rationalized way. In the process of this symbolic rationalization, Parsons believes, religion becomes more generalized and independent of other levels of action, less immediately tied to the biological world, to kinship, and to particular social functions. Yet there remains great fusion in archaic society, as Parsons demonstrates in his analysis of Egyptian kinship. Although most of the Egyptian social system was deprived of supranatural anchorage, the pharaoh was still considered divine. This society-cosmos link, moreover, was fused with the biological world, for Egyptians believed it was the union between the gods of heaven and earth which had given birth to the pharaoh. In this way, the principal representation of society, the pharaoh, was linked in a rigid, ascriptive way not only to divine mandates but, through the gods of heaven and earth, to the cyclical processes of natural and animal life.

Given this situation, the status of "community membership" in Egypt could be separated only vaguely from nonsocial, nonfunctional elements. Legal formalism developed, for example, only to a minimal degree, and the highly personalistic Egyptian bureaucracy was rooted in rigid, ascriptive controls. It is not surprising, therefore, that incest remained a vital symbolic and real element in Egyptian life, though in contrast to primitive societies it was limited to the royal family.

The crucial push toward the "historic" societies of the great empires—China, India, Rome, and Islam—came, once again, from crucial reformulations at the level of constitutive symbolism.[157] For the first time, a sharp differentiation between human and divine was established, a distinction which allowed increasing separation of the social from the biological realms in turn. Thus, Confucius, building upon China's common culture and written language, created a rationalized "philosophy" that raised religion to a new level of autonomy and generalization. As Confucian culture became the basis of education and achievement of high office, status became increasingly defined in cultural rather than in kinship terms. Moreover, while the emperor was considered to have a divine mandate, he was not considered to be divine himself. All this provided much greater distance between the sources of symbolic legitimation and social structure and, correspondingly, created greater leverage for secular, socially oriented expertise. Still, this symbolic differentiation represented more of a direction or tendency than a completed development, and Parsons demonstrates that latent kinship and notions of divine intervention continued to play crucial roles in Chinese society.

Although religious rationalization in the historic empires meant that community membership could, for the first time, now be defined according to strict and definite criteria, this achievement created sharp divisions between the elect and the masses. Parsons believes that this legitimated a two-class system which divided the community into legally defined in-group and out-group. Paradoxically, it was this sharply defined boundary which set the stage for future struggles over the broadening of solidary membership.

In analyzing the transition from historic societies to modernity, Parsons traces social development from ancient Judaism to the Greeks and Roman Christianity, and with the exception of his multidimensional digression on the failure of Roman law, his theoretical strategy remains the same.[158†] Parsons concentrates, once again, on the processes of cultural differentiation and their ramifications for the rest of society.

With the transcendent god Jahwe, Judaism severed completely the interpenetration of divine and human world, a break that not only prevented, in principle, the monopolization of earthly grace and secular prestige by kingship or social class but legitimated the purely secular regulation of the societal community by legal norms.[159] This development, in turn, differentiated for the first time membership in the solidary community from obedience to a particular political regime:

> Whatever the human organization of political authority, the fundamental normative order governing human relations was to be considered *independent* of it. The king, insofar as the kingdom was Israelite, was to act *under* the law and be the agent of its implementation, not its source and origin.[160]

This symbolic break also allowed Judaism, more than any previous religion, to eliminate from its ceremonial activity the ritualism, eroticism, and totemism which, in Parsons' terms, indicated the fusion of the cultural, social, and biological worlds.

For Parsons, the road from Judaism to Christianity led through Greece and Rome. The Greek conception of a "binding order of nature" accessible to reason amounted to a radical differentiation of nature from the metaphysical order, and Parsons analyzes the polis in terms of the way in which this cultural orientation pushed Greek life beyond traditional political forms.[161] He discusses Sophocles' *Oedipus* trilogy, for example, as presenting the conflict between a less differentiated, kinship-based order—one which, in Parsons' terms, is inevitably bound up with incestuous relationships—and a more normatively differentiated, civil society, from which incest has been strictly excluded. While Roman society later succeeded in stabilizing its territorial base in a way that Greece could not, it did so through a legal system which had systematized the Stoic philosophy of nature.[162] Parsons believes that Roman law allowed the most differentiated large-scale community yet achieved and that it produced an unparalleled expansion of the rights of citizenship to the lower classes. Though the Roman empire proved to be unstable, its legal order eventually became the basis for the canon law of the Christian church, the survival of which was so crucial to the cultural development of the West.[163†]

These are the essentially religious developments that provide the historical foundation for Parsons' vision of modern society. The cultural heritage of Israel, Greece, and Rome, surviving the Middle Ages, became revivified and even more rationalized in the Renaissance and Reformation. The Judaic and Christian differentiation of "religious community" from particular biological and social exigencies allowed an independent societal community eventually to emerge in early modern Europe, and it was from this independent normative community that the major characteristics of modernity derived.[164†] In economic life, individuals and groups gradually were freed to adopt purely economic criteria unfettered by particularistic obligations; yet, paradoxically, they remained increasingly bound by the legal norms of a universalistic community. Politically, there developed collegial, egalitarian forms of political association, which in private organizations cross-cut hierarchical bureaucratic power with horizontal professionalized authority, and in public government produced a mass democracy which cross-cut particularistic class and religious obligations. As for stratification, the fruits of premodern culture produced an increasing emphasis on internalized competence as the basis of rewards. It also created the push toward cognitive rationality, which, Parsons believes, increased equality by providing individuals with more access to what was becoming the most valued social commodity, namely, intellectual competence.

Parsons finds in these modern developments "empirical verification" for his idealized account of historical development. Premodern cultural history laid the basis for these movements toward personal autonomy, for only through this extended cultural development could individuals develop the capacity to separate value commitments from biological drives, unconscious fantasy, and particular social affiliations, and, indeed, from totalistic cultural commitments themselves. This general capacity was effectuated in the early modern community of citizenship, as individuals learned to implement autonomy in a variety of particular situations.[165] By the modern period, Parsons asserts, collective control and social responsibility rest with the individual, albeit the Durkheimian "institutionalized individual," the product of the most elaborate socialization in human history.

In this deceptively brief history of human society, Parsons has utilized the cybernetic schema to clarify some problems of extraordinary significance that remained unresolved, indeed unresolvable, in the work of his classical predecessors. Though Durkheim emphasized the importance of solidarity and its intimate relation to religious symbolization, his fundamentally valid theory of secularization was not differentiated enough analytically to distinguish the various levels of action—cultural, social, psychological, organic—which historical changes in religion and solidarity involve. Durkheim also described historical change as increasing individual autonomy, yet because he had no reference to Freud's theory of psychological growth he could not specify, as Parsons was able to, the actual social mediations upon which individualism must rest. Similarly, Parsons relies heavily on Weber's understanding of religious rationalization and its relation to increased activism and control. Yet Weber lacked not only a socialization theory but also a systematic understanding of the basis of secular as distinguished from religious community.[166†] As a result, Weber misperceived the crucial transition of secularization, the movement from the differentiating religious societies of early modern Europe to the industrial, democratic societies of the modern West. He could not comprehend that such a transition could be achieved by translating the heritage of religious rationalization into the socialization of autonomous individuals and the independence of secular solidary communities.

For all of this, Parsons has illuminated only one strand of historical development. If he has learned from Weber in certain highly significant respects, he has surely ignored him in others.[167†] To explore the full implications of this idealist rendition of history, one must examine what it finally wrought: Parsons' vision of the voluntary society.

3.2. MODERNISM AS THE VOLUNTARY SOCIETY

For Parsons, the "educational revolution"—the spread of secondary and higher education to all strata of society—presents the crucial innovation of the twentieth century, much as the political and industrial revolutions marked the eighteenth and nineteenth.[168] Not only is it mass education which provides the normative reference and context for the psychological maturation upon which the democratic autonomy of the individual is based, but it is education, particularly higher education, that provides the value of cognitive rationality upon which so much of Parsons' vision of modernity depends. It is not an exaggeration to say that for Parsons, mass education is the culmination of all previous historical development.

3.2.1. Normative Reduction and Ideological Conflation: The Modern Professions and Stratification

It is particularly in tracing the normative effects of this educational revolution that Parsons puts his disproportionate emphasis on values to the service of his ideological moderation. Through his emphasis on internalized values as the prime mover in contemporary institutions and events, he takes moral "blame" away from social authorities. In the hands of a more critical ideologist, social differentiation theory can become a tool for critique, by illuminating the monopolization of political authority, the fusion of economic and political roles, or the dedifferentiation and particularism of cultural values.[169] In the hands of the later Parsons, in contrast, the theory often becomes a vehicle for articulating the complacent faith that freedom is there for those who would take it. Because he underemphasizes coercion and the artificial identification of interest, Parsons throws responsibility back on the self, for the natural identification of interests is accomplished through value internalization alone. If society's moral authority is debased or irresponsible, the theory of internalization implies that this social failure will be visible through the weakness of the self. The society which is external to the individual in a visible, concrete sense—society, that is, in its material form—cannot, in this idealist scheme, become the object of critical attack.[170†]

This strategic utilization of modern voluntarism as an antidote to social criticism is clearly manifest in Parsons' approach to the professions. From the beginning of his efforts at empirical analysis, the professions were a vital reference for Parsons' presuppositional specification. In *Essays in Sociological Theory*, from his middle period, Parsons demonstrated the overlap between business and the "liberal professions" to argue against the primarily utilitarian approach to capitalist economic activity. In *The Social System*, the medical profession served as his principal case study for the pattern-variable schema. In the later writings, as he began to conceptualize Western development in terms of the shift from hierarchy and coercion to collegiality and voluntarism, he argued that the professions had assumed an increasingly central empirical position in modern life. The professions, Parsons argued, are the most tangible results of the educational revolution. Not only do they depend more than other kinds of work upon the socialized autonomy of the individual, but as intermediaries between the university and concrete social problems they ensure the social application of cognitive rationality.[171†]

None of these arguments, I must emphasize, is inherently idealist; the professions can indeed play a central normative role in modern society, albeit a role which is in tension with more instrumental pressures generated from within the professions and from without. It is, however, precisely such a multidimensional context that Parsons so frequently avoids. Too often, he uses the "professions" for presuppositional polemic rather than synthesis. Specifying a Durkheimian position at the expense of the Weberian, he never considers the professional monopolization of authority in anything other than a normative sense; he is unable, as a result, to identify professional self-interest in an instrumental, means-oriented way. It is not surprising, then, to find that Parsons cites the existence of modern professions as one more empirical demonstration that the socialist critique of capitalist irresponsibility is no longer relevant.[172]

But an even more striking illustration of the conflation of idealistic argument and ideological critique occurs in Parsons' theory of modern stratification. On the one hand, from the very beginning of his career, Parsons utilized his multidimensional framework to provide a synthetic reformulation of instrumental and normative approaches to class and elite behavior. This is evident, most strikingly, in the analysis of horizontal and vertical interest-polarization that informs Parsons' discussions in the early essays; it is also clear in the "functional elite" formulation which occurs in his later work.[173†] On the other hand, Parsons' thinking about stratification has, also from the beginning, been permeated by a much more idealist approach.

In his earliest essay on stratification, for example, Parsons introduces the subject by emphasizing the normative aspects of the action frame of reference.[174] From this emphasis, he reasons that stratification exists because people are concerned with making moral distinctions.[175] Insofar as these moral distinctions become collectively ordered, there develops a system of stratification that, once internalized, regulates the individual perception of instrumental interest.

> Indeed, if any given individual can be said to seek his own "self-interest" . . . it follows that he can do so only by conforming in some degree to the institutionalized definition of the situation. But this in turn means that he must to a large degree be oriented to the scale of stratification.[176]

Variation in different systems of stratification, therefore, must be explained in terms of variation in the moral orientations of different societies.

> The content of the [stratification] scale, the specific standards and criteria by which individuals are ranked, is not uniform for all social systems but varies within a wide social range. It follows from the definition of a scale of stratification adopted here that this variation will be a function of the more general variations of value orientation which can be shown empirically to exist as between widely differing social systems.[177]

To be sure, Parsons goes on to connect these normative considerations to a number of material factors, for example, to the distribution of possessions, to kinship membership, authority, and power.[178] But he argues that these factors become relevant only as the realistic objects of moral evaluation. An individual's stratification position, he asserts, "may be regarded as a resultant of the common *evaluations* underlying the attribution of status to him in each of these respects."[179]Parsons argues that the decisive criteria for the evaluation of status are provided by the pattern-variable schema, and he devotes the remainder of this essay to demonstrating how the tension between ascription and achievement values defines the fundamental difference between stratification systems. If a major problem in Weber's classic essay, "Class, Status, and Party," is the tendency to instrumentalize status variables, Parsons has inverted Weber by converting instrumental factors into moral qualities.

Fifteen years later, Parsons follows a similar strategy in his best-known essay on stratification, entitled "A Revised Analytical Approach to the Theory of Social Stratification." While he begins this essay with the multidimensional interchange model, he argues, almost immediately, that the four dimensions should be considered not as different dimensions of social activity but rather as different types of moral evaluation.[180] Utilizing the "formally deduced" pattern-variable combinations to discover the moral qualities associated with each dimension, he uses the interchange model to describe four ideal-typical kinds of stratification systems, each keyed to different moral qualities. Once again, material objects, like possessions and their modes of distribution, are treated as foci for normative evaluation, not as external factors that structure instrumental interest in their own right.[181] Parsons does, however, note a "looseness of fit" between the typical distribution of rewards and the ideal ranking of valued performance, and he discusses, in this context, the unequal allocation generated by private as compared with public occupations, the way in which safe investments keep inheritance intact, and the tendencies for wealthy or powerful families to "consolidate their position and perpetuate it as [a] hereditary 'upper class.' "[182†] But while these elements become central in his more multidimensional analyses, they are relegated here to residual status. "These factors," he writes, "are of the greatest importance for detailed empirical analysis, but [they] are secondary from the point of view of the broad characterization of our stratification system."[183†] Indeed, Parsons concludes that much more important than such material factors for explaining "looseness of fit" is the moral indeterminacy which is inherent in any attempt to establish a general evaluative standard.[184]

The same reductionist approach to stratification, with all its ideological resonance, is taken in the later "Outline of the Social System," which still presents Parsons' most systematic and elaborate discussion of his later theoretical schema. As if to emphasize the normative elements of his approach, Parsons discusses stratification as a phenomenon of the integrative subsystem itself.[185] In contrast, he considers the polarization of wealth and power as a problem for social-change theory, not as a subject for stratification analysis. Parsons then conflates this idealist reduction with an ideological justification for income inequality based on occupational achievement, arguing that the "focus of institutional stratification," qua normative evaluation, is on the "*legitimizing* of differential power and wealth."[186]

These tendencies achieve their most sophisticated articulation in Parsons' writings of the 1970s. In *The System of Modern Societies*, for example, he produces a historical account of stratification that revolves completely around shifts in evaluative perspective.[187] In the liberal capitalist ideology which was generated particularly during the English industrial revolution, individualistic morality embraced "liberty" only in the negative sense, as security from government coercion. This cultural emphasis, Parsons believes, seriously underplayed the problem of economic inequality. On the other hand, the value of political "equality," emphasized primarily by the French Revolution, not only neglected the potential problems of centralized government control but paid insufficient attention to the role which considerations of economic efficiency must have in determining the distribution of rewards. These English and French perspectives have failed to explain modern stratification, Parsons believes, because they have concentrated, respectively, only on the instrumental spheres of adaptation and goal attainment; they have ignored the central roles played by value commitment and solidarity. Only if the latter spheres are taken into account can we see that modern stratification is legitimated in a way that interweaves liberty and equality. On the one hand, since adaptive efficiency is crucial, rewards must still be distributed on the basis of individual competition. Yet this individualism, or liberty, is tempered by the supra-individual reality of individual socialization which occurs in the pattern-maintenance sphere: true individual competition is limited to the adult phase of the life cycle. In the pre-adult phases, equality is more emphasized: all children are exposed, through education, to the value of cognitive rationality. Since modern occupations are ranked largely according to levels of cognitive, or rational competence—a standard maintained by professional solidarity—Parsons believes that equal educational opportunity guarantees relatively widespread egalitarianism in the distribution of rewards. This egalitarianism, moreover, is achieved without excessive governmental intervention.

The depth of Parsons' insight here should not be overlooked. Building on the Durkheim-Freud critique of Weber's instrumental approach to education and status, Parsons has discovered a newly emergent form of legitimation, one which goes a long way toward explaining certain uniquely modern phenomena. He demonstrates, for example, that it is because access to socialization has become, with the educational revolution, radically more egalitarian that the phenomenon of socialization has become so central to the legitimation of stratification in modern society. He can also argue, quite plausibly, that if the balance between political liberty and economic efficiency is to be preserved, movements toward greater equality should aim at revising the environments of socialization rather than relying too heavily on efforts at governmental redistribution[188]—efforts which might appear to be denying the valid achievements of (socialized) individuals for the sake of "society."

Yet in making these arguments, Parsons also ignores the instrumental aspects of stratification. Mobility is not simply a matter of competitive socialization, as he implies;[189] strong economic and political constraints operate not only as contextual variables for unequal socialization but as outright attempts at the instrumental monopolization of external opportunities. A purely normative voluntaristic approach to stratification, then, simply will not do. If an individual fails to achieve high rewards, the fault cannot be placed only on an undersocialized self. It is primarily because of this fact, of course, that movements toward the equalization of status must, inevitably, rely as heavily upon governmental efforts at redistribution as upon the restructuring of socialization, despite the appearance of anti-individualistic bias this inevitably creates.

3.2.2. Affective Strain and Cultural Conflict

Yet, despite this subjectivist vision of modernity, and the ideological conservatism to which it is linked, it would be wrong to conclude that Parsons' conceptualization of a differentiated society necessarily eliminates strain and conflict. Instead of eliminating them, Parsons has simply shifted the focus of explanation.

Whereas nineteenth-century social conflicts were material in origin, the "newest phase [of social development] returns to a primary concern with cultural elements."[190] In the more fully differentiated society of the twentieth century, Parsons argues, it is "the motivational basis of social solidarity" that creates the most significant strains.[191] These strains emerge from the subjective feelings of frustration that are produced by exclusion from full social participation, whether this participation is in the symbolic or the behavioral realm.[192] This exclusion is not only ethnic and racial; it also refers to the manner in which unequal class position manifests itself in the modern, voluntaristic context. For example, the psychological strains produced by thwarted mobility can be great indeed, as Parsons demonstrates in his discussions of juvenile delinquency and xenophobic aggression.[193] And Parsons describes the conflict between egalitarian ideals and the hierarchical divisions generated by the equally high valuation placed upon efficiency as a tension which lies at the heart of most contemporary social movements.[194] But perhaps the most significant problem associated with feelings of solidary exclusion, in his view, is the motivational strain generated by demands for more direct affective community and the way these demands are frustrated by a pluralized, differentiated social context.[195]

In almost every case, Parsons believes, contemporary protest movements relate to solidary exclusion and affective alienation rather than to actual economic or political deprivation. He describes the New Left and Communist movements in Western Europe, for example, as "fundamentalist" groups, whose commitments to more narrow and secure versions of community-as-*Gemeinschaft* make them unable to accept the kinds of universalistic associations offered by a pluralist society.[196†] Yet, while he argues that "the cruder simplicities of the *gemeinschaft* school of thought cannot be institutionalized," he emphasizes that the "major problems [for modernity] lie in this *area*."[197] As Parsons wrote in an article entitled "The Problem of Balancing Rational Efficiency with Communal Solidarity in Modern Society":

> The problem is how the predominantly cognitively rational aspect of the cultural system should be fitted in with the other aspects which are important to a complete and rounded cultural system. The primary focus of [recent] dissidence is . . . the emergence of a [noncognitive] "counterculture" in the United States.[198]

More than any contemporary sociological theorist, and certainly more than any of his classical predecessors, Parsons has explored the affective deprivation generated by association in a universalistic and differentiated society.[199†] Equally important, he has systematically demonstrated how this affective deprivation creates alienating tendencies throughout the social system, from the problems generated by life-cycle transitions and inadequate socialization—which manifest themselves in juvenile delinquency, youth culture, and neurosis—to the series of structural conflicts between instrumental and expressive roles which create such "deviant" activities as gambling, eroticism, aggression, and mass spectatorship.[200†]

Of course, these analyses of conflict are all cut from the same familiar cloth. It is Parsons' very sociological idealism—his reductionist concentration on the Durkheim-Freud synthesis—that makes him so enormously sensitive to the structural vicissitudes which thwart value cathexis. While we have been reminded throughout this chapter that we must not underestimate the enormous empirical insights that Parsons generated within his idealist framework, these accomplishments should not obscure the serious distortions that this framework entails. At every point, Parsons' presuppositional errors undercut the breadth of his achievement. His accomplishments, as a result, never matched his theoretical ambition.

4. SOCIOLOGICAL IDEALISM AS THE PROPER SCOPE OF SOCIOLOGY: THE FINAL CONFLATION OF METHOD AND PRESUPPOSITION

Parsons spent most of his career attacking sectarian, or "factor," theorizing, yet the multidimensional strand of his own work is cross-cut by persistent movement toward sociological idealism. Parsons forcefully criticized Durkheim for engaging in a "crucial experiment" to prove the significance of normative elements rather than producing an analytic theory that could take a more synthetic tack. Yet his own theory, though vastly more sophisticated analytically, often exhibits precisely this Durkheimian concern, arguing by means of carefully selected examples that normative elements are, after all, more important than instrumental ones.

It seems at first glance incredible that such contradictions could permeate the work of such a self-conscious thinker. Yet, we should not really be surprised, for social theories are, in fact, rife with confusions and self-contradiction. None of Parsons' predecessors was entirely consistent. Although Marx's mature "scientific" writings were generally instrumental, his informal political writing produced vigorous theoretical counterpoint. Durkheim's scientific theory, we have seen, was torn between assertions about voluntarism on the one hand and contentions about the determinism of collective force on the other, and he allowed instrumental exigencies to intrude continually as residual categories in his work. Weber argued that comparative sociology must take a multidimensional perspective on rationality, yet his comparative work moved uncertainly between synthetic explanation and a much more materialist mode, often, indeed, within the same piece of writing.

Rather than asking how such contradictions could have occurred in Parsons' work, we might well ask how Parsons could have remained so unaware of them. Durkheim responded to the early strains in his work by moving steadily toward a more satisfactory approach to the individual/society dilemma. Though he never eliminated his residual instrumentalism, he could, however, attain an apparent consistency by conflating it with his ideological and empirical commitments. Weber, for his part, offered an empirical explanation for his inconsistencies, claiming that the world itself had experienced a deep historical rupture with the onset of industrial society. In these theoretical rationalizations, we can find implicit acknowledgement of the strains which split each classical theorists work. Parsons' work is not without similar mea culpa's. Characteristically, however, they assume a highly self-conscious, indeed systematic form.

As I have indicated particularly in chapter 2, Parsons consistently utilized his antipositivistic understanding of science to gain further insight into crucial presuppositional issues. Since science must approach the empirical world in an analytic rather than a concrete way, he asserted, science can, of necessity, consider only part of empirical reality, not the whole of it. In *The Structure of Social Action*, Parsons argued on this basis that the most apparently rational action must be scrutinized for its "concretely invisible" referents. This relationship between method and presuppositional commitment is, as we have seen, not unusual in theoretical thinking; it is similarly employed, for example, when Max Weber argues that an anti-instrumental position requires a more comparative approach to historical methodology.[201†] Yet we have seen that Parsons often goes beyond positing an interrelationship between theory and methods to asserting a truly conflationary relation between them. He argues that positivism is inherently connected to instrumentalist theorizing, that if a theory transcends positivism, its approach to order simply cannot be rationalistic.[202†]

It is through just such conflationary logic that Parsons tries to construct an implicit rationale for his idealist thrust. Since science considers the part rather than the whole, he argues, it is not unreasonable to assume that different sciences will consider different analytical elements and, indeed, that these divergent objects of analysis may be systematically related. In the movement from atomic physics to chemistry, from biology to psychology, and from psychological to social science, Parsons sees different "emergent properties" as defining each level of analysis.[203] Yet Parsons moves from this entirely plausible argument to the much less tenable claim that each of the social sciences can themselves be identified with distinctly different analytic elements, or, in his technical vocabulary, with different elements of the "unit act." Economics conceptualizes the organization of means, politics the organization of goals, and anthropology the relation of values. The domain of sociology, Parsons asserts, is norms.

This position is elaborated in the course of Parsons' writing. In *The Structure of Social Action*, when he worked primarily at the presuppositional level, Parsons identified sociology's focus simply as "common-value integration."[204] In the early part of his middle period, when his conceptual schema was still only partly distinguishable from that of classical theory, he defined sociology as the "science of institutions," these institutions, in turn, being viewed as "embodying the patterns of 'common value integration.' "[205†] With *The Social System*, Parsons can become more explicit: sociology focuses on the cathectic internalization of shared value patterns.[206] In the later writings, the interchange model allows Parsons to formulate the issue in a more systematic and precise, not to say more elegant, way. Sociology is the study of the social system's integrative subsystem, the "societal community," and of the way this solidary community seeks to institutionalize more general values and to control more specific, instrumental pressures.[207]

But this conflationary methodological rationale certainly has not been a continuous point of reference for Parsons' theoretical logic. Indeed, as the preceding discussion demonstrates, Parsons usually justifies his sociological idealism through a number of other conflationary strategies: by positing an idealist "frame of reference" valid for all social thought; by arguing that in cybernetic models systems are inevitably guided and controlled by symbolic codes; by asserting that only the internalization of these codes can sustain empirical equilibrium; by claiming for these normative arrangements an isomorphism with other well-established social "facts"; or, finally, by arguing, quite simply, that the emphasis on normative order reflects empirical-historical development itself. The methodological conflation of the sociological discipline with the focus on solidarity, however, represents Parsons' only self-conscious rationale for his idealist strain, and it surfaces periodically as a kind of "last resort" argument.[208] This strategy is most explicit in *The Social System*.

In the conclusion to that enormous, often brilliant, and seriously flawed theoretical exercise, Parsons acknowledges that "the postulate of rationality . . . occupies a somewhat curious status in the theory of action."[209] He admits, in the first place, a fact that he himself had powerfully demonstrated earlier in the book, namely, that instrumental action can be approached in a thoroughly multidimensional way. Within the context of structured motivational and value commitments, actors often take a purely "efficient" approach to their environment.[210] Parsons then discusses the three principal types of such instrumental-rational activity, which he describes as technological, economic, and political behavior.[211] He concludes, however, that these modes of behavior are outside the scope of sociological theory, and to justify this argument he returns to the importance of motivation and values. Because action theory has established that a "psychologically . . . internalized pattern is no longer an object of the situation," Parsons argues, "it is not possible to treat it as an instrumental means or condition."[212] On this basis, he concludes that "the orientation of 'instrumental rationality' *cannot* be the attitude defining the actor's orientation to internalized patterns." This fact, moreover, has "fundamental methodological significance," for "the present volume can, in these terms, be regarded rather strictly as a contribution to *sociological* theory."[213]

But what has Parsons really proved? Ostensibly, he has justified his ideal focus by suggesting that instrumental action is a contradiction in terms. But, in fact, it is not instrumental action Parsons has discussed but, rather, the status of normative orientations. That purely instrumental attitudes cannot be taken toward internalized objects is true by definition; it proves nothing about the possibility for instrumentalizing action itself, for obviously it is only the external, material location of objects that can produce pressures for efficient adaptation. The argument, in other words, is circular.

If such a definition of sociology were actually followed, it would make incomprehensible the multidimensional strand of Parsons' own work. It is interesting in this regard that if we return, for a moment, to the analysis of allocation and integration which occupied such important segments of the early chapters in *The Social System*, we find that Parsons tries, periodically, to isolate these discussions—to make significant aspects of his own sociology appear to be nonsociological. At one point, for example, after discussing the differentiated system of instrumental economic activity, he states that "the *specifically sociological* problem focus with reference to such a subsystem of social action concerns the kinds of value-orientations which are institutionalized in it."[214] Later, Parsons concludes his forcefully multidimensional analysis in *The Social System's* fourth chapter with an eight-page outline of his analytic schema. But he moves immediately to qualify this schema by arguing that sociological attention to economic and instrumental orientations is unnecessary because "obviously the subject matter under this heading has been intensively dealt with in economics and political science."[215] How can this statement be taken at face value when Parsons has just concluded an investigation of the role which the economy of instrumental orientations plays in the allocation process? Perhaps rather than as a characterization of what has preceded it, Parsons' statement should be considered as an implicit warning, for with the exception of his discussion, immediately following, of how allocative exigencies affect various empirical clusters, Parsons never returns in *The Social System* to a sustained multidimensional analysis.[216†]

But the problem here is not simply the inconsistency with which Parsons applies this argument; it is, more importantly, that the methodological rationale for idealism is impossible to sustain. This rationale errs because it employs conflationary theoretical logic: to argue from methodological to presuppositional position violates the relative autonomy of different levels of the scientific continuum. But Parsons' claim is also false in substance. If action and order are to be fully addressed, every social science must take each cybernetic dimension of society into account. Certainly, sociology has systematic differences vis-à-vis the other social sciences, but these differences lie in the substantive application of multidimensionality, not in whether or not it is operative for any particular discipline. Even if norms were to be taken as the most appropriate sociological focus, therefore, they would not be isolated from other dimensions or declared more epistemologically significant, as Parsons' idealist rationale would propose. Indeed, norms and solidary integration can be approached in a fully synthetic way, as Parsons himself at other points made perfectly clear.

This, of course, is exactly the point. By conducting a series of powerfully multidimensional arguments which are distinctly sociological—

which consider norms only as they interact with political, economic, and value exigencies—Parsons himself demonstrates the absurdity of his claims. Parsons' methodological rationale seeks to camouflage the conflicts in his presuppositional commitments. But it is on this presuppositional level and its proximate realization of multidimensional synthesis that Parsons' work must stand or fall.

Chapter Ten

CONCLUSION

Paradigm Revision and "Parsonianism"

Crucial figures in the history of social thought establish "schools," and it is by these schools that their thought is represented to following generations.[1] Yet I have argued throughout this work that the members of a sociological school change the founder's thought as much as they faithfully articulate it, and that they change it, moreover, in a manner that can be systematically related to the analytic tensions in the original theoretical position. If Engels reified Marx's positivism and determinism, it was because of the systematic ambiguity in Marx's own writings. If Mauss instrumentalized Durkheimian theory, it was to alter, without acknowledging he was doing so, Durkheim's emphasis on moral and religious control. The same is true of the tradition that must be called "Parsonianism," and I will concentrate here on Parsons' ambiguous legacy to the school that takes his name.[2†]

If a founding theory is, indeed, systematically revised in relation to its own internal contradictions—a revision, of course, always strenuously denied by the very parties who make it—this raises certain critical questions for the sociology of science.[3†] Particularly since the publication of Kuhn's work on scientific revolutions, it has been widely assumed that scientific theories are tightly integrated paradigms, that if one important part of a theory is disproved the entire paradigm will soon be relegated to the dustbin of intellectual history. The corollary to this position, which Kuhn has made explicit only in his later work, is that the carrier group for the paradigm is highly consensual.[4] Finally, Kuhn argues that the scientific change produced by such disproof is revolutionary, that one theory succeeds another in a linear progression. Throughout the present work, I have argued that each of these Kuhnian postulates—which have gained wide acceptance in contemporary social thought—is, at least for social science, false. Even the most "mature" paradigms are not so tightly integrated, nor are carrier groups so consensual, as Kuhn claims. Consequently, theoretical shifts are more piecemeal and scientific change is less linear than Kuhn proposes.

Indeed, I have maintained that since scientific theories are not tightly integrated, they must be seen as comprising a number of different components. Each component, or level, is concerned with certain distinctive theoretical problems and each, therefore, has a relative autonomy vis-à-vis the others. The most general level is concerned with presuppositions that formulate epistemological positions. Ideological orientations present a cross-cutting dimension oriented to political-evaluational questions. Methodological assumptions—both general and specific—present another independent level of theoretical decision-making, oriented to empirical practice and toward issues like induction versus deduction. Propositional elements are the most specific level of analysis, summarizing empirical observation without, at the same time, being identified with the empirical world itself; propositions reveal, for example, the theorist's vision of the world as being in equilibrium or conflict. Every theory commits itself to a position on each of these levels of sociological analysis, and the theory's position on any of the levels may be changed independently of its other commitments. It is because of the complexity and relative autonomy of the different levels and components of any scientific theory that neither paradigms nor the groups that carry them are as tightly integrated as Kuhn proposed and, further, that theoretical change is much more uneven and piecemeal than linear and revolutionary.

Great theories are, in almost every case, fundamentally ambiguous. The opposition which they generate—insofar as it is serious rather than trivial—occurs precisely in relationship to the contradictions that these ambiguities create. In championing a part of social reality that a dominant theory has ignored or downplayed, opponents are, unknowingly, setting the theory against itself. With these criticisms in mind, followers revise their theory in order to save it, and they do so by emphasizing aspects of reality that were slighted in the earlier effort. In this way, the original theory is broadened, and it is argued that such revision is perfectly consistent with the founder's intention. Whether or not it is actually considered to be so consistent by those outside the tradition, is, however, a matter that only intellectual history can decide.

1. THE HISTORICAL BASIS FOR PARSONS' SYNTHESIS AND ITS PERMEATION OF SOCIOLOGICAL TRADITION

In 1961, Parsons wrote that the "war of the schools" was coming to an end. Between the period of the turn-of-the-century theorists about whom he had written his first book and 1935—shortly before its publication—the "action frame of reference," Parsons believed, had gained an increasingly wide acceptance. The ensuing quarter-century, during which Parsons had developed his own theory, was a period of "institutionalization and crystallization" of this "action" perspective. What remained for the future of sociology—now that the basic elaboration of "action theory" had been completed—was the codification of available empirical knowledge and the closer integration of general propositions.[5]

From the standpoint of the current situation, this declaration of scientific self-satisfaction seems decidedly premature, if not positively antiquarian. "Action theory," though far from dead, has been on the defensive since the mid-1960s, and the sociological tradition has never been subject to more conflict and fragmentation. It is ironic that this situation has been generated, in part, because Parsons was himself unsure about what precisely constituted his own theoretical framework. Much more important, however, is a factor that Parsons always showed a strong tendency to overlook. Insofar as sociology relies heavily upon generalized, nonempirical assumptions, theoretical conflation and division is endemic to the enterprise itself. Still, if unanimity is impossible, objectivity is not. Because it is so ramifying and inclusive, multidimensionality is a standard which facilitates universalistic evaluation and criticism, and it is one for which sociology can strive. Whether or not it represents the course taken by sociology as a whole, theory can be further elaborated in a multidimensional way, and empirical knowledge can be increasingly codified in the context of multidimensional concepts. It is to this task, in fact, that Parsons made his most important contribution.

None of the classical theorists of sociology was able to achieve the kind of analytic synthesis which characterized Parsons' work at its best. Of course, Parsons had the great advantage of hindsight, and he was determined to capitalize upon what he viewed as the critical problems of classical thought. Parsons took the false starts and partial achievements of his classical predecessors with the utmost seriousness; he utilized them to construct a new analytic framework of his own.

Parsons' new synthesis, however, was stimulated by more than a clear-sighted reading of classical thought. It was rooted also in the course of twentieth-century history itself. As Marxists have long claimed, Marx's theory could have emerged only after economic class-conflict actually began to affect the social life of the nineteenth century, a new development that was certainly more visible in the English society of Marx's maturity than in any other nation.[6] Durkheim's focus on the independent importance of the moral community and of social solidarity, similarly, was undoubtedly linked to the way these problems emerged not just in France but throughout Western society, where societal integration became increasingly problematic in the face of rapid industrialization and secularization.[7] Finally, and most especially in Germany, the emergence of powerful bureaucracies and party systems which cross-cut classes and moral communities were new social developments that clearly lay in the background of Weber's thought.[8]

Parsons' theoretical synthesis, his analytic differentiation and interrelation of independent systems and levels of action, corresponds to similarly deep-rooted historical developments, movements which Parsons well described as growing social differentiation. Moreover, the growing pluralization of the modern social order and the increasing demands for greater integration and regulation particularly reflected the situation in mid-twentieth-century America, the nation where Parsons spent practically his entire life and which was so often the subject of his sociological concern. The intensity of this differentiation is reflected in the very range of the mutually exclusive characterizations which have been offered for "modern society." Pointing to the *economic* sphere, theorists find the "affluent society," or the "industrial society" par excellence.[9] Keying to *political* developments, writers have christened the modern West the "organizational society," the first bureaucratically regulated social life in human history.[10] To the *culturally* concerned, the West is the "active society," or the cybernetic society, the first collectivity in which culture, particularly cognitive culture, is not only widely dispersed but systematically incorporated into institutional life.[11] Finally, there is the "welfare state," the society which has undermined class conflict and fragmentation by creating the universalistic *solidarity* of citizenship.[12] Each of these theoretical formulae assumes the dominance in modern society of a different independent social sphere. Yet the very plausibility of each of them also lays the basis for an alternative theory, which, like Parsons', takes each societal dimension as an autonomous yet interrelated unit.

It is precisely such social developments, moreover, that have created the great strains which critics of modernity have so deplored. With pluralization and secularization have come the increasing isolation of the *self* and the emergence of "psychological man," who can respond to his predicament only by retiring to the comfort of the therapeutic.[13] Other critics focus on the way modernization has set the *social* adrift from its moorings in the self, decrying the oversocialized, other-directed individual.[14] There is, in addition, the *cultural* critique of the modern condition, whose spokesmen forecast the death of meaning and the vulgarization of culture by mass society.[15] In the face of these mutually exclusive claims for the significance of psychological, social, or cultural strain, it seems likely, once again, that these critical currents should be read more as responses to the tensions produced by a general process of differentiation than taken at face value as evidence of the destructiveness of any single feature of modern life. It is because of the strains introduced by the increasing separation of culture, society, and personality that Parsons' approach to the analytic autonomy of these general action systems has struck such a responsive chord. It is the historical meaning of Parsons' synthesis, the way it has captured something of the precarious newness of twentieth-century life, that largely explains its powerful impact on postwar social science, that explains why, despite the vast criticism to which his work has been subject, so much of what he has said has been incorporated into the common sense of contemporary sociology.[16†]

Any serious attempt to break through the increasingly closed schools of sociological debate—indeed, any determined attempt to expand the explanatory power of any particular theoretical tradition—must pass, I would argue, through the clarifying lens of the Parsonian vision. No modern Durkheimian theory can do without the amplification provided by Parsons' marriage of Durkheim and Freud. No Weberian analysis can advance without incorporating the analytic matrix by which Parsons interrelates individual, political, and cultural action. Contemporary exchange theory must acknowledge the insight into emergent properties which Parsons develops in his theory of values. Even conflict theory is forced, eventually, to acknowledge that the polarized factions upon which revolutionary conflict depends present "systems," which are integrated in affective and moral—that is, "Parsonian"—ways.[17†]

But perhaps the most striking illustration of Parsons' theoretical achievement can be seen in his influence on contemporary Marxism. No movement, surely, has been more radically dissociated from functionalism by Parsons' critics. Yet, even within Marxism, there are strong indications that, while some of Parsons' ideological and empirical commitments are rejected, many of his most important analytic achievements have been incorporated. Indeed, some of Parsons' key concepts have been seized upon by contemporary Marxists in their effort to transcend the limitations of Marx's original theory. Structuralist Marxists like Poulantzas, Godelier, and Althusser have taken over Parsons' functional-system model. More importantly, they have adopted Parsons' notion of the analytic division of social systems into relatively autonomous economic, political, and ideological levels, whose relation must, in any particular instance, be decided upon by empirical calculations.[18†]

Parsons' analytic influence is also effectively illustrated by his similar impact on the work of Jürgen Habermas, leading spokesman for the Frankfurt school, a branch of Marxism in most other respects inimical to the Althusserian one. From the juxtaposition of normative and instrumental kinds of action, Habermas follows Parsons in developing the distinction between activities with a goal-attainment orientation and those governed by role internalizations and socialization.[19] From here, Habermas moves to the Parsonian model of society as composed of interacting subsystems which differentially specialize in adaptive and symbolic activity, a conceptualization which he finds superior to Marx's base-superstructure model.[20] In his later work, Habermas adopts a much more explicitly functional and evolutionary approach, relying on the tension between social system, culture, and personality to locate major contradictions in contemporary capitalist societies.[21]

2. THE ELABORATION OF "PARSONIAN" SOCIOLOGY: REVISION AS RESPONSE TO INTERNAL STRAIN

Nonetheless, despite Parsons' permanent contributions to theoretical logic, no evaluation of the "fate" of his work—even a necessarily very tentative one—can be concluded on this exclusively positive note. In the first place, Parsons' synthetic approach to action and order is not a consistent one: his work evidences a significant, cross-cutting idealist slant. In this respect, his debate with Marx is crucial. Insofar as Parsons is able to address instrumental order—which means, for him, addressing the Marxian elements in Weber's work—his resolution of the classical problematic remains truly a multidimensional one. Insofar as Parsons tries simply to ignore Marx, to write him off the rolls of the "serious" sociological tradition, he avoids the instrumental elements of Weber's writing and moves inexorably toward an exclusively Durkheimian position, however refined by a Freudian addition. But Parsons' generalized ambivalence is only part of the problem, for neither of his presuppositional resolutions is carried out in a manner that is consistently sensitive to the autonomy of different levels of science, particularly to the specifically empirical elements in sociology and to the possibilities for multiple ideological commitments. Taken together, these problems have limited the impact of Parsons' work; the products of his sectarian ambition, they have certainly thwarted his ecumenical ambition as well.

Just as the generalized strains in the theories of Marx, Durkheim, and Weber have provided the motor for earlier theoretical revision and clarification—and, to some extent, continue to do so—the strains toward reduction and conflation in Parsons' writing have spurred the theoretical movement to extend the range and elaboration of his work. It is these very tensions, in fact, that have structured the course of "Parsonianism." Indeed, the most effective proof for the interpretation of Parsons' work which has been advanced in this book is that his followers have tried to revise his theory along the very fault lines which have been described. From Parsons' first students to his last, the most creative Parsonians, regardless of personal idiosyncrasy or empirical predilection, have tried to push Parsons' theory in the same directions. First, they have consistently moved to open up the closed, or conflated, aspects of Parsons' theoretical vision, in part merely to establish their own disciplinary expertise in a particular field but in part also to encompass the realistic variations of empirical phenomena. Second, and just as consistently, these students have tried to resolve the ambiguities in Parsons' attempt at presuppositional synthesis.

The first generation of Parsonian functionalists came to maturity during the early or middle phases of his work, before his theoretical system was fully developed. As a result, the permutations they introduced cannot be as systematically related to Parsons' theorizing as those of the later generation. The general direction of these revisions is, nonetheless, strikingly apparent. In terms of conflation, Merton, more than any other student of Parsons, self-consciously set out to separate the functional *model* from an overly determinate relation to more general or more specific commitments, emphasizing particularly the openness of a functional model to diverse empirical and ideological positions.[22] As for the autonomy of the *propositional* level of analysis, this position, once again, was stated most clearly by Merton, whose argument for middle-range theories reacted against Parsons' deductivist tendencies, though Merton's argument contains, in addition, a strand of unacceptably empiricist thinking.[23] The insistence on limiting the impact of generalized commitments also strikingly informed the work of Davis, Levy, Williams, and Barber, whose writings emphasized the variety of empirical outcomes and, while remaining systematic, resisted Parsons' tendency toward formalism.[24†] Among these theorists it was Williams who most self-consciously rejected Parsons' conflation of empirical equilibrium with model and presuppositional position, emphasizing the conflicts within American society not only between diverse social values but also between concrete social groups.[25]

These first-generation theorists also emphasized the instrumental elements in Parsons' *presuppositional* synthesis, avoiding much more successfully than Parsons himself the idealist dangers of the Durkheim-Freud solution. This strategy emerges quite clearly, for example, in Merton's writings on deviance, where the maldistribution of means is an important element in producing anomie.[26] In *Human Society*, Davis begins with a restatement of Parsons' means-ends schema and maintains the tension between these elements throughout, emphasizing the rational-intrinsic aspects of stratification and power, and the Hobbesian dimensions of instinctual life.[27] While Levy more explicitly follows Parsons' conceptualization of interdependent societal subsystems, in contrast to Parsons' thrust in *The Social System* he devotes *The Structure of Society* as much to processes of economic and political allocation as to those of solidarity, value integration, and emotional expression.[28]

The second generation of Parsons' students emerged in the context of the later writing; their revisions, as a consequence, can be related to the elements of Parsonian theory in a more systematic way. In terms of the conflationary problem, Smelser has addressed the deductive and overgeneralized tendencies in Parsons' work most directly. In regard to collective behavior, for example, Smelser writes that while Parsons' general conceptualization provides "a language for describing and classifying action," it is "not a direct source of explanatory hypotheses."[29†] Increasingly committed to independent conceptualization at intermediate levels of the scientific continuum, Smelser has focused on "explanation," not general theory, and on the means of bringing empirical, *propositional* evidence directly to bear on more general formulations.[30†] Thus, he criticizes Parsons' deviance theory because it "failed to specify the conditions under which empirical associations should be expected and the canons for testing such relationships."[31] Smelser also concurred with Merton in another way, by arguing, more directly than any other second-generation theorist, that the structural-functional *model* must be separated from prior commitments to *presuppositional* positions, *ideological* perspectives, and *empirical* outcomes. He demonstrates this position most effectively in an essay on the latent functional model that undergirds Marx's social theory.[32]

Parsons' second-generation students also dissented from his conflation of empirical equilibrium with more general commitments to models and presuppositions. Much more consistently than Parsons himself, the most serious Parsonian students of culture respected his injunction that values constitute a continual source of strain and conflict, emphasizing, in the process, not only culture-society conflicts but conflicts within the cultural and pattern-maintenance systems themselves. Pitts, for example, focused on the strains generated by the French Catholic formulation of grace.[33] Bellah explicated the tensions within American, European, and Japanese civil religion.[34] Lipset emphasized the conflicts between different pattern-variable combinations in European and American national cultures.[35] And Baum discussed the disintegrative tensions between the functional values of nineteenth-century Germany.[36] Such intrasystemic conflicts, of course, were precisely the kind of strain which Parsons' conflationary tendency often caused him to overlook.

Several students of the personality system, the other social-system boundary to which Parsons devoted attention, pushed his logic in a similar direction. Slater, for example, emphasized the disruptions which are inherent in the organization of symbolic internalizations by such a directly affective and organic unit as the personality; it is not surprising, therefore, that Slater approaches the socialized individual as a continuous source of socially structured strain.[37] Weinstein and Platt, similarly, take up Parsons' references to the alienative effects of affective denial, developing the psychological dimension of strain, polarization, and differentiation in a way that Parsons himself never contemplated.[38]

Parsons' students also implicitly attacked his tendency to conflate commitment to the interchange model with social equilibrium. Arguing that the completeness of differentiation cannot simply be deduced from the fact of interchange, students increasingly emphasized the "leads and lags" among societal sectors, linking this uneven differentiation to uneven development.[39] Such dislocations have been the major focus of most of Eisenstadt's work: Eisenstadt formulates a series of potential system "contradictions" which are produced, at each stage of historical development, by the possibilities for uneven differentiation among institutional spheres.[40†]

It is particularly in the process of separating the issue of empirical conflict from more general commitments that Parsons' students have, increasingly, focused on the actions of social groups and the ways in which group self-interest both structures and articulates functional exigencies. This attempt to achieve a more group-oriented focus motivated Eisenstadt's theory of "institutionalization," from which he argues, for example, that the "institutionalization of any system usually creates new collectivities and organizations" that "necessarily develop needs, actions, and orientations of their own which impinge on various other groups and institutional spheres."[41†] The same anticonflationary intention, I believe, led Keller to articulate her notion of "strategic elites."[42†] This relation between the focus on empirical conflict and that on social groups is also clearly manifest in Smelser's critical epilogue to *The American University*, where he chides Parsons and Platt for ignoring "the problems that arise in the concrete social structuring of functional activities,"[43] and it is also behind Smelser's later attempt to develop a theory of conflicting "functional estates."[44] Lipset and Rokkan modified Parsons' abstract functional model in a similar way, incorporating competing group interests into a theory of differentiating functional spheres.[45] And since his own early work with Parsons on some of action theory's most esoteric abstractions, Shils has also maintained a much more concrete, group-oriented approach to the issue of functional exchange and systemic conflict.[46]

This movement away from formalism and deduction has, finally, been manifest by an increasing tendency to open up Parsons' scheme of historical differentiation to more critical ideological perspectives. A number of second-generation students emphasized, in contrast to Parsons himself, the extent to which differentiation has yet to be completed, the drawbacks as well as the benefits of the differentiation already achieved, and the ways in which newly differentiated positions often become the objects of manipulation or the basis for new forms of exploitation. This ambiguous relation of increased efficiency and freedom is most clearly articulated in Eisenstadt's analysis of the first great bureaucratic empires, an argument which has significant implications for any perspective on the differentiation of the modern state.[47] Mayhew, in an analogous way, focuses on the potential corruption that is generated by independent agencies of social control, particularly the police.[48] Similarly, Lipset has focused, much more consistently than Parsons himself, on the way in which differentiation and rationalization generate strong right-wing opposition, a perspective that closely parallels Smelser's discussion of how privileged groups can organize to protect de-differentiated functional relationships.[49] Bellah has utilized the pattern-variable dichotomies to provide critical perspectives on antidemocratic strains in the political cultures of advanced societies; and, more recently, he and Eisenstadt both have warned about the dangers of increasing cultural universalization. On the psychological plane, Slater and Platt and Weinstein have focused on the dangers of passive regression and aggressive fantasy which are opened up by the processes of differentiation.[50]

This movement away from conflation has only been partly accompanied by a thoroughgoing critique of Parsons' idealist reduction. For Eisenstadt, a strong emphasis on instrumental action and order has grown out of his group focus, and his work consistently discusses the relationship of economic classes and political coercion to broader systemic tendencies.[51] In the process, he includes the instrumental elements of Weber's theory much more consistently than does Parsons. The other major exponent of a consistently multidimensional approach, Smelser, has emphasized the role of instrumental conditions simply by remaining faithful to the synthetic scope of the interchange model itself. Thus, in *Social Change in the Industrial Revolution*, Smelser analyzes the enormous impact of early industrial capitalism on family structure as an imbalance in the adaptation pattern-maintenance exchange.[52] As his work developed, Smelser underlined this commitment to multidimensionality by trying to integrate Tocqueville's analysis of group power and privileged estates with Parsons' analysis of functional systems.[53] The same effort has been made in less systematic but still important ways by other students. While Barber accepts Parsons' emphasis on the need for professional self-management of technical culture, he argues that it must be complemented by instrumental sanctions from extraprofessional agencies.[54] Bellah and Geertz, who focus principally on the cultural dimension, have been much more careful than Parsons to emphasize the differentiated nature of their contributions and have self-consciously distinguished the multidimensional logic involved in the study of value institutionalization from a more purely hermeneutic approach to cultural patterns.[55†]

Among writers highly influenced by Parsons, who were not his actual students, the revisionist effort to maintain a more consistently multidimensional Parsonian perspective is also apparent. Dreeben, in discussing the socialization of pattern-variable orientations in schools, views this learning process as being initiated more by new ecological arrangements than by value cathexis.[56] Similarly, Lipset combines his pattern-variable analysis of national political cultures with a structural analysis of the different class positions of national elites.[57] David Schneider draws upon Parsons' general conceptualization for his analysis of American kinship patterns, but follows this work with a discussion of the way these cultural designs are refracted by class divisions.[58]

3. PARADIGM REVISION AS BREAKDOWN OR REVIVIFICATION?

As these revisions and permutations of "Parsonianism" have developed, Parsons' original theoretical synthesis has, in an important sense, certainly been strengthened. Yet, paradoxically, these progressive developments have also broken the synthesis down. Inevitably, Parsons' students have tried to cope with the strains in his work on the basis of their scholarly expertise in particular areas. As they specialize, however, they begin to champion certain elements of the Parsonian synthesis over others. As each action level and societal subsystem is given increased autonomy—to protect it from Parsons' tendency toward conflationary and reductionistic closure—the drive for overall synthesis and integration is, correspondingly, sharply reduced.[59] In his emphasis on groups and more conditional exigencies, Smelser devotes much less attention to the social system's cultural environment than to its interpenetration with personality. On the other hand, Eisenstadt, while focusing in a similar way on groups and instrumental action, discusses culture at greater length, but refers to personality variables scarcely at all. Similarly, while differentiating the problem of concrete group solidarity and its tension with the political powers much more sharply than Parsons' himself, Shils blurs the divisions between cultural and social systems; he also relies on overly static assumptions about personality. Geertz and Bellah, while providing a much sharper analytic differentiation of culture and social systems than Parsons, only occasionally trace the interrelation of cultural patterns with concrete social and psychological processes.[60†] Weinstein and Platt, for their part, emphasize the independence of personality, arguing that evolving psychological needs provide an impetus for change overlooked by others in the Parsonian tradition.[61]

Each of these arguments, of course, is made from a position within Parsons' overall synthetic framework; indeed, the innovations introduced by each emphasis stem as much from the way they interpenetrate their analysis with those of other functional environments as from the way they allow their particular element increased autonomy. Still, this process of revision threatens Parsons' synthesis. In the process of these theoretical permutations, new fissures develop. Intra-Parsonian conflicts, like intra-Marxist ones, become as significant as those between Parsonians and those in other theoretical traditions. In fact, these fissures provide opportunities not only for continued internal development and expansion but for new cross-cuttings with other theoretical traditions as well.[62]

Despite Parsons' enduring impression on the sociological tradition, it is too early to determine the ultimate fate of his theoretical legacy. Perhaps the Parsonian synthesis will break down completely. If so, it will leave a rich inheritance for future efforts at theoretical reconstruction. On the other hand, the openings here described may lead to the development of a more loosely defined, less sectarian version of "functionalist" theory. If paradigms are not tightly integrated and their carrier groups only weakly consensual, theoretical revision will inevitably be an open-ended process.[63†]

All that can be known for certain is that these efforts will revolve around distinctive strains at each of the different levels of sociological theory, and that the most fundamental and decisive issues will continue to be defined by the presuppositional questions of action and order. Sociology has yet to produce a consistently multidimensional theory, the elements for which have certainly been provided by Marx, Durkheim, Weber, and Parsons. To do so must remain its most sought-after goal.

Appendix

CONFLATION AND REDUCTION IN THE INTERPRETATION OF PARSONIAN THEORY

In the course of this analysis of Parsons' work, I have continually noted debilitating interpretive errors both by Parsons' critics and by his sympathizers. Part of this problem can be traced to the fact that Parsons' theory is only beginning to emerge from its "charismatic," polarizing phase (see ch. 1). Yet there is, I think, another, more important reason: its interpretation has necessarily been subject to the same errors in theoretical logic that have distorted much contemporary sociological discussion. By conflating the relative autonomy of different levels of the scientific continuum (see vol. 1, pp. 36–63), contemporary theoretical logic has failed to illuminate the most generalized, presuppositional level in sociological argument. In the process, the very theoretical elements that have the broadest scope and most decisive significance have usually been ignored. Moreover, when these presuppositional assumptions have become the point of focus, their logic has often been misconstrued. Precisely such problems have distorted the debates over "Parsonianism." Because Parsons himself frequently conflated the levels of his theory and engaged in presuppositional reductionism on his own, his work has been particularly vulnerable to such theoretical errors.[1†]

1. THE CONFLATION AMONG THEORETICAL LEVELS IN PARSONIAN INTERPRETATION

1.1. *THE ANTI-PARSONIAN CRITIQUE*

Every form of conflationary argument has found its way, with a vengeance, into the contemporary critique of Parsons' work. Most pervasive perhaps is the framework established by the positivist persuasion: Is Parsons' theory true or false? That, it often appears, is the only relevant, truly scientific question. Max Black, for example, in his concluding remarks to a survey that represented, until quite recently, the most serious secondary work on Parsons, dismisses the "action frame of reference" as being not an "empirical generalization" but a mere "assumption." "That human beings often have goals or ends-in-view is not a fact," Black asserts, "but rather something that follows from our conceptions of what it is to be human." In regard to this possibility, he comments: "If this is so, the conception of the principles in question as being empirical generalizations of wide scope is an illusion." Robert Merton first canonized such an evaluative standard thirty years ago by attempting, without explicit reference to an evaluation of Parsons' work, to approach functionalism simply as a paradigmatic "codification" of accumulated empirical generalizations, a utilization of the paradigm concept that was, despite Merton's later disclaimers, quite antithetical to Kuhn's subsequent definition.[2] Hans Zetterberg took this Mertonian approach to its logical conclusion with his assertion that Parsons' four-function concept—the A-G-I-L matrix—should be viewed as providing four "master gauges" or "meter readings" for taking measurements of social life.[3] It is upon the basis of such positivist misinterpretation that Parsons' work has either been impatiently dismissed on the grounds that it is not induced directly from empirical operations—as Homans has done—or "refuted" time and time again by empirical studies that focus on particular propositional statements by Parsons on such topics as stratification, the family, the university, or social change.[4]

Such positivist interpretation assumes, of course, that no temporally prior elements intercede between the knower and the known. In arguing thus, theoretical formulation is reduced to empirical technique. Yet Parsons has simultaneously been critically evaluated from a perspective on science that is directly antithetical to the positivist one: the sociology of knowledge. According to interpreters of this persuasion, the scientific or "objective" elements of the theoretical enterprise are negligible; a theorist's ideological commitments, which can in turn be reduced to his social position, determine his scientific statements.

Alvin Gouldner's *The Coming Crisis in Western Sociology* represents the apotheosis of such ideological reduction of Parsons' theory. Gouldner runs through a mélange of social determinants which, though never systematically interrelated, cover the range of twentieth-century American conservatism: Parsons' midwestern middle-class background, his career within the socially isolating walls of the Harvard academe, his 1930s membership in a "reactionary" Harvard cabal called the "Pareto circle," his establishment position in the anti-Communist America of the cold war period. From such social commitments, Gouldner deduces Parsons' entire theoretical arsenal—his equilibrium emphasis, his normative presuppositional preference, his methodological attraction to abstract theorizing, his adoption of a systemic model.[5] Much the same simplistic account of Parsons' theory was made at about the same time by Robert Friedrichs, who particularly emphasizes the role of computer technology, cybernetics, and the cold war as the switchmen determining Parsons' ideas about conflict, ideology, model, and method.[6] T. B. Bottomore's uncharacteristically strident attack on Parsons, which appeared in 1969, perhaps best exemplifies the sectarian tone that colored so much of this genre of interpretive literature after the mid-1960s.[7] Long before its heightened politicization, however, the model for such ideological reduction of Parsons' work had been laid down by C. Wright Mills, who ascribed Parsons' penchant for "grand theory," his purported idealism, and his emphasis on social stasis to long-range processes of social bureaucratization that had transformed sociologists from social critics into deracinated, conformist academicians.[8]

Between these two extremes of scientific reduction, the positivistic and the ideological, interpreters have "explained" Parsons' thought by linking it to his theoretical commitments at more intermediate levels of the scientific continuum. Among them, the most specific, empirically oriented level concerns decisions about methodology. In his study contrasting functionalist and exchange theories, M. J. Mulkay has related every aspect of "Parsonianism" to Parsons' antipositivist approach to scientific method. If Parsons had only been more intent on producing propositions instead of precepts, Mulkay contends, he would eventually have reached the same rationalist, individualist conclusions as those obtained by proponents of exchange analysis.[9] Homans' interpretation of Parsons qualifies as a similar reduction of theory to method. If Parsons had only been acquainted with "recent philosophers of science," Homans asserts, his theory would have succeeded in "bringing men back in"; it would have adopted more individualistic presuppositions about order and more instrumental assumptions about action.[10]

Other commentators have placed the root cause of Parsons' failings at a significantly more general level, namely, in the complex propositional positions Parsons takes on the issue of empirical conflict and harmony. These commentators characterize Parsons' position on this issue, ambiguous as it may be, not as one commitment among many but as his total theory. Thus, while some theorists are "conflict theorists," Parsons is not; he is an "equilibrium" theorist. The roots of this analysis go back to Dahrendorf's first book, *Class and Class Conflict in Industrial Society*, which presents Parsons' preoccupation with equilibrium as opposed to conflict as the basis for his theoretical commitments to system, norm, and conservatism.[11] This interpretive mode became particularly important with the intensification of actual social conflict in the 1960s. Such critics as Coser and Horton utilized it to identify Parsons' ideological tendencies, while "anti-Parsonians" like Rex and Collins applied the conflict reduction more broadly to include Parsons' idealism and strong emphasis on functional models.[12†] By now, this reductionist interpretive mode, firmly linked to "Parsonian" versus "anti-Parsonian" styles of sociology, has permeated the folklore of Western sociology, functioning at the textbook level as one of the themes in theoretical instruction.[13†]

Finally, at the most general level attained by most Parsons interpretation—analysis of models—we are presented with Parsons the "functionalist." Surely this is the most omnipresent piece of conventional wisdom extent in sociological theory today. The judgment is broadcast, with little qualification, at the classroom level by Timasheff and Theodorson in their widely read introductory textbook, *Sociological Theory.* "The central theme of Parsons' social theory as it appears in his earlier works is 'the functioning of structures.' "[14] But the same reduction to model provides the theoretical linchpin for the most esoteric levels of the anti-Parsonian literature. The focus of influential analyses by Mills, Wallace, Gouldner, and Blumer—and, more recently, by Menzies, Adriaansens, and Habermas—this form of critical interpretation reaches its most elaborate form in Don Martindale's sweeping critique in *The Nature and Types of Sociological Theory.* Taking the individualism of "social behaviorism" and the sociologism of "functionalist organicism" as the two basically divergent approaches to social scientific models, Martindale connects Parsons' theory to nineteenth-century organicism, particularly its conservative ideology, static approach to process and idealist emphasis on *Geist* and tradition.[15]

As we have seen in the preceding discussion, while many of these criticisms are simply erroneous, on many specific points they are correct. Yet the points are correct only in the limited sense of accurately identifying one or another problematic dimension or theme in Parsons' theory. The criticisms are seriously in error in a broader and much more important sense. Taking the part for the whole, they have identified Parsons' entire theory with a single element in his theoretical configuration. By so drastically simplifying the rich complexity of scientific argument, a complexity that is particularly striking and particularly relevant in Parsons' case, these critiques have often grossly distorted Parsons' thought. (For a general criticism of these reductionist styles of contemporary debate—without reference to Parsons—see my discussion in vol. 1, pp. 36–63.)

To evaluate Parsonian theory purely according to its quantity of verified facts is not only to misread, rather naïvely, the complexities of scientific verification—ignoring not just postpositivism but Popperian empiricism as well—it is, more importantly, to fail to comprehend the level of generality at which Parsons' work is self-consciously aimed. To produce verifiable propositional statements was never Parsons' central intent, despite the qualifications I have discussed in chapters 6–7, nor has the achievement of such verification been the basis for his influence on Western sociological thought. Edward Devereux once put this point very clearly, if somewhat personalistically, when he wrote that despite the theory's "intricate complexities and details" and "inevitably . . . innumerable empirical generalizations," Parsons is himself "far more interested in the grand design than he is in any particular[s]."[16] As Bershady has demonstrated with great subtlety, Parsons is an analytical sociologist, not an empiricist one.[17] His intent is to provide broad structural outlines, not situationally specified causal statements. His contribution, in Menzies' terminology, amounts not to a collection of facts but to a theoretical "programme" for systematically finding out what the relevant facts are.[18]

Yet as I have demonstrated at many points in the preceding discussion, although Parsons' general statements are not induced directly from nature, they can certainly be translated into propositional terms. Accepting for the sake of argument the positivists' standard of scientific value, one could plausibly show that Parsons' statements have been verified empirically as frequently as they have been falsified, despite the fact that Parsons himself is not specifically concerned with the propositional level. A. L. Jacobson, for example, made elaborate empirical tests of Parsons' social-change theory, producing statistically substantial tests of validity.[19] Does this mean, however, that the many critiques of this change theory, proffered over the last twenty years, are incorrect? Certainly not, for Parsons' most important scientific statements in this area, as in others, cannot be accepted or discarded simply by operations at the propositional level, any more than Marx's or Freud's central notions are directly verifiable or falsifiable.[20†] Such is the nature of scientific argument. As I indicated in chapters 6–7, the degree of verisimilitude manifest in Parsons' work and the manner in which it can be made empirically specifiable are vexing problems. Nonetheless, while empirical tests may be necessary in evaluating Parsons' intellectual contribution, they are far from sufficient.

The critical interpretive efforts have been no more successful, however, when directed at the other side of the scientific continuum, when they purport to "explain" Parsons' theory by reducing it to a reflection of his ideological predilections. It is quite true that Parsons' work is permeated by ideology. What general social-scientific statement is not? It is also true that Parsons' persistent refusal to acknowledge this ideological dimension of his theory leads ultimately to internal theoretical problems of great magnitude. Yet it is just as true that the most self-conscious moments of Parsons' intellectual career have been devoted to articulating concepts that are not directly ideological. By confusing "nonobjective" thinking, or "value judgments," with ideological statements, Parsons' ideological critics indicate a severely foreshortened understanding of science. Models are not political commitments, nor are presuppositions, methods, or propositional complexes. Moreover, these critics have, for the most part, misapprehended the ideological commitments that Parsons does actually profess, misrepresenting, in the process, the very facts of his "social situation" upon which they would generalize *ad hominem*. For example, during the period when Gouldner has the young Parsons defending the status quo, he was, in fact, a democratic quasi-socialist upholding the ideal of a liberalized postcapitalist system.[21†] The middle-aged Parsons whom Gouldner paints as an anti–New Deal, laissez-faire conservative was, rather (as I have shown in ch. 5, sec. 2.1), a liberal Democrat, a staunch admirer of Roosevelt, and even, for a time, a target of McCarthyism. According to Andrew Hacker, he was "one of the liberal-intellectuals of the Democratic Party, one of the Eggheads" who were Adlai Stevenson's principal supporters.[22]

Whatever the ideological position or biographical facts, of course, they do not provide the basis for such sweeping critical generalization. Here the ideological critique of Parsons is patently in error, and its inability to develop a consistent argument makes this plain. Residual categories must be introduced—as in Gouldner's characterization of Parsons' writings on social change as not "Parsonian" but "Marxist"—to indicate that, somehow, Parsons kept two completely unconnected theoretical accounting books. Outright contradictions prove unavoidable, as when Friedrichs praises Parsons as sociology's premier anti-positivist in the second part of his book, after making Parsons the central villain of the positivist-conservative-functionalist nexus in the first.[23]

The conflation of Parsons' thought with its methodological base is even more vulnerable. It is not simply that critics like Mulkay and Homans ignore recent postpositivist developments in the philosophy of science, though this problem is quite sufficient in itself. Were the laws of Newtonian physics observed inductively from the physical data? Kant did not think so, and it is surely Kant, not Bacon, from whom Parsons' notion of science derives, as Bershady and Enno Schwanenberg have made abundantly clear.[24] Homans may invoke "real science" justification for his concrete reductionism, but Whitehead, certainly real enough as both scientist and philosopher, provided Parsons early on with a conception of science as an analytic, abstracting process, a conception that has become only more persuasive in the ensuing half century of philosophical debate.[25]

Beyond such considerations, however, the methodological critique must also overlook some overpowering empirical facts. Positivists do not necessarily agree, as Mulkay and Homans would have it, with instrumentalist and individualist generalizations about human existence. Positivism can, for example, be combined with instrumental collectivism, Karl Marx being a case in point; it may, on the other hand, be combined with normative collectivism, as the case of Durkheim well illustrates. Parsons' antipositivism, in other words, can hardly explain his presuppositional stance. No matter what our quarrel with Parsons' methodological ambivalence, we will never be in a position to deduce his theory from these methodological commitments. By attempting otherwise, Mulkay and Homans succumb, ironically, to their respective national traditions of utilitarianism and pragmatism, both of which assume that actors are proto-scientists and, further, that such actors will, unavoidably, explain human action in a rational, naturalistic way.[26]

As for the charge that we come to grips with Parsons by interpreting him as an "equilibrium theorist," it is fundamentally incorrect, despite important elements of truth. Parsons' perception of the degree of social harmony cannot, contrary to Dahrendorf, Rex, or Collins, serve as an index of his other commitments. Rosa Luxemburg and Lenin chastised Bernstein's revisionist Marxism for its equilibrium bias, yet was Bernstein not as instrumental in his presuppositions as Parsons is supposed to be anti-instrumental in his? Similarly, Goffman's approach to action and his formally antifunctionalist position contrast sharply with Parsons' presuppositions and model, yet Goffman's perception of static equilibrium in his *Asylums* is perfectly congruent with the equilibrium bias attributed to Parsons himself.[27] Nor can such essentially empirically-oriented assumptions about social harmony or conflict be linked directly to ideology, as Dahrendorf has implicitly demonstrated in his essay "Out of Utopia."[28] After all, Marx's analysis of the classless communist social system cannot be called conservative, yet it relies on equilibrium analysis as heavily as any of Parsons' works.

Equally important, however, the conflict critique is actually mistaken in its characterization of Parsons' theory. As demonstrated above, Parsons is not unequivocally committed to social harmony, as evidenced, for example, by his distinction between "static" and "moving" equilibrium, or his periodic empirical analyses of social conflict and breakdown. Moreover, far from any inevitable connection between Parsons' static equilibrium tendencies and his alleged normative-psychological emphasis, we have found that Parsons' most psychologistic, normatively centered analyses—his studies of alienation—are often his most conflict oriented. The other theoretical referents of this conflict critique are equally doubtful. Parsons is not simply an anti-instrumentalist theorist, nor is he purely a conservative one. The truth is more complicated than these conveniently reductive fictions: Parsons' position on the conflict issue can be understood only in complex interrelationship with the other levels of his work.

Finally, moving to the greater generality of the model level, to describe Parsons as a "functionalist" is surely correct, but to describe him simply as a functionalist is to employ an evaluative tool that is far too gross for the task at hand. After at least 1945, Parsons utilized a functional system model, persistently and self-consciously. Yet other, decidedly "non-Parsonian" theorists do so as well—for example, Durkheim and even Marx, though the former less systematically and the latter less persistently.[29] The French

Althusserian Marxists, too, are as functionalist as they are structuralist. The "functionalist" critique, in fact, has the situation quite upside down. What distinguishes Parsons, at his best, from other theorists employing a functional model is his clear understanding of its limits, and of the need, therefore, explicitly to clarify other levels of theoretical commitment as well. To describe, as Wallace does, Parsons' theory as "functional imperativism," as if its determinate, anti-individualistic quality could be derived simply from some gigantic reification of systematicity, is to miss the nature of the interplay between Parsons' model and the other levels of his work, both more general and more specific.[30†]

These anti-Parsonian critiques have, then, consistently made errors of principle, conflating levels of science that are relatively independent. Not surprisingly, they have also been forced into numerous errors of fact, not only by conflating levels of analysis that Parsons himself, at least as often as not, successfully differentiates, but also by misrepresenting the nature of Parsons' actual commitment at any given level. The full implications of these debates, however, can be appreciated only if it is understood that such faulty interpretations do not stem solely from a mistaken understanding of science, though such misunderstanding does have widespread repercussions. Rather, these interpretations must be seen as the theoretical arguments that they are. "Readings" are never just readings. This rule is as applicable in the case of Parsons as in that of Marx, for, as with the intra-Marxist debate, "readings" of Parsons have constituted one of the primary modes of contemporary theoretical debate in sociology.

Parsons' critics, then, take sharply polemical positions of their own; they are not simply evaluating Parsons' work. If Zetterberg insists on the factual character of Parsons' work, it is because he does not accept theoretical generality in any form, not because he has neutrally evaluated Parsons as an actual positivist. Mulkay and Homans push the determinate quality of method as much because they are arguing for a different approach to method as because they have concluded, after careful consideration, that Parsons' theory is triggered by his methodology and by little else. Similarly, it is not coincidence that, in a single book, Dahrendorf both discovers Parsons to be an equilibrium theorist and, simultaneously, presents a Hobbesian view of modern society as permeated by conflict and domination. For the same kind of reason, it is convenient for Martindale to separate radically Parsons' functionalism from the individualism, purposiveness, and conflict orientation that he calls social behaviorism, for in this manner he can argue that such emphases can be achieved only if they are divorced from any use of systemic models.[31] The case for readings as theoretical statements is much simpler to make for the ideological critique. If Parsons' theory is simply a reflection of his political evaluations, any Parsonian critique must, in turn, simply be an argument for a different ideological position.

Such ostensibly buried polemic helps explain the factual distortions of Parsons' work that undermine so much of the commentarial literature. It also indicates the error of dismissing readings as arcane and merely commentarial, as the antitheoretical proponents of the positivist persuasion would like.

1.2. THE PARSONIAN DEFENSE

That commentators sympathetic to Parsons have often engaged in the same kinds of reductive evaluation as his most severe critics testifies to the depth of conflationary thinking in the social sciences. It also points to another phenomenon that I have had occasion to refer to above, namely, the strange process of mutual reinforcement between Parsons' critics and supporters, a convergence which has the effect of furthering the critical misinterpretation of his thought.

The notion, for example, that Parsons' work should basically be evaluated in terms of its accuracy in reflecting empirical data is a position that has received periodic yet persistent support by proponents of Parsonian "action theory" themselves. During the middle phase of Parsons' development, Marion J. Levy wrote in 1952 that his *The Structure of Society*—an important work that falls, with a few significant exceptions, entirely within the Parsonian apparatus—should be viewed as "an attempt to construct [a conceptual scheme] from present knowledge of empirical materials."[32] Later, in 1959, Winston White's *Beyond Conformity* utilized both Parsons' approach to action and order and his theory of social change as structural differentiation to sharply, and quite effectively, criticize what White called the reigning "intellectual ideology" of mass society. In doing so White labeled these Parsonian constructs "facts," contrasting their objective, empirical status with what he described as the nonempirical, fanciful constructions of the ideological critics. As I illustrated in some detail in chapter 5, sec. 2, however, the Parsonian notions employed by White certainly are not simply "facts." In the first case, they are presuppositional in status; in the second, they are a complex conglomeration of Parsons' political values with the entire range of his nonempirical theoretical assumptions. The effectiveness of these concepts in White's hands lay precisely in their power as generalizing concepts, not in some pristine, nonvaluational status.[33]

More recently, the same kind of empirical reduction occurs in Guy Rocher's often insightful presentation, despite the implicit emphasis throughout the work on Parsons' use of theoretical models. Rocher writes, for example, that "the evaluation of Parsons' thinking clearly shows a direct—*and even causal*—link between his empirical studies and the development of his theoretical model." Thus, describing the A-G-I-L subsystem schema, he writes that it "*grew out of* empirical research on structure and process in small groups."[34] A much more direct kind of empiricist support for Parsons has been conducted by A. L. Jacobson, who through his methodologically oriented research "verifies" Parsons' change theory, which is treated by him as a set of directly operationalizable hypotheses and testable propositions.[35] Such an argument for the purely objective status of Parsons' work has, finally, received its most elegant and careful formulation in Victor Lidz's defense of Parsonianism against the ideological critique. Utilizing Parsons' own division of the cultural system into cognitive, expressive, moral and religious types of symbols, Lidz argues that Parsons' theory is located, contrary to the contention of the ideological reductionists, entirely within the cognitive, empirically oriented dimension.[36] In a related essay, Lidz identifies each of the different levels of Parsons' theory—system model, equilibrium assumptions, four-function interchange notion—as deriving directly from essentially empirical reasoning.[37]

There is little doubt, I think, that such interpretations have been offered as sympathetic defenses against the charges that Parsons' theory is, on the one hand, empirically irrelevant or, on the other, completely ideological. Yet in constructing such a strategy these interpreters adopt a version of positivism that misconstrues the scientific enterprise and, necessarily, Parsons' work itself. The ultimate source of Parsons' scientific contribution does not rest at this extreme level of specificity. It is one thing to emphasize the two-directionality of Parsons' work and the fundamental significance of Parsons' empirical perceptions for the theory's development; it is quite another to imply, in the manner of Zetterberg or Merton, that the theory is somehow empirically induced.

More writers in defense of Parsons have, naturally, accepted the crucial role of nonempirical inputs to his development. Yet within this realm there has still been a persistent tendency to reduce Parsons' theory to one of its parts. For example, Bershady's recent work, as noted earlier, places Parsons' epistemological assumptions at the very center of his theory, effectively refuting the positivist critique and, for that matter, the positivist defense. Yet for Bershady, Parsons' epistemological concern is limited to considerations about the nature of scientific knowledge in a purely methodological sense; it does not extend to a focus on the problem of how actors gain knowledge in a typical social situation. In other words, he does not extend Parsons' epistemological concern to what I have called the problem of action. Consequently, Bershady attempts to derive the central elements of Parsons' theory from his meta-methodological position alone, without reference to questions of model, ideology, or presupposition. He ends up, inevitably, reducing the complexity of Parsons' work despite his important insight into its methodological moorings. For example, he seeks to explain the serious inconsistencies in Parsons' analysis simply by reference to the inadequacy of Parsons' methodological position. I have argued, to the contrary (chs. 6–9), that these tensions must be traced to substantive confusion at every level of Parsons' analysis.[38]

But without doubt the most consistent form of reduction promoted by Parsons' defenders in common with his critics is the characterization of Parsons' theory as "functionalist." Even the most experienced practitioners of the Parsonian approach, who in their own empirical applications of the theory have certainly been guided by its full multilayered complexity, attribute its central distinctiveness to Parsons' commitment at the level of model. This was true, for example, in Smelser's early presentation of family-economy differentiation in his *Social Change in the Industrial Revolution*, where he argues for the existence of this differentiation on the grounds that "latency" and "adaptive" functions are separated in all living systems.[39†] It is true also for the later accounts by Rocher and Harry M. Johnson. For the latter, "Parsons' use of analytic model" is the most distinctive general aspect of Parsons' work; he presents all the central thematic elements of Parsonian theory as relatively sui generis models, without relating Parsons' understanding of these models to his other kinds of theoretical commitments.[40] Rocher's more elaborated account follows, implicitly, a similar approach, for he presents the entire range of Parsons' insights as if they were all formally derived from Parsons' conception of model. Despite his acknowledgement that "the duality of action and situation . . . is fundamental to the whole Parsonian theory of action,"[41] a duality that should be identified as a presuppositional commitment, it is the model, not the presuppositional, level that Rocher defines as crucial. He distinguishes Parsonianism from other functionalist theories simply by its systemic quality, its analytic rather than structural focus, and its evolutionary rather than historicist approach to change.[42]

Even Seymour Martin Lipset, whose own utilization of Parsons' theory has never focused on the formal analysis of functional models, has presented a variation of this reductionist appreciation. He argues for the convergence of Parsonianism and Marxism on the grounds that at the core of each there is a similar emphasis on viewing social systems as functional models.[43] This argument refutes the charges of the "functionalist critique" that Marx and Parsons have completely divergent approaches to society. Yet in so refuting the content of the charge Lipset has seemingly adopted its form. In arguing for the similarity of Parsonian and Marxist approaches, he neglects precisely the qualities that distinguish the two theories, those nonfunctionalist qualities that Lipset has so effectively applied in his own work.

This model reduction has also characterized the more specifically analytic accounts of some of Parsons' more recent students, for example, Jan J. Loubser and Rainer C. Baum, two of the editors of the most elaborate of Parsons festschrifts. It is Parsons' insight into the "functional system," they assert, not his presuppositions, ideological commitments, or propositional assumptions about equilibrium that explain his four-function theory and generalized media approach.[44] F. van Zyl Slabbert, in another sympathetic essay in this festschrift, argues directly along these same lines, attempting systematically to derive every major element of Parsons' theory from his commitment to a functionalist model. The ends/means framework, the middle period's social-system discussion, the later four-functional paradigm—all are related in detail to the type of teleological tendency that must characterize a good functionalist argument.

> Back of every attempt [by Parsons] to describe the characteristics of a social system—its structure, the processes which maintain it and change it, and the presumed laws which govern it—is the conception of a functional system.[45]

He argues, in fact, that Parsons' functionalism represents the only major thread of continuity throughout his career.

It has not been my intention here to deny the significance of such "functionalism" in Parsons' theory, nor the high degree to which his use of this model does carefully mesh with his other theoretical commitments. I have argued, however, that consideration of the model level alone is insufficient grounds for either theoretical indictment or vindication. Functional commitments do not represent the distinguishing mark of Parsons' work, nor are they the basis from which the rest of his theory is derived. Models do not provide the most important thread of his theoretical continuity, nor is his self-conscious use of them his primary distinction as an analytically sophisticated theorist.

Those who have appreciated Parsons' great significance have, then, often misrepresented the specific nature and origins of his accomplishment. In doing so, they have sometimes conflated the levels of Parsons' argument in a manner remarkably similar to that of his harshest critics. For the sake of completeness, I should add that no defenders of Parsons' theory have followed its critics in reducing its character to assumptions about the equilibrium/conflict issue or to ideological commitments. To the contrary, the very existence of guiding nonempirical assumptions in these areas has, for the most part, been denied.[46] Yet since these levels of analysis, whether recognized or not, inevitably do inform Parsons' work, such avoidance simply reinforces the conflationary tendencies I have already described, by further suggesting that the complexity of Parsons' theory can be reduced to the influence of these one or two levels alone.

In the end, however, conflation is not the most debilitating problem in such sympathetic commentary. More striking, and more disappointing, is its failure to illuminate the most generalized assumptions that inform Parsons' thought. Once again, this failure echoes problems in the anti-Parsonian critique. Both sides of the argument have generally lost sight of the essential undergirding of Parsons' thought.

2. REDUCTION WITHIN THE PRESUPPOSITIONAL LEVEL OF PARSONIAN INTERPRETATION

Since most Parsonian interpretation has been directed at the more specified levels of the sociological continuum—the empirical, ideological, and model levels—it is on one or the other of these levels that the identity of "Parsonianism" has gradually taken shape in the sociological collective conscience. In my view, however, those other levels of Parsons' thought are "presupposed" by his solutions to the generalized problems of action and order. While some interpreters have addressed this presuppositional level, the debate over Parsons' presuppositions has been distorted by the same process of "charismatic" polarization that skewed the conflationary arguments just examined. Not surprisingly, this interpretive dichotomization has been connected to serious misrepresentations of Parsons' thinking, misrepresentations based as often as not on primarily polemical intent.

2.1. THE ANTI-PARSONIAN CRITIQUE

Essentially, there are two main lines of Parsonian critique that address presuppositional issues. Although there are some points of commonality between them, they diverge widely in their principal criticism—so widely that each throws the other's theoretical legitimacy into doubt.

One large group of critics views Parsons as practicing a radical and unrealistic form of voluntarism. Parsons is seen as having fallen victim to the typical idealist faith in the freedom of human action, in the lack of constraint imposed on it by external forces. Some of these critics see this idealism as emerging from Parsons' epistemological position per se. John Finley Scott's well-known article of the early 1960s, for example, concludes that Parsons' early work, including with some equivocation *The Structure of Social Action*, is thoroughly dualistic.[47] Parsons has followed the classical phenomenological emphasis of Kant, Hegel, and the German tradition as a whole, Scott asserts, by proposing the complete, hermetic separation of ideal commitments from the pressures of material, naturalistic elements. In this way, Parsons envisions the individual as having free will vis-à-vis nature. Wolf Heydebrand took this argument a step further by attempting to portray Parsons' philosophical dualism as not limited simply to the early writings but as extending through Parsons' entire work.[48]

The main body of these critiques, however, avoids taking the idealist criticism back into Parsons' epistemology as such; most critics, indeed, implicitly employ the same kind of distinction between "philosophical" and "sociological" epistemological issues which has informed my own discussion throughout this book. They suggest that while Parsons formally acknowledges the multidimensionality of knowledge qua knowledge, his sociological theories effectively adopt a purely idealist stance by focusing solely on normative and social-psychological constraints. The classic article in this genre is David Lockwood's, "Some Remarks on 'The Social System,'" published in 1953. Lockwood finds Parsonian theory to have nothing in common with efforts that seriously consider the problem of material scarcity. Starting with the fundamental theoretical question of the relation of means and ends, and its classical articulation as the "problem of order" by Hobbes, Lockwood presents Marx and Parsons as the principal sociological representatives of the materialist and idealist positions. He finds these different presuppositional positions specified in the contrast between Marxian "mode of production" analysis and Parsonian value-pattern analysis and, further, in completely divergent understandings of the sources of social strain—exploitation for Marx, inadequate socialization for Parsons.[49]

Lockwood's analysis became incorporated in some later, better-known anti-Parsonian critiques. In the mid-1950s, for example, Mills linked Parsons to Hegel and, in turn, applied Marx's anti-Hegelian critique to Parsons;[50] yet the distinctively presuppositional aspects of Mills' argument were blurred, as we have seen, by his overarching commitment to the formative power of Parsons' ideological assumptions. Similarly, Dahrendorf adopted Lockwood's generalized orientation only to deemphasize it by characterizing Parsons' normative emphasis as an equilibrium theory. For Dahrendorf, Parsonian theory was not simply a theory of norms but of normative and social consensus. Later, Rex returned more explicitly to the means/ends generality of Lockwood's essay. He too, however, linked it directly to the conflict/harmony issue, and presented a much more ambiguous portrayal of Parsons' presuppositional position than had Lockwood.[51] Gouldner's subsequent portrait of Parsons as an idealist similarly conflated presupposition, models, and ideology.

Thus, with the outstanding exception of Lockwood himself—who, with some equivocation, argues that an ideal emphasis is a necessary component of any analysis of conflict and, at the same time, that a materialist emphasis may be combined with notions of function and system[52]—these critics utilized a presuppositional reference only to blur further the lines of Parsons' theoretical commitments. Each emphasized a less generalized problem with which Parsons' idealist commitment was considered to be completely at one. Thus Parsons is an idealist because he is an equilibrium theorist, or because he is a conservative ideologist. The weakness of such arguments is indicated by the fact that, logically, they can be turned completely upside down. This is exactly Heydebrand's approach. Every one of Parsons' theoretical characteristics, Heydebrand asserts, can be derived from his idealist dualism: his systemic-functional model, his political conservatism, his vision of empirical stability, even his analytical-deductivist approach to scientific methodology.[53] Heydebrand, in other words, accepts the conflationary argument about the relation between Parsons' presuppositions and the other levels of his thought, yet far from underemphasizing the role of presuppositions, as most such critics do, he has emphasized it with a reductive vengeance.

There is another, opposite side to the presuppositional anti-Parsonian critique. Instead of seeing Parsons as overly voluntaristic, this group of critics charges that his theory is voluntaristic in name only. Actually, they contend, Parsons has developed an anti-individualistic, deterministic theory in which external constraint completely inhibits free will. Ironically, the first well-known formulation of this argument was Scott's contrast between Parsons' early voluntarism and later behaviorism, a behaviorism that Scott himself thoroughly endorsed. Nevertheless, Scott's formulation of this contrast has been taken over by antibehaviorist critics and utilized as a normative standard to evaluate the antivoluntary behaviorist aspects of Parsons' theory. Whether this antivoluntarism characterizes Parsons' work "only" for the four decades after *The Structure of Social Action* or has been present in Parsons' work from the outset has become a major intra-group point of contention, one that has become structured along the lines of a debate over the "early" versus the "late" Parsons in much the same manner as the debate over Marx's emphasis on alienation.

Atkinson is perhaps the most effective proponent of this antivoluntary critique. While following Scott's thesis of the "epistemological break," he effectively transforms its philosophical contents into appropriate sociological distinctions.[54†] Arguing that Parsons' middle and later work has a "collectivist" emphasis, Atkinson asserts that it "views man as the plaything of social constraint, without choices and without the ability to gain control of his life."[55] The argument is particularly effective because it differentiates this presuppositional level from others. Atkinson argues throughout that his criticism applies only to Parsons' articulation of the problem of order, not to Parsons' commitment to political conservatism, equilibrium, and functional models.[56] This insight is not shared by most other critics of Parsons' anti-voluntarism. Martindale also accepts the early/late Parsons distinction, yet he follows the strategy Atkinson rejects, conflating Parsons' antivoluntarism with every other level of analysis. Wallace represents a sort of transitional figure in this respect, for while his characterization of Parsonianism as "functional imperativism" involves his recognition that functional models can be linked to a variety of presuppositional choices, the same characterization suggests that Parsons' antivoluntary "imperativism" grows, rather, from some reification of the model choice itself.[57] Blumer and Homans are much more explicit on this point, linking Parsons' "sociologistic" emphasis on supra-individual sources of order to the inherently antivoluntary qualities of "system" models.[58] Dennis Wrong, on the other hand, connects Parsons' antivoluntary stance to an ideological conservatism that produces an idealistic emphasis on "over-socialization."[59] Finally, this critique is even picked up by Friedrichs and Gouldner, despite their assertion that Parsons, simultaneously, gives voluntarism too much sway.[60]

There is, however, some methodological "logic" to this conflationary "madness." For despite their total disagreement on the issue of Parsons' voluntarism, both of the critical groups discussed above legitimate their positions by pointing to the same presuppositional problematic: Parsons' sociological idealism. The only exceptions are Sheldon Wolin—who in his highly idiosyncratic review of Parsons and Platt's *The American University* finds the origins of Parsons' inhibition of individual freedom in his adoption of an "economic model" that views interaction as "vulgar exchange"[61]—and John G. Taylor, a Marxist, who insists that this "grand bourgeois" theorist must, somehow, share the rationalism of classical political economy.[62†] Parsons as a materialist thinker is completely anomalous in this generalized strand of the secondary literature. The rest of the commentators are in agreement about the existence of Parsons' idealism, an agreement that indicates a critical consensus about Parsons' presuppositional position. Whether Parsons is viewed as overly voluntarist or antivoluntarist, however, the argument reveals fundamental theoretical confusion over what such presuppositional commitments mean.

Many of these critics of Parsons' presuppositional position are mistaken in their understanding of general theoretical logic. This problem is reflected in their tendency to conflate presuppositional position with other levels of Parsons' analysis. In addition, it is evident in the difficulties they have with the presuppositional level itself. Many misunderstand, or at least misrepresent, the sociological epistemology upon which generalized theoretical logic is based. From Parsons' emphasis on the relative autonomy of normative collective elements, members of both groups often draw erroneous, though divergent, conclusions. Those who view Parsons as antivoluntaristic assume that free will is incompatible with an emphasis on normative constraint. Those who view Parsons as overly voluntaristic often mistakenly believe that an emphasis on norms is, effectively, an emphasis on no constraint at all; they take Parsons' insistence upon the relative autonomy of the normative order as equivalent to a negation of the material one. In the terms of my discussion in volume 1, chapter 3, the former group does not understand the possibility of combining collective normative order with individual voluntarism; the latter denies the possibility of a legitimate "conditional" voluntarism—denies, that is, a truly multidimensional position.

Beyond such theoretical confusion, however, there is another, equally important source for this critical disagreement. Both types of anti-Parsonian "readings" are, simultaneously, thinly veiled theoretical arguments in their own right, arguments directed, with full theoretical clarity, against multidimensional theory itself. Critics accusing Parsons of anti-individualistic bias are actually asserting the validity of an exclusively individualistic approach to social theory, one in which any theoretical emphasis on external, supra-individual constraint is prima facie invalid. Blumer and Homans, of course, are leaders of highly individualistic schools of sociological theory; Atkinson takes a consistently existentialist position, arguing so clearly against "constraint" as such that Marx and Weber are also dismissed, with Parsons, as collectivist, anti-individualistic theorists. In turn, the critics who accuse Parsons of a purely voluntarist position are, for the most part, taking a self-consciously materialist perspective. Despite their protestations to the contrary, there is not to be found in Dahrendorf, Mills, Gouldner, Rex, or even Lockwood anything approaching a balanced acknowledgment of the equal significance and relative autonomy of order's normative components. For the most part, their abstract arguments, and their concrete examples as well, present the notion that the order of norms is really no order at all.[63†]

It is not at all surprising that, given their tendency to misunderstand presuppositional logic and their commitment to presenting independent theoretical arguments of their own, virtually all of these critics have also been drawn into serious errors of fact in their evaluation of Parsonian theory. They simply misrepresent, in an empirical sense, the nature of his theoretical commitments. As I have often pointed out, for example, Parsons' emphasis on the collective aspects of normative forces is an analytic position that focuses on emergent properties in individual interaction. Contrary to critical assertion, this position does not imply for Parsons, any more than it did for Durkheim, the rejection of individual free will. Nor does Parsons reject the particular differences that exist among individual personalities. He simply views neither of these considerations as inconsistent with the patterning of powerful supra-individual forces. His emphasis, therefore, is on the probability, not the certainty, of any concrete individual's normative conformity. Moreover, we have seen that one of Parsons' most unequivocal contributions to social theory lies precisely in the way he emphasizes the increasing autonomy of the concrete individual in Western society by analytically interweaving changing psychological, social, and cultural constraints. No clear-eyed observer, therefore, could describe Parsons as an antivoluntarist. Similarly, although Parsons' position on the multidimensional issue is far more equivocal, it is completely inaccurate to paint him simply as a sociological idealist. We have seen that a significant part of Parsons' theoretical effort must be viewed as an attempt to follow Weber in transcending the ideal/material dichotomy. To ignore this dimension of Parsonian theory is to miss an important reason for Parsons' influence in contemporary social science and, more importantly, to ignore one of the principal bases upon which his ultimate contribution to intellectual tradition depends.

2.2. THE PARSONIAN DEFENSE

As I have noted earlier, there seems to exist a strange kind of symbiotic relation between Parsons' critics and his defenders. In the process of defending Parsons against clear distortions, his sympathizers would deny the critics any validity at all. At the same time, in their own more positive assessments they often make the same kind of conflationary errors as the critics.

In analyzing the presuppositional critiques of Marx, Durkheim, and Weber, we find that the most powerful theoretical defenders of these classical theorists follow a distinctive strategy. Adopting a multidimensional perspective as the critical standard and theoretical goal of their readings, they deny that the classical theorist ever deviated from such a position. Avineri and McLellan pursue this strategy in their discussions of Marx and his critics; Lukes and Bellah treat Durkheimian theory and interpretation in much the same way; Bendix's and Schluchter's treatments of Weber's theory and its critics are also distinguished by this approach. While the power of their readings stems from the manner in which they outline the potential for multidimensional extensions of each theorist's work, its weakness, I have argued, stems from this very strength. In stretching the theory's presuppositions beyond its actual frame, they have distorted (or revised) its essential nature. These distortions have muddied the critical waters, blurring still further the lines of theoretical debate.

Just such a process occurs with Parsons' presuppositional defense. The most important Parsonian sociologists and the most articulate sympathetic commentators have continually denied any idealist cast to Parsons' theory. For example, during the middle period of Parsons' work, Robin Williams, whose critical essay represents in other respects the most objective and nuanced defense of that period, emphasizes Parsons' "continuing awareness of the massive societal impact of power, political processes, and the economy of instrumental systems of action."[64] Characterizations of Parsons' later theory in the more hostile critical environment of the 1960s were similar. In a direct response to Gouldner's attack, John K. Rhoads asserts not only that "Gouldner's evidence [for Parsons' idealism] cannot withstand criticism," which it certainly cannot, but that it is entirely without foundation. In contrast, Rhoads argues that Parsons has fully achieved a presuppositional "synthesis," a "multideterminism" in which "material factors and technology are factors of importance."[65] In a later series of articles devoted to an explication of Parsons' general framework, Harry M. Johnson makes a similar claim, contending that through such devices as his four-function schema, his interchange analysis, and his theory of generalized media, Parsons had consistently succeeded in combining the normative and material determinants of collective action.[66] Rocher, Bourricaud, and Münch also find the presuppositional critique to be without foundation; the first two interpreters present Parsons' work on the economy and polity as fully in accord with his multidimensional causality, while Münch argues that Parsons consistently interpenetrates norms and conditions.[67] Perhaps the best example of such orthodoxy is the general essay by Loubser, introducing the most ambitious Parsons festschrift. Addressing one phase of the critics' argument, Loubser dismisses it as amounting to little more than "glib phrases, stereotypes, and strawmen."[68] More generally, he asserts the unequivocal multidimensionality of Parsons' framework—"the action frame of reference avoids all forms of reductionism"[69]—and argues that the critics reject this perspective only because their ultra-empiricist standards render them unable to appreciate Parsons' level of generality.[70]

In the face of the distortions of the generalized anti-Parsonian critique, it is natural that his defenders would respond by this strategy of denial. It is natural particularly in view of the fact that of the four theorists considered in the four volumes of this work, Parsons presents the greatest advance toward a potentially multidimensional framework of analysis. Yet to suggest, for example, as Loubser does, that these presuppositional critiques are—or at least should be considered—"dead issues" or "games sociologists play," merely continues the charismatic polarization of theoretical debate that has surrounded Parsons' theory from its inception.[71] More substantively, it trivializes three decades of commentary by ignoring the serious theoretical evidence it has presented. For despite fundamental errors in their analysis, we have seen that these presuppositional critics touch important elements of truth.

It will be recalled that the attempts to legitimate Marx, Durkheim, and Weber were not exhausted by sympathetic assertions of their multidimensionality; many, perhaps most, of the defenses were actually justifications for the theorist's emphasis on one presuppositional combination over another. Thus, the later Korsch roundly defended Marx's economism; Davy stood up for Durkheim's emphasis on collective ideas; and, while Parsons spoke with approval of Weber's emphasis on the religious aspects of legitimacy, Wrong and Mills praised Weber's Hobbesian approach to political authority. It would be surprising, therefore, if the presuppositional defense of Parsons were limited to asserting his multidimensionality. It is not: within this tradition of interpretation, one strand describes his work as legitimately oriented to the overweening importance of normative over factual order. Commenting on the middle period of Parsons' work, for example, Devereux notes with approval that for Parsons social order "must rest on a core of institutionalized common values."[72] Later, reviewing Parsons' work on social evolution, Jackson Toby focuses almost entirely on the cultural aspects of change. Parsons, in his view, "uses as his pivotal concept . . . shared symbolic systems."[73] In the best brief introduction to Parsons' work, Benton Johnson argues that "the fundamental postulates in Parsons' sociology" include the assumption that "values are the key to social order."[74] And in the best monograph on Parsons' thought, Bourricaud contradicts his own multidimensional interpretation by agreeing with Parsons that "the science of action begins by the study of the norms to which actors submit, which constitute the 'structure' or the 'anatomy' of society."[75]

3. THE SOURCES OF MISINTERPRETATION IN PARSONS' THEORY ITSELF

The contemporary interpretation of Parsons poses a classical dilemma in the sociology of knowledge, the insider-outsider problem.[76] We have seen that the anti-Parsonian critiques have erred in serious and fundamental ways, yet simply by stepping outside Parsons' framework they have provided important illumination. The sympathetic defenses of Parsons' theory, on the other hand, have provided invaluable corrections to such critical errors, yet, imprisoned by Parsons' own view of his work, they ignore the serious strains that divide it against itself. In denying the internal tension in Parsons' theorizing, his defenders mistakenly simplify the complex and contradictory nature of his theoretical work. To remain completely external to Parsons' theory, then, promotes unappreciative, semi-informed kinds of critiques; to remain completely within promotes "charismatic," uncritical followership.

As in the interpretations of Marx, Durkheim, and Weber, the problems and confusions of Parsonian interpretation do not, finally, emerge only from polemical misreadings and errors in theoretical logic. They are rooted in the problems of the theory itself. Despite its one-sidedness, the idealist interpretation strikes sympathetic chords because Parsons himself is often idealist and reductive. By the same token, the defenders' contention that Parsons' theory is fully multidimensional also finds abundant substantiating evidence.

The same kind of ambiguous confirmation applies to the conflationary interpretations. Certainly the model level is not the key to Parsons' theory, yet we have seen how Parsons himself argues that the logic of his interchange formula derives from the nature of functional systems. And while there is ample evidence to refute the conflationary claims of the conflict school, Parsons himself often identifies his presuppositional commitment to norms with an emphasis on empirical equilibrium. If such an error were not pervasive in Parsons' work, the conflict interpretation would have been disregarded long ago. There are even, as we have seen, strong inclinations on Parsons' part to argue that his presuppositions prove the validity of a moderate, antiradical ideological perspective and that his general theory represents an objective reflection of the empirical world. In so arguing, he lends a certain justice to the claims of the ideological and positivist critiques. If Parsons himself equates his presuppositions with ideology, why not judge them according to the ideology alone? If Parsons himself makes the claims of empiricist objectivity, why not evaluate his work according to purely propositional standards of validity?

Like Weber's, Parsons' work is internally contradictory, and in a similar way it provides support for a variety of partial, often mutually antagonistic interpretations. The only way to overcome this problem is to step outside the problematic of both Parsons and his interpreters. By developing a standard that is broad enough to include the concerns of critics and defenders alike, a certain kind of postpositivist objectivity can be achieved. Multidimensionality is such a synthetic standard. Through its application universalistic judgments are possible. Without such a synthetic standard, the preceding analysis of conflation and reduction in Parsonian interpretation would not have been possible. Nor could the sources of such misinterpretation have been traced to the tension in Parsons' theory itself.

Notes

CHAPTER ONE

1. For the notion of theoretical "openings," see S. N. Eisenstadt and M. Curelaru, *The Form of Sociology: Paradigms and Crises* (New York, 1976). In the sense used here, theories are less open in their earlier, "charismatic" period. See my review of *The Form of Sociology* in *Contemporary Sociology* 6 (1977):658–661.

2. On Weber's relative isolation in postwar Germany, see vol. 3, ch. 1, and Fritz Ringer, *The Decline of the German Mandarins* (Cambridge, Mass., 1969).

3. See Terry Nichols Clark, *Prophets and Patrons: The French University and the Emergence of the Social Sciences* (Cambridge, Mass., 1973), for a discussion of the institutional aspects of Durkheim's great intellectual influence in the France of his day. For the intellectual impact, see Thomas M. Kando, "*L'Année Sociologique:* From Durkheim to Today," *Pacific Sociological Review* 19 (1976):147–176, and my references to the French literature in vol. 2, pp. 306–327.

4. See Steven Lukes, *Emile Durkheim: His Life and Work* (New York, 1972), esp. ch. 16, "The Reception of Durkheim's Ideas," and ch. 25, "Durkheim and His Critics," both for the depth of misunderstanding of Durkheim's ideas and the reaction against his ideas by the revolutionary elements of the French left. See also vol. 2, ch. 9, esp. pp. 323–327.

5. It is interesting that the reception of the work of another important classical sociologist, that of Simmel, does not follow this pattern. The reason is that Simmel never achieved in his own time the kind of dominant "charismatic" status of Marx, Durkheim, or Weber. Nonetheless, the reception of Simmel's work over the course of this century does show certain similarities, particularly in the manner in which key aspects of his

work have been ignored and other elements fragmented and distorted in their assimilation. The best brief case study of the assimilation of any of these classical theorists' ideas is Donald N. Levine's analysis of Simmel's assimilation in American sociology (in Levine, Ellwood B. Carter, and Eleanor Miller Gorman, "Simmel's Influence on American Sociology," *American Journal of Sociology* 81 [1976]:813–845, 1112–1130).

6. This important point is indirectly supported in the analysis by the sociologist of science, Warren Hagstrom, of Parsons' impact on American sociology. Hagstrom reminds his readers that the acceptance of a paradigm in the Kuhnian sense is not the only criterion for the theoretical acceptance of a scientist's ideas. Thus, after discussing the well-known "students" of Parsons as examples of paradigm followers, in Kuhn's sense, Hagstrom adds the following:

> The language, concepts, and to some extent the symbolic generalizations of Parsons have diffused widely in American sociology. But this has been a process of the uneven diffusions of various aspects of Parsons' thought among an unstructured set of sociologists, not the acceptance of a paradigm by a well-defined and interdependent group of investigators. ("Notes on Paradigms and Related Concepts," unpublished Ms., p. 28.)

The same basic point is made by Dick Atkinson, who, after referring to the "still considerable debate about the validity, even the morality of his [Parsons'] contributions," asserts that this has little relation to the degree of Parsons' deeper impact.

> What is clear is that followers and critics alike have accepted portions of his work. Thus such concepts as role, institution, social structure, social system, are not the subject of violent disagreement. Indeed, they are used by his critics to attack other concepts . . . which are alleged to form the substance of Parsons' work. (*Orthodox Consensus and Radical Alternative* [New York, 1972], p. 9.)

7. Thus, in the early 1960s, Bennett M. Berger wrote that "for the past twenty years systematic sociological theory in the United States has been little else than a dialogue with Talcott Parsons" ("On Talcott Parsons," *Commentary* 34 [1962]:510). More than a decade later, this point was elaborately demonstrated in Jonathan H. Turner's analysis in *The Structure of Sociological Theory* (Homewood, Illinois, 1974) of recent debates over exchange theory, conflict theory, symbolic interactionism, and ethnomethodology. Turner writes that "it is unlikely that other forms of sociological theory can be understood" without reference to Parsons' work (p. 59). Several years later, in a eulogy, Alvin W. Gouldner discussed Parsons' "very special role" in modern sociology: "It is a mark of his achievement that most of us who became sociologists after World War II felt constrained to define our own intellectual position in relation to his work"

("Talcott Parsons," *Theory and Society* 8 [1979]:299–301, quoting 300). In another eulogy, which appeared in the *Humboldt Journal of Social Relations,* Edward Tiryakian observed that while "it may be too much to say that Parsons realized with his general theory the integration of the various social sciences into a unified social science," it was true, nonetheless, that "Parsons renewed this effort and in a sense provided a basis of unification for sociology on a world-wide basis, for Parsonian sociology has been discussed, recognized, and interpreted not only in North America and Western Europe but also in Japan and even the Soviet Union" ("Post-Parsonian Sociology," vol. 7, no. 1 [Fall/Winter, 1979/80], pp. 17–32, quoting p. 21). It is quite correct that as the locus for postwar theoretical debate Parsons' work provided the single common coin not only of different theoretical schools but often of different national traditions as well.

8. For Marxism: John Rex, *Key Problems in Sociological Theory* (London, 1961); Ralf Dahrendorf, *Class and Class Conflict in Industrial Society* (Stanford, Calif., 1959); Alvin W. Gouldner, *The Coming Crisis in Western Sociology* (New York, 1970). For Weberianism, in addition to aspects of Dahrendorf's work: Randall Collins, "A Comparative Approach to Political Sociology," in Reinhard Bendix, ed., *State and Society* (Berkeley and Los Angeles, 1968), pp. 42–67, and Bendix, *Max Weber* (idem., 1978), in which a polemic against Parsonianism as a valid extension of Weber's ideas is an underlying theme; also the more positive discussion in Wolfgang Schluchter, *The Rise of Western Rationalism* (idem., 1981), esp. pp. 25–39. For Durkheimianism, see, e.g., Whitney Pope, "Classic on Classic: Parsons' Interpretation of Durkheim," *American Sociological Review* 38 (1973):399–415. For symbolic interactionism, see various themes in Herbert Blumer, *Symbolic Interactionism* (Englewood Cliffs, N.J., 1969), passim. For phenomenology, see Richard Gratoff, *The Theory of Action: The Correspondence of Alfred Schutz and Talcott Parsons* (Bloomington, Ind., 1978), and also the more sympathetic piece by Bennetta Jules-Rosette, "Talcott Parsons and the Phenomenological Tradition in Sociology: An Unresolved Debate" (Paper presented at the Forty-ninth Annual Meeting of the Pacific Sociological Association, Anaheim, Calif., April 6, 1979).

The penetration of Parsons' theorizing into contemporary antagonistic schools of thought can perhaps be no more effectively illustrated than by its impact on the Soviet Union. At least through the early 1970s, Parsons' "structural functionalism" was taken as the representative of Western bourgeois sociology, and as such the chief challenger to Soviet Marxism. Yet much like Parsons' major challengers in the postwar Western world, Soviet theorists often incorporated vital aspects of Parsonian theory even as they launched critiques to refute it. There even developed within the intellectual vanguard of Soviet sociology strands of neo-Parsonian "Marxist" analysis, as exemplified by the work of Markarian (see the discussion by Alexander Vucinich, "Marx and Parsons in Soviet Sociology," *Russian Review* 33, no. 1 [January 1974]:1–19). The impact of Parsons' theorizing, in fact, has been profound throughout the industrialized communist world—e.g., in the work of Piotr Sztompka in Poland and Nikolai Genov in Bulgaria (I refer to both these authors in later discussion). In a recent issue of *Theory and Society*, the editors published "Theses in the Syncretic Society," an article by "a fairly prominent official in one of the East European countries" (unnamed) which revealed an acute and subtle utilization of Parsonian categories (9 [1980]:233–260).

9. See n. 21 below.

10. Robert W. Friedrichs, *A Sociology of Sociology* (New York, 1970), p. 145.

11. Gouldner (n. 8 above), p. 168.

12. Ibid., p. 169.

13. Turner (n. 7 above), p. 28.

14. Atkinson (n. 6 above), pp. 2–3; Savage, *The Theories of Talcott Parsons* (New York, 1981), p. 235.

15. Rocher, *Talcott Parsons and American Sociology* (New York, 1975). For his ideological disagreement, see ibid., p. 144.

16. See my discussion (vol. 1, pp. 60–62) of the "systems" elements in the thought of this group of Marxist theorists. George Lichtheim discusses the linkage between Althusser and Parsons in "A New Twist in the Dialectic," *New York Review of Books*, January 30, 1969, pp. 33–38. Poulantzas' significant reference to Parsons and, more generally, to the "functionalist" theoretical problematic is clear throughout his *Political Power and Social Classes* (London, 1972); see esp. pp. 44–56.

For Chazel, see his *La Théorie analytique de la société dans l'oeuvre de Talcott Parsons* (Paris, 1974); for Bourricaud, see his *L'Individualisme institutionnel: Essais sur la sociologie de Talcott Parsons* (Paris, 1977); see also my "The French Correction: Revisionism and Followership in the Interpretation of Parsons," *Contemporary Sociology* 10(1981):500–505. For Touraine, see *The Self-Reproduction of Society* (Chicago, 1977).

17. For Luhmann, see his "Generalized Media and the Problem of Contingency" in Jan J. Loubser et al., eds., *Explorations in General Theory in Social Science* (New York, 1976), pp. 507–532; Niklas Luhmann and Benjamin Nelson, "A Conversation on Selected Theoretical Questions: Systems Theory and Comparative Civilizational Sociology," *Graduate Faculty Journal of Sociology* 1, no. 2 (1976):1–17; Luhmann, "A General Theory of Organized Social Systems," in Geert Hofstede and N. Sami Kassem, eds., *European Contributions to Organization Theory* (Amsterdam, 1976), pp. 96–113; and, more generally, his *The Differentiation of Society* (New York, 1982) and *Trust and Power* (New York, 1979).

For Schluchter, see n. 8 above. For Münch, see his "Talcott Parsons and the Theory of Action, I: The Structure of the Kantian Core," *American*

Journal of Sociology 86(1981):709–739; "Talcott Parsons and the Theory of Action, II: The Continuity of Development," ibid., 87 (1982):771–826; and "Socialization and Personality Development from the Point of View of Action Theory: The Legacy of Emile Durkheim," *Sociological Inquiry* 51 (1981):311–354. References to Parsons occur throughout Habermas' work, but it is in *Legitimation Crisis* (Boston, 1975) that the theoretical overlap begins in a systematic way. The quotations are from his most recent theoretical work, *Theorie des Kommunikativen Handelns* (Frankfurt am Main, 1981), 2:297, in which Parsons' work is discussed at some length (pp. 295–444).

Over the last ten years an extraordinary situation has developed: while interest in Parsons' work has rapidly declined in the United States, it has experienced a dramatic revival in Germany. The work of three of the leading younger German social theorists—Habermas, Luhmann, and Schluchter—is now suffused with Parsonian concepts. This irony was concretely represented by the fact that the first essays sympathetic to Parsons which the *American Journal of Sociology* had published in more than a decade were the work of a German social theorist in the generation younger than the theorists just cited, Richard Münch (see above). After Parsons' death, one of the major German journals, *Zeitschrift für Soziologie*, devoted a special issue (vol. 9, no. 1 [1980]) to Parsons' work, and Schluchter edited an appreciative volume of essays on his sociological contributions, *Verhalten, Handeln und System* (Frankfurt am Main, 1980). The two major American journals, in contrast, contained no official acknowledgment of his death or special discussion of his work. Another revealing irony is that, while Luhmann's work is becoming appreciated in English-speaking circles, contemporary "anti-Parsonianism" is so strong that Luhmann's Parsonian roots have been ignored by his English interpreters. E.g., Gianfranco Poggi reviews Luhmann's essays on societal media in an enthusiastic manner while hardly mentioning the tradition within which they are written (review of Luhmann's *Macht*, in *Contemporary Sociology* 5 [1976]:61–63).

For a more detailed discussion of some of these issues, see my article, "The Parsons Revival in Germany," *Sociological Theory:* 2 (1984).

18. Adriaansens, *Talcott Parsons and the Conceptual Dilemma* (London, 1980), p. 164.

19. Bershady, *Ideology and Social Knowledge* (New York, 1973); Gintis, "Alienation and Power: Toward a Radical Critique of Welfare Economics" (Ph.D. diss., Harvard University, 1969). See Parsons' reply to Gintis' use of his theory, "Commentary on Herbert Gintis' 'A Radical Analysis of Welfare Economics,' " *Quarterly Journal of Economics* 89(1975):280–290.

One should not overlook the (especially from this point of view) very interesting eulogy ("Talcott Parsons," n. 7 above) written by Alvin Gouldner, who in the later 1970s seems to have returned to the critical appreciation which characterized his important theoretical contributions of the pre-*Coming Crisis of Western Sociology* period. See also the rather sympathetic consideration for the very same morally-oriented liberal individualism that Gouldner had earlier dismissed in the chapter "Civil Society in Capitalism and Socialism" in his *The Two Marxisms* (New York, 1980), pp. 355–373.

20. What follows presents only the briefest outline of the controversy that has surrounded Parsons' work. In the Appendix to this volume, I make a much more extensive analysis of the problematics of contemporary Parsons interpretation, showing in some detail how misreadings of Parsons follow the fault-lines in theoretical logic analyzed in vol. 1; I also compare these misperceptions with the evaluations I construct in the following pages, connecting these interpretive problems to the tensions in Parsons' thinking (see esp. chs. 6–9).

21. Examples of such purely empirical approaches to evaluation abound. For critics of Parsons see the following. For an empirical evaluation of the Parsonian theory of stratification, see, e.g., J. A. Kahl, *The American Class Structure* (New York, 1957) (cf. Arthur L. Stinchcombe, "Some Empirical Consequences of the Davis-Moore Theory of Stratification," *American Sociological Review* 28 [1963]:805–808). On the family, see, e.g., Richard Sennett, *Families Against the City* (Cambridge, Mass., 1970) and "Middle Class Families and Urban Violence: The Experience of a Chicago Community in the 19th Century," in Stephen Thernstrom and Richard Sennett, eds., *Nineteenth Century Cities* (New Haven, 1968), pp. 386–420, or Philip Slater's "Parental Role Differentiation," *American Journal of Sociology* 67 (1961):269–308. On the university, see the empirically-oriented critical reviews of Parsons' and Platt's *The American University* by Joseph Gusfield and P. Sexton in *Contemporary Sociology* 3 (1974):291–300. On social change, see Anthony D. Smith, *The Concept of Social Change* (London, 1973).

For Parsons' sympathizers who argue that his theory's distinction results upon its empirical insight, see, e.g.: Marion J. Levy, *The Structure of Society*, (Princeton, N.J., 1952), p. vii; Winston White, *Beyond Conformity* (New York, 1961), pp. 70–100; Rocher (n. 15 above), pp. 127 ff.; A. L. Jacobson and Gary L. Buck, "Social Evolution and Structural-Functional Analysis: An Empirical Test," *American Sociological Review* 33 (1968):343–353; A. L. Jacobson, "A Theoretical and Empirical Analysis of Social Change and Conflict Based on Talcott Parsons' Ideas," in Herman Turk and Richard L. Simpson, eds., *Institutions and Social Exchange: The Sociologies of Talcott Parsons and George C. Homans* (Indianapolis, 1971), pp. 345–360. For the most elegant and careful defense of Parsons' work as a purely empirically-oriented theoretical exercise, see Victor M. Lidz, "Values in Sociology: A Critique of Szymanski," *Sociological Inquiry* 40

(1970):13–20, and "On the Construction of Objective Theory: Rejoinder to Szymanski," ibid., 42 (1972):51–64.

22. See Gouldner (n. 8 above), pp. 167–198; Friedrichs (n. 10 above), pp. 14–23; T. B. Bottomore, "Out of This World," in his *Sociology as Social Criticism* (New York, 1975), pp. 29–43, published originally in *New York Review of Books* 13, no. 8 (1969):34–39 (for a critical evaluation of Bottomore's efforts, see my review of *Sociology as Social Criticism* in the *American Journal of Sociology* 81 [1976]:1220-1223); C. Wright Mills, *The Sociological Imagination* (New York, 1959), pp. 29–49.

23. Max Black, "Some Questions about Parsons' Theories," in Black, ed., *The Social Theories of Talcott Parsons* (Ithaca, N.Y., 1961), pp. 282 ff.; Hans Zetterberg, *On Theory and Verification in Sociology* (New York, 1954), passim; M. J. Mulkay, *Functionalism, Exchange, and Theoretical Strategy* (London, 1971), pp. 66–93; Homans, "Bringing Men Back in," *American Sociological Review* 29 (1964):809–818.

24. Bershady (n. 19 above), pp. 125–167 and passim.

25. Dahrendorf (n. 8 above), pp. 157–240; Lewis Coser, *The Functions of Social Conflict* (New York, 1956); Rex (n. 7 above); Randall Collins, *Conflict Sociology* (New York, 1975).

26. Don Martindale, *The Nature and Types of Sociological Theory* (Boston, 1960), pp. 484–499; Mills (n. 22 above), pp. 29–49; Gouldner (n. 7 above), pp. 138–156, 246–338; Blumer (n. 8 above), pp. 57–60; Walter L. Wallace, "Overview of Contemporary Sociological Theory," in Wallace, ed., *Sociological Theory* (New York, 1969), pp. 1–59; Ken Menzies, *Talcott Parsons and the Social Image of Man* (London, 1976), esp. pp. 68–150; Savage (n. 14 above), pp. 128–235; Habermas (n. 17 above); and Habermas, "Talcott Parsons: Problems of Theory Construction," *Sociological Inquiry* 51 (1981):173–196.

27. Neil J. Smelser, *Social Change in the Industrial Revolution* (Chicago, 1959); Harry M. Johnson, "Parsons' Use of Analytic Models," *Indian Journal of Social Research*, April and August 1975, pp. 354–371; Rocher (n. 15 above), pp. 155–159; Seymour Martin Lipset, "Social Structure and Social Change," in Peter M. Blau, ed., *Approaches to the Study of Social Structure* (New York, 1975), pp. 172–209; Loubser (n. 17 above), "General Introduction," pp. 1–24; Rainer C. Baum, "Introduction to Generalized Media in Action," in Loubser, pp. 448–469; F. Van Zyl Slabbert, "Functional Methodology in the Theory of Action," ibid., pp. 46–58; Luhmann, "Talcott Parsons: The Future of a Theory," in *The Differentiation of Society* (n. 17 above), pp. 47–65.

28. John Finley Scott, "The Changing Foundations of the Parsonian Action Schema," *American Sociological Review* 28 (1963):716–735; Wolf Heydebrand, "Review Symposium," *Contemporary Sociology* 1 (1972):387–395; David Lockwood, "Some Remarks on 'The Social Sys-

tem,'" *British Journal of Sociology* 7, no. 2 (1956):137–138; Mills (n. 22 above), pp. 37–38; Rex (n. 8 above), passim; Gouldner (n. 7 above), pp. 199–245.

29. Atkinson (n. 14 above), pp. 33 ff.; Wallace, "Overview" (n. 25 above), passim; Blumer (n. 8 above); Pope (n. 8 above); Homans (n. 22 above); Dennis Wrong, "The Over-Socialized Conception of Man in Modern Sociology," *American Sociological Review* 26 (1961):183–193.

30. Edward C. Devereux, "Parsons' Sociological Theory," in Black (n. 22 above), pp. 1–63, esp. p. 16; Jackson Toby, "Review Symposium," *Contemporary Sociology* 1 (1972):395; Benton Johnson, *Functionalism in Modern Sociology: Understanding Talcott Parsons* (Morristown, N.J., 1975), p. 16.

31. Robin M. Williams, Jr., "The Sociological Theory of Talcott Parsons," in Black (n. 22 above), pp. 64–99, esp. p. 66; John K. Rhoads, "On Gouldner's 'Crisis of Western Sociology,'" *American Journal of Sociology* 78, no. 1 (1972):136–154, esp. pp. 146–150; Harry M. Johnson, "The Generalized Symbolic Media in Parsons' Theory," *Sociology and Social Research* 57 (1973):208–221, and "Parsons' Use" (n. 26 above); Rocher (n. 15 above), pp. 77–98; Loubser (n. 17 above); Bourricaud (n. 16 above).

32. In his comparison of Parsons with Marx and Weber, Atkinson (n. 14 above) is the only critic to have attempted such a theoretical comparison. His analysis differs from the present account both in method—his focus remains primarily on what I call the model level—and in his conclusion that there is a convergence among these three theories.

33. It is ironic that the only extended analysis of Parsons' relation to a theorist in the classic tradition concerns his relation to Simmel, whose work presents the only major classic tradition with which Parsons' work was not directly in dialogue. See Donald N. Levine's excellent early work, *Simmel and Parsons* (New York, [1957] 1980).

CHAPTER TWO

1. Compare this view with that of Bennett Berger, which suggests the by now standard argument that Parsons' interesting empirical essays have little connection to his "grand theory" ("On Talcott Parsons," *Commentary* 34, no. 6 [1962]:507–513).

2. Parsons' early training at Heidelberg was in economics as were his instructorships at Amherst and Harvard ("On Building Social System Theory: A Personal History," *Daedalus* 99 [1970]:826–829). As for the empirical aspect of *The Structure of Social Action*, Ken Menzies characterizes it, correctly, as in part an anti-Utilitarian "account of the rise of capitalism," noting that if "read this way, the book has many parallels with Lukács' *History and Class Consciousness*" (*Talcott Parsons and the Social Image*

of Man [London, 1976], p. 38). In the middle-period work, Parsons' empirical illuminations of the origins of fascism—based in part, obviously, on personal experience of the German situation—have been widely acknowledged (see, e.g., Arthur Mitzman, *The Iron Cage* [New York, 1970], pp. 144 ff., and Ralf Dahrendorf, *Society and Democracy in Germany* [Garden City, N.Y., 1969], pp. 52–53). In the later 1930s and early 1940s, Parsons engaged in extensive participant observation in hospital settings with an "intention to publish a major monographic study of medical practice," an intention that was never fulfilled ("On Building Social System Theory," p. 840). For Parsons' rootedness in religious studies, in addition to his writings on Weber, see "Religious Perspectives in College Teaching: Sociology and Social Psychology" (in Hoxie N. Fairchild, ed., *Religious Perspectives in College Teaching* [New York, 1952], pp. 285–337). Parsons' exposure to empirical studies of deviance occurred through close association with Merton's work and, perhaps particularly, through his supervision of the encyclopedic dissertation by Edward C. Devereux, Jr., "The Sociology of Gambling" (Harvard University, 1949). His close relation to Bales' research group is well known ("On Building Social System Theory," pp. 844–845).

3. The following is an attempt to provide simply a representative cross-section of the major efforts along this line. It is not in any sense a complete listing, and other such works will be cited in the course of this book.

Religion: Robert N. Bellah, *Tokugawa Religion* (Boston, 1957) and *Beyond Belief* (New York, 1970); Jan J. Loubser, "Puritanism and Religious Liberty: A Study of Normative Changes in Massachusetts, 1630–1850" (Ph.D. diss., Harvard University, 1964).

Deviance: Albert K. Cohen, *Delinquent Boys* (New York, 1955); Robert K. Merton, "Social Structure and Anomie," in his *Social Theory and Social Structure* (New York, 1968); Devereux, "The Sociology of Gambling" (n. 2 above); Jackson Toby, "Social Evolution and Criminality: A Parsonian View," *Social Forces* 26 (1979):386–391.

Socialization: Philip Slater, "Parental Role Differentiation," *American Journal of Sociology* 67 (1961):269–308, and "Towards a Dualistic Theory of Identification," *Merrill-Palmer Quarterly* 7 (1961):113–126; Chad Gordon, "Systemic Conceptions of Self," *Sociological Inquiry* 38 (1968):161–178.

Family: Jesse Pitts, "The Bourgeois Family and French Economic Retardation" (Ph.D. diss., Harvard University, 1958).

Economics: Neil J. Smelser, *The Sociology of Economic Life* (Englewood Cliffs, N.J., 1963).

Politics: Gabriel S. Almond, "Comparative Political Systems," *Journal of Politics* 18 (1956):391–409, and "A Functional Approach to Comparative Politics," in Almond and J. S. Coleman, eds., *The Politics of Developing Areas* (Princeton, N.J., 1960), pp. 5–64; Almond and G. Bingham Powell,

Jr., *Comparative Politics* (Boston, 1966); David E. Apter, "A Comparative Method for the Study of Politics," *American Journal of Sociology* 64 (1958):221–237, *The Politics of Modernization* (Chicago, 1966), and *Ghana in Transition* (Princeton, N.J., 1972); Samuel H. Beer et al., *Patterns of Government* (New York, 1958); David Easton, *The Political System* (New York, 1953) and *A Systems Analysis of Political Life* (New York, 1965); Karl W. Deutsch, *The Nerves of Government* (New York, 1963); Seymour Martin Lipset and Stein Rokkan, "Cleavage Structures, Party Systems and Voter Alignments," in Lipset and Rokkan, eds., *Party Systems and Voter Alignments* (New York, 1967), pp. 1–64; William C. Mitchell, "The Polity and Society: A Structural-Functional Analysis," *Midwest Journal of Political Science* 2 (1958):403–420, and *The American Polity* (New York, 1972).

Stratification: Bernard Barber, *Social Stratification* (New York, 1957); Elinor G. Barber, *The Bourgeoisie in 18th Century France* (Princeton, N.J., 1955); Suzanne Keller, *Beyond the Ruling Class* (New York, 1963); Paul B. Colomy, "Stunted Differentiation: A Sociological Examination of Virginia's Political Elite, 1720–1850 (Ph.D. diss., University of California, Los Angeles, 1982); S. N. Eisenstadt, *Social Differentiation and Stratification* (Glenview, Ill., 1971).

Revolution: Chalmers Johnson, *Revolutionary Change* (Boston, 1966); Mark Gould, *Revolution in the Development of Capitalism* (Berkeley and Los Angeles, forthcoming); David Lane, "A Paradigm of Revolution and Social Change," in Lane, *Leninism: A Sociological Interpretation* (Cambridge, 1981), pp. 110–129.

Law: Leon Mayhew, *Law and Equal Opportunity* (Cambridge, Mass. 1968); David Little, *Religion, Order, and Law* (New York, 1969); Daniel Glaser, "What Changes Criminal Law?" in his *Crime in Our Changing Society* (New York, 1978), pp. 14–34.

Psychoanalysis: Fred W. Weinstein and Gerald M. Platt, *The Wish to Be Free* (Berkeley and Los Angeles, 1969) and *Psychoanalytic Sociology* (Baltimore, 1973).

Intellectuals: Winston White, *Beyond Conformity*, (New York, 1961); Edward Shils, *The Intellectuals and the Powers and Other Essays* (Chicago, 1972); S. N. Eisenstadt and Stephen Graubard, *Intellectuals and Tradition* (Jerusalem, 1974).

Ideology: Francis X. Sutton et al., *The American Business Creed* (Cambridge, Mass., 1956); Clifford Geertz, "Ideology as a Cultural System," in David E. Apter, ed., *Ideology and Discontent* (New York, 1964), pp. 47–76.

Community studies and stratification: Edward J. Laumann and Franz Pappi, *Networks of Collective Action* (New York, 1976); Terry N. Clark, *Leadership in American Cities: Resources, Interchanges, and the Press* (Beverly Hills, Calif., forthcoming) and Clark, ed., *Community Structure and Decision-Making: Comparative Analyses* (New York, 1968).

Science: Bernard Barber, *Science and the Social Order* (New York,

1952); Robert K. Merton, *The Sociology of Science* (Chicago, 1973); Norman W. Storer, *The Social System of Science* (Irvington, N.Y., 1966); Joseph Ben-David, *The Scientist's Role in Society* (Englewood Cliffs, N.J., 1971).

Youth: S. N. Eisenstadt, *From Generation to Generation* (New York, 1956).

Collective behavior: Neil J. Smelser, *Theory of Collective Behavior* (New York, 1963); John Wilson, *Introduction to Social Movements* (1972).

Small Groups: Robert F. Bales, "The Equilibrium Problem in Small Groups," in Parsons, Bales, and Edward A. Shils, eds., *Working Papers in the Theory of Action* (New York, 1953), pp. 111–162; Morris Zelditch, Jr., "Role Differentiation in the Nuclear Family: A Comparative Study," in Parsons and Bales, eds., *Family, Socialization, and Interaction Process* (New York, 1955), pp. 307–352; W. D. Crano and J. Arnoff, "A Cross-Cultural Study of Expressive and Instrumental Role Complementarity in the Family," *American Sociological Review* 43 (1978):463–471.

Medical Sociology and Professions: Renée Fox, *Experiment Perilous* (New York, 1959); Bernard Barber et al., *Research on Human Subjects* (New York, 1973), and Barber, *Informed Consent in Medical Therapy and Research* (New Brunswick, N.J., 1980).

American Society: Robin Williams, Jr., *American Society* (New York, 1951); Kingsley Davis et al., eds., *Modern American Society* (New York, 1948); Seymour Martin Lipset, *The First New Nation* (New York, 1967).

Comparative Studies: Robert M. Marsh, *Comparative Sociology* (New York, 1967); Marion J. Levy, *The Family Revolution in Modern China* (Cambridge, Mass., 1949); Rainer C. Baum, "Values and Uneven Political Development in Imperial Germany" (Ph.D. diss., Harvard University, 1967) and *The Holocaust and the German Elite* (Totowa, N.J., 1981); Frederick W. Riggs, *Administration in Developing Countries* (Boston, 1964) and *Prismatic Society Revisited* (Morristown, N.J., 1973); Jesse R. Pitts, "Continuity and Change in Bourgeois France," in Stanley Hoffman, ed., *In Search of France* (Cambridge, Mass., 1964), pp. 249–304.

Education: Robert Dreeben, *On What Is Learned in School* (Reading, Mass., 1968).

Social Change: Neil J. Smelser, *Social Change in the Industrial Revolution* (Chicago, 1959); S. N. Eisenstadt, *The Political System of Empires* (New York, 1963); Wilbert E. Moore, *Social Change* (1963).

Organizations: Amitai Etzioni, *A Comparative Analysis of Complex Organizations* (New York, 1961).

See also the collections of topically organized essays in two of the Parsons festschrifts: Alex Inkeles and Bernard Barber, eds., *Stability and Change* (Boston, 1971), and J. J. Loubser et al., eds., *Explorations in General Theory in Social Science* (New York, 1976).

4. Guy Rocher, *Talcott Parsons and American Sociology* (New York,

1975), pp. 125 ff.; see also the discussion by Martin U. Martel, "Talcott Parsons," in *International Encyclopedia of the Social Sciences*, vol. 18, *Biographical Supplement* (New York, 1979), pp. 616–617.

5. Mulkay, *Functionalism, Exchange, and Theoretical Strategy* (London, 1971), pp. 73–74.

6. Rocher, p. 127, implies that it does.

7. Talcott Parsons, *The Structure of Social Action* (New York, [1937] 1968), p. 28.

8. Ibid., p. 29. The importance of Whitehead to Parsons' approach in his early work has generally been overlooked. It is interesting that not only does Whitehead's *Science and the Modern World* provide a justification for a theoretical, analytic focus on science but it also relates the need for such a focus to a critique of instrumentalism in the modern industrial world, a critique that relates closely to Parsons' own normative emphasis.

Schwanenberg and Bershady have written the best analytical treatments of Parsons' meta-methodological orientation (Enno Schwanenberg, "The Two Problems of Order in Parsons' Theory: An Analysis from Within," *Social Forces* 49 [1971]:569–581, and "On the Meaning of the General Theory of Action," in Loubser, *Explorations* [n. 3 above], pp. 35–45; Harold J. Bershady, *Ideology and Social Knowledge* [New York, 1973]). Both authors emphasize the central role of theory building on the most generalized level for Parsons, and Bershady (p. 84) traces the historical roots of Parsons' "analytic realism" back to the pervasive influence of the Newtonian method, drawing parallels, e.g., between Parsons and Condillac. However, these analysts underplay Parsons' presuppositional reasons for such a pursuit. This is particularly true of Bershady. (For a good critique of Bershady on this issue, see Stephen Savage, *The Theories of Talcott Parsons* [New York, 1981], pp. 39–43, 45–47.) See Jonathan Turner and Leonard Beeghley, "Current Folklore in the Criticism of Parsonian Action Theory," *Sociological Inquiry* 44 (1974):47–55, for another interesting analytical treatment of Parsons' meta-methodology, and Savage, pp. 71–81, for a critical comparison of Parsons, in regard to meta-methodology, with Weber, Merton, Mills, and Dahrendorf.

9. *Structure of Social Action*, p. 34.

10. Ibid.

11. Ibid., pp. 183–184.

12. Ibid., p. 730. See Bershady's excellent discussion of the conflict between Weber and Parsons on this point in *Ideology and Social Knowledge* (n. 8 above), pp. 51–64; for a closely related discussion, see Peter Lassman, "Value-Relations and General Theory: Parsons' Critique of Weber," *Zeitschrift für Soziologie* 9, no. 1 (1980):102–111. Hans P. M. Adriaansens shows that Parsons' demand for a still more objective antipositivist science of society vis-à-vis Weber can be seen as part of historical tradition

that began with Rickert's neo-Kantian critique of the purely "intuitionist" strand of Germany's *Geisteswissenschaft* tradition (*Talcott Parsons and the Conceptual Dilemma* [London, 1980], 14–27).

13. *Structure of Social Action*, p. 730.

14. Ibid., p. 753.

15. Ibid., p. 730.

16. Ibid. For a similar position in Parsons' later work, see *The Social System* (New York, 1951), p. 20, and his most important later discussion of theory in science, the "Introduction" to the section "Culture and the Social System" in Parsons et al., eds., *Theories of Society* (New York, 1961), pp. 963–993.

17. Parsons, "Social Interaction" in *International Encyclopedia of the Social Sciences* (New York, 1968), vol. 7, p. 436.

18. *Structure of Social Action*, p. 733.

19. Ibid., italics added.

20. Ibid., italics added.

21. Ibid.

22. Ibid.

23. Ibid., pp. 308–320.

24. For a general analysis of this problem and its relation to Parsons' work, see vol. 1, pp. 115–122.

25. This important qualifying clause—"not always unambiguously pursued"—might appear logically to nullify the preceding assertion, "Parsons tries to pursue a synthetic position." Such negation would assume, however, that theoretical ambivalence is impossible. As I noted at some length in my discussion of Empson's literary criticism in the preface to vol. 2, sociological theorists are not different in this respect from other human beings: they often hold two different attitudes toward the same fact. Because their own feelings about their ideas are not often completely resolved, such theorists often develop two implicitly contradictory lines of argument, sometimes side by side.

In vol. 2, I discussed such contradictory lines of argument in critical aspects of the works of Durkheim and Marx; in vol. 3, contradictory strains are documented throughout Weber's work. Although in contradictory theoretical work one line of argument may be less developed and only partially pursued, it is also possible that both strands can stand on their own as sui generis theoretical statements. This was occasionally true of Durkheim and Marx, and almost always true of Weber. It is also the case with Parsons. In the first half of this volume I will document and piece together an extraordinarily powerful line of multidimensional synthesis; in the second, I will demonstrate how this argument was consistently cross-cut by a more particularistic strand of more exclusively normative argument. I will, in other words, analytically separate two strands of Parsons' theorizing which are often concretely, or empirically, intertwined. This strategy is similar to that followed in much of my interpretation of Weber.

I should stress, finally, that it is not my intention to offer any real psychological explanation for theoretical ambiguity. I wish simply to document the fact that different strains exist, and to analyze them as such. Contradictory positions on presuppositional issues do not as such indicate any special psychological ambivalence in the psychoanalytic sense: epistemological questions are difficult to resolve and great theories are often fundamentally ambiguous on these points. At the same time, although such special predilections are not necessary to *explain* presuppositional positions, it is undoubtedly true that any theoretical ambiguity has some psychological reference, and the specific locus and points of theoretical ambiguity probably have an important psychological meaning for the theorist concerned.

26. Robin M. Williams, Jr., "The Sociological Theory of Talcott Parsons," in Max Black, ed., *The Social Theories of Talcott Parsons* (Ithaca, N.Y., 1961), p. 65, italics added.

27. *Structure of Social Action*, p. 747.

28. Ibid., p. 732.

29. Pitirim A. Sorokin, *Society, Culture, and Personality* (New York, 1947), pp. 44–46; F. Znaniecki, *Cultural Sciences: Their Origin and Development* (Urbana, Ill., 1952), pp. 189–190.

30. Don Martindale, *The Nature and Types of Sociological Theory* (Boston, 1961), pp. 484–493; Whitney Pope, "Classic on Classic: Parsons' Interpretation of Durkheim," *American Sociological Review* 38 (1973):399–415.

31. John Rex, *Key Problems in Sociological Theory* (London, 1961), p. 78.

32. Bloom, *The Anxiety of Influence* (New York, 1973).

33. *Structure of Social Action*, p. 17.

34. Ibid.

35. Ibid., p. 18.

36. These early critical essays are as follows: " 'Capitalism' in Recent German Literature: Sombart and Weber, I," *Journal of Political Economy* 36 (1928):641–661; " 'Capitalism' in Recent German Literature: Sombart and Weber, II," *Journal of Political Economy* 37 (1929):31–51; "Wants and Activities in Marshall," *Quarterly Journal of Economics* 46 (1931):110–140; "Economies and Sociology: Marshall in Relation to the Thought of His Time," *Quarterly Journal of Economics* 46 (1932):316–347; "Malthus," *Encyclopedia of the Social Sciences* (New York, 1933), 10:68–69; "Some Reflections on 'The Nature and Significance of Economics,' " *Quarterly Journal of Economics* 48 (1934):511–545; "Sociological Elements in Economic Thought, I," *Quarterly Journal of Economics* 49 (1934):414–453,

and "Sociological Elements in Economic Thought, II," *Quarterly Journal of Economics* 49 (1934):645–667. See Edward C. Devereux's fine brief discussion of these early essays in his "Parsons' Sociological Theory," in Black (n. 26 above), pp. 9–11.

37. *Structure of Social Action*, p. 56.

38. Parsons was well aware, then, that these and other "rationalistic thinkers" did not present—in terms of their total oeuvre—a picture of social life as completely rational and instrumental. What he insisted, rather, is that they did not systematically integrate their normative references with their instrumental theorizing, hence the former's residual status vis-à-vis the latter. Parsons insisted, also, that even their rationalistic theories—e.g., of the economy—were inadequate in themselves, for they left as parameters normative elements which had significant repercussions in the action and structure described in such rationalistic theoretical systems. (Charles Camic's critique of Parsons' early treatment of Utilitarianism, therefore, as well as his "revival" of Utilitarianism as a normative tradition of theorizing, seems completely to miss the point of Parsons' early work. See Camic, "The Utilitarians Revisited," *American Journal of Sociology* 85 [1979]:516–550.)

39. Ibid., p. 501.

40. Ibid., p. 58.

41. Ibid., p. 61, italics added.

42. Ibid., p. 66.

43. E.g., Menzies (n. 2 above) takes as his central focus the tension in Parsons' work between "action theory" and "systems theory," yet he identifies these as corresponding, respectively, with idealist and positivist methodology in Parsons' work. As a result, he never clarifies precisely which of Parsons' various theoretical commitments creates the shifts in his theory—is the central problem one of methodological ambivalence, or is it ambivalence over notions about models or presuppositions? Menzies' propensity for blurring this distinction receives its sanction, however, from Parsons' own equation of methodological and presuppositional commitment.

44. Ibid., p. 446, italics in original.

45. Ibid., p. 442.

46. Ibid., p. 446, italics in original.

47. Ibid., p. 732.

48. Ibid., p. 607.

49. Parsons, "Introduction," in Max Weber, *Theory of Social and Economic Organization* (New York, 1947), p. 15.

50. Ibid., pp. 16–17. Parsons does note, however, that Weber actually uses *Zweck* in another manner to denote a normatively regulated purpose and self-conscious action, although this is a very minor usage (p. 115, n. 38).

51. Ibid., pp. 58–60, n. 4.

52. Ibid., p. 17.

53. Adriaansens' (n. 12 above, p. 52) contention that Parsons' synthesis in *The Structure of Social Action* is concrete rather than analytic, that it merely puts factors "next to each other," completely overlooks the fundamentally analytic thrust that is basic even to this early work. The comparison of Parsons' work with Weber's reveals this contrast and underscores the originality of Parsons' formulation.

If comparison with Weber is not sufficient to show the significance of Parsons' new position, one need simply look at the pervasiveness of such "concrete" dichotomization in contemporary sociology. Although I discussed the division of contemporary theory into material and normative perspectives at some length in vol. 1 (pp. 71–112), I did not specifically address the problem of dichotomization produced by a concrete rather than analytic focus, a problem which often goes along with it. E.g., although Dahrendorf formally adheres to a multi-dimensional position, he sees normative and instrumental kinds of action as concretely divided, arguing that societies are separated into "imperatively coordinated associations," which are instrumentally coercive, and "social systems," which are normative (*Class and Class Conflict in Industrial Society* [Stanford, Calif., 1959], p. 167). The sociological division of labor, Dahrendorf believes, should follow these concrete lines, with different theorists focusing on different kinds of structures. Many of the problems in contemporary conflict theory can be associated with, although they are not caused by, such methodological errors. David Lockwood, e.g., vehemently rejects such an orientation:

> It is . . . a little surprising to find that both Dahrendorf and Rex consider it necessary to develop their antitheses to normative functionalism in a *systematic* form. These take the shape, respectively, of a "coercion theory of society" and a "conflict model of society." For this strategy they give reasons which are even more surprising. . . . Dahrendorf feels that the unification of the "integration theory" (normative functionalism) and the "coercion theory" is unlikely and probably impossible. . . . But even in situations where power is very evident and conflict endemic, it is doubtful whether the phenomena of conflict can be adequately grasped without incorporating into conflict theory many of the concepts and propositions concerning the dynamic properties of value systems (or ideologies) which have been developed, or taken over, by normative functionalism. ("Social Integration and System Integration," in Walter Hirsch and George K. Zollschan, eds., *Explorations in Social Change* [New York], 1975, pp. 247–248, italics in original.)

Even among theorists whose work does represent a thorough commitment to integrating normative and instrumental approaches to action, however, the tendency toward concrete rather than analytic frameworks creates serious difficulty. E.g., by cross-cutting several of the classical definitions of rationality, Percy Cohen develops a list of eleven different "degrees of rationality" to which any social institution may be subject (*Modern Social Theory* [London, 1968], pp. 89–90). Clearly, this is a less effective, and somewhat clumsy, approach to the problem when compared with the one Parsons recommends here.

Eisenstadt is the only interpreter of Parsons who has given systematic and detailed attention to his important emphasis on this analytic-versus-concrete division as it affects substantive, not just methodological aspects of Parsons' work. This distinction, in fact, constitutes one of the primary means by which Eisenstadt evaluates Parsons' position in the history of sociological thought (S. N. Eisenstadt and M. Curelaru, *The Form of Sociology: Paradigms and Crises* [New York, 1976], pp. 178–193). Eisenstadt takes over the distinction and utilizes it as one of his means of distinguishing among the stages of sophistication of sociological theory (pp. 88–91). See my review of this work in *Contemporary Sociology* 6 (1977):658–661. (Savage [n. 8 above, pp. 63, 83] also connects Parsons' "analytic" emphasis to his synthetic approach to the problem of action.)

54. *Structure of Social Action*, pp. 43–51. The early part of Parsons' analysis of norms is somewhat ambiguous, a problem that I will discuss below. For an attempt to clarify the voluntarism issue in its most generalized form, see my discussion in vol. 1, pp. 90–112.

55. Ibid., p. 44.

56. Ibid., p. 49.

57. Ibid., p. 732.

58. Thus, e.g., Mulkay (n. 5 above, p. 85) claims that Parsons' emphasis on normative order derives from his preference for stability, or John O'Neill claims to analyze the relation of the problems of order and rationality in "The Hobbesian Problem in Marx and Parsons" (in Loubser, n. 5 above, pp. 295–308), yet really is talking about the ideological level of theoretical commitment alone (see also the treatment by Nancy DiTomaso, "Sociological Reductionism From Parsons to Althusser," *American Sociological Review* 47 [1982]:14–28). Certainly whether Parsons feels that a good moral order can be achieved via instrumental or substantive rationality is an interesting question, and one to which Parsons implicitly addresses himself throughout his social change theory. Still, it has nothing directly to do with Parsons' direct concern in *The Structure of Social Action*. In Gouldner's *The Coming Crisis of Western Sociology* (New York, 1970) we can find an approach to Parsons' position that combines both these other levels of misinterpretation. Gouldner describes Parsons' position this way:

> To seek order is to seek a reduction of social conflict, and thus it is to seek a moratorium on such social changes as is sought through conflict or which may engender it. To seek order is to seek a predictability of behav-

> ior. . . . The commitment of those obsessed with order is not to morality as such, but only to *a* moral system that yields order. (P. 251, italics in original.)

Each of these claims, it will be argued below, ignores a significant part of Parsons' actual intent. See my general discussion of such conflationary treatments of the order problem in vol. 1, pp. 90–94; also my detailed analysis of the conflationary aspects of Parsons' critics in this volume, Appendix.

59. Among many others, see Menzies (n. 2 above).

60. *Structure of Social Action*, pp. 738–739.

61. Ibid., p. 59, italics added.

62. Ibid., italics added.

63. Ibid., p. 739.

64. Ibid., p. 740.

65. In the light of this rather clear process of logical development, it is difficult to understand the kind of interpretation to which Parsons' order emphasis has been subject by theorists of an individualistic stripe. Martindale, e.g., makes the surprising observation that "the conclusions in Parsons' *Structure of Social Action* are most noteworthy for their thoroughgoing nominalism."

> All structures [for Parsons] are merely shorthand devices of analytic utility. In principle all analyses performed by use of social structures could be made more precise by analysis into social actions [i.e., individual actions]. The only indication of a potential break from this nominalistic orientation is the suggestion that systems of social actions may have "emergent" properties not analyzable into unit acts. ("Talcott Parsons' Theoretical Metamorphosis from Social Behaviorism to Macrofunctionalism," in Herman Turk and Richard L. Simpson, eds., *Institutions and Social Exchange: The Sociologies of Talcott Parsons and George C. Homans* [Indianapolis, 1971], p. 169.)

I have argued, to the contrary, that this is precisely the opposite of Parsons' principal contention and the inverse of his application of the analytic/concrete distinction. Atkinson is one of the few individualistic critics of Parsons who perceives the true point of his order discussion, yet he, in turn, describes the normative focus as conservative and antivoluntary.

> It should be quite clear that the concept of "voluntarism" that Parsons uses does not imply what we usually mean by "freedom of choice" in everyday language, for it has quickly become interchangeable with the concept "norm," and that "subjective action" which strives to conform to "norms." (*Orthodox Consensus and Radical Alternative* [New York, 1972], p. 11.)

Rocher and Bershady more accurately perceive Parsons' point. "Parsons' critics," Rocher writes, have "too readily transposed what is essentially an analytical problem into the ideological plane" (*Talcott Parsons and American Sociology* [n. 4 above], p. 33). Bershady puts the autonomy of this presuppositional issue most sharply:

> If the ends of individual human beings vary at random, what is it that holds society together? That every society is held together in some way, that the social activities of human beings exhibit some pattern . . .—these are not mere chimeras. To understand the general principles of the "determinateness" of social life is of central concern in Parsons' thought, and it is in fact a conceptual, not a political, concern. (*Ideology and Social Knowledge* [n. 8 above], p. 42.)

Critics like Adriaansens (n. 12 above) and Jürgen Habermas ("Talcott Parsons: Problems of Theory Construction," *Sociological Inquiry* 51 [1981]:173–196) are aware of Parsons' intention to bridge the nominalist/realist gap, but they claim that in this early work Parsons' view of the actor remains an individualist one. Both, however, state the problem in an unacceptably dichotomized and concrete way, and for this reason pose the problem in a manner that Parsons' analytical framework actually superseded. Habermas (esp. pp. 79–80) poses the problem as "private individuals" versus "systems," and Adriaansens talks about "individuals" versus "institutions" (p. 13; also pp. 57, 61, 94, 99). It should be noted, however, that at other points in his discussion, particularly in reference to Parsons' later writings, Adriaansens indicates a clearer perception of the analytic perspective in Parsons' approach to order.

66. *Structure of Social Action*, p. 60.

67. Ibid.

68. Ibid., pp. 344–345.

69. Ibid., p. 91.

70. Ibid., p. 344.

71. Ibid., p. 91. Again, this linking of positivism to rationalism is true only in the limited sense that a rationalist theorist evaluates the actor as if the latter were a proto-scientist. It is not true, however, in the wider sense that Parsons implicitly argues: that only positivistic theory can produce collectivist materialist theory. Parsons' own discussion of Durkheim, and certainly the case of Comte, directly contradict this assertion. Cf. Joseph Brandon Ford, "Parsons versus Comte: On Positivism," *Indian Journal of Social Research*, 15 (1974):77–100.

72. *Structure of Social Action*, p. 345.

73. For a discussion of the occluded relation between Parsons and Halévy, see vol. 1, pp. 118–119, 198–201.

74. *Structure of Social Action*, p. 93.

75. Ibid., pp. 930–994.

76. Ibid., p. 93.

77. Ibid., p. 94.

78. Ibid., pp. 99–100.

79. Ibid., p. 106, italics added. Parsons notes that in so stipulating Malthus went beyond rationalism in important though residual ways.

80. Characteristically, Parsons is careful to distinguish here between Marx's empirical contribution, with which he disagrees, and the more generalized presuppositional issues in Marx's exploitation theory:

> The error of the many modern economists who repudiate Marx *altogether* lies in the fact that they (rightly) criticize the outworn forms of Marxian economics without going back to the *really* central proposition on which Marx's most important departures from the main trend of classical economics were based. (Ibid., p. 109, italics added.)

This presuppositional issue—Marx's collectivist attack on individualistic theory—always represented the basis of Parsons' positive attitude toward Marx. His other, negative evaluations notwithstanding, this single point of praise remained steady throughout the entirety of his career. E.g., in the 1928 article which drew on his Heidelberg dissertation, Parsons wrote as follows:

> It was one of Marx's most important contributions to socialist thought that the fault of capitalistic exploitation lay, not with the capitalist as an individual, but with the system to which he as well as everyone else was forced to conform. Thus abuses could only be remedied by changes in the fundamental basis of class interests within the system. This was a great advance on the utopian socialist view, that the remedy was the rational persuasion of the leaders of the society. (" 'Capitalism' in Recent German Literature: Sombart and Weber," *Journal of Political Economy* 36 [1928]: 659; cf. Parsons, "Some Comments on the Sociology of Karl Marx," in his *Sociological Theory and Modern Society* [New York, 1967], pp. 102–135.)

81. *Structure of Social Action,* p. 290.

82. Ibid., p. 291.

83. Ibid., p. 658.

84. Ibid., pp. 508–509.

85. Ibid., p. 576.

86. See, e.g., Parsons' emphasis on the materialist elements of Weber's analysis of India and China, ibid., pp. 542–563.

87. This connection between the Parsonian and the Marxist critique of the classical economic interpretation of the origins of capitalism is emphasized by Menzies (n. 59 above): "*The Structure of Social Action* can be read as an attack on utilitarianism in general and its account of the rise of capitalism in particular" (p. 38). Menzies also takes Parsons' argument on a generic level, utilizing it to critique contemporary exchange theorists like M. Olson (*The Logic of Collective Action* [New York, 1971]) and B. Barry

(*Sociologists, Economists and Democracy* [London, 1970]). Essentially, Menzies argues that these latter sociologists are so rooted in individualistic traditions that they can solve the "randomizing" problems only by resorting to theoretically undesirable residual categories. He points to Parsons' concept of "social ends" as a means of resolving this impasse (pp. 36–42; for a similar and more elaborate contemporary application, see Richard Münch, "From Pure Methodological Individualism to Poor Sociological Utilitarianism," *Canadian Journal of Sociology*, 8 [1983]: 45–76). An interesting connection can be made here between Menzies' argument and Peter K. Ekeh's thesis in *Social Exchange Theory: The Two Traditions* (Cambridge, Mass., 1974), because while Ekeh makes essentially the same critique of instrumentalist exchange theory, he mentions as alternatives only Durkheim and Lévi-Strauss, neglecting the important strand in Parsons' work. The link between "social exchange" and Parsons will be pursued in more detail in ch. 4. (See Edward G. Swanson, "Frameworks for Comparative Research: Structural Anthropology and the Theory of Action," in Ivan Vallier, ed., *Comparative Methodology* [Berkeley and Los Angeles, 1971], pp. 141–202, and Adrian C. Hayes, "A Comparative Study of the Theoretical Orientations of Parsons and Lévi-Strauss," *Indian Journal of Social Research* 15 [1974]:100–111.)

88. *Structure of Social Action*, p. 63.

89. Ibid.

90. Ibid., p. 64.

91. Ibid.

92. For a discussion of the historical role of this epistemological dilemma and of Parsons' critical role in making its logic explicit, see vol. 1, ch. 3, esp. pp. 67–71, 98–103.

93. *Structure of Social Action*, p. 94, italics added.

94. Ibid., p. 96.

95. Ibid., p. 97.

96. Ibid., pp. 129–177.

97. Ibid., pp. 178–300, 783–784.

98. Ibid., p. 314.

99. Ibid., p. 337; see also p. 714.

100. Ibid., p. 717.

101. Ibid., p. 81, italics added.

102. Ibid., italics added.

103. Ibid., p. 82.

104. Ibid.

105. Ibid., pp. 740–743; on the role of this concept of "means/ends chains" in Parsons, see Atkinson (n. 65 above), pp. 11–16.

106. Parsons and Shils, "Values, Motives, and Systems of Action," in Parsons and Shils, eds., *Towards a General Theory of Action* (New York, 1951), pp. 47–275, quoting p. 107, italics added.

107. Emile Durkheim, *The Elementary Forms of Religious Life* (New York, [1912] 1965), p. 262.

108. Parsons and Shils (n. 106 above), p. 105, italics added.

109. Ibid., p. 162.

110. Parsons, "The Theory of Symbolism in Relation to Action," in Parsons, Robert F. Bales, and Edward Shils, eds., *Working Papers in the Theory of Action*, (New York, 1953), p. 38, italics added.

111. Parsons, "Introduction" to the section "Culture and the Social System" in *Theories of Society* (n. 16 above), p. 963, italics altered.

112. See Parsons' distinction between social order achieved through symbolic "interpenetration" and social integration in "Social Interaction" (*International Encyclopedia of the Social Sciences* [New York, 1968], 7:429–441, esp. 437 ff.). The best discussion of the different connotations of the term "cultural integration"—ranging from actual empirical harmony to simply symbolic generalization—is Donald N. Levine's "Cultural Integration," ibid., 7:372–380. In his otherwise excellent articles on Parsons, Richard Münch, in contrast, conflates this presuppositional issue of "interpenetration" with the more specific issues of social equilibrium and human cooperation, and with "evolutionary advance" in general ("Talcott Parsons and the Theory of Action," pts. 1 and 2, *American Journal of Sociology* 86 [1981]:709–739 and 87 [1982]:771–826). Thus, less developed or more unevenly developed societies (e.g., ancient China or India) are, in Münch's view, societies where there is less interpenetration. For Parsons, however, while such societies might be more or less unorganized in empirical terms, their members would be as "interpenetrated" by symbols as members of any other society, for such interpenetration is a more generalized issue of presuppositional order itself. This conflationary approach to the problem of interpenetration corresponds with Münch's tendency to overemphasize the role of normative elements in Parsons' general theory. Though he argues strongly and persuasively for the multidimensional quality of Parsons' position as opposed to the belief that Parsons takes a purely idealist stance, he also argues that Parsons gives an epistemological "priority" to norms, in the Kantian sense of exempting them from empirical interaction. Thus, he describes Parsons' view as follows: "A social order is possible only if there is a selective principle which exempts certain means and ends from utilitarian considerations and assigns to them a permanent priority" (p. 724). Such an interpretation seems to be at cross-purposes with the argument advanced at other points in the articles that Parsons takes a fully multidimensional position; indeed, it more accurately reflects the idealist strand of Parsons' work which I will discuss in later chapters. This postulate of normative insulation clearly complements Münch's argument that interpenetration implies the successful normative regulation of conflict.

113. Parsons and Shils (n. 108 above), p. 160.

114. Parsons, "Introduction" to the section "Culture and the Social System" in *Theories of Society*, p. 975.

115. Ibid., italics added.

116. Ibid., p. 963.

117. Parsons, *Societies: Evolutionary and Comparative Perspectives* (Englewood Cliffs, N.J., 1966), p. 28.

118. Ibid., p. 11, italics in original.

119. Ibid., p. 10.

120. See, e.g., Marx's similar logic in his critique of "vulgar" or "bourgeois" communism for its emphasis on material needs and satisfactions, praising as a "higher" form communism that would focus on aesthetic needs, in the "Economic and Philosophical Manuscripts" (1844), in T. B. Bottomore, ed., *Karl Marx: Early Writings* (New York, 1963), pp. 61–219, esp. pp. 152–167.

121. A similar perception of "higher" and "lower" cybernetic positions as referring simply to qualitative differences in causation rather than to preferences for idealism over materialism is articulated by Eisenstadt and Curelaru in *The Form of Sociology* (n. 53 above), p. 182. It is also emphasized by Walter Buckley, *Sociology and Modern Systems Theory* (New York, 1967); Karl W. Deutsch, *The Nerves of Government* (New York, 1963); and Martin U. Martel, "Academentia Praecox: The Aims, Merits, and Scope of Parsons' Multisystematic Language Rebellion (1958–1968)," in Turk and Simpson (n. 65 above), pp. 174–210.

122. Parsons, *Societies*, p. 8, italics added. The fact that this apparently technical distinction between environment and determinant actually articulates fundamental theoretical issues (cf. sec. 3.3 below) is nowhere more effectively demonstrated than in the critical interpretation offered by Savage (n. 8 above). The failure to understand this merely "technical" point vitiates Savage's entire argument. From Parsons' insistence that the realm of ultimate reality lies outside of action per se, Savage claims that "Parsons precludes the possibility" of theoretical investigation of the area of cultural symbolism altogether (p. 110), and that Parsons believes values "may be subjected to scientific analysis" only if the "normative order . . . is transformed from a purely symbolic to a factual [i.e., material] order" (ibid.). On the basis of this argument, Savage assumes throughout his book that Parsons views values as effecting action in a completely indeterminate, idealistic manner, and that the investigator must himself adopt a quasi-religious faith in teleological causality if Parsons' version of value determinism is to be accepted. Yet while Parsons does differentiate the environment of ultimate reality from action and, therefore, from being the subject of scientific analysis, in no way does he exempt the cultural symbols which are derived from an orientation to ultimate reality from having a determined, patterned relation to action or from being subject to scientific analysis itself (cf. n. 131 below). Indeed, although Parsons certainly

argues that positivistic methods of value interpretation must be supplemented by hermeneutical ones, to bring social-scientific, causal analysis to bear on value configurations is one of the central ambitions of his entire work. This is the whole point, after all, of the critical position that Parsons assumes vis-à-vis the German Idealist tradition, in alliance with the criticisms which Rickert and Weber leveled against this school.

123. *Societies*, p. 8, italics in original.

124. Ibid.

125. See my discussion of this problem in Durkheim's work, without reference to the analytic-concrete distinction, in vol. 2, pp. 287–296, 304–306.

126. See my discussion of this problem in Weber in vol. 3, esp. ch. 4, sec. 1.

127. See the analysis of Marx's discussion of alienated praxis as the foundation of the economic determinism of capitalist life in vol. 2, pp. 26–35.

128. For Parsons' discussion of Marx in the terminology of the cybernetic schema including, indirectly, his use of the latter to distinguish Marx's "historical materialism" from physicalistic determinism, see "Some Comments on the Sociology of Karl Marx" (n. 80 above), pp. 102–135, esp. p. 105.

129. John Finley Scott, "The Changing Foundations of the Parsonian Action Schema," *American Sociological Review* 28 (1963):716–735.

130. Wolf Heydebrand, "Review Symposium," *Contemporary Sociology* 1 (1972):387–395, esp. p. 391. This is also the charge made by Savage (see the discussion in n. 122 above).

131. It is revealing to compare these two charges of dualism. E.g., Scott, while finding an early dualism, argues that Parsons in his subsequent work arrived at a "behavioral" position. By the latter, Scott means a theory that places norms within social interaction, not outside it, and views them as sanctions. Heydebrand, on the other hand, believes that Parsons demonstrates his idealism most sharply in this later work. This conflict reveals the confusion that lies at the heart of this attempted critique. What, precisely, constitutes "dualism"? For Scott, it implies a radical, Kantian separation of morality from empirical, interactional influence, while for Heydebrand it implies simply a strong emphasis on norms as independent causal variables. Any theory with the temerity to emphasize action's normative elements will be vulnerable to the charge of "dualism" from naturalistic critics of either a behaviorist or a materialist bent. (Although there are elements in Münch's defense of Parsons that actually support the image of radical Kantianism which Scott tries to project [see my critical discussion in n. 112 above], the main thrust of Münch's [n. 112] argument clearly demonstrates that Parsons' version of neo-Kant-

ian dualism does not in any sense preclude empirical interpenetration of "autonomous" spheres.)

One of the more interesting interpretations of Parsons' work that argues directly against the dualist criticism is Werner Stark's. In *The Fundamental Forms of Social Thought* (London, 1962), Stark describes Parsons' work as "one of the most significant attempts in recent years to fuse the Durkheimian tradition with that of Max Weber" (p. 249). In contrast to the "dualist" critics, the reason for Stark's insight on this issue is his own clarity about the presuppositional logic involved. E.g., his criticism of Tönnies' *Gemeinschaft/Gesellschaft* dichotomy amounts to a critique of dualism that closely resembles Parsons' position.

> Community and association are not, in life, separate phenomena; they are separate only in thought by virtue of definition. . . . Every social relationship is therefore bound to exhibit organism-like and mechanism-like features, though, of course, in accordance with its different proportions. (P. 212.)

Stark's understanding of Parsons may also be favorably compared with Gouldner's charge that Parsons' theoretical roots lay only in German Romanticism and French functionalism (*Coming Crisis* [n. 58 above], pp. 138–140).

132. *Structure of Social Action*, p. 349.

133. Ibid.

134. Several critics have implied that such an ambiguity exists, but none have discussed it in a precise way. Scott (n. 129 above) mentions that Parsons is not fully consistent on the voluntarism issue, but does not elaborate on the contradictory approach. Atkinson (n. 65 above, pp. 10–11) also mentions an ambiguity in Parsons' treatment, but only talks substantively about one side of the treatment.

135. This confusion goes back farther, at least to Parsons' article "The Place of Ultimate Values in Sociological Theory," *International Journal of Ethics* 45 (1935):282–316. Scott, therefore, makes a serious error in finding this earlier article the key to Parsons' basic approach to voluntarism in *The Structure of Social Action*. For an extended discussion of the distinction between a radical free-will position on voluntarism and a more modified one, see vol. 1, pp. 104–110.

136. *Structure of Social Action*, p. 44.

137. Ibid., p. 49.

138. Ibid., p. 50, italics added.

139. Ibid., p. 89, italics added.

140. Ibid., p. 90.

141. Ibid., p. 396.

142. Ibid., pp. 396–397. This clear definition of norms as involving

human desire for their realization demonstrates, I believe, that Parsons was not firmly committed to an ontological distinction between norms and conditions. He recognized that it was possible for ideal elements to be, indeed, completely external to the actor—e.g., if, while having no relation to an actor's own belief system, conduct in accordance with some other norm is forced upon the actor through the threat of material sanctions. (For evidence of Parsons' acknowledgment of such possibilities, see ibid., p. 337; see also his insistence, much earlier in the book, that his term *external* is intended "epistemologically, not spatially," and his statement that "the external world is not 'outside' the knowing object in a spatial sense. The subject-object relation is not a relation in space." [Ibid., p. 46.])

It is, of course, precisely the distinction between such a situation and the internally ordered kind of normative action that Parsons' first attempt at resolving his early ambiguity about order obscured, for if a norm is actually felt to be completely external to an actor—even if that norm was once the product of a human action—it may, in fact, play the role of a "conditional" element if it is backed up by appropriate coercive sanctions. I have tried to discuss the possibility of such a "material-like" role of normative elements in vol. 1, ch. 3, sec. 1 (see, e.g., p. 189. n. 4).

143. Gouldner, e.g., contends that "voluntarism for Parsons serves as a randomizing rather than a structuring mechanism," concluding that the concept "is thus expressive of his antideterministic intent."

> Voluntarism and morality are the equivalent of "free will" [for Parsons]; they serve not simply to qualify other theoretical models by inserting another variable into the predictive equation, but rather to undermine the entire possibility of any kind of determinism, even that of a probabilistic predictability. Moral norms are tacitly the prime starting mechanisms, the unmoved movers. (*Coming Crisis*, p. 190.)

While Scott (n. 129 above) allows that some deviant passages in *The Structure of Social Action* do not follow this form, he makes the same interpretation in a more decisive manner. Arguing that throughout most of the book Parsons takes an idealist stance, Scott claims that for Parsons voluntarism depends on individual action not being determinate "in terms of its own causes." Although such a position does occur as one strand of Parsons' early analysis, as we have noted, it certainly does not represent his major thrust. For an analysis of the presuppositional errors that inform this strand of Parsonian interpretation, see Appendix. See also the good critical comparison that Savage (n. 8 above, pp. 94–105) makes between Parsons' more qualified voluntarism and the more radical free-will positions of representatives of the individualistic position in sociology, including Blumer, Schutz, and Garfinkel and even aspects of Weber's work.

144. This connection of Parsons and Durkheim has been made, e.g., by Pope (n. 7 above) and by Martindale (n. 30 above).

145. *Structure of Social Action*, p. 354. In the following I am, of course, producing Parsons' objections to Durkheim, not my own. I am interested in this interpretation not for understanding Durkheim per se, but for understanding Parsons' theory of voluntarism.

146. Ibid., p. 348.

147. Ibid., p. 347.

148. Ibid., p. 388.

149. Ibid., pp. 440, 432.

150. Ibid., p. 439. Parsons, it should be mentioned, sees Durkheim as much more successful at this transformation of his earlier position than he actually was.

151. The analysis of Durkheim's development in vol. 2 needs a brief restatement here. Even with his strong intuitive understanding of the reconcilability of subjectivity and collective order subsequent to the publication of *The Division of Labor in Society* in 1893, Durkheim still could not develop a satisfactory theoretical understanding of how this reconciliation could be established. The writings of 1894–1897 (*The Rules of Sociological Method; Socialism; Suicide*), therefore, demonstrate extremely awkward theoretical problems, problems which have obscured the essentially normative intention of these middle-period works. At the end of this period—more accurately, what brought the period to a close and initiated the later work—was Durkheim's discovery of the phenomenon of religion as a metaphor and a sociological model of explanation. Beginning around 1897–1898, he argued that all sociological phenomena resembled religion, particularly in their ability to create voluntary compliance through the internal power of sacred symbols. In part, this revealed a true and vital element of social life; yet it also pushed Durkheim's work toward sociological idealism, as well as, even within the cultural realm itself, causing him to ignore different aspects of cultural life. In part, Durkheim turned to the religious model, then, because he did not have a sufficiently abstract understanding of the empirical processes that would allow collective and subjective force to be combined. There were, of course, other reasons: his inclination toward a purely voluntary theory, the significance of the empirical phenomenon of religion in social history, its ideological significance in Durkheim's intellectual world, and so forth.

Parsons did not understand the importance of the religious metaphor for Durkheim's later work: he saw religion as becoming important only with *The Elementary Forms of Religious Life* (1912). He was thus harder on Durkheim for being unable to portray collective voluntarism than he should have been, for this was effectively portrayed in Durkheim's use of the religious model. Still, two points must be made. First, as I suggested in vol. 2, although Durkheim utilized the religious model effectively, he still employed "society" in an often reified way. This was partly because of his continuing positivism, as Parsons rightly notes. Parsons does address a continuing problem in Durkheim's work, then, with this analysis of the failure to understand internalization. More importantly, by correcting and transcending Durkheim on this point, Parsons indirectly addresses one of the factors that forced Durkheim to move toward his exclusive and exaggerated emphasis on the religious model. The other major critical point Parsons takes up against Durkheim, which I have already mentioned and will discuss later at some length, is his idealism. Once again, as I have argued in vol. 2, Parsons interprets this idealism as emerging much later than it did and he misconceives even this later development. This misperception, as will be seen, had important repercussions in terms of Parsons' vision of his own theory. Nonetheless, Parsons did sense an idealist tendency in Durkheim, and he quite rightly embraced Weber as a means to neutralize it.

Of course, the fact that Parsons rejected Durkheim's reliance on the religious model and substituted a much more analytically sophisticated understanding of how collective facts become internalized does not mean that on a more specific and empirical model Parsons was correct in dispensing with certain religious dimensions of phenomena to the extent that he did in his later work. I will argue much later in this book that Parsons gave too little attention to expressive symbolization and to the collective-behavior or "effervescent" aspect of change, even when he described, as he often did in great detail, religious change itself. Yet this does not make his more general analytic criticism of Durkheim any less profound or less fundamentally correct.

152. *Structure of Social Action*, p. xvi.

153. Parsons, "The Superego and the Theory of Social Systems," in his *Social Structure and Personality* (New York, 1964), p. 18.

154. Parsons, "Symbolism and Its Relation to the Theory of Action," in *Working Papers* (n. 110 above), p. 42.

155. Parsons and Shils, *Towards a General Theory of Action* (n. 108 above), p. 66, italics added.

156. Ibid., p. 67.

157. Ibid., p. 66, italics in original.

158. For an elaboration of this distinction in the terminology of "formal" versus "substantive" voluntarism, see vol. 1, pp. 89, 109, and, more generally, my "Formal and Substantive Voluntarism in the Work of Talcott Parsons: A Theoretical and Ideological Reinterpretation," *American Sociological Review* 43 (1978):177–198.

159. Dennis Wrong, "The Over-Socialized Conception of Man in Modern Sociology," *American Sociological Review* 26 (1961):183–193.

160. Despite its widespread acceptance, the early/late Parsons argument has been handled in a sharply inconsistent manner, a fact that attests to the lack of theoretical precision in the charge. Gouldner considers Par-

sons to have been a radical voluntarist through the *Structure of Social Action* period (*Coming Crisis*, p. 190; cf. n. 127 above), while Scott, though agreeing that such an emphasis constitutes the main trend in the book, finds an anti-individualist trend to be a significant minor theme ("Changing Foundations of the Parsonian Action Schema" [n. 129 above; cf. n. 127]). Atkinson reverses Scott's judgment, defining the pure voluntarism position as only a minor thread in *The Structure of Social Action* (*Orthodox Consensus and Radical Alternative* [n. 65 above, p. 11]; cf. n. 54 above). Martindale, on the other hand, believes that Parsons remains a pure voluntarist, with only passing references to order's emergent properties, until the publication in 1945 of his essay "The Present Position and Prospects of Systematic Theory in Sociology" (in Parsons, *Essays in Sociological Theory* [New York, 1954], pp. 212–237). There is no evidence, however, that Martindale has examined any of the essays between 1937 and 1945 ("Talcott Parsons' Theoretical Metamorphosis" [n. 65 above]). Mullins follows Martindale's general position, suggesting vaguely that Parsons dropped the "action" theory somewhere between 1935 and 1950—before, in other words, the publications of 1951, *The Social System* and *Towards a General Theory of Action* (Nicholas C. Mullins, *Theory and Theory Groups in Contemporary American Sociology* [New York, 1973], p. 10). Walter L. Wallace adds still another twist to the "location" of this allegedly crucial transition by arguing that it was only with the introduction of the four-function schema in 1955 that Parsons actually became an antivoluntarist, that his emphasis on the pattern-variable "choices" up until this point had represented a continued commitment to voluntarism ("Overview of Contemporary Sociological Theory," in Wallace, ed., *Sociological Theory* [New York, 1969], pp. 1–59, see pp. 35–45). The position of Menzies provides a kind of summary argument in that it describes Parsons' anti-individualism bias as increasing with each stage of his theoretical development, "lock[ing] man more and more firmly into the pattern of a society" (*Talcott Parsons and the Social Image of Man* [n. 59 above], p. 110; this "incrementally increasing" position is accepted by Habermas [n. 65 above]).

What is revealing about these arguments when they are set against one another is that they disagree not simply about the timing of the purported "epistemological break" but about the nature of the theoretical commitment that brings it about. While an emphasis on collective norms per se is antivoluntary for Scott or Atkinson, for Martindale or Mullins these norms must be placed into a systems model before they became anti-freedom. While for Martindale the very mention of choices being "patterned" along five sets of dichotomous cultural axes—the assumption behind Parsons' pattern-variable usage (*The Nature and Types of Sociological Theory* [n. 30 above], pp. 487–489)—indicates a betrayal of voluntarism, for Wallace it represents voluntarism. The source of these disagreements lies, I believe, in the weaknesses of the argument itself. Because few of these critics are themselves prepared to accept the full implications of a radically voluntarist position, they "extend" the break further into Parsons' later work. Moreover, few of these critics, evidently, have read *The Structure of Social Action* closely enough to recognize that early work's firmly anti-individualistic approach to voluntarism.

The first important critical reply to this discontinuity argument which supports the position present here was Jonathan H. Turner's, which emphasizes the "enormous amount of continuity" in Parsons' work (see Turner, *The Structure of Sociological Theory* [Homewood, Ill., 1974], pp. 31–58). The focus on the unit act, Turner argues, represents a way of isolating certain elements, not the adoption of an individualist position, and he suggests that the later "systems" emphasis is a change in level of analysis rather than in basic position. In fact, Turner argues that the fact of individual negotiation is as acceptable to Parsons as to the symbolic interactionist school, a contention, I believe, that would hold true only if "individual" were modified by "concrete." The problem with Turner's presentation is his failure to identify Parsons' use of the "situation" as a material variable, with the result that he does not distinguish Parsons' position from a purely idealist one. For other discussions critical of the discontinuity thesis, see Turner and Beeghley, "Current Folklore in the Criticism of Parsonian Action Theory" (n. 8 above); Dean Robert Gerstein, "A Note on the Continuity of Parsonian Action Theory," *Sociological Inquiry* 45 (1975):11–16; Münch (n. 112 above); Adriaansens (n. 12 above); and Savage (n. 8 above).

161. Parsons, *Societies* (n. 117 above), p. 7, italics in original.

162. *Towards a General Theory of Action* (n. 108 above), p. 155, italics added.

163. Ibid., p. 156.

164. Ibid., p. 100, italics in original.

165. Ibid., italics in original.

166. Ibid., italics in original.

167. This last point indicates clearly the errors of those critics who argue that Parsons' emphasis logically eliminates "the self" from his theory. Robert W. Friedrichs, e.g., makes the charge that in *Towards a General Theory of Action* (n. 108 above), the very work from which I have drawn the preceding discussion, Parsons and Shils adopt a "startlingly mechanistic . . . image of man," one that completely eliminates the individual element (*A Sociology of Sociology* [New York, 1970], p. 235). The same problem is articulated, more seriously, by Menzies (n. 59 above), who develops the notion that Parsons' early work focuses on a radically individualist approach to the self, one derived from utilitarianism (pp. 27–53).

The "social" part of Parsons' argument, Menzies claims, enters only in his recognition that the self adopts nonindividual ends.

> What Parsons has in effect done is to see an actor with types of energy, desire, [etc.] separate from social process. These types of energy . . . are then guided by various standards. In that the actor accepts the restrictions they impose, he is tied into society. . . . The actor is using the values standards as a way of maximizing his long run gratification. Thus he is the utilitarian individual separate from social process. (P. 50.)

In the later work, Menzies believes, Parsons jettisons a conception of the autonomous self because he comes to believe that individual desire itself, not just the goals adopted by the individual, is formed through "social" objects (pp. 41–53, 110–122). This argument mistakes the fundamental direction of Parsons' argument. First, as we have seen, Parsons' internalization theory can still readily accept the notion of self in a free-will sense, as an aspect of personal motivation that is differentiated vis-à-vis the interpersonally generalized elements of interaction. But more importantly, Parsons never emphasized the utilitarian self that Menzies professes to see: he simply had not yet found, in his early work, the theoretical vocabulary to represent the process by which the "self" could "contain" extra-individual normative forces.

Commentators in the individualisitic tradition have not sufficiently recognized the extent to which Parsons' theory can allow a focus on concrete individuals and individual variation while maintaining its commitment to supra-individual normative order. In fact, Parsons' skepticism toward a more radically individualist position and his recognition of emergent properties can be viewed not as being based on some initial anti-individual bias but rather as resulting from his simply following out, in a hypothetical manner, the logic of purely individualistic interaction. Ironically, Menzies himself produces an excellent illustration of such reasoning in reference to Parsons' middle-period classification of normative order into cognitive, cathectic, and moral patterns. Menzies begins his thought experiment with two completely autonomous individuals who act from a utilitarian desire to maximize individual gratification. He then demonstrates that in order to maximize total gratification over any extended time sequence the actors will, first, differentiate these three types of cultural standards from one another and, second, institutionalize these patterns in such a manner that they are not responsive to the individual manipulation of either party (pp. 56–60). He concludes that Parsons' early collectivist focus on emergent properties is not incompatible with a thesis of voluntarism, although he implies, incorrectly, that Parsons carried through a similar line of reasoning and, therefore, at some early point in his work accepted such a social/individual interaction as a starting point.

Jonathan Turner similarly emphasizes the manner in which collective, emergent properties may be seen as developing from the interaction of previously separated actors, although he more clearly recognizes that Parsons himself deals with concrete, "socialized" individuals (*The Structure of Sociological Theory* [n. 160 above], p. 35). Ian Proctor has demonstrated this point in an elegant manner in relation to Parsons' argument in *The Structure of Social Action*. He demonstrates that Parsons conceives "effort" in that early work as the element of freedom or spontaneity which in every action mediates between the internal realm of normative order and the external realm of conditions, so that Parsons is advocating neither an anti-free-will position nor a purely voluntaristic one ("Parsons' Early Voluntarism," *Sociological Inquiry* 48, no. 1 [1978]:37–48). In arguing thus, Proctor establishes the parallel to the position I have presented in the text in discussing the "individualism" section of Parsons and Shils.

168. *Structure of Social Action*, p. 74.

169. Atkinson (n. 65 above) is a good example of a theorist who takes the exactly opposite position: that it is the fact of supra-individual constraint that is significant, not the normative-versus-material form of that constraint. Cf. Friedrichs, p. 135; Menzies, pp. 27–53.

170. Parsons, "The Present Position and Prospects of Systematic Theory in Sociology" (n. 160 above), p. 213.

171. From this position one can formulate more concretely Bershady's important insight into Parsons' similarity to Kant (*Ideology and Social Knowledge* [n. 8 above], pp. 65–81). Both theorists, Bershady argues, believe that an a priori framework is necessary for any perception of reality, and Parsons' systematic conceptual apparatus attempts to formulate social "categories" that serve the same function as Kant's more purely epistemological ones. Yet this purely methodological point that Bershady makes is not enough, for Parsons has substantive "theoretical interests" as well. The systematic sociology he produces after his early writings reflects, at every point, his commitment to carry forward his goal of presuppositional synthesis. This more substantive theoretical interest is also Kantian, and in critical respects it is Parsons' presuppositional, not his methodological, Kantianism that distinguishes his sociology from others. For a good critique of Bershady's attempt to derive Parsons' substantive sociological theory from his meta-methodological commitments, see Savage's discussion (n. 8 above, pp. 39–47); for a good discussion of Parsons' substantive sociology in terms of Kantian presuppositions, see Münch (n. 112 above, passim).

172. The word *ecumenicism* is used by Martel (n. 121 above) to describe Parsons' broadest theoretical goal. A similar argument is advanced by Adriaansens (n. 12 above, p. 33).

173. "Present Position and Prospects" (n. 160 above), p. 223.

CHAPTER THREE

1. Talcott Parsons, "The Present Position and Prospects of Systematic Theory in Sociology," in his *Essays in Sociological Theory* (New York, 1954), pp. 214–215. The essay was first published in 1945.

2. Parsons, "The Point of View of the Author," in Max Black, ed., *The Social Theories of Talcott Parsons* (Ithaca, N.Y., 1961), p. 341, italics added.

3. "Present Position and Prospects," p. 229.

4. Parsons, "Introduction," in Max Weber, *The Theory of Social and Economic Organization* (New York, 1947), pp. 19–20.

5. Ibid., p. 20. It is precisely the failure to understand the "relative" nature of the functional commitment—the reasons, in other words, for Parsons' disagreement with Weber's critique of functionalist theory—that undermines any attempt to analyze the theorizing of Parsons' middle period simply as "structural-functional" theory. Jürgen Habermas, e.g., tries to deduce all the principal defects of Parsons' later middle-period (and subsequent) work from "systems" theory as compared to "action" theory ("Talcott Parsons: Problems of Theory Construction," *Sociological Inquiry* 51, nos. 3–4 [1981]:173–196). These theories, in his view, constitute the "two paradigms" of social analysis, and where action theory is an internal perspective, systems theory is external, "based on the non-normative regulation of the action process that serves system maintenance" (pp. 175–176). But this argument is conflationary; it burdens the model commitment with presuppositional, ideological, methodological, and even empirical commitments (cf. n. 24 below). In terms of Parsons' original critique of Weber, Habermas can see "functionalist reason" (see, e.g., his *Theorie des Kommunikativen Handelns*, vol. 2, *Zur Kritik der Functionalistischen Vernunft* [Frankfurt am Main, 1981], esp. pp. 304–419) only as concerned with the external conditions of the survival of organisms. Habermas' perspective on Parsons' "functionalist" theory may have been unduly influenced by the way it is employed by his countryman Niklas Luhmann, who does, indeed, attempt to present his entire theory as derived from the imperatives of a systems analysis.

The same kind of theoretical limitation affects the analysis of Parsons' later middle-period work offered by Hans P. M. Adriaansens in *Talcott Parsons and the Conceptual Dilemma* (London, 1980), pp. 58–87. Although Adriaansens has illuminated the purely functional aspects of this phase of Parsons' work more precisely than anyone else, he, too, misinterprets this phase as expounding a functional theory that is in conflict with Parsons' earlier "action frame of reference" (p. 73).

6. The propositional and even predictive implications of Parsons' work, which certainly can be demonstrated by the empirical range of his students' writing (see ch. 2, n. 3), is forcefully articulated by Karl Deutsch:

> Parsons has sometimes been criticized for having produced a great many matrices and conceptual schemes into which all sorts of empirical data could be put, rather than giving substantive empirical data. Even if he had done no more than this, it would be no mean achievement. . . . If it were possible for a single comprehensive system to bring order into the variegated facts that are known or believed to be known about social and political behavior, a major contribution would have been rendered. . . . But Parsons has done more. An efficient conceptual scheme, like any truly efficient system of organizing information, highlights relevant connections and plays down less relevant ones. . . . It tends to highlight interesting dimensions, variables, and relevant correlations [and] suggests fruitful questions and possible discoveries. . . . Once a classification scheme or theoretical system is used to highlight particular correlations, the social scientist is already making predictions, at least in probabilistic terms. He is predicting that certain correlations are either critically high or low and that certain relationships will be significantly correlated with others. . . . In this sense, what looked like a purely formalistic system turns out to be a system that contains predictive implications when put to actual use. (Deutsch, "Integration and the Social System: Implications of Functional Analysis," in Philip E. Jacob and James V. Toscano, eds., *The Integration of Political Communities* [New York, 1964], pp. 179–208, see pp. 180–181.)

7. Parsons, "On Building Social System Theory: A Personal History," *Daedalus* 99 (1970):868. On this cognitive style in Parsons' work as it applies to the development of his recent theory of "generalized media," see the interesting discussion by Bliss C. Cartwright and R. Stephen Warner, "The Medium is Not the Message," in J. J. Loubser et al., eds., *Explorations in General Theory in Social Science* (New York, 1976), 2:648–651.

8. In view of the controversy surrounding "discontinuities" in Parsons' work, it is surprising that there are so few attempts to organize his theory into a detailed sequence. The best known is Don Martindale's, which formalizes the early-late Parsons distinction (see *The Nature and Types of Sociological Theory* [Boston, 1961], pp. 484–499, and, particularly, "Talcott Parsons' Theoretical Metamorphosis from Social Behaviorism to Macrofunctionalism," in *Institutions and Social Exchange* [Indianapolis, 1971], pp. 165–174). Martindale places phase I in the period extending through *The Structure of Social Action*, which concludes with Parsons' supposed nominalist phase; phase II extends from 1945, the date of the publication of "The Present Position and Prospects of Systematic Theory in Sociology," to 1950, and is purportedly concerned with "roles" rather than "individuals"; in phase III, from 1951 onward, Parsons is described as moving to a focus on "system" rather than "role." In addition to suffering from the kinds of presuppositional errors I ascribed to the "individualist" and "social" readings in the preceding chapter, this division simply does

not correspond to the obvious shifts in Parsons' work. Specifically, it separates the 1945–1950 essays from other essays in the early-middle period, a neglect that appears arbitrary; it also lumps together the later-middle and late, four- function writings, an association which is not warranted in view of the radical shifts the four-function model implied for the presentation of Parsons' multidimensional position.

The more recent effort at periodization in Hans P. M. Adriaansens' *Talcott Parsons and the Conceptual Dilemma* (n. 5 above), which in general is a far more sensitive treatment, also distorts Parsons' development in certain important respects. Though Adriaansens clearly identifies a "middle period" in Parsons' work, he identifies this phase almost completely with the 1951 publications alone (*The Social System* and *Towards a General Theory of Action*), ignoring the numerous and wide-ranging empirically oriented essays published in this period after the 1937 *Structure of Social Action*. This periodization allows Adriaansens to: (1) present a purely formalistic explanation of the movement between *Structure* and the 1951 publications, for he can describe the movement as following a scientific deduction from first principles rather than being influenced by a range of empirical problems, by challenges to the classical masters, and by presuppositional problems; (2) produce a much more purely "functionalist" or model-level reading of the middle period than is actually the case (see, e.g., pp. 72 and 180, n. 16); and (3) ignore, thereby, the crucial role of the interpenetration of the three systems of personality, society, and culture, which is so crucial to the middle period and which so clearly reveals its presuppositional connection. More generally, this demarcation falsely legitimates the "conceptual dilemma" which Adriaansens places at the heart of his argument (pp. 88–115), i.e., that during his middle period Parsons produced a purely functionalist and "concrete" form of theorizing which was at odds with his earlier emphasis on interpenetration and which forced the innovation that began the later period of his work.

9. Alvin W. Gouldner, "Reciprocity and Autonomy in Function Theory," in N. J. Demerath II and Richard A. Peterson, eds., *System, Conflict and Change* (New York, 1967), p. 146.

10. The relation of the pattern-variable schema to a logical dissatisfaction with Tönnies' dichotomy and to Parsons' personal experience is made, e.g., by Guy Rocher (*Talcott Parsons and American Sociology* [New York, 1975], pp. 36–37). It is also indicated by Charles P. Loomis in the Introduction to his translation of Tönnies' *Community and Society* (Lansing, Mich., 1957). It is also supported by indirect testimony from Parsons himself; see "On Building Social System Theory" (n. 7 above), pp. 836–838, and *The Structure of Social Action* (New York, [1937] 1968), pp. 686–694.

11. Alvin W. Gouldner, *The Coming Crisis of Western Sociology* (New York, 1970), pp. 154–156.

12. Parsons, "The Professions and the Social Structure," in *Essays* (n. 1 above), p. 35; this essay was first published in 1939. See also "The Motivation of Economic Activities," ibid., p. 53; first published in 1940.

An excellent example of the kind of utilitarian distinction between professions and business against which Parsons was writing—an example which indicates how it permeated critical as well as conservative thought—can be found in R. H. Tawney's *The Acquisitive Society*, first published in 1920. (Shortly after the publication of this book, Parsons was exposed to Tawney's influence at the London School of Economics. In 1927 Tawney wrote the preface to Parsons' translation of Weber's *The Protestant Ethic and the Spirit of Capitalism*.) The center of Tawney's socialist program was his proposal to make industry into a professional activity, for in this manner, he believed, its purely instrumental and, therefore, antisocial character would be overcome.

> The difference between industry as it exists to-day and a profession is . . . simple and unmistakable. The essence of the former is that its only criterion is the financial return which it offers to its shareholders. The essence of the latter, is that, though men enter it for the sake of livelihood, the measure of their success is the service which they perform, not the gains which they amass. . . . The meaning of their profession, both for themselves and for the public, is not that they make money but that they make health, or safety, or knowledge, or good government or good law. They depend on it for their income, but they do not consider that any conduct which increases their income is on that account good. (*The Acquisitive Society* [London, 1920], p. 94.)

13. "The Professions and the Social Structure," p. 37.

14. Ibid., p. 42.

15. In his critique of Parsons' pattern-variable discussion, Gouldner completely ignores this self-interest/disinterest distinction. By doing so, he is able to contend that Parsons sees no difference at all between business and the professions.

> Hitherto, says Parsons, the common view has had it that the businessman egoistically pursued his own self-interest while the professional altruistically served others. Not so, he says. . . . Assimilated to the professions, business becomes credited with the moral responsibility traditionally imputed to the professions for collective welfare. (*Coming Crisis*, pp. 155–156.)

But this is precisely the opposite of Parsons' point.

In fact, if we are interested in the ideological perspective that informs this early pattern-variable work we will have to conclude that it is far from the conservative, pro-business one that Gouldner purports to find. What Parsons sought to do, and what he in good part accomplished, was to place the traditional populist or social-gospel criticism of the selfishness of the business community into a less utilitarian analytic perspective. The first time that Parsons discusses the professions in relation to the norms which later became the pattern variables seems to be in a review in April 1937 of a work by Robert Hutchins, the president of the University of Chicago. It is clear that Parsons accepts the distinction between self-interested and antisocial business activity and socially committed activity that Hutchins draws. Parsons would, however, link this social commitment more to the impact of education and the activities of the liberal professions than Hutchins apparently allows.

Parsons, then, can draw the distinction between liberal professions and business on ideological grounds. He argues that business is separated from community interests because it is detached from the great liberal cultural tradition that regulates the professions (which can do so because of the latter's connection to the university): "Though practice certainly falls far short of the ideal, the very antithesis which is commonly drawn, not only by professional men themselves but in the general public, between the 'professional' and the 'commercial' attitudes, would indicate that in the professions and their great traditions is to be found one of the principal reserves of defense against that false conception of utility, in its close connection with the love of money, which President Hutchins so effectively attacks. That, indeed, encouragement of the professions is one of the most effective ways of promoting disinterestedness in contemporary society is one of the underlying assumptions of the present argument." ("Remarks on Education and the Professions," *International Journal of Ethics* 48 [1937]:365–369, quoting 365.) "To master [the] intellectual content of the professional tradition the liberal spirit is essential," Parsons continues, for "the man who is dominated only by the more sordid motives of gain or even the immediate success of his practical task alone is incapable of it" (p. 366). "Undoubtedly," he says, "many occupations are dignified with the name 'profession' which do not deserve it."

> Just where the line should be drawn is a difficult matter and is not the function of this brief note to discuss. But a word must be said about one group which is, in the present situation, of peculiar importance—business. It is of course true that many, perhaps most, of the traditions of business are not in harmony with professional ideals. And with the advent of business schools in the universities, the tendency has perhaps been more to regard them as schools of the art of making money than as professional schools in a strict sense. But at the same time it is generally acknowledged that business occupies a key position in contemporary society. It may be suggested that if the great cultural tradition is to be perpetuated and developed it is almost necessary that it should come to impregnate the business community. If a business education could be made a true professional education in the sense sketched here, it would be a very large step in the integration of our civilization in the sense in

> which President Hutchins desires it. Indeed, it may perhaps be said that it is the possession of a great cultural tradition which leavens the lump of the blind struggle for existence and for wealth and power in society. (Pp. 368–369.)

Parsons never gave up this criticism of the particularistic and narrow outlook of the business class, although his language later became much more moderate in tone and he wavered as to whether the "professionalization" of the business class had actually been accomplished.

16. Parsons, *The Social System* (New York, 1951), pp. 3–4.

17. Ibid., p. 5.

18. Talcott Parsons and Edward A. Shils, "Values, Motives, and Systems of Action," in Parsons and Shils, eds., *Towards a General Theory of Action* (New York, 1951), p. 177.

19. Parsons, *Social System*, p. 14.

20. Although Parsons used the cognitive-appreciative-value-oriented distinction more powerfully than any contemporary thinker, it certainly did not originate with him. Dilthey, e.g., described a similar division within his *Weltanschauung* (see "Life and the Human Studies," in H. P. Rickman, ed., *Dilthey: Selected Writings* [Cambridge, 1976], pp. 186–189; cf. Guy Swanson, "The Approach to a General Theory of Action by Parsons and Shils," *American Sociological Review* 18 [1953]:130). The distinctiveness of Parsons' usage is, first, that he utilizies this division in combination with his multidimensional presuppositional position, and, second, that he specifies it in concrete analysis of the independent exigencies of three different kinds of systems.

21. Parsons and Shils (n. 18 above), p. 165, italics in original.

22. *Social System*, p. 14.

23. Ibid.

24. This relative autonomy between personality and cultural levels has been persistently misinterpreted in the literature on Parsons, in either one of two ways: (1) as indicating a concrete distinction between individual, independent persons and cultural constraints; (2) as indicating simply an analytic distinction that is designed to integrate completely individuals and cultures (cf. n. 27 below). Ken Menzies, e.g., writes that by emphasizing the autonomy of these levels, that is, "by separating motivation from the standards that guide it," Parsons' individual "retains something . . . separate from social process" (Menzies, *Talcott Parsons and the Social Image of Man* [London, 1976], p. 51). He then argues that insofar as Parsons emphasizes internalization, "[this] distinction between the mode [of motivation] and the standard of orientation drops out of Parsons' work" (p. 60). Neither of these proposed phases of Parsons' theory, however, actually occurred. First, and most importantly, Parsons' emphasis on the autono-

my of personality level and cultural level is analytical, not concrete: it refers not to the distinction between individuals and social-cultural constraints but to the autonomy of different levels of social organization. For Parsons, the personality is always, by definition, related in its very foundation to social objects. Thus the tension between the personality and cultural levels occurs within the concrete individual, not between the individual and the society. Second, the personality-society-culture distinction is intended, from the beginning, to indicate the possibilities for internalization; it represents, after all, part of Parsons' response to the difficulty Durkheim had in locating the "social" inside the concrete actor. Menzies' interpretation illustrates the problems that beset the individualistic mode of Parsonian criticism, not just in understanding *The Structure of Social Action* but in interpreting the rest of Parsons' work as well.

While individualistic "readings" usually turn out to be presuppositional polemics for some kind of individualistic position, Jürgen Habermas' insistence on the individualism that purportedly pervades Parsons' early and middle periods is launched from a position that favors a more symbolically sensitive, collectivist stance. Habermas sees Parsons' analytical description of the actor and his situation, and of "ego" and "alter," as actually describing a society of isolated individuals who interact qua individuals; Parsons, he argues, sees "decisions as emergent of the private arbitrariness of isolated actors" ("Talcott Parsons," n. 5 above, p. 180). Because of this "highly individualistic theory," Parsons has no way of talking about order, for "one deprives oneself of a mechanism that could explain the emergence of a system of action out of unit acts" (ibid.). In this earlier part of his work, Habermas contends, Parsons develops no theory of "values as already intersubjective, shared culture" (ibid.); the pattern variables, e.g., are viewed not as referring to cultural patterning but to classifications of random individual decisions (p. 185, but see the contrary statement on p. 182). This debilitating weakness in the earlier work, Habermas can then argue, is what leads Parsons in his later writing to develop a systems theory which postulates society as an external, non-normative force and which considers only the consequences of action, not their meaning (pp. 175–176).

Yet Habermas has misconstrued the fundamental basis of Parsons' approach to order, which is consistent from the beginning of his work. Parsons never separates an analysis of action from order, and he always takes the paradigm of actor/situation, or ego and alter, in an analytical not a concrete sense. Parsons' actors, therefore, are considered to be interpenetrated by culture and society at every stage in his work: with his self-conscious utilization of systems theory, only the model for formulating this interdependence has changed. That the use of systems models is itself never separated from Parsons' cultural theory of intersubjective symbolization is clearly demonstrated by the fact that Parsons' most persistent use of these models in his middle-period work is in describing the interpenetration of social-system action by culture and personality.

25. Parsons, *Social System*, pp. 17–18.

26. Parsons and Shils (n. 18 above), p. 173, italics in original.

27. Ibid.; cf. pp. 172–179. The care Parsons takes in distinguishing the independence of the integrative standards in the three systems—and the continual possibility for malintegration which results from this independence—makes it difficult to understand Daniel Bell's contention that Parsons' "functionalism" insists upon the complete consistency of cultural and social systems (*The Cultural Contradictions of Capitalism* [New York, 1976], pp. 10–15 and passim). This criticism is especially perplexing in the light of the enormous emphasis that Parsons placed, even in the most sociologically idealist dimension of his work, on the formation of deviant or alienated subcultures in advanced societies, a topic which will be discussed in subsequent chapters (e.g., ch. 9). Stephen Savage makes the same kind of error in *The Theories of Talcott Parsons* (New York, 1981), pp. 183–188. Janet Wolff is much closer to the mark when she argues, indeed, that, in contrast to other structuralist theories of culture, Parsons' theory was unique in its emphasis on the significance of internal inconsistencies in the patterns contained in a given cultural system (*Hermeneutic Philosophy and the Sociology of Art* [London, 1975], pp. 96–97). Although it is true, as will be seen in chs. 6–9, that Parsons often does overemphasize the empirical strength of intersystem integration, the fact of autonomy is never missing on the model level, nor is the possibility for conflict ever eliminated on the empirical.

28. Geertz, "After the Revolution: The Fate of Nationalism in the New States," in Bernard Barber and Alex Inkeles, eds., *Stability and Social Change* (Boston, 1971), pp. 371–372, italics added.

29. Parsons and Shils (n. 18 above), p. 197; cf. pp. 197–221.

30. Parsons, *Social System*, pp. 117–118.

31. Ibid., pp. 119–123; cf. Parsons and Shils, pp. 199, 55.

32. It should be noted that Parsons has now employed the same term, "generalization," to indicate two distinct phenomena: symbolic interpenetration on the cultural level and differentiation of political power on the social-system level. This terminological confusion, though not particularly significant in itself, indicates a deeper presuppositional confusion, which will be addressed in detail later in my analysis.

33. *Social System*, pp. 121–126.

34. Ibid., pp. 127–132.

35. Ibid., p. 128.

36. Ibid., p. 129.

37. Parsons and Shils, p. 201.

38. *Social System*, p. 129.

39. Ibid., p. 130.

40. Parsons and Shils, p. 197.

41. Ibid.

42. Ibid., p. 203.

43. *Social System*, pp. 132–137.

44. See Parsons' elaborate classificatory schema which tries to summarize this discussion, ibid., pp. 142–150. Though it provides simply a list of logical implications, it presents an interesting indication of the course his discussion might have taken if he had pursued this line of analysis further.

45. Cf. E. K. Francis' review in 1950 of Parsons' *Essays*. Parsons' interweaving of "instrumental, situational, and integrative institutions," Francis contends, has "boldly attacked a complex of problems on whose solution depends the ultimate success or failure of sociology as an empirical science" (*Review of Politics* 12, [1950]:253–254). This judgment was somewhat premature, since the schema was greatly elaborated in Parsons' subsequent two monographs. Still, the evaluation was, in substance, correct.

46. *Social System*, pp. 154–157.

47. For a more elaborate discussion of the psychological-social-cultural origins of the incest taboo, see Parsons' later essay "The Incest Taboo in Relation to Social Structure and the Socialization of the Child," in his *Social Structure and Personality* (New York, 1964), pp. 57–77.

48. *Social System*, pp. 157–161.

49. Ibid., p. 159. Bernard Barber has greatly expanded on these two central causes of social stratification—differential responsibility and competence—and linked them to a systematic and empirically testable theory of prestige distribution. See particularly his "Stratification, Social: Introduction," in *International Encyclopedia of the Social Sciences* 15:288–296, and "Inequality and Occupational Prestige: Theory, Research, and Social Policy," *Sociological Inquiry* 48, no. 2 (1978):75–88.

50. *Social System*, p. 160.

51. Ibid., pp. 161–163.

52. Ibid., p. 162.

53. Ibid., pp. 163–167. For an elaboration of this analysis, see Parsons, "Sociology and Social Psychology," in Hoxie N. Fairchild, ed., *Religious Perspectives in College Teaching* (New York, 1952), pp. 286–337 (reprinted in William A. Lessa and Evan Z. Voght, eds., *Reader in Comparative Religion: An Anthropological Approach* [New York, 1972]). For the early roots in Parsons' interpretation of Weber and Durkheim, see his "The Theoretical Development of the Sociology of Religion" in *Essays in Sociological Theory* (n. 1 above). This essay was first published in 1944.

54. *Social System*, p. 164, italics altered.

55. In addition to the pages cited above, see ibid., pp. 169–177. On the

status of these discussions, see, e.g., the judgment of the anthropologists Lessa and Voght (n. 53 above) that "among the works of recent American sociologists those of Talcott Parsons have been of the most general significance in defining the role and function of religion in human society" (p. 88).

56. The phrase is from Parsons and Shils (n. 18 above), p. 177.

57. *Social System*, p. 173.

58. Ibid.

59. Ibid., pp. 174–177.

60. Ibid., p. 174.

61. Ibid.

62. David Lockwood, "Some Remarks on 'The Social System,'" *British Journal of Sociology* 7 (1956):134–146, quoting 140.

63. Ralf Dahrendorf, *Class and Class Conflict in Industrial Society* (Stanford, Calif., 1959), p. 165; cf. pp. 157–205.

64. C. Wright Mills, *The Sociological Imagination* (New York, 1959), pp. 35–36.

65. Judith Blake and Kingsley Davis, "Norms, Values, and Sanctions," in Robert E. Faris, ed., *Handbook of Modern Sociology* (Chicago, 1964), p. 46.

66. For an extremely perceptive analysis of Lockwood's ambivalent, neo-materialist position, see Percy Cohen's rigorous investigation in *Modern Social Theory* (London, 1968, pp. 107–121). Cohen demonstrates that although "Lockwood insists that he does not treat the two sets of factors—the structure of interests and the normative system—in terms of historical or causal primacy," his analysis still adopts the Marxian style of base-superstructure reasoning. It does so, Cohen asserts, in the following ways: (1) by simply identifying an "infrastructure" of "real," material factors; (2) by suggesting that such an infrastructure has more influence on the normative superstructure than vice versa, and that, in fact, norms are developed to conceal and assuage material conflicts; (3) by arguing that conflict originates primarily as a dispute over the distribution of material resources; (4) by linking political power to purely material, factual constraint. In my terminology, in other words, Lockwood not only has a tendency to reduce his presuppositional approach to one-dimensionality, but he tends to conflate this position with a position on empirical conflict and equilibrium. This tendency, however, is partly modified by Lockwood's later essay on "Social Integration and System Integration" (in George K. Zollschen and Walter Hirsch, eds., *Explorations in Social Change* [Boston, 1964], pp. 244–257).

67. An interesting example of the extent of Mills' misreading of Parsons can be found in this part of his argument (*Sociological Imagination*, pp. 35–44). In arguing for a more materialist approach to social values, one that examines "the legitimations of each institutional order in any given

social structure," Mills cites as his primary example of such an alternative approach *The American Business Creed* (Cambridge, Mass., 1956), by Francis X. Sutton et al. That book, however, itself represents a major application of Parsonian theory and closely follows Parsons' discussion of ideology in *The Social System*, the very work that Mills pilloried as virtually devoid of intellectual content. In addition to indicating Mills' failure to understand the actual nature of Parsons' work, this example also indicates the trouble that many analysts have had in connecting the empirical work of Parsons' students to his own more general theory.

68. For a critical discussion of this conflict school, see vol. 1, pp. 50–55. (The discussion in this section of Parsons' change theory has been published, in slightly modified form, in *Sociological Inquiry* 51, nos. 3–4 [1981]:267–280.)

69. Cf. the evaluation by Rocher (n. 10 above) of Parsons' essays of the middle period, the period which will be the major reference in my discussion which follows:

> Most of the essays deal with processes, evolution, the emergence of new phenomena, the adaptation of social structures to new situations, and with changes in functional systems. This is not surprising, for the industrialization of the western world and the transformation of political, economic and social structures have remained the central problems on which Parsons' thought was focused throughout his life. (P. 144.)

70. Parsons and Shils, *Towards a General Theory of Action* (n. 18 above), p. 229.

71. Ibid.

72. Ibid., p. 145.

73. Ibid., p. 229.

74. Ibid., p. 230.

75. Ibid.

76. Parsons, "Democracy and Social Structure in Pre-Nazi Germany," in *Essays in Sociological Theory* (n. 1 above), p. 117.

77. Parsons, "Some Sociological Aspects of the Fascist Movements," ibid., pp. 128–132. Parsons discusses in some detail these typical strains in Western development in a number of the essays included in this volume. In addition to this essay and "Democracy and Social Structure in Pre-Nazi Germany," cited above, see "Certain Primary Sources and Patterns of Aggression in the Social Structure of the Western World" (pp. 298–322), "The Problem of Controlled Institutional Change" (pp. 238–274), "Population and Social Structure of Japan" (pp. 275–297), and "Age and Sex in the Social Structure of the United States" (pp. 89–103).

78. Parsons, "Some Sociological Aspects of the Fascist Movements," pp. 127–128.

79. Ibid., p. 126. Cf. "Certain Primary Sources and Patterns of Aggression in the Social Structure of the Western World" (n. 77 above).

80. Parsons, "Social Classes and Class Conflict in the Light of Recent Sociological Theory," *Essays in Sociological Theory* , pp. 327–328.

81. Ibid., p. 329.

82. Ibid., p. 330.

83. Ibid., pp. 329–330.

84. Ibid., pp. 330–331.

85. Ibid., p. 332.

86. Ibid.

87. Parsons, "The Problem of Controlled Institutional Change" (n. 77 above), p. 265.

88. "Some Sociological Aspects of the Fascist Movements," p. 138.

89. See the essays cited in n. 77 above.

90. This summarizes the relevant parts of Parsons' argument in "Democracy and Social Structure in Pre-Nazi Germany" and "Some Sociological Aspects of the Fascist Movements."

91. "Democracy and Social Structure in Pre-Nazi Germany," p. 117.

92. Ibid., pp. 119–120.

93. Ibid., p. 120. Cf. "Some Sociological Aspects of the Fascist Movements," pp. 130–134.

94. "Some Sociological Aspects," p. 135.

95. Ibid., pp. 136–139.

96. Ibid., p. 137.

97. Ibid.

98. "Democracy and Social Structure in Pre-Nazi Germany," p. 116.

99. "Some Sociological Aspects of the Fascist Movements," pp. 139–141.

100. "Democracy and Social Structure in Pre-Nazi Germany," p. 119.

101. *Social System* (n. 16 above), ch. 11, "The Processes of Change of Social Systems."

102. Ibid., pp. 525–535.

103. See, e.g., Dahrendorf (n. 63 above), p. 120; Blake and Davis (n. 65 above), p. 472; and Lewis Coser, *The Functions of Social Conflict* (New York, 1956), pp. 20–23.

104. *Social System*, pp. 249–253, 267–296.

105. Ibid., pp. 251–256.

106. Ibid., pp. 256–267, 283–297.

107. Ibid., pp. 297–320.

108. Parsons, "The Problem of Controlled Institutional Change" (n. 77 above), p. 238.

109. Ibid., pp. 253–254. With this recommendation for situational control, it is interesting to note, Parsons follows not only Weber's multidimensional theory but his ideological prescription: Weber clearly perceived that

the Junker class's continuing hegemony posed the most drastic problems for the future of the German nation (see Weber's "Capitalism and Rural Society in Germany," in Hans Gerth and C. Wright Mills, eds., *From Max Weber* [New York, 1946], pp. 363–387).

110. Ibid., pp. 254–256.

111. Ibid., pp. 256–258.

112. Ibid., p. 271.

113. Ibid., pp. 259–260.

114. Ibid., pp. 261–262.

115. Parsons, "Social Strains in America," in his *Politics and Social Structure* (New York, [1955] 1969), pp. 163–178. Technically, this essay belongs in Parsons' later period, but for the purposes of the present discussion it has overwhelming connections to the middle-period essays on deviance and strains in Western development.

116. Ibid., p. 170.

117. Ibid., p. 177.

118. Ibid.

119. Dahrendorf, *Class and Class Conflict* (n. 63 above), pp. 160–161.

120. Mills, *The Sociological Imagination* (n. 64 above), p. 42.

121. Gouldner, "Some Observations on Systematic Theory, 1945–55," in Hans Zetterberg, ed., *Sociology in the United States of America* (New York, 1955), pp. 40–41.

122. A few analysts have drawn attention to the errors made by this conflict interpretation of Parsons' change theory. In a review of Parsons' ideologically oriented writing, Andrew Hacker, e.g., described Parsons' essay on McCarthyism as "a sophisticated analysis of tensions underlying recent American development" and as presenting society in "fundamental social disequilibrium" ("Sociology and Ideology," in Black, ed., *Social Theories of Talcott Parsons* [n. 2 above], pp. 291–292). More generally, Atkinson has recently written that "there is nothing in his [Parsons'] theory . . . which precludes the possibility of offering an explanatory model of conflict" and, after discussing a number of the middle-period publications considered here, concludes that "we can see a continuing concern for aspects of conflict" in Parsons' work (*Orthodox Consensus and Radical Alternative* [New York, 1972], pp. 24–25). He describes this change theory, however, as purely normative (p. 33). For a discussion which makes much the same point but which more accurately identifies the multidimensionality of the change theory, see Seymour Martin Lipset's excellent survey of the Parsonian literature in "The Functionalist Theory of Change," in his "Social Structure and Social Change," in Peter Blau, ed., *Approaches to the Study of Social Structure* (New York, 1975), pp. 172–209, see pp. 173–184. Finally, see Savage's quite accurate observation that "a theory of social change not only exists in the theory of the social system but is in many ways *central* to it (n. 27 above, p. 197, italics in original).

123. Indeed, the conclusion seems inescapable that Parsons' change theory, particularly in the *Essays*, actually develops a more complex, nuanced, and ultimately more satisfactory analysis of group conflict than the one developed by Dahrendorf in the later chapters of *Class and Class Conflict in Industrial Society* (for a similar point, see Peter Weingart, "Beyond Parsons? A Critique of Ralf Dahrendorf's Conflict Theory," *Social Forces* 48 [1969]:151–165). For Dahrendorf, conflict between groups will occur only vertically, and it will be based exclusively upon the rational-instrumental dimension of power differential. Although Parsons takes this dimension as one component of possible dissension, he considers empirical conflict as a variable outcome of the power relationship. First, the origins of dissensus must be broadened to include the tension with normative orders. Second, the outcomes of such strain are patterned by the nature of a particular society's psychological, cultural, and social systems. Third, because of these considerations there is a strong possibility that horizontal conflict will develop within any single hierarchical stratum, a factor further complicating the conflict generated by power. Given Dahrendorf's presupposition of collectivist rationalism, it was impossible for him to imagine such a wide range of empirical complications. That Dahrendorf—in the monograph in which he attempted to explain a major case of historical change and disequilibrium (*Society and Democracy in Germany* [New York, 1967])—follows a mode of explanation that is explicitly modeled after Parsons' own seems to be ironic verification of the viability of the change theory of Parsons' middle period (see Dahrendorf's remarks on pp. 52–53 of that work).

124. With the exception of "Age and Sex in the Social Structure of the United States," every essay cited above in n. 77 concerns the radical right, in Germany, Japan, or the United States. Scholars influenced by Parsons have carried this analysis into the discussion of the radical right in other countries. See, e.g., Jesse R. Pitts' important article on polarization in France, "Continuity and Change in Bourgeois France," in Stanley Hoffman, ed., *In Search of France* (Cambridge, Mass., 1964), pp. 249–304; Robert N. Bellah's discussions of Japan, China, Germany, France, Italy, and the United States in *Beyond Belief* (New York, 1970), and his "The Five Civil Religions of Modern Italy" in Bellah and Phillip E. Hammond, *Varieties of Civil Religion* (New York, 1980), pp. 86–113; S. N. Eisenstadt's discussions of social polarization in *Modernization: Protest and Change* (Englewood Cliffs, N.J., 1966); and S. M. Lipset's discussions in *Political Man* (New York, 1959) and *The First New Nation* (New York, 1965).

In view of this perspective on Western instability which Parsons developed in his middle-period work, and the wide-ranging empirical studies on the breakdown of modernization which this theory inspired, the critical judgment that Habermas makes on Parsons' change theory seems strikingly inappropriate: "Parsons cannot describe the rationalization of the life-world, on the one hand, and the growth of complexity of action systems, on the other, as separate . . . but frequently also conflicting processes" ("Talcott Parsons," n. 5 above, p. 193). This, it seems to me, is precisely what Parsons has done.

CHAPTER FOUR

1. The first two essays in which the four-function model appeared are "The Dimensions of Action-Space," written by Parsons with Robert F. Bales, and "Phase Movement in Relation to Motivation, Symbol Formation, and Role Structure," by Parsons, Bales, and Edward A. Shils. The first essay was written in 1951, the second in 1952; both appeared in 1953, as chs. 3 and 5 of *Working Papers in the Theory of Action*, by Parsons and Bales with Shils (New York, 1953).

2. Walter L. Wallace, "Overview of Contemporary Sociological Theory," in Wallace, ed., *Contemporary Sociological Theory* (Chicago, 1969), p. 26.

3. M. J. Mulkay, *Functionalism, Exchange, and Theoretical Strategy* (London, 1971), pp. 47–65, 91–93. Ken Menzies, *Talcott Parsons and the Social Image of Man* (London, 1976), pp. 123–150.

4. Harold J. Bershady, *Ideology and Social Knowledge* (New York, 1973), pp. 114–131.

5. Mulkay, p. 86.

6. Johnson, "The Generalized Symbolic Media in Parsons' Theory," *Sociology and Social Research* 57, no. 3 (1973):208.

7. Ralf Dahrendorf, *Class and Class Conflict in Industrial Society* (Stanford, Calif., 1959), pp. 157–240; Anthony Giddens, " 'Power' in the Recent Writings of Talcott Parsons," *Sociology* 2 (1968):257–272; Wolf Heydebrand, review of Parsons' *The System of Modern Societies, Contemporary Sociology* 1 (1972):387–395; Alvin W. Gouldner, *The Coming Crisis of Western Sociology* (New York, 1970), esp. pp. 286–338.

8. Leslie Sklair, "The Fate of the 'Functional Requisites' in Parsonian Sociology," *British Journal of Sociology* 21, no. 1 (1970):30–42.

9. Menzies (n. 3 above), ch. 8.

10. Benton Johnson, *Functionalism and Modern Sociology: Understanding Talcott Parsons* (Morristown, N.J., 1975), p. 29.

11. Edward C. Devereux, Jr., "Parsons' Sociological Theory," in Max Black, ed., *The Social Theories of Talcott Parsons* (Ithaca, N.Y., 1961), pp. 53–63; Guy Rocher, *Talcott Parsons and American Sociology* (New York, 1975), pp. 40–47.

12. Mulkay (n. 3 above), pp. 60–63, 75.

13. Sheldon Wolin, "Gilding the Iron Cage," *New York Review of Books*, January 24, 1974, pp. 40–42.

14. Wallace (n. 2 above), p. 40.

15. Martin U. Martel, "Academentia Praecox: The Aims, Merits, and Scope of Parsons' Multisystematic Language Rebellion (1958–68)," in Herman Turk and Richard L. Simpson, eds., *Institutions and Social Exchange* (Indianapolis, 1971), pp. 175–232, passim.

16. Gouldner (n. 7 above).

17. For interpretations that generally parallel the approach presented here, see Jonathan H. Turner, *The Structure of Sociological Theory* (Homewood, Ill., 1974), pp. 38–43; Karl W. Deutsch, "Integration and the Social System: Implications of Functional Analysis," in Philip E. Jacob and James V. Toscana, eds., *The Integration of Political Communities* (New York, 1964), pp. 179–208; and Richard Münch, "Talcott Parsons and the Theory of Action. II," *American Journal of Sociology* 87 (1982): 771–826.

18. These explanations are scattered through Parsons' accounts of the origins of interchange. E.g.: Parsons and Bales, "The Dimensions of Action Space," in Parsons, Bales, and Shils, *Working Papers* (n. 1 above), pp. 63–110; Parsons and Neil J. Smelser, *Economy and Society* (New York, 1956); Parsons, "An Outline of the Social System," in Parsons et al., eds., *Theories of Society* (New York, 1961), pp. 30–79; Parsons, "Pattern Variables Revisited: A Response to Robert Dubin," in Parsons, *Sociological Theory and Modern Society* (New York, 1967), pp. 192–219. In his autobiographical essay "On Building Social System Theory: A Personal History," *Daedalus* 99 (1970):844–847, Parsons reiterates these explanations of the shift to his interchange theory.

19. E.g., Harry M. Johnson (n. 6 above) writes that "in its latest version, Parsons' 'general theory of action' is a generalization of economics" (p. 208). See also Rocher's connection of interchange to Parsons' use of economic analogy, the pattern variables, and Bales' small-group research (n. 11 above, pp. 44–45, 63–67, 77 ff.).

20. Cf. Devereaux's evaluation of the reason for Parsons' later shift to the four-function schema: "So long as he had approached . . . problem[s] from the concrete institutional level, he was in constant danger of becoming involved with historically unique situations and with fantastically elaborate schemes for trying to classify them" (Devereux [n. 7 above], p. 61).

The only detailed treatment of the problems that motivated Parsons' shift from the works of 1951 to his interchange theory is Hans P. M. Adriaansens, *Talcott Parsons and the Conceptual Dilemma* (London, 1980). Adriaansens rightly emphasizes the importance of this shift and its relation to Parsons' growing dissatisfaction with the "concrete" nature of his middle-period work. Adriaansens' argument that the analytical status of interchange allowed Parsons' to achieve a more powerful synthesis (pp. 113 ff.) is also a major point I will elaborate below. The weakness with the interpretation is the precise connection Adriaansens draws between the new theorizing and the old. He describes the entirety of Parsons' theorizing between *The Structure of Social Action* (1937) and the introduction of the interchange model (1953) as utterly concrete, asserting that in this middle period Parsons failed to maintain his commitment to the analytic interpenetration of ideal and material elements which he articulated in the early work. He argues, e.g., that, although the presuppositional basis for such a theory was laid out in *Structure,* Parsons' theory contained no analysis of the symbolic interpenetration of actors and institutions until 1953 (pp. 104 ff.). The reason Adriaansens offers for such drastic discontinuity is Parsons' introduction of a purely "functionalist" position in the middle-period work. But this argument greatly exaggerates the determinant power of Parsons' model commitment, just as it greatly underestimates the continuity of Parsons' presuppositional commitment. As I demonstrated in the preceding chapter, Parsons' systems theory merely provided a more supple way of articulating his synthetic ambition, and the concern with symbolism and culture is pervasive throughout both the "early middle" essays of 1938–1950, and the "later middle" works of 1951. The "concreteness" that continued to mar this middle-period work, therefore, was a matter of degree, not kind; though it greatly elaborated Parsons' analytic position, this elaboration was not completely successful.

21. See the discussion of the effectiveness of the cybernetic schema for formulating the order problem in ch. 2, sec. 3.

22. This figure is formulated on the basis of Parsons' diagram and discussion in *Societies: Evolutionary and Comparative Perspectives* (Englewood Cliffs, N.J., 1966), pp. 28–29.

23. This diagram illustrates a number of points derived from different discussions by Parsons himself. See, e.g., Parsons and Smelser (n. 18 above) and Parsons, "Outline of the Social System" (n. 18 above). For an important argument for the close relation between the early unit act analysis and this later four-function schema, see Jonathan H. Turner and Leonard Beeghley, "Current Folklore in the Criticisms of Parsonian Action Theory," *Sociological Inquiry* 43 (1974):47–55.

24. The following analysis relies on Parsons' discussions cited above in notes 18 and 23.

25. See, e.g., Parsons, "Outline of the Social System" (n. 18 above), p. 34, and "On the Concept of Value Commitments," in his *Politics and Social Structure* (New York, 1969), pp. 439–472, esp. p. 441. For the reason why the pattern-maintenance dimension is represented by "L," see n. 29 below.

26. "Outline of the Social System," p. 39.

27. Ibid., p. 35, italics in original.

28. In the following passage, Chalmers Johnson asserts that the very existence of four dimensions testifies to Parsons' attempt to conceptualize both instrumental and normative action:

> If there were only two functional prerequisites, integration and socialization [e.g., pattern maintenance], then the need for integrative action

> would decline to the extent that socialization approached perfect efficiency. . . . However, a society must not only socialize newcomers into the value structure; it must also adapt to its environment. Adaptation itself generates conflicts of interest, which the integrative institutions must regulate. Equally important, the relationship between the particular values which are socialized into actors and the roles these actors play in adapting to the environment generates varying demands for integrative action. (*Revolutionary Change* [Boston, 1966], p. 52.)

29. In these diagrams and the following discussion I am drawing particularly on Parsons' analyses of interchange in *Working Papers in the Theory of Action* (n. 1 above), esp. chs. 3, 5; in Parsons et al., *Family, Socialization, and Interaction Process* (New York, 1955); in *Economy and Society* (n. 18 above); and in the "Outline of the Social System" (n. 18 above).

I should acknowledge here that I have exercised a certain license in my presentation of the pattern-maintenance system. First, Parsons formally identifies this dimension as "L," standing for "latency," on the grounds that values are usually latent rather than manifest in social interaction. By this he implies that values do not change as rapidly as the components of other dimensions. This identification, in other words, refers to problems of empirical equilibrium rather than to presuppositional issues, and we will see later that it reflects a common confusion on Parsons' part among different levels of his analysis. In my discussion, therefore, I will not refer to "latency" as such. Second, Parsons has often added "tension management" to "pattern maintenance" to characterize the function of the most general subsystem. By this, he indicates that the control of emotional tension occurs in institutions located in the value sphere, and that such emotional control is inevitably tied to tasks of value socialization. What this means, in effect, is that the social system's two "conditional" environments, the personality and the behavioral organism, do not affect society only through its most instrumental dimension; they are also filtered through pattern maintenance and adaptation, respectively. It is for reasons such as this that the preceding derivation of interchange from the cybernetic schema should be considered a heuristic device rather than a formal derivation.

Finally, I must acknowledge from the outset that in the sources I have mentioned, and elsewhere, Parsons persistently uses interchange for a variety of purposes other than the social-system application presented here—to analyze leadership roles, aspects of organizational behavior, phases in small groups, socialization, decision making, deviance, and social control. Though ingenious and often quite empirically effective, these uses do not, I believe, derive from the fundamental meaning of the interchange model. They are ad hoc. I will critically discuss these various non-social-system uses of the model further in ch. 6.

30. Parsons and Smelser, *Economy and Society* (n. 18 above), p. 61. Robert N. Bellah's early statement in *Tokugawa Religion* (Boston, 1957, p. 12) makes this analytic emphasis of interchange very clear.

> Functional subsystems are thought of as analytical entities rather than as concrete structures. That is, a concrete structure such as the Tokugawa government, though primarily political in function, will also have economic, integrative and motivational [i.e., pattern-maintenance] functions.

It is precisely this kind of purely analytic characterization of fundamental social forces that Mannheim set forth as the goal of social thought in *Man and Society in an Age of Reconstruction* (New York, 1940). "It is a widespread illusion that spheres of social reality are separated," he wrote. "Properly speaking," he argued, "there are no spheres in social reality—only in human activity." Given this fact, social thought should focus on the "common elements in a wide range of phenomenona which, at the level of concreteness, are still radically different from one another." Mannheim goes on to suggest that "by deepening the process of abstraction in the right way, the increasingly formal definitions embrace more and more concrete processes and phenomena which could formerly be regarded as ultimately irreducible facts." (Pp. 161–167.)

31. The great advantages of the analytic status of Parsons' interchange theory as compared with the base-superstructure division have been forcefully suggested by the British sociologist Bob Jessop:

> Marxian sociology distinguishes between the substructure and superstructure of society [but] Parsons has argued that it is based on a failure to achieve a high enough level of abstraction. . . . Only a higher level of abstraction that treats both the material base and the superstructure as particular combinations of the same analytically defined, more generalized variables can deal with such problems. . . . The infrastructure, which is the analytical equivalent of Parsons' adaptive functional subsystem, is [actually] a complex structure of all four components and is involved in interchanges with the three other functional subsystems. It is therefore fallacious to distinguish between a material substratum and cultural superstructure without also emphasizing the essential similarity of their more basic components. (*Social Order, Reform, and Revolution* [London, 1972], pp. 49–50.)

By separating the level of ideology from other theoretical considerations, Jessop conducts a neo-Marxist analysis of strain and revolution that encompasses Parson's interchange formula.

The two best general discussions of interchange theory—which emphasize the analytical and multidimensional aspects of the model—are Adriaansens' (n. 20 above, pp. 118–143) and François Bourricaud's (*L'Individualisme institutionnel* [Paris, 1977], pp. 157–218).

32. Parsons and Smelser, *Economy and Society*, p. 104; cf. pp. 105 ff.

33. Ibid., p. 121.

34. Ibid., pp. 121 ff.

35. Ibid., p. 122.

36. Ibid., pp. 108–110.

37. Ibid., p. 148.

38. Ibid., p. 105.

39. For a discussion of organization and why the factor is not accounted for within the neoclassical and classical traditions, see ibid., pp. 95–96, 105. For a discussion of the formal integrative input of laws giving property rights to individuals rather than families, see Parsons, "Durkheim's Contribution to the Theory of the Integration of Social Systems," in his *Sociological Theory and Modern Society* (n. 18 above), p. 15.

40. *Economy and Society*, p. 56.

41. Ibid., p. 75.

42. Ibid., pp. 91–95.

43. Alvin W. Gouldner, "Reciprocity and Autonomy in Functional Theory," in N. J. Demerath III and Richard A. Peterson, eds., *System, Conflict, and Change* (New York, 1967), p. 147.

44. Gouldner adds that Parsons' system theory also ignores the role of the physical environment, and the role of tools and machines. It is interesting that in the very year that this critique appeared, Smelser published his monograph *Social Change in the Industrial Revolution* (Chicago, 1959). This book, it must be emphasized, elaborates the schema he and Parsons had established three years earlier in *Economy and Society*, and it heavily emphasizes precisely such physical factors, particularly the social role of technological innovation.

For two other analyses that utilize Parsons' system theory—from a different, more critical ideological perspective—to focus on the role of material, technological pressures in societies, see Herbert L. Gintis, "Alienation and Power: Toward a Radical Critique of Welfare Economics." (Ph.D. diss., Harvard University, 1969), and Mark Gould, "Systems Analysis, Macrosociology, and the Generalized Media of Social Action," in J. J. Loubser et al., eds., *Explorations in General Theory in Social Science* (New York, 1976), pp. 470–506. Both these analyses challenge the interchange model of economic process developed by Parsons and Smelser in terms of some of its particular neo-Keynesian empirical and ideological assumptions, yet in doing so they simultaneously demonstrate its universal applicability. Cf. the evaluation by the Althusserian critic Stephen Savage: "Parsonian theory has elaborated what is undoubtedly the most rigorous and systematic analysis of the economic/non-economic relation that has been produced from within sociology" (*The Theories of Talcott Parsons* [New York, 1981], p. 166; one should note, however, that Savage excludes Marxist writing from sociology).

45. As I indicated earlier (vol. 2, ch. 8), Parsons' understanding of the

nature and locus of the idealist dimension of Durkheim's work is not always my own, even though I agree with Parsons that it definitely exists. In this instance, I would argue that Durkheim's use of "non-contractual" in *The Division of Labor* was primarily presupposed by instrumental-collective presuppositions, not by the normative ones that Parsons finds (see vol. 2, ch. 5). For the purposes of the present discussion, however, this error on Parsons' part is not relevant: there were certainly strong normative aspects of Durkheim's later and more mature thinking about the constraints on economic action, and it is precisely such a normative emphasis that Parsons is trying to synthesize with instrumentalist concepts in his interchange theory.

46. Gouldner, *Coming Crisis* (n. 7 above), p. 293.

47. John Rex, *Key Problems in Sociological Theory* (London, 1961), p. 11.

48. Giddens, " 'Power' in the Recent Writings of Talcott Parsons" (n. 7 above), p. 263.

49. Dahrendorf, *Class and Class Conflict* (n. 7 above), pp. 166–173. For an effective rejoinder to these and other critics of Parsons' writings on power, see Savage (n. 44 above), pp. 147–154.

50. Parsons, "Authority, Legitimation, and Political Action," in his *Structure and Process in Modern Society* (New York, 1960), p. 182.

51. Parsons, "Some Reflections on the Place of Force in Social Process," in his *Sociological Theory and Modern Society* (n. 18 above), p. 271.

52. "Authority, Legitimation, and Political Action," p. 182; cf. p. 176 and "Some Reflections on the Place of Force," p. 281.

53. "Some Reflections," pp. 294–295.

54. Ibid., p. 272.

55. Parsons, "On the Concept of Political Power," in his *Sociological Theory and Modern Society* (n. 18 above), p. 299.

56. Ibid., p. 340.

One of the few critics of Parsons' political theory to recognize the significance of his critique of zero-sum theory is Giddens, who describes Parsons' "typology of compliant behavior" as a device for bridging the gap between those who "assume that conformity to any specific course of social action is founded *either* on 'internalization' of appropriate moral values *or* upon some form of coercion" (" 'Power' in the Recent Writings of Talcott Parsons" [n. 7 above], p. 263, italics in original).

57. Parsons, "On the Concept of Political Power," pp. 271–272. Cf. "Authority, Legitimation, and Political Action" (n. 50 above), pp. 181–182.

58. "On the Concept of Political Power," pp. 319–321. Cf. S. M. Lipset's parallel division of power into the elements of "effectiveness" and "legitimacy" in *Political Man* (New York, 1960).

59. In addition to the essays on power and force already cited, see esp. Parsons, "The Political Aspect of Social Structure and Process," in his

Politics and Social Structure (n. 25 above), pp. 317–351, and "Polity Society: Some General Considerations," ibid., pp. 439–472.

60. Parsons and Smelser, *Economy and Society* (n. 18 above), p. 72.

61. Parsons, "The Political Aspect of Social Structure and Process," p. 345.

62. E.g., "Some Reflections on the Place of Force in Social Process" (n. 51 above), p. 284.

63. "The Political Aspect of Social Structure and Process," pp. 334–335. Cf. "Some Reflections on the Place of Force in Social Process," pp. 282–285.

64. Parsons, " 'Voting' and the Equilibrium of the American Political System," in his *Politics and Social Structure* (n. 25 above), pp. 221–222.

65. "The Political Aspect of Social Structure and Process," p. 345.

66. "On the Concept of Political Power" (n. 55 above), p. 305.

67. Parsons, *The System of Modern Societies* (Englewood Cliffs, N.J., 1971), pp. 55–63.

68. "Some Reflections on the Place of Force in Social Process," p. 293.

69. "The Political Aspect of Social Structure and Process," p. 344.

70. "Some Reflections on the Place of Force in Social Process," pp. 268, 271, 294–295. Cf. S. N. Eisenstadt's discussions of power deflation and political conflict in *The Political System of Empires* (New York, 1963), pp. 183, 315, 321. For a general utilization of this power schema to describe the process of social upheaval and revolution, see Chalmers Johnson, *Revolutionary Change* (n. 28 above), passim.

71. It is difficult to reconcile this discussion of the conflict induced by interchange with Gouldner's contention that Parsons' theory posits such perfect functional equilibrium that it contains no conception of "functional reciprocity" and of the "imbalance" that the lack of reciprocity can produce ("Autonomy and Reciprocity in Functional Theory" [n. 43 above], pp. 149, 150). Although this critical essay was first published in 1959, it follows by several years the introduction of the interchange model and the publication of a number of essays illustrating its application. There were, in addition, numerous examples of dimensional imbalance and conflict in the still earlier works of Parsons' middle period. This misreading appears to be another case of mistaking the level of generality of Parsons' work. Since Gouldner recognizes only Parsons' functionalism in his evaluation, he is able to envision a perfectly equilibrated model without attending to the tension between instrumental and normative factors, i.e., to the presuppositional level that the model often specifies.

72. Deutsch, *The Nerves of Government* (New York, 1963), p. 116.

73. Though instrumentalist critics have failed to appreciate the relevance of this interchange formula for political analysis, there is, in fact, a large body of empirical literature that effectively incorporates it. If, e.g., one examines the "functionalist" political science that Parsons has so

heavily influenced, one finds that its empirical propositions are decidedly multidimensional. In fact, to survey this literature is to trace the multidimensionality of Parsons' political theory through each of its different phases of development.

Samuel H. Beer and Adam B. Ulam's influential *The Analysis of Political Systems* (New York, 1957) is particularly interesting because it combines elements from two different phases of Parsons' work, the means-end-situation schema of his early writing and the personality-society-culture division of his middle period. Building upon these presuppositions and general models, Beer and Ulam analyze national power arrangements resulting from the interaction of particular interest-group arrangements, authority structures, and national cultural patterns (see esp. pt. 1). Referring to similar phases in Parsons' work, though in a more tentative manner, David Easton's *The Political System* (New York, 1953) proposed the systematic reorganization of political research around Parsons' actor/situation dichotomy. Defining both actor and situation in supra-individual, functional terms, Easton analysed politics as the attempt to make certain values authoritative. In a later work, *A Systems Analysis of Political Life* (New York, 1965), Easton followed Parsons into his later phase of interchange theory, utilizing, in a highly creative manner, notions of input/output and boundary analysis to discusss the interaction of diffuse support, interest-demands, political socialization, and government response.

Probably the most effective utilization of Parsons' interchange model in this literature is William C. Mitchell's *The American Polity,* which follows Easton in emphasizing the interaction of rewards, demands, and resources. Though provisional in many ways, this lengthy discussion demonstrates the empirical potential of Parsons' synthesis, particularly in its analysis of the interplay of political values and socialization with interest demands and scarce resources (New York, [1963] 1970). Cf. Mitchell, "The Polity and Society: A Structural-Functional Analysis," *Midwest Journal of Political Science* 2 (1958):403–420.

Karl Deutsch's work, particularly *The Nerves of Government,* provides an interesting contrast to these discussions. Formulated at a still later point in Parsons' development, Deutsch's book emphasizes the contrast between interchange analysis and a "narrow" version of structural-functionalism. Deutsch describes the pattern-maintenance-goal-attainment interchange as a cybernetic process through which situationally specific goals are continually reformulated through political communication.

In the field of comparative political development, Gabriel Almond's utilization of the interchange model has been particularly significant because of his important empirical specification of the inputs of political socialization and recruitment, interest articulation and aggregation, and political communication ("A Functional Approach to Comparative Politics," in Almond and J. S. Coleman, eds., *The Politics of Developing Areas* (Princeton, N.J., 1960), pp. 5–64. Cf. Almond, "Comparative Political Systems," *Journal of Politics* 18 (1956):391–409, and Almond and G. Bingham Powell, Jr., *Comparative Politics* (Boston, 1966). Less comprehensive and less directly informed by Parsons, David Apter's work, particularly *Ghana in Transition* (Princeton, N.J., 1972) connects modernization literature to concepts from the early and middle phases of Parsons' development. The work of Fred Riggs also presents creative applications of Parsons' approach to modernization (*Administration in Developing Countries* [Boston, 1954] and *Prismatic Society Revisited* [Morristown, N.J., 1973]).

In the area of political culture, Almond and Sidney Verba in *The Civic Culture* (Boston, 1963) make an important application of Parsons' cognitive-cathectic-moral division among cultural patterns. Seymour Martin Lipset's *The First New Nation* (New York, 1965) conducts an extensive historical and comparative analysis of political culture from the perspective of the pattern-variable schema. (See also Young C. Kim, "The Concept of Political Culture in Comparative Politics," *Journal of Political Science* 26 [1964]: 313–337.)

For overviews of the impact on political science of different aspects of Parsons' functionalism, see Martin Landau, "On the Use of Functional Analysis in American Political Science," *Social Research* 35, no. 1 (1968): 48–75, and Elijah Ben-Zion Kaminsky, "Talcott Parsons and the Study of Comparative Politics," *Indian Journal of Social Research* 15 (1974): 137–147.

74. Parson, "The Distribution of Power in American Society," in *Politics and Social Structure* (n. 25 above), p. 200.

75. Parsons' achievement vis-à-vis Weber's political sociology is clearly manifest in the work of his students, as, e.g., in Bellah's discussion of the religion-polity interchange in *Tokugawa Religion* (n. 30 above) and David Little's analysis of the interrelation between Puritan religion and new legal forms in *Religion, Order, and Law* (New York, 1969).

The achievement is most apparent, however, in the works that utilize the interchange framework to focus on the same political problematic that Weber addressed. In *The Political System of Empires* (n. 70 above), Eisenstadt takes on the same patrimonialism-feudalism issue that occupied so much of Weber's political sociology. He accepts Weber's basic empirical insights into the political and economic aspects of the problem, yet by utilizing the much broader framework of interchange theory he is able to interrelate these facts with religious developments in a way that Weber simply could not. In certain crucial respects, Eisenstadt's book is an outline of the book Weber would have written if he had achieved the same kind of theoretical resolution as Parsons.

Focusing on the other major area of Weber's empirical concern, the political development of early modern Europe, Lipset and Rokkan have similarly employed the model of societal interchange to interrelate factors that Weber discussed only in a dichotomized manner. They root the political cleavage structures of contemporary Europe in the peculiar national combinations of religion, class, and political nation-building strategies that emerged from the Reformation period. ("Cleavage Structures, Party Systems, and Voter Alignments," in Seymour Martin Lipset and Stein Rokkan, eds., *Party Systems and Voter Alignments* (New York, 1967), pp. 1–64, esp. pp. 1–10.) Once again, despite his insight into the political implications of comparative religious development, Weber never succeeded in combining symbolic and factual patterns in his discussions of the origins of the modern European state.

In this simplified form of presentation I am referring, of course, to the tension between Weber's political and religious writings. As noted often in vol. 3, Weber's instrumental and multidimensional tendencies actually cross-cut the empirical division into "political" and "religious" works. There were, e.g., strong elements of a synthetic theoretical position in both his religious and his historical-political work.

76. See, e.g., the Introduction to S. N. Eisenstadt, ed., *Max Weber on Charisma and Institution Building* (Chicago, 1968). Here Eisenstadt reformulates Weber's political thinking in terms of a synthesis of Parsons' and Shils' general theories.

77. See Harold Bloom, *The Anxiety of Influence* (New York, 1973).

78. In describing how Newton actually "rewrote" Galileo, instead of simply elaborating him, Kuhn has described a process in the natural sciences that is similar to the deference Parsons shows to Weber.

> Newton wrote that Galileo had discovered that the constant force of gravity produces a motion proportional to the square of the time. In fact, Galileo's kinematic theorem does take that form when embedded in the matrix of Newton's own dynamical concepts. *But Galileo said nothing of the sort.* His discussion of falling bodies rarely alludes to forces, much less to a uniform gravitational force. By crediting to Galileo the answer to a question that Galileo's paradigms did not permit to be asked, Newton's account hides the effect of [his own] revolutionary reformulation. (*The Structure of Scientific Revolutions*, 2d ed. [Chicago, 1970], p. 139, italics added.)

Parsons similarly credits to Weber an answer that Weber's presuppositional limitations prevented him from making in anything like a consistent way. This "accumulationist" bent in Parsons' thought—which runs contrary to the thrust of his anti-empiricism—will be examined at some length in ch. 6.

Parsons' abnegation in regard to Weber's political sociology has allowed some of the recent Weberian analysts who rely heavily on Parsonian concepts to argue that they utilize these concepts merely to elaborate

Weber's fundamentally multidimensional work (e.g., Wolfgang Schluchter's position in his important book, *The History of Western Rationalism: Max Weber's Developmental History* [Berkeley and Los Angeles, 1981]). In fact, however, it is Parsons' reconceptualization of Weber's thought which has provided the framework within which such contemporary "elaborations" have been conducted. See my discussion of such recent Weber interpretations in vol. 3.

79. Parsons, " 'Voting' and the Equilibrium of the American Political System," in his *Politics and Social Structure* (n. 25 above), p. 219.

80. Ibid., pp. 214, 218.

81. Ibid., p. 218.

82. Ibid.

83. Parsons, "On the Concept of Influence," in his *Sociological Theory and Modern Society* (n. 18 above), p. 368.

84. Parsons, *The System of Modern Societies* (n. 67 above), p. 41.

85. Ibid., p. 43.

86. "On the Concept of Value Commitments" (n. 25 above), p. 436.

87. Ibid., pp. 437–438. Cf. *System of Modern Societies*, pp. 12–17.

88. Ibid., pp. 10–28.

89. Ibid., p. 92.

90. Ibid., p. 51. Cf. Parsons, "Full Citizenship for the Negro American?" in his *Sociological Theory and Modern Society* (n. 18 above), p. 424.

91. *System of Modern Societies*, p. 31.

92. Ibid.

93. Ibid., p. 36.

94. Throughout the following discussion I am referring to the critically important fourth chapter of *The System of Modern Societies*, pp. 50–70.

95. For Parsons' analysis of how this blocked situation created great problems for Austria and Germany when they later faced the industrial revolution, see *System of Modern Societies*, pp. 71–74. Surely this analysis of Counter-Reformation Europe indicates that Parsons' evolutionary theory does not adopt a purely linear view of Western progress, as is claimed, e.g., by Wolf Heydebrand (review of *The System of Modern Societies* [n. 7 above]), and Anthony D. Smith (*The Concept of Social Change* [London, 1973]).

96. *System of Modern Societies*, p. 15.

97. Ibid., p. 56.

98. Ibid., pp. 58–61.

99. Ibid., pp. 64–67.

100. Judith Blake and Kingsley Davis, "Norms, Values, and Sanctions," in Robert E. L. Faris, ed., *Handbook of Modern Sociology* (Chicago, 1964), pp. 462–468.

101. Heydebrand (n. 7 above). Indeed, in his long review essay on *The System of Modern Societies*, Heydebrand writes as if ch. 4, from which I have drawn most of the preceding analysis, simply does not exist:

> [Parsons] starts with the "cultural revolution" of the Protestant Reformation and essentially deduces, in familiar "Weberian" fashion, the entire gamut of economic, political, and cultural changes characterizing European historical development (p. 388).

Viewing Parsons simply as an idealist, Heydebrand never mentions the central theoretical innovation in the book: the utilization of interchange theory to differentiate social solidarity in a multidimensional fashion.

102. Most of Parsons' followers, unfortunately, have discussed either the more general "value" dimension, or the more instrumental and specific examples of solidarity, particularly the law. But there are a few exceptions. See, e.g., Rainer Baum's interesting article on the historical evolution of solidarity, "The System of Solidarities," *Indian Journal of Social Research* 16 (1975):307–352. The article which exemplifies the empirical and theoretical potential of Parsons' conceptualization of solidarity as an independent dimension is Lipset and Rokkan's "Cleavage Structures, Party Systems, and Voter Alignments" (n. 75 above).

103. It should be noted, however, that although Durkheim does often speak of solidarity in this kind of diffuse way—a diffuseness which is necessitated by his failure to achieve a multidimensional perspective that fully differentiated normative and conditional elements both in terms of the culture/social-system distinction and within the social system itself—there is a very real sense in which he implicitly recognizes levels of generality and specificity *within* the normative and solidary spheres. It was precisely these intranormative differentiations that I sought to emphasize in my presentation of Durkheim's later "idealist theory of society" (in vol. 2, ch. 8, esp. pp. 261–263). I described this theory as placing abstract and "civilizational" cultural patterns like individualism at the top, concrete groups like families and occupational groups at the bottom, and entities like education, law, and the state in between. This implicit hierarchy is partly motivated by Durkheim's recognition of the different organizational and material exigencies of different groups, and in this sense it corresponds to Parsons' differentiation of institutional spheres. The two approaches, nonetheless, differ in substantial ways. First, Durkheim does not explicitly "theoretize" instrumental pressures, but leaves them as residual categories, so his valid understanding of the different levels and kinds of solidarity is never explained in depth (it is the description and analysis of the solidarities, and their interrelations, that interests him). Second, the actual hierarchy that Durkheim so describes is not a hierarchy from culture to instrumental conditions, even though it is informed by some sensitivity to these issues, but rather is a hierarchy from universalistic culture to particularistic. Thus it is a normative hierarchy of cultural and ideological evaluation, not a true analytical hierarchy. There is a very similar cultural and ideological hierarchy which is implicit in Parsons' work, but it is more clearly differentiated from analytic concerns.

104. There is some indication, of course, that Weber was aware of the significance of the solidarity variable. He makes several important references to the Indian caste system's failure to universalize solidarity, or to develop "fraternization," in *The Religion of India* (see esp. ch. 1, pt. 7, "Caste and Guild"), and in *The Sociology of Religion* he refers periodically to the great achievement of Christianity as creating a universal brotherhood of man. Unfortunately, these references are unsystematic and remain undeveloped. Also they are not connected to his discussion of law in *The City,* which I analyze as a strongly multidimensional strand of Weber's work in vol. 3, ch. 2, sec. 5.

105. It is interesting in this regard that the only analysis in the Weberian tradition that attempts to deal with solidarity as an independent variable, Guenther Roth's *Social Democrats in Imperial Germany* (Totowa, N.J., 1963), is forced to go beyond Weber's concepts to Durkheim's. Roth produces a fine analysis of the isolation of the German working class in the Bismarck period, which he describes not only as the result of religious, economic, and political discrimination, but also as reinforced, on the other side, by the exclusivist solidarity of the Marxist German working class. He describes the situation of the latter as "negative integration." Of course, as a major Weberian "revisionist," Roth insists he is merely following out the path that Weber laid down, not making up for weaknesses in Weber by turning to Durkheim. (For an excellent general discussion of Weber's failure to appreciate the solidary dimension of contemporary political life, and the difficulties this creates for a Weberian political sociology in contrast to a Durkheimian one, see Jeffrey Prager, "Moral Integration and Political Inclusion: A Comparison of Durkheim's and Weber's Theories of Democracy," *Social Forces* 59 [1981]:918-950.)

106. Parsons and Gerald M. Platt, *The American University* (Cambridge, Mass., 1973), p. 41.

107. Parsons, "On the Concept of Value Commitments" (n. 25 above), p. 440.

108. Ibid., p. 452.

109. Parsons and Platt, *The American University,* p. 35.

110. "On the Concept of Value Commitments," pp. 447, 451.

111. Parsons and Smelser first wrote about functional values as related to the economic system—"economic values"—in *Economy and Society* (n. 18 above), pp. 175-176. Bellah writes about the functional, "political" values of Tokugawa Japan in *Tokugawa Religion* (n. 30 above), ch. 1. In *The Political System of Empires* (n. 70 above), Eisenstadt writes about the conflict between different functional values—cultural, political-collective, and economic—in the ancient empires (pp. 222-253). Rainer Baum uses the functional approach to value analysis in "Values and Democracy in Imperial Germany," *Sociological Inquiry* 138 (1968):179-196; cf. the more elaborate treatment in his "Values and Uneven Political Development in

Imperial Germany" (Ph.D. diss., Harvard University, 1967). In an ideological critique, Daniel Foss accuses Parsons of arguing that functional values completely regulate the economic subsystem, excluding the influence of material facts. Although there are elements of this, Foss completely ignores the meaning of the interchange problem. ("The World View of Talcott Parsons," in Maurice Stein and Arthur Vidich, eds., *Sociology on Trial* [Englewood Cliffs, N.J., 1963], pp. 96–126.)

112. See n. 111.

113. Parsons and Platt, *The American University,* pp. 42–43.

114. Ibid., p. 44.

115. Ibid., p. 45.

116. Ibid., p. 120.

117. Ibid., p. 46, italics in original. Chs. 2–3 of *The American University* are devoted to elaborating the nature of this cognitive rationality value and the cultural basis for its autonomy.

118. Ibid., pp. 45–55. The following argument refers to this section.

119. Ibid., pp. 53–54.

120. Ibid., pp. 53–55.

121. Ibid., p. 81.

122. Ibid., pp. 231–232.

123. Ibid., p. 228.

124. Ibid., p. 263, n. 24.

125. Ibid., pp. 273–276.

126. Ibid., p. 273.

127. Ibid., italics added.

128. Ibid., pp. 267–303.

129. Ibid., p. 275.

130. Ibid., p. 212.

131. Ibid., p. 204.

132. Ibid., pp. 214–215.

133. Ibid., p. 168.

134. Ibid., p. 169.

135. Parsons, "On the Concept of Value Commitments" (n. 25 above), p. 455.

136. On this problem, see Parsons and Platt, ch. 7, "Dynamic Process in the University System: The Nature of the Crisis," pp. 304–345.

137. This interpretation has been made, e.g., by Joseph R. Gusfield in his review of *The American University* in *Contemporary Sociology* 3 (1974):291–295.

138. For Parsons, *Moral Education* represented Durkheim's last major normative work before his final work, *The Elementary Forms of Religious Life.* Hence Parsons did not discuss *The Evolution of Educational Thought* or the writings on political or legal rationality. Nonetheless, the basic presuppositional issue that Parsons is dealing with here—implicitly,

to be sure—still holds good as a critical response to the idealist tendency in Durkheim's writing on moral rationality.

139. This rewriting of Weber does not rely only on Durkheim's more normative approach to rationality, of course, but on Parsons' much clearer understanding of secularization as the abstraction and generalization of religious values. This aspect of the Durkheimian legacy to Parsons, and the use he makes of it vis-à-vis Weber, is discussed in my analyses of social change below, chs. 5, 9.

140. Parsons rarely distinguished, as I have done here, between the analytic usage of interchange and its concrete application to individual and unit interaction. The reasons for his failure to offer such a distinction are complex and any substantive discussion must be deferred until later in my analysis. Briefly, the problem can be traced to Parsons' attraction to formal analogy. E.g., insofar as he analyzed interchange and generalized media as if they presented one single matrix of input-output analysis—insofar as he did not differentiate, in other words, between the construction of analytic dimensional pressures and the production of concrete media—he could construct an exact sociological parallel to macro-economic analysis, and this "isomorphism" was, for a number of reasons, very important to him. (See, e.g., p. 353, fig. 3, in his *Sociological Theory and Modern Society* [n. 18 above].) Since this commitment to formal analogy has usually been shared by those who have applied and elaborated interchange theory, the distinction between medium and analytic dimension has continued to be obscured by later developments in Parsonian theory.

In the preceding discussion I have intermixed a strictly analytic approach to interchange with concrete references to the media of interaction. In view of Parsons' own interchangeable references, a more "purified" method would have been unwieldy. I hope, nonetheless, that the theoretical point is clear.

141. In this analysis of the media theory, I am drawing on Parsons and Smelser, *Economy and Society* (n. 18 above); on Parsons, "Some Reflections on the Place of Force in Social Process" (n. 51 above), "On the Concept of Political Power" (n. 55 above), "On the Concept of Influence" (n. 83 above), and "On the Concept of Value Commitments" (n. 25 above); and on Parsons and Platt, *The American University* (n. 106 above).

142. "On the Concept of Influence," pp. 369–370.

143. "On the Concept of Value Commitments," p. 461.

144. Ibid., pp. 446–447. Cf. Parsons, "Social Structure and the Symbolic Media of Interchange," in Peter M. Blau, ed., *Approaches to the Study of Social Structure* (New York, 1975), p. 98.

145. Parsons and Platt, p. 71. The manner in which this theoretical distinction between code and base relates to Parsons' broader multidimensional purpose is clearly articulated in Bourricaud's discussion (n. 31 above, p. 17):

> Can one juxtapose an interpretation of power in "real" terms to an interpretation in "symbolic" terms? In every case, to be sure, one must begin by distinguishing the field and range of application of the one and the other. But these fields are not closed and inpenetrable domains; they are, rather, interconnected levels whose relation is articulated by a hierarchy of reversible controls.

146. Ibid., p. 25.

147. This skeletonized version of Parsons' media theory—I am more concerned here, as elsewhere, with the theory's most abstract theoretical implications than with an exposition of the theory as such—may make the notion seem much more esoteric than it actually is. In fact, the conception of general media of exchange implicitly informs a variety of well-known discussions of the structure and processes of modern life. Below I will note the media analysis of Marx. Here might be mentioned the centrality of the concept of generalized communication and trust in the writings of George Herbert Mead. Even in a society which is complex and specialized, Mead believed, it is possible for members of the same society to "recognize others as members, and as brothers." This "universal society" will occur to the degree to which "all can enter into relationship with others through the medium of communication." This community will be based, in other words, "simply on the ability of all individuals to converse with each other through use of the same significant symbols." (*George Herbert Mead on Social Psychology*, ed. Anselm Strauss [Chicago, 1964], pp. 257, 281.) Parsons' notion of the significance of such generalized communication is much the same, but it is specified in a much more complex, systematic, and empirical way, and related also to historical and comparative perspectives.

148. See Parsons and Platt, ch. 7, "The Dynamic Process in the University System: The Nature of the Crisis," pp. 304–345.

149. Probably the most important empirical discussion of media, interchange, and the multidimensional sources of conflict is Chalmers Johnson's *Revolutionary Change* (n. 28 above). Other insightful treatments are Neil J. Smelser's "Stability, Instability, and the Analysis of Political Corruption," in Bernard Barber and Alex Inkeles, eds., *Stability and Social Change* (Boston, 1971) pp. 7–29, and François Bourricaud's "Penury and Deficit, or the Problems of Political Underutilization," in Loubser et al., *Explorations* (n. 44 above), pp. 557–578. The notion of media "entrepreneurs" was introduced by S. N. Eisenstadt, who relies heavily on the general media analysis to develop an analytic approach to concrete interaction. See, e.g., his *The Political System of Empires* (n. 70 above), *Essays in Comparative Institutions* (New York, 1965, particularly pts. 1, 3), and "Social Change, Differentiation, and Evolution," *American Sociological Review* 29 (1964):275–286.

150. This is one of the major points made by Rainer C. Baum in his essays "Introduction to Generalized Media in Action" and "On Societal

Dynamics," in Loubser et al., pp. 448–469, 579–608. (Baum is influenced here by the approach to media taken by Niklas Luhmann, whose own essays on "generalized media," though generally derived from Parsons' work, strongly emphasize the central role of stability; see, e.g., his *Trust and Power* [New York, 1980].) The legitimation of equilibrium is also cited as the major source for media theory by Bliss C. Cartwright and R. Stephen Warner in their critique of media theory, "The Medium Is Not the Message," in Loubser, pp. 639–660.

151. Baum also very closely relates media theory—as does Luhmann—to Parsons' particular conception of functional models ("Introduction to Generalized Media in Action"). Harry M. Johnson argues that it is derived directly from Parsons' effort to isomorphize economic theory ("The Generalized Symbolic Media in Parsons' Theory" [n. 6 above]).

152. This is a primary argument in Wolin (n. 13 above); in Gouldner, *Coming Crisis* (n. 7 above), pp. 291 ff.; and in Jürgen Habermas, "Talcott Parsons: Problems of Theory Construction," *Sociological Inquiry* 51 (1981):173–196, see p. 190.

153. Terence S. Turner makes this assertion in his otherwise excellent "Parsons' Concept of 'Generalized Media of Social Interaction' and Its Relevance for Social Anthropology, *Sociological Inquiry* 38 (1968):121–134. The same kind of approach is made in Baum's "Communication and the Media," in Loubser, pp. 533–556, as it is by Luhmann in "Generalized Media and the Problem of Contingency," ibid., pp. 507–532.

154. See, e.g., Giddens' interpretation of Parsons' theory of political media: "Parsons does not suggest any answers to why power deflations occur. . . . Power deflation [for Parsons] is deviance writ large. . . . Thus the possibility of explaining power deflation in terms of the mutual interaction of interest-groups is excluded [and] the process of power deflation is conceived purely as one of psychological 'loss of confidence' in the existing system." ("'Power' in the Recent Writings of Talcott Parsons" [n. 7 above], pp. 266–267.) Such a statement can only be made if the relationship between media theory and interchange is completely ignored.

155. Parsons, "Levels of Organization and the Mediation of Social Interaction," in Turk and Simpson [n. 15 above], p. 26, italics in original. This is the fundamental point, of course, that informed Parsons' principal polemic in *The Structure of Social Action.* Such an intimate connection between his first book and one of the major innovations of his later writings is yet another example of the strong continuity, in terms of presuppositional emphasis, between the early and later work.

156. Ibid., pp. 26–27, italics in original.

157. See Marx, *Capital,* vol. 1, pt. 1, and the present work, vol. 2, pp. 168–171.

158. The implications for Marxist theory of Parsons' generalized media analysis are explored in Bob Jessop's extremely interesting mono-

graph, *Social Order, Reform, and Revolution* (London, 1972). Using the four media and interchange analysis, Jessop redefines Marx's discussion of exploitation and class hegemony in a neo-Marxist effort to rid Marx's original theory of its rationalist bias.

In contemporary sociology, rational collectivist theorists continue to ignore the possibility of noninstrumental media and of equal legitimacy for both the symbolic and intrinsic aspects of social sanctions. E.g., in a critical review of Parsons' essay on the media of influence, James Coleman interprets Parsons' position as arguing that influence can get results only if actors are subject simultaneously to monetary sanctions (*Public Opinion Quarterly*, Spring 1963). See Walter L. Wallace's critique of this rationalist bias in Coleman's "action theory" in "Structure and Action in the Theories of Coleman and Parsons," in Blau, *Approaches to the Study of Social Structure* (n. 144 above), pp. 121–134.

159. Peter K. Ekeh's *Social Exchange: The Two Traditions* (Cambridge, Mass., 1974) traces the conflict between the rationalist approaches to exchange and the Durkheimian ones. He writes, e.g., that the latter's "morality of generalized exchange" emphasizes a "trust of others" that leads actors to "discharge their obligations to the enrichment of society rather than for their exclusive narrow self-interest" (p. 59). Yet Ekeh sees Lévi-Strauss as the only major contemporary theorist who develops a normative alternative to instrumental and individualistic perspectives on exchange. Surely Parsons presents another such example. Cf. Guy Swanson, "Frameworks for Comparative Research: Structural Anthropology and the Theory of Action," in Ivan Vallier, ed., *Comparative Methods in Sociology: Essays on Trends and Applications* (Berkeley and Los Angeles, 1971), pp. 203–263, and Adrian C. Hayes, "A Comparative Study of the Theoretical Orientations of Parsons and Lévi-Strauss," *Indian Journal of Social Research* 15, nos. 2–3 (1974):101–111. I would also qualify Ekeh's normative-ideal evaluation of the Durkheimians, for, as I suggest in vol. 2, ch. 9, this was much the same motivation that led Mauss to combine generalized symbolic concerns with instrumental ones through his own use of exchange. Because Mauss was a reviser in spite of himself, however, he produced a profoundly ambiguous theory of generalized exchange, one that vacillated between obeisance to Durkheim's idealistic reliance on symbolism and a quasi-utilitarian, even quasi-Marxist instrumentalization of primitive political and economic life. Because Parsons was much more theoretically self-conscious than Mauss, and also, obviously, so much more temporally differentiated from Durkheim, his effort to combine symbolic generalization with concrete, instrumentalizing exchange could be more successful. Still, as will be noted below, Parsons' attempt does not, in the end, avoid profound ambiguity any more successfully than Mauss's (see chs. 8, 9).

160. Jeremy Bentham, *An Introduction to the Principles of Morals*

and Legislation, ch. 4, "Of the Four Sanctions or Sources of Pain and Pleasure."

CHAPTER FIVE

1. Although I am writing in this chapter only about Parsons' later socialization writings, this later period includes most of his work on socialization. With the exception of ch. 6 of *The Social System* (New York, 1951) and sections of pt. 2, sec. 2, of his and Edward A. Shils' *Towards a General Theory of Action* (New York, 1951), all of his writing on socialization occurred in the later period, primarily in two publications, Parsons and Robert F. Bales, eds., *Family, Socialization, and Interaction Process* (New York, 1955), and Parsons, *Social Structure and Personality* (New York, 1964).

2. For the conflict critique of Parsons' socialization theory, see Alvin W. Gouldner, *The Coming Crisis of Western Sociology* (New York, 1970), pp. 219–220; for the model critique, see Richard Sennett's writings, e.g., *Families against the City* (Cambridge, Mass., 1969), pp. 62–68; for the ideological critique, see Dennis Wrong, "The Over-Socialized Concept of Man in Modern Sociology," *American Sociological Review* 26 (1961):183–193.

3. See Gouldner, pp. 219–220, and J. P. Scott, "The Changing Foundations of the Parsonian Action Schema," *American Sociological Review* 28 (1963):716–735. More recently, see Stephen Savage's analysis in *The Theories of Talcott Parsons* (New York, 1981), which claims that "Parsons does not provide a theory of the *mechanism* by which the ego is formed" (p. 126, italics added) and, further, that for Parsons "the process of learning is not a mechanism by which the personality is formed but is a process of *realisation* of an immanent capacity" (ibid., italics in original). In this way, Savage claims, Parsons' socialization theory returns "to the idealism which the theory of action explicitly attempted to avoid" (ibid.).

4. For such a sympathetic emphasis on Parsons' focus on socialization and values as an alternative to a focus on material conditions and conflict, see, e.g., Jackson Toby's *Contemporary Society* (New York, [1964] 1971) and Benton Johnson's *Functionalism in Modern Sociology: Understanding Talcott Parsons* (Morristown, N.J., 1976).

5. For an analysis of these middle-period concepts, see ch. 3, sec. 3.2.

6. For an analysis of this earlier discussion of internalization as it relates to Parsons' presuppositional position on voluntarism, see ch. 2, sec. 4.

7. See Parsons and Neil J. Smelser, *Economy and Society* (New York, 1956), pp. 139–143.

8. See ch. 4, sec. 2.

9. See "The Superego and the Theory of Social Systems," in Parsons, *Social Structure and Personality*, pp. 17–33.

10. *Social Structure and Personality*, p. 257, and passim.

11. Ibid., p. 24, italics altered.

12. Ibid., pp. 23, 30.

13. Parsons, "Family Structure and the Socialization of the Child," in Parsons and Bales, *Family, Socialization, and Interaction Process* (n. 1 above), pp. 35–132, see p. 56.

14. Most psychoanalytic social theory still has not absorbed this point, despite the work of such "Parsonian" psychoanalytical sociologists as Fred Weinstein and Gerald M. Platt, and others, to be discussed below. For a critical discussion of a recent exercise in psychoanalytic social theory, in which many of the points mentioned here are elaborated, see my review of Leo Rangell, *The Mind of Watergate* (New York, 1980), in *The New Republic*, March 29, 1980, pp. 38–39.

15. Parsons, "Family Structure and the Socialization of the Child," p. 42.

16. Ibid., p. 65.

17. Parsons, "The Superego and the Theory of Social Systems," in his *Social Structure and Personality* (n. 1 above), p. 29.

18. Ibid.; Parsons, "Social Structure and the Development of Personality: Freud's Contribution to the Integration of Psychology and Sociology," ibid., pp. 78–111, see pp. 86–87; "Family Structure and the Socialization of the Child," p. 42.

19. "Social Structure and the Development of Personality," p. 87.

20. "Family Structure and the Socialization of the Child" and Parsons, "The Organization of Personality as an Action System," in Parsons and Bales (n. 1. above), pp. 35–186, passim.

This relationship between cultural and psychological generalization, general role understandings, and the evolution of individual autonomy is well articulated by François Bourricaud in *L'Individualisme institutionnel: Essai sur la sociologie de Talcott Parsons* (Paris, 1977). For Parsons, Bourricaud writes, socialization "provides us with a stock of schemas, of very simple formulas which we can by generalization apply to a great variety of situations, permitting us to identify ourselves with others, but also to distinguish ourselves from them." Rather than instilling particular procedures which would bind us irrevocably to particular acts or persons, Parsons realized that socialization provides individuals with "the general aptitude to apply, to interpret, even to innovate from schemas that are transposable from the situation in which they have been learned to situations that are objectively comparable or symbolically analogous." (P. 134.)

21. Parsons, like Freud, spends more time on the socialization of the male child, although he does provide the outlines of a separate, and more tenable, approach to female socialization. See "Age and Sex in the Kinship Structure of the United States" in his *Essays in Sociological Theory* (New York, 1954), pp. 89–103; "Certain Primary Sources and Patterns of Aggression in the Social Structure of the Western World," ibid., pp. 298–322; and

"Family Structure and the Socialization of the Child" (n. 13 above), pp. 94–104. Also see n. 31 below.

22. Parsons, "Social Structure and the Development of Personality," p. 118, italics in original.

23. Ibid., p. 89.

24. Parsons, "The Father Symbol: An Appraisal in the Light of Psychoanalytic and Sociological Theory," in *Social Structure and Personality* (n. 1 above), pp. 34–56, see pp. 40–41.

25. "Family Structure and the Socialization of the Child," p. 52. It is the central significance that such "structural configurations" of the life cycle play in Parsons' understanding of value socialization that is completely ignored by critics (and sympathizers) who interpret the socialization theory as having a completely cultural and idealist slant. Savage (n. 3 above), e.g., describes the theory as if it spoke only about the relation of personality and cultural systems (pp. 121–127); he makes no reference to the critical role, in the theory, of the child's actual experience of concrete role situations.

26. "Family Structure," p. 114.

27. Ibid., p. 52.

28. Ibid., p. 117. See Robert Dreeben, *On What Is Learned in School* (Reading, Mass., 1968), and Parsons and Gerald M. Platt, *The American University* (Cambridge, Mass., 1973).

Although Parsons' theory has often been criticized for ignoring the level of individual interaction and the processes of active intentionality, it should be clear from this account that they both play a crucial role in his theory of socialization. When Bourricaud (n. 20 above) makes his strong case for the active and vigorous qualities of "*homo parsoniensis*," it is clearly this theory of socialization that he has firmly in mind, for Parsons' theory both describes and presumes a wide range of interactional consequences and individual activity. In the first place, Bourricaud writes, *homo parsoniensis*

> is an acting individual as a sensitive being; he experiences pleasure and pain—not only from the presence of physical objects, but also from the actions of his partners. In the second, the *homo parsoniensis* chooses. . . . To say that the individual is sensitive is to say that he is not indifferent, that he does not give to every event the same value; he has a capacity for evaluation. But to say that the *homo parsoniensis* chooses can signify also that he is provided with a capacity to combine, that he decomposes and recomposes the elements of his situation, according to the laws of the logic which is furnished him by the variables of [cultural] configuration. (P. 118.)

In fact, there are very strong similarities between the account Parsons presents of generalization in the socialization process and George Herbert

Mead's account—taken as the prototype of social interactionism—of the origins in early life of the notion of the "generalized other." "By generalizing these individual attitudes of . . . organized society or social group . . . as a whole," Mead writes, the individual must "act toward different social projects which at any given time it is carrying out, or toward the various larger phases of the general social process which constitutes the group's life" in terms of differentiated, less concrete beliefs. Like Parsons, moreover, Mead insists that this ability to take a more generalized attitude toward particular events and life experience is inherently tied to the very development of the "self": "Only insofar as he takes the attitudes of the organized social group to which he belongs toward the organized, cooperative social activity or set of such activities in which that group as such is engaged, does he develop a complete self or possess the sort of complete self he has developed." (*George Herbert Mead on Social Psychology*, ed. Anselm Strauss [Chicago, 1964], p. 219 and passim.) Parsons' account of the actual contents of the interaction which produce this generalization is, however, more empirically specific than Mead's and, through his incorporation of Freudian theory, more sensitive to emotional rather than simply moral and cognitive dimensions. Parsons also ties this conception of generalization more directly to institutional, comparative, and historical considerations.

29. "Family Structure and the Socialization of the Child," pp. 115, 121–123. S. N. Eisenstadt has elaborated this in great detail in *From Generation to Generation* (New York, [1956] 1971).

30. See the evaluation of the social psychologist Baldwin that Parsons' socialization theory represents "the most ambitious attempt yet made to encompass" the relational aspects of socialization. "[Parsons demonstrates] that socialization pressure on the child is not merely an antecedent variable whose consequence is personality. The whole process is the behavior of a social system with various feedbacks and other patterns of interrelationships." (Alfred L. Baldwin, "The Parsonian Theory of Personality," in Max Black, ed., *The Social Theories of Talcott Parsons* [Ithaca, N.Y., 1961], p. 178.) The best overall discussion of the relationship between Parsons' socialization theory and other, more traditional approaches to the problem is Jesse Pitts, "Introduction to Personality and the Social System," in Parsons et al., eds., *Theories of Society* (New York, 1961), pp. 685–716.

31. Cf. the object-relations theorist Roy Schaffer's judgment that Parsons' approach to personality formation "adds a major dimension to the theory of internalization" by demonstrating, while remaining within the psychoanalytic framework, that "much learning does take in what is offered from the environment" (*Aspects of Internalization* [New York, 1968], p. 9). Parsons' critique of Freud's "drive theory" can be viewed as opening up important ideological possibilities in the debate over the psychology of women. Miriam M. Johnson, e.g., demonstrates that by separat-

ing cultural from physical determinants Parsons' theory makes it possible to rewrite Freud's approach to feminine personality. Unlike Freud, Johnson contends, Parsons sees male and female children as possessing equally strong superego structures. Sexual differentiation occurs, therefore, in the variation of early object choice, a variation that Parsons views as produced by the sexual division of occupational roles ("Misogyny and the Super-Ego: Chauvinism in the Moral Sphere," *Indian Journal of Social Research* 16 [1975]:372-383). For another recent feminist work that relies heavily (although not exclusively) on the "object relations" psychoanalytic sociology opened up by Parsons' work, see Nancy Chodorow, *The Reproduction of Mothering: Psychoanalysis and the Sociology of Gender* (Berkeley and Los Angeles, 1978). In *The Wish to Be Free* (idem, 1969; ch. 6), which is based on Parsons' personality theory, Weinstein and Platt also discuss the relation between social change and sex-role variation. Their *Psychoanalytic Sociology* (Baltimore, 1973; esp. chs. 1–2) presents the best analysis of the implications of Parsons' analysis of personality and socialization for linking psychoanalytic and sociological frameworks.

32. See Menzies' judgment as to Piaget and Parsons: "Each partially confirms the other. . . . Parsons can be used to help explain some of Piaget's work [and] some of Piaget's work is needed to supplement Parsons." (Ken Menzies, *Talcott Parsons and the Social Image of Man* [London, 1976], p. 105.) See his detailed comparison of Piaget and Parsons (pp. 105–109).

For a sophisticated and insightful discussion of the point-by-point relationship between Parsons' work and the discoveries of Piaget's developmental tradition, see Richard Münch, "Socialization and Personality Development from the Point of View of Action Theory, the Legacy of Emile Durkheim," *Sociological Inquiry* 51 (1981):311–354, esp. pp. 323 ff.

33. Richard Sennett's writings on the family provide a good illustration of such misunderstanding. Though Sennett praises Parsons "brilliant perception of the [socialization] process," at the same time he characterizes this perception as indicating "a process wherein the young man learned to see how fragmented his power was in the world." Parsons was led to this view, Sennett argues, because his functionalism allowed him to see only the individual's bureaucratic subservience to the needs of the "system," blinding him to the possibilities for socializing "self-sufficient competence and activity." (*Families against the City* [Cambridge, Mass., 1969], p. 67, cf. pp. 62–68.) See the similar conclusion in Sennett's "Middle Class Families and Urban Violence: The Experience of a Chicago Community in the 19th Century," in Sennett and Steven Thernstrom, eds., *Nineteenth Century Cities* (New Haven, Conn., 1969), pp. 386–420.

But Parsons' vision of socialization does not emphasize passivity. He sees socialization, to the contrary, as providing the capacity to cope with fragmentation as part of growing ego autonomy, and he views lengthy pre-adult internalization as integral to this process.

A similar misreading based on presuppositional error can be found in Gouldner's analysis. After describing Parsons' socialization theory as intrinsically conformist, Gouldner offers the following alternative:

> The very nature of primary socialization . . . serves not to provide well-tooled parts for any one specific group, but to ensure a measure of functional autonomy for the *individual* by virtue of preparing him to participate in various different groups. . . . The development of self involves development of the discriminating processes which perceive likeness and differences. It is not, however, the likenesses but the differences that become crucial in distinguishing the self from others. (*Coming Crisis* [n. 2 above], pp. 219–220.)

It would be difficult, indeed, to find a more succinct summary of what Parsons' own socialization theory actually says. Preparation for individualizing participation in various groups is the whole point of Parsons' analysis of role internalization, and the child's perception of differences rather than likenesses is crucial for Parsons' theory of the emergence of universalism. Gouldner is forced into this major interpretative distortion because he insists on viewing any internalization as per se opposed to individual freedom.

34. For a general discussion of this presuppositional point, see vol. 1, pp. 104–110; for its relation to Marx's writings, see vol. 2, pp. 203-205.

35. Fred Weinstein and Gerald Platt have utilized Parsons' personality theory to relate Marx's lack of insight into socialization to his ambivalence about working-class alienation. They argue that Marx implies both that alienation destroys the worker's autonomous will—thereby creating passivity—and, simultaneously, that alienation creates sufficient resentment to produce revolutionary aggression. Against this ambiguous position, derived from a purely economic analysis, they emphasize the increasingly universalistic socialization of the European working classes in the nineteenth century. It was because of this psychological fact that workers had, in fact, sufficient will, or ego strength, to create independent and critical opposition to capitalist exploitation at an early stage of industrialization. Such a strong response, they believe, fostered reform rather than the kind of revolutionary activity that Marx had envisioned as the long-range fruits of alienation.

> Marx's point of view . . . cannot clarify the relationship of the individual . . . to reality or specify the modes by which the individual makes reality his object. . . . In the absence of such notions as identification, internalization and the like Marx could not possibly have understood . . . why the workers could not act as he predicted [i.e., in a revolutionary manner] despite the presence of all the conditions for action he specified. Above all, he consistently failed to observe the positive aspects of [psychological] support that were available to the workers. ("Alienation and the Problem of Social Action," in Edward A. Tiryakian, ed., *The Phenomenon of Sociology* [New York, 1971], p. 297.)

Although this analysis limits the problem in Marx's thought to his psychological theory, it does indicate how political assumptions about the independence and critical behavior of oppressed and dominated groups rely heavily on an implicit theory of socialized autonomy.

36. Emile Durkheim, *Moral Education* (New York, 1961), p. 115. For a discussion that explores the relation between Parsons' socialization theory and Durkheim's moral theory in more detail, from much the same perspective presented here, see Münch (n. 32 above), esp. pp. 315–323.

37. In another context, I have used the distinction between the "formal" and "substantive" elements in Parsons' work as a guide to the relations between his general—presuppositional and model-oriented—theory and his more specific analysis of change, particularly as this centers on the fate of "voluntarism." See my "Formal and Substantive Voluntarism in the Work of Talcott Parsons: A Theoretical and Ideological Re-Interpretation," *American Sociological Review* 43 (1978):177–198.

38. The ideological, or normative, approach to "freedom" obviously is complex, and in the following discussion I am drawing upon several different strands of analysis. Freedom can, of course, be viewed as natural or given, as simply an attribute of any individual action. Beyond this individualist position, however, freedom can be viewed as dependent either upon external, supra-individual circumstances, or upon conditions internal to the individual. Hobbes points to external circumstances when he writes that a "freeman is he that, in those things which by his strength and wit he is able to do, is not hindered to do what he has a will to do" (*Leviathan*, pt. 2, ch. 21). For those in the internalist tradition, however, it is precisely the nature of this will which is at issue, not the circumstances that hinder it. Thus, as Marcus Aurelius said, influenced as he was by the Stoics: "It is possible to live well even in a palace." Or as Jesus proclaimed, "Ye shall know the truth, and the truth shall make you free." Freedom, in other words, is a matter of the quality of insight and perception. I will argue that Parsons draws on both these traditions.

Within each of these general traditions there are various more specific controversies. Does external freedom depend on the acquisition of individual liberty or on equality? Does internal freedom depend on the acquisition of "virtue," particularly by grace, or on the development of reason? Although I do not investigate Parsons' positions on these various specific controversies in great detail, I do refer to them in the following discussion of his relationship to Puritanism and to the political options of laissez-faire liberalism, radical socialism, and fascism. (For a broad discussion of these general and specific controversies, see Mortimer J. Adler, *The Idea of Freedom* [New York, 1958]).

As a sociological theorist, however, Parsons' major contribution to the discussion of freedom lies, as does Weber's, in his translation of normative arguments into historical-empirical frameworks. Parsons' contribution rests, in other words, with his argument that the internal and external conditions of freedom can be viewed as based upon the extension of what I will identify shortly as "cultural, social and psychological differentiation." (In *The Structure of Freedom* [Stanford, Calif., (1958) 1970], Christian Bay provides an important philosophical argument that emphasizes the relation between empirical, or positive, approaches to freedom and normative theories. His outline of freedom's psychological and social requisites—proposed as an empirical argument and informed by a synthesis of normative idealism and utilitarianism—relies extensively on Parsons' middle-period formulations about the nature of functional systems.)

39. I am rejecting here the Leninist and Romantic interpretations of Marx's perception of freedom, both of which emphasize a de-differentiated approach. As for the Leninist—which I do not think Marx himself ever self-consciously embraced (see Shlomo Avineri, *The Social and Political Thought of Karl Marx* [Cambridge, 1968], and George Lichtheim, *Marxism* [New York, 1965])—the conception emphasizes that individual freedom is dependent upon a fusion of state and society, which is still an "externalist" view but one with a decidedly different emphasis from that given by Marx. On the other hand, though Marx did clearly embrace elements of the Romantic vision of freedom as the end of separation between the self and the environment—a view quite contrary to the Enlightenment vision emphasized here—this was not the central thrust of his normative argument. More importantly, it was not an argument that he empirically specified in his historical theory of socialism. Only by understanding Marx's socialist vision as based on increased social differentiation can we understand his insistence on distinguishing between the "division of labor in manufacture," which he continually condemned as the dominant mode of differentiation in capitalist society, and the "division of labor in society," a situation which he viewed not simply as indicating the precapitalist economic situation but also as outlining basic elements in the postcapitalist one. In comparing the two notions, Marx contrasts the difference between capitalism as a dominant social form and the public, political discipline of economic life that characterizes a democracy.

> Division of labour within the work shop implies the undisputed authority of the capitalist over men, that are but parts of a mechanism that belongs to him. . . . The same bourgeois mind which praises [such] division of labour in the workshop, life-long annexation of the labourer to a partial operation, and his complete subjection to capital, as being an organization of labour that increases its productiveness—that same bourgeois mind denounces with equal vigour every conscious attempt to socially control and regulate the process of production, as an inroad upon such sacred things as the rights of property, freedom and unrestricted play for the bent of the individual capitalist. It is very characteristic that the enthusiastic apologists of the factory system have nothing more damning to urge

> against a general organization of the labour of society, than that it would turn all society into one immense factory. (*Capital* [Moscow, n.d.], 1:356.)

I am grateful to Dietrich Rueschemeyer for pointing out this passage in his excellent article "Structural Differentiation, Efficiency, and Power," *American Journal of Sociology* 83, no. 1 (1977):1–25. For another discussion of Marxism within the context of differentiation theory see Bob Jessop, *Social Order, Reform and Revolution* (London, 1972).

Marx never fully reconciled his continued links to the Romantic critique of alienation with this much more successfully systematized commitment to "differentiation." The separation he postulated later in life between early and later periods of socialism—the distinction that his followers turned into the contrast between socialism and communism—dramatically testifies to this ambivalence.

40. Most of these democratic ideas are contained in one form or another in Marx's "Critique of the Gotha Programme" (*Selected Works of Marx and Engels* [Moscow, 1962], 2:13–37). For the specific case for an autonomous electorate and an independent law, see his "Contribution to the Critique of Hegel's Philosophy of Right," in T. B. Bottomore, ed., *Karl Marx: Early Writings* (New York, 1963), pp. 41–60. For a general discussion of the importance of liberal perspectives on freedom in the socialist tradition, see Irving Howe, "Socialism and Liberalism: Articles of Conciliation?" *Dissent* (Winter 1977), pp. 22–35. See also Bottomore, "Karl Marx: Sociologist or Marxist?" in his *Sociology as Social Criticism* (New York, [1969] 1974), pp. 72–84, and Avineri, *The Social and Political Thought of Karl Marx* (n. 39 above).

41. Michels, *Political Parties* (New York, 1962); Marshall, *Class, Citizenship, and Social Development* (New York, 1965). For an article which implicitly links Marshall to the theory of differentiation, see Seymour Martin Lipset's "Introduction" to the latter work (pp. 15–39). Marshall's precursors in British political history, the radical Utilitarians and Fabians, would also be considered part of this tradition. For the classical discussion of the former, see Elie Halévy, *The Growth of Philosophic Radicalism* (New York, [1901–1903] 1972).

42. On the Judaic and Christian notions of divine law and the natural-law traditions of the French Enlightenment, see, e.g., Max Weber, *Ancient Judaism* (New York, 1952) and *Law in Economy and Society* (Cambridge, Mass., 1954); Benjamin Nelson, *The Idea of Usury* (Chicago, [1949] 1969); Carl L. Becker, *The Heavenly City of the Eighteenth Century Philosophers* (New Haven, Conn., 1935). For the Protestant notion of the sanctity of individual conscience and the legitimation of doubt, and its secular expression in theories of democratic rights, see Weber, *The City* (New York, 1958) and *The Protestant Ethic and the Spirit of Capitalism* (New York, [1927] 1958); Parsons, *The Structure of Social Action* (New York, [1937]

1968), pp. 51–58; David Little, *Religion, Order, and Law* (New York, 1969); Michael Walzer, *The Revolution of the Saints* (Cambridge, Mass., 1965); Edward A. Tiryakian, "Neither Marx Nor Durkheim . . . Perhaps Weber," *American Journal of Sociology* 81 (1975):1–33, esp. 24–30). For the various conceptions of freedom tied to the autonomy of secular intellectual ideas, from classical thought to modern science, see Eric Voegelin, *Order in History* (Baton Rouge, 1956), vols. 1–2; Leo Strauss, *Natural Right and History* (Chicago, 1953); Edward A. Shils, *The Intellectuals and the Powers and Other Essays* (Chicago, 1972).

43. Parsons and Platt, *The American University* (n. 28 above), p. 1. For Parsons' discussion of "institutionalized individualism," see "Durkheim's Contribution to the Theory of Integration of Social Systems," in his *Sociological Theory and Modern Society* (New York, 1967), pp. 3–34.

44. "From what source is this vital ingredient, voluntarism, obtained? . . . The inspiration for the term has its roots in Puritan social thought. To be sure, Weber and Troeltsch, whom he had studied intensively, are European intellectual influences that may have contributed to Parsons' theoretical formulation of voluntarism, but his cultural heritage is probably the primordial factor underlying the emergence of the concept. . . . [Parsons'] early critique of utilitarianism in *The Structure of Social Action* is highly consonant with the Puritans' awareness of the societal dysfunctions of economic individualism, of money making as an end in itself; however much support Protestantism gave to economic conduct, the Puritans disapproved of merchants seeking their own enrichment" (Tiryakian [n. 42 above], pp. 28–29). See Guy Rocher, *Talcott Parsons and American Sociology* (New York, 1975), pp. 1–5, and my discussion of Parsons' first critical analyses of the business community (ch. 3) in connection with the origins of the pattern-variable schema. If these cultural roots of Parsons' ideology were to be followed up—in contrast to the mainly analytical treatment in the text—Parsons might justly be discussed as one of the most distinguished representatives of the third great wave of the Protestant, moralistic, and middle-class "protectionist" response to the development of capitalist society. The first response was made by the early English Utilitarians, who insisted, more than many of their socialist confrères, that protection and democratization would have to occur in such a way as to maintain individual freedom. The second major wave of protectionist response maintained this liberal emphasis, though it reacted against the greater alienation of industrial capitalism by rejecting Utilitarianism's instrumental theory. This late nineteenth-century protective reaction can be traced throughout the major nations of the West: in the work of men like Brentano and Weber in Germany, in the movement initiated by T. H. Green and his followers in England, in the Durkheim-Bouglé-solidarist movement in France, and in the "social control" theorists in the United States. In each of these movements intellectuals stressed the need to con-

trol external conditions through moral commitments which could be seen as this-worldly or secular manifestations of religious grace. True citizenship would be created only if industrial society were changed so that discipline was internalized and order became the result of self-generated action by mutual agreement. As a more or less secularized religious response to the devastating effects of early industrialism, each movement sought to combine solidarity with voluntarism, though each differed in terms of its confidence in the state's ability to initiate such reform.

Parsons may be seen as carrying this reaction through in the third phase of capitalist society, in a situation which was far more complex and in which there had already been extensive regulation of earlier industrial excesses. The reforming impulse is still there, as is the desire to effect this reform through voluntary and internal constraint and through the construction of solidary community. What Coser has written of the early American theorists of social control—consciously echoing the "calling" of early Puritan divines—may well be said of Parsons: "The deep-rooted reformist interests of the day demanded in their forceful implications the systematic, rational, and empirical study of society and the control of a corrupt world" (Lewis A. Coser, "American Trends," in Tom Bottomore and Robert Nisbet, eds., *A History of Sociological Analysis* [New York, 1978], pp. 287–320, quoting p. 290).

The Anglo-Saxon tradition of social control can be traced back to the Scottish moralists of the eighteenth century, and as Allan Silver rightly insists, this tradition reflected the particular situation of Anglo-Saxon society. The Scottish moralists so emphasized voluntarism and self-control because "the institutions of church and state could not readily be invoked as causal sources of moral order" ("Small Worlds and the Great Society: The Social Production of Moral Order," Paper presented at the Seventy-fourth Annual Meeting of the American Sociological Association, Boston, 1979, p. 5). In relative terms, of course, Parsons must have experienced much the same situation in the American Depression years of the 1930s. Faced with a need for social reform, but also with a weak state and no institutionalized church, Parsons envisioned a reformed society as one of voluntarily cooperating and solidary individuals for whom the state would play a rather secondary role. Instead of seeing this as a grave weakness, moreover, Parsons made this necessity into a virtue, universalizing these American characteristics into the basis for democratic society in general. This is much the same transformation that Tocqueville made in the early years of the American republic, but more to my present point it is precisely the same path which the first generation of American sociologists took as well. For thinkers like Albion Small, Lester Ward, and Edward Ross, democratic reform and the good society would be achieved in much the same way. As Coser writes of Ross's work: "In contrast to those regulative institutions that operate largely in terms of outside controls on component individuals, there are, according to Ross, means of control that become effective through persuasion instead of constraint [and,] among other things, [through] public opinion, education, the emulation and imitation of extraordinary moral figures, and the creation of ideal images by artists who invite the public to live up to moral and aesthetic ideals" ("American Trends," p. 302).

Although Coser himself has usually described Parsons' work as inimical to this American reform tradition, Parsons' very different mode of theorizing should not be allowed to camouflage the striking similarities. Parsons' background, like that of these American sociological forebears, was rooted in the Social Gospel and Protestant reform movements, and his ideological emphasis, like theirs, must ultimately be traced back to Puritan roots. Silver articulates this religious connection very well in reference to the early American sociologists:

> The notion that there is something sacred, something irreducibly ultimate, about the moral texture of . . . voluntary personal relationships resonates with the tenets of free church theology and congregational theories of church government; namely, that the church is in its essence composed of compacts made among freely choosing persons in whose relationships, in the ideal case, no distinction can be made between the institutional and personal aspects. The American social control theorists, though rejecting the churches as an institutional source of moral order, nonetheless envisaged the relationship between the private, civic sphere and the Great Society in terms analogous to certain churchly doctrines: the former was to moralize the latter, by creating standards of judgment, moral personalities and value aspirations—much as free will theologies seek to penetrate unredeemed society by the force of influence and voluntary consent rather than the sacerdotal role of a formally authoritative church. ("Small Worlds," p. 9.)

Precisely the same may be said for the ideological aspirations that informed Parsons' analytical work, with two qualifications: (1) Parsons was more sympathetic to collective structures like the state than many of these American sociological pioneers; (2) this critical spirit was modulated in the later Parsons by a more quiescent ideological inclination. Yet, even in the later period, this quiescence did not exhaust Parsons' political commitment.

45. Parsons and Platt (n. 28 above), pp. 40–41.

46. This theme of the religious roots of modern individualism—as an empirical fact and a normative goal—is the thesis of Robert N. Bellah's seminal essay "Civil Religion in America" (in his *Beyond Belief* [New York, 1970], pp. 168–169). Parsons cited this essay more than any other statement on twentieth-century culture. Bellah and Parsons, of course, both have drawn on Durkheim for their conception of modern secular individualism.

47. See, e.g., Parsons, " 'Capitalism' in Recent German Literature: Sombart and Weber, I and II," *Journal of Political Economy*, no. 36 (1928) and no. 37 (1929), and "Some Reflections on the Institutional Framework of Economic Development," in his *Structure and Process in Modern Society* (New York, 1960); also Parsons and Smelser, *Economy and Society* (n. 7 above).

Cf. Enno Schwanenberg:

> The basic, and at the same time, moral supposition of the [Parsonian] theory in the face of the idea of the Hobbesian "war of all against all" is that order in modern industrial society is possible only when individuals internalize social values to eliminate destructive self-interested motivation, the crucial and most basic premise being that the values are those of a good society (Schwanenberg, "The Two Problems of Order in Parsons' Theory: An Analysis from Within," *Social Forces* 49 [1971]:569–581, quoting p. 580).

48. For Parsons' discussion of religious and cultural fundamentalism, see his middle-period essays on the radical right—e.g., "Certain Primary Sources and Patterns of Aggression in the Social Structure of the Western World," in his *Essays in Sociological Theory* (n. 21 above), pp. 298–322; for his perspective on McCarthyism, see "Social Strains in America," in his *Politics and Social Structure* (New York, 1969), pp. 163–178.

It should also be noted (see Bourricaud [n. 20 above], pp. 246–251, 271–274) that this criticism of ideologies which castigate modern societies as completely individualistic, amoral, and even degenerate also applied, in Parsons' view, to the kind of "aristocratic conservatism" (the phrase is Bourricaud's) espoused by thinkers like Pitirim Sorokin (e.g., in *Social and Cultural Dynamics* [New York, 1937], vol. 1, pt. 1) and David Riesman (e.g., *The Lonely Crowd* [New Haven, 1950]), who criticized twentieth-century capitalist societies for their self-indulgence and for their individuals' lack of moral character. (For Parsons' critical discussion of Sorokin, see "Christianity and Modern Industrial Society," in his *Sociological Theory and Modern Society* [n. 43 above], pp. 385–421; for his criticism of Riesman, see his article with Winston White, "The Link between Character and Society," in *Social Structure and Personality* [n. 1 above], pp. 183–235.) More recently, such "aristocratic conservatism" has informed the writings of some American neo-conservatives, e.g., Daniel Bell, *The Cultural Contradictions of Capitalism* (New York, 1976).

49. For his views on fascism and communism, see "Social Strains in America"; "Certain Sources and Patterns of Aggression . . ."; "Democracy and Social Structure in Pre-Nazi Germany," in *Essays in Sociological Theory*, pp. 104–123; "Some Sociological Aspects of the Fascist Movements," ibid., pp. 124–141; "The Distribution of Power in American Society," in

Politics and Social Structure, pp. 185–203; "Some Comments on the Sociology of Karl Marx," in *Sociological Theory and Modern Society* (n. 43 above), pp. 102–135.

50. "The Distribution of Power in American Society."

51. On this point, as on most others, Parsons' ideological position has often been more explicitly stated by his students than by himself. In *The American Business Creed* (Cambridge, Mass., 1956), Francis X. Sutton et al. produced an extended critique of the individualistic, laissez-faire ideology of American businessmen. Although they attack it as "unscientific," this judgment should also be taken as a value judgment reflecting a position that Parsons also shared (see n. 35 above; see also Sutton's Ph.D. thesis, "The Radical Marxist" [Harvard University, 1950]). Winston White's *Beyond Conformity* (New York, 1961) employs Parsons' structural differentiation theory as an argument against the mass-society ideology—in both its individualistic and neo-Marxist forms—that views the modern individual as isolated and helpless because of the overwhelming domination of impersonal institutional rationalization. Once again, this argument is consistent with Parsons' perspective on the place of "institutionalized individualism" in modern life (see Parsons and White, "The Mass Media and the Structure of American Society," in Parsons, *Politics and Social Structure* [n. 48 above], pp. 241–251).

A good example of Parsons' acceptance of the social-democratic tradition of T. H. Marshall—a connection which certain of Parsons' critics, like T. B. Bottomore, have denied on the grounds of Parsons' purportedly pro-capitalist "conservatism" ("Out of This World: The Sociological Theories of Talcott Parsons," in Bottomore's *Sociology as Social Criticism* [n. 40 above], pp. 29–43)—is his essay "Full Citizenship for the Negro American?" in Parsons, *Sociological Theory and Modern Society* (n. 43 above), pp. 422–465. Thus, in arguing for the extension of social as well as legal and political rights to Negro Americans, Parsons takes what he calls the "idealists" to task for ignoring the material rewards which are necessary to realize abstract legal guarantees to freedom. Parsons' commitment to political activism and reform within the parameters of his antiradicalism is clearly stated by Jackson Toby, when he characterizes the impact of Parsons' differentiation theory as follows:

> Consider one implication of this differentiation. . . . Cultures and personalities can be critical of their host societies in a way that is literally unimaginable with less differentiation. Personality systems are relatively free of social, cultural, and even organismic involvements. (Toby, review of Parsons' *System of Modern Societies* in *Contemporary Sociology* 1 [1972]:395–401, quoting 397.)

52. On the one hand, ideological critics have attacked Parsons for being anti-individualist and organicist. Thus Daniel Foss writes:

> We know that in the Parsonian world the individual doesn't have a chance. He [Parsons] instead advocates a set of assumptions which assert the desirability . . . of positive social organization. (Foss, "The World View of Talcott Parsons," in Maurice Stein and Arthur Vidich, eds., *Sociology on Trial* [Englewood Cliffs, N.J., 1963], pp. 96–126, quoting p. 112.)

Peter K. Ekeh, on the other hand, relates Parsons' conservatism to precisely the opposite problem, his individualism and anticommunitarianism: "Even though Parsons may be less individualistic than Homans, his sociology is not as Durkheimian as appearances make it seem" (Ekeh, *Social Exchange: The Two Traditions* [Cambridge, Mass., 1974], p. 12). This kind of polarization unknowingly presents the extremes which Parsons tried to bring together, a compromise that he tried to effect between the ideological poles of individualism and collectivism, freedom and tradition. It is this middle position that is effectively captured by Ken Menzies:

> Accepting a social image of man, Parsons is not a typical liberal. Rather than rooting his social philosophy in an individual seen as independent of society, Parsons sees society as central. [But] he wants a society that creates men who value individualism. (Menzies, *Talcott Parsons and the Social Image of Man* [n. 32 above], p. 122.)

Gouldner's designation of Parsons as "conservative" is based on an antihistorical, nonstructural approach to the nature of political ideology. On the one hand, he argues, a theory is conservative if it "treats institutions as given and unchangeable in essentials." On the other hand, it is still conservative if it "proposes remedies for them so that they may work better," just as long as these remedies are not "alternatives." If a theory suggests such nonalternative remedies, it "counsels acceptance of or resignation to what exists." (*Coming Crisis* [n. 2 above], p. 332.) Such a vague and diffuse definition covers everything from other-worldly mysticism and traditionalism and right-wing capitalism to Marxist social-democracy. It relates the ideological appellation not at all to class position or value commitment. When Gouldner does get down to specifics, moreover, he is often simply factually incorrect. E.g., he describes Parsons as "laissez-faire" in the 1920s and 1930s, when in fact he was something of a democratic socialist in the first decade and a strong New Dealer in the second. (For an interesting evaluation of these factual errors in Gouldner's political description of Parsons, see Seymour Martin Lipset and Everett Carll Ladd, Jr., "The Politics of American Sociologists," in *Varieties of Political Expression in Sociology* [Chicago, 1972], pp. 67–104.) Gouldner's judgments in this regard were reflective of the intensely politicized environment of the late 1960s; he seems to have significantly qualified and refined his views since.

53. Parsons, "Evolutionary Universals in Society," in *Sociological Theory and Modern Society*, pp. 490–520.

54. This point is made persuasively by Anthony D. Smith in *The Concept of Social Change* (London, 1973).

55. As I mentioned at the beginning of the preceding section, Parsons never explicitly acknowledged the ideological component of his change theory, burying his normative commitments in the argument that differentiation occurs simply for "adaptive" reasons. S. N. Eisenstadt has characterized such neglect of ideological issues in a survey of postwar modernization literature:

> Modern societies were seen as . . . coping with a continuously wider range of internal and external . . . problems. . . . Although not entirely neglected, the other qualities of modern order—rationality and extension of liberty—were seen as, or implicitly assumed to be, either following naturally from the capacity to grow and absorb change or tantamount to it. (*Tradition, Change, and Modernity* [New York, 1973], p. 14.)

Yet such ideological commitments do, in fact, structure Parsons' change theory; they simply do so in an unacknowledged way. Leon Mayhew has proved this in an ingenious way in "Ascription in Modern Societies" (*Sociological Inquiry* 38 [1968]:105–120). Taking systemic adaptation and efficiency as the sole criteria by which social structures are produced in social evolution, Mayhew indicates that on these grounds ascriptive, particularistic, and diffuse patterns are bound to be maintained—and have in fact been so—in every institutional sphere. The fact that Parsons generally ignores the continuing significance of such "conservative" structures indicates the manner in which his change theory is as much normative advocacy for universalism as empirical description of its fate.

56. Parsons, "Evolutionary Universals in Society," passim.

57. Ibid., p. 507.

58. Parsons, *The System of Modern Societies* (Englewood Cliffs, N.J., 1971), e.g., pp. 98–101.

59. For an interesting discussion of the continuum of strains that can initiate structural differentiation and social conflict, see Jan J. Loubser's "General Introduction" in Loubser et al., eds., *Explorations in General Theory in Social Science* (New York, 1976), pp. 4–5.

In the following discussion I am drawing on Parsons, "Some Considerations on the Theory of Social Change," in S. N. Eisenstadt, ed., *Readings in Social Evolution and Development* (Oxford, 1970), pp. 95–122; Parsons, "Comparative Studies and Evolutionary Change," in Ivan Vallier, ed., *Comparative Methods in Sociology* (Berkeley and Los Angeles, 1971), pp. 97–139; and Parsons and Smelser, *Economy and Society* (n. 7 above), pp. 252–284.

60. Parsons and Bales, "Conclusion: Levels of Cultural Generality and the Process of Differentiation," in their *Family, Socialization, and Interaction Process* (n. 13 above), pp. 353–396, see pp. 389–391.

61. Parsons, then, generalizes from his discussion of deviance (see ch. 3, sec. 4) to describe the actual process of differentiation. But the two processes are clearly different, a fact that Parsons' "conflict" critics have usually failed to observe. In 1956, Lewis A. Coser argued in an influential study that Parsons viewed social conflict only as deviance, that he focused only on "adjustment" and not on "structural reform" (*The Functions of Social Conflict* [New York, 1956], pp. 19 ff.). But, as my analysis indicates, this argument is inaccurate. The judgment has perhaps more relative validity when applied only to *The Social System* rather than to Parsons' work taken as a whole, for this book concentrated on change and conflict less than any of his other works. Yet even here Coser overly concentrates on the deviance chapter (ch. 7), whereas the systematic discussion of social change occurs in ch. 9, "The Processes of Change of Social Systems." Moreover, Coser's criticism ignores *Towards a General Theory of Action*, published simultaneously in 1951, and the change essays of Parsons' "early middle" period (see ch. 3). The more systematic theory of social change which Parsons began to develop in the mid-1950s represents a sophisticated extension of this earlier work, not a radical departure.

62. Parsons, "Some Considerations on the Theory of Social Change" (n. 59 above), p. 116.

63. Parsons, *The System of Modern Societies* (n. 58 above), pp. 74–78.

64. Parsons, "Some Reflections on the Institutional Framework of Economic Development," in his *Structure and Process in Modern Society* (n. 47 above), pp. 98–110.

65. Parsons and Smelser (n. 7 above), pp. 263–274.

66. The historical processes by which successful economic differentiation and the expansion of the scope of action have been achieved, and through which successive noneconomic differentiation has in turn been produced in response to the market's suppression of pre-industrial modes of societal integration, have been the main concern of Neil J. Smelser's discussions of modernization (*Social Change and the Industrial Revolution* [Chicago, 1959] and *Essays in Sociological Explanation* [Englewood Cliffs, N.J., 1968, chs. 6–8]). Parsons, White, Smelser, and Barber have compared the degree of individual freedom promoted by a differentiated economy with the pre-industrial, undifferentiated situation: Parsons and White, "The Mass Media and the Structure of American Society" (n. 51 above); Parsons and Smelser, *Economy and Society* (n. 7 above); and Bernard Barber, "The Absolutization of the Market: Some Notes on How We Got from There to Here," in G. Dworkin et al., eds., *Markets and Morals* (Washington, D.C., 1977; pp. 15–31). Jonathan Turner has applied the differentiation schema to the entire course of economic development from primitive bands to postindustrial economies in *Patterns of Social Organization* (New York, 1972), pp. 17–54.

It should now be clear that much of my analysis of the interchange model in the preceding chapter drew upon the more specific empirical and ideological commitments of Parsons' change theory, not just the presuppositions. Parsons' development of the interchange model was so thoroughly intertwined with his development of differentiation theory that such an overlap is unavoidable. In chs. 6–7, I will indicate, indeed, that this intertwining of different levels of analysis creates serious problems in Parsons' work.

67. Parsons, *The System of Modern Societies* (n. 58 above), pp. 56–64.

68. Eisenstadt's writing on the historical empires represents the broadest empirical analysis of this kind of interrelationship (*The Political System of Empires* [New York, 1963]). In discussing the differentiated conditions necessary for the democratic competition of political elites, Lipset and Rokkan have moved beyond the rationalistic formulations of Michels and placed that central ideological issue on a different plane of analysis ("Cleavage Structures, Party Systems and Voter Alignments," in Seymour Martin Lipset and Stein Rokkan, eds., *Party Systems and Voter Alignments* [New York, 1967], pp. 1–64, and Lipset, "Introduction," in Michels, *Political Parties* [n. 41 above], pp. 15–39). More recently, Rokkan has employed Parsons' multidimensional model to help create a new model of Western nation-building in the early modern period ("Dimensions of State Formation and Nation-Building: A Possible Paradigm for Research on Variations within Europe," in Charles Tilly, ed., *The Formation of National States in Western Europe* [Princeton, N.J., 1975], pp. 562–600). Smelser has analyzed the political forces that maintained a condition of functional de-differentiation in the California system of higher education in the 1960s ("Growth, Structural Change, and Conflict in California Public Higher Education, 1950–1970," in Neil J. Smelser and Gabriel Almond, eds., *Public Higher Education in California* [Berkeley and Los Angeles, 1974], pp. 9–141). On the same theme of political de-differentiation, Samuel P. Huntington has used Parsons' functional model to argue that the American political system is less independent vis-à-vis other social sectors than the European ("Political Modernization: America versus Europe," in his *Political Order in Changing Societies* [New Haven, Conn., 1968], pp. 93–139). This general perspective has also been pursued at length within the functionalist tradition of political science. For a discussion of this work, see ch. 4, sec. 3.

69. *The System of Modern Societies* (n. 58 above), pp. 50–70. For a detailed discussion of this process in terms of the interchange model, see ch. 4, sec. 4.3.

70. Ibid., pp. 87–114, and Parsons, "Full Citizenship for the Negro American?" (n. 51 above), pp. 422–465.

71. Parsons, *Societies: Evolutionary and Comparative Perspectives* (Englewood Cliffs, N.J., 1966), pp. 87–93.

72. "Full Citizenship for the Negro American?" In addition to Parsons'

discussion of the differentiation of solidarity, the writings of Little and Mayhew trace a continuum from the first delineation of distinctive secular legal rights to the successive attempts at their real institutionalization (David Little, *Religion, Order, and Law* [New York, 1969]; Leon Mayhew, *Law and Equal Opportunity* [Cambridge, Mass., 1968]). Lipset and Pitts implicitly have used the notion of integrative de-differentiation to trace the manner in which dominant class, political, and solidary groups have skewed European social developments toward fascism or communism (Seymour Martin Lipset, *The First New Nation* [New York, 1967], ch. 7, 9; Jesse R. Pitts, "Continuity and Change in Bourgeois France," in Stanley Hoffman, ed., *In Search of France* [Cambridge, Mass., 1964], pp. 249–304).

73. In a series of essays on Japan, Turkey, the countries of Western Europe, and the United States, Bellah has traced the effect of religious particularism and universalism on the possibility for achieving democratic political activism (*Beyond Belief* [n. 46 above], pt. 2). Lipset's *The First New Nation* is the most important application of the pattern-variable schema to the specific question of the impact of different kinds of Western political structures on the possibility for structural reform and the expansion of freedom.

74. Parsons, "Comparative Studies and Evolutionary Change" (n. 51 above), p. 127.

75. Ibid., pp. 127–128; Parsons, "Introduction to Culture and the Social System," in Parsons et al., *Theories of Society* (n. 30 above), pp. 976–979. This problem of value generalization is the central focus of Parsons' *Societies* (n. 71 above).

The way that this relationship between cultural generalization and the growth of individual autonomy "secularizes" Weber's Protestant ethic theme, and provides further evidence of Parsons' ideological roots in American Puritanism, has been put extremely well by Bourricaud (n. 20 above):

> Just as God acts through the general will and through impersonal commandments, society sets out the rules of the game, but it leaves to each actor the task of playing his proper role. It imposes on him nothing in detail, it does not regulate the sequence of his acts, the only obligation which it lays on him is to be autonomous, that is to say to assure the realization of his own individuality under the Law, without preventing alter [the other person] from realizing his own autonomy as well. (P. 250.)

Bellah's essay "Religious Evolution" represents the classic formulation, couched within the general framework of Parsons' multidimensional theory, of the relation between the stages of religious transcendence, social reform, and the achievement of individual freedom (*Beyond Belief*, pp. 20–50; also in William A. Lessa and Evon Z. Vogt, eds., *Reader in Comparative Religion: An Anthropological Approach* [New York, 1972], pp. 36–50). Bellah uses the concepts of symbolic differentiation, objectification, and generalization to discuss how the movement from ritual, to sacrifice and worship, and finally to prayer and religious law has contributed to the modern conception of the bounded self. On a more specific level, symbolic differentiation has been dealt with in terms of the differentiation of specialized types of cultural patterns. E.g., Parsons, Platt, Eisenstadt, Geertz, and Barber have analyzed the significant social leverage provided by the emergence of the secular morality called ideology (Parsons, "Introduction to Culture and the Social System," pp. 963–993; Parsons and Platt, *The American University* [n. 28 above], ch. 6; Eisenstadt, *The Political System of Empires* [n. 68 above], pp. 64–70, and "Religious Organization and Political Process in Centralized Empires," in his *Tradition, Change, and Modernity* [n. 68 above], pp. 169–200; Clifford Geertz, "Ideology as a Cultural System," in his *The Interpretation of Cultures* [New York, 1973], pp. 193–233; Bernard Barber, *Science and the Social Order* [New York, 1952], chs. 2, 11).

76. "Comparative Studies and Evolutionary Change," p. 127.

77. Parsons, "The Father Symbol" (n. 24 above), p. 46.

78. Parsons, "Social Structure and the Development of Personality" (n. 18 above), pp. 104 ff.

79. Parsons and Platt, *The American University*, pp. 209–215.

80. This interweaving of the Freudian understanding of individual personality growth with the ideological theory of institutionalized individualism as the product of cultural and structural differentiation has been most developed by Weinstein and Platt. In *The Wish to Be Free* (n. 31 above), they contend that it was the development of structural differentiation that eventually created in nineteenth-century Western society the opportunity for successful Oedipal rebellion and separation from social and familial authority. In turn, they argue that this expansion of the developmental process and increase in psychological autonomy were themselves crucial and independent variables in the subsequent development of freedom in other social spheres. Such a historical analysis of the interplay between psychic and social differentiation has also been pursued by Bellah in a suggestive essay, "Father and Son in Confucianism and Christianity" (*Beyond Belief*, pp. 76–99). Bellah follows Erik H. Erikson in describing how universalistic developments in the religious sphere provide a point of leverage for the development of greater psychological control over primary object relations, particularly over those objects associated with authority and domination. The emerging autonomy of families, peer groups, and schools, and their relation to the expansion of individual control, has been discussed, respectively, by Smelser (*Social Change in the Industrial Revolution* [n. 66 above]; by Eisenstadt (*From Generation to Generation* [n. 29 above] and Parsons ("Youth in the Context of American Society," in his *Social Structure and Personality* [New

York, 1964], pp. 155–182); and by Robert Dreeben (*On What Is Learned in School* [Reading, Mass., 1968]), Parsons ("The School Class as a Social System," in his *Social Structure and Personality* [n. 1 above], pp. 129–154), and Parsons and Platt (*The American University*).

81. This historical discussion of the lengthening and internal differentiation of the socialization process provides the same kind of sociology-of-knowledge perspective on the Resource Chart (see sec. 1.1 above) as the discussion of social differentiation provides for the interchange model. Though the sequential "production" of individuals is an inevitable part of any society, institutional organization around these imperatives only occurs with increased social differentiation. The theoretical understanding of the Resource Chart could, therefore, only occur at a certain stage of historical development. This reasoning applies also to the relationship between the theoretical understanding of interchange and the actual differentiation of the social system.

The distinction I am making between a general multidimensional perspective on order and the specific historical form that order takes in a more differentiated society points to a difficulty in Richard Münch's account of Parsons' change theory, which in many other respects is an extremely illuminating one. Münch argues that in Parsons' theory it is greater "interpenetration," not greater "differentiation," that characterizes evolutionary development (see, e.g., "Talcott Parsons and the Theory of Action, I: The Structure of the Kantian Core," *American Journal of Sociology* 86 [1981]:709–739, esp. pp. 718–727). By interpenetration, Münch means, in general, the interrelation of values and interests and, more specifically, the interchange and mutual control of societal subsystems. I have argued above (see ch. 2, secs. 2.2, 3.1) that such interpenetration must be viewed as a presuppositional commitment. To try to use it simultaneously to describe an empirical-historical situation—not to mention an ideological or moral ideal—is to conflate different levels of analysis and to create some otherwise avoidable theoretical confusion.

In terms of these issues, the view I have presented in the present discussion is as follows. Parsons viewed interpenetration as a historical constant. What he regarded as variable, as subject to change, were the normative and structural standards according to which each interpenetrating dimension and system was defined. Would the interpenetration of dimensions and systems all be geared to the same standard—e.g., the standards supplied by kinship in primitive societies—or would they interpenetrate on the basis of more differentiated, relatively autonomous criteria? To cite a specific dimension: in all societies there is interpenetration between cultural and noncultural systems in an analytical sense; the important question for social change is how universalistic are the cultural norms that interpenetrate with this society.

Thus, it is true that in Confucian and Hindu societies the universalistic ethical order does not permeate the entire social order: these religions are confined to a narrow elite and grace is distributed differentially according to status. Yet this is an empirical statement: *all* the actors and strata in the society are, nonetheless, still thoroughly interpenetrated by *some* cultural system, whether it is the high culture of Confucianism and Hinduism or not. To have the kind of thoroughgoing ethical interpenetration of the society which Weber considered so important, one must have an extraordinarily differentiated and abstract cultural system. Yet cultural systems, Parsons believed, could not contest and criticize cultural order—in Münch's terms, could not "interpenetrate" with it—unless they were firmly independent and differentiated from it in an empirical sense.

It is revealing, in this context, that toward the end of his second article on Parsons' change theory Münch acknowledges that Parsons himself did not actually use the term *interpenetration* in the manner he proposes: "Parsons tended to write as if every concrete action had to be thought of as a product of the interpenetration of subsystems" ("Talcott Parsons and the Theory of Action, II: The Continuity of the Development," *American Journal of Sociology* 87 [1982]:771–826, quoting 791, n. 13). He did so, I would argue, precisely for the reasons presented here. Münch's dismissal of the differentiation concept has, it seems to me, more to do with the internal German debate than with its actual use in Parsons' work. It is clear that Münch is in a debate with Niklas Luhmann, whose own theory of differentiation severely underestimates the continuing role of cultural systems, i.e., the fact of interpenetration in Münch's sense.

82. Thus Parsons writes that in modern societies "the mobility of resources, and of agent-product relations associated with high levels of societal differentiation," necessarily introduces "factors of instability . . . which were not equally prominent in less 'advanced' societies." And again:

> With differentiation of a system into kinds of units, which contribute differentially to the meeting of the various functional exigencies of the system, a new order of mechanisms of integration and of adaptation *must* emerge. . . . The "solution" of this dilemma lies in the institutionalization of *generalized* normative patterns which are compatible with adaptive flexibility in particular situations. ("The Point of View of the Author," in Black, *The Social Theories of Talcott Parsons* [n. 30 above], pp. 343–344, italics in original.)

Bourricaud (n. 20 above) writes perceptively about Parsons' sensitivity to the greater potential for instability of a differentiated order. Parsons realized, Bourricaud writes, that "internalized values are at once too general, too ambiguous, too badly sanctioned to assure a perfect equation between their ideal exigencies and our actual behavior" (p. 290). Social integration in a modern society, then, cannot be an "expressive totality" in which social-system parts articulate some overarching value system, in a

Hegelian sense; rather, integration must be perceived "as an effort at *compatibilisation* . . . among partial orders" (p. 21). While differentiation can, in principle, contribute to "a world of equilibriated and balanced activities, [it can] just as easily . . . place us in a disarticulated world of partially isolated and conflicting activities" (p. 334). It is to this possibility of disarticulation that Parsons directed his theory of media generalization.

83. Parsons, "On the Concept of Value Commitments," in *Politics and Social Structure* (n. 48 above), pp. 439–472. For a discussion of the need for "generalized media" in his middle-period work, before the concept was formally introduced, see Parsons and Shils, *Towards a General Theory of Action* (n. 1 above), p. 216.

The German sociological theorist Niklas Luhmann has elaborated at great length upon this relationship between the individualizing changes that make modern society more complex and differentiated and the need for generalized media that generate trust without eliminating the reality of choice. In Luhmann's translation of Parsons' insight, generalized media are necessary because modern life is more than ever "contingent." "A fact is contingent," Luhmann writes, "when seen as selection from other possibilities which remain in some sense possibilities despite a selection," and as examples of such modern contingencies he points to "the objective world, the concrete self with its biography, conscious life, decisions and expectations and other persons with their experiences and choices" ("Generalized Media and the Problem of Contingency," in Loubser, *Explorations in General Theory in Social Science* [n. 59 above], pp. 507–532, quoting p. 508). The phenomenon of "generalization," according to Luhmann, is developed to "solve" the problem of contingency by "reducing the complexity" of the world faced by any individual actor.

> [Media] employ their selection pattern as a motive to accept the reduction, so that people join with others in a narrow world of common understandings, complementary expectations, and determinable issues. Media are not only words, symbols, or codes; they are meaningful constellations of combined selectivity which can be signified by words, symbolized, and codified legally, methodologically, or otherwise. (P. 512.)

Because of the primacy of his emphasis on contingency (see also his *Trust and Power* [New York, 1980]), Luhmann brings out more strongly than Parsons himself the relation between the normative generalization of media theory and the individualistic dilemmas emphasized in such a quintessentially modern philosophy as existentialism. (In the essay just cited, e.g., Luhmann insists at one point that "we should try to link the concept of generalized media more directly to the central problem of the subjective contingency of orientation and choice" ["Generalized Media," p. 507].) I will indicate below, however, that he does so partly at the expense of the multidimensional and systemic potential of Parsons' original work.

84. Parsons, "On the Concept of Influence," in *Politics and Social Structure*, pp. 405–429.

85. Parsons, " 'Voting' and the Equilibrium of the American Political System," in *Politics and Social Structure* (n. 43 above), pp. 204–240, quoting p. 222.

86. I am generalizing here from Parsons' scattered writings on elites, particularly on the following: "A Revised Analytical Approach to the Theory of Social Stratification," in *Essays in Sociological Theory* (n. 21 above), pp. 386–439; "The Distribution of Power in American Society," in *Politics and Social Structure*, pp. 185–203; *The System of Modern Society* (n. 58 above), pp. 86–121; and Parsons and Smelser, *Economy and Society* (n. 7 above), pp. 246–294.

87. For the sociological studies that have elaborated and refined this notion of functional elites, see, most importantly, Suzanne Keller, *Beyond the Ruling Class* (New York, 1963); see also A. Etzioni, "The Fundamental Differentiation of Elites in the Kibbutz," *American Journal of Sociology* 64 (1959):476–487.

88. "The Distribution of Power in American Society."

89. Implicit in Parsons' argument is the notion that the "personalistic" or biographical approach to elites has obscured the crucial, functional reference to their actual performance. Given the fact of structural differentiation, it is possible in principle for members of the same social class, as defined by background and birth, to carry out opposed and conflicting social functions. Smelser, although he rarely speaks of classes and elites in this way, provides an important illustration of this point in his *Social Change in the Industrial Revolution* (n. 66 above). Smelser discusses, e.g., the crucial role of the British parliamentary commissions in providing early reform of industrial capitalism. By responding quickly to crisis, the commissions proposed and legitimated factory reform and child labor acts, the effect of which was to take some of the edge off the radical labor protest of the day. Yet participants in these commissions were often—in terms of birth and social network—members of the same upper class whose industrial capitalists staunchly opposed these reforms in the economic realm. The commissioners had created reform, in other words, because of their differentiated function in a democratic, constitutional state. Because of its differentiation, the state was bound not to respond simply to economic developments but to religious dissent, legal sanctions, and political protest.

This discussion illustrates the error made by critics who have argued that Parsons wanted to erect a new, politically-based ruling class (Andrew Hacker, "Sociology and Ideology," in Black, *The Social Theories of Talcott Parsons* [n. 30 above], pp. 307–308, and Daniel Foss, "The World View of Talcott Parsons" [n. 52 above]). Parsons' occasional calls for a "political class" are, rather, directed toward the creation of a more powerful, differentiated political elite that would more effectively hold its own, as a representative of the "whole," against other dimensional interests and elites. (See my discussion of Parsons' analysis of the roots of American McCarthyism, in ch. 3, sec. 4.)

This debate between the personalistic and functional approaches also occurs in both the Marxist and the non-Marxist radical critiques of elite domination. See, e.g., the debate over Mills' personalistic approach between Andrew Hacker, William Domhoff, and Maurice Zeitlin in *The New York Review of Books*, May 1, 1975, pp. 9–13 and July 17, 1975, pp. 45–46. See also the controversy, conducted more completely from within Marxism, between Nico Poulantzas and Ralph Miliband in Miliband, *The State and Capitalist Society* (New York, 1969), and Poulantzas, *Political Power and Social Classes* (London, 1972), and Poulantzas, "The Problem of the Capitalist State," and Miliband, "Reply to Poulantzas," in Robin Blackburn, ed., *Ideology in Social Science* (New York, 1973), pp. 238–253, 253–262. It should be clear that the argument for "functional elites" addresses the same issue of personalism versus institutional responsibility. As Keller writes in the work which developed the implications of Parsons' class, or elite, theory more than any other:

> In constructing his model of the social system by means of analytical rather than historical building blocks, Parsons has avoided the pitfalls of various determinist explanations of the social order in which certain social factors are overemphasized because they loom large in the mind of the observer (*Beyond the Ruling Class* [n. 87 above], p. 93).

This argument about the relation between structural differentiation and the differentiation of elites also has significant repercussions for the analysis of non-capitalist elites. The British political sociologist David Lane has used the more complex structure of Parsonian theory to insist that neither the Weberian-inspired "totalitarian" models of socialist industrial society nor the Marxist-inspired "new ruling class" models are correct. Both imply the complete domination of complexly differentiated societies by a single group, a situation only somewhat less empirically unlikely in industrially Communist societies than the absolute domination of capitalist societies by a ruling class. Lane insists, therefore, that Communist states must be considered within the framework of differentiated industrial societies, in which "ruling groups become dependent on the various functional groups and have to take account of their interests."

> It becomes more difficult [in the industrial situation], not less, for the ruling groups to maintain effective control of the population. Communications, for example, are international and transcend geographical areas and political boundaries. Universal literacy which characterises industrial states gives far greater access to science, cultural and "deviant ideas" than that known in pre-modern society. In practice, it is impossible for

> governments to encapsulate their citizens and it is notoriously difficult for them to root out either political or criminal deviance. (*The Socialist Industrial State* [Boulder, Colo., 1976], p. 49.)

Only by acknowledging the elements of pluralism in such Communist societies, Lane suggests, is it possible to recognize the sources and patterns of strains that can lead to change. Such strains exist because the political systems of party-domination occur in relatively functionally differentiated social systems with relatively autonomous elites.

> In terms of the Parsonian interchange model, exchange between the various sub-systems is controlled by the polity [in Communist societies]—though there is feedback between it and the other sub-systems. This exchange (or lack of it) has varied over time and directs attention to tensions in the social system. The model includes not only tensions between ideal goals (such as egalitarianism) and economic efficiency (the need for income differentials), but also helps one to identify conflicts between various institutional interests—those concerned with value articulation (party ideologists), enforcement (police), goal attainment (government industries) and the economy (managerial groups). (Ibid., p. 67.)

Lane argues for the Parsonian over the Marxist model of elite conflict on the same grounds, that it points to the more realistically diverse sources of systemic strain. "A Parsonian model," he suggests in a criticism of Marxist analyses of the Soviet Union, "would point to unreciprocated, and unequal and exploitative exchange relationships, rather than a class conflict dichotomy" ("Towards a Sociological Model of Socialist Society," Paper presented in the Ninth Annual Meeting of the International Sociological Association, Uppsala, Sweden, 1978, p. 21, n. 5).

For another empirical application of this analytic approach to stratification, see, e.g., Amitai Etzioni, "The Functional Differentiation of Elites in the Kibbutz" (n. 87 above), and also Alvin Boskoff's argument that interfunctional mobility has been unduly ignored in more traditionally Weberian approaches to mobility ("Stratification, Power, and Social Change," in Herman Turk and Richard L. Simpson, eds., *Institutions and Social Exchange* [Indianapolis, 1971], pp. 289–308). The most detailed empirical application of this functional elite theory, which also breaks some new theoretical ground in terms of the processes by which the differentiation of elites may or may not occur, is Paul B. Colomy, "Stunted Differentiation: A Sociological Examination of Virginia's Political Elite, 1720–1850" (Ph.D. diss., University of California, Los Angeles, 1982).

90. Coser, *The Functions of Social Conflict* (n. 61 above), p. 21. But see also the relatively anomalous position of *The Social System* (n. 61) in this respect.

91. Coser, p. 154. Cf. John Rex, *Key Problems in Sociological Theory* (London, 1961), pp. 116 ff.

92. Coser, p. 154.

93. Ibid., pp. 15–31; Rex, pp. 131–135; Dahrendorf, *Class and Class Conflict in Industrial Society* (Stanford, Calif., 1959), pp. 120–123.

94. This is the principal criticism against functionalist change theory leveled by Anthony Smith in *The Concept of Change* (London, 1973); it is also a major point in Alejandro Portes, "On the Sociology of National Development: Theories and Issues," *American Journal of Sociology* 82 (1976):53–85. Robert A. Nisbet placed this antifunctionalist critique in the broadest perspective in *Social Change and History* (New York, 1969; esp. pp. 223–239, 251–266). The fact that such antithetical complaints could be made against "functionalist" reasoning about change suggests, of course, that there is nothing intrinsically functionalist about internalist versus externalist understandings of system change. It also suggests, I think, the kind of radical misunderstandings to which Parsons' change theory has been subject. The opposing evaluations, it should be emphasized, do not reflect changes that actually took place in Parsons' theory, for though intrasystem differentiation becomes more explicit in the later work, an enormous amount of attention was paid to internal sources of change in the middle-period writings, including *The Social System* (pp. 249–325, 505–535). The striking divergence of interpretations represents, instead, selective attention and misunderstanding on the part of the interpreters themselves. This is nowhere more clearly demonstrated than in Hermann Strasser and Susan C. Randall's *An Introduction to the Theories of Social Change* (London, 1981), where Parsons' theory is accused of being both too intrasystemic and too extrasystemic.

> The model of a stable equilibrium in particular leaves only "one point of view from which the problem of structural change can be analyzed—by relating it to the *influence of powerful exogenous forces*" [M. Guessous, "A General Critique of Equilibrium Theory," in W. E. Moore, R. Cook, eds., *Readings on Social Change*, Englewood Cliffs, N.J., 1967, p. 27, original ital.]. [Parsons] expresses this idea in system-theoretical terms. (P. 81.)

> [Because] functional analysis places emphasis on the interdependence of a system's parts and their role in producing change, it seems to have the (desired) effect of excluding the randomness of change sources located outside the system (p. 141).

95. Dahrendorf, *Class and Class Conflict*, p. 268.

96. Ibid., pp. 268, 270, italics added.

97. Ibid., pp. 272–276.

98. Weinstein and Platt have criticized Dahrendorf's pluralization theory on other grounds. They argue that, because it ignores the role of socialized values, it traces effects whose causes it cannot explain.

> Dahrendorf indicates that institutionalization began with the process of [working-class] inclusion in both economic and political spheres. . . .

> However, the concept of institutionalization is misleading in this context unless it includes the concept of internalization. . . . It was the internalization of these [inclusive] values, not merely their institutionalization, which inhibited conflict in capitalist societies. (*Psychoanalytic Sociology* [n. 30 above], p. 26, n. 42.)

Because Marxism is the quintessential "conflict theory," it is revealing, for similar reasons, to compare Parsons' differentiation theory with the approach to change taken by Jürgen Habermas, the Frankfurt school neo-Marxist. The purpose Habermas has set for himself—to preserve Marx's ideological commitment to freedom while transforming the instrumentalism of his theoretical apparatus—leads him ineluctably to a change theory that resembles Parsons'. Differentiation theory, however, clearly can be viewed as subsuming Habermas' theory of communication distortion. In working out the latter idea (*Knowledge and Human Interest* [Boston, 1973], p. 315), Habermas' intention is to construct a theory of human "evolution toward autonomy and responsibility" keyed to the ideal of increased "freedom from domination." In order to do so, he realizes that his theory must measure progress toward "human adulthood" on the psychological level, and he incorporates Freudian and Piagetian concepts to accomplish this (*Towards a Rational Society* [Boston, 1970], p. 119; *Theory and Practice* [Boston, 1973], p. 256). Habermas acknowledges further that, in addition to including the structural emphasis of Marx, he must address the problem of the historical development of moral systems (*Theory and Practice*, pp. 2–3) and the preconditions of an autonomous public opinion, one with the capacity to mediate between a society and its social values (*Towards a Rational Society*, pp. 72–74). Despite the often brilliant texture of his argument, however, Habermas has failed, until recently, to make significant empirical progress on these questions. This failure can be linked, I believe, to his insufficient regard for the complexity of social life. In addressing the issues of institutional interrelation and the relation of institutions and personality, Habermas has simply lacked the theoretical vocabulary to distinguish the complex causal processes involved. On the issue of moral and symbolic development, moreover, he has had no substantive theory at all. Only in his most recent work (*Legitimation Crisis* [Boston, 1975]) has Habermas begun to surmount these difficulties. It is far from accidental that he has done so only by drawing extensively on Parsons' theoretical system.

See the concluding words in Münch's work on Parsons' change theory: "There is no comparable theory in sociology today which has established such a depth and breadth in the understanding of change, conflict, power, authority, and other areas of study which have been favored by 'critical' sociologies" ("Talcott Parsons and the Theory of Action, II: The Continuity of Development" [n. 81 above], p. 819).

99. But this concept was implicit in all of Parsons' previous discussions

of change and conflict. For explicit reference to differentiation in these works, see *The Social System* (n. 1 above), pp. 174 ff., and *Essays in Sociological Theory* (n. 21 above), p. 133.

100. Gouldner, *The Coming Crisis in Western Sociology* (n. 2 above), pp. 199, 214-215. By this time (1970), however, it was becoming so difficult to maintain this fallacious position that Gouldner was forced to introduce residual categories into his analysis whenever he wrote directly about Parsons' work. Indeed, Gouldner must characterize even the middle-period discussions of change—of which he identifies only a few—as "non-Parsonian" and Marxist (pp. 354–357). As for differentiation itself, he seeks to convince his reader that this entire theory of change somehow did not represent Parsons' real theoretical ideas. He writes about the "Parsons-Marx Convergence" (pp. 357–370) as if this later change theory was residual to Parsons' theoretical development. I have shown in this section, to the contrary, that the theory follows directly from Parsons' middle-period writing and from his ideological commitments, and that it is firmly rooted in his conception of social-system interchange as well.

101. It is ironic that the best succinct response to these conflict critics can be found in the work of a critic of Parsons who is more committed to orthodox Marxist analysis than his earlier conflict critics. John G. Taylor exposes the fallacy of the conflict critique—how it wrongly conflates ideological criticism with empirical commitment—in his *From Modernization to Modes of Production* (London, 1979):

> The various "conflict theorists" (notably, Dahrendorf, Rex, and Lockwood) argued that structural-functionalism was incapable of analysing the emergence of social conflict, and, more particularly, that form of disruptive conflict which produced fundamental changes in the functioning of the social system. Yet, if we refer to sections of *The Social System* that analyse social change, or to Parsons and Smelser's formulations in *Economy and Society*, or Smelser's analysis of the Industrial Revolution in *Social Change and the Industrial Revolution*, it is clear that they do provide an account of conflict arising as a result of changes produced in the social structure by transformations in the operation of its various sub-systems. They also provide analysis of the effects of this conflict on the continuing reproduction of the structure, showing how this necessitates fundamental changes in its reproduction. Because the various sub-systems must fulfill particular functions in order that society can reproduce itself, and because, in order to do this, there must be constant interchanges between systems which develop unevenly, there is a constant basis for the generation of conflict. Contrary to the conflict critics' conclusions, it is the very relations which they criticise between sub-systems and structural reproduction that generate conflict. Furthermore, the "disruptive" conflict which the critics view as a crucial omission, can also be analysed from within structural-functionalist theory. The uneven devel-

> opment of sub-systems and their elements can generate strains which then provide the basis for a generalized conflict which can only be resolved by major transformations in the dominant value-system or economic structure. Such disruptive conflict, which induces fundamental changes in the reproduction of the structure and its elements, is, for example, the object of Smelser's analysis in *Social Change*. The criticisms of the conflict theorists can, it seems, be met from within Parsonian theory. (Pp. 4–5.)

Taylor's comments indicate, once again, the greater theoretical sophistication which is often exhibited by Marxist theorists relative to conflict theorists. A good Marxist theorist will be compelled, indeed, to reject the theoretical rationales which have been the major legitimations for conflict theory—the claim, e.g., that system or equilibrium models are inherently committed to empirical stability, or the notion that only instrumental, antinormative action can be tied to the depiction of antagonistic and disruptive social groups. I have made this point at greater length in the conclusion to vol. 2.

102. Parsons and Smelser (n. 7 above), p. 292.

103. The best presentation by Weber of this multidimensional approach to rationalization is the "Author's Introduction" to his essays in the sociology of religion. Though one of the last essays Weber wrote, it is published in English with *The Protestant Ethic and the Spirit of Capitalism* (New York, 1927), pp. 13–31.

104. Thus Smelser has placed the arguments Weber made about rationalization in the concluding pages of *The Protestant Ethic and the Spirit of Capitalism* into the context of "economic differentiation":

> Weber notes that, at the beginning of the twentieth century, when the capitalistic system was already highly developed, it no longer needed the impetus of ascetic Protestantism. By virtue of its conquest of much of Western society, capitalism had solidly established an institutional base and a secular value system of its own—economic rationality. Its secular economic values had no further need for the "ultimate" justification they had required during the newer, unsteadier days of economic revolution. Such lines of differentiation constitute the secularization of religious values. In the same process, other institutional spheres—economic, political, scientific, etc.—become more nearly established on their own. (Neil J. Smelser, *Essays in Sociological Explanation*, Englewood Cliffs, N.J., 1968, p. 135.)

It should be clear from this statement, however, that Smelser is arguing that Weber himself actually makes this point, that "differentiation" is simply a direct translation of Weber's ideas rather than a theoretical reconstitution and synthesis of the Weberian theory. This approach to Weber's change theory, of course, follows Parsons' own lead, for Parsons continually denied that he had altered Weberian analysis in any substantial way. This is as true for his treatment of Weber's change theory as for his analysis of Weber's general political and religious sociologies.

Despite the fact that at every point differentiation theory actually transforms Weber's rationalization theory by relating it to different presuppositional and ideological propositions, Parsons argues that his theory merely provides a more effective way of expressing Weber's insights. In one sense, this disavowal represents Parsons' deference to "traditional" intellectual authority, a response which I have noted at various points. In another sense, the identification represents an attempt to rewrite the history of sociological theory according to the convergence thesis. Finally, the argument that Weber's path was really his own also constitutes a subtle form of rebellion on Parsons' part. It is precisely this ambiguity, as manifest in the poetic sphere, that has been so effectively articulated by Harold Bloom:

> [Among the great poets, there is] the triumph of having so stationed the precursor, in one's own work, that particular passages in his work seem to be not presages of one's own advent, but rather to be indebted to one's own achievement and even (necessarily) to be lessened by one's greater splendor. . . . The mighty dead return, but they return in our own colors. . . . In the exquisite squalors of Tennyson's "The Holy Grail," as Percival rides out on his ruinous quest, we can experience the hallucination of believing that the Laureate is overly influenced by [Eliot's] *The Waste Land*. (*The Anxiety of Influence* [New Haven, Conn., 1973], pp. 141–142.)

In reading Weber's *Protestant Ethic*, Parsons and Smelser would have us believe, we are actually reading about the changes they describe in their own *Economy and Society*.

105. The positive and negative elements are captured in Eisenstadt's description of the strains that produced imperial bureaucracy. In his translation of Weber's patrimonialism-feudalism theory into Parsons' differentiation approach, he writes that, "as the major social spheres and groups became increasingly autonomous and differentiated from other institutional systems and groups, as they became less embedded in one another, their interaction could no longer be regulated only or mainly by their internal, common, or complementary mechanism." Autonomy and increased freedom occurred because "the integration of any group into the total society and its loyalty to the society" was not nearly "so self-evident as in less differentiated societies." At the same time, however, it was "the emergence of different types of groups, each with different structure and problems, which precluded uniform regulation of their interrelations" (*The Political System of Empires* [n. 68 above], pp. 95–96).

106. Parsons, "Authority, Legitimation, and Political Action," in his *Structure and Process in Modern Society* (n. 47 above), pp. 170–198.

107. Parsons, *The System of Modern Societies* (n. 58 above), pp. 56–64.

108. Parsons, "Introduction," in Max Weber, *The Sociology of Religion* (Boston, 1963), pp. ix–lvii. Here—once again, implicitly—Parsons ties Weber's discussion of the historical development of religion to his own theory of cultural differentiation and social evolution. In terms of Parsons' statements about cultural development and his characterization of his relation to Weber's theory, this is one of his most important essays.

109. In his essay "Rationality and Freedom: Max Weber and Beyond," Donald N. Levine puts this problem in Weber's work very well.

> [The] Weberian argument seems most wanting in its inattention to the social psychological context of autonomous decision-making. . . . The most profound correction of his vision may perhaps lie in the incorporation of those hypotheses which thinkers like Aristotle and Durkheim considered bedrock: that the human capacity for autonomous moral judgment must be based on nonrationally grounded habits of character instilled well before humans are fully capable of mature deliberative choice, and that continuing social support is of the greatest relevance to the capacity for subjective rationality and freedom. (*Sociological Inquiry* 51 [1981]:5–25, quoting 23.)

Parsons' socialization theory, which built upon the synthesis of Freud and Durkheim, is the most precise and far-reaching attempt to supplement Weber's theory of individual autonomy in this way.

110. See Philip Rieff's comparison of these works in *Freud: The Mind of the Moralist* (New York, 1959), pp. 281–328.

111. At this point it should not be necessary to point out that Parsons always camouflaged these confrontations with his classical predecessors by "reading" them in ways that made them complementary to the analysis I have presented in this final section as his own original contribution. This reading was, e.g., the purpose of Parsons' "Introduction" to his translation of Weber's *Theory of Social and Economic Organization* (New York, 1947), as it was also the buried aim of his "Durkheim's Theory of the Integration of Social Systems" (n. 43 above), written in 1960. While these essays stand as two of the most brilliant interpretations of the founders of sociology, they must also be seen as sociological theories of change in their own right. The fact that these imposing "interpretations" have spawned generations of Weberian and Durkheimian interpreters who have argued over the meaning of the classics on the grounds that Parsons himself set—and thus, implicitly, in terms of Parsonian theory itself—has made the originality and distinctiveness of Parsons' interpretations difficult to see. The most impressive examples of such Parsonian-inspired secondary interpretation are, in relation to Durkheim, Bellah's "Durkheim and History" (*American Sociological Review* 24 [1959]:447–461) and the Introduction to his selections, *Emile Durkheim on Morality and Society* (Chicago, 1974), and, in relation to Weber, Wolfgang Schluchter's on Weber's theory of historical rationalization (e.g., "The Paradoxes of Rationaliza-

tion" and "Value-Neutrality and the Ethic of Responsibility" in Guenther Roth and Schluchter, *Max Weber's Vision of History: Ethics and Methods* [Berkeley and Los Angeles, 1979]), and S. N. Eisenstadt's Introduction to his selections, *Max Weber on Charisma and Institution Building* (Chicago, 1965). The work of these seminal interpreters is directly filtered through Parsons' differentiation theory. In this sense they can be seen as elaborations, although at the same time each goes beyond Parsons' framework in significant ways.

CHAPTER SIX

1. Talcott Parsons, "The Present Position and Prospects of Systematic Theory in Sociology," in his *Essays in Sociological Theory* (New York, 1954), pp. 238–274.

2. The best historical discussion of the struggle to maintain an open, multilevel approach to theorizing in sociology is S. N. Eisenstadt and M. Curelaru, *The Form of Sociology: Paradigms and Crises* (New York, 1976). See my review in *Contemporary Sociology* 6, no. 6 (November 1977):658–661.

3. See also, later in Parsons' career, *The Social System* (New York, 1951), pp. 335–348.

4. See the discussion of these thinkers in vol. 1, pp. 20–30.

5. For an analysis of this strand in Parsons' discussion, see ch. 2, sec. 1.

6. Parsons, *The Structure of Social Action* (New York, [1937] 1968), p. 11.

7. Ibid., p. 4.

8. On this point, see Ken Menzies, *Talcott Parsons and the Social Image of Man* (London, 1977), p. 16.

9. *Structure of Social Action*, p. 11.

10. Ibid., pp. 347, 362, italics added.

11. Ibid., p. 362, italics added.

12. Ibid., italics added.

13. Ibid., p. 347, italics added.

14. For a discussion of the "accumulationist" perspective on theoretical transformation in science and its important role in the contemporary positivist position, see vol. 1 (e.g., pp. 6–8, 181–182).

15. *Structure of Social Action*, p. 52, italics added.

16. For a technical discussion of the differentiation of logical empiricist from logical positivist thought, see vol. 1, pp. 19 ff. The logical empiricists—of whom Karl Popper may be considered an illustrious though in some ways maverick illustration—broke from the strict correspondence model proposed by the Vienna positivists because they came to realize the impossibility of verifying a general law through concrete and specific pieces of empirical evidence. The logical empiricists allowed more general

conceptual development and proposed to close the gap—for verification purposes—between general laws and specific cases through "bridging" principles of various types. They strongly maintained, nonetheless, that the differentations between theories and facts were plain to see, and that the one could cleanly test the other once and for all. Popper realized that verification as such would be impossible, and proposed that the bridging principles were useful only to falsify general laws and schemas. While Popper's "falsificationism" was more realistic than the "verificationism" of his empiricist colleagues, he continued to maintain the untenable theory/fact distinction. I am suggesting here that Parsons wavers ambiguously between this general "empiricist" position and the genuinely post-positivist position—where the objectively based theory/fact distinction is broken down—which I presented in vol. 1 (pp. 18–30). Stephen P. Savage writes in a similar way about the "paradox" of Parsons' theory of knowledge in *The Theories of Talcott Parsons* (New York, 1981). Refering to Parsons' theoretical insistence on systemic models, Savage asks: "How do we know that action takes the form of systems?—because sociology [i.e., theory] informs us that that is the case. But then we are also told that the [real] factual order (systems of action) is the *condition* of that knowledge." (P. 88, italics added.)

17. The best historical documentation of this generational perspective is in H. Stuart Hughes, *Consciousness and Society* (New York, 1958). Though this work is strongly influenced by Parsons' *Structure of Social Action*, it takes a very different view of the intellectual history of this period.

18. *Structure of Social Action*, p. 14, italics added.

19. The artificial quality of this convergence thesis is no more effectively illustrated than in *Theories of Society* (New York, 1961), which Parsons edited with Edward A. Shils, Kaspar D. Naegele, and Jesse R. Pitts. This enormous reader organizes all pre-Parsonian social theory as anticipations or adumbrations of different parts of Parsonian "action theory." As a compilation of different theoretical statements, this book is not without interest, and one could make the argument that, properly conceived, the most important elements of earlier theory can "fit" at various points into Parsons' synthetic framework. But this is an analytic, not a historical argument. Given Parsons' empiricist search for convergence, however, the argument in *Theories of Society* has a definite historical aspect: through empirical and conceptual advances, earlier social theories gradually worked up to modern, Parsonian theory. Parsons was, of course, aware that this argument implied a kind of theoretical consensus which did not, as yet, completely exist. But instead of relating extant contemporary conflict to competing presuppositional commitments, he attributed it simply to the temporal lag between his own theoretical discoveries and developments in sociological subfields. As he put this issue in 1959, in his

essay "An Approach to Psychological Theory in Terms of the Theory of Action":

> As the sciences of behavior mature, they will not continue to be the province of a plurality of competing "schools" of theoretical interpretation, but will tend to converge on a logically integrated but also highly differentiated conceptual scheme. . . .What at one time have been considered competing and incompatible schools of theory in a special field will be shown to be special cases of a more general theory, each of which is fruitfully applicable within the range of its own limitations. (In Sigmund Koch, ed., *Psychology: A Study of a Science* [New York, 1959] 3:703.)

20. *Structure of Social Action*, ch. 17.
21. Ibid., p. 697.
22. Ibid., p. 721.
23. For a postpositivist understanding of scientific objectivity, see my discussion in vol. 1, pp. 113–126.
24. Parsons, "Introduction to Culture and the Social System," in *Theories of Society* (n. 19 above), pp. 963–993, quoting p. 965, italics added.
25. Ibid., italics added.
26. Parsons, "The Point of View of the Author," in Max Black, ed., *The Social Theories of Talcott Parsons* (Ithaca, N.Y., 1961), pp. 311–363, quoting p. 340, italics added.
27. Ibid., p. 339.
28. Black, "Some Questions about Parsons' Theories," ibid., pp. 268–288, quoting p. 265.
29. See, e.g., Arthur L. Stinchcombe, *Constructing Social Theories* (New York, 1968), p. 6.
30. Parsons, "The Prospects of Sociological Theory," in his *Essays in Sociological Theory* (n. 1 above), pp. 348–369, see p. 352. Originally published in Georges Gurvitch and Wilbert E. Moore, eds., *Twentieth Century Sociology* (New York, 1945).
31. Parsons, "Positions and Prospects of Systematic Theory" (n. 1 above), pp. 216–217.
32. Parsons and Edward A. Shils, "Values, Motives, and Systems of Action," in Parsons and Shils, eds., *Towards a General Theory of Action* (New York, 1951), pp. 37–278, see p. 50.
33. Ibid., p. 60.
34. For a description of this alternative approach to "systematic theory" which informs Parsons' work, see ch. 2, sec. 5.
35. Parsons and Shils, p. 50.
36. Parsons, "Positions and Prospects" (n. 31 above), p. 216, italics added.
37. Parsons and Shils (n. 32 above), pp. 50–53.
38. Ibid., pp. 50–52.

39. See my discussion of this movement away from Parsons' earlier, more concrete theory to his more generalized and more original conceptualization in ch. 3, sec. 1. For the relevance of this movement to the specific emergence of the interchange model, see ch. 4, sec. 1.

40. Parsons and Robert F. Bales, "The Dimensions of Action Space," in Parsons, Bales, and Shils, *Working Papers in the Theory of Action* (New York, 1953), pp. 63–110, esp. pp. 102–103.

41. Ibid., p. 109.

42. Parsons, "An Approach to Psychological Theory in Terms of the Theory of Action," in Koch, *Psychology* (n. 19 above), 3:709, italics added. This quotation occurs in an essay published six years after Parsons' breakthrough to interchange, but it still represents, in a highly graphic way, the attitude of naturalistic discovery that Parsons adopted toward the new theory from the outset. This attitude is also strikingly expressed in the first essay in which interchange theory ever appeared. Here, the analogue to classical mechanics is completely explicit:

> If we have succeeded so far in defining a space, the units which must be located in that space, the nature of change of location in the space and finally of the systems of units which are conceived as moving interdependently with respect to location, direction and rate of change of location as systems, the question next arises as to whether we are in a position to state any general conditions governing the equilibrium of such systems. This is essentially what is meant by the statement of the "laws" of a system, namely certain fundamental generalizations about the nature of the equilibriating processes such that it is possible, by applying them, to deduce the nature and directions of the changes which will take place in systems. (Parsons and Bales, "Dimensions of Action Space" [n. 40 above], p. 99; cf. p. 345.)

Eight years later, Parsons described interchange in terms of the "three fundamental laws" of action, but the mechanical analogy remained the same ("The Point of View of the Author" [n. 26 above], p. 344).

43. Ibid.

44. Parsons and Bales (n. 40 above), p. 103.

45. "The Point of View of the Author," pp. 345–346.

46. "An Approach to Psychological Theory in Terms of the Theory of Action," pp. 702–704. By S-R-S, Parsons refers to the level of stimulus-response.

47. Bershady characterizes this ambition well when he describes Parsons' attitude toward his interchange theory:

> It must . . . produce sufficient conditions, explanations, of all the "objects"—the units and systems—of his [Parsons'] concern, and show that these explanations are . . . unthinkable without his framework. And he must be able to do all of these without adding "underived" basic categories to his framework, or else the entire point of the framework will be

> lost. (Harold J. Bershady, *Ideology and Social Knowledge* [New York, 1973], p. 124.)

48. For an analysis of the socialization theory in these terms, see ch. 5, sec. 1.

49. For discussions of Parsons' approach to political and integrative interchange in terms of references at different levels of generality, see ch. 4, secs. 3, 4.3.

50. For a discussion of Merton's ambiguous recognition of the need for generalized theory, see vol. 1, pp. 11–15.

51. Robert K. Merton, "On Sociological Theories of the Middle Range," in his *On Theoretical Sociology* (New York, 1967), pp. 39–72, see p. 45.

52. Wolf Heydebrand articulates this problem well—albeit in a highly polemical fashion—when he describes Parsons' "identification of the *conceptual* system of analysis with the [*empirical*] *object* of analysis" as creating the "reification of historical and experiential processes with *logical* ones."

> The analysis of concrete historical societies and processes becomes, therefore, an exercise in "systems analysis," a mere symbolic transformation of a complex of pre-defined concepts and of preformed structures. (Review essay on *The System of Modern Societies*, in *Contemporary Sociology* 1, no. 5 [1972]:391, italics added.)

Yet Heydebrand fails to recognize that although this describes a tendency in Parsons' work, it certainly does not exhaust his methodology as a whole, a qualification which, it is to be hoped, the preceding five chapters of my analysis amply demonstrate. Such one-sidedness is true of virtually all of Parsons' meta-methodological critics, who while often making valuable points ignore the two-directional aspects of Parsons' approach, the very segment which certainly represents his most lasting sociological contribution.

On the other hand, sympathetic interpreters of Parsons' meta-methodology usually come down too hard on the other side, ignoring the tensions in Parsons' position and their often destructive results. Until recently, most of these sympathetic commentators have simply accepted Parsons own self-description as an empirical scientist (see, e.g., Winston White, *Beyond Conformity* [New York, 1961], pp. 70–100; cf., the Appendix to this volume, "Conflation and Reduction in the Interpretation of Parsonian Theory"). Jonathan Turner produced one of the earliest defenses of Parsons that took a more sophisticated position. He argued that, far from failing to achieve the positivists' stringent standards, Parsons asserts from the outset that science must first gain "systemic conceptual coherence" by producing an inclusive analytic scheme. Only subsequent to this scheme could empirically testable propositions be produced. (*The Structure of Sociological Theory* [Homewood, Ill., 1974], pp. 29–30.) Yet this description misses the other part of Parsons' ambition, his contention that, at least with interchange analysis, his categorial system has also become propositional and law-like. A similar problem occurs in Enno Schwanenberg's penetrating critique of the positivist attack on Parsons' attention to generalized theory. It is true that Parsons eschews the positivist criteria of verification for the criteria of theoretical convergence and internal coherence ("The Two Problems of Order in Parsons' Theory: An Analysis from Within," *Social Forces* 49 [June 1971]:569–581, esp. 571). Schwanenberg ignores, however, the enormous problems that such efforts at nonempirical "verification" create, i.e., the tendency toward formalism and deductivism that I describe in the present chapter.

Harold J. Bershady's defense of Parsons' meta-methodology is perhaps the most forceful recent interpretation (*Ideology and Social Knowledge* [New York, 1973]). He demonstrates that Parsons' theoretical emphasis is, indeed, consistent with one particular approach to scientific explanation, that of the "covering law" model. Yet Bershady does not fully appreciate the problems with this position when it is carried out in a formalistic, deductivist manner. Certainly, as Bershady argues, there must be some correspondence established between theoretical a priori and empirical reality, but the crucial point is that this cannot be done directly, in a conflationary way. Bershady ignores, in other words, the "level" problem in Parsons' utilization of a priori reasoning. He agrees too readily with Parsons' claim that Newton's mechanical laws are similar to those of the "action frame of reference." This identification, however, confuses an essentially philosophical, or presuppositional framework with a much more propositionally-oriented one, and it is precisely this confusion of levels that gets Parsons into so much trouble. Parsons' goal is indeed similar to Kant's synthetic a priori, because he believed, with Kant, that an a priori can be objectively true. Yet this Kantian model cannot be as easily applied to action theory as to Newtonian laws: their respective levels of generality are too divergent. It is not, therefore, simply that a covering-law model is itself inadequate, as Bershady argues, but that Parsons' utilization of it has been confused. Furthermore, Parsons did, in fact, combine this empiricist pursuit of a covering law with a strong element of postpositivist emphasis on the relative autonomy of purely theoretical and generalized argument.

In his more recent interpretation, Ken Menzies argues, somewhat along these lines, that to emphasize Parsons' scientism and his pursuit of a "covering law" is, in view of the impossibility of such an empiricist model of science, ultimately a waste of time. He chooses instead to emphasize the dimension of Parsons' work that presents what he calls an "open program," in the nonpositivist sense of Wittgensteinian philosophy or, more recently, of Imre Lakatos. (*Talcott Parsons and the Social Image of Man* [n. 6 above], pp. 1–26.) Yet by ignoring the other, neopositivist dimension of Parsons' meta-methodology, Menzies ignores a major element of confusion in Parsons' work. Menzies does discuss "positivism," but only as a form of presuppositional rationalism.

It may be noted, finally, that toward the end of his career, in the mid-1970s, Parsons ostensibly rejected the deductivist approach to theory which he held for nearly forty years ("Afterword," in Max Black, ed., *The Social Theories of Talcott Parsons* [reissue, Carbondale, Ill., 1976], pp. 364–370, and the review of Bershady's *Ideology and Social Knowledge* in Parsons, *Social Systems and the Evolution of Action Theory* [New York, 1977], pp. 122–123). Yet, while he rejects a linear approach to scientific growth for a more ad hoc, trial-and-error course, he still maintains that every level of his theory is, ultimately, deducible from the more general concepts which he had previously enunciated ("Afterword," p. 366).

53. Alfred W. Baldwin, "The Parsonsian Theory of Personality," in Black (n. 26 above), pp. 153–190.

54. On this peculiarity of Durkheim's style, see Steven Lukes, *Emile Durkheim* (New York, 1972), p. 31; for synecdoche in Freud, see Philip Rieff, *Freud: The Mind of the Moralist* (New York, 1959).

55. Parsons, Bales, and Shils, "Phase Movement in Relation to Motivation, Symbol, and Role Structure," in *Working Papers* (n. 40 above), pp. 163–269, quoting pp. 164–165. This remarkable discussion has not entirely escaped notice. See, e.g., Leslie Sklair's remark that it represents "a bad attack of scientism" ("The 'Functional Requisites' in Parsonian Sociology," *British Journal of Sociology* 21, no. 1 [1970]:30–42, quoting 36). But Sklair errs by viewing this essay as completely idiosyncratic—"perhaps encouraged by contact with the experimentally-minded Bales" (ibid.)—rather than as exemplifying a systematic problem that pervades Parsons' work. Baldwin (n. 53 above) also sharply criticizes Parsons for his analogic isomorphism, although this critique is limited to Parsons' *Family, Socialization, and Interaction Process* (New York, 1955).

56. "Phase Movement," in *Working Papers*, pp. 189–202, passim; see also Bales, "The Equilibrium Problem in Small Groups," ibid., pp. 111–162.

57. Parsons, "An Outline of the Social System," in *Theories of Society* (n. 19 above), pp. 30–79, see pp. 60–66, quoting p. 60; Parsons and Neil J. Smelser, *Economy and Society* (New York, 1956), pp. 1–8 and passim.

58. Thus, following Parsons' lead, Harry M. Johnson introduces a discussion of Parsons' media theory by describing it as "a *generalization* of economics" ("The Generalized Symbolic Media in Parsons' Theory," *Sociology and Social Research* 57 [1973]:208–221, quoting 208, italics added).

59. Parsons, "Social Structure and the Symbolic Media of Interchange," in Peter M. Blau, ed., *Approaches to the Study of Social Structure* (New York, 1975), pp. 94–120, quoting pp. 94–95. This article is reprinted in Parsons, *Social Systems and the Evolution of Action Theory* (n. 52 above).

60. See, e.g., Parsons, "On the Concept of Political Power," in his *Poli-*

tics and Social Structure (New York, 1969), pp. 352–404; I quote from pp. 397–404. For more recent technical exercises of this type, see, e.g., Parsons and Gerald M. Platt, "Technical Appendix: Some Theoretical Paradigms," in their *The American University* (Cambridge, Mass., 1973), pp. 423–447.

61. Robert F. Bales, *Interaction Process Analysis* (New York, 1951).

62. It was originally presented in 1953 in *Working Papers* (n. 40 above), whereas *Economy and Society* was not published until three years later.

63. For a good discussion of the differences between this economic analogy and its application to the political medium, see Bliss C. Cartwright and R. Stephen Warner, "The Medium Is Not the Message," in Jans J. Loubser et al., eds., *Explorations in General Theory in Social Science* (New York, 1976), pp. 639–661, esp. p. 645.

64. Parsons and Smelser, *Economy and Society* (n. 57 above), pp. 69–70.

65. For a discussion of these aspects of Parsons' pattern-variable usage, see ch. 3, secs. 2, 3, and ch. 5, sec. 2.

66. For this derivation, see Parsons and Bales (n. 40 above), passim, and Parsons, Bales, and Shils (n. 55 above), pp. 163–269. See also Parsons, "Pattern Variables Revisited: A Response to Robert Dubin," in his *Sociological Theory and Modern Society* (New York, 1967), pp. 192–220.

67. Early tendencies for this kind of formalistic reduction of the pattern variables can be seen in Parsons, *The Social System* (n. 3 above), p. 347, and in Parsons and Shils, *Towards a General Theory of Action* (n. 32 above), pp. 86 ff.

68. In fact, the only empirical discussions where the pattern variables have been presented as dimensions of an interchange system have been analyses of cultural configurations (Robert N. Bellah, *Tokugawa Religion* [Boston, 1957]; Rainer C. Baum, "Values and Democracy in Imperial Germany," *Sociological Inquiry* 38 [1968]:179–186; Menzies, *Talcott Parsons and the Social Image of Man* [n. 6 above], pp. 68–89). Even in the context of interchange analysis, in other words, the pattern-variable combinations still retain their cultural reference; they have no intrinsic relationship to a multidimensional model like interchange. One indication of the superfluous relationship of the pattern variables to interchange can be seen in the fact that after 1960 Parsons never referred to the variables in his systemic writings. Thus, in the important essay, "An Outline of the Social System" (in *Theories of Society* [n. 19 above], pp. 30–79), Parsons conducts a detailed explication of interchange without reference to the basic pattern combinations from which it is alleged to have been derived.

69. For what I believe is a more accurate, less formalistic analysis of the transition from the middle-period work—of which the pattern-variable scheme is an important part—to the later writings, particularly the interchange model, see my discussion in ch. 4, sec. 1.2.

70. George A. Lundberg, "The Natural Science Trend in Sociology,"

American Journal of Sociology 61 (1955):191–212; William Catton, *From Animistic to Naturalistic Sociology* (New York, 1966), pp. 225–231.

71. Helmut R. Wagner, "Displacement of Scope: A Problem in the Relation between Small-Scale and Large-Scale Sociological Theories," *American Journal of Sociology* 69 (1964):571–584.

72. William Gamson, review of *Politics and Social Structure*, in *American Sociological Review* 36 (1971):523; Cartwright and Warner (n. 63 above), passim.

73. Parsons, "Pattern Variables Revisited" (n. 65 above). For Dubin's original article, see "Parsons' Actor: Continuities in Social Theory," *American Sociological Review* 25 (1960):457–466.

74. As Dubin first put the issue, with interchange Parsons "turned his attention to analyzing the social act from the standpoint of social system problems." Whereas the pattern-variable schema " 'looks out' to the social system from the vantage point of the actor," the later interchange model " 'looks down' at the individual actor from the perspective of the social system." The latter perspective, Dubin maintained, "attempts to establish a direct and imperative connection between the social system and the individual actor." ("Parsons' Actor," pp. 462–463.) The influence of this initial misunderstanding—itself partly the result of Parsons' own empiricist-inspired strategy of "internal manipulation"—can be seen from the fact that more than twenty years later Jürgen Habermas cited Parsons' transformation of the pattern-variable schema and, indeed, Dubin's original discussion, as evidence of Parsons' turn away from hermeneutics toward objectivist systems theory. "Parsons decided to allocate the analytical components of action," Habermas writes, "to one of the basic functions." This decision, he insists, "made the reinterpretation of the hitherto central pattern variables inevitable," adding that Parsons "accomplished that revision in the course of his debate with Dubin." He continues:

> These abstract decision alternatives [i.e., the pattern variables] had been introduced in order to explain how cultural values could be reduced to a finite number of preference patterns from a universal perspective. After Parsons abandoned the perspective of action theory, the pattern variables lost this particular meaning. Now the question was no longer one of the cultural determination of action orientations. Now the question was how the actor's decisions could be derived directly from system formation processes. ("Talcott Parsons: Problems of Theory Construction," *Sociological Inquiry* 51 [1981]:173–196, quoting 189.)

Even Niklas Luhmann, a systems theorist himself, has been misled by the pattern variable derivation argument. Attempting to interpret interchange in terms of the internally manipulated pattern-variable combinations, Luhmann concludes, quite rightly in my opinion, that something important about the understanding of meaning has been lost when the interchange-pattern-variable model is compared with the earlier, simpler pattern-variable schema. "The problem is not whether the connections represented by the grid [i.e., by interchange] exist or can be shown to be necessary," Luhmann writes. "Rather, we must ask in what way they are made accessible to theory by being put into the form of a grid." To define these connections, he turns, following Parsons' derivation, to the pattern-variable schema: "In this light, the critical point appears to be the position occupied by the pattern variables, or constructive dichotomies," for "they indicate how the squares in the grid are to be interpreted." He concludes, however, that with the new interchange position of the pattern variables, "we lose the ability to use them inside the grid in a unified way," and that, for this reason, "the clear dichotomies begin to dissolve" ("Talcott Parsons: The Future of a Theory," in Luhmann, *The Differentiation of Society* [New York, 1981], pp. 47–65, quoting pp. 56–57). This is one of the major stated reasons for Luhmann's rejection of the interchange model.

75. Savage (n. 16 above), p. 164.

76. Walter L. Wallace, "Overview of Contemporary Sociological Theory," in Wallace, ed., *Sociological Theory* (Chicago, 1969), pp. 1–59, see pp. 40, 44.

77. Menzies (n. 6 above), p. 73, italics added.

78. Ibid., p. 77; see also pp. 83–86.

79. Leon Mayhew, "Ascription in Modern Societies," *Sociological Inquiry* 38 (1968):105–120, quoting 107.

CHAPTER SEVEN

1. For an extended discussion of the concept of "conflation" and its relation to issues in current debates over the philosophy and sociology of science, see vol. 1, pp. 24–63. For the widespread recourse to conflationary strategy in contemporary theoretical debate among non-Parsonians, see ibid., pp. 64–112. For a relatively brief summary of these earlier statements about conflation, see the Preface to the present volume. For conflation in the interpretation of Parsons' theory, see the Appendix.

2. See the discussion of this approach to functionalist analysis in ch. 3, sec. 1. The 1945 essay is "The Present Position and Prospects of Systematic Theory in Sociology," in Parsons, *Essays in Sociological Theory* (New York, 1954), pp. 212–237.

3. Parsons, *The Social System* (New York, 1951), pp. 26–36; David F. Aberle et al., "The Functional Prerequisites of Society," *Ethics* 9 (1950):100–111.

4. Parsons and Neil J. Smelser, *Economy and Society* (New York, 1956), p. 16.

5. For an analysis of Parsons' view of interchange as the specification of his presuppositional synthesis, see ch. 4, sec. 1.3.

6. Parsons and Gerald M. Platt, *The American University* (Cambridge, Mass., 1973), p. 10.

7. Ibid.

8. Ibid.

9. Ibid., p. 11, italics in original.

10. Ibid., p. 12.

11. Ibid., pp. 13–16. For similar arguments that place the Adaptation–Goal-Attainment–Integration–Pattern-Maintenance framework in the context of systemic models per se, see Parsons, "An Outline of the Social System," in Parsons et al., eds., *Theories of Society* (New York, 1961), pp. 60–79, and "Some Problems of General Theory in Sociology," in his *Social Systems and the Evolution of Action Theory* (New York, 1977), pp. 229–269.

12. For "conditions" and "ultimate reality" as the external environments of action and order, see ch. 5, sec. 3.2.

13. For an analysis of Parsons' discussions of these prerequisites of institutionalized individualism, see ch. 5, secs. 2.1 and 2.3.2.

14. Menzies ingeniously illustrates this confusion by showing how Parsons continually shifts back and forth between systemic and individual references in his explications of the interchange model (Ken Menzies, *Talcott Parsons and the Social Image of Man* [London, 1977], pp. 151–153). He connects this individualistic reference to the idealization of Parsons' system language. I would contend, to the contrary, that both the idealism and the individualism emerge from other, more fundamental strains in Parsons' work.

The clearest exposition of Parsons' interchange theory as embodying phase movements related to an "individualized," means-ends choice is Dean R. Gerstein, "A Note on the Continuity of Parsonian Action Theory," *Sociological Inquiry* 45, no. 4 (1975):11–16. Contrary to the perspective set forth here, however, Gerstein views this phase movement emphasis as consistent with the rest of Parsons' usage.

15. For Parsons' criticism that Weber's understanding of functionalism ignored the variability in the relation between models and frames of reference, see ch. 3, sec. 1.

16. Parsons, *The Social System* (n. 3 above), ch. 10. See also Edward C. Devereux's discussion of this chapter in "Parsons' Sociological Theory," in Max Black, ed., *The Social Theories of Talcott Parsons* (Ithaca, N.Y., 1961), pp. 1–63.

17. See Martel's criticism that "ambiguities permeate much of the Parsonian scheme and lead to characteristic exaggeration of its effective empirical scope." This results, Martel believes, in Parsons' failure to "consider . . . the classificatory operations for singular cases," his "general neglect of the entire problem of the relations between theoretical and factual statements on the workaday level of empirical investigation." (Martin U. Mar-

tel, "Academentia Praecox: The Aims, Merits, and Scope of Parsons' Multi-systemic Language Rebellion (1958–1968)," in Herman Turk and Richard L. Simpson, eds., *Institutions and Social Exchange: The Sociologies of Talcott Parsons and George C. Homans* (Indianapolis, 1971), pp. 175–211, quoting p. 180, n. 6.

18. For an analysis of this conception of psychological, social, and cultural systems, see ch. 3, sec. 3.1. For the articulation of the boundary relations between these systems in cybernetic terms, see ch. 4, sec. 1.3.

19. This interchange arrangement of the four general action systems was first discussed in Parsons, *Societies: Evolutionary and Comparative Perspectives* (Englewood Cliffs, N.J., 1966), pp. 28–29. It was first presented in schematic form in "Some Problems of General Theory in Sociology" [n. 11 above], an article first published in 1970.

20. In the late 1960s, Parsons began to formalize this "general action" interchange by specifying the actual input-output relations (*The American University* [n. 6 above], esp. pp. 33–102, 423–447; also Parsons, "Some Problems of General Theory in Sociology" [n. 11 above]). While the results are often extremely illuminating in empirical terms, the kinds of problems noted here seriously detract from such "general action" analysis.

21. See my discussion of this presuppositional reference for the cognitive-expressive-moral division in ch. 3, sec. 3.1.

22. This interchange arrangement of the elements of culture was first suggested in Parsons' narrative discussion in "Introduction to Culture and the Social System," in Parsons et al., *Theories of Society* (n. 11 above), pp. 963–993, see pp. 964–970, 982–984, and first presented schematically in Parsons and Platt, *The American University*, p. 436.

23. The same can be said for those efforts at cultural analysis which have relied on the formal interchange model, conducted by Parsons' students. Dean R. Gerstein's "Cultural Action and Heroin Addiction" (*Sociological Inquiry* 51 [1981]:355–370) draws upon Parsons' interchange theory of culture and is a remarkable analysis of the cultural dimensions of heroin addiction. (See, more generally, his 1975 doctoral dissertation, "Heroin in Motion: A Working Paper in the Theory of Action" [Harvard University].) Yet while one can see that the A-G-I-L schema allowed Gerstein to tease out different dimensions of cultural experience, the substantive, presuppositional logic of Parsons' original interchange model is nowhere in evidence.

For an example of the problems presented by this formalist camouflage, one need only compare Clifford Geertz's essays "Religion as a Cultural System" and "Ideology as a Cultural System" (in his *The Interpretation of Cultures* [New York, 1973], pp. 87–125, 193–233) with Parsons' earlier article, "Introduction to Culture and the Social System" (n. 19 above). Geertz, in his now famous discussion, relies almost entirely on Parsons' conceptual distinctions regarding symbolism and the cognitive-cathectic-moral distinction; he also follows Parsons' empirical discussion of historical process as cultural differentiation among these elements. Yet Geertz's essays stand in sharp contrast to Parsons' because he does not reify his argument by encapsulating it in the interchange model; as a result, Geertz can remain closely connected to the actual empirical and presuppositional logic involved. Robert N. Bellah's work on religion presents another revealing contrast to Parsons'. In an early essay, "The Systematic Study of Religion," written in 1955 but first published in his *Beyond Belief* (New York, 1970, pp. 260–288), Bellah followed Parsons' conflationary bent and applied multidimensional, functionalist reasoning to culture through the formalization of the interchange model. In his later essays, Bellah abandoned this formalism while maintaining not only Parsons' presuppositional and model commitments, but also the concern with differentiation among both cultural and social components (see, e.g., "Religious Evolution," ibid., pp. 20–50).

24. Parsons and Platt, *The American University*, p. 65.

25. Parsons, "The Position of Identity in the General Theory of Action," in C. Gordon and K. J. Gergen, eds., *The Self in Social Interaction* (New York, 1968), pp. 1–23.

26. This same point—that interchange analyses of personality produce important insights despite the formal characteristics of the model rather than because of it—applies to much of the work done by some of Parsons' later students and followers. See, e.g., the extremely interesting discussion by Chad Gordon, "Systemic Sense of Self" (*Sociological Inquiry* 38 [1968]: 161–178), and the ambitious and far-reaching integration of different developmental theories by Richard Münch, "Socialization and Personality Development from the Point of View of Action Theory, the Legacy of Emile Durkheim" (*Sociological Inquiry* 51 [1981]: 311–353).

For an analysis of some of the substantive insights generated by the later, formal personality theory, see Guy Rocher, *Talcott Parsons and American Sociology* (New York, 1975), pp. 99–123.

27. Parsons, "A Sociological Approach to the Theory of Organizations" and "Some Ingredients of a General Theory of Formal Organizations," in his *Structure and Process in Modern Societies* (New York, 1960), pp. 16–58, 59–96.

28. "A Sociological Approach," p. 56, italics added.

29. Once again, this is not to imply that sociologists have been unable to apply interchange directly to the empirical study of organization in interesting ways (see, e.g., R. Jean Hills, "The Organization as a Component in the Structure of Society" and "The Public School as a Type of Organization," in J. J. Loubser et al., eds., *Explorations in General Theory in Social Science* [New York, 1976], pp. 805–828, 829–856). The use of interchange in such institutional work, however, does not have any logical relationship to the model's use in macro-societal theory. Such work does not, e.g.,

approach organizational process and differentiation in terms of cybernetic, presuppositional issues. In contrast, this is precisely the approach taken by Amitai Etzioni, who follows a Parsonian approach to organizations in a more general sense (*A Comparative Analysis of Complex Organizations* [New York, 1961]).

30. Parsons and Smelser, *Economy and Society* (n. 4 above), pp. 41–44.

31. Parsons, *The System of Modern Societies* (Englewood Cliffs, N.J., 1971), pp. 71–74. Cf. his "Comparative Studies and Evolutionary Change," in Ivan Vallier, ed., *Comparative Methods in Sociology: Essays on Trends and Applications* (Berkeley and Los Angeles, 1971), pp. 97–139, see pp. 108–111; reprinted in Parsons, *Social Systems and the Evolution of Action Theory* (n. 11 above).

32. It is precisely this arbitrary quality that so often detracts from the work most directly influenced by interchange theory, work which in other respects is often highly successful. The significant empirical and theoretical insights generated by Smelser's *Social Change in the Industrial Revolution* (Chicago, 1959) certainly do not depend upon his differentiation of the internal workings of industries and families according to the interchange model. But this application, nevertheless, occupies a good deal of Smelser's attention, resulting in a series of technical, formalistic discussions which often appear rather arbitrary. E.g., Smelser defines the pattern-maintenance activities of factories as involving low-level technical workers (pp. 24–25), a characterization that has little relation to the generalized definition of this dimension as the carrier of cultural values; indeed, it seems motivated as much by the need to fill an empty box as anything else. Smelser's later delineation of family functions seems similarly arbitrary, more influenced by his empirical focus on economic theory and labor supply than by any independent consideration of the family in the context of the generalized reference of interchange theory (pp. 160–163).

At about the same time, William C. Mitchell attempted a similar formalization of the internal operation of the American political system. Arguing that "the polity is simply a micro-community of the social system," Mitchell applies interchange to political activities in an equally arbitrary manner. Thus, legislation performs the "integration" functions of securing support while the executive functions provide the actual power mechanisms of goal attainment ("The Polity and Society: A Structural-Functional Analysis," *Midwest Journal of Political Science* 2 [1958]: 403–420). Neither of these political subsystems, however, can be differentiated from the other by virtue of presuppositional reference, and no interchange actually occurs between them.

Bellah's highly technical explication of the interchange model applied to "religious action"—where ethics, systems of worship, faith, and modes of religious therapy are systematically assigned functional meanings—operates at a similar distance from the model's more generalized implications and significance (*Beyond Belief* [n. 23 above], pp. 260–288). Lipset and Rokkan's effort to construct the internal, functional referents of the integrative subsystem reveals similar problems ("Cleavage Structures, Party Systems and Voter Alignments," in Lipset and Rokkan, eds., *Party Systems and Voter Alignments* [New York, 1967], pp. 1–64). The true substance of their classificatory scheme—the distinction between territorial and cultural lines of national conflict—is more obfuscated than clarified by formalizing it within the language of interchange; the generalized referents of interchange simply cannot be directly operationalized as territorial and cultural polarization.

The basic irrelevance of such conflationary efforts is, in effect, confirmed by the way these theorists have abandoned such formalist schemes in their subsequent work. After his first book, Smelser never again applied interchange within a specific institutional level. Mitchell in *The American Polity* (New York, 1962), four years after his initial classificatory effort, abandoned the technical detail and employed interchange to study the political system in a much more generalized and satisfactory manner. Bellah in his much better-known later essays on religion never built directly upon his earlier formal analysis. He characterized this earlier essay (n. 23 above) as "an effort to think through the main theoretical problems in the scientific study of religion at a point when I was still caught in the unfolding of the Parsonian theoretical scheme" (*Beyond Belief*, p. 260). Similarly, Lipset and Rokkan rarely refer to the technical functional apparatus outlined in their introductory presentation in their substantive discussion, later in the essay, of the origins of modern Europe's political cleavages (see pp. 9–64).

Yet these less formalistic renderings are still informed by the substantive insights generated by the interchange theory, a fact which those who simply dismiss interchange as pure formalism do not understand. Niklas Luhmann, e.g., rightly criticizes the ad hoc, free-floating quality of Parsons' use of interchange, attacking the apparently endless "need to repeat the gridwork within each of the squares of the original grid" and asking, quite rightly, "how far can this process be repeated?" ("Talcott Parsons: The Future of a Theory," in Luhmann, *The Differentiation of Society* [New York, 1982], pp. 47–65, see pp. 57–58). Yet Luhmann does not see the presuppositional reference of Parsons' interchange work as it applies to the social system, arguing that interchange is derived simply from systems thinking rather than from any understanding of action (p. 54). One must note, however, that Parsons' conflationary tendency encouraged precisely this kind of misunderstanding.

33. Parsons and Robert F. Bales, *Family, Socialization, and Interaction Process* (New York, 1955), esp. pp. 35–41; Parsons, Bales, and Edward A. Shils, *Working Papers in the Theory of Action* (New York, 1953), esp. pp. 63–70.

34. For this analysis, see ch. 5, sec. 1.1.

35. Parsons, "Family Structure and the Socialization of the Child," in Parsons and Bales (n. 33 above), pp. 35–132, see pp. 39–41.

36. Parsons and James Olds, "The Mechanisms of Personality Functioning with Special Reference to Socialization," ibid., pp. 187–258, see p. 198.

37. See ch. 3, sec. 4.3.

38. Parsons, Bales, and Shils (n. 33 above), pp. 237–245, and Parsons, "Family Structure" (n. 35 above), pp. 39–41.

39. See ch. 3, sec. 4.2.

40. See ch. 5, sec. 1.2.

41. This formalism is clearly manifest in Parsons' rhetoric. In describing the phase patterns of socialization, e.g., he talks about "fitting them in" to the exchange model he had conceptualized several years earlier (Parsons and Bales [n. 33 above], p. 40).

This general analysis of Parsons' conflationary formalism helps explain the discomfort often noted by social psychologists otherwise sympathetic with the substance of Parsons' analyses. As Baldwin, e.g., writes about a section of *Family, Socialization, and Interaction Process*:

> All through his portion of the argument, it is almost impossible to escape the feeling that Parsons makes the developmental process fit the theoretical model only by straining the normal meaning of terms beyond reason. . . . What seems especially unfortunate is that the isomorphism is not necessary for the fruitfulness of the conceptualization. . . . The strenuous attempts to realize complete analogy hide the contributions to the picture of socialization that Parsons does make. . . . The false orderliness and isomorphism is an all too effective camouflage for what values are inherent in the general scheme. (Alfred L. Baldwin, "The Parsonian Theory of Personality," in Black [n. 16 above], pp. 153–189, quoting pp. 167, 170–172.)

A sympathetic British commentator, W. J. H. Sprott, puts his exasperation more bluntly. After reviewing what I have called the presuppositional reference of interchange theory, Sprott comments on Parsons' later socialization analysis:

> My trouble is that all too often it happens I am confronted with a square divided into four boxes, with the appropriate letters in the corners, and I read in, say, the pattern maintenance box words which don't seem to me to have anything to do with pattern maintenance at all. I cannot help feeling that Parsons is so sold on his squares that when he is dealing with any topic he divides his material into four groups and shoves them into the most plausible boxes. ("Principia Sociologica, II," *British Journal of Sociology* 14 [1963]: 307–320.)

On occasion, Parsonian formalism can become almost fetishistic. E.g., in the period of intensive elaboration on the interchange model among Parsons and his co-workers, the number seven is applied to virtually every aspect of social development. In 1955, Bales argues in *Family, Socialization, and Interaction Process* (n. 33 above) that there are seven phases in group decision-making, from the suggestion of a problem to its final resolution ("Role Differentiation in Small Decision-Making Groups," pp. 259–306). In a subsequent essay in the same publication, Parsons and Bales argue that this group phenomenon parallels the seven stages involved in the creation of norms in the socialization process, where personality moves from dissatisfaction to new internalization of parental objections ("Conclusion: Levels of Cultural Generality and the Process of Differentiation," pp. 353–396). In the same year, in an article published in *Scientific American* 192, no. 3 (1955):31–35, Bales argues that a parallel "interlocking series of seven steps" describes the information processing and decision making involved in the radar identification and interception of enemy planes by the national air defense system. In 1956, Parsons and Smelser claimed that the "Resource Chart" (see ch. 4, sec. 2)—composed of the life-cycle stages from birth to adult participation in the labor force—also involves seven steps that are parallel, or "cognate" with small-group and socialization processes (*Economy and Society* [n. 4 above], p. 122). Finally, in 1959 and 1962, Smelser expanded this proposition by arguing that every component of action (values, norms, goals, and facilities) has seven levels of generality and by asserting that every sequence of structural differentiation—from dissatisfaction and social control to structural change—also involves seven distinctive phases (*Social Change in the Industrial Revolution* [n. 32 above] and *Theory of Collective Behavior* [New York, 1962]). Far from reflecting true empirical reality, this series of references seems rooted in numerology.

42. See Arthur L. Stinchcombe, "A Parsonian Theory of Traffic Accidents," *Sociological Inquiry* 45(1975): 27–30. For interchange and Parsons' conceptualization of the human condition, see his *The Human Condition* (New York, 1978), pp. 352–433.

43. E. P. Thompson, "Preface," in *The Making of the English Working Class* (New York, 1966).

44. Smelser, *Theory of Collective Behavior* (n. 41 above); Chalmers Johnson, *Revolutionary Change* (Boston, 1966).

45. This point must be particularly insisted upon in light of the criticism which will follow. Parsons always very explicitly utilized an "equilibrium" form of systems model, more specifically what he called a "moving equilibrium" model. In these terms, equilibrium is an analytical concept derived from postulated characteristics of what a system would have to do to maintain stability or integration. (I have indicated above that conflict per se is not inconsistent with the maintenance of moving equilibrium, and that if the system reference is the cultural level, even societal disequilibrium may be consistent with it.) Equilibrium, then, is a point with which to compare the processes of the empirical world, not a commitment to em-

pirical stability in itself. It has been argued, indeed, that Marx himself had a strong system model which heavily if implicitly relied on a notion of the requirements of equilibrium in a capitalist society (see vol. 1, pp. 60–62). In fact, it is a Marxist theorist, John G. Taylor, who has recently put the differentiated quality of Parsons' "equilibrium" concept in its clearest form.

> The criticisms made by writers, such as Barrington Moore, Foss, and C. Wright Mills, that the centrality of the concept of equilibrium to Parsonian theory reproduces an inherently conservative approach, in which order and stability are held to exist empirically at the outset of structural-functionalist analysis, are . . . misplaced. . . . Parsons repeatedly criticises the notion of a unitary correspondence between theoretical concepts, facts and actual phenomena. As with all his concepts, the notion of equilibrium has an essentially heuristic status; it is not a readily observable phenomenon, but rather a means of structuring reality for the purposes of empirical investigation. Far from taking societal equilibrium as a given, Parsons' project is to examine how, given the conflicts perpetually engendered in and by social action and interaction, societies can reproduce themselves whilst retaining relative stability. Concepts such as equilibrium are theoretical means for posing such a question. . . . Consequently, the conclusion that Parsonian theory, by its very content, must necessarily produce a static and conservative bias, due to one of its major concepts, equilibrium, is clearly inadequate. (*From Modernisation to Modes of Production* [London, 1979], p. 5.)

In the preceding analysis, of course, I have given ample evidence of how Parsons' utilization of an equilibrium model in no way prevented him from recognizing and often brilliantly explaining empirical conflict and upheaval. What I will speak about below, then, amounts to the elimination in Parsons' work of the analytical status of the equilibrium concept. Taylor recognizes that this slippage does occur, acknowledging that "Parsons' use of the [equilibrium] concept does, at times, blur the epistemological distinction he has established between phenomena and concepts that provide a theoretical knowledge of these phenomena" (p. 5).

46. For the contrast between focusing on a concept like exploitation and one like equilibrium, see Alvin W. Gouldner, "The Norm of Reciprocity: A Preliminary Statement," *American Sociological Review* 25 (1960):161–178.

47. See ch. 2, sec. 2.2.

48. Parsons and Edward A. Shils, eds., *Towards a General Theory of Action* (New York, 1951), p. 107, italics added.

In the purely presuppositional strand of his argument, Parsons contrasts "interdependence of parts"—which is one way he conceptualizes collective "order"—with randomness, a condition of non-order that he attributes to individualistic theories. In this presuppositional argument, then, he does not equate such nonrandom order, or interdependence, with any particular model. Instead, he leaves this question open and acknowledges, indeed, that an institutional approach to collective order, like that of Malthus or Marx, can be just as nonrandom as a functional approach like that of Durkheim. (See my analysis of this aspect of Parsons' order discussion in ch. 2, sec. 2.) In the argument I have reproduced in the text, however, Parsons negates this logic, asserting that nonrandom order must be associated with a particular kind of model, namely, system-functional ones. He is, therefore, conflating two levels of analysis which should be distinct.

49. Ibid., p. 107.

50. Parsons, "From the Point of View of the Author," in Black (n. 16 above), p. 337.

51. Ibid., pp. 337–338. This empirical reduction becomes fully transparent when Parsons writes on the next page: "But social disorder certainly exists: witness the conditions of the ex-Belgian Congo in the late summer of 1960" (p. 339). According to his presuppositional definition, of course, the social conflict in the ex-Belgian Congo is certainly not an example of disorder—when order is taken, that is, in the sense of nonrandom social arrangements.

52. Ibid., p. 336.

53. Parsons and Smelser (n. 4 above), p. 16, italics added.

54. Ibid., italics added.

55. Parsons, Bales, and Shils (n. 33 above).

In the 1970s, Parsons relabeled the pattern-maintenance system as the "fiduciary system" rather than the latency system. This identification also imparts a distinctive empirical connotation of stasis and equilibrium. E.g., as he and Platt write in the Introduction to their *The American University* (n. 6 above; p. 8n): "The fiduciary subsystem of a society acts as a trustee of some interests in the society. . . . We shall be dealing in this volume with the portion of the fiduciary subsystem concerned with trusteeship of the cognitive culture dimension."

56. Parsons and Smelser (n. 4 above), p. 17, italics added.

57. Parsons, Bales, and Shils (n. 33 above), p. 210.

58. Ibid., italics in original.

59. Parsons and Smelser, p. 50.

60. Ibid., p. 18.

61. In addition to *Economy and Society*, this same empiricist approach to integration in terms of equilibrium is taken in Parsons, Bales, and Shils (n. 33 above) and in Parsons, "An Outline of the Social System" (n. 11 above).

Hans P. M. Adriaansens, then, is wrong to suggest that Parsons' misleading identification of the analytical categories of systems theory with empirical equilibrium is restricted to the middle-period work, touching not at all the systems conceptualizations in the early and later phases. In regard to the later work, e.g., he writes that "the concept of function, as it is used here, lacks the typical structural-functional connotations of stability and homeostasis" (*Talcott Parsons and the Conceptual Dilemma* [London, 1980], p. 111). I have tried to show, to the contrary, that this conflationary strategy creates ambiguity throughout Parsons' writing.

62. Devereux (n. 16 above), pp. 34–37.

63. Benton Johnson, *Functionalism in Modern Sociology: Understanding Talcott Parsons* (Morristown, N.J., 1976), p. 29.

64. Harry M. Johnson, "The Generalized Symbolic Media in Parsons' Theory," *Sociology and Social Research* 57 (1973):208–221, see 212.

65. Chandler Morse, "The Functional Imperatives," in Black (n. 16 above), pp. 100–152, quoting p. 144.

But see Robin Williams' evaluations of Parsons and, more recently, Guy Rocher's. While Williams argues that "Parsons repeatedly and emphatically calls attention to 'strains' and 'inconsistencies' within each of these four analytically separable systems," he goes on to assert that

> It remains true that the main preoccupation of the body of theory under examination is to account for order, stability, and equilibrium rather than for disruptive or violent change. The basic model from which analysis departs is that of a boundary-maintaining system in which small changes are counteracted in such a way as to restore the prior state of affairs, or else to produce "orderly" change (presumably, gradual and nonviolent). (Robin M. Williams, "The Sociological Theory of Talcott Parsons," ibid., pp. 64–99, quoting p. 71.)

And while Rocher points out Parsons' frequent utilization of interchange to describe social conflict, he acknowledges that Parsons has not "pursued a dynamic analysis of [the] various contradictions he himself brought into his system" (Guy Rocher [n. 26 above], p. 166; cf. Dick Atkinson, *Orthodox Consensus and Radical Alternative* [New York, 1971], pp. 21–22). For an illuminating discussion of Parsons' confusion of the terms "equilibrium" and "order," see Keith Dixon, *Sociological Theory: Pretense or Possibility?* (London, 1973), pp. 41–44. However, like most other critics, Dixon explains this problem not in terms of fundamental methodological problems but in terms simply of Parsons' terminological vagueness. Bershady makes a similar response: after calling attention to this terminological confusion, he dismisses it as purely "lexical" (Harold J. Bershady, *Ideology and Social Knowledge* [New York, 1973], p. 97).

66. For an analysis of this approach to institutionalization, which includes coercion (Parsons also calls it the "integrative problem"), see ch. 3, sec. 3.2. For Parsons' discussion of institutionalization in the more purely presuppositional sense—as the intermediate, value level between social and cultural system—see ch. 4, sec. 5. For the specific utilization of the

phenomenon of symbolic institutionalization to explain conflict rather than stability, see the discussion of Parsons' and Shils' analysis, ch. 3, sec. 4.1.

67. Parsons and Platt (n. 6 above), p. 34.

68. For a discussion of the voting essay in these terms, see ch. 4, sec. 4.1.

69. Parsons, " 'Voting' and the Equilibrium of the American Political System," in his *Sociological Theory and Modern Society* (New York, 1967), pp. 223–263.

70. These empirical specifications are discussed in Parsons' essays on the radical right in *Essays in Sociological Theory* (n. 2 above) and the essay on McCarthyism, "Social Strains in America," in his *Politics and Social Structure* (New York, 1969).

71. See my discussion on this point in ch. 5, sec. 2.3.2.

72. For an example of an empirical discussion of the role of symbolization in creating contrasting solidarities and normative arrangements, see E. E. Evans-Pritchard's discussion of "refraction" and the problem of order in "The Nuer Conception of Spirit in its Relation to the Social Order," *American Anthropologist* 55 (1953):201–214. In *Orthodox Consensus and Radical Alternative* (n. 65 above), Atkinson shows how some of Parsons' conflict critics, notably Rex and Dahrendorf, have implicitly adopted a "Parsonian" emphasis on consensus while linking this symbolic factor to conflicting subgroups rather than total societies (ch. 5). For a general critique of Parsons' inability to relate symbolization to subgroups rather than total societies, see Thomas Burger, "Talcott Parsons, the Problem of Order in Society, and the Program of Analytic Sociology," *American Journal of Sociology* 83 (1977):320–354.

73. Parsons, "Social Structure and the Symbolic Media of Interchange," in Peter M. Blau, ed., *Approaches to the Study of Social Structure* (New York, 1975), pp. 94–120, quoting p. 96.

74. Ibid., p. 98, italics added.

75. Ibid., p. 96.

76. Ibid., p. 99.

77. The same kind of confusions enter Parsons' discussion of solidary "influence" and value "commitments," but I reserve comment on these media for the analysis of ideological reduction which follows in sec. 3.

78. For this conception of interchange as simply an aggregating device, one which does not imply the absence of groups and group conflicts, see Mark Gould, "Systems Analysis, Macrosociology, and the Generalized Media of Social Action," in Loubser (n. 29 above), pp. 470–506, see p. 470.

79. Parsons, "From the Point of View of the Author" (n. 50 above), p. 234.

80. The closest Parsons and Platt come in *The American University* (n. 6 above) is in the section "The Deflationary Panic" (pp. 339–345), which

describes the conflict between students and faculty within the university. Yet even in this discussion they portray conflict as between two different societal functions rather than between different functional parts of the university itself: the students represent the particularistic demands of the societal community, while the faculty's commitment to universalistic cognitive rationality represents the needs of the society's pattern-maintenance system.

81. Hermann Strasser clearly articulates just this problem when he writes that "functionalists have dealt with social systems almost exclusively on an analytical level focusing on variables, relations, roles, statuses, subsystems, etc., rather than in concrete terms such as people, their interactions, collectivities, groups, classes, needs, and the like." "Functionalists," he suggests, "have maneuvered themselves too often into a scientific dilemma by converting the methodological necessity of employing the system concept into a theoretical virtue, supposedly resulting in social knowledge with immediate empirical reference" (Strasser and Susan C. Randall, *An Introduction to Theories of Social Change* [London, 1981], p. 144). Yet this insight is not precise enough, for Strasser relies on the conceptual vocabulary of conflict theory. It is not the use of functional models per se that draws "functionalists" like Parsons away from groups, but rather the conflationary approach to internal unity generated by a neopositivist ambition.

82. This analysis of the theoretical weaknesses of the earlier essays is made in ch. 4, sec. 1.2.

83. Although the main body of this essay, "Social Strains in America" (n. 70 above, pp. 163–178), was actually written at the beginning of the period I have identified as Parsons' late period, Parsons scarcely refers to the interchange model; as a result, he can maintain much of the emphasis on internal fragmentation and group conflict that characterized his earlier essays on the radical right.

84. Parsons, "Postscript to 'Social Strains in America' " (n. 70 above), pp. 179–184.

85. The charge that Parsons ignores groups for "functions" has often been made by his critics, although this criticism has almost always failed to acknowledge that such conflict between abstraction and concreteness is not an inherent aspect of Parsons' theorizing. E.g., one of the implicit polemics in Reinhard Bendix's *Max Weber* (New York, 1960) is directed against the failure of Parsons' "system theory" to emphasize concrete groups and the conflicts groups engender (pp. xxii, 257–268; see also n. 81 above). The most effective criticism of Parsons' inattention to groups and internal conflict—an argument which, singularly, does not link this failure to the problem of Parsons' abstraction as such—is Atkinson's discussion in *Orthodox Consensus and Radical Alternative* (n. 65 above). In characterizing Parsons' general theory, Atkinson writes that "it seems important to

emphasize that there is nothing in his theory . . . which precludes the possibility of offering an explanatory model of conflict. It is quite reasonable to imagine two or more opposed groups, each integrated in exactly the same way, in place of the assumption of a single unified [sub]system" (p. 25). Atkinson shows, e.g., how Parsons describes pattern-maintenance failures as producing a systemic shift toward political coercion (in my terms, as producing boundary tension and conflict between the subsystems of values and politics). An alternative approach, Atkinson argues, would be to discuss such pattern-maintenance problems in terms of internal-value disputes.

> Parsons insists that a slackening of ultimate-end control [i.e., pattern-maintenance stability] calls only for the sanction of "unpleasant, external consequences," or force [in] the pure Hobbesian state employing force in order to gain cohesion and order. This is most certainly not the only possible case and a "slackening of ultimate-end control" can imply value conflict and, therefore, individual or group conflict. This would imply adherence to or acceptance by the actor of alternative, new, and clashing values. It is at this point that Parsons is attacked for, amongst other things, omitting an analysis of power *within* and *between* institutions. (P. 15, italics added.)

Atkinson actually relates this problem to the kind of meta-methodological confusion I have identified as conflation.

> Because Parsons has no exact method of empirical reference, he systematically confuses his abstract model, and the diffuse idea of power and authority which is built into it, with the power, authority and action of particular groups of men. (P. 33.)

This same general point has been made by Parsons' more sympathetic interpreters. Thus, Martel called on Parsons to produce a "clear specification of the population and subgroups for which various norm scripts [i.e., the integrative and pattern-maintenance functions] apply" and for a "clarification of the breaking points in social system commitment levels [i.e., values] for various units of interest . . . along with much more attention to group structure as a phenomenon in its own right" ("Academentia Praecox" [n. 17 above], p. 209). Martel also links this problem to Parsons' methodological failure to provide independent, intermediate levels of theoretical analysis.

This problem has been emphasized at various times by some of the students and co-workers of Parsons who have made the most important contributions to "Parsonianism"—such as S. N. Eisenstadt, Neil J. Smelser, Edward A. Shils, Jesse R. Pitts, and Leon Mayhew, each of whom has sought to reemphasize the group level of systems analysis (see ch. 10, passim).

86. In the earlier discussion of the empirical and ideological "specifications" of Parsons' change theory (ch. 5, secs. 2.1, 2.2), I did not make the precise relation between these lines of argument explicit. My purpose was simply to demonstrate that these two more specific lines of argument represent significant aspects of Parsons' theory of social change.

87. Karl Popper, *The Poverty of Historicism* (Boston, 1957); see also Harold J. Bershady, *Ideology and Social Knowledge* (n. 65 above), and Barclay D. Johnson, "Some Philosophical Problems in Parsons' Early Thought" (Ph.D. diss., University of California, Berkeley, 1975).

88. Parsons, "The Prospects of Sociology Theory," in *Essays* (n. 2 above), pp. 348–369.

89. Talcott Parsons, Edward A. Shils, Gordon W. Allport, Clyde Kluckhohn, Henry A. Murray, Robert R. Sears, Richard C. Sheldon, Samuel A. Stouffer, Edward C. Tolman, "Some Fundamental Categories of the Theory of Action: A General Statement," in Parsons and Shils (n. 48 above), pp. 3–29, quoting p. 3.

90. For Parsons' critique of Weber's meta-methodology as insufficiently analytic, see ch. 2, sec. 1.

91. Parsons, "Evaluation and Objectivity in Social Science: An Interpretation of Max Weber's Contribution," in *Sociological Theory and Modern Society* (n. 69 above), pp. 79–101.

See Bershady's excellent discussion of the "anti-historicist" origins of this new, more explicitly functionalist phase of Parsons' theorizing (*Ideology and Social Knowledge* [n. 65 above], pp. 93–124). As my discussion in the preceding chapters should indicate, however, this ideological reference is only one among several rationales for the evolution of Parsons' theoretical development, and not nearly so important, I believe, as Parsons' continuing effort to refine and specify his presuppositional solutions.

92. This argument occurs throughout the following: "The Distribution of Power in American Society," in Parsons, *Politics and Social Structure*, (n. 70 above), pp. 185–203; " 'Voting' and the Equilibrium of the American Political System" (n. 69 above); Parsons and Smelser, *Economy and Society*, (n. 4 above); Parsons, *The System of Modern Societies* (n. 31 above).

93. Parsons and Smelser, *Economy and Society*, pp. 56–59.

94. Ibid., pp. 156–157.

95. Parsons and Smelser evidently were vaguely aware of this latent internal contradiction in their argument, for they introduced a residual category to cover for it.

> The *control* of economic productivity [by political power] is, in the absence of salient collective system goals, often latent. In periods of domestic and international quiescence the rights and interests of the political authority in the productivity of the economy may be so seldom exercised as to appear not to exist. (Ibid., p. 59, italics in original.)

But in resorting to residual categories, as Parsons himself so acutely analyzed them in *The Structure of Social Action*, theorists try to conceal theoretical weakness by relying on concepts which are actually not intrinsic to a theoretical system's internal logic.

There are other cases of polity-economy fusion which Parsons and Smelser have ignored by assuming complete differentiation. One example is the role of oligopoly in late capitalism, which, as Smelser pointed out in a later work, cross-cuts purely economic decisions—those governed by economic efficiency alone—with the political control of markets by corporate actors (see his *The Sociology of Economic Life* [Englewood Cliffs, N.J., 1963], pp. 44–55). See Menzies' comment that "[a] laissez-faire economic structure where there are numerous small firms securing bank loans is more differentiated than a situation where oligopolies control their own financing" (*Talcott Parsons and the Social Image of Man* [n. 14 above], p. 143).

96. Parsons and Smelser, *Economy and Society*, pp. 56–59.

97. See Menzies, p. 143. Indeed, if Parsons were really to take seriously his conflationary equation of evolutionary adaptation and the growth of individual freedom (see the introduction to this third section), he would have to argue, simply on logical grounds, that Communist industrial societies must be not only relatively differentiated but also more free than less successfully adaptive societies. Since Parsons manifestly did not believe that the latter was true—he argued that such societies were not adaptive in the long run—his correct description of some of the "fused" elements of Communist industrial societies further demonstrates the fallacy of his conflation of normative and empirical considerations. David Lane brings out this very point when he argues that "both China and the Soviet Union are prime examples of societies which have successfully enhanced adaptive capacity while suppressing individual choice expressed through elections and the free play of the economic market" ("Towards a Sociological Model of State Socialist Society" [Paper delivered at the Ninth Annual Meeting of the International Sociological Association, Uppsala, Sweden, 1978], p. 19). Throughout Lane's work one can find a concerted effort to "de-ideologize" Parsons' interchange theory. Lane demonstrates that Parsons' identifications of inputs/outputs were geared toward specifically American conditions, showing how very different terms would be necessary for analysis of Soviet society. While Lane's "Amended Model" of interchange seems to lean, in turn, too much toward Marx (see his *Leninism: A Sociological Interpretation* [Cambridge, 1981], pp. 115–119), his emphasis on generalizing the interchange model is well taken.

98. See, e.g., Polanyi, *The Great Transformation* (Boston, 1957), and George Dalton, ed., *Primitive, Archaic and Modern Economies: Essays of Karl Polanyi* (Boston, 1968).

99. Terence H. Hopkins, "Sociology and the Substantive View of the

Economy," in Polanyi, Conrad M. Arensberg, and Harry W. Pearson, eds., *Trade and Market in the Early Empires* (Boston, 1957), pp. 271–306, and Harry W. Pearson, "Parsons and Smelser on the Economy," ibid., pp. 307–319.

100. Neil J. Smelser, "A Comparative View of Exchange Systems," *Economic Development and Cultural Change* 7 (1959):173–182. But Smelser later used the same framework to adopt some of the more important aspects of the Polanyi position in his "Re-examining the Parameters of Economic Activity," (Paper prepared for the Conference on "Business and Society," Berkeley, March 1975), pp. 1–57.

101. On Parsons' side-stepping of the capitalist-socialist controversy, see the criticism by Rocher, a sympathetic interpreter:

> Parsons has limited his field of study to capitalist industrial society [and] has scarcely stepped outside the narrow framework of the capitalist world of North America. . . . Parsons seems not to have taken any interest in comparative analysis of socialist and capitalist countries. They both appear much the same to him, in that they are both industrialized; only their political regimes distinguish them. (Rocher [n. 26 above], p. 144.)

Although Rocher inexplicably ignores Parsons' vast comparative and historical work, he is right about the failure to consider seriously the differences between capitalist and socialist societies in the economic sphere.

Since I have discussed Parsons' difficulties with the economic aspect of the capitalist-socialist distinction primarily in terms of his ideological concern to criticize Communist industrial states, it should be noted that his conflation of the epistemological differentiations of the interchange model with the reality of capitalist industrial society creates simple empirical distortions of Communist societies as well. The empirical categories that Parsons chooses to identify as the interchanges between adaptive and pattern-maintenance and between adaptive and goal-attainment subsystems, e.g., correspond, contrary to his universal claims, only to the empirical situation of Western capitalist societies. For socialist industrial states, the specifications of interchange would have to be substantially different. David Lane outlines what such different correlations might entail: "Money, for instance, does not control labour and capital as the primary factors; it does not have the same role in a planned economy as in a market one." Referring to similar discrepancies in the political systems, Lane adds that " 'interest demands' in the USSR do not '*define the situation* for political decision-making' . . . as does the infra-structure and pressure group process in the USA." ("Towards a Sociological Model" [n. 97 above], p. 18; see also, in the same note, the discussion of Lane's *Leninism*.)

102. Parsons, "The Political Aspect of Social Structure and Process," in his *Politics and Social Structure* (n. 70 above), pp. 317–351, see p. 334.

103. Ibid., p. 335.

104. Ibid., p. 338.

105. Ibid., p. 335.

106. Ibid., p. 338, italics in original. It is revealing that this statement is followed by several pages of purely generalized presuppositional argument.

107. Ibid. See also " 'Voting' and the Equilibrium of the American Political System" (n. 69 above).

108. See ch. 4, sec. 4.3.

109. This line of argument is developed further in my "Core Solidarity, Ethnic Outgroup, and Social Differentiation: A Multidimensional Model of Inclusion in Modern Societies," in Jacques Dofny and Akinsolo Akiwowo, eds., *National and Ethnic Movements* (London, 1980), pp. 5–29.

110. Perhaps particularly because of his reliance on the pattern variables, Parsons was more sensitive to the variation in national political cultures in his early and middle period essays. This is, e.g., a major theme in his early discussions of the radical right. After the appearance of interchange theory, and the jettisoning of the pattern-variable schema, his conflation of concrete cultural development with the analytic differentiation of his interchange schema becomes much more pronounced. Once again, Parsons' students and co-workers have often resisted this trend, choosing less formalistic frameworks and concentrating more on the uneven, often particularistic development of national political cultures. See, e.g., Robert N. Bellah's essay "Religion in the Modernization Process," in his *Beyond Belief* (n. 23 above), pp. 53–189); Jesse R. Pitts, "Continuity and Change in Bourgeois France," in Stanley Hoffman, ed., *In Search of France* (Cambridge, Mass., 1964), pp. 249–304); Rainer C. Baum, "Values and Democracy in Imperial Germany," *Sociological Inquiry* 38 (1968):179–196); and Seymour Martin Lipset, *The First New Nation* (New York, 1965).

111. Parsons and Platt (n. 6 above), pp. 346–388.

112. Neil J. Smelser, "Epilogue: Social Structural Dimensions of Higher Education," in Parsons and Platt, pp. 389–422, and "Growth, Structural Change, and Conflict in California Higher Education, 1950–1970," in Smelser and Gabriel Almond, eds., *Public Higher Education in California* (Berkeley and Los Angeles, 1974), pp. 8–141.

113. Parsons and Winston White, "The Mass Media and the Structure of American Society," in Parsons (n. 70 above), pp. 241–251.

114. It is in regard to this strand of Parsons' writing—which certainly does not represent his treatment as a whole—that Gouldner's ideological critique has clear merit. See particularly Gouldner's argument that Parsons minimizes the tensions between "functional autonomy," "functional reciprocity," and "functional domination" (Alvin W. Gouldner, "Reciprocity and Autonomy in Functional Theory," in L. Gross, ed., *Symposium on Sociological Theory* [White Plains, N.Y., 1959], pp. 241–270). See also Ralph Dahrendorf, "Out of Utopia," *American Journal of Sociology* 64, no. 2 (1958):115–127.

115. Parsons and Platt, p. 291.

116. Ibid., p. 290.

117. A similar ideological reduction cross-cuts the argument Parsons and Platt make in *The American University* that social conflict is produced by the empirical disbalance between cognitive and noncognitive cultural concerns in the university's interchange with other, more instrumental functional exigencies. Parsons and Platt argue, e.g., that the university's radical critics are wrong because they want to "repudiate" the cognitive dimensions altogether (p. 274). Since the cognitive dimension is rooted in the very "epistemological" structure of action itself, they can proceed to argue against these critics not on their empirical or ideological merits but on purely generalized, analytical grounds. At other points in their argument, however, they do take a more empirical tack, as when they try to demonstrate that cognitive disbalance is only a temporary historical aberration.

118. Parsons, "The Distribution of Power in American Society," in *Politics and Social Structure* (n. 70 above), pp. 185–203.

119. Ibid., pp. 195, 197.

120. For an analysis of Parsons' middle-period discussion of historical variation in the development of Western elites, see ch. 3, sec. 4.2.

121. Ibid., p. 202.

122. Ibid., pp. 199–200.

123. A good example of such a radical ideological critique leveled from a more sophisticated analytic position can be found in some of Gintis' work. Gintis adopts Parsons' analytic perspective, and on the basis of the differentiation between cultural, social, and psychological systems adopts a much more voluntaristic perspective on social contradictions than more traditional Marxist-oriented critics. Yet on the basis of his particular ideological commitments and empirical findings, Gintis still argues for the dominance in American society of narrowly economistic imperatives. (Herbert Gintis, "A Radical Analysis of Welfare Economics and Individual Development," *Quarterly Journal of Economics* 86 [1972]:572–599; see also Gintis, "Alienation and Power: Towards a Radical Critique of Welfare Economics," Ph.D. diss., Harvard University, 1969.) It is interesting, in this regard, that in his commentary on Gintis' article Parsons adopts a much less conflationary position than in his reply to Mills, concentrating on more directly empirical and ideological responses ("Commentary on Herbert Gintis," *Quarterly Journal of Economics* 89 [1975]:281–290). For another leftist critique that is couched within a quasi-Parsonian analytic framework, which uses a different ideological position to develop similarly anti-Parsonian empirical propositions, see Bob Jessop, *Social Order, Reform, and Revolution* (London, 1972). The most direct attempt at fusing Marxian ideological and empirical positions with Parsons' analytic framework is Mark Gould, "Systems Analysis, Macrosociology and the Generalized Media of Social Action," in Loubser (n. 29 above), pp. 470–506.

124. See the discussion in ch. 5, sec. 2.1.

125. Parsons uses this empirical development as a critical "proof" of the differentiation of family from economy in the following: "Some Reflections on the Institutional Framework of Economic Development" and "Some Principal Characteristics of Industrial Societies," in his *Structure and Process in Modern Societies* (n. 27 above), pp. 98–131, 132–168; *Economy and Society* (with Smelser, n. 4 above), pp. 246–294; "The Distribution of Power in American Society" (n. 118 above); *The System of Modern Society* (n. 31 above), pp. 86–121.

126. "The Distribution of Power in American Society," p. 188.

127. *The Social System* (New York, 1951), pp. 157–171. For an analysis of the way Parsons develops this argument in *The Social System*, see ch. 5, sec. 2.1.

128. For critical comments on this aspect of Parsons' work, see Alvin W. Gouldner, *The Coming Crisis of Western Sociology* (New York, 1970), pp. 320–323, and Theodore D. Kemper, "On the Nature and Purpose of Ascription," *American Sociological Review* 39 (1974):844–853.

129. Parsons, "From the Point of View of the Author" (n. 50 above), pp. 343–344.

130. Parsons, "The Political Aspect of Social Structure and Process" (n. 101 above), p. 345.

131. For Parsons' more differentiated, nonconflationary analysis of the phenomenon of political generalization, see ch. 4, sec. 6.1.

132. "Political Aspect," p. 333, italics in original.

133. Chalmers Johnson uses media "inflation" and "deflation" in precisely this way in his *Revolutionary Change* (n. 44 above), indicating how it is often corrupt and traditionalistic political regimes that become deflated in response to growing demands for legitimate action. Similarly, one of the principal points in S. N. Eisenstadt's *The Political System of Empires* (New York, 1963) is that the generalization of political power can actually create increased movement toward barter and destabilization; these movements often increase, in fact, at the same time that legitimate power becomes increasingly separated from more ascriptive and less differentiated commitments (see p. 344).

134. The conflationary aspect of Parsons' presentation of his media theory is discussed in an extremely interesting, quasi-biographical way by Bliss C. Cartwright and R. Stephen Warner ("The Medium Is Not the Message," in Loubser [n. 29 above], pp. 639–661). They show that Parsons arrived at his definition of "generalized media" after a series of important empirical and ideological encounters. (1) Parsons' critical attitude toward populist notions of direct democracy—which he tried to justify in a purely analytic way—may have been strongly affected by Shils' argument that McCarthyism derived from the overly populist ideology of American politics, an ideology which prevented the kind of toleration for secrecy exhib-

ited by the more elitist politics of England (Parsons' discussions appeared after Shils', and he and Shils were close co-workers at the time); (2) Parsons' critical confrontation with Mills' power-elite theory, which increased his suspicions of the kind of "utopian," individualistic ideologies of direct control that, he believed, underrepresent the needs of the collectivity as a whole; (3) Parsons' empirical understanding of fascism and American right-wing movements as presenting type cases of undifferentiated, deflated political systems. "What later appear ostensibly as derivations from the [media] concept," Cartwright and Warner conclude, "were earlier derived from [these] more particular substantive premises" (p. 648).

> It would seem that under the rubric of "generalization," an attribute of money as a medium, Parsons has included a number of attributes of 'power' in his more special [i.e., empirical and ideological] sense. . . . One gets the feeling that Parsons has somehow overloaded a valuable heuristic model with theoretical burdens it was never meant to carry. (Pp. 647, 656.)

Another, more indirect argument for Parsons' "overloading" of the media concept—what I would call its conflationary treatment—is presented by Terrence S. Turner in "Parsons' Concept of 'Generalized Media of Social Interaction' and Its Relevance for Social Anthropology" *Sociological Inquiry* 38 [1968]: 121–134). Turner argues, quite legitimately, that the "prestation gifts" of primitive societies are generalized media of exchange in the strict analytic sense in which Parsons' defines that concept. Yet such gifts enforce highly ascriptive, traditionalistic sanctions, which, in empirical and ideological terms, place strong limits on individual and societal freedom. The degree of generalized exchange in such societies, therefore, is highly restricted. This points to precisely the point I have just made: more empirical specification is needed for any ideological evaluation of the political process to be made. Arguing that a societal process involves generalized media does not demonstrate the ideological and empirical points that Parsons' conflationary argument implies.

135. For this approach to the influence media, see ch. 4, sec. 6.1, and ch. 5, sec. 2.3.2.

136. Parsons, "On the Concept of Influence," in his *Sociological Theory and Modern Society* (n. 69 above), pp. 355–382, see pp. 368–370.

137. Parsons, "Postscript to 'On the Concept of Influence,'" in his *Politics and Social Structure* (n. 70 above), pp. 430–438, see p. 434.

138. Parsons' confusion on this point helps explain the extraordinary difficulty he had in defining a base, or "intrinsic persuader," for the influence medium. He moved forth and back from the neutral concept of "information" or "solidly verifiable information" to the conflationary concept of "*Gemeinschaft*" or "diffuse solidarity." His overlapping ideo-

logical and empirical ambitions kept him from achieving the kind of analytic sophistication he desired (see, e.g., "Postscript to 'On the Concept of Influence,' " pp. 432–433).

139. Parsons, "On the Concept of Value Commitments," in his *Sociological Theory and Modern Society* (n. 69 above), pp. 439–472, see pp. 457, 472.

140. For this substantive, as contrasted to formal, aspect of "value generalization," see ch. 5, sec. 2.3.2.

141. "On the Concept of Value Commitments," pp. 455–456.

142. Ibid., pp. 467–472.

143. Parsons can thoroughly misconstrue the implications of his own empirical work if it implies a negative, pessimistic prospect for historical development. An example is his evaluation of the future of student conflict in *The American University* (n. 6 above). Parsons and Platt repeatedly assert that such conflict and unrest should be viewed in the context of "typical" reactions to new structural differentiations, in this case the differentiation of the cognitively specialized American university system. Relating their work to Smelser's analysis in *Social Change in the Industrial Revolution*, they compare contemporary student reactions to those of the working classes in nineteenth-century England, who reacted with violent dissatisfaction against the differentiation of home and work place. Student unrest, they contend, is formally parallel, a reaction against the increased demands for tolerance of the impersonal, cognitively specialized activity embodied in the modern university. Once such tolerance is developed, this conflict will disappear. In this way, Parsons and Platt can view student unrest as epiphenomenal, as a phase which has no long-term, systematic historical roots. Yet this analogy with Smelser's findings is thoroughly misleading. According to Smelser, worker discontent and unrest were mitigated only after extensive *additional* structural differentiations had occurred. In response to worker protest, fundamental changes in family structure and work arrangements were made; indeed, totally new institutions, like trade unions, schools, and credit associations were developed to soften the impact of the earlier differentiation and to make the factory workers' environments more integrated and secure. It is quite possible, of course, that some parallel changes have been initiated in the student environments, but Parsons and Platt never address this question. Parsons avoids this focus because it would be inconsistent with the relatively quiescent liberalism of his later work and the conflationary ambition of his theoretical strategy, according to which he must argue that essential differentiation has been completed.

144. Parsons and White (n. 113 above). For a detailed and highly original statement of this position, which relies on Parsons' theory of structural differentiation, see Winston White, *Beyond Conformity* (New York, 1961).

145. Parsons, *Societies* (n. 19 above), pp. 22–23.

146. See, e.g., Philip Selznick review of Black, ed., *The Social Theories of Talcott Parsons*, in *American Sociological Review* 26 (1961):932–935.

147. E.g., Benton Johnson (n. 63 above), p. 60.

148. For Parsons' earlier criticism of the positivist error of "misplaced concreteness," see ch. 2, sec. 1.

This same criticism has been leveled by Loubser in his "General Introduction" to the two-volume festschrift prepared by Parsons' students (*Explorations in General Theory in Social Science* [n. 29 above], pp. 1–22). While arguing that Parsons' critics have judged his analytic theory by an overly specific, realistic empirical standard, Loubser adds that "Parsons himself has not consistently adhered to *analytical* realism and has fallen on occasion into the same fallacy" (p. 3, italics added). Moreover, Loubser implicitly relates this "theoretical reification" to Parsons' problems with the "weighting of factors" (i.e., his propensity for idealism), his problems with social change, and his overly positive attitude to American society (pp. 3, 5). Unfortunately, Loubser does not pursue this line of critical analysis. For this reason he fails to connect such "misplaced concreteness" to the serious internal strains that permeate Parsons' work.

CHAPTER EIGHT

1. Talcott Parsons, *Societies: Evolutionary and Comparative Perspectives* (Englewood Cliffs, N.J., 1966), p. 113.

2. For Parsons' analysis of this rationalist-collectivist tradition, see *The Structure of Social Action* (New York, [1937] 1968), esp. pt. 1. For my earlier discussion, see ch. 2, sec. 2.

3. Ibid., pp. 59–60.

4. Ibid., p. 110, italics added. This is the same error that informs Louis Dumont's otherwise penetrating analysis in *From Mandeville to Marx* (Chicago, 1977).

5. Parsons, *Structure of Social Action*, p. 93.

6. Ibid., pp. 91–92; see also p. 346, n. 2.

7. Ibid., p. 362, italics added.

8. Ibid., p. 89. R. Stephen Warner has acutely described this contradictory conflation of order with presuppositional and empirical criteria in "Toward a Redefinition of Action Theory: Paying the Cognitive Element Its Due," *American Journal of Sociology* 83 (1978):1317–1349.

9. *Structure of Social Action*, pp. 96–97.

10. Ibid., pp. 97, 100–102. For Elie Halévy's discussion of Locke, see his *The Growth of Philosophic Radicalism* (New York, [1901–1904] 1972), pp. 5–6, 43–44, 137–138.

11. Parsons uses the term *positivism* instead of *rationalism* because he has conflated his methodological and presuppositional critiques. This conflation helps justify his earlier argument that factual, or material, order is

not satisfactory; since it describes order only in a statistical, or scientific, sense, it commits not only the individualistic error, but the methodological error of positivism as well. Since positivism is clearly inadequate on the methodological level, Parsons can reason that rationalist-collectivist theories must be rejected on these grounds alone. For my discussion of this tendency to conflate rationalism and positivism, see ch. 2, sec. 2.1.

12. *Structure of Social Action*, pp. 99–125.

13. Ibid., pp. 124–125, 129.

14. Ibid., p. 96, n. 2.

15. Halévy (n. 10 above), pp. 75–87, 120–203.

16. See the more accurate historical account in H. Stuart Hughes, *Consciousness and Society* (New York, 1958).

17. In addition to legitimating the idealist strand of Parsons' theoretical reading, this reading of Western intellectual history offers an important secondary gain because it also supports Parsons' latent positivism. Parsons paints a linear picture of Western theoretical development as accumulation, as opposed, e.g., to an understanding which emphasizes the crucial fact of revolutionary, often unpredictable breakthroughs. If, in contrast, Parsons had described Durkheim as in direct conflict with Spencer or Marx, rather than as completely superceding them, it would have been more difficult for him to conflate his presuppositional argument with a methodological one. For my analysis of "history" in theoretical argument, see vol. 2, ch. 1.

18. *Structure of Social Action*, pp. 52–69; see also p. 91, n. 1.

19. For a general discussion of the conflation of order and action, and the manner in which it justifies one-dimensional arguments for sociological idealism or materialism, see vol. 1, pp. 115–122.

20. Parsons, "Social Classes and Class Conflict in the light of Recent Sociological Theory, in his *Essays in Sociological Theory* (New York, [1940] 1954), pp. 323–335, quoting p. 323. It is for this reason that Mark Gould, in arguing against Parsons' exclusion of Marx from the "founding fathers" discussed in *Structure*, criticizes Parsons' equation of utilitarianism with a random understanding of order. In arguing that Parsons should have included Marx in his analysis of the sociological critique of individualism, Gould insists, quite rightly, that a utilitarian "may attribute an order to ends within a system of interactions, not because the ends are regulated by social values, but because mutually interrelated actions define the conditions for mutually related unit acts, thus limiting what ends are attainable." He concludes that "a simple version of such a theory is based on a Hobbesian sovereign." ("Parsons versus Marx: 'An earnest warning . . .,' " *Sociological Inquiry* 51 [1981]:197–218, quoting 201.) Yet Gould errs, it seems to me, when he suggests that Marx should have been included in *Structure* as an earlier representative of "voluntaristic theory." Marx's "base" is Hobbes' sovereign in another form: Marx must be

seen, therefore, as a contributor to one side of the dialectic out of which a voluntaristic, multidimensional theory would have to be built.

21. *Structure of Social Action*, p. 345.

22. Ibid., p. 346.

23. Ibid., p. 404.

24. For my earlier discussion of Parsons' critique of Durkheim's idealism, see ch. 2, secs. 2, 4.

25. Ibid., pp. 444–446.

26. For the distinction between sociological and epistemological idealism, see vol. 1, pp. 69–71.

27. Ibid., p. 465.

28. Ibid., pp. 58–69.

29. For Parsons' writing on this aspect of Weber's work, see my discussion in ch. 2, sec. 2.

30. Ibid., pp. 658–672.

31. Ibid., pp. 343–375, 441–450.

32. Ibid., pp. 601–609.

33. Parsons, "The Motivation of Economic Activities," in *Essays in Sociological Theory* (n. 20 above), p. 62.

34. This approach to the pattern variables, I should emphasize, is contrary to the multidimensional argument which Parsons establishes in these same essays (see ch. 3, sec. 2). In this more satisfactory treatment, he criticizes the conception of instrumental, self-interested economic action not only as an inadequate approach to order, but, more importantly, as an inadequate understanding of action. To correct this approach to action, Parsons argues that the conception of self-interest must be expanded. Because moral internalization profoundly influences motivation, he contends, the perception of conditional structures must be filtered through normative order.

35. See ch. 3, sec. 3.1.

36. Parsons, *The Social System* (New York, 1951), pp. 4–5. See also Parsons and Edward A. Shils, "Values, Motives, and Systems of Action," in Parsons and Shils, eds., *Towards a General Theory of Action* (New York, 1951), pp. 47–248, see pp. 57, 103.

37. For a discussion of Parsons' middle-period critique of the culture-personality school, see ch. 3., sec. 3.1.

38. This movement toward a one-dimensional argument is explicitly formulated in Parsons' and Shils' early discussion in *Towards a General Theory of Action* (n. 36 above). They focus here on the inadequacies of biological and behaviorist approaches to action. Because survival or physical pleasure becomes the principal criterion for individual choice, these theories ignore the plurality of options that a social environment presents to an actor; concomitantly, they ignore the importance of individual intentionality. But Parsons and Shils then move from this perfectly legitimate

critique of instrumentalism to the argument that it is normative elements that principally structure individual intentionality: "Survival is *not* the sole ground of this selection; on the contrary, we hold that internalized cultural values are the *main* grounds of such selection" (p. 63, italics added). The argument that biological or instrumental conditions are not the "sole" criterion, however, in no way justifies the conclusion that noninstrumental values are themselves the "main" grounds of the social environment. This is a false dichotomy which marks a deviation from multidimensional thinking.

39. Parsons, *The Social System*, pp. 28–29.

40. Ibid., p. 37.

41. Ibid., pp. 40, 37.

42. Ibid., pp. 29, 40.

43. Ibid., p. 42, italics added.

44. Ibid., p. 36.

45. Ibid., pp. 30, 41; see Parsons and Shils (n. 36 above), pp. 191 ff.

46. In W. G. H. Sprott's detailed summary of this argument, published as a kind of "primer" to *The Social System* ("Principia Sociologica," *British Journal of Sociology* 3, no. 3 [1953]:203–221), this conflationary logic is more direct than in Parsons' more complex and obscure treatment. After describing Parsons' discussion of the subjective orientations of interacting individuals, Sprott writes that "Ego must therefore conform," and concludes that "we have now *derived* the normative element from the nature of interactive systems" (p. 203). Sprott follows Parsons, in other words, by equating normative action with stable, hence conforming interaction.

My criticism of Parsons on this point is complementary to Gouldner's important argument in "The Norm of Reciprocity" (*American Sociological Review* 25 [April 1960]:161–178) that Parsons takes complementarity as dependent solely upon normative constraints. At the same time, however, Gouldner completely ignores the other side of Parsons' argument, which attends more closely to multidimensionality (pp. 164, 167, 173). Even within this purely normative description, moreover, Gouldner overstates his case by claiming that Parsons assumes that equilibrium among actors is maintained without any outside intervention, a statement that ignores Parsons' great emphasis on deviance and normative social control.

47. Parsons, *The Social System*, p. 43.

48. Ibid., pp. 69–73.

49. Ibid., p. 74.

50. Ibid., pp. 38, 46.

51. Ibid., pp. 82–88.

Rex catches this abrupt shift in emphasis very well:

> We are told that "every social system must have mechanisms for the allocation of possession of facilities, because their possession is desirable and they are inherently limited in supply relation to demand. . . . Now we

> might expect this to lead to a discussion of the struggle for power in social systems. But in Parsons the discussion does not take this course. The scarcity of facilities imposed by the unequal distribution of power is something to which the social system has to be adapted. . . . Thereafter discussion of power drops into the background and the system is discussed as though it were integrated purely in terms of value-patterns. (John Rex, *Key Problems in Sociological Theory* [London, 1961], p. 110.)

52. *The Social System*, p. 88.

It is their failure to understand the *sociological* form of Parsons' idealism that has led so many commentators to argue, erroneously, that his social theory is concerned only with cultural regulations. Thus, Timasheff writes in his well-known textbook on sociological theory:

> Culture, as Parsons stresses frequently, is internalized by those who share it, and when thus internalized it becomes a learned behavior tendency that is as real as any kind of potential energy. Thus, there is no substantial difference between culture and social system, if, as Parsons argues, the latter is identified with a network of role expectations. (Nicholas S. Timasheff and George A. Theodorson, *Sociological Theory* [New York, 1976], p. 259.)

This is not, however, Parsons' point, for even in his idealist strand he argues that the social system provides independent structuration of roles. Yet by arguing that these roles are always institutionalized within value arrangements which can themselves be logically deduced from the pattern variables, Parsons writes "as if" the social-system level did not really matter. This qualifying "as if," of course, is precisely what distinguishes sociological from epistemological idealism.

The only way to avoid this "as if" reduction is to construct a truly multidimensional analysis of role distribution. Parsons does in fact accomplish this in *The Social System* (ch. 4–5) and even more impressively, perhaps, in his parallel discussion with Shils in *Towards a General Theory of Action* (pp. 209–212). Parsons and Shils describe role differentiation as being based on the "functional prerequisites of order." These functional tasks are defined by the tasks of allocation and integration, as the latter are modified by interaction with the overarching cultural order that is established by dominant pattern-variable combinations. Parsons and Shils define roles, furthermore, as institutionalizing each of the three fundamental dimensions of instrumental, expressive, and integrative orientations. Yet this discussion, too, is cross-cut by an idealist approach, for Parsons and Shils tend to subsume the problems of exchange within value standards rather than interweave them in a balanced way. (Pp. 213–218.) For other discussions of the tension between objectivist and subjectivist aspects of Parsons' analysis of social roles, see Ken Menzies, *Talcott Parsons and the Social Image of Man* (London, 1977), pp. 65, 71, and S. N. Eisenstadt and

M. Curelaru, *The Form of Sociology: Paradigms and Crises* (New York, 1976), pp. 273–274.

53. For Parsons' discussions of allocation and integration and the central role they play in the multidimensional strand of his theory, see ch. 3, sec. 3.2.

54. See the similar phenomenon noted in my analysis of Weber's work (e.g., in *The Religion of China*) in vol. 3, ch. 3, sec. l.

55. *The Social System*, pp. 51–52.

56. Ibid., p. 55.

57. Ibid., p. 93.

58. Ibid., pp. 174 ff.; see also pp. 100–101.

59. Ibid., pp. 74, 114, 416.

60. For Parsons' multidimensional approach to institutional differentiation, which occupies the first two-thirds of ch. 5, see my discussion, above, in ch. 3, sec. 3.3.

61. Parsons, *The Structure of Social Action*, pp. 689–691.

62. Ibid., p. 550.

63. I should add that this ambivalence about the pattern-variable schema can be found in the early middle period as well. On this point, see the discussion of Parsons' early essays in this chapter (sec. 1).

64. For this multidimensional approach to the ascriptive and achievement complexes, see ch. 3, sec. 3.4.

65. Sprott's "primer" to *The Social System* (n. 46 above), once again, demonstrates this ambivalent approach to the pattern variables in an unusually clear way. On the one hand, Sprott presents the pattern variables as introducing a "further set of limitations [on institutions] worked out deductively" from cultural affinities; on the other hand, he presents them as being generalized from the actual "empirical clusterings" of institutions (p. 215). But the pattern variables cannot, of course, be both of these at the same time.

This internal contradiction reaches into the most technical, esoteric level of Parsons' argument. In one aspect of his analysis in *The Social System*, e.g., the pattern-variable combinations are derived indirectly by interweaving the three modes of orientation (cognition, cathexis, and morality) with the three levels of order (personality, culture, and society). It is in reference to the latter orders, particularly in terms of the influence of social-system scarcity, that the "structural" relevance of the pattern-variable schema arises. In Parsons' idealist analysis, however, the pattern variables are derived by interrelating cognitive, cathectic, and moral considerations with psychological and cultural exigencies alone. They are not related, in other words, to the tension created between culture and personality, on the one hand, and the conditional exigencies of society, on the other (see *The Social System*, chs. 2, 3, 5).

66. Parsons and Shils (n. 36 above), pp. 76 ff.

67. *The Social System*, p. 184.
68. Ibid., p. 185.
69. Ibid., pp. 182–199; cf. Parsons and Shils, pp. 80–88.
70. See these observations by Menzies:

> Normally, theories in the idealist tradition focus on unique clusters. [But] while still accepting the subjective point of view and the use of "verstehen," Persons sees the orientations of actors as being of a limited range of types which he classified in terms of the pattern variables. . . .
>
> [This] is in direct opposition to Winch's position that the form of life of a society can be described only in terms participants use themselves . . . and in direct contradiction to the claim, of some, that seeing action as meaningful precludes scientific laws. Parsons' claims to provide universally meaningful categories, and laws about actions described in terms of them, eliminates one major source of embarrassment for people who want to argue against Winch and still remain within the idealist tradition. They [now] have examples to illustrate their positions. If these examples are accepted, the debate is over. (Menzies, *Talcott Parsons and the Social Image of Man* [n. 52 above], pp. 160, 89; see also pp. 71–88, passim.)

For the same kind of interpretation, see Martel's discussion of Parsons' advances within the idealist tradition of social thought:

> The pattern variable formulation is significant because it suggested that important content differences between societal values and institutions—often thought of before in more historically restricted terms—could be viewed nomothetically as variations on common human themes apparent even in the smallest acts; rather vague theoretical ideas were converted into more succinct variables with definite classificatory categories and some unit anchorage; and . . . by making the jump from societal patterns to elementary actions, an opening was made for further extensions to intermediate levels with some content continuity. (Martin U. Martel, "Academentia Praecox: The Aims, Merits, and Scope of Parsons' Multi-Systemic Language Rebellion, 1958–1968," in Herman Turk and Richard L. Simpson, eds., *Institutions and Social Exchange: The Sociologies of Talcott Parsons and George C. Homans* [Indianapolis, 1971], pp. 175–211, quoting p. 192.)

Most of the extensive case studies that have utilized the pattern-variable schema may be viewed precisely in this manner, as vital advances within the idealist tradition, cultural studies that go beyond the idiographic to establish systematic cultural laws in different kinds of social situations. (See, e.g., the work of Robin Williams, Samuel Stouffer, Jackson Toby, Robert Merton, Kingsley Davis, William Goode, Marion Levy, William Moore, Robert Blau, Robert Bellah, Neil Smelser, Rainer Baum, and Seymour Martin Lipset). A few of the utilizations of the pattern-variable schema, however, extend beyond the idealist tradition and follow Parsons' more multidimensional usage, using the patterns both as cultural inputs and also as ways of characterizing patterns established by economic, political, and ecological situations. In this context, see, e.g., Lipset's analysis of class relationship and value patterns in West European nations in *The First New Nation* (New York, 1963), ch. 6, and Robert Dreeben's analysis of the relation between ecological patterns and values in early education (*On What Is Learned in School* [Reading, Mass., 1968]).

71. *The Social System*, p. 207.

72. Ibid., p. 208.

73. Ibid., pp. 216 ff.

74. Ibid., p. 238. In terms of its description of the process of socialization itself, however, this analysis remains multidimensional.

75. See ch. 3, sec. 4.3. and ch. 5, sec. 2.

76. Ibid., p. 251.

77. Ibid., pp. 251–252. For a general discussion of the multidimensional aspects of Parsons' treatment of the origins of deviant activity, see ch. 3, sec. 4.3.

78. Ibid., p. 250, italics added.

79. On this point even Sprott, certainly a friend to Parsons' theory, takes exception: "What, however, one cannot quite allow to pass is the absence of any reference to the repercussions of action on non-action variables, e.g., population structure, material resources, etc." ("Principia Sociologica" [n. 46 above], p. 220).

80. *The Social System*, pp. 267–272.

81. Ibid., p. 252.

82. Ibid., pp. 252–267: see also p. 292.

83. See especially, ibid., pp. 286 ff.

84. Ibid., p. 277.

85. Ibid., p. 278.

86. Ibid., p. 278, italics added.

87. Ibid., pp. 274, 276. Most of Parsons' conflict critics have erred by making the claim that his deviance theory, because it relies heavily on psychological variables, is individualistic. Referring to Parsons, e.g., Coser writes that in "the dominant trend of contemporary American sociology, the psychological subsumes the structural and hence individual malfunctioning subsumes social conflict," and he notes what he believes to be Parsons' "conviction that psychoanalysts and other mental health specialists can play a significant role in reducing deviance" (Lewis Coser, *The Functions of Social Conflict* [New York, 1956], pp. 20, 23). This same position is presented in Ralf Dahrendorf, *Class and Class Conflict in Industrial Society* (Stanford, Calif., 1959), pp. 157–240; Judith Blake and Kingsley Davis, "Norms, Values, and Sanctions," in Robert E. L. Faris, ed., *Handbook of Modern Sociology* (Chicago, 1964), pp. 456–484; and Dennis Wrong, "The Over-Socialized Conception of Man in Modern Sociology," *American Sociological Review* 26 (1961):183–193.

This critique accuses Parsons of making an individualistic explanation of deviance, of making an argument for individualistic as opposed to collectivistic approaches to order. To the contrary, Parsons' error derives from making an idealistic approach to collectivist order itself. Parsons' emphasis on the psychological aspects of deviance, in other words, is always made within the context of his Durkheimian critique of Freudian theory. He never puts this distinction more clearly than when he emphasizes, in *The Social System*, that "we are speaking here of regression in relation to the order and conditions of acquisition of value-orientation patterns, not of [regression in relation to] object attachments as such" (p. 233). It is for this reason that his deviance theory can utilize concepts like emotional regression without invoking psychologistic explanations.

88. For Parsons' multidimensional analysis of the left-right polarization, see ch. 3, sec. 4.2.

89. Ibid., pp. 295 ff.

90. Ibid., p. 293; see also pp. 522 ff.

91. Another problem in Parsons' treatment of radical and conservative deviance, and one which has generally been overlooked, is presented by his contention that deviance is an inherently disequilibriating phenomenon. This bias allows Parsons to overlook the kind of deviance—often committed by elites—which has become successfully institutionalized in a system's dominant value-system. In such situations, deviant values actually play an important part in maintaining a system's equilibrium. This kind of deviance—e.g., the partial institutionalization of racist or elitist values in a politically democratic nation—may itself be the target for radical attacks which disequilibriate the social system. Yet, strictly speaking, such radical attacks should be considered no more deviant, and sometimes less so, than the system's antidemocratic values which are their target.

Parsons' failure to distinguish between deviance per se and disequilibrium allows him to conflate further his deviance analysis with ideological judgments. (A good example of how Parsons' deviance model can, in fact, be applied to deviations within *institutionalized* value systems can be found in Francis X. Sutton et al.'s discussion of the American business ideology, *The American Business Creed* (New York, 1956).

92. For the multidimensional use of these sanctions, see ch. 3, sec. 4.3.

93. *The Social System*, p. 299.

94. Ibid., pp. 299–302.

95. Ibid., pp. 317–318.

96. See ch. 5, secs. 2.3.3 and 2.4.

97. Parsons and Shils (n. 36 above), p. 230. For this multidimensional listing of strategies of social control, see ch. 3, sec. 4.3.

98. The manner in which Parsons' students and coworkers have utilized his theory to treat deviance in a more multidimensional way constitutes indirect corroboration of the argument here presented. It

demonstrates, in the first place, the kind of deep-rooted ambiguity that pervades Parsons' model; it also indicates, more incidentally, the manner in which scientific paradigms adapt and respond to internal presuppositional strains. (Compared with most of the rest of Parsons' writing, the deviance model does constitute an empirically related exemplar in Kuhn's technical sense of that term.)

In terms of the sources of deviance, the outstanding example of a multidimensional treatment is Merton's discussion of the innovative deviance which is created by the scarcity of means rather than the disequilibrium of ends (Robert K. Merton, "Social Structure and Anomie," *American Sociological Review* 3 [1938]:677–682). Almost two decades later, Sutton et al. (n. 91 above) placed role conflict at the heart of their discussion of the deviance represented by the American business ideology, but they viewed this conflict as generated by "realistic," conditional factors, rooted in the industrial economy as much as in the conflict between different kinds of pattern variables. Shortly afterward, William J. Goode formulated a conception of role strain that actually emphasized the individual's rational manipulation of scarce resources ("A Theory of Role Strain," *American Sociological Review* 25 [1960]:483–496). At about the same time, Robin Williams called attention to the fact that, contrary to the gist of Parsons' own deviance analysis, role complementarity "may be subject to endemic strain because of the difficulty of 'equating' exchanges of gratification and because of the likelihood of 'egoistic' tendencies on the part of the interacting parties." He argued that any focus on this lack of complementarity would involve emphasis on "differences in power, in the sense of unequal capacities to control the exchange relationship." (*The Sociological Theory of Talcott Parsons* [Ithaca, N.Y., 1961], p. 86.) Later, in "Norms, Values, and Sanctions," Blake and Davis (n. 87 above) argued, in effect, that Parsons' deviance paradigm does not inherently exclude an emphasis on illegitimate instrumental means to achieve acceptable goals (pp. 472–474).

As for the control of deviance, in both of his major works Smelser has applied the "therapy" model to the political control of conflict in a way that emphasizes the instrumental and coercive aspects of the "rewards" and the "withdrawal of reciprocity" (*Social Change in the Industrial Revolution* [Chicago, 1959], p. 15, and *Theory of Collective Behavior* [New York, 1962], passim). For a broad discussion of Parsons' students' adaptation to the strains in his work, see ch. 10 below.

99. I will discuss this meta-methodological strategy for legitimating Parsons' idealist emphasis in ch. 9, sec. 4.

100. *The Social System*, pp. 14–17, 490, 539 (n. 2).

See Edward C. Devereux's description of Parsons' attack on the idealism of the culture and personality school in "Parsons' Sociological Theory" in Max Black, ed., *The Social Theories of Talcott Parsons* (Ithaca, N.Y., 1961), pp. 1–63, see pp. 17–18. Devereux, however, accepts this attack on idealism at face value, failing to make the distinction between epistemological and sociological idealism.

101. Parsons, "The General Interpretation of Action," in Parsons et al., eds., *Theories of Society* (New York, 1961), pp. 85–97, quoting p. 93.

102. Rex, *Key Problems* (n. 51 above), pp. 106 ff; David Lockwood, "Some Remarks on 'The Social System,' " *British Journal of Sociology* 7, no. 2 (1956):144 (n. 17), 145, and idem, "Social Integration and System Integration," in G. K. Zollschan and W. Hirsch, eds., *Explorations in Social Change* (London, 1964), pp. 245–257, see pp. 242–252.

103. For the "misreading" argument, see Rainer C. Baum, "The Generalized Media in Action," in J. J. Loubser et al., eds., *Explorations in General Theory in Social Science* (New York, 1976), pp. 448–469, esp. p. 454. For the general argument that Parsons has maintained a consistent multidimensional perspective throughout his work, see, e.g., Harold J. Bershady, *Ideology and Social Knowledge* (New York, 1973), and Loubser, "General Introduction," in Loubser et al., *Explorations*, pp. 1–25, esp. pp. 4–5.

104. See, e.g., Enno Schwanenberg, "The Two Problems of Order in Parsons Theory: An Analysis from Within," *Social Forces* 49 (1971):569–581.

105. Lockwood, who calls for a synthesis of normative and factual theories, includes Durkheim in his own theoretical argument, and criticizes the conflict school for an excessively rationalistic position ("Some Remarks on 'The Social System' " [n. 102 above], pp. 140–143, and "Social Integration and System Integration" [n. 102 above]). Yet he argues, at the same time, that strains toward such conflict emerge only from the material substratum ("Some Remarks," pp. 136–137). His illustrations of social change, furthermore, leave normative elements out completely, drawing only upon Marx's economic theory and the instrumental aspect of Weber's political sociology ("Social Integration," pp. 250–256). Similarly, Rex responds to Parsons' lack of attention to the material order by proposing an alternative in which society is divided into groups whose ends are entirely separated and where instrumental interest alone divides the participants in any conflict (*Key Problems* [n. 51 above], pp. 102 ff.).

106. Devereux presented an early influential position that confuses the presuppositional issue by arguing for Parsons' multidimensionality and idealism at the same time. He states, e.g., that for Parsons, order "could not be a resultant either of rational self-interest or of externally imposed sanctions *alone*, but must rest on a *core* of institutionalized common values" ("Parsons' Sociological Theory" [n. 100 above], pp. 11–12). Or again, while arguing that Parsons synthesized utilitarian and idealist positions, he also asserts that for Parsons "psychological and motivational factors provide the forces, strains, and tensions with which he likes to deal" (p. 52). Benton Johnson presents a similarly ambiguous picture in *Functionalism in Modern Sociology: Understanding Talcott Parsons* (Morristown, N.J., 1975),

pp. 10–16, as does François Bourricaud in *L'Individualisme institutionnel: Essai sur la sociologie de Talcott Parsons* (Paris, 1977). The latter work is particularly interesting in this regard, not just because it is the finest work yet published on Parsons' thought but also because Bourricaud, at certain points in his discussion, makes a strong case for the multidimensionality of Parsons' thought and a strong critique of those who accuse him of idealism. Yet alongside this discussion, Bourricaud paradoxically writes—as Parsons does himself—that "the science of action begins by the study of the norms to which actors submit, which constitute the 'structure' or the 'anatomy' of society" (p. 33). Following Parsons' own idealist turn, he goes on to define Parsons' "sociological theorem" as the contention that norms cannot be reduced to conditions (p. 41), and he follows one of Parsons' rationales for this idealism by equating Parsons' support for objective scientific method with an emphasis on the importance and autonomy of objective material conditions (p. 42). Yet the external conditions to which Bourricaud often refers in his analysis of Parsons' theory are merely the subjective evaluations by alter of ego's acts (e.g., pp. 72–73, 102). The ambiguity of Bourricaud's sympathetic analysis, in other words, closely follows the ambiguity in Parsons' own work.

To my knowledge, only one interpreter, Ken Menzies, has recognized the internal ambiguity of Parsons' theory. In *Talcott Parsons and the Social Image of Man* (n. 52 above), Menzies sees Parsons as torn between his idealist "theory of action" and his positivist "systems theory." Despite this important insight, Menzies' analysis suffers from serious conflationary strains. He never specifies precisely the theoretical properties to which these central antinomies refer, whether the action-system conflict is over (1) an individual-versus-collective emphasis in a presuppositional sense, (2) a normative-versus-instrumental perspective, (3) an institutional-versus-functional approach to questions of model, or (4) a meta-methodological conflict between idealism and positivism. These fundamental distinctions are insufficiently clarified because Menzies evidently assumes that all these levels—the presuppositional questions of action and order, the problem of model, and the issue of methodological assumptions—vary together. He also fails to recognize the significant elements in Parsons' work where a true theoretical synthesis is achieved.

CHAPTER NINE

1. For this analytical justification of the differentiation of pattern maintenance and integration as an argument for multidimensional theorizing, see ch. 4, sec. 1.3.

2. For Parsons' rejection of Durkheim's strategy of crucial experiment as the source of his idealist tendencies, and his justification for systematic theory as a strategy for achieving multidimensionality, see ch. 2, sec. 5. In

the terms developed in the preceding chapter, interchange theory can be identified as a more satisfactory—more sophisticated and secularized—version of Durkheim's religious model of modern life.

3. See ch. 4, sec. 2.

4. Talcott Parsons and Neil Smelser, *Economy and Society* (New York, 1956), pp. 89, 91.

5. Ibid., p. 90.

6. Ibid., p. 53.

7. Ibid., p. 54.

8. Ibid., p. 222, italics added; see also pp. 221–232.

9. Ibid., p. 223.

10. Karl Marx, *Value, Price and Profit* (New York, 1969), p. 57.

11. For an analysis of the "Resource Chart" in terms of its multidimensional function in Parsons' work, see ch. 4, sec. 2.

12. Parsons and Smelser, *Economy and Society*, p. 121.

13. Neil J. Smelser, *The Sociology of Economic Life* (Englewood Cliffs, N.J., 1959), p. 160.

14. It seems likely that another reason for this reduction is Parsons' search for formalism: by describing the integrative-adaptive interchange in this manner he can portray it as perfectly isomorphic with Schumpeter's formal discussion of the entrepreneurial function in economic production.

15. Parsons and Smelser (n. 4 above), p. 66.

16. Ibid., pp. 75–76, 91–92.

17. I have dealt here with the idealist tilt in *Economy and Society* primarily in terms of the interchange model. Yet while the book taken as a whole deals with more than interchange, its other sections reflect a similar pattern of cross-cutting references. In ch. 3, Parsons and Smelser deal with the problem of the institutional structure of the economy, primarily in terms of the structure of contracts and the problem of imperfect markets. Although they begin with a multidimensional approach to the former, they qualify this synthetic aim by arguing that the normative sources of contract constitute their primary concern (p. 105). In their analysis of imperfect markets, trade unions and the supply of executive and professional labor occupy their principal attention. Although they mention the problem of the ways in which imbalances in power and money create instrumental pressures, they argue that unions exist largely for noneconomic, solidary reasons (p. 249). This uneven treatment is even more clear in Parsons' and Smelser's discussion of the supply of executive and professional labor, where they argue that the monopolistic, noncompetitive aspects of the markets stem primarily from the particular cultural demands of these occupational roles (pp. 151, 153). In ch. 4, Parsons and Smelser counterpose another multidimensional aspect of their analysis (pp. 196–218) by arguing that the most interesting aspect of the consumption and invest-

ment functions is the manner in which the residual categories of neoclassical theory can be redefined as functions of integrative and pattern-maintenance processes (pp. 219–245).

18. See ch. 4, sec. 3.

19. Parsons, "On the Concept of Political Power," in his *Sociological Theory and Modern Society* (New York, 1967), pp. 297–354, see p. 308.

20. Parsons, "The Distribution of Power in American Society," in his *Politics and Social Structure* (New York, 1969), pp. 185–203, quoting p. 200.

21. Thus, as Percy Cohen has written, while "Parsons does not necessarily neglect this [power] problem within his system . . . he tends to view it as a resource for maintaining a system of guiding changes within it, rather than as a device for imposing certain characteristics on it" (*Modern Social Theory* [London, 1968], p. 121).

22. I am grateful to Allan Kitner for demonstrating the logical possibility of this point in an undergraduate seminar at the University of California, Berkeley.

23. For a discussion of the collegial-bureaucratic split in the content of Parsons' multidimensional analysis, see ch. 4, sec. 3.

24. Parsons, "On the Concept of Political Power" (n. 19 above), p. 332.

25. Parsons, "The Political Aspect of Social Structure and Process," in his *Politics and Social Structure* (n. 20 above), pp. 317–351, see p. 338.

26. "On the Concept of Political Power," p. 323.

27. Ibid., p. 332.

28. Ibid., pp. 318–319; see also "The Political Aspect of Social Structure and Process," pp. 327–328.

29. "Political Aspect," pp. 323–324.

30. Ibid., p. 324.

31. Ibid., p. 325.

32. "Concept of Political Power," p. 323.

33. "Political Aspect," p. 326.

34. Parsons, *The System of Modern Societies* (Englewood Cliffs, N.J., 1971), p. 105.

35. "Political Aspect," p. 338, italics in original; see also Parsons, "Some Reflections on the Place of Force in Social Process," in *Sociological Theory and Modern Society* (n. 19 above), pp. 264–297, see p. 284.

In an interesting empirical application generated by this theory of collegial authority, Parsons and Platt explain the contrast between the bureaucratic atmosphere of high schools and the freedom of college life in terms of contrasting membership criteria. While colleges emphasize normative selectivity and, therefore, the importance of prior socialization and internalized skills, high school attendance is legally mandated for every American citizen, that is, enforced rather than voluntary. (*The American University* [Cambridge, Mass., 1973], pp. 209–215.)

36. *The System of Modern Societies*, p. 106, n. 40. It is the growing awareness of the freedom which is allowed highly skilled, professional labor power that has generated the movement within Marxism away from Marx's purely instrumental analysis of labor exchange and organizational authority toward "new working class" theories which emphasize the worker's subjective feelings of alienation rather than his objective exploitation. This approach to alienation focuses, in Parsons' terms, on the value-oriented, internalized elements of workers' actions. See, e.g., the references to internalization by the "new working class" theorist André Gorz, in his *Strategy for Labor* (Boston, 1967).

37. Probably the most clear-cut emphasis on the Protestant ethic as a crucial comparative factor in allowing Western labor to be "formally free" can be found in Weber's *General Economic History* (Glencoe, Ill., 1950).

38. It is true that Weber viewed the English style of modern politics as more substantively democratic than the purely formal mass democracy of, e.g., America, citing England's strong party organization which disciplined Caesarism. Still, this part of Weber's analysis was never integrated with his systematic discussion of the normative historical roots of democratic political behavior. See vol. 3, ch. 5.

39. Max Weber, "Bureaucracy," in Hans Gerth and C. Wright Mills, eds., *From Max Weber* (New York, 1958), pp. 196–244, see pp. 240–243. See also my discussion of the bureaucracy essay in vol. 3, ch. 5.

40. Parsons sharply criticized Weber for ignoring the role of professional competence in his important introduction to Weber's *Theory of Social and Economic Organization* (New York, 1947), pp. 58–60, n. 4.

In view particularly of this long-standing critique of Weber's excessive emphasis on hierarchy and involuntary control, it is surprising that so many of Parsons' critics have argued that he accepts authoritarian political organization as the norm of modern life. Gideon Sjoberg and Leonard D. Cain, e.g., claim that Weber's view of modern bureaucratic society is "accepted uncritically by Parsons ("Negative Values, Countersystem Models, and Analysis of Social Systems," in Herman Turk and Richard L. Simpson, eds., *Institutions and Social Exchange* [Indianapolis, 1971], p. 227). To the contrary, Parsons places the ideological issue of individual freedom from hierarchical control at the center of his political theory. Indeed, with the help of his presuppositional bias toward voluntarism, Parsons often bends his empirical vision to accommodate voluntarism in an overly optimistic fashion.

41. Parsons, "Political Aspect" (n. 25 above), p. 326.

42. In terms of the kinds of internal strains that have created conflict and revision among Parsons' students, it is revealing to compare Smelser's approach to collegiality with that of Parsons. Referring to collegial bodies as "estates" in the medieval sense, Smelser emphasizes the oppressive, expropriative aspects of contemporary faculty associations:

> As an "estate," the faculty retained control of all the main educational functions—research, graduate training, upper-division education, and lower-division education—but much of the work in all these categories was actually done by those in roles that were something less than that of faculty members. . . . These role-incumbents were asked to perform duties associated with faculty roles but were not given the same degree of formal responsibility or the same kinds of rewards. (Neil J. Smelser, "Growth, Structural Change, and Conflict in California Public Higher Education, 1950–1970," pp. 9–141 in Smelser and Gabriel Almond, eds., *Public Higher Education in California* [Berkeley and Los Angeles, 1974], pp. 9–141, quoting p. 29.)

Parsons, in contrast, confines the problem of monopoly only to the form of organization represented by economic markets, accepting the feudal connotations of collegial estates with equanimity:

> [Although] the collegial-associational type . . . has scarcely surfaced in ideological discussions yet, negative characterizations . . . tend either to treat [collegial-association organizations] as bureaucracies or as monopolies, the latter being a version of the economic model. Perhaps the feeling remains that as estates, collegial associations are medieval and have no place in the modern world. (Parsons and Platt, *The American University* [n. 35 above], p. 284, n. 26.)

It is this kind of ambiguity that makes Parsons' contribution to a theory of the modern professions such an uneven one. On the one hand, the normative strand of his analysis has made his theory of the professions the primary target for recent instrumentalist critics, who view the professions simply as means to maintain professional dominance (e.g., Eliot Freidson, *Professional Dominance* [New York, 1970]). At the same time, however, Parsons' multidimensional theory offers the basis for a much more synthetic approach to the role of professions in modern life. His analysis of the increasing importance of collegiality in bureacracy demonstrates the historical basis for the professions' voluntaristic and democratic impact, and the intrinsic connection between the enlargement of this impact and the growth of technical knowledge. In principle, this recognition need not be combined with the denial of professionalism's more instrumental features. For a recent example of this more balanced perspective, one which converges with a more balanced kind of Parsonian view, see Thomas L. Haskell, "Power to the Experts," *New York Review of Books*, October 13, 1977, pp. 28–33, and Bernard Barber, *Informed Consent in Medical Therapy and Research* (New Brunswick, N.J., 1980).

43. For a discussion of interest groups in Parsons' approach to political interchange, see ch. 4, sec. 3.2.

44. "Political Aspect" (n. 25 above), pp. 333, 335, 338. At times Parsons' reduction of politics to influence is put quite bluntly. Thus, his essay "Culture and Social System Revisited" (in Louis Schneider and Charles Bon-

jean, eds., *The Idea of Culture in the Social Sciences* [Cambridge, 1973], pp. 33–46) seems to place politics directly in the value rather than the conditional realm. The "crux of the interest problem and the integration of interest with the institutionalization of values," he says, "lies at the level of the political interest struggle" (p. 42). On the basis of this definition, Parsons proceeds to a rather peculiar explanation for the great concern with political equality in modern Western society. Whereas the instrumentalist tradition attributes the attention to political inequality either to Hobbesian political conflicts or to the division of property, Parsons attributes it to the needs of the value system, particularly to the widespread acceptance of achievement norms, "the expectation that social system units will contribute to the best of their abilities." "Since it cannot be assumed that capacities are equally distributed", he reasons, "the outcome of the achievement emphasis . . . tends to produce what is felt to be . . . inequality" (pp. 42–43). Although this statement is, in itself, unexceptionable, it presents a one-sided account of the origins of political inequality. There is a vast difference between this explanation, where Parsons feels compelled to choose between the material and ideal positions, and e.g., his multidimensional approach to political conflict which links the continuing focus on inequality to the inherent tension between utopian value legitimation and the facts of scarce political power.

45. Alvin W. Gouldner in *The Coming Crisis of Western Sociology* (New York, 1970) argues that Parsons ignores the dialectic between power and morality (pp. 292–297), discusses Parsons' lack of attention to the Michelsian tradition of organizational analysis (pp. 298–299), and criticizes the "collectivist" reference of Parsons' political sociology and its failure to emphasize the interplay of rational and nonrational factors (p. 264). Ralf Dahrendorf's discussion in *Class and Class Conflict in Industrial Society* (Stanford, Calif., 1959) remains the best critique of Parsons' failure to incorporate the instrumental elements of the Weberian tradition in his political theory (pp. 164–179). Both these critiques, however, fail to attend to the more multidimensional elements of Parsons' arguments. Anthony Giddens' insightful criticisms of Parsons' idealist treatment of politics is similarly intertwined with an erroneous contention that Parsons never pays any attention to the instrumental inputs to political process (" 'Power' in the Recent Writings of Talcott Parsons," *Sociology* 2 [1968]:257–272, esp. 264–268).

46. Harry M. Johnson, "The Generalized Symbolic Media in Parsons' Theory," *Sociology and Social Research* 57 (1973):208–221, see p. 214.

47. William C. Mitchell, *The American Polity* (New York, 1972), pp. 39, 45–46. Parsons' insistence on placing both "demands" and "support" in the integrative subsystem—though correct in the technical sense that demands are not instrumental sanctions in themselves—represents another example of formalism obscuring substance. Easton, who actually originat-

ed the demand-support terminology, does not even try to locate these inputs in a dimensional subsystem. Because he eschews such formalism, he can more easily articulate the economic and instrumental aspects of demands on the political system. See David Easton, *A Systems Analysis of Political Life* (New York, 1965).

48. S. N. Eisenstadt, *The Political System of Empires* (New York, 1969), pp. 8, 14, 19, 26, 110, 198–210, 315; also Eisenstadt's "Institutionalization and Change," *American Sociological Review* 29 (1964):235–247. Smelser has also come to emphasize the role of groups in initiating the process of interchange; see, particularly, "Growth, Structural Change, and Conflict in California Public Higher Education, 1950–1970" (n. 42 above).

49. Seymour Martin Lipset and Stein Rokkan, "Cleavage Structures, Party Systems, and Voter Alignments," in Lipset and Rokkan, eds., *Party Systems and Voter Alignments* (New York, 1967), pp. 1–64.

50. For Parsons' multidimensional approach to the cybernetic schema, see my discussion of his refinement of his presuppositional synthesis in ch. 2, sec. 3.2.

51. Parsons, *Societies: Evolutionary and Comparative Perspectives* (Englewood Cliffs, N.J., 1966), p. 16, italics altered.

52. Ibid., pp. 16–17.

53. Ibid., p. 113, italics added.

54. Ibid., p. 116.

55. Ibid., p. 114, italics in original.

56. For Parsons' multidimensional approach to "generalization-specification," see ch. 2, sec. 3.1.

57. Parsons, "Culture and Social System Revisited" (n. 44 above), p. 37, italics added.

58. For the multidimensional approach to "institutionalization," see ch. 4, secs. 1.3, 5.1.

59. Ibid., p. 41, italics added.

60. Ibid.

61. See, e.g., Parsons' statements about his revised understanding of the importance of law as the core of Weber's sociology in "Evaluation and Objectivity in Social Science: An Interpretation of Max Weber," in his *Sociological Theory and Modern Society* (n. 19 above), pp. 79–101, see pp. 92–96. For his own work, see his statement that "what we have been treating as the societal normative order comes very close to what is generally meant by the concept of law" and his general analysis of the role of law in society in *The System of Modern Societies* (n. 34 above), pp. 18–20. For his final statement, see "Law as an Intellectual Stepchild," *Sociological Inquiry* 47, nos. 3–4 (1977):11–58.

62. Parsons, *Societies* (n. 51 above), p. 16.

63. Ibid., p. 17. For a much more balanced, multidimensional approach to force, see Parsons' essay "Some Reflections on the Place of Force in Social Process" (n. 35 above).

64. It is ironic that one of the most succinct refutations of this one-sided approach to law comes from Weber, upon whom Parsons professes to have drawn for his own emphasis. "There has recently appeared," Weber writes in his most famous methodological essay, "the attempt to 'refute' the 'materialistic conception of history' by a series of clever but fallacious arguments which state that since all economic life must take place in legally or conventionally *regulated forms*, all economic 'development' must take the form of striving for the creation of new *legal* forms." Weber's response to this argument follows:

> [But] the cultural significance of normatively regulated legal *relations* and even norms themselves can undergo fundamental revolutionary changes even under conditions of the formal identity of the prevailing legal norms. Indeed, if one wishes to lose one's self for a moment in phantasies about the future, one might theoretically imagine, let us say, the "socialization of the means of production" unaccompanied by any conscious "striving" towards this result, and without even the disappearance or addition of a single paragraph of our legal code; the statistical frequency of certain legally regulated relationships might be changed fundamentally, and in many cases, even disappear entirely; a great number of legal norms might become *practically* meaningless and their whole cultural significance changed beyond identification. ("Objectivity in Social Science and Social Policy," in Max Weber, *The Methodology of the Social Sciences* [New York, 1949], pp. 49–112, quoting pp. 82–83, italics in original.)

For an approach to legal development and institutionalization within the Parsonian framework which follows the more multidimensional strand of Parsons' analysis, see Leon Mayhew, *Law and Equal Opportunity* (Cambridge, Mass., 1969).

65. Parsons, "The Point of View of the Author," in Max Black, ed., *The Social Theories of Talcott Parsons* (Ithaca, N.Y., 1961), pp. 311–363, quoting p. 342, italics in original.

66. *Societies*, pp. 18–20, and Parsons, "An Outline of the Social System," in Parsons et al., eds., *Theories of Society* (New York, 1961), pp. 30–79, see pp. 40–41.

67. *Societies*, p. 19.

68. Ibid. Although this schema of "components" does not play a large role in Parsons' theory, it does constitute a major reference in Smelser's. In part, the subjectivist bias that this scheme produces presents a confusing counterpoint to Smelser's much more multidimensional analysis. E.g., Smelser identifies the goal-attainment, or "collectivity" function as concerned with the "motivation" to participate in collectives rather than with organizational problems as such. This disparity between the four-component scheme and the interchange model created significant logical problems for the formal continuity of the Parsonian scheme. It was partly because of this discontinuity that Smelser's elaborate discussions of the

"Resource Chart" and collective behavior were never related formally to the scheme of interchange analysis which occupied most of Parsons' own theoretical attention.

69. Judith Blake and Kingsley Davis, "Norms, Values, and Sanctions," in Robert E. L. Faris, ed., *Handbook of Modern Sociology* (Chicago, 1964), pp. 456–484, see pp. 458–464.

70. Wolf Heydebrand, review of *The System of Modern Societies, Contemporary Sociology* 1 (1972):387–395. Similarly, it is precisely Parsons' identification of the four "structural components of action" with interchange products that provides the rationale for the Bulgarian theorist Nikolai Genov to identify his work as a form of "idealistic monism" ("The Problem of Social Interaction in Bourgeois Sociology," *Bulgarian Journal of Sociology* 1 [1978]:61–71, see 70).

71. Jackson Toby, review of *The System of Modern Societies, Contemporary Sociology* 1 (1972):395–401, see 397–399.

72. Guy Rocher, *Talcott Parsons and American Sociology* (New York, 1975), p. 51.

73. S. N. Eisenstadt and M. Curelaru, *The Form of Sociology: Paradigms and Crises* (New York, 1976), pp. 182–183.

The prime exception among Parsons' sympathetic interpreters is Martel, who argues in his excellent essay that Parsons' cybernetic hierarchy is not only overly generalized but, because of its idealist strain, grossly misleading (Martin U. Martel, "Academentia Praecox: The Aims, Merits, and Scope of Parsons' Multisystematic Language Rebellion [1958–1968]," in Turk and Simpson [n. 40 above], pp. 174–209, see p. 195, n. 28). Martel calls for "removal of the 'invidious' control-versus-condition impediment from the hierarchy model, so that two-way interactions are freely explored" (p. 209). See also Guy Rocher's evaluation of Parsons' cybernetic conceptualization, where he concludes that Parson has "made too limited a use of his idea of cybernetic hierarchy."

> He *uses* only the hierarchy of controls and leaves out the hierarchy of conditioning factors. Taken as a whole, allowing for the "upward" effects of conditions as well as the "downward" effects of controls, the cybernetic idea would probably provide Parsons with a more complex model capable of encompassing more features of reality. (*Talcott Parsons and American Sociology*, p. 72, italics added.)

74. "On the Concept of Value Commitments" (n. 19 above), pp. 440, 445.

75. Ibid., pp. 442–443, italics added.

76. This use of the notion of "implementation" is implicitly legitimated by the way that Parsons confuses the analytic and concrete levels of analysis, a confusion I discussed at some length in chs. 6–7. Thus, Parsons often uses "implementation" to refer to the manner in which actors exchange

values for more conditional kinds of resources; in this way, Parsons holds, concrete actors utilize their newly gained resources to "implement" their values. In writing about the "interchange that operates between the pattern-maintenance system and the societal community," e.g., Parsons argues that "in terms of combinational logic, this involves the acceptance of the normatively-primary social (as distinguished from political and economic) conditions of effective value-implementation. The individual unit no longer 'goes it alone' but adopts associational status, which gives him expectation of solidarity with fellow-members of the community or collectivity in question." (Ibid., p. 461.) In terms of concrete individual actors, of course, it is perfectly plausible to speak of implementation as the principal focus of value analysis. However, when the concept applies to the analytic process of value interchange, it implies a distinctly idealist approach.

77. For the utilization of "scope" and "responsibility" in a multidimensional manner, see ch. 4, sec. 5.1.

78. Ibid., p. 445, italics altered.

79. Ibid., p. 447.

80. Menzies claims, in fact, that the primary function of Parsons' interchange schema is to develop a systematic model of four kinds of prototypical social values (Ken Menzies, *Talcott Parsons and the Social Image of Man* [London, 1977], pp. 73–89). Yet Parsons' utilization of interchange for the sole purpose of value exposition is actually quite unusual.

81. See, e.g., Robert N. Bellah's contrast between Japan's more collectivist values and America's more instrumental activism in *Tokugawa Religion* (Boston, 1957), ch. 1.

82. Parsons and Smelser, *Economy and Society*, (n. 4 above), p. 178.

83. Parsons, "A Revised Analytical Approach to the Theory of Social Stratification," in his *Essays in Sociological Theory* (New York, 1954), pp. 386–439, quoting p. 415, italics added.

84. See, e.g., "Certain Primary Sources and Patterns of Aggression in the Social Structure of the Western World," ibid., pp. 298–322.

85. See also Martel's criticism that "seemingly, the key idea is that ends having strongest commitments also have greatest causal force; so that economic factors weigh largest, for example, where achievement values as goals predominate" ("Academentia Praecox" [n. 73 above], p. 201).

86. *The American University* (n. 35 above), p. 45, italics in original.

87. Ibid., pp. 120–121.

88. Ibid., pp. 163–224.

89. E.g., ibid., pp. 228–230, 245–246, 257.

90. Ibid., pp. 327–330.

91. Ibid., pp. 274, 292.

92. Ibid., p. 314.

93. Ibid., pp. 313–316.

94. Ibid., pp. 275, 283, 314–316, 326–327.

95. Ibid., pp. 275, 283, 314–316.

96. Ibid., pp. 258, 264.

97. Ibid., pp. 337–339.

98. Ibid., pp. 165, 315, 324.

99. In relating the inflation-deflation spiral to actual social protest by students in the 1960s, Parsons and Platt adopt what they call a cybernetic perspective, yet they do so only in the cybernetic schema's idealist form (ibid., pp. 325–339). While discussing six different levels of causation, they rank them in terms of importance, with cultural strains on top of the cybernetic hierarchy and political-economic strains on the bottom. Thus, instead of producing a multidimensional analysis, they actually are simply tracing out the effects of cultural strain on a number of more specific levels. The instrumental and conditional sources of the student rebellions are reduced to an epiphenomenal status.

100. Parsons, *The System of Modern Societies* (n. 34 above), p. 99.

101. Parsons and Platt, *The American University*, pp. 276–279.

102. Ibid., pp. 80–86.

103. Ibid., p. 261. It is difficult, then, to accept the claim by R. Stephen Warner that Parsons' action theory has consistently ignored the cognitive element in favor of the moral ("Toward a Redefinition of Action Theory: Paying the Cognitive Element Its Due," *American Journal of Sociology* 83 [1978]:1317–1349). I earlier mentioned (ch. 7, n. 134) that I am in agreement with Warner's discovery of a normatively reductionistic element in Parsons' work, particularly his media theory (although I would insist that this is only one strand), and the present discussion should indicate why. I would insist, however, that in both his multidimensional and his idealist discussions Parsons gives the relatively autonomous cognitive element its "due." Normative reduction means, in Parsons, explaining action by reference to value causation, and the latter can be of either the cognitive, expressive, or moral (i.e., normative) type. In practice, it is usually either cognitive or moral, expressive symbolism being treated with less enthusiasm and relatively less insight.

There is a technical problem in Warner's interpretation which may help to explain such a serious interpretive error in what is in other respects such an intelligently and lucidly argued paper. Parsons does insist on "normative" determinism, from *The Structure of Social Action* to the middle-period work and in the later writings as well. But in this normative or moral dimension of the cultural system he always includes *each* of the three dimensions of cultural life: cognitive, expressive, and moral. By normative, in other words, Parsons is simply stipulating the collective, socially sanctioned pattern among the range of cognitive, expressive, and moral patterns that exist in any cultural system. It is these normative, mandated patterns that correspond to institutionalized values.

Warner's emphasis is primarily on *The Structure of Social Action*, and he accuses Parsons of reducing cognitive patterns to the asocial, pseudo-scientific framework that the utilitarian positivists assumed. This reduction, however, is actually the polemical target of Parsons' analysis, and he is critical of the role of cognitive inputs only as they are framed within an instrumentalist perspective. As Warner himself acknowledges, there are, in fact, many elements in Parsons' accounts of Durkheim and, especially, Weber which praise them for emphasizing the normative structuring of cognitive perception.

As I have tried to indicate in ch. 3, the notion that cognitive culture functions to independently structure the object world—that what "is" is not automatically given in objects themselves—was an absolutely fundamental theoretical position of Parsons' middle-period work. This position occurred within the critique not of scientific rationality per se but of the reductionistic, instrumental perspective on this rationality. The pattern-variable schema is the best example of the attention Parsons gave, theoretically and empirically, to the problem of cognition. Such tensions as specificity versus diffuseness and universalism versus particularism clearly relate to the problem of cognitive valuation. But *The American University*, the principal cultural work in the later period, presents the single piece that is most clearly devoted to how the cognitive element comes to be structured and institutionalized in an advanced industrial society. Certainly one of the primary points in the book is the continuing conflict between relatively autonomous cognitive emphases and relatively autonomous moral and expressive ones.

One reason, perhaps, for Warner's inattention to this cognitive element is that Parsons has almost always dealt with the cognitive dimension in terms of the "rationality" value. It is conceivable, therefore, that Parsons could be read as continuing a quasi-utilitarian approach, though I hope to have demonstrated that this is emphatically not the case. Because of this focus on rationality, Parsons never expanded his study of cognitive culture into the realms that have been explored, e.g., by Lévi-Strauss and the structuralists, by Harold Garfinkel in his earlier work, and by ethnomethodologists and phenomenologists more generally. Parsons does not do so, perhaps, because in contrast to these traditions he is fundamentally interested in linking his investigation of cognitive culture to historical and comparative generalizations about societal development; he is interested, i.e., in treating cognitive culture as a diachronic, not a synchronic system. In terms of such diachronic and historical analysis, of course, the relative universality and rationality of culture become especially crucial questions; in this respect Parsons clearly follows Weber.

Finally, Warner may have been inclined to attack Parsons on this issue because of what seems to be his own tendency to identify the lack of an instrumental and material emphasis with the neglect of the cognitive element. In Parsons' case, however, these emphases do not go together. Parsons always emphasized the importance of the independent structuring of cognitive rationality, e.g., in the detailed attention to cognitive development in his socialization studies. The variation occurred in whether he focused on the cultural or social-system aspects of this commitment, i.e., on the belief itself or on the objects to which it referred and which it brought into "rational" focus. In his idealist strand, Parsons elaborately described cognitive rationality but he did not talk about the objects which such rationality allowed the actor to efficiently manipulate, or the pressures which the ordering of such "rationally related to" objects produce.

Thus, rather than there being one "cognitive sociology," as Warner implies, there are actually two, corresponding to the possibilities of a more cultural or more social emphasis. Utilitarian and Marxist sociology, and the instrumentalist strands of Weberian and Simmelian sociology, are cognitive only in that they assume a cognitive rationality as the major form of orientation to the object world; they do not focus on the subjective structuring of this orientation to objects. In contrast, the other "cognitive sociology," i.e., structuralism and phenomenology, focuses on the cultural patterns but not on the instrumental pressures of the ordered subjects.

104. For the contributions he made within the multidimensional framework, see ch. 4, sec. 5.4.

105. Parsons' analysis of the modern university and of the role of cognitive rationality in modern integration constitutes a fundamental dialogue with the concerns of one strand of modern Marxism, the Frankfurt school, whose principal theorists are Adorno, Horkheimer, Marcuse, and Habermas. Frankfurt theorists view the culture of modern industrial society, both capitalist and socialist, as dominated by a "technical rationality" which makes action purely instrumental and which allows individuals and groups to be coercively determined by external forces. Parsons has demonstrated, to the contrary, that the most modern capitalist societies depend heavily on nontechnical expressive, moral, and religious symbolization. Moreover, he has demonstrated that even the cognitive values of such societies—those which are most devoted to purely technical processes of reasoning—depend heavily on support from noncognitive sources. On the other hand, by arguing that the relationship between cognitive and noncognitive values depends purely on cultural patterns, as he does in the idealist strand of his analysis, Parsons ignores the economic and bureaucratic demands for technicism that the Frankfurt school emphasized.

Gianfranco Poggi refers to the "basic ambivalence" that Parsons manifests about the "systematic position to be allotted to cognitive processes in general, and rational cognitive ones in particular, in the orientation of action" ("Parsons's *Structure of Social Action* Reconsidered," *Canadian Journal of Political and Social Theory*, forthcoming). Despite this accurate and telling reference to ambivalence, however, Poggi writes as if Parsons had actually adopted a completely idealist approach to cognition and "interested" action, which I hope I have shown was not the case. Warner's criticism (n. 103 above) suffers from a similar exaggeration of Parsons' idealization of the cognitive element.

106. See ch. 4, sec. 4.3.

107. *The System of Modern Societies* (n. 34 above), pp. 12–14. Thus, Parsons writes in 1973: "In my theoretical conception of society I have come increasingly to follow the lines of analysis put forward by Durkheim. Relative to non-members, which category may be very important in its environment, a society exhibits the property Durkheim called solidarity. It is this solidarity, he concludes, that gives the collectivity "some kind of relatively definite identity." ("Culture and Social System Revisited" [n. 44 above], p. 34.)

108. *The System of Modern Societies*, pp. 12–13.

109. Ibid., p. 13.

110. Ibid., p. 16.

111. Ibid., p. 17.

112. Ibid., pp. 30–34.

113. Ibid., pp. 37–38.

114. Ibid., pp. 38–39.

115. Ibid., pp. 39–40.

116. Ibid., pp. 79–84.

117. For this conflation of model and empirical levels of analysis, see ch. 7, sec. 1.

118. In my earlier discussion of the multidimensional treatment of Parsons' theory of integrative interchange (ch. 4, sec. 4.3) I have relied heavily on this chapter in *The System of Modern Societies.*

119. Ibid., pp. 87–94.

120. Ibid., pp. 94–101.

121. Ibid., pp. 106–114.

122. For such an emphasis, see, e.g., Lipset and Rokkan (n. 49 above) and my "Core Solidarity, Ethnic Outgroup, and Social Differentiation: A Multi-Dimensional Model of Ethnic Inclusion," in Jacques Dofny and Akinsola Akiwowo, eds., *National and Ethnic Movements* (London and Beverly Hills, 1980), pp. 5–28.

123. See my criticism of this tradition on this point in vol. 3, ch. 6. I also argued, however, that a more solidaristic approach to modern citizenship is implicit in Weber's discussion of "fraternization." It is also an important, though not explicitly articulated, factor in Reinhard Bendix's writings on the origins of modern citizenship, particularly insofar as he emphasizes that the origins of Western citizenship depended in important ways on the Christian notion of universal community (*Nation-Building and Citizenship*, 2d ed., rev. [Berkeley and Los Angeles, 1976]). It should also be emphasized, in this context, that T. H. Marshall explicitly takes solidarity into

his account of the origins of the social phase of citizenship, particularly in his discussion of the role of social sentiment (*Citizenship and Social Development* [New York, 1962]). Parsons himself, as noted earlier (ch. 4, sec. 4.3), relies heavily on Marshall for his analysis of citizenship.

124. For an interesting critical analysis of the idealization of Parsons' writing on solidarity—which, however, ignores the cross-cutting multidimensional element in Parsons' analysis—see Heydebrand's review of *The System of Modern Societies* (n. 70 above). It is revealing that even Jackson Toby, a sympathetic interpreter, views Parsons' principal emphasis in this book as one of "shared symbolic systems" ("Parsons' Theory of Social Evolution," *Contemporary Sociology* 1 [1972]:395–401).

125. For the multidimensional element in Parsons' media analysis, see ch. 4, sec. 6.1.

126. Parsons and Platt, *The American University* (n. 6 above), p. 24, italics in original.

127. *Societies* (n. 19 above), p. 20, italics added.

128. Parsons, "Social Structure and the Symbolic Media of Interchange," in Peter M. Blau, ed., *Approaches to the Study of Social Structure* (New York, 1975), pp. 94–134, quoting p. 101.

129. "Political Aspect" (n. 25 above), pp. 333, 338.

130. Parsons, "Social Structure and the Symbolic Media of Interchange," p. 98.

131. For the multidimensional aspects of this treatment of American instability, see ch. 3, sec. 4.3.

132. This transition from the 1955 essay "Social Strains in America" (Parsons, *Structure and Process in Modern Societies* [New York, 1969], pp. 226–249) to the later "Postscript," first published in 1963 (*Politics and Social Structure* [n. 20 above], pp. 179–184) is not intended to attribute any temporal sequence to Parsons' media idealization. First, when Parsons wrote "Social Strains" he had not yet developed the media theory. Second, I would maintain that the media theory is ambiguous throughout the course of its development.

133. See, in this context, Cartwright's and Warner's assertion that in Parsons' theory "the very control mechanism and inputs and outputs are symbolic and are, in their very essence, constituted by consciousness (Bliss C. Cartwright and R. Stephen Warner, "The Medium Is Not the Message," in J. J. Loubser et al., eds., *Explorations in General Theory in Social Science* [New York, 1976], pp. 639–660, see p. 652). Such a position, they argue, ignores the "structural attributes of levels of mobilization" (p. 643). The problem with this critical analysis, however, is that Cartwright and Warner take this idealist strand of Parsons' media analysis for the whole. Further, although they argue successfully for the importance of structural inputs to media process, they never demonstrate their claim that symbolic trust is not also a critical independent variable. They also fail to recognize

the importance of a "circulating medium" per se, which acts as a buffer and as a means of communication between institutional structures, both subjective and objective.

Parsons' often restricted use of the term "generalization" should be compared with Eisenstadt's utilization of the term as a pivotal concept in *The Political System of Empires* (n. 48 above). For power to remain generalized, Eisenstadt emphasizes, the state must struggle to maintain its autonomy not only against the economic pressures of social classes but also against the self-interested intrigues of the administrative apparatus itself. This approach to political generalization, in other words, rejects the idealization which distorts Parsons' account; it maintains a more fully multidimensional utilization of the interchange model.

134. Parsons, "Levels of Organization and the Mediation of Social Interaction," in Turk and Simpson (n. 40 above), pp. 23–35, see pp. 29–30.

135. This model of the general action media is presented, e.g., in Parsons and Platt, *The American University* and in Parsons' essays "Social Structure and the Symbolic Media of Exchange" (n. 128 above), "General Introduction" (in his *Social Systems and the Evolution of Action Theory* [New York, 1977], pp. 1–16), "The Present Status of Structural-Functional Theory in Sociology" (ibid., pp. 100–117), and "Some Problems of General Theory in Sociology" (ibid., pp. 229–269).

136. For this understanding of media theory as a way of concretizing the analytic interchange model, see ch. 4, sec. 6.

137. For one of the most illuminating of these recent attempts, see Dean Robert Gerstein, "Heroin in Motion: A Working Paper in the Theory of Action" (Ph.D. diss., Harvard University, 1975).

138. "Social Structure and the Symbolic Media of Exchange" (n. 128 above), p. 109.

139. Even in this empirical sense, the problem remains that this interrelationship among the four systems is formalistically presented in terms of an A-G-I-L interchange system. I have criticized this conflation of general action and interchange (ch. 7, sec. 2.1), and the criticism certainly applies to the formulation of the "media of general action" as well. While it is convenient to conceptualize culture, personality, and behavior organism as environments or boundaries of the social system, these do not have the precise kind of cybernetic relationship to one another that informs Parsons' synthetic framework for the analysis of boundaries within the social system. Indeed, Parsons has elaborately discussed the "boundary relationships" between these general action systems throughout his career—long before he ever systematized them in an A-G-I-L framework. (See, e.g., affective crises induced by the social structure of socialization in his *Social Structure and Personality* (New York, 1964). By "systematizing" these relationships, Parsons exposes these formulations to a dangerous simplification by funneling the variety of boundary strains into four specific kinds

of media. There are, of course, distinctive advantages to be gained from such systematization. These benefits can be gained, however, only by removing the discussion from the formalistic framework of interchange.

140. E.g., Giddens, " 'Power' in the Recent Writings of Talcott Parsons" (n. 45 above). For similar evaluations, see also Walter L. Wallace's discussion of Parsons' media theory in "Structure and Action in the Theories of Coleman and Parsons," in Blau (n. 28 above), pp. 121–134, and Cartwright and Warner, "The Medium Is Not the Message" (n. 133 above).

141. Enno Schwanenberg, "The Two Problems of Order in Parsons' Theory: An Analysis from Within," *Social Forces* 49 (1971):569–581, see 579.

142. Rainer C. Baum, "Communication and the Media," in Loubser et al. (n. 133 above), pp. 533–556, quoting p. 533.

143. Ibid., pp. 535, 538. In this discussion, Baum seems to be following the interpretive lead of Niklas Luhmann, who has taken off from Parsons' media theory in creative and elaborate ways (see my reference to Luhmann's work in ch. 5, n. 83). Luhmann, also, focuses only on the "trust" aspect of media and its relation to symbolic generalization, neglecting tension between the symbolic element and the medium's more instrumental, intrinsic persuader. It is possible that he leans too far in this direction because he writes primarily of social "systems" rather than of parts of systems, that is, of particular institutional subsystems with differentiated and often particularistic interests. In Luhmann's terms, "systems" reduce complexity through institutionalizing symbolically generalized mediums. But what about the institutional "parts," e.g., political bureaucracies, which would use these media for their own institutional interests? It is often precisely through such particularistic media use that trust is deflated to instrumental persuasion.

144. Rainer C. Baum, "On Societal Media Dynamics," in Loubser, pp. 579–608, see pp. 592–606. Baum writes, e.g., that "recognizing that analytically the values medium controls the other media cybernetically, the introduction of empirical variation in substantive societal values should help in approaching the prediction of the inflation-deflation potential in media in general" (p. 579).

145. Three good examples of such multidimensional analysis of media are Chalmers R. Johnson, *Revolutionary Change* (Boston, 1966), esp. pp. 28–32; François Bourricaud, "Penury and Deficit, or The Problems of Political Underutilization," in Loubser, pp. 557–578; and Neil J. Smelser, "Stability, Instability, and the Analysis of Political Corruption," in Bernard Barber and Alex Inkeles, eds., *Stability and Social Change* (Boston, 1971), pp. 7–29.

146. Parsons, "The Problem of Controlled Institutional Change," in his *Essays in Sociological Theory* (n. 83 above), pp. 238–274, see p. 241.

For a discussion of Parsons' writing in this period on vested interests, see ch. 3, sec. 4.2.

147. Parsons, *The Social System* (New York, 1951), p. 492, italics added.

148. *Societies* (n. 51 above), p. 23, and *The System of Modern Societies* (n. 34 above), p. 101.

149. *Societies*, pp. 12–14.

150. "An Outline of the Social System," in Parsons et al. (n. 66 above), p. 73.

151. Insofar as Parsons' interpreters have recognized this idealist strain in his later change theory they have, once again, viewed it as if it were perfectly consistent with the rest of his analysis. This is the position not only of Parsons' critics, like Gouldner and Heydebrand, but also of his sympathizers, like Benton Johnson (*Functionalism in Modern Sociology: Understanding Talcott Parsons* [Morristown, N.J., 1975], p. 45) and Jackson Toby (review of *The System of Modern Societies* [n. 71 above]). In a typical strategy adopted by this kind of sympathetic approach, two English analysts, Atkinson and Menzies, have pointed to Parsons' frequent emphasis on "vested interest" as an example of his continuing concern with processes of change and polarization (Dick Atkinson, *Orthodox Consensus and Radical Alternative* [New York, 1971], p. 110; Ken Menzies, *Talcott Parsons and the Social Image of Man* [n. 80 above], pp. 111–115). In making this point, they have helped to clarify the enormous confusion in the critical literature, which sees Parsons' change theory as simply nonexistent. Both contend, however, that Parsons describes vested interests only as ideal interests; as a result, they ignore the important multidimensional approach to interest which Parsons establishes in his middle-period work.

152. The most well known of these shorter essays is "Some Considerations on the Theory of Social Change" (*Rural Sociology* 26 [1961]:219–319). The more recent is "Comparative Studies and Evolutionary Change" (in Ivan Vallier, ed., *Comparative Methods in Sociology* [Berkeley and Los Angeles, 1971], pp. 97–139). In the Vallier piece, e.g., not only is there a disproportionate emphasis on "value generalization" and "normative inclusion," but "adaptive upgrading"—which by definition should refer to economic or even political rationalization—is treated primarily in terms of historical improvements in biological health and psychological self-sufficiency. In the light of my earlier criticism of Parsons' utilization of the "general action model," it is interesting that he justifies this anomalous treatment of adaptive upgrading by arguing that he has shifted his consideration of adaptation to the level of general action. On this level, he argues, adaptation concerns the status of the behavioral organism, hence the legitimacy of his account of increases in biological and psychological health. This is a typical instance of the way that formalistic reasoning can disguise a shift in presuppositional emphasis. In this entire later essay on social change, Parsons devotes only one paragraph to early modern shifts in economic structures.

153. For this analysis of value generalizations, see ch. 5, sec. 2.3.2.

154. *Societies* (n. 51 above), pp. 26, 34.

155. Ibid., pp. 30–50.

156. Ibid., pp. 51–62.

157. Ibid., pp. 69–94.

158. For this multidimensional approach to Roman law, see ch. 5, sec. 2.3.2.

159. Ibid., pp. 96–102.

160. Ibid., p. 99, italics added.

161. Ibid., pp. 86–93.

163. In this monograph there are two significant counter-examples to Parsons' idealization of premodern change. The first is his analysis of the actual process of transition from advanced primitive to archaic societies, which focuses on the emergence of the first ruling classes. Parsons describes the process in terms of the interrelationship of resource competition, the expansion of solidarity, and religious rationalization (*Societies*, pp. 42–59; see also Anthony D. Smith's discussion of this section in *The Concept of Social Change* [London, 1973], pp. 45–46). This anomalous treatment presents a parallel to ch. 4 in *The System of Modern Societies*, though it is not nearly as central to Parsons' argument. The other exception is the analysis of the strains in the Roman Empire, where Parsons describes strains caused by the uneven development of each of Roman society's different subsystems (see ch. 5, sec. 2.3).

Despite its idealism, the general analysis in *Societies* demonstrates quite clearly that Parsons does not conceive of the influence of religion and culture in a passive, unfolding way. He does not, to use Gouldner's phrase, emphasize the Platonic one-ness of morality and society (Gouldner [n. 45 above], pp. 267–273). To the contrary, Parsons conceives the religious dimension in an extremely active manner, and he finds in religious development the roots not of one-ness but of social differentiation and discontent. Gouldner is certainly correct, on the other hand, in his argument that Parsons' conception of modern society is excessively voluntaristic (pp. 155, 254–257). On this, see sec. 3.2.

164. *The System of Modern Societies*, pp. 71–121, 138–142. See also ch. 4, sec. 4.3.

165. Ibid., pp. 29–70, and Parsons, "Durkheim's Contribution to the Theory of Integration of Social Systems," in *Sociological Theory and Modern Society* (n. 19 above), pp. 3–34. See also, for this general point, Fred Weinstein and Gerald M. Platt, *The Wish to Be Free: Society, Psyche, and Value Change* (Berkeley and Los Angeles, 1969).

166. In addition to the discussion in vol. 3 (ch. 5), see, particularly, my "Max Weber, la théorie de la rationalisation et le marxisme," *Sociologie et Sociétés* 14 (1982): 33-43.

167. It is characteristic that Parsons himself insisted that his account of

the historical emergence of a voluntaristic society—one dependent principally upon institutionalized ideals—was actually derived from Weber's work. A personal letter written toward the end of his life indicates a belief that Weber in the later years of his career had rejected his conception of modern society as an amoral "iron cage." He wrote that Weber's last article, the "Author's Introduction" which he added to *The Protestant Ethic and the Spirit of Capitalism* in 1920, "mitigated the pessimism about the iron cage which he [Weber] expressed in the closing paragraphs of *The Protestant Ethic.*" Parsons follows this interpretation—for which, I believe, there is no strong textual or biographical evidence—with the revealing observation that this ideological shift in Weber paralleled a change in his own evaluative outlook. "All of this is of course in close accord with my own development as a student and interpreter of Weber's work. I have been moving toward a substantially more optimistic, if you will, interpretation of modern industrial society than is the predominant vogue among sociologists and related types of intellectuals. At the same time, I have maintained my basic confidence in Weber's work and the extraordinary levels of insight he attained." ("Letter from Parsons to Edward Tiryakian," *Sociological Inquiry* 51 [1981]:35–36.) Parsons' optimism about modern society undoubtedly helped produce the growing idealization of his social change theory, for his optimism was rooted in the growing conviction that modern society allowed voluntary action without significant constraint.

By drawing the negative contrast between Parsons' historical theory of Western development and Weber's, I do not wish to give the impression that Parsons has, in contrast, incorporated Durkheim's insights in a completely successful way. Although he goes beyond Durkheim's religious model of normative order in fundamental respects, there is one respect in which he would have done well to maintain the earlier theorist's model of symbolic-ritualistic association rather than simply to transcend and discard it. This is in the area of collective behavior, particularly the phenomenon of creative, "effervescent" movements. Although Parsons, like Durkheim, focuses heavily on the role of religious change in history, his analysis is too categorical and abstract—too focused on the level of model and on the empirical problem of historical stages—to illuminate the concrete symbolic processes involved in the breakthroughs and transitionary movements. Although he notes, following Weber, that these movements were often prophetic movements, he concentrates far more on the internal symbolic structure or on the social and psychological effects of various religious systems than on the actual religious processes. It is a striking fact, indeed, that while religion is as central to certain parts of Parsons' theorizing as it was to Durkheim's later work, Parsons never engaged, as Durkheim certainly did, in a detailed analysis of the nature of religious life per se.

168. *The System of Modern Societies* (n. 34 above), pp. 94–98. See also

Parsons, "Equality and Inequality in Modern Society; or, Social Stratification Revisited," in *Social Systems and the Evolution of Action Theory* (n. 135 above), pp. 321–380; "On Building Social System Theory: A Personal History," ibid., pp. 22–76, see pp. 62–66; Parsons and Platt (n. 35 above), passim.

169. For some critical applications of this structural differentiation notion, see, e.g., Smelser, "Growth, Structural Change, and Conflict in California Higher Education" (n. 42 above); Jesse R. Pitts, "The Hippies as a Counter-Meritocracy," *Dissent*, July-August 1969, pp. 305–316; Robert N. Bellah, *Beyond Belief* (New York, 1970); S. N. Eisenstadt, *Tradition, Change, and Modernity* (New York, 1973), pp. 231–257; and my "Core Solidarity, Ethnic Outgroup, and Social Differentiation" (n. 122 above) and "The Mass News Media in Systemic, Historical, and Comparative Perspective," in Elihu Katz and Thomas Szecsko, eds., *Mass Media and Social Change* (London, 1981), pp. 17–52.

170. There is a certain sense, therefore, in which the idealist strand of Parsons' analysis of modern society coincides with Rieff's analysis of "psychological man" (Philip Rieff, *Freud: The Mind of the Moralist* [New York, 1959], ch. 10, and *The Triumph of the Therapeutic* [New York, 1966]). Given the centrality of cathectic internalization, social problems will inevitably affect the psychological as well as the moral self, or, in Parsons' technical vocabulary, the personality as well as the cultural levels of action. Yet Parsons focuses on this problem in a more sophisticated way, for he relates the sense of individual malaise, at every point, to precise, historically based developments in the social structure. I will refer to these developments in the following discussion.

171. See my earlier discussion of the ambiguities of Parsons' analysis of the professions in n. 42 above.

That this kind of normative reduction and ideological conflation is not inherent in the Parsonian framework is implicitly demonstrated by Bernard Barber's work on professional irresponsibility, which has appeared over the last decade. Arguing that the doctor-patient relationship must be viewed as a social system in the fullest sense, Barber emphasizes that the stratification and power relations within this system must be taken into account. As a result, the internal control over information which is legitimately generated by expert collegiality must be balanced by the external, more instrumental controls of the state.

> Because of the character of the professions . . . as social groups which command powerful, relatively esoteric knowledge and which make claims to use that knowledge in the service of society, social control of the professions must be a mixture of internal and external control. Internal control is essential because, to a considerable degree—although a degree which is often exaggerated—only the professions themselves can know in terms of their esoteric knowledge how to exercise control for good and

> ill. External control is important because no powerful social role can be left entirely in the hands of its occupants. (Barber, "The Social Control of the Professions: Toward a Solution of an Ethical Crisis," in *Seminar Reports*, Columbia University, vol. 3, no. 7 [1975], pp. 128–133, quoting pp. 129–130.)

For a fuller explication of this position, see Barber's extremely insightful *Informed Consent in Medical Therapy and Research* (New Brunswick, N.J., 1980).

172. *The System of Modern Societies*, pp. 105–106. See also Parsons, "Professions," in *International Encyclopedia of the Social Sciences* (New York, 1968), and Parsons and Platt (n. 35 above), pp. 267–303.

173. For Parsons' discussion of horizontal versus vertical elite polarization, see ch. 3, sec. 4.2. For his analysis of "functional elites," see ch. 5, secs. 2.3. and 2.4.

174. Parsons, "An Analytical Approach to the Theory of Social Stratification," in *Essays in Sociological Theory* (n. 83 above), pp. 69–88, see p. 70.

175. Ibid., p. 74.

176. Ibid.

177. Ibid.

178. Ibid., pp. 75–76.

179. Ibid., p. 76, italics added.

180. "A Revised Analytical Approach to the Theory of Social Stratification" (n. 83 above), p. 394.

181. For possessions and their mode of distribution by the market, see, ibid., pp. 403, 411.

182. Ibid., p. 428–432. One is struck, in this essay as well as in Parsons' other references to stratification by class, by the insistence that "class" becomes operative only insofar as it is linked directly to kinship through explicit norms of ascription rather than achievement. In *The Social System*, e.g., Parsons treats class as a particularistic grouping that is parallel, in form and impact, to ethnic group (*The Social System* [n. 147 above], pp. 171–174; see also "An Outline of the Social System" [n. 66 above], p. 59, and *The System of Modern Societies*, p. 92). Yet, in a market-oriented economy, class advantage actually operates through universalistic and achievement-oriented norms, not against them. Parsons' failure to recognize this fact represents one of the few instances where he returns to a version of laissez-faire liberalism, ignoring the kind of market critique offered by the socialist left, Marxist and non-Marxist.

183. "A Revised Analytical Approach," p. 421. It is Parsons' critics, of course, who have produced the most consistent analyses of this essay's idealist qualities (e.g., C. Tausky, "Parsonian Stratification: An Analysis and Critique," *Sociological Quarterly* 6 [1965]:128–138). Yet, taking the part for the whole, they have consistently neglected the multidimensional strand of Parsons' stratification theory. On the other hand, Parsons' sym-

pathetic interpreters—even those who are themselves committed to a synthetic analysis—have, for the most part, refrained from criticizing this analytic essay for its idealist tendencies. Boskoff, e.g., has written a highly positive account not only of Parsons' general stratification theory but of the multidimensional elements in this essay in particular. Only in a casual aside does he acknowledge that Parsons' theories of power and stratification have been developed "in relative conceptual isolation from one another" (Alvin Boskoff, "Stratification, Power, and Social Change," in Turk and Simpson [n. 40 above], pp. 289–308, quoting p. 290). In his own stratification theory, Boskoff brings these two strands together to highlight the multidimensional strand in Parsonian stratification theory. Keller follows an essentially similar strategy in her analysis of elites (Suzanne Keller, *Beyond the Ruling Class* [New York, 1963]).

184. "A Revised Analytical Approach," p. 421.

185. "An Outline of the Social System," pp. 59–60.

186. Ibid., italics in original.

187. See, e.g., *The System of Modern Societies*, p. 95.

188. Parsons, "Equality and Inequality in Modern Society" (n. 168 above), pp. 340–346.

189. Parsons, "The School Class as a Social System: Some of Its Functions in American Society," in *Social Structure and Personality* (n. 139 above), pp. 129–154, and "Equality and Inequality in Modern Society," p. 327.

190. *The System of Modern Societies*, p. 99.

191. Ibid., p. 143, italics added.

192. Ibid., p. 115.

193. See, e.g., Parsons, "Certain Primary Sources and Patterns of Aggression in the Social Structure of the Western World" and "Social Classes and Class Conflict in the Light of Recent Sociological Theory," in *Essays in Sociological Theory* (n. 83 above), pp. 298–322, 323–335.

194. Parsons, "Equality and Inequality in Modern Society."

195. *The System of Modern Societies*, pp. 116–118, 143.

196. See, in this context, the relevance of Foss's wildly exaggerated remark that "Parsons rarely if ever attributes political radicalism or political action to direct confrontations of interest within the social structure" (Daniel Foss, "The World View of Talcott Parsons," in M. Stein and A. Vidich, eds., *Sociology on Trial* [Englewood Cliffs, N.J., 1963], pp. 96–126, quoting p. 108).

197. *The System of Modern Societies*, p. 143, italics in original.

198. Parsons, "The Problem of Balancing Rational Efficiency with Communal Solidarity in Modern Society," in Japan Economic Research Institute, *International Symposium on "New Problems of Advanced Societies"* (Tokyo, 1973), pp. 9–14, see pp. 13–14.

199. See, e.g., Gouldner's remark that despite what he regards as the

problematics of Parsons' theory, it still has focused attention on some of the new sources and sites of social change in the modern world. Thus, Gouldner continues, "it was not the Marxists but Talcott Parsons and other functionalists who early spotted the importance of the emerging 'youth culture,' and at least lifted it out as an object for attention." (Alvin W. Gouldner, "Toward a Radical Reconstruction of Sociology," *Social Policy* 1 [1970]:18–25, quoting 21.) But this sensitivity to subjective strains rests upon the intricate scaffolding which Parsons has built for his specification of the Durkheim-Freud synthesis, an achievement Gouldner notes only in a negative sense.

200. For the life cycle, see Parsons, "Youth in the Context of American Society," in *Social Structure and Personality* (n. 139 above), pp. 155–182, and Parsons and Platt, *The American University*; for inadequate socialization, see Parsons, "The School Class as a Social System" (n. 189 above); for neurosis and its genesis in socially structured strains in the life cycle, see Parsons, "Toward a Healthy Maturity," "Definitions of Health and Illness in the Light of American Values and Social Structure," and "Mental Illness and 'Spiritual Malaise': The Role of the Psychiatrist and of the Minister of Religion" in *Social Structure and Personality*, pp. 236–254, 257–291, 292–324; for an exposition of the way in which the conflict between instrumental roles creates such "deviant" activities as gambling, eroticism, aggression, and mass spectatorship, see Parsons and Shils, "Values, Motives, and Systems of Action," in Parsons and Shils, eds., *Towards a General Theory of Action* (New York, 1951), pp. 47–275, see pp. 212–218, and Parsons, "Certain Primary Sources and Patterns of Aggression in the Social Structure of the Western World" (n. 193 above). For a historical discussion of the continuing role of regressive eroticism in societies and its social structuring, see Parsons, "Kinship and the Associational Aspects of Social Structure," in Francis L. K. Hsu, ed., *Kinship and Culture* (Chicago, 1971), pp. 409–438. The last general discussion Parsons published on the way in which a differentiated and universalistic society creates affective strains and frustrated emotional needs—in which he also speculates about future associational changes which may be linked to this tension—is his "Belief, Unbelief, and Disbelief," in Rocco Caporale and Antonio Grumelli, eds., *The Culture of Unbelief: Studies and Proceedings from the First International Symposium on Belief, Held in Rome, March 22–27, 1969* (Berkeley and Los Angeles, 1971), pp. 207–245.

201. See vol. 3, ch. 2, sec. 2.

202. For a discussion of this argument, see ch. 2, sec. 1.

203. Parsons, *The Structure of Social Action* (New York, [1937] 1968), pp. 754–755; see also pp. 34–36, 82–86.

204. Ibid., p. 768.

205. Parsons, "The Present Position and Prospects of Systematic Theory in Sociology," in *Essays in Sociological Theory* (n. 83 above), pp. 212–

237, quoting p. 235. As I mentioned in vol. 2 (pp. 259–263), a similar definition of sociology as the study of normative institutions emerged with the idealist phase of Durkheim's work.

206. *The Social System* (n. 147 above), pp. 251–252.

207. *The System of Modern Societies* (n. 34 above), pp. 10–11; see also Parsons and Platt (n. 35 above), pp. 287–288.

208. Emerson has shown that last-resort arguments are offered by institutions for actions which can't be justified in rational and consistent ways. See Robert M. Emerson, "On Last Resorts," *American Journal of Sociology* 87 (1981):1–22.

209. *The Social System*, p. 549.

210. Ibid.

211. Ibid., pp. 549–551.

212. Ibid., p. 551.

213. Ibid., italics in original, and p. 552, italics added.

214. Ibid., p. 74, italics added.

215. Ibid., p. 147.

216. See ch. 8, sec. 2.

CHAPTER TEN

1. This chapter was first published, with a somewhat different introduction and conclusion, in the *Canadian Journal of Sociology* 4 (1979):343–357.

2. There is some controversy over what precisely constitutes a school in science as compared, e.g., with a tradition or simply a theoretical tendency. I do not intend to enter into this controversy. In my use of the term, it is synonymous with tradition as generally defined. Compared with Durkheim, Parsons did not establish a school, both because he did not exercise the kind of administrative control over appointments that Durkheim commanded, and because he never established a powerful journal to carry on his ideas. On the other hand, in contrast to Weber, Parsons definitely established a coherent group of sociological followers.

3. I pursue these critical questions at some length in vol. 1. See also my contribution to the debate which followed publication of my *Canadian Journal* article (n. 1 above): "Kuhn's Unsuccessful Revisionism: A Reply to John Selby," ibid., 7 (1982):66–71.

4. Thomas Kuhn, *The Structure of Scientific Revolutions*, rev. ed. (Chicago, 1970), Postscript. For more elaboration of these points, and a detailed examination of Kuhn's "Postscript," see my article cited in n. 3.

5. Talcott Parsons, "Comment," on Lewellyn Gross, "Preface to a Metatheoretical Framework for Sociology," *American Journal of Sociology* 67 (1961):136–140.

6. For the argument about the emergence of class conflict in general,

see Roger Garaudy, *Karl Marx: The Evolution of His Thought* (New York, 1967), pp. 16–18. For the argument relating Marx to the specifically English context of economic class-struggle, see Anthony Giddens, *Capitalism and Modern Social Theory* (London, 1971), pp. 185–190.

7. For the relation between Durkheim's moral analysis and the climate of the French Third Republic, see Lewis Coser, *Masters of Sociological Thought* (New York, 1971), pp. 156–163.

8. For this aspect of the social background for Weber's analytic theory, see Fritz K. Ringer, *The Decline of the German Mandarins* (Cambridge, Mass., 1969), pp. 176–177.

9. John Kenneth Galbraith, *The Affluent Society* (Boston, 1958).

10. Robert V. Presthus, *The Organization Society* (New York, 1962).

11. Amitai Etzioni, *The Active Society* (New York, 1968).

12. T. H. Marshall, *Class, Citizenship, and Social Development* (Garden City, N.Y., 1965).

13. Philip Rieff, *Freud: The Mind of the Moralist* (Garden City, N.Y., 1959) and *The Triumph of the Therapeutic* (New York, 1966).

14. David Riesman, *The Lonely Crowd* (New Haven, Conn., 1950); William H. Whyte, Jr., *The Organization Man* (Garden City, N.Y., 1956); Herbert Marcuse, *One Dimensional Man* (Boston, 1964).

15. Bernard Rosenberg and David Manning White, eds., *Mass Culture* (Glencoe, Ill., 1957).

16. See, e.g., S. N. Eisenstadt and M. Curelaru's assessment of the impact of Parsonian structural-functionalism in the 1950s and 1960s:

> The impact of the broad structural-functional paradigm and its analytic concepts and orientations impinged on many areas of research. Hardly any area of research remained unaffected. . . . In almost all fields of sociology, the structural-functional approach not only provided a general view, image, or map of the social system, but gave hints about more analytic specifications that could become foci of research. In such areas of research as stratification, political organization, educational sociology, and the study of deviance, many specific paradigms and research programs were related to or derived from the structural-functional framework. In other substantive fields, as in studies of public opinion and voting behavior, which had developed strong concentrations on middle-range theories, not only were the concepts those that had been developed in the structural-functional model [but] this model also provided the basis for a broader analytic orientation. . . . The influence of this model also spread to other disciplines. (*The Form of Sociology: Paradigms and Crises* [New York, 1976], p. 185.)

On the extent of the incorporation of Parsons' work into contemporary thought, see also the comments by Dick Atkinson:

> There is still considerable debate about the validity, even the morality of his contribution, [but] followers and critics alike have accepted portions

> of his work. Thus such concepts which he develops as role, institution, social structure, social system are not the subject of violent disagreement. Indeed, they are used by his critics to attack other concepts . . . which are alleged to form the substance of Parsons' work. (*Orthodox Consensus and Radical Alternative* [New York, 1971], p. 9.)

17. In part because of the very influence of Parsons' work (for a fuller discussion, see vol. 2, pp. 306–327), there is not a distinctively Durkheimian tradition in modern American or English sociology, although the tradition of symbolic anthropology represents a Durkheimian school in a neighboring discipline (see, e.g., the works of Victor Turner, esp. *The Ritual Process* [Chicago, 1969]). The work in symbolic anthropology would be enormously clarified by the kind of insights Parsons has generated about the analytic differentiation of personality, society, and culture. (Clifford Geertz's *The Interpretation of Cultures* [New York, 1973] moves precisely in this direction.) One extremely interesting attempt to create a less dichotomized, more continuous Weberian theory of society through the incorporation of Parsonian conceptualization is S. N. Eisenstadt's essay "Charisma and Institution Building: Max Weber and Modern Sociology," in Eisenstadt, ed., *Max Weber on Charisma and Institution Building* (Chicago, 1968), pp. ix–lvi. Wolfgang Schluchter's work represents more recent important work in the same direction (see his essays in Guenther Roth and Schluchter, *Max Weber's Vision of History: Ethics and Methods* [Berkeley and Los Angeles, 1979] and his *Max Weber's Developmental History* [idem, 1981]). For a good illustration of the movement within exchange theory toward the inclusion of a more Parsonian emphasis, see Peter M. Blau, "Mediating Values in Complex Structures," in his *Exchange and Power in Social Life* (New York, 1964), pp. 253–282, and, more recently, William J. Goode, *The Celebration of Heroes: Prestige as a Social Control System* (Berkeley and Los Angeles, 1979). For the overlap that develops between "conflict theory" and Parsons' conceptualization when the former is forced to consider problems of intragroup cohesion, see, e.g., John Rex, *Race, Community, and Conflict* (London, 1968), and Ralf Dahrendorf, *Essays in the Theory of Society* (London, 1968) and *Class and Class Conflict in Industrial Society* (Stanford, Calif., 1959), pp. 206–299. Atkinson's commentary on this phenomenon is relevant here.

> [The conflict theorists'] explanation of the structure of relations within any one class, or of the structure of orderly Western industrial societies, implied either rejection of the analysis of conflict (Dahrendorf), or a static view of conflict (Rex and Marcuse). . . . The analysis of any one class taken separately or of a total, integrated or bourgeois society specifically assumes the need for concepts which are equivalent to those required by Parsons for the analysis of the whole of society. They include role, status, status structure, authority, and, finally, their relation together in a social system of unintended consequences. Marcuse, Dahrendorf, and Rex all

> converged towards this Parsonian position. . . . Their analysis involved a view of the normative integration of institutions, of dominant values, their voluntary acceptance by actors, and integration of all three levels of analysis in the concept of the "social system." (*Orthodox Consensus and Radical Alternative*, pp. 113, 115.)

18. These three levels, of course, represent Althusser's, not Parsons', rendering of the analytic divisions of social life. See Louis Althusser, "The Errors of Classical Economics," in Althusser and Etienne Balibar, *Reading "Capital"* (London, 1970), pp. 96–100, 104–105, 107–108, and, in the same book, "Marx's Critique"; also "Contradiction and Over-Determination," in Althusser, *For Marx* (London, 1966). Althusser traces his innovation to Mao and to Freud. His actual reliance on Parsons, however, is visibly apparent, as the critics of such structuralist Marxism are quick to point out (e.g., George Lichteim in *The New York Review of Books*, January 30, 1969.) The Parsonian reference of structuralism is more clearly revealed in the work of Althusser's students e.g., Nicholas Poulantzas, *Political Power and Social Classes* (London, 1972), and Maurice Godelier, *Rationality and Irrationality in Economics* (London, 1971), particularly Godelier's introductory essay "Functionalism, Structuralism, and Marxism," and the later section "The Idea of a 'System.' "

Of course, this discussion of the reliance on Parsons by the structuralists, and the discussion of his influence on Habermas which follows, must not be taken as an indication that such an incorporation is totally effective. As I indicated at some length in my discussion of Marx in vol. 2 (see ch. 10, sec. 2), the continued commitment of these and other writers to Marx's presuppositional framework pushes their theoretical revision into inevitable compromises with instrumental rationality and antivoluntarist determinism, or else leads them into residual, ad hoc formulations.

19. Jürgen Habermas, "Technology and Science as 'Ideology,' " in his *Towards a Rational Society* (Boston, 1970), pp. 81–127, see pp. 92–93.

20. Ibid., pp. 93, 114.

21. Habermas, *Legitimation Crisis* (Boston, 1975).

22. Robert K. Merton, "Manifest and Latent Functions" (1949), in his *On Theoretical Sociology* (New York, 1967), pp. 73–138.

23. Merton, "On Sociological Theories of the Middle Range" (1949), ibid., pp. 39–72. See my discussion of this aspect of Merton's work in vol. 1, pp. 11–15.

24. Kingsley Davis, *Human Society* (New York, 1949); Robin W. Williams, Jr., *American Society* (New York, 1951); Marion J. Levy, Jr., *The Structure of Society* (Princeton, N.J., 1952); Bernard Barber, *Social Stratification* (New York, 1957). See also the introductory materials in Davis, Levy, and Harry C. Bredemeirer, eds., *Modern American Society* (New York, 1946).

Though Barber, like so many of these other Parsons students, has never publicly challenged Parsons' theory, a statement he made more recently illustrates the kind of strains that have led these students toward implicit "rebellion" in a more propositional direction.

> Parsons showed no intensive and systematic awareness of the "measurement problem" in social science; he did not have that problem "in his guts." None of his great mentors had a strong concern for [it] and Parsons never impressed any awareness of it on his students or readers. Neither as his undergraduate student in the 1930's nor later as his graduate student in the 1940's did I ever hear anything about the "measurement problem." Indeed, it was only when I began on my own in the later 1940's to read the work of Paul Lazarsfeld and then when I became his colleague at Columbia University that I even became aware that there was such a problem, that for every concept there must be an indicator, a measure. . . . My own growing awareness of the problem and of its complexities not only influenced my own work, not only pushed me strongly to connect empirical data to any and all theorizing, but increasingly made me aware of how lacking it was in the work of Parsons. ("Theory and Fact in the Work of Talcott Parsons," in Samuel Z. Klausner and Victor M. Lidz, eds., *Talcott Parsons on the Social Sciences*, forthcoming.)

Barber's judgment at the time of this later writing is explicit and harsh: "Although he very much acknowledged the importance of empirical research and encouraged it, from a relatively early stage of his career, Parsons seems to have lost the capacity for being continuously and systematically influenced by the facts accumulated by intensive empirical research. . . . Eventually only very close students of the theory found it possible to bring it into easy relationship with empirical research" (Ibid.).

Barber's statement also raises the question of the role of "outside influences"—in this case, Lazarsfeld—on revision. For a discussion of this problem, see n. 55 below.

25. Williams, *American Society.* In the second edition of this book (1963), see, e.g., ch. 10, "Institutional Variation and the Evasion of Normative Patterns," and ch. 13, "Interrelations of Major Institutions and Social Groupings."

26. Merton, "Social Structure and Anomie," *American Sociological Review* 3 (1938):677–682.

27. Davis (n. 24 above), pp. 120–146, 175–184, 364–391, 435–506.

28. Levy (n. 24 above), pp. 389–503.

29. Neil J. Smelser, *Theory of Collective Behavior* (New York, 1963), p. 383.

Smelser recalls his first recognition of this problem in Parsons' theory in an autobiographical discussion of his theoretical development:

> As I began my work on the theoretical aspects of collective behavior, I wanted to make my account of the field not only "consistent with" but also more nearly "derived from" the theoretical framework [i.e., Parsons'

> theory] within which I was working. To explore this possibility, I undertook to refine some of the ingredients of the theory of action—in particular the "resource table"—and to attempt to derive from it some empirical propositions concerning the causes underlying collective outbursts and collective movements. I spent several months trying systematically to exploit these ingredients of the theory of action. Much of this work was rewarding, [but] that framework was not helpful in providing variables that might identify the determinants of these kinds of episodes. The lack of success—and the accompanying frustration—of this search led me to develop the value-added model. ("Some Personal Thoughts on the Pursuit of Sociological Problems," *Sociological Inquiry* 39 [1969]: 155–167, quoting 163.)

30. The contrast between the titles of Smelser's and Parsons' collections of essays is instructive. Cf. Parsons, *Essays in Sociological Theory* (New York, 1954) and Smelser, *Essays in Sociological Explanation* (Englewood Cliffs, N.J., 1968). For Smelser's increasing concentration on the relation between empirical evidence and theory, see his *Comparative Methods in Social Science* (Englewood Cliffs, 1976).

31. Smelser and R. Stephen Warner, *Sociological Theory* (Morristown, N.J., 1976), p. 204.

32. Smelser, *Karl Marx on Society and Social Change* (Chicago, 1973). See the similar argument by Seymour Martin Lipset, "Social Structure and Social Change," in Peter M. Blau, ed., *Approaches to the Study of Social Structure* (New York, 1975), pp. 172–209.

33. Jesse R. Pitts, "Continuity and Change in Bourgeois France," in Stanley Hoffman, ed., *In Search of France* (Cambridge, Mass., 1964), pp. 249–304.

34. Robert N. Bellah, *Beyond Belief* (New York, 1970), pp. 53–189, and "The Five Civil Religions of Italy," in Bellah and Phillip Hammond, *Varieties of Civil Religion* (New York, 1980), pp. 86–118. See also Bellah's discussion of American civil religion in *The Broken Covenant* (New York, 1975).

35. Seymour Martin Lipset, *The First New Nation* (Garden City, N.Y., 1967).

36. Rainer C. Baum, "Values and Democracy in Imperial Germany," *Sociological Inquiry* 38 (1968):179–196.

37. Philip E. Slater: "Parental Role Differentiation," *American Journal of Sociology* 67 (1961):296–308; "Towards a Dualistic Theory of Identification," *Merrill-Palmer Quarterly* 7 (1961):113–126; "On Social Regression," *American Sociological Review* 28 (1963):339–364; and *Microcosm* (New York, 1966).

38. Fred Weinstein and Gerald M. Platt, *The Wish to Be Free: Society, Psyche, and Value Change* (Berkeley and Los Angeles, 1969) and *Psychoanalytic Sociology* (Baltimore, 1973).

39. For the term "leads and lags," see Ivan Vallier, "Empirical Comparisons of Social Structure: Leads and Lags," in Vallier, ed., *Comparative Methods in Sociology* (Berkeley and Los Angeles, 1971), pp. 203–263, and Neil J. Smelser, "Stability, Instability, and the Analysis of Political Corruption," in Bernard Barber and Alex Inkeles, eds., *Stability and Change* (Boston, 1971), pp. 7–29.

40. See, e.g., S. N. Eisenstadt, "Social Change, Differentiation, and Evolution," *American Sociological Review* 29 (1964):375–386, and *The Political System of Empires* (New York, 1963).

The same empirical specificity, one might add, leads Eisenstadt to emphasize much more than Parsons the variable outcomes of national paths toward modernization. See, e.g., his *Tradition, Change, and Modernity* (New York, 1973) and *Modernization: Protest and Change* (Englewood Cliffs, N.J., 1966); also Eisenstadt and Yael Azmon, eds., *Socialism and Tradition* (New York, 1973). For an extended discussion of Eisenstadt's work as revisionism, see Jeffrey C. Alexander and Paul Colomy, " 'Institutionalization' and 'Collective Behavior': Points of Contact between Eisenstadt's Functionalism and Symbolic Interactionism," in Erik Cohen et al., eds., *Comparative Social Dynamics: Essays in Honor of S. N. Eisenstadt* (Colorado, 1984).

41. Eisenstadt, "Institutionalization and Change," *American Sociological Review* 29 (1964):235–247, quoting 246. See also Dietrich Rueschemeyer, "Structural Differentiation, Efficiency, and Power," *American Journal of Sociology* 83 (1977):1–25, and my own "The Mass News Media in Systemic, Historical, and Comparative Perspective," in Elihu Katz and Thomas Szecsko, eds., *Mass Media and Social Change* (London, 1980), pp. 17–52.

Eisenstadt was influenced in this more group-oriented approach by the work of Shils, with whom he has been closely associated. Eisenstadt's term for members of groups that specify functional exigencies is "institutional entrepreneurs" ("Social Change . . ." [n. 40 above]).

42. Keller's explanation for her focus on groups is particularly instructive:

> [One] problem which arises in applying Parsons' analytical categories to current institutions stems from the fact that institutions themselves are abstractions. Institutions never act or deliberate or have crises of conscience or hostile impulses. The assignment to them of functional responsibilities therefore leads to reification of the social order. The normative order becomes confounded with the factual order. Unwittingly, the implication that the state or the economy or the family ought to do such and such leads to the assertion that they do such and such. . . .
>
> In the absence of such a correspondence, some individuals must assume responsibility for translating functional prescriptions into workable rules. The individuals who do this for the social system are, in our view, the strategic elites. . . . By shifting the level of analysis from norms and insti-

> tutions to elites, the problem of reification disappears. These elites never act solely in accordance with the functional requirements of their status. The moral and personal imperfections of men, the temptations of their surroundings, and also the characteristics of the social structure in which men participate prevent them from doing so. (Suzanne Keller, *Beyond the Ruling Class* [New York, 1963], pp. 94–95.)

Although this rationale conflates the problems of empirical representation with the problem of presuppositional idealism, it well illustrates the kind of frustrations that have led to the increasing emphasis on groups among certain representatives of the Parsonian tradition.

43. Neil J. Smelser, "Epilogue: Social Structural Dimensions of Higher Education," in Parsons and Gerald M. Platt, *The American University* (Cambridge, Mass., 1973), pp. 389–422, quoting p. 394.

44. Smelser, "Growth, Structural Change, and Conflict in California Higher Public Education, 1950–1970," in Smelser and Gabriel Almond, eds., *Public Higher Education in California* (Berkeley and Los Angeles, 1974), pp. 9–141.

45. Seymour Martin Lipset and Stein Rokkan, "Cleavage Structures, Party Systems and Voter Alignments," in Lipset and Rokkan, eds., *Party Systems and Voter Alignments* (New York, 1967), pp. 1–64. See also Rokkan, "Models and Methods in the Comparative Study of Nation-Building," in T. J. Nossiter and A. H. Hanson, eds., *Imagination and Precision in the Social Sciences* (New York, 1972), pp. 121–156, and "Dimensions of State Formation and Nation-Building: A Possible Paradigm for Research on Variations within Europe," in Charles Tilly, ed., *The Formation of National States in Western Europe* (Princeton, N.J., 1975), pp. 562–600.

46. Shils, *The Intellectuals and the Powers* (Chicago, 1972) and *Center and Periphery: Essays on Macrosociology* (Chicago, 1975).

47. Eisenstadt, *The Political System of Empires* (n. 40 above).

48. Leon H. Mayhew, "Stability and Change in Legal Systems," in Barber and Inkeles (n. 39 above), pp. 187–210.

49. Seymour Martin Lipset and Earl Raab, *The Politics of Unreason* (New York, 1970); Smelser, "Growth, Structural Change, and Conflict . . ." (n. 44 above).

50. See Slater (n. 37 above, all works cited) and Weinstein and Platt (n. 38 above, both works). For other critical discussion of the differentiation concept, see Rueschemeyer (n. 41 above) and also my "Formal and Substantive Voluntarism in the Work of Talcott Parsons: A Theoretical and Ideological Reinterpretation," *American Sociological Review* 43 (1978):177–198, and "Core Solidarity, Ethnic Outgroup and Structural Differentiation: Toward a Multidimensional Model of Inclusion in Modern Societies," in Jacques Dofny and Akinsola Akiwowo, eds., *National and Ethnic Movements* (London, 1980), pp. 5–28.

51. Eisenstadt, *The Political System of Empires* and *Tradition,*

Change, and Modernity (both, n. 40 above); also Eisenstadt and M. Curelaru, *The Forms of Sociology: Paradigms and Crises* (New York, 1976).

52. Smelser, *Social Change in the Industrial Revolution*, (Chicago, 1959).

53. Smelser, "Growth, Structural Change, and Conflict . . ." (n. 44 above).

54. Bernard Barber, "Control and Responsibility in the Powerful Professions," *Political Science Quarterly* 93 (1978/79):599–615. Barber's *Informed Consent in Medical Therapy and Research* (New Brunswick, N.J., 1980) is the very prototype of "revisionist" Parsonianism. Utilizing the multidimensional apparatus of Parsons' general theory to criticize and revise his theory of the medical profession, Barber, like all significant revisionists, successfully turns the master's theory against itself.

55. Bellah, *Beyond Belief* (n. 34 above), e.g., pp. 114–145, and Geertz (n. 17 above), pp. 87–125, 142–169, 193–233.

Both these former students have, in addition, tried to redefine the relation of Parsons' theory to the Durkheimian tradition. While both accept the multidimensional critique that Parsons launched vis-à-vis Durkheim, neither completely accepts the manner in which Parsons rejected the "religious model" as a reference for social theorizing. I have noted earlier (ch. 9, n. 167) that although the idealist strand of Parsons' theorizing made religious change as central for him as for Durkheim, Parsons did not, because of his greater abstractness and concern for delineating historical stages, reveal as clearly as Durkheim the effervescent element which religious consciousness contributes to historical development. In this particular and specific sense, Geertz and Bellah have moved back to Durkheim, having done so under the influence of symbolic anthropologists and symbolically sensitive literary critics. In the same vein, and influenced by similar considerations and thinkers, is the recent statement about the direction in which Parsonian sociology should move made by Edward A. Tiryakian, another former student of the same period as Geertz and Bellah. In a eulogy for Parsons, Tiryakian writes: "Post-Parsonian sociology has a further need of giving increased attention to non-institutionalized phenomena, or perhaps I should say to collective behavior marked by a high intensity of affect and a low degree of institutionalization." He goes on to argue, implicitly, for the renewed vitality of Durkheim's reliance on the religious model.

> The phenomena of "high energy," capable of collective mobilization, are closely related to the religious sector, and I would suggest are derivatives of religious representations and conditions such as asceticism, pollution, purification, salvation, etc. I would suggest that a great deal of the political phenomena that cause such discontinuities in our contemporary world are in fact religious phenomena that attend the "explosion" of core meaning-patterns of the societal community. I view a great deal of the

> political phenomena that appear as discontinuities in our contemporary world as manifesting fundamental religious dimensions . . . that in earlier periods may have been for the most part contained in collective rituals.

Tiryakian concludes with the argument that "it is my reading of Durkheim, Weber, and Parsons that we can best obtain clues as to the next round or next phase of modernity by further research and integration of the sociology of religion and general sociological theory." ("Post-Parsonian Sociology," *Humboldt Journal of Social Relations* 7 [1979/80]:17–32, quoting p. 29.)

The case of these more Durkheimian-oriented students of Parsons, and of the impact on them by currents in symbolic anthropology, raises an issue which should be mentioned in a more general way though I will not investigate it at great length. First, to the degree that revisions are introduced into Parsons' theory in either a more symbolic or a material direction, these revisers will make greater reference to classical theorists who represent different traditions. Thus, just as Weber's followers divide into those who push Weber more toward Marx or toward Durkheim, Parsons' students, in the course of their revision, tend to move toward Durkheim, or Weber, or Marx. Eisenstadt, e.g., has pushed Parsons toward Weber; Smelser has implicitly drawn at great length on Marx; Geertz and Bellah, as just noted, have pushed in a Durkheimian direction. A second point is related to this first and more general one: to the degree that the students revise Parsons' theory in specific ways, they have usually done so under the influence of other teachers whose positions differed from Parsons' in the same way as the revisions these students later introduced. Bernard Barber, e.g., was highly influenced by Lazarsfeld (personal communication). Merton was also affected by Lazarsfeld, and earlier by Sorokin. A more detailed sociology of scientific revisionism would follow out these networks while placing them within the kind of general analytic framework of theoretical differentiation and strain I have described in this chapter.

56. Robert Dreeben, *On What Is Learned in School* (Reading, Mass., 1968).

57. Lipset, *The First New Nation* (n. 35 above), pp. 237–283.

58. David M. Schneider and Raymond T. Smith, *Class Differences and Sex Roles in American Kinship* (Englewood Cliffs, N.J., 1973).

59. For the notion of theoretical "closure," see Eisenstadt and Curelaru (n. 51 above).

60. When Geertz talked about noncultural processes in his monograph *Agricultural Involution* (Berkeley and Los Angeles, 1963), he did so in a manner that avoided an attempt at direct material-ideal synthesis. In Geertz's *Negara: The Theatre State in Nineteenth-Century Bali* (Princeton, N.J., 1980), culture and social structure are relegated to different sections

of the book, and though their interpenetration is formally stressed, there is little substantive elaboration of the actual relationship between them.

61. For their direct critique of Parsons on this count, see Weinstein and Platt, *Psychoanalytic Sociology* (n. 38 above), pp. 30–33.

62. Eisenstadt and Curelaru (n. 51 above) emphasize the cross-cuttings between these internal dynamics of the functionalist tradition and recent developments in non-Parsonian theoretical traditions (pp. 245–375).

63. At the time of this writing, the best known and most influential members of the Parsonian tradition have almost all ceased to frame their work within the Parsonian framework in a strict and literal sense: this is precisely the point I try to make in the present chapter. There are still, however, some accomplished practitioners of the Parsonian schema in what I have here called its late and sectarian form. I am thinking particularly of some of Parsons' distinguished students from the 1960s: Mark Gould, Victor Lidz, Rainer Baum, Jan Loubser, and Dean Gerstein. These students have not been as productive as the earlier generations of Parsons' followers, and their impact on sociological theory has not been anywhere near as great. The latter fact can be traced to Parsons' diminished stature in the sociological discipline, to the major and rather public revisions introduced by earlier generations of Parsonians, and—not least of all—to the most recent generation's diminished scholarly productivity in relation to its predecessors. Even these students, however, have subtly revised Parsons' work, as I have noted at various points in the preceding pages. Nonetheless, they apply "Parsonianism" in a purer form than theorists who still work within the tradition more broadly defined. So far, it is not clear whether this small nucleus of sophisticated followers will be able to sustain a "strict" version of the Parsonian tradition. Whether they will do so depends less on the intrinsic value of their work than on the intellectual, social, and cultural framework of the discipline of sociology itself.

As for more loosely defined versions of "functionalist" theorizing, in addition to the efforts discussed in this chapter one would want to look at two other developments. There are, first, the movements toward the "Parsonianization" of earlier classical traditions, not just by theorists in the Parsonian tradition (efforts I have discussed earlier in this chapter), but by those who actually write within other theoretical orientations. In the Marxist tradition, e.g., Habermas's work (n. 21 above) and the structuralists' (n. 18) can be viewed as developing different strands of Parsons' theoretical legacy; in the Weberian tradition, the same might be said for the writings of Schluchter (n. 17). The second development is the national differentiation of the loose Parsonian tradition, where significant segments of Parsons' original theory are "selected out" by contemporary controversies in various national traditions. This may be developing in France (see my "The French Correction: Revisionism and Followership in the Interpretation of Parsons," *Contemporary Sociology* 10 [1981]:500–505, an essay review of François Bourricaud's *L'Individualisme institutionnel* [Paris, 1977]). It is certainly evident in Germany, with Luhmann, Habermas, Schluchter, and Münch all developing different German variations of Parsonian theory (see my "The Parsons Revival in Germany," *Sociological Theory* 2 [1984]).

APPENDIX

1. If the polarization created by the charismatic period of Parsons' theorizing were the principal reason for the misinterpretation of his thought, one would expect that the "routinization" of this charismatic period would significantly diminish interpretive distortion. To some degree this may be the case: a few of the most recent interpretive works have cautioned explicitly against theoretical reduction. Hans P. M. Adriaansens concludes his basically sympathetic work by arguing against the "average criticisms" of Parsons as follows: "The arguments which form the basis of the line of interpretation are often founded on the *confusion between various principally distinguishable levels of theory*" (*Talcott Parsons and the Conceptual Dilemma* [London, 1980], p. 173, italics in original). Yet Adriaansens makes a number of conflationary analyses in the course of his interpretation, e.g., analyzing the middle phase of Parsons' work in purely functional terms (pp. 58–87). Similarly, Stephen P. Savage begins his critical analysis with a perceptive and extensive argument against reductionist interpretation (*The Theories of Talcott Parsons* [New York, 1981], pp. 1–61). He attacks the conflation of most anti-Parsonian criticism with "extra-discursive" considerations—including in this attack criticisms of Parsons' conservatism, functionalism, and abstraction—and he suggests, much as I am suggesting here, that such reductions assume that Parsons' theory is unified into what Althusser calls an expressive totality. The problems presented by Savage's analysis are, first, that he develops no systematic criteria for differentiating the various levels of extradiscursive commitment and, second, that his central positive concept, discourse, is defined only in the residual sense of referring to everything that is not extradiscursive. Rather than any substantive criteria for defining a theoretical text, he offers a purely formal one that refers simply to coherence: "*Discourse*. . . must be specified as a set of concepts and the relations between them in which the relations that can be demonstrated are strictly *logical* ones" (p. 58, italics in original).

Savage claims, in other words, that he can adopt a purely internalist analysis which employs no standards of criticism other than those employed by Parsons himself. Yet to argue in this way implies a kind of interpretive positivism, for it would allow interpretation to be itself without presuppositions—a possibility, indeed, that Savage explicitly upholds (p. 4). Thus, while he rightly criticizes the relativism of extradiscursive critiques, his internalist stance would imply an even greater relativity, for it can be carried out only within the terms set by the author himself. Not surprisingly, however, Savage does bring his own presuppositions to bear; they are simply more obscure and less visible than the criticisms he is arguing against. Throughout his discussion there is a persistent naturalistic bias. He reads Parsons' argument for the relative autonomy of norms, e.g., as an idealist argument for the absolute status of culture as a determining element (e.g., pp. 229–230), and he argues in principle (p. 47) and in relation to Parsons' theory (p. 122) that the "mutual determination" of norms and interests is impossible. His underlying assumption, in other words, is that a multidimensional theory is not viable or legitimate, a position in which he clearly follows Althusser.

It would seem from even these most recent and most sophisticated interpretations, therefore, that there are sources of interpretive error other than the polarization inspired by personal and political antagonism. These errors stem from the interpreters' own confusions about theoretical logic and from the confusions that exist within Parsons' work.

2. Black, "Some Questions about Parsons' Theories," in Black, ed., *The Social Theories of Talcott Parsons* (Ithaca, N.Y., 1961; reissued with an "Afterword" by Parsons, Carbondale and Edwardsville, Ill., 1976), p. 282; Merton, "Manifest and Latent Functions," in his *On Theoretical Sociology* (New York, [1949] 1967), pp. 39–72. For a discussion of Merton in this positivist context, see vol. 1, pp. 11–15. For Kuhn, see vol. 1, pp. 24–30.

3. Zetterberg, *On Theory and Verification in Sociology,* 3d ed. (New York, 1965). For my discussion of Zetterberg's positivist persuasion, see vol. 1, pp. 6–8.

4. George C. Homans, "Bringing Men Back in," *American Sociological Review* 29 (1964):809–818. The examples of propositional refutations are numerous and scattered throughout the sociological literature. For such purely empirical evaluations of the Parsonian theory of stratification, see, e.g., J. A. Kahl, *The American Class Structure* (New York, 1957), and Arthur L. Stinchcombe, "Some Empirical Consequences of the Davis-Moore Theory of Stratification," *American Sociological Review* 28 (1963):805–808; of the family, see, e.g., Richard Sennet, *Families Against the City* (Cambridge, Mass., 1970) and "Middle Class Families and Urban Violence: The Experience of a Chicago Community in the 19th Century," in Stephen Thernstrom and Sennet, eds., *Nineteenth Century Cities* (New Haven, Conn., 1968), pp. 386–420, or Philip Slater, "Parental Role Differentiation," *American Journal of Sociology* 67 (1961):269–308; of the university, see the empirically oriented critical reviews of Parsons and Platt's *The American*

University by Joseph Gusfield and P. Sexton in *Contemporary Sociology* 3 (1974):291–300; of social change, see Anthony D. Smith, *The Concept of Social Change* (London, 1973).

5. Gouldner, *The Coming Crisis in Western Sociology* (New York, 1970), esp. pp. 167–198.

6. Friedrichs, *A Sociology of Sociology* (New York, 1970), e.g., pp. 11–30.

7. Bottomore, "Out of This World: The Sociological Theories of Talcott Parsons," in his *Sociology as Social Criticism* (New York, 1975; originally in *The New York Review of Books*, vol. 13, no. 6 [1969]). See my review of Bottomore's book in *American Journal of Sociology* 81, no. 5 (1976):1220–1223.

8. Mills, *The Sociological Imagination* (Oxford, 1959), pp. 29–49.

9. Mulkay, *Functionalism, Exchange, and Theoretical Strategy* (London, 1971), pp. 66–93.

10. Homans (n. 4 above).

11. Dahrendorf, *Class and Class Conflict in Industrial Society* (Stanford, Calif., 1959), pp. 157–240.

12. Lewis A. Coser, *The Functions of Social Conflict* (New York, 1956); John Horton, "Order and Conflict Theories of Social Problems as Competing Ideologies," *American Journal of Sociology* 71 (1966):701–713; John Rex, *Key Problems in Sociological Theory* (London, 1961); Randall Collins, "A Comparative Approach to Political Sociology," in Reinhard Bendix, ed., *State and Society: A Reader in Comparative Political Sociology* (Berkeley and Los Angeles, 1968), pp. 42–67. For a general discussion of these theorists, differentiated from their particular relation to Parsons, see vol. 1, pp. 50–55.

13. There are a number of recently published introductory textbooks, otherwise excellent, which organize every chapter around the misleading conflict/order debate and its connotations of parallel divisions over ideology and presuppositions. Such "anti-Parsonian" styles of textbook presentation may be compared with such a "Parsonian" text as Jackson Toby's *Contemporary Society* (New York, 1971). This now well-established folklore extends into specialized textbooks as well. In what is probably the most sophisticated textbook on social change, Herman Strasser introduces a key chapter as follows: "A social theory based on the concepts of order, equilibrium, and integration is unrealistic; two facts make it so: conflict and change. . . . In the context of this study, therefore, the order or integration vocabulary of social explanation will be regarded as a substantive requisite for functional analysis and as synonymous with equilibirum theory with respect to the study of change phenomena" ("The Structural-Functional Theory of Social Change," in Strasser and Susan C. Randall, *An Introduction to Theories of Social Change* [London, 1981], pp. 130–191,

quoting p. 132). Strasser clearly conflates presuppositional understandings of order, models of society (e.g., functional analysis), and propositional statements about empirical conflict and change.

14. Nicholas S. Timasheff and George A. Theodorson, *Sociological Theory* (New York, 1976), p. 255.

15. Martindale, *The Nature and Types of Sociological Theory* (Cambridge, Mass., 1960), pp. 484–499. For Gouldner and Mills, see nn. 5, 8 above; for Wallace, see his "Overview of Contemporary Sociological Theory," in Wallace, ed., *Sociological Theory* (Chicago, 1969), pp. 1–58; for Blumer, see his *Symbolic Interactionism: Perspective and Method* (Englewood Cliffs, N.J., 1969), esp. pp. 57–60; for Menzies, see *Talcott Parsons and the Social Image of Man* (London, 1977), pp. 110–159; for Adriaansens, see n. 1 above, pp. 58–87; for Habermas, see "Talcott Parsons: Problems of Theory Construction," *Sociological Inquiry* 51 (1981):173–196.

16. Devereux, "Parsons' Sociological Theory," in Black (n. 1 above), p. 3.

17. Harold J. Bershady, *Ideology and Social Knowledge* (New York, 1973).

18. Ken Menzies (n. 15 above), pp. 6–26.

19. Jacobson, "A Theoretical and Empirical Analysis of Social Change and Conflict Based on Talcott Parsons' Ideas," in Herman Turk and Richard L. Simpson, eds., *Institutions and Social Change: The Sociologies of Talcott Parsons and George C. Homans* (Indianapolis, 1971), pp. 345–360; also Gary L. Buck and Alvin L. Jacobson, "Social Evolution and Structural-Functional Analysis: An Empirical Test," *American Sociological Review* 33 (1968):343–353.

20. Herminio Martins has put this issue very clearly in his criticism of the attempts that have been made to challenge Parsons' theory by criticizing the kinds of pattern-variable combinations Parsons thought occurred in modern societies. "It is curious to note," Martins writes, "that although there has been much discussion in the sociological literature of the ascription-achievement pattern-variable or structural distinction it has been largely empirical and polemical rather than conceptual."

> Probably the main pattern of argument has been the attempt to show how far short of the achievement-oriented ideal actual advanced industrial societies fall. To bring out the resilience of structural, institutionalized racism in such societies, the relative inefficacy of the educational system in operating as an agency of intergenerational vertical mobility, at least in a secularly increasing way, the rigidity in the pattern of the distribution of wealth despite fiscal and other would-be equalizing mechanisms, etc., is extremely valuable. But such findings would not actually impair the conceptualization itself, only the empirical scope of its application and location. ("Time and Theory in Sociology," in John Rex, ed., *Approaches to Sociology* (London, 1974), pp. 246–294, quoting p. 259.)

21. In fact, a critique of the negative aspects of late capitalism was one of the major themes in Parsons' earliest scholarly articles, derived from his Heidelberg dissertation (" 'Capitalism' in Recent German Literature: Sombart and Weber, I–II," *Journal of Political Economy* 36 [1928]:641–666, and 37 [1929]:31–51). In these articles Parsons is critical of Sombart and Weber precisely because of their pessimism about the possibilities for significant, qualitative social change. These facts are in sharp contrast with Gouldner's distorted analysis of Parsons' early ideological position (*Coming Crisis* [n. 5 above], pp. 182–185). Gouldner rested his case for the early Parsons' conservatism partly on biographical facts, as well as on his interpretation of Parsons' works. For the former he relied on an article by his student Barbara S. Heyl, "The Harvard 'Pareto Circle' " (*Journal of the History of the Behavioral Sciences* 4 [1968]:316–334). Yet Heyl herself makes no claims for Parsons' conservatism in this article; to the contrary, she suggests that Parsons was quite peripheral to the study group on Pareto, which was organized by L. J. Henderson, an outspoken conservative, but whose members were of different political stripes. For a general discussion of the errors in Gouldner's biographical analysis, see Seymour Martin Lipset and Everett Carll Ladd, Jr., "The Politics of American Sociologists," in Robert K. Merton et al., *Varieties of Political Expression in Sociology* (Chicago, 1972), pp. 67–104.

22. Hacker, "Sociology and Ideology," in Black (n. 1 above), p. 291.

23. Gouldner, *Coming Crisis*, pp. 351–368; Friedrichs (n. 6 above).

24. Bershady (n. 17 above), pp. 65–81; Schwanenberg, "The Two Problems of Order in Parsons' Theory: An Analysis from Within," *Social Forces* 49 (1971):569–581, and "On the Meaning of the General Theory of Action," in J. J. Loubser et al., eds., *Explorations in General Theory in the Social Sciences* (New York, 1976), pp. 35–45. For Homans and Mulkay, see nn. 4, 9 above.

25. Parsons, *The Structure of Social Action* (New York, [1937] 1949), pp. 27–41, and "On Building Social System Theory: A Personal History," *Daedalus*, no. 99 (1970), pp. 826–881, see p. 830; Schwanenberg (n. 24 above), passim; Thomas J. Fararo, "On the Foundations of the Theory of Action in Whitehead and Parsons," in Loubser (n. 24 above), pp. 90–122.

26. See Noel Annan's excellent account of the role of positivism and individualistic rationalism in British social thought in his Hobhouse Memorial Lecture, *The Curious Strength of Positivism in English Political Thought* (London, 1959), pp. 2–21. Basically, Annan takes over Parsons' framework from *The Structure of Social Action* and applies it to the particular circumstances of the British case.

27. Erving Goffman, *Asylums* (New York, 1961).

28. Ralf Dahrendorf, "Out of Utopia," *American Journal of Sociology* 64 (1958):115–127.

29. See my references to the system aspect of Marx's work in vol. 1, pp. 60–63.

30. Wallace, "Overview" (n. 14 above), pp. 25–28. Much the same can be said for Habermas's interpretation (n. 15 above). Insofar as Habermas sees Parsons' later theory as consistently functionalist, he seeks to deduce all of its principal characteristics from this model assumption. Because Parsons is a functionalist, Habermas reasons, his theory is burdened with a certain ideology, method, presuppositional position. Yet even when he views Parsons' later theory as inconsistent, Habermas still poses the inconsistency as one between "action theory" and "systems theory," writing, e.g., about the "two paradigms" which are in tension in Parsons' work (pp. 174–176). Though Habermas cites the (similarly reductionist) interpretation of the later work by Menzies (n. 15 above), it would seem that he has also been influenced in his interpretation of Parsons by the example of his colleague Niklas Luhmann, who claims at once to articulate a version of Parsonian theory and to be purely a systems theorist.

I have suggested throughout this study, to the contrary, that everything that is particular and specific to Parsons' theorizing emerges not from his "functionalism" but from the manner in which this model is complexly articulated and concretized with other scientific levels. For these reasons, to equate Parsons' functionalism with nineteenth-century organicism, as, e.g., Martindale (n. 15 above) does, is to misread Parsons' entire theoretical project. The early Gouldner perceived very clearly the dangers in such an interpretation, noting that organisms are examples of particular types of systems, not the only type of systemic models available. Moreover, Gouldner writes, with the transition to the twentieth century, "the need to distinguish between the concrete case, namely the organism, and the thing it was a case of, namely a 'system,' became increasingly evident to functional theorists" ("Reciprocity and Autonomy in Functional Theory," in N. J. Demerath III and Richard A. Peterson, eds., *System, Change, and Conflict* (New York, 1967), p. 142. It has, of course, "been easier to unravel the implications of system thinking by the direct inspection of a concrete example," Gouldner acknowledges, rather than "to analyze formally the implications of the concept of a system treated in full abstraction" (ibid.). Yet this should not allow the critical equation of the two. While Martindale admits no such distinction, and the later Gouldner has apparently forgotten it, such an analytic isolation of the system concept is one of the driving forces in a major segment of Parsons' work.

31. Martindale (n. 15 above), passim. It is this perspective of "social behaviorism" that informs Martindale's work, e.g., *Social Life and Cultural Change* (New York, 1962).

32. Levy, *The Structure of Society* (Princeton, N.J., 1952), p. vii.

33. White, *Beyond Conformity* (New York, 1961), pp. 70–100.

34. Rocher, *Talcott Parsons and American Sociology* (New York, 1975), p. 127, italics added.

35. Jacobson in Buck and Jacobson (n. 19 above).

36. Lidz, "Values in Sociology: A Critique of Szymanski," *Sociological Inquiry* 40 (1970):3–25.

37. Lidz, "On the Construction of Objective Theory: Rejoinder to Szymanski," *Sociological Inquiry* 42 (1972):51–64.

38. Bershady (n. 17 above), pp. 125–167.

39. Neil J. Smelser, *Social Change in the Industrial Revolution* (Chicago, 1959). I am not referring here to Smelser's argument about the historically increasing autonomy and separation of family and industrial enterprise, but rather to his justification for the analytic separation of the family economy and industrial economy as societal subsystems, a phenomenon that in his opinion is universal. Smelser's argument for the latter as deriving from the characteristics of "systems" per se occurs in pp. 10–14 of that book.

40. Harry M. Johnson, "Parsons' Use of Analytical Model," *Indian Journal of Social Research*, April-August 1975, pp. 354–371.

41. Rocher (n. 34 above), p. 29.

42. Ibid., pp. 155–159.

43. Lipset, "Social Structure and Social Change," in Peter M. Blau, ed., *Approaches to the Study of Social Structure* (New York, 1975), pp. 172–209.

44. Loubser, "General Introduction," and Baum, "Introduction to Generalized Media in Action," in Loubser (n. 24 above), pp. 1–24, 448–469.

45. Slabbert, "Functional Methodology in the Theory of Action," ibid., pp. 55–56.

46. Lipset and Ladd's discussion (n. 21 above) of Parsons' political commitments is an outstanding exception to this general rule.

47. Scott, "The Changing Foundations of the Parsonian Action Schema," *American Sociological Review* 28 (1963):716–735.

48. Heydebrand, "Review Symposium," *Contemporary Sociology* 1 (1972):387–395.

49. Lockwood, "Some Remarks on 'The Social System,'" *British Journal of Sociology* 7, no. 2 (1956):137–138.

50. Mills, *The Sociological Imagination* (n. 8 above), pp. 37–38.

51. John Rex, *Key Problems in Sociological Theory* (London, 1961), passim.

52. The exceptional character of Lockwood's position becomes much more explicit in his devastating critique of "conflict theory" in his "Social Integration and System Integration," in George K. Zollschen and Walter Hirsch, eds., *Explorations in Social Change* (Boston, 1964), pp. 244–257.

53. Heydebrand, "Review Symposium" (n. 48 above).

54. "Epistemological break" or "rupture" is the term introduced by Louis Althusser to describe what he views as the crucial transition in Marx's thought which, in 1845, marked the emergence of the "mature" as compared with the early Marx (*For Marx* [London, 1969], pp. 21–86, 153–160.) I have argued in vol. 2 (chs. 2, 3, 6) that no such epistemological break occurred for Marx; rather, Marx altered his understanding of the translation of his basic epistemological position into sociological terms. In the growing commentarial literature on the early versus the late Parsons, a similar break is postulated by critics who, like Althusser, also have a distinctly polemical animus. Yet, as my discussion in the preceding chapters should amply indicate, no such break exists in Parsons' work, not even in the realm of his "sociological epistemology."

55. Dick Atkinson, *Orthodox Consensus and Radical Alternative* (New York, 1973), p. 33.

56. Ibid., pp. 9–33.

57. Wallace, "Overview" (n. 30 above).

58. Blumer (n. 14 above); Homans (n. 4 above).

59. Wrong, "The Over-Socialized Conception of Man in Modern Sociology," *American Sociological Review* 26 (1961):183–193.

60. Gouldner, *Coming Crisis* (n. 5 above), pp. 199–285; Friedrichs (n. 6 above), pp. 12–16.

61. Wolin, "Gilding the Iron Cage," *New York Review of Books*, January 24, 1974, pp. 40–42.

62. Taylor, *From Modernization to Modes of Production* (London, 1979). "Parsons has abstracted this notion of rational organization of means to achieve ends from the discourse of neo-classical economics [and] then elevated it to the status of a concept with universal application, gradually discarding the limits placed on its application by neo-classical economic theory" (p. 9).

The interpretations of Taylor and Wolin are as far from empirical accuracy as it is possible to get. It is as if Marx or Bentham were accused of proposing a religious or idealistic conception of capitalistic motive.

63. For general discussion of the problems of such arguments, see vol. 1, pp. 94–110.

64. Williams, "The Sociological Theory of Talcott Parsons," in Black (n. 1 above), pp. 64–100, quoting p. 66.

65. Rhoads, "On Gouldner's 'Crisis of Western Sociology,' " in Merton et al., *Varieties of Political Expression in Sociology* (n. 21 above), pp. 146–150.

66. Johnson, "The Generalized Symbolic Media in Parsons' Theory," *Sociology and Social Research* 57 (1973):208–221, and "Parsons' Use of Analytic Model" (n. 40 above).

67. Rocher (n. 34 above), pp. 77–98; François Bourricaud, *L'Individualisme institutionnel: Essai sur la sociologie de Talcott Parsons* (Paris,

1977), pp. 157–218; Richard Münch, "Talcott Parsons and the Theory of Action, I–II," *American Journal of Sociology* 86 (1981):709–739, 87 (1982):771–826.

68. Loubser, "General Introduction" (n. 44 above), p. 15.

69. Ibid., p. 5.

70. Ibid., p. 2.

71. Ibid., p. 12.

72. Devereux, "Parsons' Sociological Theory" (n. 16 above), p. 16.

73. Toby, "Review Symposium," *Contemporary Sociology* 1 (1972):395.

74. Johnson, *Functionalism in Modern Sociology: Understanding Talcott Parsons* (Morristown, N.J., 1976), p. 16.

75. Bourricaud (n. 67 above), p. 33.

76. Robert K. Merton, "Insiders and Outsiders: A Chapter in the Sociology of Knowledge," in Merton et al., *Varieties of Political Expression in Sociology* (n. 21 above).

Works of Parsons

Following are the works cited in the text and notes, listed chronologically according to date of original publication or, if unpublished, date of composition. I have included the original language edition only when it was a primary reference.

" 'Capitalism' in Recent German Literature: Sombart and Weber, I," *Journal of Political Economy* 36 (1928): 641–661.

" 'Capitalism' in Recent German Literature: Sombart and Weber, II," *Journal of Political Economy* 37 (1929): 31–51.

"Wants and Activities in Marshall," *Quarterly Journal of Economics* 46 (1931): 101–140.

"Economics and Sociology: Marshall in Relation to the Thought of His Time," *Quarterly Journal of Economics* 46 (1932): 316–347.

"Malthus," *Encyclopedia of the Social Sciences*, 1933 ed.

"Some Reflections on 'The Nature and Significance of Economics,' " *Quarterly Journal of Economics* 48 (1934): 511–545.

"Sociological Elements in Economic Thought, I," *Quarterly Journal of Economics* 49 (1934): 414–453.

"Sociological Elements in Economic Thought, II," *Quarterly Journal of Economics* 49 (1934): 645–667.

"The Place of Ultimate Values in Sociological Theory," *International Journal of Ethics* 45 (1935): 282–316.

"Remarks on Education and the Professions," *International Journal of Ethics* 48 (1937): 365–369.

The Structure of Social Action, [1937], 1968.

"The Professions and the Social Structure," [1939], in Parsons, *Essays in Sociological Theory*, 1954.

"An Analytical Approach to the Theory of Social Stratification," [1940], in Parsons, *Essays in Sociological Theory*, 1954.

"The Motivation of Economic Activities," [1940], in Parsons, *Essays in Sociological Theory*, 1954.

"Age and Sex in the Social Structure of the United States," [1942], in Parsons, *Essays in Sociological Theory*, 1954.

"Democracy and Social Structure in Pre-Nazi Germany," [1942], in Parsons, *Essays in Sociological Theory*, 1954.

"Some Sociological Aspects of the Fascist Movements," [1942], in Parsons, *Essays in Sociological Theory*, 1954.

"The Theoretical Development of the Sociology of Religion," [1944], in Parsons, *Essays in Sociological Theory*, 1954.

"The Present Position and Prospects of Systematic Theory in Sociology," [1945], in Parsons, *Essays in Sociological Theory*, 1954.

"The Problem of Controlled Institutional Change," [1945], in Parsons, *Essays in Sociological Theory*, 1954.

"The Prospects of Sociological Theory," [1945], in Parsons, *Essays in Sociological Theory*, 1954.

"Certain Primary Sources and Patterns of Aggression in the Social Structure of the Western World," [1946], in Parsons, *Essays in Sociological Theory*, 1954.

"Population and Social Structure of Japan," [1946], in Parsons, *Essays in Sociological Theory*, 1954.

Introduction to *The Theory of Social and Economic Organization*, by Max Weber, 1947.

"Certain Primary Sources and Patterns of Aggression in the Social Structure of the Western World," [1947], in Parsons, *Essays in Sociological Theory*, 1954.

"Social Classes and Class Conflict in the Light of Recent Sociological Theory," [1949], in Parsons, *Essays in Sociological Theory*, 1954.

The Social System, 1951.

Towards a General Theory of Action (ed. with Edward A. Shils), 1951.

"Some Fundamental Categories of the Theory of Action: A General Statement," in Parsons and Shils, eds., *Towards a General Theory of Action*, 1951.

"Values, Motives, and Systems of Action," in Parsons and Shils, eds., *Towards a General Theory of Action*, 1951.

"Sociology and Social Psychology," [1952], reprinted in William A. Lessa and Evan Z. Voght, eds., *Reader in Comparative Religion: An Anthropological Approach*, 1972.

"The Superego and the Theory of Social Systems," [1952], in Parsons, *Social Structure and Personality*, 1964.

Working Papers in the Theory of Action (with Robert F. Bales and Edward A. Shils), 1953.

"The Dimensions of Action-Space" (with Bales), in Parsons, Bales, and Shils, *Working Papers in the Theory of Action*, 1953.

"Phase Movement in Relation to Motivation, Symbol Formation, and Role Structure" (with Bales and Shils), in Parsons, Bales, and Shils, *Working Papers in the Theory of Action*, 1953.

"The Theory of Symbolism in Relation to Action," in Parsons, Bales, and Shils, *Working Papers in the Theory of Action*, 1953.

"A Revised Analytical Approach to the Theory of Social Stratification," [1953], in Parsons, *Essays in Sociological Theory*, 1954.

Essays in Sociological Theory, 1954.

"The Father Symbol: An Appraisal in the Light of Psychoanalytic and Sociological Theory," [1954], in Parsons, *Social Structure and Personality*, 1964.
"The Incest Taboo in Relation to Social Structure and the Socialization of the Child," [1954], in Parsons, *Social Structure and Personality*, 1964.
Family, Socialization, and Interaction Process (ed. with Robert F. Bales), 1955.
"Conclusion: Levels of Cultural Generality and the Process of Differentiation," in Parsons and Bales, eds., *Family, Socialization, and Interaction Process*, 1955.
"Family Structure and the Socialization of the Child," in Parsons and Bales, eds., *Family, Socialization, and Interaction Process*, 1955.
"The Mechanisms of Personality Functioning with Special Reference to Socialization" (with James Olds), in Parsons and Bales, eds., *Family, Socialization, and Interaction Process*, 1955.
"The Organization of Personality as a System of Action," in Parsons and Bales, eds., *Family, Socialization, and Interaction Process*, 1955.
"Social Strains in America," [1955], in Parsons, *Politics and Social Structure*, 1969.
Economy and Society (with Neil J. Smelser), 1956.
"Definitions of Health and Illness in the Light of American Values and Social Structure," [1958], in Parsons, *Social Structure and Personality*, 1964.
"Social Structure and the Development of Personality: Freud's Contribution to the Integration of Psychology and Sociology," [1958], in Parsons, *Social Structure and Personality*, 1964.
"An Approach to Psychological Theory in Terms of the Theory of Action," in Sigmund Koch, ed., *Psychology: A Study of a Science*, 1959.
"The School Class as a Social System: Some of Its Functions in American Society," [1959], in Parsons, *Social Structure and Personality*, 1964.
" 'Voting' and the Equilibrium of the American Political System," [1959], in Parsons, *Politics and Social Structure*, 1969.
Structure and Process in Modern Societies, 1960.
"Authority, Legitimation, and Political Action," in Parsons, *Structure and Process in Modern Societies*, 1960.
"Some Ingredients of a General Theory of Formal Organization," in Parsons, *Structure and Process in Modern Societies*, 1960.
"Some Principal Characteristics of Industrial Societies," in Parsons, *Structure and Process in Modern Societies*, 1960.
"Some Reflections on the Institutional Framework of Economic Development," in Parsons, *Structure and Process in Modern Societies*, 1960.
"A Sociological Approach to the Theory of Organizations," in Parsons, *Structure and Process in Modern Societies*, 1960.
"The Distribution of Power in American Society," [1960], in Parsons, *Politics and Social Structure*, 1969.
"The Mass Media and the Structure of American Society" (with Winston White), [1960], in Parsons, *Politics and Social Structure*, 1969.
"Mental Illness and 'Spiritual Malaise': The Role of the Psychiatrist and the Minister of Religion," [1960], in Parsons, *Social Structure and Personality*, 1964.
"Toward a Healthy Maturity," [1960], in Parsons, *Social Structure and Personality*, 1964.
"Durkheim's Contribution to the Theory of Integration of Social Systems," [1960],

in Parsons, *Sociological Theory and Modern Society*, 1967.
"Pattern Variables Revisited: A Response to Robert Dubin," [1960], in Parsons, *Sociological Theory and Modern Society*, 1967.
Comment on "Preface to a Metatheoretical Framework for Sociology," by Lewellyn Gross, *American Journal of Sociology* 67 (1961): 136–140.
"Some Considerations on the Theory of Social Change," *Rural Sociology* 26 (1961): 219–319.
Theories of Society, 1961.
"The General Interpretation of Action," in Parsons et al., eds., *Theories of Society*, 1961.
"Introduction to Culture and the Social System," in Parsons, ed., *Theories of Society*, 1961.
"An Outline of the Social System," in Parsons, ed., *Theories of Society*, 1961.
"The Link between Character and Society" (with Winston White), [1961], in Parsons, *Social Structure and Personality*, 1964.
Afterword to *The Social Theories of Talcott Parsons*, ed. by Max Black, [1961], 1976.
"The Point of View of the Author," in Max Black, ed., *The Social Theories of Talcott Parsons*, [1961], 1976.
"Social Strains in America: A Postscript—1962," in Parsons, *Politics and Social Structure*, 1969.
"Youth in the Context of American Society," [1962], in Parsons, *Social Structure and Personality*, 1964.
"Christianity and Modern Industrial Society," [1963], in Parsons, *Sociological Theory and Modern Society*, 1967.
"On the Concept of Influence," [1963], in Parsons, *Sociological Theory and Modern Society*, 1967.
"On the Concept of Political Power," [1963], in Parsons, *Sociological Theory and Modern Society*, 1967.
Social Structure and Personality, 1964.
"Evolutionary Universals in Society," [1964], in Parsons, *Sociological Theory and Modern Society*, 1967.
"Some Reflections on the Place of Force in Social Process," [1964], in Parsons, *Sociological Theory and Modern Society*, 1967.
"Evaluation and Objectivity in Social Science: An Interpretation of Max Weber's Contribution," [1965], in Parsons, *Sociological Theory and Modern Society*, 1967.
"Full Citizenship for the Negro American?" [1965], in Parsons, *Sociological Theory and Modern Society*, 1967.
Societies: Evolutionary and Comparative Perspectives, 1966.
"The Political Aspect of Social Structure and Process," [1966], in Parsons, *Politics and Social Structure*, 1969.
Sociological Theory and Modern Society, 1967.
"Some Comments on the Sociology of Karl Marx," in Parsons, *Sociological Theory and Modern Society*, 1967.
"The Position of Identity in the General Theory of Action," in C. Gordon and K. J. Gergen, eds., *The Self in Social Interaction*, 1968.
"Professions," *International Encyclopedia of the Social Sciences*, 1968 ed.

"Social Interaction," *International Encyclopedia of the Social Sciences*, 1968 ed.
"On the Concept of Value Commitments," [1968], in Parsons, *Politics and Social Structure*, 1969.
Politics and Social Structure, 1969.
"Polity and Society: Some General Considerations," in Parsons, *Politics and Social Structure*, 1969.
"Postscript to 'On the concept of Influence,'" in Parsons, *Politics and Social Structure*, 1969.
"Belief, Unbelief, and Disbelief," [1969], in Rocco Caporale and Antonio Grumelli, eds., *The Culture of Unbelief: Studies and Proceedings from the First International Symposium on Belief*, 1971.
"On Building Social System Theory: A Personal History," *Daedalus* 99 (1970): 826–881.
"Some Considerations on the Theory of Social Change," in S. N. Eisenstadt, ed., *Readings in Social Evolution and Development*, 1970.
"Equality and Inequality in Modern Society, or Social Stratification Revisited," [1970], in Parsons, *Social Systems and the Evolution of Action Theory*, 1977.
"Some Problems of General Theory in Sociology," [1970], in Parsons, *Social Systems and the Evolution of Action Theory*, 1977.
"Comparative Studies and Evolutionary Change," in Ivan Vallier, ed., *Comparative Methods in Sociology*, 1971.
"Kinship and the Associational Aspects of Social Structure," in Francis L. K. Hsu, ed., *Kinship and Culture*, 1971.
"Levels of Organization and the Mediation of Social Interaction," in Herman Turk and Richard L. Simpson, eds., *Institutions and Social Exchange*, 1971.
The System of Modern Societies, 1971.
The American University (with Gerald M. Platt), 1973.
"Culture and Social System Revisited," in Louis Schneider and Charles Bonjean, eds., *The Idea of Culture in the Social Sciences*, 1973.
"The Problem of Balancing Rational Efficiency with Communal Solidarity in Modern Society," in Japan Economic Research Institute, *International Symposium on "New Problems of Advanced Societies,"* 1973.
"Commentary on Herbert Gintis' 'A Radical Analysis of Welfare Economics,'" *Quarterly Journal of Economics* 89 (1975): 280–290.
"Social Structure and the Symbolic Media of Interchange," in Peter M. Blau, ed., *Approaches to the Study of Social Structure*, 1975.
"The Present Status of 'Structural-Functional' Theory in Sociology," [1975], in Parsons, *Social Systems and the Evolution of Action Theory*, 1977.
Social Systems and the Evolution of Action Theory, 1977.
"General Introduction," in Parsons, *Social Systems and the Evolution of Action Theory*, 1977.
"Law as an Intellectual Stepchild," *Sociological Inquiry* 47, nos. 3–4 (1977): 115–18.
Action Theory and the Human Condition, 1978.
"Letter from Parsons to Edward Tiryakian," *Sociological Inquiry* 51 (1981): 35–36.

Author-Citation Index

This index is intended as a combination bibliography/name index. Every article and book referred to in the text and notes is included here (with the exception of works by Parsons), but authors are included only if their work is specifically cited. If the work of an author mentioned in the text is cited only in the notes, the page of both text and note references is indexed.

Subject Index